THE BUILDINGS OF ENGLAND

SUSSEX

IAN NAIRN AND
NIKOLAUS PEVSNER

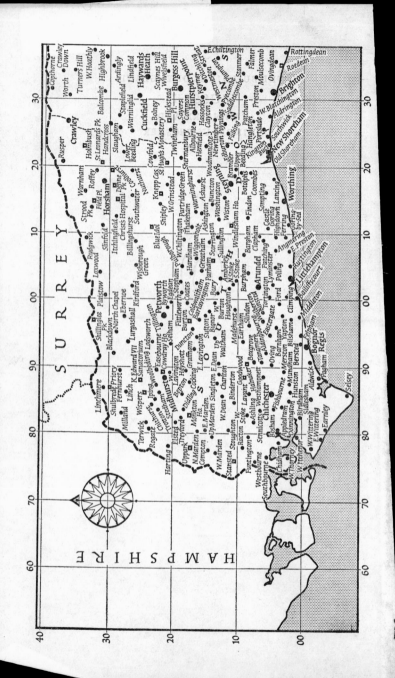

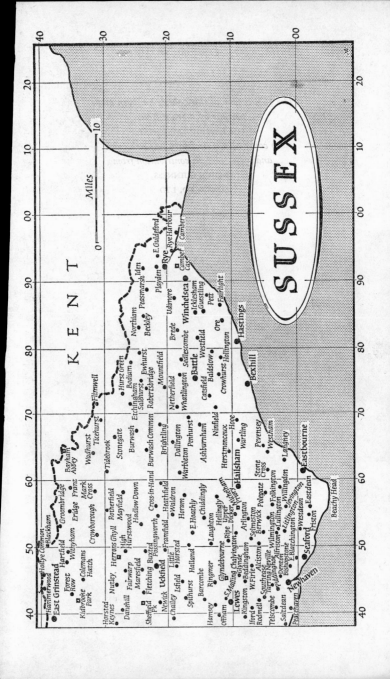

*The publication of this volume has been made
possible by a grant from*
THE LEVERHULME TRUST
*to cover all the necessary research work
and by a generous contribution from*
ARTHUR GUINNESS,
SONS & CO. LTD

THE BUILDINGS OF ENGLAND

Sussex

BY
IAN NAIRN AND
NIKOLAUS PEVSNER

*

PENGUIN BOOKS

Penguin Books Ltd, Harmondsworth, Middlesex, England
Penguin Books Inc., 7110 Ambassador Road, Baltimore, Maryland 21207, U.S.A.
Penguin Books Australia Ltd, Ringwood, Victoria, Australia

—

First published 1965
Reprinted 1973

—

ISBN 0 14 071028 0

—

Copyright © Ian Nairn and Nikolaus Pevsner, 1965

—

Made and printed in Great Britain
by William Clowes & Sons, Limited, London, Beccles and Colchester
Gravure plates by Clarke and Sherwell, Limited
Set in Monotype Plantin

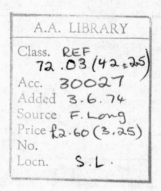

CONTENTS

*

Map References

*

The numbers printed in italic type in the margin against the place names in the gazetteer of the book indicate the position of the place in question on the index map (pages 2–3), which is divided into sections by the 10-kilometre reference lines of the National Grid. The reference given here omits the two initial letters (formerly numbers) which in a full grid reference refer to the 100-kilometre squares into which the country is divided. The first two numbers indicate the *western* boundary, and the last two the *southern* boundary, of the 10-kilometre square in which the place in question is situated. For example Horsham (reference 1030) will be found in the 10-kilometre square bounded by grid lines 10 and 20 on the *west* and 30 and 40 on the *south*; Hastings (reference 8000) in the square bounded by grid lines 80 and 90 on the *west* and 00 and 10 on the *south*.

The map contains all those places, whether towns, villages, or isolated buildings, which are the subject of separate entries in the text.

FOREWORD

FOREWORD

The regular users of The Buildings of England *are very much a
family, and so I feel encouraged to take them into my confidence
and tell them of a matter concerning the innermost family circle.
Some of the most recent volumes suffer in one way from a distrust
I harbour in my longevity. As there are still some twenty volumes
to come, what if I can't keep it up? So I decided to go to others for
help and to split volumes between two authors, one of them being
myself. In Lincolnshire the division was between ecclesiastical and
secular, the secular being seen and described by Mr John Harris.
In Surrey it was a topographical division. Mr Ian Nairn did about
two-thirds or more of the area, I the rest. It worked superbly well,
as users and reviewers seem to agree. So I turned to him for Sussex
and in this case the whole of Sussex. He agreed, but then, when he
had completed West Sussex, he found that he could no longer bear to
write the detailed descriptions which are essential in* The Buildings
of England. *His decision filled me with sadness, but I had of course
to carry on, and thanks to Mrs Helen Hill's (then Miss Helen
Davey's) excellent preparation, I could. But I know only too well
that it is is not the same as if he had done the whole book.*

*As things were, the volume called for two introductions, one to
West Sussex, one to East, unavoidable because neither could Mr
Nairn introduce what I had travelled and docketed nor could I
introduce a part of the county which I had only studied in a selected
fifty or sixty items and places suggested to me by Mr Nairn. They
included, of course, Chichester Cathedral, Boxgrove, the Shore-
hams, and Arundel, and in these cases I have even, though in
minor ways, taken the (agreed) liberty of some interference with
Mr Nairn's text. Whether this is an asset remains to be seen. I also
wrote most of the account of Crawley. Mr Nairn, on the other hand,
wrote the villages of outer Brighton and two or three others for me.
I am only too well aware of the fact that our texts and introductions
differ in certain ways already noticeable in the Surrey volume.
Mr Nairn has a greater sensibility to landscape and townscape
than I have, and he writes better than I could ever hope to write.
On the other hand, those who want something a little more cata-
loguey and are fervently interested in mouldings and such-like
details, may find my descriptions more to their liking.*

However that may be, the final result cannot be of the best vintage. There are other shortcomings as well. One concerns timber-framed cottages and smaller houses, the other the deplorable, ever-spreading commuters' belt. As for the timber-framed houses, so important a contribution to the Sussex scene, we have not been able to attempt completeness nor can we hope to have achieved a reliable selection. Often the internally most interesting are unpromising externally, and unless experts have published them, they would necessarily slip through the meshes of our net. Often also the externally most attractive may be less deserving from the historical and strictly architectural point of view. So all I can say is that we have tried to work to a compromise.

Regarding the Commuters' Belt the problem was different. In Sussex, as in Surrey, Victorian and post-Victorian architects built a great deal and often on a lavish scale. Where we had records of architect, place and fairly accurate location, we went, saw, and decided on inclusion or exclusion. But where the record just gave the architect and the place and no name of the house or its location? How is one to spot Townsend's hand behind the rhododendron bushes? Or what if one knows the name given a house in 1890, and it changed its name twenty years later, that is at a time beyond the memory of the most experienced of post office sorters, police officers, or librarians? So again, often one had to give up, and work of great intrinsic interest may never have been seen by us, effectively hidden by its leafy screen.

Where such shortcomings mar this volume, let it be said at once that they are not the fault of any want of help. On the contrary, as we nearly always find with The Buildings of England, *everyone we approached was ready to help, and some even whom we did not approach. Foremost among these is Mr George McHardy, who offered once again to go and spend his weekends on tours around with our typescript, watchful of errors and omissions: his help is a considerable asset to this volume. Then we had the benefit of Mr R. B. Pugh's kindness in allowing us access to unpublished Sussex material ready for the Victoria County History, and as always of the Ministry of Housing and Local Government (here abridged M H L G), whose lists were liberally at our disposal, of the National Buildings Record (NBR), and of Mr Peter Ferriday's index of Victorian church restorations (PF), which he has actually loaned to* The Buildings of England. *In the Victorian field, moreover, Mr Geoffrey Spain has been providing us gradually with lists of tenders published in the technical press, and what we owe him is marked here G S. Then there is the Goodhart-Rendel index of*

Victorian churches (GR) *and Sir Thomas Kendrick's index of Victorian glass* (TK). *For personal help we are indebted to many, and we think we ought to start the list with our thanks to Clifford Musgrave at Brighton and Dean Hussey at Chichester, and (in alphabetical order) Rupert Gunnis, Rodney Hubbuck, David Lloyd, Harold Taylor, Nicholas Taylor* (NT). *From the knowledge of both the county archivists, R. F. Dell at Lewes and F. W. Steer at Chichester, we have profited much, and what would we have done without the help of the librarians, especially at Bexhill (Miss M. L. Butler), Chichester (H. K. Gordon Bearman), Crawley (D. E. Plunkett), Crowborough (W. Bennett), Eastbourne (A. G. S. Enser), East Grinstead (Miss C. Ellis), Forest Row (Miss P. Walker), Hastings (Mrs L. D. O'Nions), Horsham (H. J. N. Watson), Lewes (Miss E. Clarke and R. F. G. Rowsell), Rye (G. M. Johnson), and Worthing (L. M. Bickerton). To theirs we want to add the names of Mr Austin Blomfield, of Mr A. E. Allison of Christs' Hospital, of W. A. Whitty, who took us round Arundel Castle, of R. W. J. Tridgell, Clerk of the Crawley Council, and of F. R. Steele, the county architect. Nor must we forget to put on record the fact that the prehistoric and Roman antiquities were entirely in the hands of Mr Derek Simpson, and that once again rectors and vicars have on the whole been very helpful in answering letters and checking proofs. Owners and occupiers of houses have allowed us access when we asked for it, and we feel we must protect them from importunity by stating that by no means anything like all the houses mentioned in our gazetteer are open to the public.*

The principles on which inclusion in the gazetteer is based are by now familiar, illogicality and all. We have ourselves seen everything that we describe. Where this is not the case, the information obtained by other means is placed in brackets. Information ought to be as complete as the space of the volume permits for churches prior to c.1830 and all town houses, manor houses, and country houses of more than purely local interest. Movable furnishings are not included in secular buildings, though they are in churches. Exceptions to the latter rule are bells, hatchments, chests, chairs, plain fonts, and altar tables. Royal arms, coffin lids with foliate crosses, and brasses of post-Reformation date are mentioned occasionally, church plate of after 1830 only rarely. Village crosses are omitted where only a plain base or a stump of the shaft survives. As for churches and chapels of after 1830, we had to make a selection, and this is dictated by architectural value or by significance otherwise in the light of architectural history. The same applies to secular buildings of the C19 and C20. In churches, incidentally, where they are not correctly orientated, W always means ritual W, i.e. what ought to be W, E means ritual E, etc.

Finally, as in all previous volumes, it is necessary to end the foreword to this with an appeal to all users to draw our attention to errors and omissions.

INTRODUCTION

GENERAL

BY IAN NAIRN

'GOOD old Sussex by the Sea': the words come from a popular parody, but the basic truth is undeniable. Whether in the 1060s or the 1960s, Sussex depends on its sea; and even though most of its visitors and an ever increasing number of its residents work in London, it is still facing outwards, away from the metropolis. And north Sussex is always looking south, to the line of the Downs which becomes a firmer guarantee of the sea beyond than an uninterrupted view would have been.

Compared with Surrey, most of which is fatally turned towards London, the difference is huge. The physical terms of the commuters' equation may be the same, especially in mid-Sussex on either side of the Brighton line, yet the feeling is quite different. It becomes a kind of contract between equals, rather than Surrey's meek subjugation. And at the eastern and western ends there is mile after mile of unspoilt countryside. Be in no doubt that it is preserved countryside, bolstered by a multitude of healthy bank balances; but the unseen hand rarely patronizes or forces a false conformity – Sussex is a good place both for modern houses and for unspoilt village pubs. Equally it is a good place for half-timbered houses in genuine condition, and rump steaks in saloon bars.

This is the pattern of affluence working to conserve and create rather than destroy and level down. It is a pattern which will rapidly extend to more and more of Britain, for better or worse: as a pointer to the future, much of Sussex is as hopeful as anywhere in the country.

It is a comfortable size for a comfortable county: fourteenth in area, thirteenth in population. It is in the seaside towns today where the population of Sussex grows fast. In 1961 Brighton was the biggest town, with 163,000 inhabitants, the only one over 100,000, and as Hove is Brighton that makes it 235,000. Next in size is Worthing in West Sussex with 80,000, and then Hastings with 66,000, or, as Hastings and Bexhill are now one, i.e. run into each other without any break, the figure is 95,000. After that comes Eastbourne with 61,000, and only then

Crawley, away from the sea, with 54,000, though Crawley in its special New-Town way has a chance of outpacing some of the others. Not that everything in the Sussex garden is rosy. As the figures might indicate, the coast is almost gone, and the original sea-sprayed countryside can only be felt patchily around Cuckmere Haven, or between Bognor and Littlehampton, or on the cliffs of the chalk (Brighton to Eastbourne), and the slides and landslips of the sandstone (Hastings to Rye).

This has brought in GEOLOGY. All the strata run east–west, parallel to the Channel, but the coast slopes up to intercept them. Southernmost is the alluvial plain of the Selsey Peninsula, still being eroded by both man and nature. Bent-over trees, and farmhouses in windbreaks show just how bleak this part of England was before the C19. Behind the plain are the indes-
2a tructible chalk Downs, only a few miles thick but as impressive as the Alps.* Still free from building, in most places – with those parts unfortunate enough to be within the Brighton boundaries as a terrible exception. The Downs stub out the plain near Shoreham and are themselves stubbed out at Beachy Head after an adventurous see-saw between cliff and haven.

To the N, there is first of all another strip of level ground, narrow in West Sussex, widening at the E end between Eastbourne and Bexhill to become a miniature edition of Romney Marsh. Then, behind it, the sandstone hills begin; tumbled and intricate at the western end, growing into a surprisingly wild and heathy moor at Ashdown Forest, then running out *diminuendo* in long parallel ridges towards Hastings and Rye. In between the ridges are more levels which become part of Romney Marsh at the eastern end. This is the site of the Wealden iron industry which culminated in the C16 and C17,
2b and has left its mark on the landscape in many hammer-ponds. But it has done little to art and architecture, except for the not
42b very frequent cast-iron tomb-slabs. In the C17 one would not have said that smelting had not affected the scenery; for forests were used up by the ironmasters to the detriment of the ship-builders and the hillsides. The government decreed a halt, and the iron industry decreased. The end, however, came only when coke replaced wood for smelting and the North replaced Sussex. The last furnace, the Ashburnham Furnace near Penhurst (E),‡

* Crowborough Beacon in the Weald is 792 ft high, Ditchling Beacon in the South Downs 823 ft.
‡ Throughout the volume, (E) refers to places in East Sussex; those in West Sussex are the ones not specially distinguished.

ceased work only after 1800. By then the denuded hills had been replanted by improving squires, John Evelyn's *Silva* of 1664 having made the first plea, and the scene had become the English park landscape so much admired by foreign visitors.

The BUILDING MATERIALS reflect this geology. Flint on the Downs* and the coastal plain, with occasional incursions a mile or two N into the Weald. Sandstone in the Weald itself, usually buff-coloured from Horsham eastwards, nutty and brown in the hills around Pulborough, greenish in the NW corner, N of Midhurst, where it is the same as the Burgate stone of Surrey. And after that, of course, brick everywhere; first seen at Herstmonceux Castle (E) in the mid C15, now over the whole county, usually a cheerful vermilion. Brighton and Lewes (E), different as usual, developed their black-glazed bricks for a few years at the end of the C18 and then, sadly, abandoned them in favour of stucco. Roofing in the S was of tiles or thatch; in the N of Horsham slates, i.e. split slabs of sandstone.

PREHISTORIC AND ROMAN ARCHAEOLOGY

BY DEREK SIMPSON

Sussex prehistory is richly endowed with finds of all periods. Nearness to the continent, coupled with favourable soil conditions, made it particularly subject to invasion and settlement. New cultures, however, were often absorbed and developed a distinctly local flavour. Many of the sites are worth a visit both for their archaeological interest and for their excellence as vantage points, providing splendid views of the surrounding downlands.

The earliest conclusive evidence for settlement of the county by Man comes from the second or Great Interglacial period (*c*.400,000 B.C.). The melting of the ice sheet brought about a rise in sea level and the formation of beaches some distance inland from the present coastline. The raised beaches were subsequently buried beneath a deposit of chalk sludge – Combe Rock – and can now only be seen where exposed in the sections of gravel pits. The most important of these gravel pit sites which have produced evidence of Palaeolithic man is in the NW corner of Slindon Park.

At this point one must mention one of the greatest hoaxes in British archaeology – Piltdown Man. In 1908 gravel digging

* And cobbles, i.e. beach stones, in the pre-Regency buildings around Brighton, where they were often tarred against the wind and weather.

near the hamlet of Piltdown (E) produced a small fragment of human skull of unusual thickness. Excavations conducted in the area over succeeding years revealed further fragments of skull and part of a lower jaw, all apparently from the same spot in which the initial discovery was made. The work also brought to light the teeth of elephant, mastodon, hippopotamus, rhinoceros, and beaver and a crude tool made from the thigh bone of an elephant. The reconstructed skull and lower jaw in combination represented so many unusual features that a new genus within the family Hominidae was proposed. Intensive tests carried out on the bones since the last war, however, have shown that the skull, although ancient, was not fossilized as previously thought, while the lower jaw is quite modern and is that of an ape. Both skull and jaw had been artificially stained with sulphate of iron to match the bones with the soil conditions in which they were supposed to have been found. Similarly the teeth of the extinct mammals 'found' in the vicinity of the skull were proved to have in fact come from areas as far away as Sicily and Tunisia. Although conclusively shown to be fraudulent, however, the ghost of Piltdown Man has not yet been laid and, like Stonehenge and the Druids, is exceedingly difficult to erase from the public memory.

About 3000 B.C. or a little before, Sussex, along with the other areas in lowland Britain, was settled by the first Neolithic colonists, coming probably from northern France and bringing with them cereals and domesticated herds. The culture of these first farmers, named after the site of Windmill Hill, Wiltshire,* is in Sussex confined to the chalk areas where three characteristic forms of field monument are to be found – causewayed camps, flint mines, and long barrows. The causewayed camps, of which there are four known examples in the county, consist of roughly oval or circular areas on hilltops bounded by one or more concentric banks and ditches. The latter were dug as a series of disjointed trenches with unexcavated areas between, suggesting the work of individual gangs of labourers. They may be regarded as seasonal gathering places for neighbouring tribes, serving both as commercial and social centres where cattle and other goods might be exchanged, and also possibly as religious foci for a given region. The evidence for feasts, the careful burial of animal bones – in some cases, as at Whitehawk, of whole animals – and, again at Whitehawk, human interments, all suggest the mixed purpose which this type of site served.

* See *Buildings of England: Wiltshire*; Archaeological Introduction.

Faced with the obstacle of encroaching forests which had to be cleared for their crops and herds, the Neolithic farmers employed flaked and polished axes of flint. To obtain the superior flint which occurred in buried seams as much as 50 ft below the ground, organized mining was developed. Seven of these mining sites have been identified in the county, of which five have been proved by excavation. All now appear as areas of downland, generally on or near a hilltop, covered with low mounds and depressions – the filled-in mine shafts with their accompanying dumps. Probably the best known of these mining sites is that at Cissbury (*see* Findon), where over two hundred shafts have been identified. At the base of each shaft galleries radiate horizontally, following the flint seams and in many cases linking up with radial galleries leading off from another vertical shaft, so that in plan the whole presents a warren-like effect. In addition to enormous quantities of waste material and complete or partially finished flint tools in the galleries and in the area surrounding the shafts, there were found numerous antler picks and shovels made from the shoulder blades of oxen, pig, and red deer, used in excavating the shafts. In one of the mine shafts on Church Hill, Findon, were found traces of the wooden ladder used by the miners to descend to the galleries, while at Harrow Hill, Angmering, the soot from the miners' lamps could still be seen on the roof of the galleries.

Contact between the Windmill Hill groups and indigenous hunter-fisher communities led to the adoption of farming techniques by the latter and the emergence of hybrid, Secondary Neolithic Cultures. The causewayed camp at Combe Hill, Jevington (E), appears to have been built by people of this hybrid culture. A temporary encampment was also discovered at Selmeston (E). The flint mines continued to be worked by these people, and some at least were exploited too by the Beaker folk who represent the last waves of Neolithic immigrants to settle in Britain.

The Beaker folk, who began to settle in Britain about 2000 B.C., were invading pastoralists from the Rhineland and Low Countries, their cultures being named after the characteristic S-profiled drinking cups which they buried with their dead beneath round barrows. Both the form of the barrow and the nature of the burial rite – generally individual – represent an important break with the funerary tradition of Neolithic Britain. The material equipment of these invaders, which includes archers' wrist guards, barbed and tanged arrowheads, and rare copper daggers, is also of a more warlike and aristocratic character than that of the Windmill Hill peasants. About a dozen Beaker sites have been recorded in Sussex.

In the Early Bronze Age in Sussex (c.1600 B.C.) two main elements are detectable: on the one hand, a native tradition of cremation burial in a collared urn, which represents a continuation of Secondary Neolithic ceramic fashions; and on the other, a foreign element characterized by exotic objects placed in graves with the dead. The finest grave group in the whole county is undoubtedly that which was found in a wooden coffin beneath a now destroyed round barrow at Hove. Here the burial was accompanied by a bronze dagger, perforated whetstone, stone shaft-hole battle axe, and an amber cup – the raw material for the latter being imported from the Baltic, probably via Germany. Many of the large number of round barrows on the Downs must be of this period. Most show signs of having been dug into, but there are no records of these early excavations and nothing is known of their contents. The bowl barrow, a round barrow with ditch running round the edge of the mound, introduced by the Beaker folk continued to be erected over Early Bronze Age burials, but new forms were also introduced. Most important as regards Sussex are the bell barrows, generally very large barrows separated from their surrounding ditch by a flat platform or berm (e.g. Waltham Down, Stoughton, and Bow Hill, Up Waltham).

About 1200 B.C. fresh settlers arrived on the S coasts of Britain, bringing with them a new form of agriculture which was to provide the basic system of economy until Roman times. A number of farmsteads of this period with their associated field systems occur in Sussex, of which the Plumpton Plain settlement (E) is the best known. Other important farmsteads occur at Park Brow Sompting, Barn Down, and Blackpatch.

About 500 B.C. or a little before, southern Britain was extensively settled by large numbers of iron-using Hallstatt immigrants from the Low Countries and northern France. This first Iron Age culture in Britain is termed Iron Age A. These newcomers mingled with the Bronze Age stock, and many of the farmsteads, such as Park Brow, continued to be occupied by iron-using peoples. The rural economy and Celtic field system remained unchanged.

A second wave of Iron Age invaders from northern France settled in southern Britain and Yorkshire c.250 B.C., bringing

with them elements of the continental La Tène culture. The
arrival of these Iron Age B settlers in Sussex is marked by hill-
fort building, and many of the most spectacular prehistoric
monuments in the county are the work of these people. The
initial settlement was on the Downs of West Sussex, where a
number of very large hill-forts (e.g. The Trundle, Goodwood,
and Cissbury, Findon) were constructed, all bearing a number
of structural features in common – contoured plan, massive
ramparts and ditches with counterscarp banks on the outside of
the ditches, and inturning of the ramparts at the entrances.
Sussex E of the Adur remained the stronghold of Iron Age A
peoples until the end of the C2, when the West Sussex peoples
began to push E and N across the Weald, doubtless attracted by
iron ore deposits.

Around 100 B.C. the first of two main waves of Belgae introduced the Iron Age C culture into south-eastern Britain, this
early occupation being concentrated in Kent. These aristocratic
invaders brought with them wheel-turned pottery, gold coinage,
and a new agricultural system based on the heavy wheeled
plough. They established themselves as overlords, grouping the
small tribal units into larger confederations. A change of settlement pattern too is perceptible as the more heavily wooded
soils – clays and loams – which had resisted the primitive agricultural techniques of their predecessors, were drained and
cultivated with the new plough. Belgic suzerainty was not
established firmly in Sussex, however, until the great revolt in
Gaul against Roman authority in 53–52 B.C., when Commius,
king of the Gaulish Atrebates, fled with his followers to Britain,
where they established a kingdom in the south-west. He was
followed by his sons, one of whom, Verica, ruled the tribe of
the Regni in Sussex. The latter used on his coins the title *rex*,
which suggests some form of Roman recognition. The location
of the tribal capital is unknown, although the scatter of Belgic
finds in the neighbourhood of Selsey may indicate its site.

Following the Roman invasion of South-East Britain in A.D.
43 the Regni, under their king Cogidumnus, were quick to treat
with the invaders, and as a reward Cogidumnus received
suzerainty over at least two other tribes and the unique title of
Rex et legatus Augusti in Britannia. Other settlers in Sussex did
not submit so readily, however. The Caburn (Beddingham; E)
hill-fort was strengthened by the provision of a second massive
rampart and very broad, flat-bottomed ditch encircling the earlier
fortifications. These last minute alterations were of no avail, how-

ever; the site was sacked and the timber gate structure burnt down. Following the siege the site was abandoned.

The Roman capital for the district was established at Chichester, which must then have been occupied by Cogidumnus and his court also. Chichester, or Regnum, is the only Roman town in Sussex, the other domestic sites in the county consisting of villas (e.g. Angmering, Bignor, Fishbourne) – the provincial Roman economic unit – and the ubiquitous farmsteads. The iron ore deposits of East Sussex continued to be worked, and over a dozen Roman bloomeries have been located in the NE part of the county.

About A.D. 200 the walls of Chichester were erected, probably as a reaction against the collapse of the N frontier and invasion of northern England. From now on the story in Sussex is one of increasing unrest and pressure both on the N frontier and, later in the C3, from the increasing threat of Saxon raids. At the end of the C3 the hill-forts of Highdown Hill, Cissbury, and the Caburn, Beddingham, were re-fortified, strengthening bastions were added to the walls of Chichester, and the fort of Anderida was built at Pevensey (E), forming one of a series of powerful Saxon shore defences in South-East Britain.

The Roman practice of employing foreign mercenaries was continued into the period after the withdrawal of the legions, most notably by the British chieftain Vortigern, who employed Saxons against the Picts and Scots. These mercenaries rebelled against their employer, however, and were joined by more and more of their countrymen, who began to expand rapidly over eastern and southern England. The first entry in the Anglo-Saxon Chronicle relating to Sussex is for the year A.D. 477 and records slaughter at Cymensore, which was on the coast between Selsey and Wittering and has since been destroyed by erosion, and then even more slaughter inland at Andredsceaster (probably Anderida, i.e. Pevensey, E). With that inauspicious beginning prehistory ends and the traveller can begin to look above ground for his evidence.

Here the introduction splits in two. West Sussex follows immediately, East Sussex begins on page 42.

WEST SUSSEX

BY IAN NAIRN

To begin West Sussex with ANGLO-SAXON ARCHITECTURE is to jump off into a tricky current. There are many bits and

pieces, and few firm dates; the whole situation was complicated
by the many buildings put up in the late CII – the 'Saxo-
Norman overlap' – in which old and new styles marched side
by side. The earliest kind of building is represented best by the
foundations at Bargham which include both a W apse and N
and S 'porticus'. Whatever stood on top was almost certainly
tall and narrow, a literal reaching up to God which still moves
the visitor wherever it survives intact. Woolbeding and Lyminster keep these proportions, West Dean reflects them in a plain
doorway which is thirty-two inches wide and nine feet high.

There are more elaborate things too. The biggest is the
astonishing tower of Sompting, still with its pyramidal cap or 10a
'Rhenish helm', sturdy and rough but far from crude. The
tower arch inside has this same quality and ability to reach to
the expressive essence, reflected too in a rougher way in the
chancel arch at Botolphs. And, above all, there is the chancel
arch at Bosham, florid yet tense, the thick strips and heavy 10b
imposts speaking a completely developed architectural
language.

Bosham appears on the Bayeux Tapestry as the point from
which Harold sailed to Normandy in 1064 and brought on himself an unwelcome return visit two years later. Immediately
after the Conquest a great deal seems to have been done in
West Sussex; and the results are much less straightforward than
in most of England. Churches still keep their tall proportions
and have often survived intact without the need for later alteration: Chithurst, Selham, Stopham, Hardham, Buncton,
Stoughton. The doorways at Stopham and particularly the
grand chancel arch at Stoughton use roll-mouldings in a broad,
personal way much nearer to Bosham than to the impressive
rigour of true Early Norman buildings. The arch at Selham
has crazy capitals which seem to combine Saxon fragments with 12
much later work and can only really be explained as the work
of a clever arranger of the mid C12. Yet at the same time features
appeared which are traditionally accepted as Norman, e.g.
herringbone masonry in stone at Elsted and Chithurst, and in
re-used Roman brick at Westhampnett. And there are also a
couple of straightforward Early Norman pieces as they might
be found anywhere in the country: the chancel arch at Eartham
and the capitals at Bramber.

This last example is understandable enough; for Bramber
was one of the newly built CASTLES. Nothing is left now but
the motte, though Arundel has an CII gatehouse and the C12

shell keep as well as the earthworks, now all hedged around by the preposterous trappings of the late C19.

After a few years, NORMAN ARCHITECTURE became as standardized here as in the rest of the country. The biggest example was, of course, the new cathedral at Chichester, begun c.1090. It represents an absolute dead level of competence and impersonality with all the virtues and vices of official architecture. This can fully be seen now only in the transepts and part of the choir, for the designers who rebuilt after the fire of 1187 could not stomach this impassivity and embroidered it; but the bones remain, and set the tone for the whole cathedral, judicious and surprisingly humane. There can be good committees, too.

This style and scale was not repeated, or at least, if it was, then nothing has survived. Instead, there are innumerable 6a village churches – a majority of the old churches of West Sussex – whose bones are still the simple plan of nave and square-ended chancel. Small parishes and lack of later expansion have ensured their survival. Compared with the C11 the proportions have become less exaggeratedly tall, and one or other variety of standard Norman ornament replaces the wayward and intriguing rag-bag of the earlier buildings. Often enough there was no ornament and no moulding to the arches: Coates is a good complete example. Occasionally there is an apse also, applied to a single-cell church at North Marden, to a double-cell church in the most delightful way at Up Waltham.

Very few churches aspired to more. Wisborough Green was later rebuilt but keeps fragments to a big scale of a style hardly met with elsewhere in the county, with windows framed in a double order of unmoulded and uninterrupted arches. Shipley, 15a well up in the Weald, is a complete church of the less common type where a central tower without transepts separates nave and chancel. This was apparently built c.1125 by the Knights Templars, and they should have been *au fait* with the changes of fashion; yet Shipley still keeps the double-splayed windows which are usually regarded as a Saxon trademark.

The style gradually quickened and became more luxurious. LATE NORMAN had a splendid run in Sussex, but before that there are gradual indications of the retreat from austerity: doorways at Tortington and East Lavant, a chancel arch at Amberley, especially rich, and the tower arches at Old Shoreham, especially varied both in ornamental and figure carving. The naves of Boxgrove and New Shoreham are both of this period, say 1120–

50; both ruined and recognizable only by fragments, and both originally of high quality.

Then, around 1160, the style escaped from custody. Chevron ornament is thrust out at 90 degrees to the arches, sometimes even sprayed on top of the other mouldings (Burpham). Diamond mouldings appear on the soffits of arches (Broadwater). Zizgag enfolds complete windows (Climping) or wraps itself around a door (Arundel Castle). The best places to go are those mentioned, especially Climping, and also two churches where the style is 17a more than a matter of isolated ornamental fireworks: the nave of Steyning and the choir of New Shoreham. Here the whole 18 space is inflected by this red-blooded piling on of ornament; particularly at Shoreham and particularly in the N aisle, it is 17b done as well as anywhere in the country.

This aisle at Shoreham has pointed arches and alternate round and octagonal piers. Gothic forms were appearing even though the spirit was purely Norman. West Sussex has more of these TRANSITIONAL hybrids than most counties.* They mostly looked forward rather than back, to a new simplicity and chasteness. The biggest by far is the highly sophisticated vamping-up of Bishop Luffa's work at Chichester after the fire of 1187. 19 Purbeck marble mouldings and shafts are delicately but insistently attached to the old carcase, and the cathedral was reroofed throughout with one of the new quadripartite vaults (there is another at Sompting, see footnote). Under direct influence from Chichester are a few details in the churches around: Aldingbourne, East Dean, Yapton, Burpham. Capitals turn vegetable, first to crockets or water-leaves and then to the stiffest kind of stiff-leaf. Arches can be pointed or round almost indifferently. Vault ribs occasionally include chevron ornament on a tiny scale, almost as a nostalgic souvenir (Aldingbourne, Boxgrove). The most solid piece is the crossing tower at Box- 23a grove; and that, appropriately, has round arches in the belfry but pointed arches inside, supported on conservative scallop capitals.

Norman CHURCH FURNISHINGS should be gathered up here. There are a good many types of fonts, some of them crudely ornamented, and a few with arcaded bowls. One is made of lead (at Edburton). The wall paintings at Hardham and

---

* And also one example of a completely different 'Latest Norman' style, more like what happened in South-West France at the end of the C12. This is the remodelling of Sompting by the Templars after 1184, including an exquisitely detailed apse in the S transept.

Coombes are dealt with on page 44. Two piscinas, at Up Waltham and Bosham; one delightful reliquary of Limoges 15b enamel at Shipley, and the truly great pair of sculptured Lazarus 14 panels at Chichester – great in the country, not only the county, telling their austere story of death and resurrection with an intense sympathy for the whole of creation

EARLY GOTHIC as a style, as distinct from an intermittent 20 use of pointed arches, begins c.1200 with the retrochoir of Chichester Cathedral. With only two bays and the E wall, and under the necessity to keep the Norman proportions of arcade, gallery, and clerestory, the designer achieved a classic balance. Fluent and comfortable, speaking in an easy southern way quite different from the contorted strivings of e.g. Lincoln, he juggled expertly with the mixture of pointed and round arches, forced by the need to match the older work. It is amazingly mature, and the best proof is the way in which the later sculpture (perhaps added at the translation of St Richard in 1256) has been added without any sense of a change in style.

This balance and freedom from the need for experiment is typical of all E.E. architecture in West Sussex. It found its mode of expression straightaway and saw no need to modify or develop it. The quality was remarkably high; Chichester retrochoir was obviously something special, but the style had enough collective virtues to carry along even an indifferent designer. 21 This is well proved in the choir of Boxgrove of c.1220, where the detailed design is muddled and unsatisfactory yet the overall impression is still happy and stable.

Boxgrove was a MONASTIC church of the Benedictine order. Fragments of four Augustinian monasteries show the adaptability and unfailing elegance of this C13 style: a Buttery and Lavatorium at Shulbrede, part of the cloister at Easebourne (a nunnery), fragments of the church at Tortington, and best of all, the measured and subtle *ordonnance* of the entrance to the 23b chapter house at Hardham, which resolves perfectly the difficult job of harmonizing a central doorway with side openings.

If more than fragments remained, then C13 students might well come to the Sussex abbeys as they do to those of Yorkshire. 6b As it is, the C13 is best represented in its PARISH CHURCHES, probably the high-point of medieval architecture in the county. Starting from what might seem to be the simplest of styles, every building seems to have some new inflexion; and there are dozens of these churches, substantially unaltered. Lancet windows, austere proportions, arcades of a standard pattern

(round piers, round abaci, two orders of chamfered arches):*
very little more than that. Yet they are always combined
differently. Sometimes the church is a simple rectangle (Tangmere), sometimes cruciform and unaisled (Oving, complete but
over-restored), sometimes with big arcades (Bersted, and Yapton
which keeps its huge roof and tiny side walls no more than 5 ft
high). The bigger churches have a clerestory too (Horsham,
West Tarring, Boxgrove). Sidlesham, unexpectedly, has transepts with E aisles. The E end was given two lancets in the hum-
blest buildings (e.g. Coates or Barlavington), or more usually
three lights, diversified in all kinds of ways, with shafts around
the rere-arches (Appledram, East Preston, Pagham) or continuous mouldings (Donnington, Wisborough Green). Bosham,
already notable, has five noble lancets. Occasionally parishioners
could provide something more, like the vaulted chapel at Burpham. All of them are worth seeing, but two of these C13 churches
are exceptionally moving: Climping for the consistence and 22
purity of its design, and Up Marden for an atmosphere of un- 7
disturbed holiness which is as tangible as the most fulsome
decoration.

Naturally enough, with this inner austerity, there are not
many FITTINGS and ORNAMENTS worth mentioning. No fonts,
carving only at North Stoke (lovely), Boxgrove (discordant), and 25a
in the Bishop's Chapel at Chichester. This has the only notable
wall painting, an exquisite roundel of the Virgin and Child,
c.1250, as delicate as a water colour. Decoration in woodwork
was equally spare, either in the numerous kingpost roofs (e.g.
Yapton and Patching) or in the occasional survival of early pews
or benches (Didling and Loxwood). Climping has a chest which
permits itself a doiley pattern or two.

This style continued well into the C13, and a visitor from
Picardy might well have been puzzled by those intractable
lancets. Experiments in tracery progressed slowly, e.g. in the
chapel at Petworth, where only the openings remain. But the 42c
half-century is better summed up by the chancel of the Greyfriars church at Chichester, built between 1269 and 1282: the
side windows have twin lancets under a quatrefoil – a minimum
concession, grudgingly given. But the E window simply has five
lancets, still impressively sheer in the jaded surroundings of a
C20 public park.

It might be expected that this simplicity would find itself
opposed to the emerging style of DECORATED architecture.

* This type is called standard in the gazetteer.

And so it proved. After a century of achievement followed a
century of inertia. There was less building to be done, admittedly,
for Sussex like the rest of southern England had no equivalent
to the late medieval expansion of East Anglia and the Cots-
wolds; but this does not explain the utter lack of conviction
with which the late C13 and early C14 builders set out their
unwontedly increased elaboration.

27a   Nothing shows this better than the extended Lady Chapel of
the Cathedral, built *c*.1300. The widened openings are stamped
cheerlessly into the walls, and filled by what are in effect compositions of lancets slightly elaborated around the head. The
few Dec churches and parts of churches in West Sussex have
just this same uninspired feeling. The proportions still remain
firmly C13, whatever the windows do, whether geometrical
(Trotton, *c*.1300) or reticulated (Sutton chancel, *c*.1330) or
curvilinear (Felpham chancel, after 1345, and Rudgwick, with
a variety of window heads, including the perplexing 'Kentish
tracery' with downward-pointing cusps). But a complete rebuilding such as Ifield, Crawley, technically 'Decorated', did
little more than cusp the ends of the lancets attached to a morose
Wealden hulk. Easily the best building of these years is not
strictly a church at all: the enchanting St Mary's Hospital at
Chichester, of *c*.1290–1300, where the 'nave' housed and still
houses the almspeople and the 'chancel' – in the style of the
Lady Chapel – was the hospital chapel. Britain has a lot of
medieval monuments, but not many living medieval buildings
like this one.

FURNISHINGS, although minor, were less likely to produce
these clashes between style and temperament. There are several
curly tomb recesses, the best at Didling, and several good
effigies, beginning with the supposed Maude Countess of
Arundel † 1270, at Chichester, continuing with Bishop Langton
† 1337, also at Chichester, the sophisticated and mannered pair
26a
& b at Ifield, Crawley, *c*.1340–50, and then Bishop Stratford † 1362,
back at the cathedral.* Wooden screens start with that at St
Mary's Hospital, Chichester, still rigid and spiky and really
good. Then there is a modest set with a band of ornament across
the top – quatrefoils at Bignor, oculi at West Thorney and in
the Bishop's Palace at Chichester. The delicate iron screen to
the Lady Chapel at Chichester is also worth mentioning here.
And in the metallic vein, the mid C14 lead font at Parham is a
rarity. But small beer, all this, after the C13.

* And one big and lively early brass – to Lady Camoys † 1310, at Trotton.

DOMESTIC ARCHITECTURE in the C13 and C14 is no more exciting. Quite a few early houses survive in one form or another – at Lodsworth, Nyetimber Barton (Pagham), Cakeham (West Wittering), and Sutton, and what might be called an early bonded warehouse at Shoreham: The Marlipins. None of them is fortified, and all that remains of defensible architecture is the plain late C13 barbican at Arundel. But in the mid C14 a new threat – that of sea invasions by the French – caused the construction of two new castles at the highest navigable points of the Rother in East Sussex (Bodiam) and the Arun in West Sussex (Amberley, constructed after 1377 around an earlier house). Amberley has the regular quadrilateral plan which became standard in Britain after the Welsh castles were built in the C13, and it still looks very impressive in its placid site beside a river that will now hardly support rowing boats. 31b 31a

Amberley is technically PERPENDICULAR, that is the next development of medieval architecture. In West Sussex it must have felt more like a happy reversion to plain-speaking. There is not much Perp work in the county, but it is always honest, solid, and sensitive within its limited vocabulary. Most of it is in the Weald, which was now at last responding to large-scale cultivation, though the roads remained notoriously bad until the days of the turnpikes. At the cathedral it is represented by the cloisters,* built c.1400, unconventionally arranged around the s transept to fit in with the existing buildings – there is a lot of fitting-in at Chichester. From this Early Perp period there is Arundel, after 1380, still with a few Dec reminiscences like the quatrefoil clerestory, then the chancel of Westbourne, c.1390, with windows under segmental heads like the contemporary remodelling of Winchester Cathedral, then Kirdford and Pulborough, early C15, admirably straightforward yeoman buildings. After Amberley the most notable Early Perp secular building is the remodelling of the Bishop's Palace at Tarring,‡ then the unshowy but beautifully designed tower house of Rymans at Appledram. For the rest of the C15 there was very little church-building;§ then at the very end of the Middle Ages a few more jobs were undertaken, in a Perp whose inspiration 27b 32b

* And also by the C15 spire, now a replica, which makes a splendid show without ever asserting its own personality, and by the detached bell tower, which is all self-assertion and nothing else.

‡ The bishop of Canterbury, not Chichester. The details are near enough to Yevele's work on Canterbury Cathedral.

§ In fact, several C13 churches lost aisles in the late Middle Ages: Compton, West Thorney (2), Barlavington (2, one rebuilt), and Barnham.

had slackened yet which showed no signs of taking up Renaissance ideas, even in their most superficial form. Occasionally,
though, this C16 Perp replaced force by subtlety, as in the tower
of Angmering, rebuilt in 1507 by Syon Abbey in Middlesex.
The other jobs are the nave and tower of Westbourne, probably
again connected with Winchester, and the tower of Birdham,
34a as late as *c*.1545. Subtle also the main secular job, the Chichester
Market Cross of 1501.

Perp FITTINGS are diverse but not numerous. No fonts
worth notice; two stone pulpits, one plain (Climping) and one
34b fancy, Gothick before its time (Arundel); the stone Arundel
Screen at Chichester, of *c*.1460–70, recently re-instated; one
wooden screen worth noticing, at Burton, and quite a lot of
miscellaneous woodwork: belfry framing at Rogate, Stoughton,
and Itchingfield (this last one very like an Essex belfry, covered
with shingles instead of weatherboarding). Porches at Wisborough Green and West Grinstead. Roofs in the cathedral
cloister (very subtle wagon roof) and in two alarming village
churches, Ashurst and Findon, where the builders kept an
earlier arcade and laid timbers across it to roof the former nave
and aisle in one span. Equally alarming are the contrivances
used in the kitchens of the Bishop's Palace at Chichester to
28 cover the big square room with a timber roof and central louvre
to let out the smoke.

Sculpture is represented by two pieces only: St Genevieve
at Barnham, probably French, and the splendid Spanish Crucifix at Arundel.* But there are more MONUMENTS, including
p. 357 some good C15 brasses († 1419 at Trotton, † 1426 at Wiston,
† 1432 at Broadwater) and one of superb quality, that to Thomas
p. 200 Nelond † 1433 at Cowfold. Three-dimensional effigies come in
a variety of materials: one example in wood (C16, at Slindon),
several in stone (Burton, Horsham), and others in alabaster – at
Easebourne, and also at Arundel, where the set of Fitzalan
monuments is worth a special visit: John † 1435 for the splendid
stone cadaver underneath the conventional alabaster effigy, and
35a William † 1487 for the bewilderingly frothy canopy which any
C16 Spanish designer would have been proud to own.

In the C16, there is an odd local set of small monuments
which are in the form of a Pietà, not at all what you would
expect from Tudor England. Most of them were later defaced,
and some of them used Renaissance ornament and come in later.

* Another Spanish crucifix, from Toledo, late C15, at Lancing College
is one of the few accessible examples of old Sussex PLATE.

The best of the pure Gothic examples is at West Wittering, then Selsey † 1537 and Westhampnett c.1535. And at the other end of the religious scale, the worldly Bishop Sherbourne † 1536 is commemorated at Chichester Cathedral by a showy monument which is completely Gothic and completely soulless.

So that is the Middle Ages. Here is probably the best place to tot up the score of VERNACULAR BUILDING, whereby medieval traditions were prolonged as late as the C18. Several half-timbered cottages are clearly medieval in date too, most commonly in the Weald, such as Capon's Farm at Cowfold, and especially the astonishing survival of the Old Shop at Bignor, which is the Kentish type with overhanging first-floor wings and a recessed centre (also at Fogdens, Bury, and Sands Farm, Warnham). The best close timbering in terraces is in Church Street, Steyning, a very fine sequence, and 6–10 High Street, West Tarring (Worthing). The best farm building is the aisled barn at Sullington, perhaps dated 1685: other good groups are at Coldharbour, Wisborough Green (tile and tarred weather-boarding, like Sullington), and at Woodmansgreen Farm, Linch (tile and sandstone). The best windmill is at Shipley.   8b

To see vernacular buildings in larger groups, the best towns are Petworth (Lombard Street, especially), Horsham, and Mid- 4 hurst; the best villages, and amongst the best in the south of England, are Lurgashall, Wisborough Green, Amberley, and the group round the churchyard at Cowfold. Finally, there is a set of demure medieval bridges over the Rother near Midhurst, and one more memorable bridge of 1423 at Stopham near 33 Pulborough.

To return to the formal design, the RENAISSANCE appeared first in monuments. Sometimes it would be a tiny touch like arabesque ornament on the Pietà monuments mentioned earlier (e.g. at Clapham † 1526 and West Wittering † 1545). More often it was a boisterous mixing up of motifs on a larger scale, sometimes crude (Arundel † 1524, Burton † 1553, and Broad-water (Worthing) † 1524). Occasionally it would be more refined (Broadwater † 1554), and once it is downright delightful, in the De la Warr Chantry at Boxgrove, † 1526 and † 1532, 35b which is like a miniature building and mixes up Gothic and Renaissance details in the naughtiest and most disarming way.

There was nothing naughty about the C16 houses in West Sussex. They all belong to the TUDOR style at its most sober: that is, a simplified Gothic with window tracery reduced eventually to simple mullions and transoms, elevations largely symmetrical and becoming more and more so throughout the century, and elements such as the gatehouse, which had been a serious matter for the Middle Ages, gradually reduced to display features. The tower of *c*.1520 at the Bishop of Chichester's manor at Cakeham, near West Wittering, still means business, certainly, and its complicated pentagonal shape is still medieval. 36b But the gatehouse at Cowdray, which is the best Tudor house in the county, gives off a comfortable unmilitary air, although it could have been defended. Cowdray was built *c*.1530–40, and it alone contains a few Renaissance details, e.g. under the gatehouse. Halnaker may have had more but nothing can be seen now. Bishop Sherbourne's rooms in the Palace at Chichester, as comfy as a Pall Mall Club, are resolutely old-style.

This sobriety carries through to the end of the century, i.e. Elizabethan and Jacobean architecture, in what would in other counties be a show of cresting and bulbous cupolas. Wiston 38a *c*.1575* has shaped gables, Parham of 1577 does not even have that. Both have a simple and very effective grid of mullion-and-transom windows, both are entered symmetrically through a central porch, but this in the usual Elizabethan way leads to a passage with the hall reached from one side of it. And the style carried through into the C17, still plain, still 'Tudor' – the 38b apogee of this is Danny in East Sussex. The most that is allowed is an occasional shaped gable to a porch (Coke's House, West Burton, 1610), or tiny mannerisms like the group of manor houses around Petworth which sport brick mullions in a stone carcase (Dean House, Tillington, Tillington Manor House, Coates Manor House). Through to Ecclesden Manor, Angmering of 1634 and Blackdown of 1640 the unemphatic progression continues,‡ a remarkable proof of how self-contained the county still was; and this when it was in the middle of its 'Industrial Revolution', the time when the Weald was being cut down to provide ships' timbers and also charcoal for iron smelting: the only relics now are names on maps like Hammer Farm, occa-2b sional sleepy ponds, and very occasional early uses of iron (*see* East Sussex). The one exception to this sobriety is as late as 41 1653, the grimly accoutred Somerset Lodge at Petworth; compact and punchy, sporting its shaped gables and ball finials

---

* A three-part ornamental frontispiece at Wiston is nearer the traditional conception of Elizabethan architecture. But it is brought in, and the original source is unknown.

‡ Echoed of course in all the smaller stone houses, like Langhurst Farm at Balls Cross, Kirdford. Half timber was no more exuberant.

with self-confidence. With its dark stone it could fit easily into the West Riding or Northumberland.

Nor did the new brick style of 'Artisan Mannerism' have much more luck. Imported from Holland via London, it travelled extensively in Surrey and then seems to have got bogged down in the Weald. s of the Downs there is only the really handsome Barnham Court, *c*.1640, which with its pilasters, 39b window surrounds, and shaped gables is very like Kew Palace in Surrey.* One staircase is worth mentioning here also, at Lordington, Racton, which has carved panels containing strapwork and swags instead of the more usual banisters.

That takes us up to 1660 with houses. There is no more enterprise in C16 CHURCH ARCHITECTURE, though that might have been expected. What jobs needed to be done were done in a minimum Gothic. As in most counties, there is more than you might expect at first: after all, buildings continued to fall down whatever the King and Pope did. South Harting was repaired *c*.1576, with quite personable ornamented roofs that are recognizably Elizabethan. Steyning got a w tower about the same time. Egdean was rebuilt in 1622 and is terribly spoilt, Milland Old Church must be about the same date and is now on its last legs – a real tragedy, this. Burton was repaired in 1636 and assertively royalist Royal Arms provided at the same time. Church towers continued to be more or less Gothic until well after the Restoration – Stedham, 1673, and Woolbeding as late as 1728.

CHURCH FITTINGS have more to show, but not much more. In many ways Sussex went doggo from 1500 to 1800. The Bishops of Chichester employed *Lambert Bernard* to paint deplorable large panels of Kings and Bishops, now in the transepts of the cathedral; and also, much more happily, to decorate the vaults with jolly trails of heraldry and foliage. Only one bay of the Lady Chapel remains; but the similar sequence at Boxgrove is nearly complete, and a very attractive Spenserian 21 dream-world it makes. There is some C16 glass, made in foreign lands and brought in from foreign places at Woolbeding and Pagham. The Flemish glass at Stopham of *c*.1600, signed by *Roelant*, may just possibly have been made for the church, and if so would be quite a rarity. Only one pulpit is worth recording, which is an extraordinary dearth – at Botolphs, *c*.1630. And monuments can provide nothing more than standard work at

* Continued after the Restoration at South Mundham (1671) and Shipley (1683).

Shipley † 1616, and a dismembered example at Easebourne † 1592 by *Richard Stevens*, which might have been impressive originally (cf. Titchfield, Hants).

The 'new style', that is Inigo Jones's style, of stricter classicism and simpler, smoother design, came into Sussex first with MONUMENTS.* One very severe tablet at Arundel † 1633, and a monument by *Edward Marshall* at Horsham † 1654, up to his standard of competent unimaginativeness, sum it up. Back in domestic architecture, this new style, apart from isolated buildings by Jones and his friends, gradually became assimilated into a tide of simplicity and straightforwardness whose apogee was Wren. Inigo's inspiration was Italian; this broadening and loosening of his ideas came from Holland: comfortable burgher, not Capulet-and-Montagu. With two exceptions, it came into the county at the lower levels, that is through fashion-conscious masons. This can be tracked down at Blackdown (Upper Roundhurst House), at Donnington (Church Farm, 1677), and at Field Place (1678). It is impossible to miss at Westgate House, Chichester (1696), heavily handsome with its heavy cornice and window openings filled with mullion-and-transom crosses. The attribution to Wren would have surprised him more than it does us. Pallant House at Chichester, *c*.1712, also has a Wren myth attached to it and in fact applies the same simple-mindedness to the next generation of classical detail.

The exceptions are Petworth and Uppark. The enigmatic
43b Petworth, which was built in 1688–96, puzzled Horace Walpole and has puzzled people ever since. The key, perhaps, is the missing central dome. With it, the long low front and the crimped patrician vertical strips of windows linked by ornament begin to make sense. The designer is unknown; but there is a clear connexion‡ between it and Drayton House, Northants. So it was probably designed by *William Talman* or one of his associates. It still feels as strange as one of Purcell's excursions into the minor keys, touched not with anachronism but with a quintessential remote tension. It is only a matter of time before psychiatrists begin to analyse it. Locally, it set off a mason's style: at Treyford, Midhurst (Spread Eagle), both *c*.1700, and Lodsworth Dower House, 1728. Uppark of *c*.1690 is also con-
43a nected with *Talman*, though here the style is much more conventional – basically a Wren box with a little more stone

* And a good, mannered STATUE of Charles I on the Market Hall at Chichester.

‡ As Mr John Harris was not slow to point out to me.

trim than Wren would have given it. It is not really a success
as a design, and its remarkable atmosphere is due to the lonely
and lovely site, and the completeness of its c18 fittings.

The inside of Petworth is nobody's problem. Maladjustment
would be a word that *Grinling Gibbons* would not have understood. His lime-wood miracles spray over the Carved Room – 42a
and are trumped in the rest of the house by the estate carpenter,
John Selden: not in technique but in creative expressiveness.
In the chapel, especially, his understanding of children has 42c
transformed what might have been conventional cherubs' heads
into universal types of behaviour. With its sham theatre curtain
around the w gallery, it is one of the most attractive of Baroque
re-fittings.

Otherwise, CHURCH REFITTING after 1660 was confined to
a pair of fonts – dull at North Chapel (1662), and alarming at
Lurgashall (1661), covered in rustication like a liturgical arma-
dillo. But the NONCONFORMISTS were beginning to come in,
with chapels that looked as much like cottages as possible: the
Quakers at Ifield (Crawley; 1676), Horsham, and with overpowering simplicity and dignity at Blue Idol near Coolham; the
Unitarians in the c18 with churches at Billingshurst and Horsham. But in Anglican terms the c18 was a comfortable snooze,
broken by no more than the decent humble fittings at Warminghurst, a pulpit at Kingston Buci, and a Queen Anne 'tympanum',
or piece of plaster stage-scenery where the chancel arch should
be, at Racton.

The Baroque and c18 expressed itself a little more fully in
STATUES and MONUMENTS. At Chichester, Bishop Grove
† 1696 is commemorated with a cheerfully extrovert bust and
surrounding cherubs, and there are good carved cartouches at
Lurgashall, Warminghurst, and Chichester again (Mrs Miller
† 1701). For statues there are pieces at Christ's Hospital brought
from their original site in Newgate Street, London, and one
almost unknown and anonymous* masterpiece – the haunting,
swirling bust of William III on the side of Petworth Town 45a
Hall.

The change to a colder, more classical style for monuments
came early in Sussex. That to Sir William Morley at Boxgrove,
erected in 1728, has already a handsome but cold-hearted urn.
When feeling was added to this strictness the results could be
lovely: the busts of Susan Cook, undated, at Goring and Sir

---

* Dr Whinney suggests *Honoré Pelle*, the sculptor of a gorgeous bust of
Charles II now in the Victoria and Albert Museum.

Charles Nicoll † 1733 at Racton. Both are unsigned. Sir Charles
has what one would describe as a Rysbrack bust, and in fact is
much better than the only actual *Rysbrack* monument in West
Sussex – at West Grinstead † 1746. After 1750 sentiment crept
into monumental art, fresh at first, slowly to decline into stale
sentimentality. The true freshness is beautifully illustrated by
Mary Countess of Derby † 1752 at Boxgrove, with an (unsigned)
relief worthy of van Gelder. After this there is one more good
humanitarian bust at West Grinstead † 1787, and then the steep
and slippery slope. *Nollekens* at Westbourne; *Flaxman* at Petworth, Chichester, Eartham, and West Grinstead;* *Chantrey*
well after the turn of the century at Easebourne – a long catalogue of talent without any urgency or creative necessity. At the
end, in the mid C19, there is the conscientious lifelessness of
Carew, mostly at Petworth. Amongst all this, there are one or two
better things: a decent bust by *Joseph Towne* at Chichester
(Bishop Otter † 1844), a delightful pair of busts at Donnington,
c.1840, and the English rarity of a tablet by *Thorwaldsen* († 1814,
in Slindon R.C. church).

   The equivalent in architecture of this new austerity was the
PALLADIAN style. It also appeared very early in West Sussex,
mainly through the various works carried out by *Roger Morris*
for the Duke of Richmond. *Lord Burlington* himself is credited
with Fox Hall, Charlton, of 1730, with a circumstantial first-
floor room. *Morris*, with much more application than talent, did
the Council House at Chichester, 1731–3, and Carne's Seat at
Goodwood of 1743. The style caught on immediately, and the
earlier part of Shillinglee, built by the local man *Thomas Steel
Jun.* in 1735, has no backward glances at the Baroque – unlike
comparable work in e.g. Yorkshire or Bristol. Midhurst, Petworth, and Chichester are the best places to pick up the equivalent idiom in town houses.

   Gradually, through the C18, the details became more polished;
Shillinglee is a good place to check the difference, by comparing
the additions of 1776 with the original work of 1735. Big names
are absent, except for the grandly aloof and understated stables
at Goodwood, built in 1757–63 and designed by *Sir William
Chambers*. The style continued even more attenuated, into the
1790s, at Findon and East Lavington.

   Inside, this was reflected in decoration which started in a
pretty Rococo vein and slowly turned to copy Adam's filigree

* Most of his early work was done in Sussex, and several tablets show
the influence of his friend, William Blake.

games with neo-Etruscan ornament. Uppark has rooms in both styles, possibly by *Paine*, *c.*1760. Chichester has the staircase of the Ship Hotel, unexpectedly rich for the plain exterior. But there is really not much to see.

The next stage is better provided for. About 1780 a group of architects decided that the existing styles needed a shot of robustness and found it by going back again to Roman proto-types and beyond them to Greece. The result was the NEO-CLASSICAL style, which rapidly became the Greek Revival. The biggest example was *Wyatt*'s Goodwood of *c.*1795, but Goodwood is incomplete and unsatisfactory. A better example is the s front of Castle Goring by the local man *Biagio Rebecca,* 47 *c.*1790. Castle Goring is far better inside, too, with such up-to-date touches as fluted Greek Doric columns supporting the vestibule on the ground floor. And a small but splendid example is the vestibule of the Bishop's Palace at Chichester, *c.*1800, which might be by *Wyatt* also.

Castle Goring's real claim to fame is not its neo-classical detailing, but the fact that the N front, designed by the same 46 man at the same time, is determinedly GOTHICK.* *Rebecca*'s split mind extended as far as designing a corridor which was Gothick at one end and classical at the other. But Gothick of course had been used by designers for half a century before, as a relief from the mandatory classical style. Most of the early attempts were connected with landscape ornaments in country gentlemen's parks, all of which were more or less FOLLIES.‡ Hence there is the Grotto at Goodwood (*c.*1740), the Vandalian Tower at Uppark (1774, by *Henry Keene*), the very jolly Racton Tower (1772, by another *Keene*), the surprisingly scholarly tower at Arundel by *Hiorn*. Follies could be classical, too, and Petworth has a complete set. It also has the best landscaped park in the county, a lovely example in *Capability Brown*'s serpentine style.

So by 1800 Gothic and several varieties of classicism were thought to be equally valid styles. The disintegration began here, not with the Victorians. Houses could be Greek – Burton Park, 1831 by *Henry Bassett*, with a splendid and heartless earlier staircase of *c.*1800 brought in, and *Smirke*'s much duller Walberton of 1803. Corn Exchanges could be very Greek indeed, like the example in Chichester done by the local architect

---

* Castle Ward, in Ulster, does the same thing.
‡ Occasional appearances in houses (Wiston, North Street, Chichester) and in one very humble church, St Pancras at Chichester, of 1750.

Elliott in 1832. But much more often, in Sussex, the new houses were Gothick. There is a whole crop, ranging from the genuinely ingenious stage-scenery of *Nash* himself (West Grinstead, *c*.1806, worth keeping as a ruin, and Knepp Castle, 1809) to lesser men like *P. F. Robinson* (Coolhurst, 1833, and perhaps Warnham Court, 1828) and *Francis Edwards* (Holmbush, 1823), and then to inanities like Hayley's own house at Felpham which is called The Turret and looks it.

CHURCHES were equally susceptible to fashionable whim. After a long gap through the C18 they began to appear again in West Sussex. Selecting *à la carte*, you could dress your house of God in modest classical (St Bartholomew, Chichester, 1832), slightly Soanic (St John, Chichester, 1812–13 by *Elmes Sen.*, which has preserved an extraordinary and complete low church interior), or fighting Greek (St Paul, Worthing, 1812 by *Rebecca*). If your religion wore a pointed hat you could choose plain (Sennicotts, 1829) or fancy (Stansted Chapel, a delightful comfit, 1812–15). If a skyline inflection was needed, what better than a Scots Crown or openwork spire – and there it is at Tillington, 1807, peering over into the Petworth landscape. Nature has confounded the landscape gardener, here, by growing its rude trees too high: but it remains a pretty idea.

Worthing was a new church, and it was part of what was for Sussex a much more important process than the languid selection of styles. This was the first stage of SEASIDE DEVELOPMENT: and for this West Sussex has always been secondary to the glories of Brighton. It was not all imitation; an ambitious entrepreneur began to set out Hothampton in quite a grand way with The Dome and Spencer Terrace in 1787. It never really came to anything, possibly because he built a little back from the sea front, refusing to look the briny in the face, and the other developments at what became first Bognor and then Regis were later and further west. A pair of names tells a lot: Waterloo Place and Steyne (in imitation of Brighton). Littlehampton made one attempt in *c*.1800 (South Terrace) which for fifty years must have been out in the country; Worthing went about things in a more regular way so that a complete small town was in being by 1830. The ubiquitous *A. H. Wilds* built Park Crescent in 1829, a heavily classical crescent with not one but two Swiss Cottages attached; the unknown *Henry Cotton* provided Liverpool Terrace in the same years, an impressively grouped design with plenty of sheer stucco which is the only thing in West Sussex up to the Brighton level. The rest of the Sussex coast was still a bleak windswept collection of fishermen's cottages, more like Aldeburgh than the comfy mellowness it has today. This can still be felt at New Shoreham, and in the single precious gap of countryside between Selsey and Brighton, at Climping.

The Victorians carried on the spirit of these seaside enterprises but dropped any pretensions to elegance. But in VICTORIAN CHURCHES the pretensions mounted steadily. At first, the Gothic Revival was simply a skimpy dress given to the provision of the greatest area of pews under a wide roof. The most typical example is Christchurch, Worthing (*John Elliott*, 1841); and a national figure like *Decimus Burton* could do no better at Goring in 1838. When self-respect seeped in, it took a sensible and sensitive form, free from Pugin's hysteria. New churches were common-sense buildings in local Gothic style and most restorations were common-sense too. Men like *Butler* of Chichester must have saved dozens of village churches, and are rewarded with obscurity, whilst the self-important meddlers are well known. The national architect who expressed this attitude best was *R. C. Carpenter*, and some of his best buildings are in Sussex. If he had not died in mid-career (at only forty-three, in 1855), the whole course of the Gothic Revival might have been different. His is the discriminating church of St Peter, opposite the cathedral, of 1850. His also are the original buildings of Lancing College* (designed in 1848) built for Nathaniel 54b Woodard as one of a set of Anglican public schools. The others – Hurstpierpoint and Ardingly – are in East Sussex. Lancing is remembered mostly for its melodramatic chapel, built from 54a 1868 by *Carpenter*'s son. It is splendid at a distance, but close to the detail has none of the mature restraint and true originality of the rest. Otherwise there is very little in West Sussex: one good church by *Butterfield* (West Lavington, 1850, with an 57a impressive rectory) and one good church by *Ferrey* (Slinfold, 1861). Later on, there is the *tour de force* of the R. C. church at Arundel, by *Hansom*, 1868 – like Lancing, it is best seen at a distance – and the extraordinary and insensitive buildings provided for the Carthusians at St Hugh's Monastery (Parkminster) by *Monsieur Norman* of Calais in 1875–83. Of Victorian FITTINGS no more need be mentioned than the glass at Arundel R. C. church by *Hardman* and at Horsham by *Heaton*; one monument in Chichester Cathedral (by *Sir Gilbert Scott*, to

---

* *Butler* began Bishop Otter College at Chichester in the next year.

Dean Hook † 1875, very rich and dignified); and – stretching
the category a bit – *Woolner*'s sentimental but pretty statue in
the quad at Christ's Hospital, of 1875.

DOMESTIC ARCHITECTURE is equally uneventful. The hard,
confident style of the mid-century is perfectly represented by
P. C. Hardwick's Sompting Abbots and also, much later, by the
truly horrifying remodelling of Arundel Castle by *C. A. Buckler*,
who created nearly all of what oppresses today's visitor so heavily.
Then a more thoughtful, less crass style set in, which began as
neo-Tudor and ended as neo-Queen Anne. The leader here
was *Norman Shaw*, and he has three jobs in West Sussex:
Wispers, 1876, heavy and hearty, and two small, more sensitive
commissions – at Rustington, 1879, and the additions to
Adsdean, Funtington, 1877. Other architects imitated *Shaw*
very quickly; *Salvin* decently at Fernhurst (1878) and *E. C. Lee*
delightfully in the cottages on St Ann's Hill, Midhurst.

One building and one object take one into the c20. The
building is West Sussex's only memorable railway station, at
61a Christ's Hospital (1899), which is quite untouched and a perfect
anthology of railway forms. The object is a terrifyingly curly
56 lampstandard in the road opposite Petworth church. The
designer turns out to be *Sir Charles Barry*, of all people, and
heaven knows what he had in mind. It looks as though he were
trying to hack his way single-handed into an Art Nouveau style.

Art Nouveau itself passed the county by. In the early
TWENTIETH CENTURY, the worthwhile buildings were mostly
in one variety or other of FREE TUDOR. Gabled, adaptable,
comfy, and cosy, as mellow as the West Sussex scenery, which
must have been at its best in the years just before 1914: only
the great red elephant of Christ's Hospital, by *Aston Webb*, 1893
onwards, strikes a discordant note. Sometimes the transcriptions
were literal: Clock House, Cowfold, 1913 by Unwin's partner
Barry Parker, or The Slip, Bosham, by *Imrie & Angell*, of the
same year. Sometimes there was more originality; the personal
60b mannerism of *Lutyens*'s only house in the county – Little
Thakeham, 1902, with its dramatic Vanbrugh-like interior.
There is less personal and in the end more worthwhile originality in the young *Charles Holden*'s King Edward VII Sanatorium
near Midhurst, begun in 1903, which was really breaking
through to a new style – the true modern architecture which
we are still fumbling for sixty years afterwards.

The immediate future was with the classicists, now headed
by that ingenuous renegade Sir Edwin. Before NEO-GEORGIAN

settled down into plain stodge* it put up a dashing convalescent
home at Rustington and also some dashing Westminster Banks,
e.g. at Horsham and Petworth, all by a local man, *Frederick
Wheeler*, and a sober, dignified house (Ivorys, Cowfold) by the
Yorkshire architect *Walter Brierley*. Meanwhile, neo-Tudor
bowed out with some mad farm buildings at Wappingthorn
near Steyning by *Maxwell Ayrton*, and finally and gloriously
with the astonishing mirage of Bailiffscourt, immaculately C15 62a
in its honey-coloured stone, surrounded by genuine transplanted
buildings. Dornford Yates, if you like; but done with panache
and sensitivity.

Bailiffscourt dates from 1935, designed by *Amyas Phillips*. By
then many other things had sprayed on to the Sussex coastline.
Among them were the first examples of MODERN ARCHITEC-
TURE: weird boxes, undigested essays in cubism, their concrete
blotched and stained now. A true, responsible modernity only
started after the war with bungalows by *Powell & Moya* in
Chichester, schools at Bognor (County Council) and Worthing
(Ministry of Education), many good houses, e.g. at South
Harting and Slindon, and of course at Crawley New Town.
There, where the new and old shopping centres dovetail per-
fectly, there is a good deal of unnecessary dullness but also many
felicitous touches and very many trees – Crawley is the leafiest
of the New Towns. And few counties could finish a survey of
buildings with one as original and as finely detailed as *Powell &
Moya*'s Festival Theatre in Chichester (1961).

West Sussex is lucky, in many ways. It is prosperous and
sophisticated enough to commission good new buildings, and
to hang on to most of its good old buildings. Yet it is far enough
from London to avoid being swamped, as Surrey is. The coastline is gone, but it was a lost cause before the war; the rest has
changed surprisingly little in twenty-five years of unprecedented
expansion in the South-East. Here, you get a glimpse of how a
new C20 pattern could emerge: fully motorized, fully affluent,
yet aware of the need to keep countryside green, suburbs leafy,
and towns compact. It may not come about, but at least the
possibility is there: and that, in Britain, is something to shout
about. God bless the sensitive stockbrokers of West Sussex.

* Slightly fancy stodge is the County Hall at Chichester, by *C. G. Stillman*, 1936. But the siting, screened from Westgate, is brilliant.

EAST SUSSEX

BY NIKOLAUS PEVSNER

East Sussex in the last hundred and especially the last fifty
years has changed its character entirely. Today the Weald is –
except for some precious enclaves – commuters' country. The
trees have survived, but one can rarely get away from the well-
to-do habitation. In some parts generous private grounds follow
generous private grounds, in others ample gardens follow ample
gardens. Wherever there is a suitable railway station, cars wait
during the day in the large parking places for their masters
returning at six or seven in their town clothes. At the same
time fast trains have opened up the seaside places to Londoners
63 – Brighton, Hastings, and the others – and there it is the blocks
of flats which betray their presence and their readiness to pay
high prices for cramped living conditions.

Brighton was a very small town when its seaside development started, but Hastings was one of the Cinque Towns and
became (later) the premier town of the five. It is the only one
of the five in Sussex (the others – New Romney, Hythe, Dover,
Sandwich – are in Kent), but Winchelsea and Rye were soon
recognized as members and Pevensey and Seaford at least as
non-corporate members. The importance of these ports lay
in their proximity to the Continent, with its commercial peacetime and its naval war-time consequences. The towns had to
supply, furnish, and man ships and they also ran the herring
fishery off the Norfolk coast. It culminated in the C13 and C14
and declined from the C15. In 1444 the Five Towns did full
service for the last time. The end came in the C16 and C17 for
all except Hastings with the silting-up of the river mouths. So
one will look to these towns for castles, walls, and prominent
buildings of the High Middle Ages. In fact East Sussex is
altogether poor in prominent buildings of before the C12.

Of ANGLO-SAXON ARCHITECTURE the only example any
national survey would have to include is Worth, with its grand
11b proportions, powerful details, its two-light nave windows, its
transepts and its apse. Worth is C11, and so is the equally
powerful chancel arch of Clayton. Bishopstone of the C10 has
its s *porticus* preserved and has long-and-short quoins, as has
Arlington too. Arlington as well as Jevington near by used
Roman tiles for what they thought would make window voussoirs.
The tower at Jevington has the familiar turned baluster shafts
for the bell-openings. There is at Jevington also a very good

relief of Christ wearing only a loin-cloth and standing amid
interlace of the wild Urnes type. The only other piece of
sculpture worth recording is a coped coffin-slab with interlace
decoration at Bexhill. Add to this the re-set doorway at St John-
under-the-Castle at Lewes and the interesting inscription there
to an anchorite Mangnus of royal Danish blood, and the survey
is concluded.

Of EARLY NORMAN WORK there is much more, but nearly
all of it is minor. The only nationally significant building is the
keep of Pevensey Castle, built about 1100, a keep entirely 9
different from the standard types which the Normans had
brought from France, i.e. the tower keep and the hall keep,
both rectangular, with thick walls and shallow buttresses.
Pevensey instead added to its rectangular interior enormous
spurs or buttresses reaching out some 30 ft beyond the walls
and being over 20 ft thick without any hollowing out. They are
set in various directions with no principle apparently guiding
them. The builders must have believed that thickness of
masonry is all. At Lewes Castle also there are Early Norman
remains, especially the inner gateway and the shell keep, and at
Hastings Castle some walling and some of the collegiate church
which formed part of it are Early Norman. It must have been a
strange building, as the Norman builders gradually developed
it, apparently with a cloister walk along the s side and a w
narthex with one, if not two, flanking towers, not really belonging
to any of the known Norman church-planning schemes.

Most of the NORMAN CHURCHES of which we have evidence,
and there are plenty, were of the simplest kind, usually just a
nave and a chancel, or occasionally a central tower between
them, or – rarer still – transepts as well. In addition there are
Norman w towers and Norman aisles. Only few comments are
needed. Apses were never as usual in England as in France.
But in Sussex, as in Kent, both being near France, they do
occur, as one did already at Worth (Newhaven, Keymer). At
Westham, i.e. probably in what was the church of the Hospital
of St Cross outside Pevensey Castle, there was not only one main
apse, but there were transepts as well with their apsed E chapels.
Rye church, being from the start on a monumental scale, had
both proper transepts and aisles. Other transepts were lower
than nave and chancel, i.e. still reminiscent of Saxon *porticus* or
at least of Worth. This is the case at Horsted Keynes and
Pevensey. At Bishopstone we have the interesting case of various
Norman additions to the Saxon church, at Icklesham an un-

commonly complete sequence of Early to Late Norman events.
Among W towers three are round, i.e. of the East Anglian rather
than South-East English type. They are Piddinghoe, Southease,
and St Michael at Lewes.

Lewes of course in the Middle Ages possessed one of the
grandest Norman buildings of East Sussex, its priory, the earliest
Cluniac house in England – one of the two grandest, I should
have said, the other being Battle Abbey. But in both cases
nothing Norman survives *in situ* which can conjure up the past
majesty. The plans are known from excavations. Otherwise at
Lewes there are only crags of masonry and a number of splendid
13b capitals in the Lewes Museum and the British Museum, whereas
at Battle there is much more, but of a later date. Norman Lewes
had two sets of transepts like the new abbey at Cluny itself, going
up at the very same moment. Norman Battle had an ambulatory
and radiating chapels like the majority of the great French Romanesque churches. In the church of Southover at Lewes which
was probably the *hospitium* by the gatehouse to the priory is the
11c beautiful black marble tombstone or memorial stone to Gundrada, wife of the founder, with its symmetrical foliage decoration.* Otherwise little of NORMAN SCULPTURE is preserved:
a slab with St Michael at Seaford of the same date as, and in a
style similar to, that of the Chichester reliefs, and the font of
13a St Nicholas, Brighton, a drum-shaped piece with excellent,
highly disciplined representations of the Last Supper, the
Baptism of Christ, and scenes from the life of St Nicholas. St
Nicholas at Brighton depended on Lewes Priory, and such a
dependence has also been made responsible for the exceptionally
high standard of NORMAN WALL PAINTING in Sussex. The
p. principal places, Hardham in West Sussex and Clayton in East
473 Sussex, did indeed belong to Lewes, but other places with wall
paintings of the same style did not, and the style is not really
specially Cluniac. What parallels have been adduced are more
with St Savin in Poitou and with Sicilian mosaics than with
French Cluniac illumination. The group dates from *c.*1125
(Hardham) to *c.*1150 and is characterized by long, gaunt,
extremely small-headed figures, strange headgear, and odd
architectural walls round scenes, like play-pens seen from above.
At Hardham all the walls of nave and chancel are covered, at
Clayton nearly so. Minor work in East Sussex is at Plumpton,
and more existed at Slaugham and Westmeston, but it has

11a   * A good somewhat later Norman coffin-lid, small, with fine representations of the cross, the lamb, and two birds is at Bishopstone.

perished. Of other Norman work inside churches only FONTS need a word. They are frequent, as they are all over England, perhaps because there was no reason for replacing them once they had been installed. That at Brighton already mentioned is easily the best. The next in quality is the lead font at Pyecombe, not as crisp as some others of lead, but delicately and competently composed all the same. Competently composed also is the stone font of St Anne, Lewes, though nothing special as ornamental invention. It was copied at Denton and Eastdean. The so-called Purbeck fonts, so called although in Sussex they are (or may be) often of Sussex marble, on the other hand, are minimum as far as invention goes: square, on five supports, and with, as their decoration, just very shallow, entirely un-moulded arcading. Only occasionally do other motifs come in – an elongated fish e.g. at Slaugham.

The greatest era of parish church building in East Sussex is from LATE NORMAN to EARLY ENGLISH, i.e. from c.1170 to the early C13. Churches during that time received aisles if they had not had any or replaced aisles only recently built. They also expanded otherwise, e.g. by chancel chapels. The signs of the transition are many, and they do not all run strictly parallel. In fact very often more advanced and more conservative details will be found side by side. The signs are these: arches pointed and no longer rounded, arch mouldings with slight chamfers and no longer plain steps or thick rolls, and then with proper standard chamfers, stop chamfers along the edges of square piers, round piers with round abaci, and capitals turning from multi-scalloped to single flat, stylized, upright leaves (e.g. Herstmonceux N, Bexhill), rarely in East Sussex to waterleaf, and then to crockets and to stiff-leaf in its earliest form, i.e. with one row of small, not-much-overlapping leaves at the top of the bell and the rest of the bell left uncovered (Eastbourne, Seaford, Herstmonceux, etc.). At Beddingham, St Anne Lewes, 13c and Rodmell the capitals have stiff-leaf corbels or head corbels to support them, an unusual and pretty motif. At Seaford one capital, instead of foliage, has lively religious scenes with tiny figures. The chancel of Hellingly is an excellent, much shafted piece of these same years, i.e. c.1200.

When the EARLY ENGLISH STYLE settles down, the standard details of the arcades are round piers or octagonal piers and normally double-chamfered arches. With octagonal piers, this standard remains that of Dec and Perp, and dating is as a rule hard. There is plenty of enjoyable E.E. work in East

Sussex, chancels especially, which were now often lengthened or rebuilt, but little that must be singled out, indeed hardly more than the work at Bayham Abbey and Battle Abbey. Bayham is not only impressive but also instructive, in so far as the church was built c.1210 etc. and enlarged c.1260–70 and as the older parts were not pulled down for the enlargement. The case is similar to that at Canterbury Cathedral between c.1070 etc. and c.1100 etc. So one can at Bayham compare the plainly moulded capitals of the early with the rich mature stiff-leaf capitals of the later C13. The polygonal apse at Bayham is a great exception at its date in England and must be of French derivation. At Battle the most prominent remaining part is the dormitory range with its vaulted undercroft and its beautiful 24 group of lancet windows in the end wall, and the W wall of refectory and cloister with bar tracery of a kind made normal in England by Westminster Abbey in 1245 to c.1260.

Battle Abbey, to look now to its MONASTIC ASPECTS, was Benedictine, i.e. belonged to the oldest of Western orders. It was founded by William the Conqueror to commemorate the battle of Hastings and the place where Harold had fallen. The church was consecrated in 1094. Minor Norman fragments remain to the l. and r. of the later gatehouse. Of the C13 are the extended E end of the church, the undercroft of whose polygonal radiating chapels has been exposed by the excavators, parts of the abbot's quarters, later much added to and especially the chapel, and the amazing undercroft of the guest-house with its eight tunnel-vaulted compartments en enfilade. The only other Benedictine house of which fragments survive is Wilmington, a cell of Grestain in Normandy which never got so far as a church of its own or any claustral arrangement of its buildings. They belong to the C13 and C14. Lewes Priory, we have seen, was Cluniac, that is of the first reformed Benedictine order. The remains comprise the SE corner of the refectory, still with herring-bone masonry, the undercroft of the dormitory, traces of the reredorter and the infirmary chapel, and a fragment of the SW tower of the church. The guest-house is now Southover church. At Langney outside Eastbourne is the C14 or C15 chapel of a grange of Lewes. The Augustinian Canons had Michelham Priory, founded in 1229, where, apart from a later gatehouse, there are C13 remains of the refectory and the W range, partly C13, partly C15. Warbleton was Augustinian too, transferred here from Hastings in 1413. Little of it is visible. The only house of the Cistercians in Sussex, the next reformed order after the Cluniacs, is Robertsbridge, founded in 1176. Of the mid C13 abbot's house the undercroft and part of the large W window of the hall can still be seen, and fragments of the refectory, the warming room, and the dormitory undercroft. Bayham was Premonstratensian, and the Premonstratensians being the order of canons created to follow the reforms of the Cistercians, the explanation of the polygonal apse of its later C13 extensions is probably such French Cistercian houses as Obazine and Fontfroide. Of the living quarters the most prominent frag-ment is the chapter house. There are also parts of the vaulting beneath the former refectory and in the range W of the cloisters, and there is the gatehouse, interfered with in the C18 to make it a picturesque object. At Otham, near Polegate, which was a grange of Bayham, the chapel with pretty early C14 windows is preserved. So, to round off this survey of the work of the orders, even if it takes us beyond the C13, here is what existed or exists of the FRIARS. They represent the last reform of monas-ticism before the Reformation and were a creation of the early C13. They settled in towns, not in the countryside, and so houses of friars were established at Winchelsea (Franciscans, Dominicans), Lewes (Franciscans), and Rye (Austin Friars, Friars of the Sack).* Architectural remains are the polygonal chancel of the Greyfriars, i.e. the Franciscans, at Winchelsea of c.1310–20, the chapel of the Austin Friars at Rye, early C14 in style though probably of after 1378, a doorway of the Greyfriars at Winchelsea and one of the Greyfriars at Lewes, and an un-determined building of the Friars of the Sack by the church at Rye.‡

After this detour we must return to the E.E. style and note what little has to be noted of C13 CHURCH DECORATION AND FURNISHINGS. It is very little indeed: Wall Paintings at Patcham (Brighton) of c.1230 and at Rotherfield of c.1300, the one much restored and hence readable, the other quite well preserved, a splendid late C13 Chest at Buxted, and nothing else. Nor is the harvest spectacular if we anticipate and take in every-thing to the end of the Middle Ages. What is there that qualifies for this survey? Of Wall Painting only the work at Preston (Brighton), a little later than Rotherfield, of Stained Glass the

* Apart from the Dominicans and Franciscans at Chichester and the Carmelites at Sele and Shoreham, all in West Sussex.

‡ Medieval hospitals of which traces remain are at Westham, i.e. probably the Hospital of the Holy Cross at Pevensey, to whose plan reference has already been made, and at Winchelsea, where one wall stands of the Holy Cross Hospital.

delightfully drawn birds of *c*.1400 at Salehurst, of Fonts nothing, of Metalwork some Patens of *c*.1500 with the Vernicle engraved (e.g. Southease), of Woodwork some C14, i.e. Dec, Screens (Rodmell, Playden, two at Eastbourne, Penhurst) apart from many later ones of no special interest,* the Stalls at Etchingham, late C14 with Misericords, the Pulpit at Rye with linenfold panelling, i.e. end of the Middle Ages, and three Font Covers of the polygonal kind with doors that open. One of them, at Sedlescombe, has linenfold panels too, the second, at Ticehurst, has quite splendid Flamboyant tracery, of the Late Gothic French or Flemish rather than the Dec kind. The third, at Rotherfield, dates from 1533, and its panels have Early Renaissance motifs. But that is really anticipating too far; for we have left the survey of churches before the year 1300.

Of churches in the DECORATED style East Sussex has only one of the first order, New Winchelsea, built, by the king no doubt, as part of the splendidly conceived new town. Only the chancel remains, partly on a rib-vaulted crypt, and its aisles, and the lower parts of the transepts. The scale of the chancel is cathedral-like, the date must be about 1290–1310. The architectural details are pre-ogee, but have as an equally enterprising motif Kentish (i.e. barbed) tracery instead and an extreme exuberance of cusping. Inside, on the other hand, the ogee comes in, and in the Sedilia and Piscina of the S aisle and the five MONUMENTS displays all the glories it was capable of. The small figural sculpture too around the monuments, including a crouching figure as an image bracket, is of the very best. So are the foliage and the lavish diapering.

p. 632

There is nothing of much splendour in later C14 and PERPENDICULAR churches in East Sussex. The two old parish churches of Hastings are Perp, one of after the French raid of 1377, the other of shortly before 1436, and uneventful. St Nicholas Brighton of the C14 is restored out of existence and can never have been up to much. The most interesting and indeed very dignified later C14 churches are a group of three, cruciform as though they were much earlier and carrying on the dignity of that earlier conception. They are Etchingham, begun before 1369 and in its details still entirely Dec (*see* e.g. the flowing tracery of the five-light E window),‡ Alfriston where

---

* But Fletching has six-light divisions, which is unusual.

‡ Another instance of the long survival of flowing tracery is the Austin Friars at Rye, to which reference has already been made. They moved to their present site only in 1378.

purely Dec and purely Perp windows are standing side by side, and Poynings where nearly all is Perp. At Etchingham the monument to the founder survives, who died in 1389. The inscription says that he *fecit istam ecclesiam de novo re-edificare.* The monument is a brass and, as is true of all England, BRASSES up to the early C15 are as a rule the best. In Sussex the earliest is in the West (Trotton *c.*1310). In East Sussex the best are perhaps (in chronological order) at Bodiam, Herstmonceux († 1402), Buxted († 1403), Ore (*c.*1430) and Warbleton († 1436). Of MONUMENTS other than those with brass effigies the best is Sir G. Oxenbridge at Brede. Effigy and tomb-chest are equally convincing. He died in 1537, but there is no sign yet of the Renaissance. Nor is there in any of the East Sussex monuments of the frequent type with a tomb-chest in a recess, a very flat arch over the recess, and a top cresting. Such are at Brede († 1482), and then at Selmeston (an Easter Sepulchre), at Isfield († 1527), at Herstmonceux (Lord Dacre † 1533, the only really swagger one of the group*), at Hamsey († 1538), at Slaugham († 1547), and again at Isfield. This second one at Isfield is to Edward Shurley who died in 1558, and yet there is again not a Renaissance detail.

PERPENDICULAR CHURCHES have nothing as ornate in their architecture as these monuments. The only work to be recorded is the Perp remodelling of the nave at Bayham Abbey, and a group, chiefly of towers, paid for by a Pelham and as a sign of this carrying the badge of the Pelhams, a buckle granted them after the Battle of Poitiers. The badge occurs at Ashburnham, Chiddingly, Crowhurst, Dallington, East Hoathly, Halland Park Farm, Laughton, Ripe, Wartling, and also on the font at Burwash. The towers are solid but not outstanding.‡

On the whole this survey of medieval churches has probably convinced most readers that East Sussex is not a church county. If one thinks back of them in mass the picture conjured up is one of small or medium-sized buildings with modest shingled

---

* But the group ought of course to be seen in conjunction with West Sussex.

‡ A Pelham was Constable of Pevensey Castle under Henry IV. The family remained in the county, though one branch moved N, into Lincolnshire, and is now represented by the Earls of Yarborough. The Sussex Pelhams became barons early in the C18, intermarried with the Holleses, Dukes of Newcastle, and became Dukes of Newcastle. The title became extinct in 1768, and the line split into the Earls of Lincoln outside Sussex and the Earls of Chichester in Sussex. Their house was Stanmer, outside Brighton.

broach spires* and large roofs, often covering in one sweep the
nave and an aisle or at least with only a change of pitch. Towers
are uncommonly often in positions other than at the w end of
the nave. Small but telling specialities of churches are very rare.
Eastbourne has a sacristy at the E end behind the altar, an East
Anglian motif. Penhurst is exceptionally unspoilt by restoration
and by the removal of furnishings.

It is curious that brick plays no part in East Sussex church
36a building of the late C15 and early C16; for with Herstmonceux
Castle of 1440, the county has one of the earliest really ambitious
brick structures in England. But then one will find throughout
medieval building in the county that the secular work is more
ambitious and more significant than the ecclesiastical or at least
parochial. We have so far touched SECULAR ARCHITECTURE
only in the Norman castles, but there is a good deal more to be
said on fortified as well as unfortified domestic building. The
growth of CASTLES followed a pattern which is the same in
other parts of the county, in West Sussex e.g. at Arundel. If
you take Arundel and take Lewes, you will see that the Norman
shell-keep and the Norman inner gate were followed by C13
additions of towers to the keep and by work on the wall and its
towers and then by an early C14 outer gateway, at Lewes the
famous barbican. At Hastings and Pevensey also the C13
strengthened the walls and added well defendable gatehouses.
At Pevensey in addition a chapel of plain nave and chancel was
built in the middle of the inner bailey, apparently late in the C13.
Only its plan survives. At Rye the Ypres Tower, i.e. a keep
with four round turrets, was built as late as the C14.

The job of fortress walls and gatehouses is exactly the same
for the defence of a castle and a town. So a word must now be
said on TOWN DEFENCES; for Lewes, Rye, Winchelsea, Hastings
were towns of importance and had to be made secure. At Lewes
comparatively much of the wall can still be followed, and one
C13 gate, the Westgate, can at least be traced. At Hastings all
that survives is a short stretch, a few courses high, of the late
C14 sea wall. But Rye has, apart from stretches of the wall and
the Ypres Tower, a C14 gatehouse, the big Landgate with
machicoulis, and Winchelsea has three gates, all of the early
p.
632 C14. For Winchelsea was New Winchelsea, and a NEW TOWN,

5   * There are only five stone spires in Sussex. They belong to Chichester
Cathedral and East Preston in West Sussex, and Chiddingly, Dallington,
and Northiam in East Sussex. Only that of the cathedral remains in one's
memory.

i.e. one of the made towns of which so many surviv[e]
The French call them bastides, and the most famou[s]
Aigues Mortes. New Winchelsea, built to replace a [Win]-
chelsea which had been destroyed by the sea, was laid out in
1283 as grandly and as regularly as Aigues Mortes. But after a
few glorious decades of building, epitomized by the church and
the Court House (too much restored to be of value now), New
Winchelsea ceased to grow, and more than half the area set
aside for it, over 100 acres, was never built up. It included what
was intended to be the market place and the town hall. New
Winchelsea was laid out by three men who came together for
the purpose. They were the Warden of the Cinque Ports, the
Mayor of London, and *Itier Bochard* of Angoulême, builder of
bastides. The plan is as elementary and reasonable as that of
the bastides – simply a grid of streets, all meeting at r. angles
and one block spared for the church. This is what the Greeks,
what the Jesuits, and what the North American and Commonwealth colonizers did in comparable situations.

Winchelsea now would strike no naïve visitor as a medieval
town. Apart from the court house, the wall, and the gates, medieval work is confined to vaulted cellars and some of their visible 25b
outside masonry. Winchelsea has over thirty of them, tunnel-
or rib-vaulted. There are some at Rye as well (e.g. Mermaid
Hotel) and an occasional one at Eastbourne (if it still exists) and
at Seaford (where they seem to have been let go). Otherwise
we know nothing of the c13 town-house in East Sussex.

We are much more fortunate regarding MANOR HOUSES.
Here also, of course, West Sussex and East Sussex ought to be
taken together, and the evidence of Amberley Castle e.g. is
more telling than in the houses now to be named. The VCH
suggests that in a wall of South Malling Manor House, just
outside Lewes, c11 work survives, Portslade (Brighton) has
remains of a manor house of the late c12, Charleston Manor
Westdean and Swanborough Manor Iford of *c.*1200, Crowhurst
of the late c13. In addition Westdean and Denton parsonages
are of the late c13. With the exception of Swanborough the
hall, i.e. the main living room, was in all of them on the first
floor. At Crowhurst we can still trace a large window with geometrical tracery. The pattern of the abbot's quarters in MONAS-
TERIES was clearly the same, as the evidence at Battle and at
Robertsbridge shows, both of upper-floor halls of the c13. At
Battle the abbot's private chapel remains in addition.

The concern with the trustworthy gatehouse also finds its

parallel in the abbeys. At the time when the barbicans were built
30 at Lewes and at Arundel, Battle received its mighty gatehouse,
broad, high, and both strong and rich. The decoration, lacy and
dainty, bears out the date when the abbot received his licence to
crenellate: 1338. Gatehouses were also built in the C14 at
Bayham and in the C15, tall and broad, at Micheham. Finally,
at Battle, also in the C15, the abbot found his hall inadequate
and built himself a new one, on the ground floor now, and
impressive today more by its size than by details, which are
nearly all victorianized.

By far the most imposing medieval hall in East Sussex is that
32a of the Archbishops of Canterbury in their palace at Mayfield. It
was in ruins, was restored, and is now the chapel of a convent,
but its principal motif is original: the pointed transverse stone
arches which run across. They are of great force and majesty.
There is no exact date for this hall, but the details of the tall
transomed two-light windows and the diapering formerly
behind the archbishop's seat and also of the arches themselves
are clearly of the early C14, the years of Winchelsea church. To
go on with major LATER DOMESTIC BUILDING, it is impossible
in Sussex to separate the castle from the manor house; for
whereas in most parts of England by the later C14 the manor
house, only lightly fortified or not fortified at all, had replaced
the castle, the proximity to France kept castles a going concern
in Sussex right to the C16. So of major work in manor houses
no more need be remembered than C15 Brede with its hall, its
chamber and its solar, and its attached chapel and attached to
that its sacristy and priest's room, a very interesting survival,
and the mighty hammerbeam roof above the later hall at Firle
Place, West Firle.* The key CASTLES of the C14 to C16 in East
Sussex are three, all of far more than local interest. The first is
31b Bodiam Castle licensed in 1385, one of the most gripping
castles in England, by its absolute symmetry, and its placing in
a wide moat. The type seems externally that of the Edwardian
castle of Harlech, i.e. of the early C13 Louvre of King Philip
Augustus of France and of his Dourdan, but whereas in these
earlier buildings the symmetry was confined to the walls with
the corner and gate towers, with most domestic accommodation
being placed in less order against these walls, Bodiam is a fortified courtyard house, i.e. has (like e.g. Bolton in Yorkshire of
the same time) four proper ranges of building round a courtyard.

* The stone hall-house next to Eastbourne parish church is of the early
C16 and was probably the priest's or priests' house.

Both hall and chapel are still easily recognized. The decorative
details, oddly enough, are nearly a hundred years out of date.
Then, fifty years after Bodiam, followed Herstmonceux Castle, 36a
of brick now, which was quite an innovation for England; for
though English bricks seem to have existed in the C12 and even
earlier, they were not used with any conviction until the mid
C15. It is true that Hull parish church had made use of bricks
already in the C14, but that does not alter the fact that one has
to go to Caister Castle in Norfolk of the 1430s, to Faulkbourne
in Essex of the 1440s, and indeed to Herstmonceux of 1440 to
find a real appreciation of brickwork. Herstmonceux is even
larger than Bodiam, and its exterior looks more palatial and less
fortress-like. Its long façades are treated absolutely symmetrically, but inside instead of one courtyard there were originally
four. In fact the interior has been too much altered to be
archaeological evidence now, but the machicolated gatehouse
and the apsed chapel forming a polygonal projection in the
middle of the E wall are still there. Another sixty years later
(1511–14), and at Camber a round tower was built, and this in 37a
& b
1539–43 Henry VIII used as the centre of one of his new castles
against the French menace, the first castles built in England
for defence by firearms exclusively, i.e. low, with platforms on
which to mount cannon. These Henrician castles, which
stretched from Kent to Cornwall (Deal, Walmer, Sandgate, St
Mawes, Pendennis) were given curiously symmetrical – mostly
lobed – shapes, patterns of a regularity to please the Renaissance
mind. At Camber it is an earlier circular core surrounded by a
dodecagon with five lobes.

So much of castles and stone-built manor houses. But in
Sussex, the county being a county of woods and forests, the
smaller manor house, especially of the Weald, was a job of
TIMBER-FRAMING throughout the Middle Ages and later. The
framing has closely set studding between the main posts in the
C14 and C15. Later the infill panels are wider. The plan type is
standard, the HALL-HOUSE, i.e. a house with its hall in the
middle, open to the roof – usually a tie-beam-and-kingpost roof,
which is also the standard Sussex church roof – and with chamber
and solar above at one end, the services at the other. Both wings
are two-storeyed. Many of these houses survive, far more than
the gazetteer of this book can mention, and far more than
external appearance might lead one to assume. An external
feature characteristic of a number of hall-houses in Sussex and
the adjoining counties is the arrangement of the roof in such a

way that in spite of the slight projection of the wings and recession of the hall a straight eaves line is observed. This is done by means of usually curved braces running in front of the upper part of the hall parallel to its front wall and rising towards the wings. These braces support the part of the eaves projecting in front of the halls. Houses with this arrangement are known as Wealden houses. Sussex hall-houses can be divided by the type of hall into the few with aisles (Capons at Cowfold, the Rectory at Sutton, both in West Sussex), with one aisle (38 High Street, East Grinstead; Priory Cottage, Bramber, West Sussex; Apple Tree Cottage, Henfield, West Sussex), with no aisle but a spere-truss at the end (Tickeridge, West Hoathly, of the early C14, Chelwood Vachery, Forest Row, of the C15). Houses with aisleless halls specially well preserved or well restored are e.g. the Clergy House at Alfriston, the first property ever bought by the National Trust, the Pilgrims' Rest at Battle, Stonehill House Chiddingly (a Wealden house), Great Dixter Northiam. Uncommonly large and spectacular is Horselunges Manor near Hellingly, uncommonly ornate the Ship Inn at Alfriston. Villages with an uncommonly large number of timber-framed 29a houses are Lindfield, East Grinstead, and Crawley in West Sussex. In two cases complete timber-framed houses from outside Sussex have been re-erected in the county and attached to bigger houses. One case is a house from Benenden in Kent at Great Dixter, the other is a house from Cheshire at Dutton Homestall, Forest Row. The timber-framed house goes on, 29b externally little changed, into the Elizabethan and Jacobean Ages, though inside the standard procedure now was to divide the hall into two storeys and put a large fireplace into one of its end walls. Externally in the ELIZABETHAN AGE some patterning by means of diagonal, usually curved braces came in, forming lozenges or concave-sided lozenges or a kind of reticulation unit in the panels. Dated Elizabethan examples of these patterns are the Middle House Hotel at Mayfield of 1575, East Mascalls, Lindfield of 1578, and Yeomans, Hamsey of 1584. And so timber-framing went on throughout the C17. Brickwall, Northiam is the example of a large symmetrical Jacobean and later façade (dates 1617, 1633) all timber-framed, and Rampyndene, Burwash is a proper William and Mary brick house of 1699 all timber-framed behind. But that admittedly is an extreme case.

However, timber-framing, being out and out conservative, is not the best introduction to the Elizabethan Age. In other works of architecture the principal characteristic of the age is the synthesis of traditional forms with the new forms of the Renaissance, and so the first question to be answered is where and how the RENAISSANCE got into East Sussex. The first dated appearances seem haphazard. At Rotherfield the Font Cover of 1533, already mentioned, is the earliest piece of all. At Laughton Place, the original Pelham House, in 1534 a tall, quite medieval brick tower was given small-scale decoration in terracotta including Renaissance arabesques. The material also was of Italian introduction and specially fashionable just during those years (see Layer Marney in Essex and a group in Suffolk round Old Shrubland Hall). More of this terracotta decoration survives at the second Pelham House, Halland, but there no doubt at some stage brought from Laughton. Of 1536–7 is the painted frieze in the Flushing Inn at Rye, which has sturdy Renaissance putti but still black-letter inscriptions. Of about the same time may be the perfectly preserved room in Court Lodge, Hooe, which has a frieze of the unmistakable heads in medallions, but still linenfold panels. The earliest monuments with Renaissance details are the Oxenbridge Monument at Brede of 1537 with pilasters against the back wall and the monument to Sir Antony Browne and his wife at Battle parish church. She died in 1548. The second Shurley monument at Isfield, as has already been said, has nothing of the Renaissance, though he died in 1558, but it must of course not be forgotten that the de la Warr Chantry at Boxgrove in West Sussex has plenty, though its date 35b is 1532.

The standard type of ambitious MONUMENTS of the mature Elizabethan and Jacobean Age is that with recumbent effigies on a tomb-chest, columns l. and r. of a back wall with inscription, a coffered arch, and a top achievement. To this type conform more or less the monuments at Fletching († 1596), Willingdon († 1619), and Isfield († 1631). At Pevensey († 1616) the effigy is not recumbent but lying on its side. Kneeling figures, also an accepted type, are at Slaugham († 1579), Friston († 1613), and Westdean († 1639). At Chiddingly in the Jefferay and 39a Montagu monument with the operative date of death 1578 there are, a unique motif, l. and r. of the recumbent effigies two standing figures. Few monuments of these years can be given to sculptors whose names we know. In East Sussex there are only a certain *Flynton*, who made the monument of 1579 at Slaugham, and *Gerard Johnson*, who, according to the surviving contract and drawings of 1595, made the three Gage monuments at West Firle. The interesting allegorical slate plate at Cuckfield († 1628) has been attributed for good reasons to *Epiphanius Evesham*. A conceitism starts here which belongs to the C17 rather than the C16. A yet earlier example of conceitism is the monument to Margaret Jefferay at Chiddingly – she died in 1618 – where a skull is placed in a recess in an urn.

The coming of the ELIZABETHAN COUNTRY HOUSE is marked in East Sussex by the extremely interesting Chiddingly Place, once much larger than it is now, where the remaining windows still have uncusped arched lights, a Henry VIII motif which, however, stayed long in Sussex, but where there are fluted lintels above the windows. This also occurs at Little Hammond's Farm, Burgess Hill of 1566. Here the porch has pilasters as well, i.e. a Renaissance motif, and at Chiddingly Place, moreover, the spandrels of the doorways to kitchen, buttery, and pantry have allegorical figures in the Renaissance taste. This is probably of *c.*1550–60. Of 1569 is the gatehouse of Glynde Place and the plainly gabled front in which it is placed, but most of the rest of the Elizabethan work must be later. The ruins of Slaugham Place do not connect with a date either. The splendid, lively staircase is now in Lewes Town Hall. It is too reminiscent of Hatfield and Blickling not to be of *c.*1610–20 too. But what may be the date, or indeed the original appearance, of the two loggias ? Wakehurst Place, Ardingly of 1590 is remarkable for still having the arched lights of Henry VIII's time. Danny Park, Hassocks, brick, of *c.*1582–93 and Gravetye, West Hoathly, stone, with dates 1598 and 1603, are much more Late Elizabethan standard, Danny Park quite monumental with its E front and large windows. It has its parallels in West rather than East Sussex (Wiston e.g.). Cuckfield Park with dates 1579 and 1581 has a delightful detached brick gatehouse.* Inside Cuckfield Park is the best Elizabethan plaster ceiling of East Sussex and a gorgeously carved screen. Rich panelling in a room of Pelham House, Lewes, too. This is of 1579. Cuckfield has also one of the two noteworthy secular Jacobean buildings, other than houses, the Grammar School by the church, of six bays, i.e. quite stately. But the other is far statelier, Sackville College at East Grinstead of 1619, an almshouse round a spacious quadrangle with gables to the front and a chapel still with arched lights. This conservatism or moderation remains typical of Sussex. No Elizabethan or Jacobean prodigy houses, and no early enthusiasm for Inigo Jones's and his circle's exacting

* Another, clearly earlier, is at Bolebrooke, Hartfield.

classicism. Brambletye, Forest Row of 1631, though in ruins, gives an illuminating illustration of this conservatism. The porch still has a Gothic rib-vault, and the whole front range has a rib-vaulted undercroft – reached from outside incidentally by a tunnel-vaulted ramp. Houses like Batemans, Burwash of 1634 and Great Wigsall, Salehurst of 1641 also remain essentially Jacobean, even if cross-windows begin to take the place of mullioned and mullioned and transomed windows and the façades tend to become more even and symmetrical. One can watch that in several minor houses: Possingworth Old Manor of 1657, a house belonging to St Francis Hospital, Haywards Heath, of 1660, the Deanery at Battle of 1669, Buckholt Farm Bexhill of 1670, Littlemark Farm Hurstpierpoint of 1677 (with shaped gables, i.e. a Jacobean motif), Filsham Farm Hastings of 1683, where only the circular windows are typical of the date, Lower Standard Hill Farmhouse at Ninfield of 1702, still with mullioned windows, though with a bolection moulding round the doorway, and Spraysbridge Farm at Westfield of 1690, also with mullioned windows, still not wholly symmetrical and still with a kind of shaped gable, although nationally the shaped gable had already two generations before been replaced by the Dutch gable, i.e. shaped gable crowned by a classical pediment, as a token recognition of the Palladian style of the court. There is one building in East Sussex which has such gables and in addi- 40 tion another motif, indicative of the same hesitating acceptance of court innovations: giant pilasters along the front. It is Peacock's School at Rye, established in 1636. Even for London this date would be quite early; for the first giant pilasters seem to have been on Lindsey House, Lincoln's Inn Fields and a terrace of houses in Great Queen Street, both of the mid thirties; whereas the Dutch gable made its first appearance on a house in Holborn in 1618. Both motifs on the whole were favoured more by the builders than the architects, the City than the Court, and therefore the provinces as well. Even so, for Sussex, Peacock's School was a piece of remarkable enterprise.

It was in complete contrast to the attitude of those building CHURCHES IN THE SEVENTEENTH CENTURY. Hardly any were built, and they, as well as added chapels or pieces of interior equipment, remained entirely Gothic. This applies to South Malling and Ashburnham churches, of 1626–8 and 1665 respectively, to the Sedilia and Piscina at Buxted (a church with a very attractive Jacobean chancel ceiling), and to the Sackville Chapel at Withyham of after 1663.

The conservatism is particularly unexpected there, because in the chapel stands a monument which is one of the first in England trying to be Baroque in the Italian or Flemish sense. We have seen that MONUMENTS went on in their Jacobean way well into the middle of the C17.* The first sign of a wish to develop new types, and one which is to be seen at the same moment all over England, is the frontal bust in an oval recess. In East Sussex this appears at Ringmer with a date of death 1642, at Berwick with a date of death 1656. But there is all the difference in the world between so modest an innovation and the Sackville
44a Monument at Withyham which was commissioned from *Cibber* in 1677. Its only parallel in England is also in East Sussex, the
44b Ashburnham Monument at Ashburnham by *Bushnell*, with the date of death 1675. Cibber's is the far more competent and convincing job, Bushnell's as usual is awkward, but as compositions both are equally daring. At Withyham two parents, life-size, kneel on the floor mourning their son, who is lying on the tomb-chest. At Ashburnham the husband kneels on the tomb-chest on which his wife reclines. The freedom of both these schemes, the independence of the universally accepted funerary traditions, was something completely new for England, even for London. The source is the Italian Baroque which Bushnell knew personally but Cibber only in its Netherlandish transformation. Both monuments will be remembered for their flow of feeling and pathos of gesture.

There is nothing in CHURCH FURNISHING as novel as this. In fact there is very little of the C17 one need refer to at all:‡

* This is the place, perhaps, where a note may be appended on CAST IRON TOMB SLABS. The Sussex iron industry reached its peak in the C16 and C17. The earliest iron instead of stone slab in the county is as early as the C14. It is at Burwash and has just a small cross and an *Orate* inscription. The next is of 1570, at East Grinstead, and this has an inscription along the slab. Others are at West Hoathly (1619, 1624), at Wadhurst (over thirty,
42b from 1617 onwards), Bepton (w), Maresfield, Mayfield, Salehurst, Streat, and Uckfield. The earliest at Wadhurst have only small shields, at Rotherfield is one of stone with an iron cross let in. The others have inscriptions along or more frequently across the slab. The latest is at Wadhurst and has the date 1799. But on the whole they cease after about 1710. Otherwise the iron industry has left few products. The STOCKS at Ninfield, all of iron, are an exception.

‡ Of the later C16 the only dated piece of interest is German – the pulpit of 1577 at Worth, fully carved, also with statuettes. This leaves out CHURCH PLATE, where, as in most counties, the Elizabethan Settlement brought a rush to replace plate destroyed under Henry VIII and after. The *annus mirabilis* was 1568. In that year and the years around dozens of cups and covers were ordered and made. Only one is post-Reformation and older: a very good cup of 1552 at Battle.

the West Gallery at Worth of 1610 with the usual vertically symmetrical balusters, familiar from staircases in houses, and a number of Pulpits with dates 1620 (Lewes, St Anne, unusual in the details), 1623 (Eastdean), 1636 (Pyecombe). They and a number of undated ones go in for flat arabesque carving rather than the stubby blank arches favoured in most other counties. The only really splendid pulpit is undated, that at Rotherfield. Add to these two of the typical Fonts made immediately after the Restoration and recognizable by their elementary geometrical motifs or plain initials (Upper Dicker 1663, Mayfield 1666), and you have seen all that could be of interest.

In LATER SEVENTEENTH CENTURY HOUSES much more was happening. They are the parallel to the monuments, only progress here led to the classical, not the Baroque. First the style of Peacock's School was enthusiastically carried on. As in Surrey, giant pilasters became a favourite of the mid and later C17. At Albourne Place they appear together with some very weird and irregular brick details, typical of what Sir John Summerson has christened the Artisan Mannerism of the mid C17. In connexion with this one ought also to look again at the Deanery at Battle of 1669, where the details of the doorway are Artisan-Mannerist, though the rest is, as has already been said, traditional Jacobean, symmetricized. Later C17 giant pilasters, or rather pilaster strips, at Halland in what is now a barn, and at Newick Park. Nothing exists in East Sussex of the fully classical type and date of Coleshill or Eltham Lodge, nothing of the more domesticated classical type and date of Denham Place and Belton, and one has to wait to the very end of the century to find the standard classical brick house of the kind as it existed in all parts of the country. The best examples are Stone Hall, Balcombe, of brick, the South Malling Deanery, also of brick and with giant pilasters, and Rampyndene, Burwash of 1699 with a brick front and sumptuously carved door-hood, but the windows still of the cross-type, Shelley's Folly at Barcombe, also brick and also with wooden cross-windows, and the swagger Hailsham Vicarage, again brick and again with giant angle pilasters. The finest interior work, even if of course not up to the class of Grinling Gibbons's work at Petworth, is the open-work-acanthus staircase and the door surrounds at Herstmonceux bought at Doncaster, some details at Glynde Place, and the stucco ceilings at Rampyndene and at Brickwall, Northiam.

The transition from 1700 to EARLY GEORGIAN is gradual, and such houses as Malling House, South Malling of 1710 or

Cralle Park, Warbleton of 1724 and the new s front of 1728 at
Danny (Hassocks), both with angle giant pilasters, continue the
type of the Malling Deanery. The s side of Danny has segment-
headed windows, a favourite Early Georgian motif which recurs
e.g. at Hye House, Crowhurst of 1744. Hye House also still
keeps the motif of very narrow windows l. and r. of the doorway,
on the Queen Anne rather than Early Georgian pattern, a motif
occurring not infrequently in Sussex. Segment-headed windows
also in *Andrews Jelfe*'s Town Hall at Rye of 1743. It is here, as
befitted a town hall, combined with a cupola and the traditional
open arcading on the ground floor. Typical restrained Early
Georgian is Kidbrooke Park, or was when it was originally built
probably in 1724–c.30, ashlar, with no enrichment but its
pediments. The ashlar-faced vicarage at Crowborough, dated
1744 and with a Gibbs surround to the doorway and a broken
three-bay pediment, may find its place in this context too.*

The English Baroque, i.e. the style of Vanbrugh, Hawksmoor, and Archer, is almost non-existent. The only sign is the
entrance side of Herstmonceux Place with its crowding of
motifs. Equally rare is early pure Palladianism, i.e. the Campbell–
Burlington style, though *Colen Campbell* himself designed
Compton Place, Eastbourne (1726). But the exterior of Compton
Place was much changed about 1800. Inside, however, there
45b are some fine *ensembles* of c.1730–50, but they are too exuberant to go as Palladian. The same is true of interiors at Firle
Place, West Firle, of c.1740, especially the staircase. The typical
reticence of the Burlingtonian taste, however, does appear in
two MONUMENTS of these same years, monuments without the
Baroque swagger of e.g. the Sergison Monument at Cuckfield
of c.1732 (by *Thomas Adye*). One of the two, at Waldron († 1722),
is purely architectural and has no figures at all, the other, at
Warbleton († 1740), by *Rysbrack*, has an outstanding bust, but
is also architectural otherwise.‡

As regards the LATER GEORGIAN style, there is far more in

---

* At the same time the CHURCH at Crowborough was rebuilt. But it was
so much altered in the late C19 that only its plain tower remains evidence of
1744. No other church of these decades exists in East Sussex, though
St Michael at Lewes was remodelled in 1748 and then received its symmetrical doorways from the street and the odd wooden piers with columnar
capitals inside. On the Brightling porch of 1749, *see* below. Of early C18
CHURCH FURNISHINGS hardly anything deserves attention either, though
one comes across charming pulpits of simple forms but with pretty inlay.

‡ For minor works by *Green* of Camberwell and by *William Palmer see*
the index of artists and architects.

East Sussex, both of monuments and of buildings, though of
neither is there anything in the very first class. A survey might
start from the anonymous work in the streets of towns like
Lewes and Rye and villages like Lindfield and Mayfield. The 3a
picture is of course a composite one, with some timber-framing
and quite some Early Georgian work, but the principal contribution is that of the late C18 and early C19, and these streets are
by and large still an undisturbed joy. They are never quite
straight, and they have as a rule some changes of level too. So
the vistas gradually shift, and further variety is added by the
manifold materials, brick, red and grey, the mathematical tiles
of Lewes,* red tile-hanging, white weatherboarding. It is all
cheerful, and all much alive. Individual buildings in these
towns and villages need no reference here, and what individual
buildings are now to be listed will be in an order appropriately
varied too.

First of all the classical style now begins to find a competitor
in the Gothic Revival, still picturesque and not at all concerned
with antiquarian accuracy. Its first signs are the s porch of
Brightling church with the date 1749 in florid figures in a
Gothic quatrefoil and a handsome monument at Eastbourne
with the date of death 1764 and a bust in front of a Gothic recess.
The only purely classical church in East Sussex is Glynde,
1763–5, designed by *Sir Thomas Robinson,* more like a private
chapel than a church. It was provided by Bishop Trevor of
Durham in conjunction with some classicizing of Glynde Place,
where the fine stables and gatepiers and e.g. the entrance hall
of 1758 are his. Then both the Gothic and the Classical got into
their stride, and several major works were undertaken in the
1770s and 1780s. Of the two major Gothic Revival houses of
these years Eridge Castle of 1787 has alas been pulled down,
but Sheffield Park by *James Wyatt,* of before 1779, remains in
its entirety, with Gothic turrets and oddly Gothick gables and
with some very fine classical interiors. James Wyatt also rebuilt,
in 1785–9, the parish church of East Grinstead, quite large and
not at all fanciful. At the same time (1777) *Samuel Wyatt*
added the neatly proportioned classical and unadorned garden
range to Herstmonceux Place. Two classical houses of about
1793–4 are by a famous architect hardly otherwise represented
in England, *Benjamin Latrobe,* whose fame is the buildings he

* An uncommonly large front to be faced with mathematical tiles is
Patcham Place, Brighton. An uncommonly distant place from Lewes and
Brighton is Theobalds, Wivelsfield.

designed in America, after he had emigrated in 1795. In Sussex he built Hammerwood House and Ashdown House, Forest Row, the latter with an exquisite round porch, semicircular with columns to the outside and semicircularly recessed into the façade. The Doric columns of the attached pavilions of Hammerwood House are patently inspired by the then very recent work of such men as Ledoux and Brongniart. Finally one building by *Robert Adam* and one by *Henry Holland*, Marlborough House Brighton and the Prince of Wales's massive Pavilion also at Brighton, both of 1786. Marlborough House survives, of Holland's Pavilion we have, as everyone knows, only a ghost.

So to Brighton and SEASIDE SUSSEX. The Pavilion and Marlborough House faced the Steine, i.e. the Common, and not the sea. They were not the start of the career of Brighton, rather its confirmation, for already in 1766 and 1767, two inns, the Castle and the Ship, had provided uncommonly large and expensive ballrooms or assembly rooms. The turn to the sea and to the kind of compositional ambitions for which Bath was famous throughout England came with the Royal Crescent, i.e. in 1798–1807. The houses were faced with mathematical tiles, and each had its canted bay window. But it is the bow window which Brighton made her own and which hence became the hallmark of seaside England. It probably came from the two bows of Holland's pavilion, even if for the garden sides of West-End houses in London ample bows had become fashionable already in the 1770s.* After the Royal Crescent things speeded up, though the great Brighton monumentality belongs only to the twenties. This being so, Jane Austen seems remarkably prophetic in what she wrote in her unfinished novel *Sanditon* in 1817:

'A very few years ago [Sanditon] had been a quiet village of no pretensions; but some natural advantages in its position and some accidental circumstances having suggested to [Mr Parker] and the other principal Land Holder, the probability of its becoming a profitable Speculation, they had engaged in it, and planned and built, and praised and puffed, and raised it to a something of young Renown'.

Mr Parker – 'Everybody has heard of Sanditon – the favourite – for a young and rising Bathing-place, certainly the favourite spot of all that are to be found along the coast of Sussex; – the most favoured by nature and promising to be the most chosen by Man' –

'Yes – I have heard of Sanditon', replied Mr Heywood – 'Every five years, one hears of some new place or other starting up by the

---

* Can the pair of bows of East Hill House, Hastings really be of 1762?

sea, and growing the fashion – How they can half of them be filled, is the wonder! *Where* people can be found with Money and Time to go to them! – Bad things for a Country; – sure to raise the price of Provisions and make the Poor good for nothing – as I dare say you find, Sir.'

'Not at all Sir, not at all' – cried Mr Parker eagerly. 'Quite the contrary I assure you – A common idea – but a mistaken one. It may apply to your large, overgrown Places, like Brighton, or Worthing, or East Bourne – but *not* to a small village like Sanditon' . . .

. . . 'I do not mean to take exceptions to *any* place in particular Sir', answered Mr H. -- 'I only think our Coast is too full of them altogether' . . .

– 'Our Coast too full' – repeated Mr P. – 'On that point perhaps we may not totally disagree; – at least there are *enough*. Our Coast is abundant enough; it demands no more – Everybody's Taste and everybody's finances may be suited – And those good people who are trying to add to the number, are in my opinion excessively absurd, and must soon find themselves the Dupes of their own fallacious Calculations – Such a place as Sanditon Sir, I may say was wanted, was called for – Nature had marked it out – had spoken in most intelligible characters – The finest, purest Sea Breeze on the Coast – acknowledged to be so – Excellent Bathing – fine hard sand – Deep Water 10 yards from the shore – no Mud – no Weeds – no shiney rocks – Never was there a place more palpably designed by Nature for the resort of the Invalid – the very Spot which Thousands seemed in need of – The most desirable distance from London! One complete, measured mile nearer than East Bourne . . . But Brinshore Sir . . . – the attempts of two or three speculating People about Brinshore, this last Year, to raise that paltry Hamlet, lying, as it does between a stagnant marsh, a bleak Moor, and the constant effluvia of a ridge of putrifying sea weed, can end in nothing but their own Disappointment. What in the name of Common Sense is to *recommend* Brinshore ?' . . .

'Our Ancestors, you know, always built in a hole – Here were we, pent down in this little contracted Nook, without Air or View, only one mile and three quarters from the noblest expanse of Ocean between the South Foreland and the Land's End, and without the smallest advantage. You will not think I have made a bad exchange, when we reach Trafalgar House – which by the bye, I almost wish I had not named Trafalgar – for Waterloo is more the thing now. However, Waterloo is in reserve – and if we have encouragement enough this year for a little Crescent to be ventured on – (as I trust we shall) then, we shall be able to call it Waterloo Crescent – and the name joined to the form of the Building, which always takes, will give us the command of Lodgers'.

. . . In ascending, they passed the Lodge Gates of Sanditon House, and saw the top of the House itself among its Groves. It was the last

Building of former days in that line of the Parish. A little higher up, the Modern began; and in crossing the Down, a Prospect House, a Bellevue Cottage, and a Denham Place were to be looked at by Charlotte with the calmness of amused Curiosity . . . Trafalgar House, on the most elevated spot on the Down, was a light elegant building, standing in a small Lawn and with a very young plantation round it, about an hundred yards from the brow of a steep, but not very lofty cliff – and the nearest to it, of every Building, excepting one short row of smart-looking Houses, called the Terrace, with a broad walk in front, aspiring to be the Mall of the Place. In this row were the best Milliner's Shop and the Library – a little detached from it, the Hotel and Billiard Room – Here began the Descent to the Beach, and to the Bathing Machines – and this was therefore the favourite spot for Beauty and Fashion . . .

At Brighton the time for 'a little crescent' was nearly over by 1817. In 1823 Kemp, part-lord of the manor and Nonconformist preacher, began Kemp Town E of Brighton, in 1825 the Hove
3b seaside development was started. Both looked to Nash's Regent's Park terraces, begun in 1821, rather than to Bath, i.e. the façades
50a were stuccoed, and the length and the height grew, to thirty
&51 and more bays for one terrace, and to four, then to five storeys. The architects were *Amon Wilds* and *C. A. Busby* and Wilds's son *Amon H. Wilds*. The Wildses had come from Lewes, where in 1806 Amon Senior built the long and not specially interesting church of All Saints and where in a house called Castle Place in 1810 he introduced that hallmark of the Wildses' work, the ammonite capital. He took it over from Dance no doubt because of his name Amon, an irrelevance characteristic of an architect who had rarely anything like the panache of Nash and never a feeling for the finesses of proportions and accentuation. In fact, with a few lucky exceptions, the terraces of Brighton and Hove are on the coarse side, impressive to the *hoi polloi* rather than the connoisseur. But impressive they were, and they found their
50b followers at once. Pelham Crescent at Hastings, though, cannot be called a follower. For *Joseph Kay* began it in 1824 and finished it in 1828 together with the church of St Mary-in-the-Castle, a fine climax with its portico and its more-than-semicircular auditorium. But St Leonards was started by James Burton, the London builder, with his son *Decimus Burton* as his architect, immediately after the first of the grand Brighton terraces in 1828. The scheme was excellent, with a big hotel as its centre – at Brighton the first hotels on the new scale and in the seaside style were the Royal York of 1819, the Royal Albion of 1826, and, the most remarkable of them architecturally, the Bedford

of 1829. At St Leonards the hotel had long terraces l. and r., a great Doric assembly room in axis behind (at the height of fashion, but yet rather an exacting style to choose), and, again in axis, the S lodge to a picturesque park in a rocky quarry with picturesque villas around, a variation on the theme of the Regent's Park villas, which themselves were actually partly designed by Decimus and built by James Burton from 1818 onwards. At Brighton something very similar was begun in 1829: Queen's Park, laid out by *Charles Barry*, also with lodges and also intended to have villas. Barry built only one, for Mr Attree, and that is highly memorable, because it was the first villa in England in the revived Quattrocento style.

So we get on to the splendours and miseries of HISTORICISM. Brighton had had a good foretaste of it already; for at one time the Regent, rather belatedly, had fallen for chinoiserie and in 1802 converted Holland's chaste interior in that Rococo way. Then he fell for the Moorish style, and this time it was not a whim to pass so quickly. It passed only after *Porden* had built for him the very large domed stables and riding school in 1804–8 and after *Nash* had converted Holland's Pavilion into that folly 48b of all follies that it is now – Moorish (Hindoo-Gothic, they said) &49 outside and a mixed Sino-Mahometan cum pre-Victorian drapes and *grossièretés* cum cast iron exposed in the staircase and the kitchen shafts inside. Nash's wizardry spread over the years 1815 to 1822. There were few in the county who felt inclined to go Moorish too – such outlandish borrowings were in fact C18 rather than C19 in attitude – but at Brighton *A. H. Wilds* was moved to build himself a little pavilion all his own, the Western Pavilion, *c.*1827, and Kemp in 1819 built for himself the Temple, another folly, to the measurements of King Solomon's temple and with columns all round of unmistakable Pavilion inspiration.*

To the classical, the Gothic, and the Moorish aberration, *Barry*, as we have seen, now added his neo-Quattrocento. He used it at the same moment in a very similar way in London for the Travellers' Club, but he had used it in fact already a little earlier at Brighton itself – and that really is the *locus classicus* – for a church façade, St Andrew Waterloo Road at 52a Hove, which was built in 1827–8.

* While we are on FOLLIES, outside Brighton the following few may merit listing: Lord Heathfield's substantial Gibraltar Tower at Heathfield of 1792, a charming Gazebo with shell-grotto interior at Willingham House, Ringmer, and Mad Jack Fuller's Sugar Loaf at Dallington and 65 ft obelisk at Brightling and perhaps also his pyramidal Mausoleum at Brightling.

Perhaps a few lines should here be interpolated on the new churches of Brighton and Hove, erected in these very years of hectic terrace building. But the best church of the 1820s is not
5ob at Brighton, but at Hastings, St Mary-in-the-Castle of 1828 by *Joseph Kay* which has already been mentioned in connexion with Pelham Crescent and which, with its composition of circle and portico, belongs to a great Continental tradition (S. Francesco di Paola, Naples, 1816–24, Canova Temple, Possagno, 1819–22, etc.), and the most interesting church of the same years is not at Brighton either: the parish church of Frant, by *J. Montier*, of 1819–22, which has long, segment-headed Perp windows of the Commissioners' type with cast-iron tracery and slender piers of cast iron with remarkably knowledgeable Perp details – an anticipation of the antiquarian attitude of the Vic-
52b torians. *Barry*'s St Peter in Brighton of 1824 on the other hand has a w tower (i.e. really s tower) which is archaeologically quite unjustifiable, but has inventiveness and zest. The rest is large and in its proportions again of the Commissioners' kind. Otherwise the Brighton churches are classical. St George's Chapel by *Busby* of 1824–5 is a typical example, Regency in style and very similar to the Nonconformist chapels of the same years. In fact it may well be considered characteristic of the attitude to religion in the early C19 that so little difference in style, scale, or arrangement existed between church and chapel. Details vary from Late Georgian to severe Doric Grecian. The latter is used, e.g. outside the Unitarian Chapel in New Road of 1820 by *A. H. Wilds** and inside St John Evangelist Carlton Hill of 1840 by *Cheeseman*. But Cheeseman's Christ Church Montpelier Road of 1837–8 is Gothic, and still Gothic of the uninformed kind (as is his St John-under-the-Castle at Lewes of 1839). The turn to a real respect for the Middle Ages and consequently to accuracy in its imitation came, nationally speaking, only with Pugin and George Gilbert Scott, i.e. round about 1840.

But before we are ready for this, a few lines on the MONU-MENTS of these churches and these years. They go perfectly with them: classical and some Graeco-classical, with standardized motifs: the urn, the mourning woman, the sarcophagus, an allusive still-life. The motifs and the gradual dilution by sentimentality – the spray of weeping willow – are familiar. In East

---

* On the whole NONCONFORMIST CHAPELS in East Sussex are, though frequent, undistinguished. For reasons other than architectural one may be recorded: the chapel at Wivelsfield of 1780, because it was Selina, Countess of Huntingdon's own. She lived at Wivelsfield.

Sussex there are few monuments of about 1800 and up to about 1835 which a traveller would remember, though the names of the best sculptors are all represented: *Flaxman*, *Westmacott*, then *Chantrey*. If two or three have to be singled out, they might be *Nollekens*'s at Withyham (1802), with charming putti by the conventional urn, *Flaxman*'s also at Withyham († 1815) with an all-too-Grecian female but an excellent portrait in a medallion, and *Rouw*'s at Brightling – actually Mad Jack Fuller's († 1834) – with an eloquent bust. Rouw's is not a familiar name, but it is an experience everywhere in England that in Georgian sculpture it is not necessarily the most famous names that produce the finest work. Take *J. E. Carew*'s Baptism of Christ as an example, in 53 St John Baptist, Brighton, of 1835. This could hold its own anywhere on the Continent – even if perhaps suitable compari-sons might have to be one or two generations earlier – yet who knows Carew?*

The churches of Brighton which have so far come into the picture were nearly all close to the seafront, but St John Evange-list and Christ Church are farther inland, and indeed the town planning pattern of Brighton with its terraces and crescents spread N in the 1840s and 1850s. Montpelier Crescent, of the 1840s, is an example of this, still orderly, still within a mannered spread. The idiom was still essentially that of the Regency, but one can watch at the W end of Hove, in Montpelier Road and in the villas round the new picturesque parks, how the Tudor and the Jacobean with their gables, straight or shaped, come in to disrupt the Georgian unity. Even a little earlier that fundamental change of taste had expressed itself in a few country houses: Buckhurst, Withyham by *Repton*; and a remarkably correct, unfanciful lodge to Ashburnham House – both of the 1830s.

So there starts the VICTORIAN AGE, the Victorian fancy-dress ball. We can follow it through all its intricacies and fancies in walking the fronts of the other East Sussex seaside resorts. Eastbourne, where large-scale development began in 1851, still kept at first, oddly late, to the Brighton-Regency pattern. But soon, and of course entirely at Bexhill, which only got going in the 1880s, the Italianate, the Frenchy, the Sir-Ernest-Georgian–

---

* And, while we are concerning ourselves with the Georgians, let it not be forgotten to build a little niche for *Jonathan Harmer* of Heathfield, who made sweet terracotta plaques for head-stones or sarcophagi in graveyards, emigrated to America in 1796, and returned in 1800. Many of his plaques are to be found at the Cade Street Chapel near Heathfield, at Heathfield, Herstmonceux, and Mayfield.

Netherlandish C17 appeared, and they will all be found and recognized everywhere, as intruders at Brighton of course as well.

There is an extraordinarily interesting contrast in English architecture and in architects' and clients' attitudes towards architecture between the domestic and the ecclesiastical: in the one irresponsibility, fancifulness, licence, in the other (with exceptions) high-minded earnestness which could result merely in a respectful faith in the derivative but also in a disciplined exacting originality. Brighton's spread continued after 1850. The population had been 7,339 in 1801. It was 65,569 in 1851, and 99,091 in 1881. And Brighton was on the whole a wealthy place. Churches were needed, and BRIGHTON CHURCHES were built to a generous scale with no cheese-paring in materials and finishes. The change from the fancy-Gothic to the serious Gothic at Brighton was due in the first place to the Rev. H. M. Wagner asking, as early as 1846, *R. C. Carpenter* to design a new church, St Paul. Carpenter's work is always grave, humble, self-effacing, and utterly without frills. He made his name later with St Mary Magdalene, Munster Square in London of 1849–52, one of the foremost churches of the Ecclesiological Movement. This got into its stride at just this time – the Cambridge Camden Society had been founded in 1839 – and stood for a Catholic (as they called it) ritual. These were of course also the years of the Oxford Movement and Newman's return to Rome (which took place in 1845). H. M. Wagner's son was Arthur Wagner, an ardent High Anglican much attacked for these convictions of his. High Anglican also was Nathaniel Woodard, and it was Woodard (1811–91) who started Hurstpierpoint College in 1851, Lancing College in 1854 (*see* p. 39), and Ardingly College in 1864. *R. C. Carpenter* designed Lancing and Hurstpierpoint, his son *R. H. Carpenter* the Lancing chapel and (with his partner *Slater*) Ardingly. The buildings of Hurstpierpoint and Ardingly are grave, somewhat gloomy, except for the chapels, where a great *excelsior* was attempted and at Lancing gloriously achieved.

Altogether Sussex is a county of schools, colleges, convent schools, and the houses of various orders, High Anglican and Roman Catholic. For schools of course it is the seaside places that have it, and he would be a bold man who would try to count how many there are at Eastbourne and Seaford. *Scott* built Brighton College in 1848 etc. and *Sir T. G. Jackson* added in a far more lively Gothic to it in 1886. *Simpson* at Roedean in

1898 turned away from the Gothic altogether to a more cheerful and also a daintier Jacobean. Convents and the houses of orders, teaching or otherwise, often took an existing house, converted it, and added to it. But *Street*'s impressive premises for the Sisterhood of St Margaret at East Grinstead, founded by Neale, one of the founders of the Cambridge Camden Society, are buildings on a virgin site. The chapel is the climax, as it is in 55 the case of *Whelan*'s chapels for the Novitiate of the Fathers of Charity at Wadhurst (1881), polygonal like a chapter house, and for the Salesian Novitiate at Burwash (1887), a chapel of church size, which is vaulted throughout. Holy Cross Convent, Haywards Heath has a chapel by *Tower*, Kempe's partner (1902–6), his unquestionable *chef d'œuvre*, the Heritage Crafts School at Chailey Common a noble chapel by *Comper* (1913).*

The Christian zest reflected in these buildings found a most moving expression in Father Wagner's work at Brighton. With his own money he built five churches‡ – of which, alas and to the shame of this century, three have meanwhile disappeared. *Bodley*, who had already built the small initial building of St Michael in 1858–61, built him St Mary Magdalen (1864; de-molished) and probably the Annunciation (1864), *R. H. Car-* See p. *penter* the Resurrection (demolished), *Somers Clarke* (1874–5) the 691 uncompromising, almost ruthless St Martin in memory of H. M. Wagner, and *Edmund E. Scott*, a local architect, St Bartholomew (1872–4), which is one of the most tremendous C19 churches in the world – brick, 135 ft in height, i.e. higher than Chartres Cathedral, with sheer outer and sheer inner walls of brick.

Bodley, who had an unerring sense of noble and appropriate CHURCH DECORATION and nothing of the puritanism, if the word is permissible in this context, of Carpenter, got *William Morris* to provide stained glass for the Annunciation and for St Michael in the early sixties too. The glass in both cases is 57b exquisite, strong, clear, eloquent, and not at all sentimental. *Rossetti* did much of the figure designing. There is later Morris glass at Rotherfield, quite outstanding, and much at Rotting-

---

* Other colleges and houses of orders are Worth Priory, the Convent of Notre Dame at Forest Row, Mayfield College, the Convent of the Holy Child Jesus at Mayfield (in the former Archbishop's Palace), the Convent 32a of the Holy Child Jesus at Hastings, Holy Cross Convent at Haywards Heath, the Priory of Our Lady of Good Counsel at Haywards Heath, St Joseph's College Mark Cross, St Mary's House Burgess Hill, St George's Retreat Burgess Hill.

‡ Or rather four and a half.

dean, of the nineties, all designed by *Burne-Jones*, who had a
house there.* Morris glass stands out among all Victorian glass
and that by *Kempe*, often mentioned side by side with Morris's,
never reaches its height. Kempe, a pupil of Bodley, lived at
Lindfield and did more windows for Sussex than can be listed
in the gazetteer of this volume. For the years of his partnership
with Tower no attempt is made; but most of the earlier glass
will be found mentioned. It starts with Cuckfield, 1875, and
St Nicholas Brighton, 1878, but, apparently earlier still, Kempe
had painted the chancel of Staplefield. He also did the excellent
wall paintings at St Nicholas Brighton (to designs by *Somers
Clarke*). Hardly any other church decoration calls for a record:
just some terrible gaudy glass by *Capronnier* of Brussels which
makes Kempe's shine like so many Aladdin's lamps, and the
interesting neo-Trecento wall paintings of 1873 in Holy Trinity,
Hastings.

But against that scarcity stands a glut of VICTORIAN
CHURCHES and among them some of a quality almost a match
for St Bartholomew. Brighton of course has more than any other
town, but several good ones are in the villages too. How are we
to arrange them ? First the left-overs of the pre-ecclesiological,
pre-antiquarian approach: *Basevi* in 1833–6 built St Andrew,
Church Road, Hove in a neo-Norman, an early case, as Norman
became fashionable (for a short time) only in the 1840s, at the
time when *Donthorne* built the neo-Norman Upper Dicker
(1843), and even *Carpenter* did a neo-Norman church (Catsfield,
1845). The Baptists of Lewes built themselves one in 1843, and
a neo-Norman funerary chapel was added to St John Evangelist
Southover, Lewes, in 1847. *William Moseley*'s churches of the
same years are also still pre-antiquarian and tend to be rather
spindly (e.g. Forest Row, 1836). *Barry*'s pre-antiquarian St
Peter has been introduced earlier on, his church at Hurstpierpoint of 1843–5 is large, in the late C13 style and not in any way
remarkable. Of the first antiquarian generation *Scott* built no
church in East Sussex, but Brighton College, as we have seen,
and the former Library at Lewes (1862), both of course Gothic.
His son *John Oldrid Scott* built the church of St Mary at Chailey
Common with a forceful central tower (1876). What Goodhart-
Rendel called the Rogue Architects had few Sussex clients. Only
Teulon could show a little of his idiosyncrasies – not much – at

* He also painted the altar triptych or retable for St Paul at Brighton.
This is a very early work of his, and the commission was again due to
Bodley's recommendation.

Rye Harbour (1848) and Holy Trinity Hastings (1851–9). During the same years the church at Tidebrook was built by *T. H. Rushforth*, and it turned out to be an excellent, quite individual, yet not at all mannered job. *Street*'s Convent of St Margaret at East Grinstead (1865–70) has been referred to. It has a chapel with a powerful chancel. He also built the excellent 55 St Saviour, Eastbourne (1867–8), brick, with a noble steeple. *Burges* designed the superb, cathedral-like enlargement of St Michael at Brighton which was executed in 1893, i.e. after his death. *James Brooks*'s St Peter Hastings (1885) is not one of his best, but the pier shape is highly interesting. *Bodley*, apart from what has already come into this survey, is represented by the early Haywards Heath (1863–5) with a good, oblong central tower, and the serious Danehill (1892). Superb and cathedral-like are also the words for *Pearson*'s All Saints, Hove (1890–1). His St Matthew, Hastings (1884) is impressive, but no more, and St Barnabas, Hove (1882–3) is nothing really special. The Victorian church of Hastings which everyone will remember is St Mary Star of the Sea by *Champneys* (1882), towering externally, though without a tower, and fully vaulted inside. *Slater & Carpenter*'s church at Burwash Common (1867) is E.E. and has chancel and apse vaulted. *John Norton*'s St Matthew, Brighton deserves notice, because it is of mass concrete, *A. P. Strong*'s All Souls, Eastbourne, because it is Italian Romanesque, with a campanile, at a time (1882) when nobody was interested in that style, and the grand E end of St Peter's Brighton by *Somers Clarke & Micklethwaite*, because it marks the return to Perp at the end of the C19 (1900–6). It was now often treated more freely than these two archaeological architects would have permitted themselves, especially when it was handled by architects who had taken to the Arts and Crafts. Sedding's is the most important name here. He is not represented in Sussex, but his favourite pupil, *Henry Wilson*, is, with the magnificent decoration of St Bartholomew at Brighton, partly Early Christian in derivation, but partly also of that completely original kind of metalwork which is England's equivalent to the Continental Art Nouveau. The work dates from *c.*1900, but before the C20 can be rounded up, a survey is still needed of SECULAR NINETEENTH-CENTURY WORK. Secular of course includes public and commercial buildings as well as domestic, but of the former so unindustrial, uncommercial, unurban a county has produced little: the Old Prison at Lewes of 1793 with its Vanbrughian entrance, the modest Old Town Hall at

Hastings of 1828, the Grecian Town Hall of Brighton by
T. Cooper of 1830–2, the oddly monumental, though small,
former station at Lewes of 1846, *Waterhouse*'s red and unmistakable Hove Town Hall of 1882, and not one commercial, not
one industrial building.*

For VICTORIAN HOUSES what followed after the Tudor of
Buckhurst and the Quattrocento of Barry's Attree villa?
Dawkes's Tudor Gothic of Horsted Place, Little Horsted of
1850–1, *Clutton*'s varied and picturesque Tudor Gothic of Balcombe Place of 1856, *Matthew Digby Wyatt*'s colossal and joyless
Tudor Gothic of Possingworth (1866), and *Vulliamy*'s plain and
joyless Italianate of Shernfield Park, Frant (1853) with its
gargantuan portal, and so on to that epitome of High Victorian
showiness and licence, *E. M. Barry*'s Wykehurst, Bolney of
1872, in a kind of French château style. The reaction was on its
way then, initiated by Devey, by Philip Webb, and by Norman
58 Shaw. By *Shaw* Glen Andred near Groombridge, one of his
first mature works, of 1867, moderate in size, varied in materials,
domestic in character, inventive and not at all demonstrative.
Of the more famous neighbouring Leyswood of 1869 only a
fragment has been preserved, still reminiscent of High Victorian historicism. The one masterpiece of *Philip Webb*'s in East
59& Sussex is a late work, Standen near East Grinstead of 1891–4,
60a which combines a relaxed exterior with strong, vigorous interior
features. A few years later *Aston Webb*, before he turned classical
and conventional, did a flamboyant Arts and Crafts extension
to *Salvin*'s Tudor Paddockhurst, Worth (Worth Priory) of
1869–72. The extension is of 1897 and contains a sumptuous
61b dining room with memorable and entertaining decoration by
Walter Crane. Remarkably early does the turn to the so-called
Queen Anne appear in Sussex; the turn which one usually
connects with the names of Nesfield and Shaw. An architect
whose name it has not been possible to find designed Crabbet
Park Worth in 1873, and the Queen Anne vocabulary is used so
perfectly that the house at first may well take in even the expert.

* Unless one calls WINDMILLS industrial. They do exist, more than are
listed, and nearly all out of action. The best-looking ones in East Sussex,
still with sails, are the post-mills of Argos Hill Rotherfield, Hog's Hill
Icklesham, Nutley, and Clayton. The post-mill at Clayton is of 1821 and
8a stands close to a tower-mill of 1876. They are known as Jack and Jill.
Other tower-mills are at Polegate (1817) and Patcham (Brighton). Smock-
mills are at Rottingdean (C18), Battle (1810), Chailey, Cross-in-Hand, and
West Blatchington (Brighton), the latter of 1724 and oddly mounted on an
L-shaped barn which contains the machinery.

The neo-Queen-Anne or neo-William-and-Mary then, as everyone knows, became the universal neo-Georgian of the C 20.

So into the TWENTIETH CENTURY and first this very
neo-William-and-Mary and neo-Georgian, exemplified by *Smith
& Brewer*'s Ditton Place, Balcombe of 1904 and several houses
by *Sir Reginald Blomfield*, e.g. Saltcote Place, Rye of 1900–2
and much of Heathfield Park, Heathfield of 1898–1910. One
of the best of the neo-Georgians would undoubtedly have
been *Alwyn Ball*, who designed Houndsell Place outside
Wadhurst, if he had not fallen in the First World War in 1918.
Lutyens did a great deal in East Sussex, and it ranges from the
neo-Tudor of Barton St Mary, Forest Row of 1906 and the
reconstruction and sensitive additions to Great Dixter, Northiam
of 1910, to The Hoo, Willingdon of 1902, a house in the village
street by the church, ingeniously altered, and to the brilliantly
semi-classical entrance range of Plumpton Place of 1927–8.

Only a few years later and the INTERNATIONAL MODERN was
beginning to find its missionaries in England. *Frank Scarlett*'s
Starlock, Rye, designed in 1929, is the first of the white and cubic
buildings in Sussex and one of the first in England. Historians
ought not to neglect it. Then came *Colin Lucas* to raise the
battle-cry Le Corbusier. Yet his Sun House, Chelwood Gate,
Forest Row, of 1931, seems now no more than a modest box.
Saltdean House of 1934 by *Connell & Ward*, soon to be
partners of Lucas, is more of a composition. But even this
remains elementary compared with what was soon to come:
Serge Chermayeff's house at Halland of 1934* etc. and *Erich
Mendelsohn*'s Bexhill Pavilion of 1933–6, done in partnership 62b
with *Serge Chermayeff*. Both are accomplished works, resourceful in their grouping and in the relations between solid
and glazed, and the Bexhill Pavilion has aged admirably and
is as exhilarating today as when it was new and a revolution for
the English seaside. *Francis Lorne*'s St Dunstan's, Rottingdean
of 1937–9, though also entirely International Modern, is much
more conventional, with its symmetrical façade and its yellow
brick walls. *Goodhart-Rendel*'s St Wilfred, Brighton, of 1933–4,
on the other hand, is highly remarkable for being entirely un-
imitative, un-historicist, and yet entirely un-International-Mod-
ern as well. It had nothing like the effect of the Bexhill Pavilion
and remained in fact pretty well unnoticed. However, the Pavilion
as uncompromisingly modern seaside architecture had actually
been anticipated by a little by *Wells Coates* who, fresh from his

* 1934 is the date when plans were submitted.

Lawn Road flats, built Embassy Court at Brighton in 1934–5, with the radical white bands of balconies and stair parapets the ruthlessness of which is coming back now in some work of the last few years.*

The building in which this revival of ruthlessness, this disregard for any prettiness made its spectacular appearance in 64 East Sussex is *Sir Basil Spence*'s University of Sussex at Falmer outside Brighton, which was begun in 1960. The individual motifs, chunky slabs of concrete and shallow concrete vaults, may not be as original as were the motifs of Coventry Cathedral – they were contributed to the international architectural arsenal by Le Corbusier with his Jaoul houses and his buildings for Chandigarh – but Sir Basil Spence has certainly made them his own and composed them at Falmer with a most impressive counterpoint of voids – whole parts of storeys of a square block with a spacious inner courtyard left open as terraces. This reaction towards what has been termed brutalism must be understood in juxtaposition with a certain prettiness that had come in, partly from Sweden, immediately after the Second World War and still goes on in many of the private houses designed and built now. So we have a situation at present – and this is the end of the survey – when the stalwarts of the International Modern of the thirties still go on vigorously, e.g. much of the curtain-walled or not-curtain-walled shopping centre of Crawley New Town, and the well composed, not at all cheerless new theatre of Eastbourne by *Bryan and Norman Westwood & Partners*, when the private house is much more ingratiating than it was in the thirties (e.g. a house by *Neville Conder* at Hassocks and one by *Leslie Gooday* at East Grinstead), when this sense of the accommodating, the playful, one is inclined to say, appears even in major buildings (*Brian O'Rorke*'s Royal Observatory, Herstmonceux) and when against this a bolder, more expressive, more plastic style, that of the University of Sussex, just begins to make itself felt. That is the situation, and no one can say whether any of these trends will wane or which of them will dominate in the years to come.

FURTHER READING

This annotated list applies to West as well as East Sussex. Sussex is divided into six Rapes, three w, three e. They are

* Marina Court, St Leonards, by *Dalgliesh & Pullen*, 1937–8, is a vulgarized version of Embassy Court.

strips running N–S. Of these the *Victoria County History* has done three and the town and cathedral of Chichester (1935). The rapes covered are Chichester (1953), Lewes (1940), Hastings (1937). They are covered in great detail, and the VCH forms the basis of what our gazetteer contains. In addition, as early as 1907, the VCH (vol. II) gave a survey of architecture and church furnishings etc. in the whole county. This was done by P. M. Johnston and, though naturally no longer up-to-date, is still very valuable. It is a good deal more detailed than our introductions. As a more general and popular guide to the architecture of Sussex the *Little Guide* holds first place. It is by R. F. Jessup and F. G. Brabant, came out originally in 1900, and has had its most recent revision in 1949. J. R. Armstrong's *A History of Sussex*, 1961, is an excellent brief introduction and should not be missed, especially as our gazetteer does so little for history. The old *Cambridge County Geography* volume (by G. F. Bosworth, 1909) also still has its value. So have the essays assembled by P. D. Mundy as *Memorials of Old Sussex* (1909).

Antiquarian research is concentrated in the *Sussex Archaeological Collections* (here abbreviated SAC), the *Sussex Notes and Queries*, and valuable articles on houses are also to be found in the *Sussex County Magazine* (here abbreviated SCM), apart of course from the articles on houses in *Country Life*. Among those whose names should be watched for because of the particular merit of their work are foremost the late Walter Godfrey and Mr R. T. Mason. The former has written many papers on individual Sussex churches and also many guides to churches, all models of their kind, the latter specializes in timber-framed houses. His most important papers are in SAC, vols. 95 and 96. Manuscript material, and especially water-colours of churches in their pre-Victorian state, are in the British Museum (Burrell and Dunkin Collection),* in the Lewes Museum (Sharpe Collection), and in the Bodleian Library in Oxford (Gough Collection). Of other literature the most important is still Horsfield's *History of Sussex*, published in 1835.

On individual towns the most copious literature is of course that referring to Brighton. Here the following, all recent, are to be recommended: A. Dale: *Fashionable Brighton*, 1948, *The History and Architecture of Brighton*, 1950, and *About Brighton*, 1951, the latter a perambulation like ours; C. Musgrave: *Royal Pavilion*, 1951, and the current edition of his guide to the

---

* A catalogue was published in SAC, vol. 28, and 191 illustrations in the jubilee edition volume of the Sussex Record Society ,1951.

Pavilion. In addition, much older, H. S. Goodhart-Rendel on the Victorian churches of Brighton, in *The Architectural Review*, vol. 44, 1918, three articles. On the growth of Brighton an article in *The Builder*, 1885, II, pp. 111 etc., is also valuable.

On medieval funerary monuments there is a special book by H. R. Mosse (*Sussex Brasses and Effigies*), on church plate a series of papers by J. E. Couchman (SAC, vols. 53–5). In addition there are of course books collecting certain types of works of art and architecture nationally, such as Aymer Vallance for church screens, Mill Stephenson for brasses, Tristram for wall-paintings of the C12, C13, and C14, E. Croft-Murray for decorative painting, etc.

For the prehistory and early history of Sussex much material also is contained in papers and reports in the SAC. An inventory of Roman sites is included in vol. III of the *Victoria County History*, and a study of the Pagan Saxon period in vol. I. For the prehistoric period the best general account is E. C. Curwen's *Archaeology of Sussex* (2nd ed., 1954).

WEST SUSSEX

*

In the plain E of Chichester, and much less spoilt than most of
the surrounding villages: unpretentious thatched flint cottages,
no particular group. Remote and sequestered as long as the
aircraft from Tangmere are not flying, for it is almost on the
airfield boundary. Most of the village is at NORTON, ½ m. N,
with pleasant flint barns and cottages.

ST MARY. Do not be put off by the horrible restoration of 1867
by *Ewan Christian* which has left the outside maimed and
valueless, the hard windows stamped into the walls with real
hatred. All that was spared was the odd battlemented brick
wall of the S aisle and the crowstepped post-Reformation S
transept gable. Inside, there is still a lot of worthwhile and
unrestored work at Aldingbourne, and to a much bigger scale
than in most of the village churches around. The nave S wall
comes first, with one blocked Norman window above the
doorway and the blocked three-bay arcade of a former N aisle.
They are early C12, still with some geometrical painted decoration which was probably a commonplace over most walls in
most churches. Noble five-bay S arcade, of *c.*1170 or 1180,
the round piers looking earlier than the arches. They are the
standard type of *c.*1150 with round scalloped or fluted capitals,
whereas the arches are pointed of two orders, the inner order
chamfered, and must be *c.*1200. But Boxgrove has this combination of scalloped caps and pointed arches too. A little
later the S doorway was inserted and the easternmost bay of
the aisle given a rib-vault – beautifully carved in hard chalk,
probably done by masons from Chichester, as the cathedral
held the advowson. The S doorway is the type which has E. E.
mouldings and spirit but keeps to the round arch (like the
cathedral retrochoir). Two orders, with roll-mouldings and
jamb shafts, and an outer label with dogtooth. The vaulted
bay has its ribs elegantly enriched with dogtooth also; the
arch into it is carried on two shafts with capitals very similar

to late C12 work at the cathedral: one is crocketed, the other has been given beautifully resilient stiff-leaf carving. The arch above is perplexingly plain, round-arched and unchamfered, and must be re-used.* But why was that bay vaulted? Just lavishness for a chapel, or a plan to put the tower here, before it was decided to build a N tower? In the event, the N tower went up, E.E., and with a blocked W arch and a blocked N arch at the E end of the N arcade to prove that the tower was connected with the old N aisle. The only other detail left by the Victorians is the twin SEDILIA, an ambitious design of c.1230 with jamb shafts at the sides and a central corbel with two orders of dogtooth ornament that is exactly like a section in a textbook of medieval mouldings. Perhaps it was a worked stone not wanted elsewhere. – FONT. Standard, crude c.1200: square arcaded bowl on stem and four shafts. – ROYAL ARMS of William III. – CHAIR. In the chancel. As a rule chairs do not go into *The Buildings of England*, but this is a special chair. With its very rustically carved emblems, it is certainly Catholic and certainly outlandish. Could it come from the Colonies? The date looks early C19. – PLATE. Cup and Cover, 1568; Cover, 1679–80.

ALDINGBOURNE HOUSE, 1 m. N. Built c.1800 as a rather mannered stock-brick villa, perhaps an imitation of Goodwood. W front with five bays – two curved bays at the ends, a Venetian window inboard of that, and the centre blank – a puzzling and not very satisfactory design. The S front has a curved central bow window, and in front of it is the nicest part, presumably belonging to the additions made after a sale in 1814: an enormous two-storey iron veranda, the whole height of the house, the ground floor much taller than the first. The effect, very disarming, is just as if a Regency seafront hotel had been moved bodily three or four miles inland.

9090   # ALDWICK

Immediately W of Bognor Regis: a few old cottages and many more new ones, mostly in expensive semi-private estates running down to the sea. The biggest, the ALDWICK BAY ESTATE, is lush and thickly planted like a miniature Bournemouth. Most of the houses are cosy, e.g. a big group, weatherboarded and thatched like overblown strays from an Essex village, in THE

* If it were not, it would have to be the arch from a S transept to an apse or chapel.

FAIRWAY: but there are also a few 1930 modern buildings,
e.g. BEACH HOUSE, on the shore.

ST RICHARD. The most debilitated kind of Gothic Revival,
1933 by *F. G. Troup*. Horrible.

NEALS FARM, ¾ m. N, beside B2166. A good example of a C16
half-timbered farm in its original condition – roughcast and
thatched, with tiny windows. Worth any number of cosified
cottages.

AMBERLEY

0010

At the N end of the Arun gap, and one of the show villages of
Sussex, achieved without any single worthwhile building and
without any definite focus either. The plan is a quadrilateral of
lanes on a low ridge, with one of them prolonged as a cul-de-sac
leading to the church and castle. The site is so definite and
striking – all the views S upwards to the Downs, all the views N
slightly downwards to the Wild Brooks and across them to the
Weald hills – that it defines the village shape as sharply as a
green or market place would have done. Long, pretty, irregular
perspectives of cottages, beautifully kept, with something like a
formal tree-lined approach up to the church. An anthology of
building materials – thatch and tile, brick, flint, half-timber, and
Burgate stone, and also just a little clunch. The nearest things to
formal architectural detail are actually the Moorish windows of
*c.*1880 on the house next to the Congregational Church, and
the regular brick and half-timber cottage (PANEL COTTAGE)
next door to that.

ST MICHAEL. Just outside the castle walls, with its tower overlooking the courtyard and making nonsense of the defensive
scheme. The framework is Norman, a church initially with
the usual small windows (one remains on the N side) and given
a bigger scale *c.*1150–60. It probably had three chambers
(aisleless nave, chancel, and apse), which would account for
the shortness of the C12 masonry incorporated in the later
chancel: the division is clear outside. Thumping great windows, to a cathedral scale on the N and W sides, the W window
now inside the plain C13 tower. Outside, the windows are
unusually set in a taller and wider blind arch; inside they have
thick nook-shafts carrying a thick roll moulding. The blocked
doorway in the N wall is large too. The chancel arch has the
same overall scale and proportions, spoilt by a tragic difference
in scale of the detail. Triple responds, huge and forceful, each

with shafts, the two outer carrying volute capitals, the inner
capitals which could be described as stylized Corinthian or a
scallop made up from leaf shapes. They were of course
originally pointed. The mason would doubtless be amazed at
either category. These huge details support a three-order arch
which alas is full of finicky zigzag ornament, almost em-
broidery, even on the soffit. The effect is as incongruous as
Adam trying to imitate Vanbrugh. The style is like Tortington, or some of the latest Norman parts of Chichester Cathedral. Simple, sober additions; C13 lancet chancel with a
triplet at the E end, big three-bay S arcade with standard
details, and the tower. The S doorway is c.1300, and is lavish
for a parish church but not good. Complex mouldings bent
awkwardly round the arch, which looks like the C13 one redecorated. Two orders, capitals covered by arch vegetable
growths which are beginning to spread on to the jambs. –
FONT. Square, C12, with the usual shallow blank arches,
four in this case. – WALL PAINTINGS. All but gone, so that
there is no point in recording them.* – PLATE. Cup, dated
1567; Paten, 1754. – MONUMENT. Brass to John Wantele
†1424. Effigy, 28 in. high, much more vivid and forceful than
most surviving C15 examples.

AMBERLEY CASTLE. A magnificent sight from the S, stretched
along a ridge with the church and village at one end. Equally
impressive from the N across the watermeadows of Amberley
Wild Brooks. All this is part of a rectangular curtain wall put
up c.1380 (licence to crenellate 1377). Exactly contemporary
with Bodiam and perhaps put up for a similar reason – i.e.
at the upper end of a then navigable river, the Arun, running
into the Channel.

    In fact the site contains things much older. It belonged to
the bishops of Chichester throughout the Middle Ages, and
was, before it became a castle, a much humbler manor house.
This survives in the SE corner and through alterations probably no firm date will ever be found for it. It is L-shaped
with one wing running W–E and the other projecting S from
the E end. In the N wall of the W wing is a rich Late Norman
doorway, in the same style as the chancel arch of the church,
i.e. of c.1150–60. Jamb shafts, scallop capitals, one order of
zigzag in the plane of the doorway, one order jutting forward
from it. Only the stumps of the arch remain, alas. So some-

* The Rev. E. N. Staines kindly tells me that more of the painting s of
the chancel arch has been exposed, revealing a Crucifixion.

thing was here then, but whether it was the present building or not, that is whether it is *in situ* or not, nobody can say. What the present building stands for is more easily grasped. The forms are of the early C13, again with details that can easily be matched in Sussex churches. In the W end wall is a twin window with a long shaft, in the S wall of the W wing a lancet and a mysterious giant arch now partly blocked and evidently later, round the corner in the S range, facing W, is another twin window, and a third is in a N attachment (of which more presently) facing W. This has a kind of rough quatrefoil above the twins and an arch around them. All these windows are on the upper floor, and they represent an upper hall of the early C13, with appendages, something of the Boothby Pagnell or Aydon kind.

Then Bishop Rede came along and decided to make this a castle on a monumental scale. So up went the curtain wall, up went the gatehouse (not centrally placed as at Bodiam), and up [31a] went a new great hall with its own appendages, including among these the old manor. The hall does not look quite like a hall now; for of the original four bays the third has gone completely, the fourth (N) is ruined, the first two (S) are restored and altered to make up the N part of the present house. Its S part is the Chamber and Solar of the hall range, which contains no features of 1380. The services extension of the hall range on the other hand can at least be seen in its location. As one enters the ruined part through what was the main doorway of the hall (with complex arch mouldings and label stops of a king and bishop which were clearly very good but are now badly weathered), one has to one's l. the three arches to pantry, kitchen, and buttery, chamfered and plain. As a large N window of the hall has left traces above the middle doorway, the passage to the kitchen must have been low. The doorway, unlike the early C13 details, could hardly be paralleled in a church of its date – it looks, like so much at Bodiam, much out of date. Bishop Rede also converted the hall range of the manor house into his chapel. He did this by taking out the hall floor and putting in a tall S window. The chapel PISCINA survives. Reactionary again the curtain wall – e.g. the two traceried windows in the N side (two lights and a quatrefoil, with the lines still flowing, not up-and-down). Life had begun to have compartments. These windows lit what was presumed to be guest chambers, either side of a massive projecting garderobe, whose bottom openings would then have discharged into water. Otherwise, the curtain is severely military: original cross-slits in the N side, square corner towers flush with the wall, semicircular towers to the gatehouse. None of the original battlements remain – those on the gatehouse are a restoration of 1908–13, when a good deal of the s front was refaced, but not aggressively.

Bishop Sherbourne early in the C16 used Amberley and made additions which include windows at the SE corner and a big and rather odd five-light window in the W side of the chamber (the heads of the centre lights are a restoration). He also had *Lambert Bernard* paint eight (originally nine) wooden panels of the Heroines of Antiquity (!) and Cassandra. They are in the early C13 hall. The castle was probably sacked in the Civil War and reoccupied on a smaller scale afterwards. From the late C17 remain the simple staircase with its twisted balusters, a jolly and naïve hunting scene painted on the plaster of one of the upper rooms, and panelling in another room which was cleverly and subtly grained. This catalogue does little to suggest the happy, lived-in feeling of curtain wall and house, and the cheerful jostling of details of all dates. Amberley is not nearly so well known as it ought to be.

w of the castle a good big BARN. Tile roof (originally thatched) and weatherboard walls. Built in two parts, one with a queenpost roof, the other with a variant whereby the queen-posts become arched braces instead of straight members.

AMBERSHAM COMMON *see* HEYSHOTT

oooo
ANGMERING

NE of Littlehampton, but inland from the coast and hence without the worst effects of C20 building. Expansion is going on rapidly at the moment but seems comparatively careful. Angmering is built on two little hills with a small green between: its potentials or 'capabilities' are great and have not been removed so far by modern houses. They depend, oddly enough, on what in most villages would be disastrous – enlarging, opening out, and unifying the central space so that it and the streets leading into it can read as one unit.

ST MARGARET. The body of the church restored by *S. S. Teulon*, 1852–3. Experienced users of *The Buildings of England* will know that this is likely to be the most important visual fact about the church. It is: Teulon had a field day, renewing

all the windows and the arcades, leaving medieval fragments
around like flotsam on the beach. What remain are the elegant
and complex keeled mouldings of the chancel arch, *c.* 1200,
the plainer arch to the Gratwick Chapel s of it, and the E.E.
s door of two orders, which was moved and does not look
very trustworthy. Teulon could design remarkable and
original new churches, but was at his worst in this kind of
sack of an old building. What we have in exchange are the
incredibly naturalistic capitals (carved by Mr *Forsyth*) and
the incredibly pious angels of the nave arcades, which have
some life of their own.

Luckily for us, Teulon left the tower alone. It is a good,
bulky design of 1507, built by Syon Abbey, Middlesex –
there is a dated carved inscription over the w door, something
very typical of 1500 as against any earlier century. Squat and
positive: big square stair-turret on the NE side, diagonal buttresses, plain oblong two-light bell-openings – the details
bluff and simple to match the proportions. Better than many
taller and more ornate towers. – FONT and COVER. Very
much Teulon: praised by the *Ecclesiologist*.

The church is on top of one of Angmering's hillocks. Immedi-
ately outside it, everything is *Teulon* again: SCHOOL and
VESTRY HALL, done at the same time as the church, crow-
stepped and gabled and not very good. From here a pretty,
unpretentious set of terraced cottages runs down BAKERS
LANE to the green, and continues beyond on the s side of
HIGH STREET. E, along this, around the junction with
Weaver's Hill, several more worthwhile cottages: CHANTS
COTTAGE has a brick and half-timber front, quite rare in this
part of Sussex, with a good barn behind – tarred weatherboarding, thatched, on a flint base. A little way down Weaver's
Hill, CRESSINGHAM COTTAGE, thatched flint, makes a good
group with another similar barn. From here a cul-de-sac runs
E to ECCLESDEN MANOR, a long, low, comfortable, Tudor-
looking building as they occur in almost every English county.
It was in fact built as late as 1634, and it takes a keen eye to
spot the tiny C17 touches. Flint with a few brick dressings,
seven bays, plain four-light mullioned windows, one central
gable above a two-storeyed porch with a plain classical doorway, four other small gables – dormer gables, where a real
Tudor house might have had them larger. The game is given
away only in the complicated shaped gable at the w end, and
perhaps in the elegant ball finials.

NEW PLACE FARM, ¾ m. N. As so often, the name signifies late medieval or Tudor buildings. Fragment, probably one wing, of a house built by Sir Thomas Palmer in the C16. The design can only be guessed at; brick, of three storeys, most of the detail on the N side, the second floor with one six-light mullion-and-transom window, the first floor with four-centred Tudor arches, probably relieving arches for smaller windows rather than blocked windows themselves.

ROMAN VILLA, ¾ m. W of the church. In the C19 a bath house and hypocaust system were uncovered. The villa proper lies some 100 ft W of the bath house. Finds of Samian ware from the latter building suggest a date in the C1 and early C2 A.D. The bath house had a pavement of *opus sectile*, composed of pieces of stone cut into shapes and bedded in cement – a form of flooring rarely found in Roman buildings in Britain. The stone for this floor was imported from northern Italy.

S and W of the villa is a DITCH which has produced Iron Age A pottery, including haematite coated wares. At first flat-bottomed, the ditch was later recut with a V-section.

HARROW HILL FLINT MINES. A large group of mine shafts: some are simple pits sunk to a depth of 6 or 8 ft and worked on an 'open cast' technique; others are over 20 ft deep and have galleries at their bases which radiate in all directions, following the buried flint seams. The site appears to have been worked primarily by people of the Early Neolithic, Windmill Hill Culture.

Also on the hill lies a small, roughly rectangular HILL-FORT, defended by a single rampart and ditch. It overlies the flint mines. There appear to be original entrances on the NE corner and W side. Excavation revealed that the rampart had been faced with vertical timber uprights, and evidence for a stout wooden gateway supported on four large posts was recovered from the W entrance. The site is to be dated to the first half of the C3 B.C.

ANGMERING ON SEA see EAST PRESTON

8000

APPLEDRAM

A church and two old houses in the fields SW of Chichester, a few yards from the upper end of Chichester Harbour. The original port was immediately W of the church and has vanished completely. It was replaced in the C17 by DELL QUAY, ½ m. S, an enchanting group of boatyards and cottages. The nicest thing at Dell Quay, the splendid visual foil of a white house and a row of poplars, was destroyed by the mutilation of the trees a few years ago.

ST MARY. Originally a chapel of ease to Bosham. All plain C13 from the outside, an earlier date showing only in stones of the former E end in the N side of the chancel. Nave, chancel, and three-bay S aisle with a coarse restoration of 1877 by *Lacy W. Ridge*: pitch-pine roofs and a fussy bell-turret. The inside, which was sensitively restored by *Butler* in 1845 (NT), is a surprise, one more variation on Sussex's inexhaustible repertoire of elaborated C13 chancels. Here, triple lancets are gathered together with shafting and wall arcading, one in the E wall, one each in the N and S sides – the effect rich and austere at the same time, and very exciting in the otherwise plain space. Purbeck shafts, circular abaci, complex arch mouldings. The arcade is the usual type, double-chamfered arches on circular piers with circular abaci. The lowest altar step is paved with C14 TILES: four tiles make up two types of circular pattern. – SCREEN (S aisle). C14, crude but complete. Six bays, including a two-bay central door, each bay with single ogee head and quatrefoils in the spandrels.

MANOR HOUSE. Mid-C17, very much altered. Stone with brick dressings, the N end made up into a big thin Dutch gable containing a blocked architectural frame of pilasters and entablature.

RYMANS, SE of the church. A delightful small C15 manor house 32b with a very unusual plan, quite clearly a deliberate and subtle design, not the result of happy accident. It was built for William Ryman some time after 1410 and consisted of a three-storey central tower with a pair of two-storey wings forming an L-shape. The tower and one arm of the L remain, stone built; the other arm was replaced in the C17. This contained the two-storey great hall, which presumably had a gallery connecting it with the solar on the first floor of the tower. Above this a bedroom, reached by a spiral staircase projecting from the SW corner of the house; opening off it in the existing C15 wing the master's bedroom. The ground floor of this wing was some kind of workshop and had no direct connexion with the rest of the house. In the tower big two-light windows, square-headed, with beautifully managed reveals; in the wing smaller one- and two-light windows without reveals. The tower top now has a C17 pyramidal cap, above an elegant concave string course.

This bald catalogue can give very little idea of the extreme delicacy of the planning – perhaps an odd word to use of a medieval house. It is best seen in the wing, with its built-in garderobe, and three windows of graduated size facing E, S, and W to admit different amounts of light to workshop and bedroom. Here the C15 was considering the quality of life with as much care as the most painstaking C20 designer. The bedroom has all three windows in authentic condition and an original fireplace.

The plan is not unique, but is very unusual in Sussex. It looks in an odd way like the gentle southern equivalent of a Northumbrian bastle-house. All the stone was brought by sea, from the Isle of Wight and Normandy.

0000   ## ARUNDEL

Arundel seen from a distance is one of the great town views in England, although very un-English: castle and dramatic pinnacled church at either end of a long ridge, backed by the Downs, with mellow brick houses tumbling down to the river Arun. At closer view however, the two accents are demonstrably C19 and demonstrably mock-medieval, and as soon as this can be seen the views somehow become compromised, a piece of elaborate open-air fancy dress, rather as Wyatville's bogus medievalisms at Windsor infect the perfectly genuine domestic fabric of the town. This is accentuated because Arundel, like Windsor, has no real central space and seems just an appendage to the castle, and also, to some extent, because a good deal of the domestic rebuilding by the Norfolk estate has been in the overtly picturesque styles of the last hundred years.

27b ST NICHOLAS. Rebuilt all of a piece after 1380, a good harmonious example of what the Early Perp style meant in South East England – firm masculine proportions and detail, no flights of fancy but no hesitation or confusion either. It cannot be appreciated properly because, although it appears from outside as a straightforward aisled nave and chancel with central tower, the eastern half or Fitzalan Chapel with the Lady Chapel to the N was in fact collegiate and was originally separated from the parochial nave and tower by an iron grille. This was augmented by the C19 Dukes of Norfolk with a wall, making nonsense of the design: the Fitzalan Chapel can now only be reached through the castle grounds. The college was founded in 1380, and building started from the E, but it

is all of a piece, the style of Yevele at Canterbury and Westminster and Wynford at Winchester. Piers with four shafts
and in the diagonals four hollows, round bases, and octagonal
abaci (the responds have three shafts, the tower arches five),
setting up a fine large-scale rhythm through the church; the
arches with double-hollow-chamfers augment this. The
tracery takes a variety of forms but always keeps in the same
spirit. The grandest is the E window: seven lights and panel
tracery, made up of two subdivisions of three lights each
separated by a single light running to the apex of the arch.*
The S side of the Fitzalan Chapel has four-light windows with 27b
tracery heads of three quatrefoils and two quatrefoils above
that, an expansion of one of the commonest Early Perp types;
the N side has clerestory windows with four plain lights under
a segmental head and may be a C15 alteration (the ornate
external cresting to the Lady Chapel, incidentally, is C19).
The nave windows are plainer, the familiar three-light panel
tracery but set internally in recesses in the wall, as in some
East Anglian churches, which accentuates the already strong
rhythms of the church. The clerestory windows are, unexpectedly, quatrefoils, normally a motif of *c.*1300: it is worth
looking at them closely to see how in fact every trace of Dec
sinuousness has been removed – an echo of what Yevele did
when he completed the nave of Westminster Abbey, with the
C13 forms altered in detail but significantly. Finally, the squat
central tower, which is the least effective part of the church,
ornamented with two tiers of two-light bell-openings under
segmental arches and in very deep concave reveals: it seems
somehow curt and mean after the amplitude of the rest. – FONT.
Perp, octagonal, but decorated with pairs of trefoil-headed
panels instead of the usual rosettes. – PULPIT. It looks a per- 34b
fect piece of about 1800, in light and elegant Gothick stonework. In fact it is Perp also, though dressed up in the C19.
Three-arched ogee canopy going up to frilly cresting and
crockets which are oddly like Dec motifs carried on without
gusto. As it carries no more conviction than a *c.*1800 Gothick
pulpit would, the first intuition is right after all, in a way. –
WOODWORK. The Fitzalan Chapel was originally vaulted.
The vault was taken down in 1782, but many of the roof
BOSSES remained and were incorporated in the present vault

---

* Inside, close to this E window, a narrow staircase comes down into the
church from the master's lodging in the college. On the college, *see* below,
p. 90.

of 1886. They are very good. – In the Lady Chapel a few old
STALLS, with good faces on the arms, and one original
MISERICORD among a great deal of renewal. – In the Fitzalan
Chapel a CRUCIFIXUS, life-size, probably Spanish C15 and
very good indeed; Late Gothic tragedy and intensity without
any Late Gothic neurosis or self-pity. – METALWORK. The
original grille separating nave and Fitzalan Chapel is still *in
situ* behind the reredos, and is quite a rarity. Repeated pattern
of thin uprights with trefoil heads under a thicker battlemented horizontal member, a nervous, flickering design. –
WALL PAINTING. Seven Deadly Sins and Seven Works of
Mercy, in a wheel pattern. Very faded, but clearly of the time
when the church was being completed. – MONUMENTS. The
Fitzalan Chapel has a remarkable set of Norfolk monuments.
Sculpture and brasses are separated, and the order in both is
that of the descriptive leaflet. – Thomas Fitzalan, 5th Earl of
Arundel, † 1415 and his wife † 1439. Recumbent effigies with
canopies on elaborate tomb-chest, all alabaster, probably from
Chellaston in Derbyshire. Ornate and competent but circum-
scribed by the need for official portraits; hence the best
touches are in the details; the faces of the weepers, the details
of the Countess's upswept headdress, and the supporting
angels. – John, 6th Earl, † 1421. Tomb-chest with elaborate
side panels, quatrefoils with a trefoil inside each lobe. No
effigy. Sussex marble. – John, 7th Earl, † 1435, the 'English
Achilles', killed at Beauvais when in charge of the English army.
Tomb-chest, effigy above, cadaver below, the one stiff and
official, the other grimly expressive, especially around the
face with the lank hair spilling out across the shroud, the
shroud-end itself curled over with macabre elegance. –
35a   Chantry and tomb of William, 9th Earl, † 1487 and his wife
† 1462. Sussex marble, very large, of three bays, with a big
solid top and all over every surface a brilliant and bewildering
display of skin-deep Gothic motifs, clearly ripe for the
Renaissance. The display is doubly bewildering, because it is
not at all certain what belonged originally to the chantry.
Clearly the four detached twisted shafts capped by pinnacles
and acting as a parody of flying buttresses to the hugh canopy.
On its high wall a pattern of big flat ogees among a riot of
oculi, lozenge panelling, and other motifs, all in very low
relief. The ogee and oculi repeat in the back wall below the
canopy. The tomb-chest also stands where it should stand
and looks as it might look. But is the more shrine-like tomb-

chest put on top of the first *in situ*? The female figure right
on top clearly is not. She would never contemplate the canopy
so closely, and she is of a different stone too. What does belong
is more like the Late Gothic of Portugal or Spain than of
Sussex, and is in fact remarkably successful – it is far better
to express a truly felt attitude to Gothic ornament than to
stick at the mechanical repetition of forms which have lost
their meaning, which was what the c15 so often did. – Thomas,
10th Earl, † 1524 (and the 11th † 1544 and 12th † 1580). Here
the Renaissance, or something like it, has indeed arrived, though
in an incredibly gauche and naïve way. There is no comparison
with the de la Warr chantry at Boxgrove except in the
Plateresque mixture of Gothic and Renaissance detail. Tripartite canopy supported on columns which are an indes-
cribable mixture of motifs. Each bay has two squat ogees with
pendants, above that a coat of arms, above that a cresting of
small semicircular ornaments. The ceiling inside is both
coffered and has pendants, the back wall is panelled with trefoils, roundels, and the weirdest kind of adaptation of *grot-
tesche*. The table-tomb inside and the stone railing between
the bays have arches which are more like Italian Romanesque
than anything else; in fact, most of the ornament would not
be out of place on a Romanesque font. It is an astonishing and
endearing effort. – Henry, 12th Earl, † 1579. Rather odd
for the date: big, severe, reredos-like monument with Corinthian pilasters, the type of *c.*1700, but also a little strapwork.
– Robert Spyller † 1633. Very plain, very Roman architectural
frame with open segmental pediment and in the opening a
bust in a shell surround. It is surely by *Inigo Jones* or someone
very near him. – Lord Henry Howard † 1842. Big black marble
tomb, Gothic Revival, no effigy. – Henry, 14th Duke of
Norfolk, † 1860 and his wife † 1886. Pious, unrevealing effigies;
sculptor unknown. – Henry, 15th Duke, † 1917. Bronze, not
stone, a patriarchal figure with robes slipping down over the
black marble tomb. By *Sir B. Mackennal*. Rich, polychrome,
and impressive in a purely Edwardian way – the spirit of
Kipling's Recessional – which is after all a legitimate part of
the c20.

Now, the BRASSES. At the W end, two c15 figures of
priests, one full length, the other half length, roughly but
vividly engraved like the figure at Poling. – Further E, Thomas
Salmon † 1430 and his wife † 1418, the former very incomplete.
Big figures under canopies. – S of this John Threel † 1465.

Rather charming small figure in frilly armour. – In the N chapel, a group of indifferent small late C15 brasses. – Robert Ward † 1474, half length. – John Baker † 1456, full length, and Esperaunce Blondell, half length.

Immediately SE of the church, forming a quadrangle with the S side of the Fitzalan Chapel, is ST WILFRED'S PRIORY, a C19 reconstruction of the original collegiate buildings. A few simple windows remain (square-headed, of one and two lights) but the predominant effect is of a bit more of Arundel's Gothic Revival. Much of the S range and the W wall standing without rooms behind are in fact old.

ST PHILIP NERI (R.C.). Designed in 1868–9 and built in 1870–3 by *J. A. Hansom & Son* at the expense of the fifteenth Duke, to commemorate his coming of age. The feeling of *ecclesia triumphans* which Catholics during those very years must have had could not have found a more elated expression. This even more than the castle gives Arundel its exciting, un-English skyline. At the highest point of the town, tall and apsed, with a flèche over the crossing. French Gothic style of *c.*1300. A NW tower was intended but not built, so the distant effect is that of a building like Beauvais or even Mont St Michel, with the little town huddling around it.

It would be easy if description could stop there. The trouble is that the reproduction of a French Gothic church five hundred years after the event has made the detail so mechanical and so shallowly felt that a close look at the outside is a tragic anti-climax. The key is in the sickly and vapid figure sculpture. Inside, the detail is no more convincing, but the proportions and space do impress. Tall narrow aisles, no triforium, clerestory with doubled tracery. Piers of great height, with eight shafts, on the pattern of Bourges. Enormous crocket capitals taken from French cathedrals of these same years. Stone-vaulted all through, naturally enough. It is a real puzzle – a moral puzzle – to decide how far the good qualities can be ascribed to the C19 at all, how far they are simply a pallid reflection of the C13. After all, we do not suggest that a strict Greek Revival public building is a faint echo of the C6 or C5 B.C. If this was in fact genuine, how would we regard it? With an architect like Pearson – this is superficially like a Pearson church – there would be no doubt: he was a C19 man who chose to speak a Gothic language. But this replica architecture is a much harder business. Certainly, it cannot be dismissed as valueless. To do this would be to perjure one's eyes,

because the spaces *are* impressive however one may deplore
the attitude of mind that created them.* The FITTINGS
generally are terribly weak. They do not help the viewer's
moral dilemma. – STAINED GLASS. Easily the best part of the
decoration. Mostly by *Hardman*. The bright, hard style of
the mid century deepened and enriched. Plenty of reds and
purples, vigorous design. Best in the main windows of the
apse and, especially, the lancet windows high up on the E sides
of the transepts.

Big PRESBYTERY to the SE.

CONGREGATIONAL CHURCH, Tarrant Street. Flint-fronted,
Romanesque, not good.

CASTLE. There is no getting away from the fact that Arundel
Castle is a great disappointment. The fault is that of the C19,
which would not leave well alone, and to a humble mixture of
medieval ruins and C18 brickwork added first of all silly but
spirited Gothic additions of 1791–1815 by *Abraham*. A century later there was an almost complete rebuilding in an
unfeeling Windsor Castle style by *C. A. Buckler*, 1890–1903,
which neither amuses nor convinces. That anybody, Duke or
Banker, could as late as 1890 have embarked on the pretty
complete building of an imitation castle, remains a puzzle
anyway, though for the historian of society rather than the
architectural observer. After all, during the decade when the
Duke had done with it, Lutyens started on Holy Island and
Castle Drogo.

The fragment to which these fruits of misdirected energy
were applied was a big late C11 castle, built by Roger Mont-
gomery, Earl of Shrewsbury, immediately after the Conquest
in an admirable tactical position.‡ Its plan was a familiar one:
a big motte and two baileys N and E of the motte. Only the
gatehouse remains of Roger's time. Then Henry II, between
1170 and c.1190, put a shell keep on top of the motte, de-

---

* A baffling fact which must not be left unnoticed is how incorrect much
of the detail is and how unconcerned Hansom was as to whether he took
from France or England. Incorrect e.g. the motifs of much of the geometrical
tracery and especially the N transept E window, and most incorrect of all the
frieze of quatrefoils inside, taking the place of a triforium. Incorrect also but
original enough to be valid in its own right the relation of the two E chapels
to the great apse with its narrow ambulatory. They have just two sides of an
octagon with two windows. English rather than French the W portal with its
stiff-leaf capitals and much of the blank arcading.

‡ The view from the keep is as lovely as the distant view of the castle
from the marshes.

veloped the curtain wall which must have existed under Roger already, and added other towers (e.g. the surviving Bevis Tower) and grander domestic premises. Under Edward I the higher Well Tower was added to the keep and the barbican was built outside Roger's gatehouse – but the castle was almost ruined in 1643–9 and everything else is now C19.

The detailed description follows the visitor's route. What he sees first as he walks up to the castle is the appalling s front, all by Buckler. But it includes first one Norman window, near the N end, and that makes one regret the original Arundel very much: two lights under a relieving arch, joined by coupled columns, admirably sturdy, yet decorative, of the time of Henry II. The path winds round the W side and enters at the BARBICAN, which is of 1295, two towers close together with a deeply recessed centre between them and windows with shouldered lintels (Caernarvon arches). Beyond is the INNER GATEWAY, convincingly C11, two massive un-moulded arches with plain imposts. The portcullis groove remains. The gatehouse was heightened in the late C13, and then the enormous NW buttress was built up. On the l. is the KEEP. This is nearly circular (59 by 67 ft), with flat buttresses and battlements. It has no windows to the outside, but there is plenty of evidence that there were buildings of two storeys leaning against its wall – perhaps of timber. The wall-walk has a Norman doorway to a garderobe, and there is also a small Norman doorway at ground-floor level to the well, i.e. the later well-house; and there is finally also curiously enough at ground-floor level – a rarity, but cf. Bamburgh – a big blocked doorway on the E side, clearly of the 1170s, one order of zigzag and one roll-moulding sweeping from floor to floor without capitals. In the middle of the open space left in the keep is an underground store-room with a pointed tunnel-vault with plain transverse arches and a ridge-rib. Attached to the s side is the late C13 WELL TOWER, plain as the barbi-can and also with the motif of the window with shouldered lintel. Its upper part is of 1890 etc. Beyond the keep to the N is the BEVIS TOWER, originally late C13 with the upper part again of 1890 etc. It has a garderobe shoot. The curtain wall surrounding the bailey is mostly of 1890 too.

The interiors are entered to the r. of the barbican and inner gateway from a depressing courtyard, all of 1890 etc. The interiors, unless stated, are 1890 too. First the CHAPEL, vaulted and apsed, with lots of Purbeck and stiff-leaf, a cross between Canterbury and Lincoln, vitiated by complete lack of feeling. Good set of STAINED GLASS by *Dunstan Powell* of *Hardman's*. Then the BARONS HALL, 133 ft long, 50 ft high, with two huge fireplaces, quite dead: again the best thing the STAINED GLASS on the W side, historical scenes in good overall colour patterns, also by *Hardman*, freer and livelier than church glass would have been. A corridor and the staircase under its high, lantern-like tower follow in the same style, then the Queen Victoria Room, with early C19 decoration, no more feeling but a good deal more fun, and then the LIBRARY, at last a room worth a look in its own right. It dates from 1801. It is all mahogany and planned like a complete hall-church with crossing and flattened wooden sexpartite vaulting. The result is neurotic but impressive, rather like Soane at his creepiest, though not using a Soanic vocabulary. Space seesaws and tiptoes from side to side, always looking over its shoulder. Beyond this everything is again 1890.

The most impressive Norman, i.e. Henry II, part of the castle is buried below this ducal show and not seen by visitors. It is a very large undercroft with a round tunnel-vault, single-chamfered arches, and two windows to the N. These give now on a basement corridor, but were originally outer windows. So they tell us the width of the Norman apartments above, about half, if that, of the present width, and as all this is below the present hall, we have here some indication of the hall of the 1170s which we are at liberty to endow with decorative riches on the image of Bishop Pudsey's hall range at Durham Castle. For it must of course always be remembered that the keep served as living quarters only in an emergency. For peacetime use less cramped space was provided.*

In the park N of the house HIORN'S TOWER, built in 1790 by *Francis Hiorn*. A skittish C18 shape – triangular, with octagonal corner-turrets – but in spite of that a very serious and sober piece of Gothic, in the style of the C14 parts of Arundel Castle, convincing at a distance. Flint and stone in chequer pattern.

Just S of this ARUNDEL PARK, the new house of the Duke of Norfolk, 1960 by *Claud Phillimore*, disappointingly dumb

* PLATE kept at Arundel Castle: Chalice and Paten of *c*.1500, the paten with the Vernicle. Very fine and large gilt Lamp of 1700.—Six Candlesticks, by *Ambrose Stevenson*, 1710. – Holy-water Bucket with Sprinkler, by *Frederick Kandler*, 1735. – Lamp, in the Adam style, 1789.

Neo-Georgian. Centre and wings, painted white, and none of the elegance of a really clever pastiche.

ST MARY'S GATE. In the kitchen garden of the castle, W of the church. Made up in the C19 from fragments of a medieval gate. Only the jambs of the arch were left by 1780.

Two more lodges in the NW corner of the park. Both are mid-C19, soberly designed. WHITEWAYS LODGE is at the join of A29 and A284, the other lodge is ¾ m. S on the road to Arundel. On the other hand, SWANBOURNE LODGE, of the same date, NE of the house, is fussy Jacobean, like a railway station on a branch line.

PERAMBULATION. This is best started from the station, ½ m. E of the town, as this gives the right distance and scale to see Arundel at its best. Immediately E of the station is what is left of CALCETTO PRIORY. All that remains is the bottom of a flint C13 tower, unbuttressed and without any medieval detail, made into the core of an C18 farmhouse. It was a house of Augustinian Canons, dedicated to St Bartholomew in the mid C12. Going W into the town, nothing much until the BRIDGE itself, a decent three-arched rebuilding of 1935. Immediately on the r. what is left of the MAISON DIEU, a hospital or almshouse founded in 1395, dissolved in 1546: a roofless rectangular building of clunch and flint with all the dressed stones removed. It was apparently the W side of a quadrangle: it is now, rather oddly, a rose-garden. The main road splits around one island of buildings (the kind of opening out so dear to traffic engineers might be an improvement, here, as it would give Arundel a focus) and reunites as a steep triangular open space leading up to the walls of the castle grounds all known as HIGH STREET. It contains a good deal of fussy C19 building, but also a study sequence of plain, un-reflective C18 buildings on the E side (Nos 26–34), all in warm red brick, all following the pattern of the NORFOLK ARMS at the downhill end of the group, a splendid example of a coaching inn, five bays and three storeys with the hotel name in splendid gold early C19 Egyptian lettering on a white ground, holding the little space together. More plain C18 houses higher up on the W side: No. 57 early C19 and stock-brick, No. 61 late C18 and red brick.

W of the High Street three roads run off parallel and make up the rest of the town. The first is TARRANT STREET, which starts modest and becomes a bit grander further W, with the VICTORIA INSTITUTE, a sober stucco front of c.1840, then

plain c18 and c19 houses, with something like a formal street
(ARUN STREET) running off l. down to the river. It ends by
running into the main Chichester road at almost the end of
the town, and by turning r. It can be followed back to the
High Street by way of the second of the three streets,
MALTRAVERS STREET. It begins with stuccoed cottages and
some of the ubiquitous late c19 half-timber,* then develops
quite impressively as an undulating street with pavements and
sometimes service roads high above the heavy traffic, with
views up to the Catholic church and down to the river: Arundel here begins to fulfil the promise of the first distant glimpses.
On the s side Nos 57 and 59–61 are big and very blank late
c18 builders' houses, both with Tuscan doorcases, twelve
bays altogether. Further E there is early c19 stucco on the s
side (Nos 45–49) and quite a showy Roman Doric porch on
the N side (No. 26) flanked by a pair of bay windows. None of
this is more than an agreeable background to a town walk,
something provided also by the cottages of BAKERS ARMS
HILL, running back downhill on the r. to Tarrant Street. The
street continues on the N side with a pair of c18 houses with
weatherboarded bay windows, then runs down to the High
Street via the gloomy COUNCIL OFFICES, c.1836, only too
clearly by the same (unknown) architect as the Congregational church.

Turn l. at the end, then, after a brush with the familiar neo-
Gothic of Castle Lodge, you are in LONDON ROAD, the
third of the parallel streets. It is an oddly chilling feudal
experience, with the feudalism largely reinterpreted in terms
of the c19. On the r. there is the castle wall, the church (*see*
p. 86), then the castle wall again. On the l. there is first a piece
of Gothick that must date from the early c19 work at the
castle (TOWER HOUSE; stock brick with a stone octagonal
tower at the E end) and then the pretentious Catholic church,
then, beyond, a whole set of late c19 Tudor cottages and a
former school by *Hansom*, 1880. The simple early-c19 flint
terraces running s from here towards a tributary of the Arun
(BOND STREET and MOUNT PLEASANT) come as a distinct
relief after this, and are in fact almost the nicest part of
Arundel.

PARK FARM, ½ m. w. Largely early c19, with handsome barns.
(But the N front, invisible from the road, is c16, with a five-
light bow window. MHLG)

* Nos 40–44 by *Hansom*

1010
ASHINGTON

A long straggle down the London–Worthing road a little way N
of the Downs. No group, and too much new building, particularly bad on the lane leading to the church.

ST PETER AND ST PAUL. Disastrously treated in 1872 by
Robert Wheeler of Tunbridge Wells, with a big new aisle. A
few simple Perp details remain, like the E and W windows and
the stoup reset in the aisle near the S door.

The nicest cottage in the village is BROADBRIDGE FARM, on
the main road opposite the lane to the church. Two gables,
stone with brick dressings, simple C17 refronting on an older
frame which still shows on the r. gable. Good unrestored
textures.

8000
ASHLING

Two hamlets, East and West, without a church, in flat wooded
country NW of Chichester, seeming much further than they
actually are from the suburbanized ribbon along A27. East
Ashling has pretty timber-framed cottages on a cul-de-sac
running W from the main road; West Ashling has two good
timber-framed cottages among a lot of pretty ones: HILLS
COTTAGE on the N side of the road, thatched, regularly
framed, with herringbone brick-nogging, probably C17; and
OLD QUINNINGS, similar but with overhanging first floor,
hence perhaps a little earlier, and very similar to the cottage
at Nutbourne (*see* p. 332).

1010
ASHURST

In the Weald N of Steyning, and much more remote than the
villages around it. A look at the map shows the amount of woodland remaining. The long, quiet views, backed by Downs to the
S, have a lot of charm. No real centre.

ST JAMES. By itself on a remote by-road, and from the N one
of the prettiest village exteriors in Sussex, with shingled
broach spire at the SW end, lean-to to the N of this, then the
much taller W gable of the nave. Flint, although the Downs
are four miles away. Usually, the local stone took over immediately. Yet the roof is Horsham slate and the nave gable is
tile-hung, a cheerful mixture. Inside, what happened is a
smaller edition of the goings-on at Findon – i.e., a big kingpost roof spanning both nave and aisle and resting on top of
the arcade. Here, with everything so much more irregular, it
does not look so bizarre, and provides all sorts of cosy diagonal

views. The N wall of the nave is probably early C12, with a plain blocked round-headed doorway. Tower and aisle must have been begun by 1200, but it is impossible to say just how and in what order. The arch from tower to old nave is still round, to the aisle it is pointed. The arcade arches are all pointed. Where chamfers occur they are all slight. The piers are round, the capitals mostly moulded, but those of the arch between chancel and aisle have stiff-leaf in that early form where there is only one row of small leaves and much of the bell remains visible. All this is c.1180–1200 in character. The only thing which would make one think of a much later date – and wrongly, apparently – is the width of the aisle. The change from narrow to wide aisles came usually only later in the C13. The low lean-to which forms the W part of the nave and makes such an attractive silhouette outside must also be of the same build as the rest. Chancel C13 with trefoil-headed lancets, arch from aisle to chancel probably C13 too, corresponding to a lengthening of the aisle. Most windows on the s side 1877. – FONT. Square C13 bowl, plain except for a lively arcade incised on one side as though it were a mason's blueprint. – VAMPING HORN. – PLATE. Chalice and Paten, late C18.

SW of the church, PEPPERS FARM is quite a big black and white building, regularly framed. Dated 1611 on the N porch. To the E is the main hamlet of the village. Just N of the Fountain pub is BLOCQUES, a good, unrestored half-timber cottage. C16, L-shaped, with a pronounced lean.

Further N, BINES GREEN is good and rough, hardly altered in the last hundred years. Scattered cottages around a big open space. One of the best places in this part of Sussex to see the whole repertoire of cottage building. Half-timber, tile-hanging, weatherboarding, and even a little flint. Across the Adur, both BINES FARM and BRIGHTHAM'S FARM have good groups of barns – again, in every kind of material. The houses are brick or tile-hung with the usual earlier timber frame underneath.

ATHERINGTON see CLIMPING

BAILIFFSCOURT

What on earth can a topographer committed to a C20 style of architecture, yet committed also to recording the memorable without fear or favour, say about Bailiffscourt ? It was originally the house of the bailiff of the abbey of Séez, in Normandy, and from this the CHAPEL remains: a late C13 building, a simple rectangle with lancet side windows and a three-light E window, with, inside, carved foliage capitals to the rere-arch. All the rest dates from 1935, built by Lord Moyne and his architect, *Amyas Phillips*, and it poses a moral problem which is not at all simple. What they did was to create one big house and several smaller ones in a medieval style and medieval way of design which is absolutely indistinguishable from old work. Nearly all the details are original work imported piecemeal: where they have to be matched or recreated the result is completely authentic in texture as well as style. So what does the critic do? Is he to disown the whole thing and perjure his own eyes – because Bailiffscourt is a lovely house – or to accept wholeheartedly the result as a kind of dream or flashback to the C15 whilst being dubious about the motives which led to its being built?

However, once it has happened, to adapt the proverb, one can only lie back and enjoy it. The main building is a compact but irregular quadrangle in the (accurate) style of a Somerset manor house, warm limestone with a roof of Horsham slate. Asymmetry, enclosure, and texture are recreated rather than reproduced, quite clearly a labour of love. Inside, several medieval roofs from buildings in Somerset. Close to the house two more detached blocks, limestone and thatch, in the style of an early medieval house like Boothby Pagnell: further E beside the original chapel is an early type of thatched cottage (from Bignor) and a complete brick and half-timber gatehouse, the back with timbers widely spaced, the front impressively close-timbered with central entrance arch under an overhang (from Loxwood). Attached to it another good cottage (from Old Basing, Hants.). All are completely convincing, and in fact are simply transplanted to form an open-air museum like St Fagan's or Skansen.

The key to this superb performance is perhaps in the mind of Mr Phillips, and his flair for asymmetrical and eclectic design. Twenty years later, it could well have led him into designing some of England's best schools.

BALLS CROSS *see* KIRDFORD

BARGHAM

CHURCH, 2 m. N of Angmering. A wonderful remote situation

on the s slopes of the Downs, with one good flint farm as the
only building near. Flint foundations only, movingly overgrown, excavated in the 1950s. The results showed a complicated and interesting building, of several dates. It starts with
the very unusual feature of a w apse, including Roman brick
fragments, which may be Romano-British; then an Early
Saxon rectangular nave and chancel, then later Saxon N and
s porticus. The building was given three apses in the C12 (to
chancel and to N and s porticus), and converted again to a
rectangular E end in the C13. The church was demolished
c.1500: all the changes can be followed out on the ground,
which makes the site worth a visit.

BARKFOLD HOUSE see KIRDFORD

BARLAVINGTON   9010

s of Petworth: a church, a farmyard, and a magnificent view of
wooded downs, here in unexpected perspective as the scarp
becomes a vast natural amphitheatre to the s of Bignor.

ST MARY. Complete humble village E.E., as usual in West
Sussex. The outside renewed, the inside surprisingly coherent
and effective. The utter simplicity of these C13 village
churches is remarkable. Nave and chancel, and two-bay aisles.
The N is still blocked, the s was unblocked in 1874. All of
c.1200 or shortly after. E end with two lancets, still round-
headed, instead of three, arcades with round piers, square
abaci, and obtusely pointed arches, i.e. slightly earlier than
the usual run in Sussex.

BARNHAM   9000

In the plain between Arundel and Bognor Regis. Most of Barnham is 'Barnham Junction', where the trains for Bognor leave
the main line, and not very attractive, but church and manor
house are by themselves to the s. The junction was suburban by
c.1900, so it wears a heavily landscaped Wimbledonian air which
is rather weird.

ST MARY. Like Ford, one of Sussex's nicest exteriors; patched
flint walls, mellow tile roofs, and a white-painted wooden
bell-turret. The inside lightly restored but rather empty: a
single room with wood and plaster tympanum instead of
chancel arch. The nave walls are Norman, as usual, see the
windows high up on the s side. An aisle was thrown out from

(or rather, crude pointed openings pierced in) the N side
c.1180, and blocked later, probably before the end of the
Middle Ages. Arch of the same date on the N side of the
chancel, now unblocked and leading to the vestry. Chancel
details E.E., with three noble lancets in the E end and very
crude attempts at plate tracery in the S side: two lancets close
together with an irregular lozenge in the spandrel between
them. Elegant, simple trefoil-headed PISCINA. The W window
is Perp, and a rather odd design: two lights and an arched head
fitted into a square frame with the spandrels glazed. – SCULP-
TURE (chancel, S side). First-rate French C15 figure of St
Genevieve, painted wood, the colours (a subtle combination
of olive and dark green) still vivid. Face and draperies stiff
but not at all expressionless, a kind of dumb humility that is
very touching. – PLATE. Upper half of thurible of Limoges
enamel, pre-Reformation; Cup, 1779.

39b BARNHAM COURT. A very good brick house of c.1640, the best
of its date in the county, so similar to Kew Palace in Surrey
that the same designer must surely have been responsible.
He achieved an effect of all-over magnificence combined with
precision and elegance in the details. Barnham, like Kew, was
probably built for a rich merchant or yeoman-farmer and the
style is known as Artisan Mannerism: his aristocratic counterpart would have employed Inigo Jones or one of his group.
The front has only five bays and two and a half storeys, yet is
more effective than many palaces. The two main floors have
pilasters (Doric below, Ionic above – leaving the angles free),
splendid cornices, and a very splendid Doric pedimented
doorcase on a rusticated surround. The attic has three pedimented (i.e. Dutch) gables with a window in each, the ratio
of 3 above to 5 below not seeming at all awkward; the main
cornice is strong enough to separate the rhythms. The back
much plainer with two bigger shaped (i.e. unpedimented)
gables; the inside plain also, with a simple contemporary staircase, the balusters on the way from Jacobean to the later
C17 dumb-bell shape. The brickwork is laid in English bond,
whereas Kew Palace started Flemish bond in England.

BEEDINGS see PULBOROUGH

8010

BEPTON

Scattered village under the Downs SW of Midhurst, the cottages
still largely sandstone and half-timber rather than flint. The

original group of church and farm is by itself on a knoll with a superb view s to Bepton Down, half a mile away. As usual this has a scale and majesty quite out of proportion to the actual height of the hills.

ST MARY. Originally simple C13 but very much restored; new chancel and chancel arch, new or renewed lancet windows. The squat tower with pyramidal cap (and inside, with the simplest sort of tower arch, pointed and single-chamfered but unmoulded) is the best part. The inside impression all C19. – PLATE. Cup and Paten, 1625. – MONUMENT. Niche in the chancel above a damaged tomb, very much better and more alive than usual. Probably c.1300, exactly balanced between E.E. and Dec, using the new forms but keeping the earlier rigidity and force. Triangular arch with crocketed sides, stalky vegetable finial on top, enclosing a trefoil and then a cinquefoil. In the little church it radiates energy as though it had an electric charge: it shows perfectly that rough carving with life is better than mechanical perfection without it. Damaged Lombardic inscription below: RADO. DE. LAHEDOL. GIT. ICY. DEU. LY. RNDE. MERCY. RYCH. – In the churchyard, several late C19 iron headstones, the effect still delicate and pre-Victorian. Where were they cast?

BERSTED

The original village of Bognor, now caught up in the flood of houses spreading inland. Two hamlets, South and North, both with a few old cottages but not much recognizable village character. North is better than South, and SHRIPNEY, a little further NE, is better than either.

ST MARY MAGDALENE, South Bersted. Hard and rebuffing outside, all renewed in 1879–81 by *Ewan Christian*; only the plain C13 W tower with its prodigious later W buttresses is easy on the eye. The inside has a quite unsuspected scale and effectiveness, even though the chancel is rebuilt, due to the narrow aisles and the big five-bay arcades, c.1240, of the standard type, but nicely done, the piers alternately round and octagonal, the responds delicately scalloped. The tower is evidently a little older, c.1200, see the tower arch (and the fact that the tower buttresses show inside the church). – STAINED GLASS. E window, given in 1880, by *Powell's*. Good; weak drawing but first-rate colour composition using deep blues, greens, and reds and treating the whole group of lancets as one unit. It adds a lot to the interior. – MONUMENT. Decent bust, above the N door. It represents Dr A. C. Tait, Archbishop of Canterbury, who died in 1882. The surround and inscription have disappeared.

Several good bulky thatched COTTAGES at North Bersted, ½ m. NW and almost in the country.

BIGNOR

Small village around a quadrilateral of lanes between Petworth and Arundel. No group, but an exhilarating view near the church into an amphitheatre of the Downs.

HOLY CROSS. Plain lancets outside, renewed by *Street*, who added the fussy bell-turret, out of key. Impressively big inside, like a barn, with a solidarity and sense of space which is out of all proportion to the simple details. The plainest possible Norman chancel arch – an unchamfered arch on plain imposts. All the rest is C13 work – chancel with three lancets in the E end, narrow lean-to aisles with double-chamfered arches, circular abaci. The responds of the inner order have their own abacus and shaft on the S side, abacus and bracket on the N side, which may be slightly later. The odd W window, three lancet lights with quatrefoils between, is presumably Street's. – SCREEN. Terribly made over, but basically Dec, similar to West Thorney: the original parts mainly the band of cusped quatrefoils forming the heads of the lights.

THE OLD SHOP. On the E side of the quadrilateral. Deservedly famous C15 cottage, illustrated time and again: half-timbered and thatched, the sides with a first-floor overhang and wooden spandrels in front of the recessed centre – the usual type of yeoman's cottage in Kent. Brick infillings in the centre, flint stone and plaster at the sides. The mixture of textures is captivating, and it has somehow remained unrestored.

BIGNOR PARK. Plain and decent white stuccoed box by *Henry Harrison*, 1826–31.

ROMAN VILLA. The site, which lies to the E of the village and N of the road from Bignor to Bury, is of one of the largest villas in Britain. The villa was of the courtyard type, surrounded by a wall enclosing an area of 4½ acres. The inner courtyard, some 250 ft by 144 ft, was surrounded by corridors off which rooms opened on the N, S, and W sides. The N wing contained the principal rooms, many decorated with floor mosaics. These mosaics are of the very highest quality and are notable for their detail and the minuteness of the tesserae employed. Among the most interesting is the 'Venus and Gladiator' mosaic, from an apsidal room, consisting of a lunate panel in the apse with a central circle containing the head of Venus flanked by peacocks and to the s a panel depicting cupids engaged in gladiatorial display. A large and elaborate bath suite consisting of dressing room, hot, warm, and cold rooms was in the s wing. The inner courtyard is reached through an outer, larger court containing barns and the dwellings of estate workers. Early finds from the villa suggest occupation from the c1 to the c4, and recent excavations (as yet unpublished) have revealed a number of building phases and structural alterations.

CAUSEWAYED CAMP, 1¼ m. sw, on Bignor Hill. A Neolithic causewayed camp consisting of a roughly oval enclosure defined by a ditch with slight internal bank. Gaps or causeways through bank and ditch are traceable in the N and E sectors of the camp.

BILLINGSHURST

Billingshurst, although the map calls it a village, looks and feels like a small town. One long curving street, the main London to Bognor road, with very much of a coaching air. Hence it has adapted fairly easily to motoring. Bright, with good serpentine street views, but not many individual buildings.

ST MARY. Above the road at the s end of the townlet. The w tower is the best part, dour even in the context of Sussex steeples, with clasping buttresses and heavy broach-spire. Originally it must have been almost without windows. One c13 lancet opening remains on the s side (is the odd detail inside it original?). The other tower windows look c16, and the pretty brick and timber w porch must be c.1600. The tower arch is hard to date: an outer continuous chamfered order, and an inner chamfered order resting on shafts with octagonal abaci but round bases. It looks as though the c15 interfered with the c13 here. Restoration has not left the rest with much interest. s chancel chapel c13, arcades probably c.1300, as rough as they would be in Cornwall: octagonal piers and double-chamfered arches, the s arcade almost rebuilt. Good c15 windows in the s aisle, skimpier c16 windows in the N aisle. The whole E end is of 1866 and rather disastrous, especially from outside. The nave has a C15 wagon roof with a pattern of square panels and carved bosses at the intersections. – PLATE. Cup and Flagon, 1631; Almsdish, 1640; Paten, 1720. – MONUMENT. Brass to Thomas Bartlet † 1499 and wife. Effigies 2 ft 6 in. high, the usual Late Gothic lifelessness in the etching (nave).

The long main road is called High Street and South Street. In High Street nothing worth a special look: interest starts only at the church, with a nice build-up of humble cottages to the churchyard entrance, 15 ft above the road level. On the opposite side, the OLDE SIX BELLS, C16 half-timber, with an overhang along the whole first floor, the framing becoming regular. Nicely set back from the street, as is the other thing to see, a little further S, the UNITARIAN CHURCH of 1754, like a demure Georgian cottage. Although the architecture is utterly self-effacing, it lies on a knoll in a surprisingly big churchyard, so makes a display in spite of itself.

In East Street one good C16 farm (GORE FARMHOUSE). Half-timber frame, tile-hung front with a half-hipped gable at the w end: very pretty. Opposite, alas, the deplorable brand-new CATHOLIC CHURCH by *H. Bingham Towner* of Uckfield.

GREAT DAUX FARM. Good C16 timber-framed house in an unlikely situation by the railway just E of Billingshurst station.

OKEHURST, 1 m. N. Picturesque agglomeration of house and farm buildings, the most prominent part stone-built, two-storeyed, probably C16. Small half-timbered granary on the N side. The Weald landscape near here is splendidly unspoilt, a continuously changing pattern of copses and small fields.

9000   BILSHAM

¾ m. SW of Yapton

Secluded set of farms and barns just off the Bognor Road, including a C13 CHAPEL, used as a shed. One single room, original two-light windows on the N side (*c.*1260) and at the E end (early C14).

8010   BINDERTON

1 m. N of Lavant

CHAPEL. Beside the main road: tiny oblong of flint with brick dressings, probably late C17. Never consecrated, already a barn by the C18. Now roofless, the inside quite choked with trees, sad and neglected. Round-arched w door; nothing else can be deciphered.

BINDERTON HOUSE. Fragment of a house built in 1677 in the form of a half- H with exceptionally long wings. The N wing and the centre are complete; plain two-storey brickwork, partly roughcast. Late C18 additions, e.g. the central porch. (Inside a good late C17 staircase. VCH)

BINES GREEN see ASHURST

BINSTED

9000

No village; a handful of secluded cottages w of Arundel at the point where the carefully preserved estate countryside runs into the cheerful, over-built Sussex plain.

ST MARY. Small, with a shingled bell-turret and no aisles; given a rough and ready restoration in 1867 by *Sir T. G. Jackson*. The masonry and three windows Norman. In the splay of one of them C12 WALL PAINTING, badly faded, of St Margaret and a weird three-headed Tree of Life. No chancel arch; simple timber-framing indicates the division, almost identical to that which holds up the bell-turret. – FONT. Late Norman, a bit more elaborate than usual in Sussex. Bulgy arcaded bowl on thick round stem. – STAINED GLASS. E window panels by *Henry Holiday*. In grisaille pattern designed by *Jackson*. All made by *Powell's*, 1869.

BIRDHAM

8000

SW of Chichester, and near enough to be slowly filling up with new houses. No group, and nothing nearly as architectural as the splendid patterns made by the moored yachts in the big square harbour, as formal as a parade ground. Two of the modern houses near it are worth a look. One to the w was built in 1939 by *Davies & Moro*, a big, spreading, two-storeyed house, flat-roofed, with a garden screen of rubble stonework. The other, to the E, is called WILLOW END and was built in 1960 by *Higgins & Ney*: a simple house on stilts, the first floor with all the living rooms and weatherboarded, the ground floor taken up with car ports enclosed by purple brick walls. Refreshing and witty, with no silly mannerisms.

ST JAMES. Bulky, as Selsey churches go, and built of ragstone like Sidlesham. It was terribly restored in 1882 by *G. M. Hills*

and the impression, especially inside, is terrifyingly harsh. All
nave windows renewed and new chancel. The chancel arch
remains, early C14, with complex arch mouldings dying into
the imposts. The tower is old too, a bulky design that can be
dated *c.*1545, with single square-headed bell-openings. The
tower arch is rather a puzzle. It has a convincingly Perp
hollow-chamfered arch, but it rests on clustered shafts which
are too small for it and look C14. Was a smaller tower projected, or built and replaced?

BLACKDOWN

1 The twin to Hindhead in Surrey, a great whalebacked sandstone
hill, 918 ft high, immediately s of Haslemere. Splendid views
from it.

BLACKDOWN HOUSE. 500 ft up on the s slope: no views from
the house itself but an abundance of them from the grounds.
The nucleus is a handsome plain stone manor house of 1640 in
the usual Sussex continuation of the Tudor style. But it has
been so hedged around by alterations, first of 1844–6 by
Salvin and then of 1891, that it is difficult to appreciate it any
more. The original work has not been tampered with, just
embroidered at the edges – the bargeboards to the gables e.g.
The old part is the centre of the s front; five- and three-light
mullion-and-transom windows, two-storeyed porch, gabled
and dated with a four-centred entrance arch. The hood-
moulds to the windows have an odd and attractive trick in
that two courses of very thin tiles are inserted between them
and the stonework above, an effect Lutyens would have enjoyed. The style is really extraordinarily serviceable and handsome, more so than that of better known Cotswold manor
houses. Inside simple early C17 staircase and fireplaces.

ALDWORTH HOUSE. High up on the E side of Blackdown; built
for Tennyson by *Sir James Knowles* in 1869 as a summer
retreat when Farringford on the Isle of Wight became too well
known. Choice of architect and style do not add much to one's
opinion of the poet; the result is a fussy small hotel half-way
between the French and English C16 style.

UPPER ROUNDHURST HOUSE. Lovely situation immediately
under the E slopes, at Roundhurst Common: small late C17
house of the newly arrived Wren or Hugh May type which is
quite rare in the Weald (and in Sussex generally). The style is
inevitably mixed with a few earlier reminiscences and these

give it a good deal of its charm. Five bays, hipped roof, ashlar front. The windows have stone surrounds and (wooden) mullion-and-transom casements; the doorway has a bulgy frieze and a cornice. But the cornice turns out to be a section of the string course between the floors, brought down rather naughtily for the purpose. Good late C17 GATEPIERS in front. The plainness and simplicity must have seemed extraordinary, after five hundred years of complicated mouldings. It still does, come across suddenly in this close intricate landscape of gables and tile-hanging.

BLACKPATCH HILL *see* PATCHING

BLUE IDOL
2 m. SE of Billingshurst

FRIENDS MEETING HOUSE. A lovely, remote site, at the end of a cul-de-sac turning of A272 between Billingshurst and Coolham. The meaning of the name is unknown. The meeting house is simply one wing of a half-timbered cottage, the framing so regular that it is probably C17. It was converted, for Penn, in 1691. One room going up two storeys, a plain gallery and the plainest kind of furniture. Like everything Quaker, it has a wonderful feeling of honesty and wholeness. This must have been how the Cistercians felt when they began to build.

BOGNOR REGIS

Bognor is an oddly disconnected place because everything has grown up piecemeal: the parts of the town never seem to be where you expect them. The original village was at Bersted, a mile from the coast, having as little as possible to do with an eroded coastline. In the 1780s Sir Richard Hotham, a wealthy hatter of Southwark, descended on it and started an ambitious scheme, including a hotel and assembly rooms. These he built between Bersted and the sea, but, very typically, not on the seafront itself. The scheme and the name – he tried to call it Hothampton – were in fact too ambitious, and seaside Bognor developed in the 1820s almost a mile away and on a quieter scale, frankly an imitation of the bigger resorts. It was probably the original of Jane Austen's 'Sanditon', and its piecemeal appearance was remarkable even in the seaside boom of the early C19. *The Beauties of England and Wales* said in 1813: 'it consists of several rows of elegant brick structures, but so detached that the place is at least a mile in length, erected with the professed design of making Bognor the resort of more select company than is to be found at other bathing places'. In other words, only carriage owners encouraged. The town did not finally fill up until the c20, and the prevailing character is a cheerful jostle of *c.*1910, very suited to the seaside: the Regis followed in 1929 after King George V's convalescence. Much of the original building near the pier disappeared in the war or soon after, and on its site is a big new scheme which has at last given Bognor a focal point, albeit a crude one.

ST JOHN THE BAPTIST, London Road. Big, hard, and heartless, by *A. W. Blomfield*, 1882. Polychrome brick inside, as a reminiscence of the handful of sincere buildings he put up in his youth.

ST JOHN THE BAPTIST, Steyne. Old church, built by *Daniel Wonham* in 1821 as a speculation. Only the tower remains, erected in 1833. Stucco Gothick, cheaply done.

ST WILFRED, Victoria Drive. Hard and heartless also, by *G. H. Fellowes Prynne*, 1908. Unfinished: no loss. The inside brick and stone, and better.

TOWN HALL, Clarence Road. 1929 by *C. Cowles-Voysey*. Lutyens's Neo-Georgian style on a splayed corner: the syntax a bit confused, but could be worse.

GRAMMAR SCHOOL, Pevensey Road (on the edge of the town, w of Bersted). By the *County Architect's Department*, 1958. Good, unaffected example of a kind of school design that will later be immediately recognizable as coming from the 1950s: largely glass curtain walls, multiple thin uprights, a delicate brittle character like a piece of machinery. (The 1960s schools have already become thicker and more emphatic, as can be seen in the junior school to the SE of this.) Three-storey main block with a deep top cornice, two-storey gymnasium ditto. Humane materials – stock brick and cedar boarding – and a good deal more care and thought given than to the average curtain-walled school.

The seaside centre of Bognor is by the PIER of 1910, quite a good date for piers. Not much of the original early C19 building is left, and what does remain, as in most of the small Sussex resorts, is not really attractive, trying to outdo Brighton with insufficient means. To the E is the CARLTON HOTEL, with big balconies, opposite the pier WATERLOO PLACE, with stuccoed and balconied detached houses too close to one another, and at the N end, well designed FLATS of 1910. Immediately W of this is STEYNE, in imitation of Brighton, and undoubtedly the best part of seafront Bognor: a long square open to the sea, with a nice jostling variety of two- and three-storey houses, bow-fronted and balconied, the epitome of an English seaside, set off nicely by the brick and flint Gothic front of a chapel. West again, the ROYAL NORFOLK HOTEL, nine stucco Italianate bays, set back grandly.

N of Waterloo Place the new QUEENSWAY scheme, by *Donald Harwin & Partners*, 1960–2. This includes a fifteen-storey block of flats and has given the town a focus, but the details, alas, are terribly thick. To the E is Station Road, and the shopping centre of Bognor, mostly with a cheerful 1920 flavour.

From there HIGH STREET runs NE to the original late C18 buildings of Hothampton. There is enough on the way to make a connected walk possible. First, two bow-fronted houses (VALHALLA and MANORA), semi-detached at the corner of Lyon Road. Then on the l. SUDLEY LODGE, built by *John Shaw* in 1827 and intended to be the first of a series, a plain villa half-way between Regency and Italianate. The next building is HOTHAM HOUSE in a sizeable park, built by Sir Richard Hotham for himself in the 1790s – a big, plain, ten-bay house. The nicest part, which must be early C19, is the extremely prettily and elegantly detailed two-storey veranda on the E side: trellis ironwork above supported on a chaste and almost Florentine Doric loggia. On the other side of the road, as a contrast, BUTLIN'S HOLIDAY CAMP, 1960. Curtain-walled communal buildings, and long two-storey terraces of chalets with overhanging balconies. Designed by *Sir Billy Butlin* himself.

Here the walk turns l. along UPPER BOGNOR ROAD. At the intersection first ST MICHAEL'S, a long confused stucco front, and then, much more remarkable, THE DOME, the 48a only one of Bognor's old buildings worth a special visit. It was built as Hothampton Crescent *c.*1787, apparently as an inducement to George III to desert Weymouth, and consists of three houses forming centre and wings (the two end houses seem to be original but look like afterthoughts, and the design is certainly better without them). The centre has five bays and three storeys, the centre pedimented and crowned by a saucer dome on a slate-hung drum. The style loosely Late Palladian, but with all sorts of odd quirks which make it look as though it were done, very successfully, by a local man.

Arcaded ground floor, overscale central doorcase made into one composition with the window above by a blind arch; lunette above that. The designer has rung the changes expertly on three different colours of brick – yellow, grey, and vermilion – exactly in the way a local mason would do; and he has given the stock-brick string course between first and second floors a naughty upward quirk under each window so that it becomes the sill.

The next house is MORDINGTON, stuccoed and plain, then THE WARREN of c.1830, and finally NORTHCLIFFE SCHOOL, built as Spencer Terrace in 1787, perhaps by the same architect as The Dome. Here, the character is quite different: fourteen bays of plain red brickwork as they might have been on any of the roads out of London, punctuated only by big porches with Doric columns carrying segmental arches. A very nice building to have in a town. From here the centre can be reached via Station Road or by a long bosky footpath just E of it.

BORDEN see ROGATE

8000

BOSHAM

Deservedly, the best known village around Chichester Harbour: a close-packed huddle of cottages at the waterside, as intricate as a Cornish village, but built to a softer Sussex colour scheme – flint, brick, tile, and tile-hanging. Bosham has a delightful plan: it is a dead end between two inlets of the sea. The very tip is a field, Quay Meadow, and the village extends NE from it, turning its face out to the harbour (a road along the edge which is flooded at high tide) whilst its real everyday axis is a very narrow lane (High Street) at the back. Boats everywhere, and a smart place to be, except that sailing, like flying, can mercifully never be truly 'smart'. Everything but essential road traffic ought to be kept out, as in Clovelly, as a matter of sheer physical necessity. The best view of all, and a splendid counterpoint after walking in the village, is of the whole waterfront seen from across the inlet to the S, spread out and backed by the Downs.

HOLY TRINITY. Again the Sussex habit of being humble outside and majestic inside. Bosham was an important place in Saxon times; there was already a monastery here in the C7 and the church is said to be on the site of a Roman basilica, with bases of a Roman arch still *in situ* beneath the chancel

arch. Later it was probably the chief seat of Earl Godwin;
Harold sailed from here in 1064 on his ill-fated voyage to
Normandy, and hence Bosham church appears, convention-
ally, on the Bayeux tapestry. Tower and chancel arch are in
fact pre-Conquest: the tower is unbuttressed and plain, and
its age can best be seen on the N side with a blocked two-light
window, and inside in the small plain tower arch a triangle-
headed window above and yet higher up an asymmetrically
placed window. The top stage is C15 and has a small shingled
broach-spire. The chancel arch is much grander, one of the 10b
best Saxon arches in England, giving tremendous scale to the
interior (and incidentally making a perfect match for the long
E.E. chancel and five-light E window: the same rich simplicity
permeates both). It has almost exactly the dimensions of the
Early Norman arch at Stoughton, and it must date from well
into the C11. A base like a millstone, three orders with deeply
cut tubular roll-mouldings becoming shafts of the same size.
The abaci are in two stages, a bold square slab on top of
another millstone, with the top of the shafts below given crude
grooving and necking. This has the effect of tying the orders
together, and with the slight horseshoe shape of the arch
gives a vivid expression of tension and holding in of an arch
as the balance of forces. It is a very good refutation of the
theory that the Saxons could not create architecture: very
few arches built since have the architectural presence of this
one. Saxon Bosham must have been as a space something
moving too – wide indeed but high to a degree we cannot
easily visualize now that there are arcades l. and r. The Saxon
roof-line appears on the W wall at half the height of the topmost window.

The westernmost part of the chancel walls is pre-Conquest
too, with one blocked window on the N side and herringbone
masonry. It was lengthened in the C12, and lengthened again
in the early C13, making it as long as the nave. This work,
which must be of c.1230, is very grand: coupled lancets on
the side walls under a rere-arch with Purbeck shafts, and a
splendid set of five graduated lancets in the E window, separated by free-standing Purbeck shafts under a stilted four-
centred rere-arch with shafts of its own. To preserve the
architectural syntax the outer edges of the outermost splays
are not given shafts; instead the roll-moulding is carried down
to the sill without interruption – a nice touch. Double-trefoil-
headed PISCINA with a short octagonal column between. The

two-storey sacristy on the N side was also originally C13 but
has been very much altered.

The C13 also carried out wholesale rebuilding of the nave,
putting in four-bay aisles in the usual Sussex way (round
piers, round abaci, double-chamfered arches)* with the N side
a little earlier than the S (renewed). Both arcades have elegantly moulded bases with spurs at the corners. The N arcade
has above it three plain circular windows said by the VCH to
be pre-Conquest but more probably of the time of the arcade
(see how they line up with the spandrels below), and a C13
PISCINA using a C12 pillar piscina as its drain; the S has the
height of its two E bays reduced by the insertion underneath
of a crypt – a charnel or treasury – which is thus half above
ground. It has a thick quadripartite rib-vault springing from
corbels. Wholesale widening of the aisles in the C14. The N
aisle is authentic, the matching windows in the S aisle are
modern, and so is the geometrical window at the E end, imitated from Oundle at a restoration of 1845. – FONT. c.1200,
with familiar plain arcading, but octagonal, not square, and
four corner shafts on a good marble base. – PLATE. Cup,
given 1675; Paten, 1692. – STAINED GLASS. Fragments in the
S aisle, four roundels of angels: originally from Norwich
Cathedral. – MONUMENTS. Moving mutilated early C14
effigy of a lady, N side of chancel, 2 ft high; originally of good
quality, quite different from the usual hack Perp work. –
Recess in the S aisle, early C14 flat cinquefoil-headed arch
with big carved heads at the ends of the cusps. (The VCH says
probably C15.)

Bosham was a collegiate foundation, and masonry from the
college has clearly found its way into the OLD MANOR HOUSE,
N of the churchyard, and into the cottage to the W of it.
Nothing more definite remains, however (the Manor House
has in its garden a small plain building with C12 or C13 rubble
walling). W of this again, at the edge of the harbour is THE
SLIP, by *Imrie & Angell*, 1913, flint and tile-hung, very sensitive in both massing and detail. It has set the tone for the C20
at Bosham, which is on its best behaviour without being genteel. S of the church in the High Street is BROOK HOUSE with
a plain front of 1743. The walk back from the Quay is quite
delightful whether down the High Street or around the fore-
shore: there is nothing else quite like it in Sussex, and the
total effect of the tiny cosy houses is much greater than any

* The spurs on the pier bases deserve a look. One has monster-heads.

individual design. The road leading out to the N is Bosham Lane: in it a pleasant CONGREGATIONAL CHURCH of 1837, and many pleasant cottages, either C17 with thatch or C18 with brick and tile.

Bosham lies on an irregular peninsula jutting into Chichester harbour. At its S end, in thick woodland, is an admirable true suburb with each house invisible from the next. Most of the houses are cosy and thatched, but one is modern: UPPER WOLVES, by *Kenneth Capon* of *Architects' Co-Partnership*, built for himself in 1957. First floor only, on stilts with a car port underneath: simple wood construction, simple landscaping.

BOTOLPHS   *1000*

At the N end of the Adur gap, s of Steyning. A tiny, depopulated flint-built hamlet which has had the C19 and C20 thrown at it – the railway a few yards away, cement works down the valley, pylons on the hill-crest, and the northward view built up, at Bramber and Beeding. The contrast of extreme rurality and the C20 is effective, but for all that Botolphs would have been better left to itself.

ST BOTOLPH. Simple, mellow, lightly restored. Nave, chancel, and C13 tower with a pert pyramidal cap. Inside, there is a telling reminder that the place has shrunk, in the big and well-detailed mid C13 arcade, now blocked. Three bays, the two-order arches crisply stop-chamfered. In fact the chancel wall is Late Saxon, and so is the chancel arch. Touchingly crude, with a roll moulding on the soffit and responds, jabbed at rather than carved. It is a much rougher edition of the Sompting tower arch. C11 window in the S wall. E window of *c*.1310. – PULPIT. Jacobean, and notable in a county which is poor in C17 fittings. Sounding-board and everything covered with thin incised abstract patterns – no strapwork or wild men. Not quite enough force. – WALL PAINTINGS. Fragments which look as though they could be part of a cycle like Coombes, which is the next village. – PLATE. Cups, 1683 and 1704.

BOW HILL see STOUGHTON

BOWLEY FARM see MUNDHAM

BOXGROVE   *9000*

NE of Chichester where the Downs slip into the plain, sur-

prisingly small and quiet compared with the size of its church.
One rambling, pretty street of flint and brick houses.

ST MARY AND ST BLAISE. The chancel is, after Chichester
the most important E.E. building in Sussex. There was a lot
of influence back and forth between here and Chichester (not
always the case between cathedrals and near-by monasteries –
St Augustine's and Canterbury Cathedral, e.g.), so that Boxgrove seems like the natural continuation of the Chichester
retrochoir. But what at Chichester had been a most beautiful
balance between round and pointed arches – a moment which
could not be repeated – was attempted at Boxgrove to be
carried through into the C13. It is as though the nave of Lincoln had tried to incorporate round arches. The choir of what
has now become Portsmouth Cathedral has the same scheme
as Boxgrove, and one of them is as near to a straightforward
copy as the Middle Ages got. The task was impossible, and
so Boxgrove, strictly, is a failure, a failure of unresolved
grammatical construction in the most syntactical of all styles.
But England is never really strict and rigid, and Boxgrove in
the end is a very happy building, through a mixture of time
and accident.

Boxgrove Priory was founded from Lessay in Normandy
c.1117. What survives is part of the nave, and crossing, transepts, and chancel complete, plus a C14 room serving as a
porch and a C15 vestry. From the early C12 building only
the transepts with their arches into nave and chancel and
some blocked windows are preserved, plain and unremarkable.
Just a little later, the first two bays of the nave (the only part
of it now roofed): no aisle on the N side, presumably to preserve an earlier cloister, two round-headed arches of two
slightly chamfered orders on round piers with round scalloped
capitals and scalloped abaci. Above them, now blocked, the
original clerestory windows. The rest of the nave followed on
from this c.1170, and enough of it is left to show that it must
have been a lovely, sturdy design. The same basic pattern is
followed for the arcades, except that the arches have become
pointed. But alternate piers now have a complex Greek cross
shape with attached shafts (there would have been eight altogether, if we had a complete pier) and leaf-crocket capitals;
and it is these piers which carried the vault enclosing a single
clerestory light. So the whole thing was organized into double
bays, a classic solution without any fumbling or imprecision,
perfectly Gothic in its consistent and ordered use of the

pointed arch. The vaulting-shafts and vault are almost identical with those of the choir, i.e. quadripartite bays with ribs
ornamented with dogtooth. This must be early C13. But the
intention is quite clear in the work of c.1170 and a vault must
have been intended from the beginning. One bay remains on
the s side, four (blank, because there is no aisle) on the N: the
original total length was twelve bays, and from the place
where the present blank arcade ends the N arcade became a
real one, i.e. there was an aisle. It was destroyed at the Dissolution with the whole W part of the church, as the parishioners preferred to use the choir. The old pulpitum with two
doorways was converted into the W wall of the shortened church.

At the same time the low central tower was rebuilt or
possibly remodelled, with new crossing arches put under the
existing bell-stage. The outside has pairs of big round-headed
bell-openings with nook-shafts and roll-mouldings much as
at Chichester, comfortably spread; the inside has splendidly
ample crossing arches, the best single detail in the church.
They are tall and wide, with complex arch mouldings and
very unusual piers and capitals. The piers have clustered
shafts, circumscribing 270 degrees altogether: two small and
unkeeled, three much more massive and keeled. Round, i.e.
three-quarter round, bases and round, i.e. three-quarter
round, abaci. The capitals are very unusual, a kind of development and quickening of Norman scallop capitals which occurs
in just one place at Chichester, the part of the Lady Chapel
built before the fire of 1187. The scallops remain but are
decorated with frills and grooving in a way which changes
their character completely. Above is arcading, two twin bays
to each side, in which earlier shafts, square abaci, and certainly
capitals have been re-used. One especially, with rudimentary
volutes, cannot be much later than the foundation.

The rest of Boxgrove is all of a piece, all c.1220, following
on directly from the Chichester retrochoir. It consists of six
aisled bays with a square end (three double bays, as they had
been in the nave and as they are at Chichester). It needs to be
seen from outside first, where it seems placidly spread out and 23a
English, a far cry from Gothic verticality. Plain and simple,
but very satisfying. One tall lancet in each clerestory bay, two
small ones in the aisles, immensely solid comfortable flying
buttresses reaching half-way up the clerestory. Flint walling
and tile roofs. Only the E end has a little more detail, string
courses with dogtooth ornament. It is the austere structural

system of a French Cistercian abbey like Pontigny given humanity and humility. As early as this, it is clear that English Gothic could never become a rigid system used as an end in itself.

21   The interior, also, could only be English: Purbeck marble shafts and angular shapes are everywhere. But it has none of the calmness and certainty of the outside. It has happy proportions, and it has the unexpected Spenserian fantasy of the PAINTING on the ceiling, heraldry and foliage all intertwined, done in the mid C16 by *Lambert Bernard*. But the bay design, and hence the overall rhythm, is jagged and inharmonious, a too-experimental mixing of round and pointed arches. Each vault bay comprises two arches of the arcade. They are sharply pointed with multiple mouldings and are surmounted by a single wide round-headed blind arch, with one small quatrefoil in the spandrel; an unlovely conjunction of shapes. Above that is a single clerestory light, a wall passage, and three-light clerestory arcades on the inner wall plane consisting of one stilted arch and two much lower triangle-headed ones. It seems an awkward, botched job to fit the shape of the vault. The vault itself rests on triple wall shafts, the middle one with a fillet, standing on corbels carved with mannered sharp-featured faces, staring-eyed and ungentle. The ribs with their dogtooth enrichment are exactly like those of the S transept at Chichester. The E end has three tall lancets. The details throughout have an almost indiscriminate use of Purbeck marble to enliven them, noticeable most of all in that part of the design not yet described: the arcade piers. At the W end they are octagonal with the capitals only of Purbeck marble; the third pier from the W is round and entirely Purbeck, the other four are variations on the theme of the Chichester central core and surrounding shafts. The piers carrying the vault and the E respond have a limestone core, four attached limestone shafts, four attached Purbeck shafts. The piers are actually twelve-sided, a nice conceit. The intermediate piers have a core with four shafts free-standing around it, all Purbeck marble and very elegant, almost identical with the retrochoir piers at Chichester, only reduced in scale.

Later medieval additions are confined to the plain porch room S of the E end of the nave and the plain Perp sacristy on the N side. Dec and Perp windows in the aisles and transepts, and the division of the latter into two storeys with C15 wooden floor and a traceried wooden screen towards the crossing.

FURNISHINGS. FONT. The usual Perp type, octagonal with shields inside quatrefoils. – TILES. Medieval tiles with lions, stags, etc. in the s chancel aisle at the E end. – STAINED GLASS. E window by *O'Connor*, 1862. Vivid reds and purples, very effective as a pattern and as a foil to the sober colours of the church. – MONUMENTS. Several indifferent Perp tomb-chests and recesses, s transept, s aisle, N aisle: the various tracery patterns help little in dating. – De la Warr Chantry 35b (for Lord de la Warr † 1526 and his wife † 1532). A very different thing, like a complete and improbable casket set down in one bay of the choir. It is the only complete chantry chapel in Sussex, and one of the very few really successful marriages of Gothic and Renaissance ornament anywhere in England. It is only skin-deep, of course: this was not the time or place for deeply religious feeling. But within those limits it is delightful, an expert confection of witty details, almost self-mocking, and carved with a quality far above the usual naiveté of such compromises. Deep canopy supported on seven piers and the solid E wall, with a pendant vault underneath and elaborate niches all round it, twice twelve altogether. To stand inside is to get the queerest effect of a church within a church. Entirely covered with carving whose details the visitor can enjoy at leisure, e.g. shield-bearers that are alternately sim-pering angels and robust putti, the corner piers with their men in armour and vertical parables, the fan-vault with its intricate oculi and its angels (standing on their heads!) on the central pendant. It is a delighful performance, and it could so easily have become gross and weary. – Sir William Morley, erected 1728 (N transept). A cold but grand urn on a boldly carved plinth, with all trace of the Baroque style gone. – Mary Countess of Derby † 1752 (N transept). A lovely monument in the style of *c*.1770, with a big sarcophagus. On it, an exqui-sitely crisp high relief of the Countess giving alms to the poor, as Van Gelder might have done it. Although one can see how this led to sentimentality there is not a trace of it here, and the composition and execution are splendid. Mrs Esdaile suggests *Thomas Carter*, and the relief is indeed entirely in the style of the best reliefs on chimneypieces. – Admiral Nelson-Ward † 1937, by *Cecil Thomas* (s aisle). Recumbent figure in uniform. Oh dear!

MONASTIC BUILDINGS. Not much is left of the monastic buildings at Boxgrove. The cloister was on the N side and the nave seems to have been built to fit around it. Part of the E side remains, being an entry to the chapter house, and this is in style the oldest part of Boxgrove. Early C12, consisting of a central doorway and a window on either side subdivided into two with a thick central shaft: the details badly weathered but stumpy and primitive looking, all the responds consisting of one large and two small shafts. Scalloped capitals. The only other building, well N of this and separate from the claustral premises, is the Guest House of c.1300, roofless but with N and S gable walls standing to their full height, plain and impressive. It was originally two-storeyed with a vaulted undercroft, and some of the corbels for this remain.

In the main street the DERBY ALMSHOUSES of c.1740, a half-H of cottages with a taller pilastered centre, too much altered to be really attractive; just S of them NIGHTINGALE COTTAGE, dated 1641, a very pretty mixture of flint, half-timber, and weatherboarding all under a shaggy thatched roof. More good cottages in the lane leading up to the church.

1010

BRAMBER

Next to Steyning, and originally a sizeable port on the river Adur. This and the easily defensible natural mound made it an early centre of Norman administration. When the river silted up, so did Bramber. For the authors of *The Beauties of England & Wales*, in 1813, it was a 'mean village' with twenty-two houses, ninety-one inhabitants, and two MPs, something which was not cleared up until 1832. Elections, according to Defoe, were 'scandalously mercenary'. Now, it consists of one short weatherbeaten street harried by traffic, stretching from the church and castle at one end to St Mary's at the other. Nothing to see otherwise, apart from the weird Victorian MUSEUM of taxidermy – a kind of museum among museums.

ST NICHOLAS. Built partly as a chapel to the castle, and given to the abbey of St Florent at Saumur c.1075. The building must date from the very first few years after the Conquest – or rather, what is left of it; for it shared both the general decline of the town and the particular depredations of the C17. It was used as a gun emplacement for attacking the castle in 1642. It had to be patched up in the late C18 (by the Rev. T. Green – *see* below) and the hollow top of the tower dates from then. The C11 plan was aisleless and cruciform. That is, saving the big blocked arch on the N side of the nave. What was it? Chan-

cel and transepts have gone, and the repair is now not pretty
and late C18 (there was an *Eginton* E window) but bungling
and late C19. So, visually, Bramber is no fun at all; but historically the crossing capitals, some of them recently uncovered, are a perfect illustration of Early Norman naïveté.
Not only crude volutes, but also carved heads and (very rare)
what seems to be a fox-and-goose. 'Seems to be', because the
carving is so crude that it is difficult to say – and not a strong,
moving crudeness, either. Shapes are spattered over the capital as though the carver had only a few hours of life left and
desperately wanted to record some or any message. This is
a steep decline from the expressiveness and inventiveness of
Late Saxon art, at least in Sussex.*

CASTLE. The mound looks as though it might be a gargantuan
motte, like Ongar or Thetford, but is in fact natural. On top
of it a smaller motte (pre-Conquest) and then a huge fragment
of a tower-keep which served also as a gatehouse. This is
supposed to be late C11 (i.e. like Rochester and the Tower)
and the scale of what is left, 76 ft high, suggests that it was
worth looking at. William de Braose took over the site immediately after the Conquest. No recognizable detail except one
splay. Low fragments of the bailey around the top of the
natural mound also. Owned by the National Trust, which
keeps the site overgrown and romantic. The Ministry of Works
could learn a lot from it on the treatment of the true spirit –
as distinct from the mere physical facts – of ancient sites.

ST MARY'S. Probably one wing of a courtyard, built in the C15
as a home for the Wardens of the Bridge, monks from Sele
Priory at Beeding. Timber-framed, except for the S wall,
simple and honest – close timbers, with an overhanging first
floor, on N and E sides. The W side, originally facing into the
courtyard, is a patchwork of additions. The type is as wide-
spread in timber areas as a grain silo in the Middle West of
America. Inside, simple C16 staircase, Elizabethan overmantel in the hall, and one first-floor room with jolly perspective paintings on the panelling. It is graded 1 by the
MHLG.

BROADWATER *see* WORTHING, p. 390

* Further C11 indications are the herringbone masonry of the tower, the
single-step arches, and the plain billet hood-mould of the S doorway. The
position of the doorway is odd. It is almost immediately W of the tower. In
the W addition put up in 1931 a later Norman shaft found on the site was
built in.

BUCKINGHAM HOUSE see OLD SHOREHAM

BUCKS GREEN see RUDGWICK

1010

BUNCTON

Church and a few cottages directly opposite Chanctonbury Ring.
Very remote, though only a few yards from main roads.

ALL SAINTS. Delightful approach down into a wooded ravine
and up again. Unrestored Norman nave and chancel, with
the C19 represented only by a bellcote. Tall Norman nave
with tiny windows very high up, probably C11. Short, tall
chancel with lancets and a C14 E window. An extraordinary
set of arches built into the outside wall on the N side. They are
of c.1160, one with formalized beakheads, another with intersecting mouldings. Where do they come from? Equally inexplicable the various blocked arches on the S side of the nave,
inside. But the main impression is of orange plaster, high,
narrow proportions, and a building which has been left to
itself for eight hundred years. This Sussex can provide as
consistently as can anywhere else in the country. Plain two-
order chancel arch with shafts and crude figures worked into
the N impost. C14 PISCINA which manages to get a lot of
character into tiny dimensions.

S of the church, MANOR FARM is a good unrestored C15 or
C16 farm, plastered and tile-hung. Originally moated.

0000

BURPHAM

A lush, sequestered, exciting village, exciting not through any
formal design but in the way that it is loosely spread over half a
dozen hillocks with water meadows in between that were originally branches of the Arun. It is in fact half-way up the Arun gap
and hence has views both of the Downs and of the skyline of
Arundel itself. As it is at the end of a three-mile cul-de-sac road,
it stands a good chance of keeping its romantic leafy complexity.

ST MARY. Deceptively demure from outside. It is largely an
impressive church of 1160–1220, at a time when architecture
in Sussex, in maturity and sure-footedness, was among the
best in England. It is no accident that the inside with its
vaulted chancel could be easily imagined as being a few miles

from Caen rather than Arundel. Although, from the point of view of style, parts are 'Late Norman' and parts 'Early English', the overall spirit is astonishingly similar, a matter of rich yet not decadent multiplicity of mouldings rather than the ornament which the mouldings bear. The detailed story here, however, is complex in a way which few Sussex churches are. The easiest way to start is by discounting first of all the C19 additions; S transept and S aisle walls and chancel arch, all cleverly done in 1869 by *Sir T. G. Jackson*, in a style which is hard to tell from the original and which in fact adds a lot to the church. The original S transept and aisle were taken down in 1800; the chancel arch was originally plain Norman and was replaced as unsafe. The story then starts in a familiar way with the N wall of the nave, Norman and probably C11. One blocked window and N doorway remain. Norman also the N transept, with two original windows and also one of c.1250, two-light with a quatrefoil above, plate tracery. The opening into the nave is plain and looks early C12, with a single chamfer on the arch and stop-chamfers on the jambs.*
That into the S transept is also Norman but very different – rich, ornate work of c.1160 which is Late Norman at its best, exploration and elaboration of multiple space without any of the meanness of Late Norman in the West Country. The sequence from here to Broadwater, New Shoreham, and then into the C13 at Chichester and Boxgrove is all of a piece. Two orders, the inner with a triple roll-moulding, the outer with, on the N side, zigzag parallel with and perpendicular to the wall, a typical trick of the mid C12 to articulate space. On the S side an even clearer expression of the desire for exploration and probing into space: deeply cut chevrons following each other round the arch, as at St Mary at Ely, very unusual in Sussex; around it a hood-mould with grotesque heads as stops. Each order has its own jamb shafts and scalloped capitals, making three on each side, one big and two small.‡

The next inevitable step in development was the use of the pointed arch, and this can be exemplified straightaway in the two arches now forming the S aisle. Which came first – or were they done at almost the same time by men of different temperament? The easternmost is almost a literal transcription of

* The blocked arch in the E wall indicates a former E chapel or E apse.
‡ There is a puzzle here; this is a very ornate arch to open merely into a transept. Was there originally a central tower of which this was the arch to the nave?

the Norman arch, with the ornamental enrichment gone and deeply cut pointed mouldings replacing it, the label stops now of crudely carved foliage, the capitals still scalloped except on the S side, where again there is crude foliage which seems trustworthy. The other arch, quite different in detail, manages to be the same in general feeling: single order with only one roll-moulding, plain soffit and plain jambs except for small shafts at the corners with single waterleaf capitals. There is a little plain wall left between the two arches. Was the W bay then a lengthening almost immediately resolved on?

That takes us to *c.*1180. The chancel is a little later, a complete spatial unit: two bays with quadripartite vaulting, beautifully proportioned and detailed, defining space subtly, precisely, and elegantly, resting on corbels at the four corners and roughly carved piers at the mid-sides made up of three keeled shafts under thick generalizations of waterleaf capitals. One of the four corbels is still scalloped. That corresponds exactly to the situation in the Lady Chapel at Chichester, i.e. before 1185. A string course runs round the whole chancel just below the capitals. Original E end with three widely splayed, widely placed lancets: PISCINA and DOUBLE AUMBRY with the same rich plainness.

The rest of the story is simpler: C14 windows in the chancel and a plain Perp tower which looks *c.*1400. Three-light W window, arch dying into the jambs without capitals. – FONT. Perp, the familiar national type with octagonal bowl with rosettes in quatrefoils and panelled octagonal stem. – COMMUNION RAIL. Early C17; multiple, thin, turned balusters. – CHANDELIERS. Three, of brass, late C17 or early C18. – PLATE. Chalice, 1568. – STAINED GLASS. Small window, N side of nave, by *Leonard Walker*, 1930, a nice object lesson to the W window (*Kempe*, 1900), the E window (*Wailes*), and the S aisle (three of 1875 by *Powell*). Complex fluctuating colours, the pattern of eagles filling the shape of the window naturally, not seeming arbitrarily contained.

(S of the church are the vast earthworks of the SAXON BURH, enclosing a promontory overlooking the river and facing its successor, Arundel Castle. It was one of a series on the South Coast; cf. Porchester, Hants, and Berwick, in East Sussex. NT).

Nice flint and brick cottages everywhere, mostly thatched, the best at WEPHAM, which is SE of the main village. One of them is half-timbered with flint infilling. 1 m. further S at

WARNINGCAMP there is another agreeable and unaffected street of flint cottages and barns.

BURTON

9010

No village; church and house only, a mile from the Downs s of Petworth.

CHURCH. Close to the house, a lovable, unrestored building, one of the mellowest in Sussex. Norman nave and chancel, as usual, with some herringbone masonry in carstone. No Norman detail; a wholesale repair was ordered by Archbishop Juxon in 1636, and the windows must be part of this, square-headed, with hood-moulds and a single mullion. A dumpy bell-turret to complete the ensemble. The C19 dealt mercifully with Burton, and only the E window jars a little. Delightful crowded interior, looking like a Welsh border church before the restorers got there: rood screen, plaster tympanum above with Commandments, monuments. – BENCHES. Linenfold panels re-used in modern benches. – SCREEN. Simple Perp, complete with its battlemented rood beam still with traces of decoration. East Anglia or Devon are a long way away here: long narrow lights with spindly ogee-headed tracery, and plain coving. – WALL PAINTING. In the splay of a N window; a female martyr, upside down – ROYAL ARMS. A very rare example: Charles I, dated 1636, painted on the s wall. The text above, a sign of the times, says curtly: Obey them that have the rule over you. – MONUMENTS. Recess, s side of chancel; crocketed ogee arch flanked by pinnacles enclosing a delightfully stylized stone effigy of a lady, 40 in. high. Probably C15. – John Goring † 1521, s wall of nave. Brass, 14 in. high, in a mechanically designed recess. – Sir William Goring † 1553 and his wife † 1558, N wall of nave. Only the wife's effigy remains, again in brass, 14 in. high. Very typical canopy of Sussex marble, mixing up Gothic and Renaissance motifs like the contemporary monuments at Arundel: attached demi-shafts with floral decoration, central pendant, fantastic tracery shapes around it – shapes exactly half-way between Gothic oculi and the pattern of a Jacobean ceiling. Typical also in its slapdash quality: it might as well have been stamped out of leather.

BURTON PARK. Built in 1831 by *Henry Bassett*, who was then aged 28, and very much a clever young man's building (he was an R.A. Gold Medallist). Determinedly Grecian, with all kinds of ornamental tricks. Unhappily, and perhaps inevitably, a rather heartless building also.

The tone is set firmly by the entrance front, with its four-column Ionic portico *in antis*. Three storeys and five main bays, with an elaborate blind half-bay between outer windows and portico. Very Grecian doorcase and pierced balustrade – that is to say very C19 Grecian, the incredibly ingenious adaptation of Greek forms of a building like St Pancras New Church. Burton outdoes even this in its outsize foot-scrapers, made up of anthemion and Ionic capitals. The s front has five narrower bays and another pierced parapet; the E front had to be asymmetrical to fit the plan and does not look nearly so clever – though some of the ground-floor pilaster details are perverse enough to be worthy of Lutyens. All stuccoed.

No Grecian interiors, except the plain entrance hall and the corridor leading from it. But the STAIRCASE is remarkable. It was brought to Burton from Michelgrove near Arundel, which was demolished in 1828, and was originally built in about 1800 (perhaps by *Byfield*, who did work there in 1800). It starts as one arm, returns as two, and has extraordinary banister details: openwork bronze panels, one to each tread, alternately wide and narrow (the adjustment to the equal width of the treads is ingenious). The wide bays have a chained greyhound under a big leaf-motif, the narrow bays have pairs of crescent moons separated by another leaf pattern. The ends of the treads are ornamented, and even the underside has a complex moulding. The oddest thing is that it is all heartless and ostentatious, what might have been expected as the spirit of 1850 rather than 1800: Georgian England was not invariably tasteful and discreet.

The walled GARDEN to the E looks as if it dates back to the earlier house, which was by *Leoni* and was burnt down in 1826.

BURY

Under the Downs at the N end of the Arun gap, opposite Amberley. Pretty and leafy without being remarkable. Most of the cottages along two lanes, one N–S and the other at r. angles running down to the church and river. More than half are built of sandstone, and hardly any of flint or clunch, although the chalk is only a mile away.

ST JOHN THE EVANGELIST. A very typical beetle-browed exterior: plain tower with shingled broach-spire, a continuous roof sweeping down without openings to a low aisle. In this, like the cottages of Bury, it belongs to the Weald, although it is almost under the Downs. The bones look all C13, but this is probably deceptive: the tower base seems Norman with its pattern of plain round-headed windows and doorway, and the N wall of the nave by its proportions is C12 as well. Simple single-chamfered pointed tower arch of *c.*1200, and then an impressive arcade in a completely different style. Arches of two orders, the inner chamfered and the outer with continuous mouldings. Round piers and abaci, stylized foliage capitals, not yet wind-blown. The responds have not one capital and abacus but three, a very unusual detail, and on the E respond, there is a tiny sigh of movement in the leaves. Various late medieval windows, a good simple Tudor S porch and inner doorway. The chancel arch C14, the chancel of 1855. As in so many village interiors, the arcade dominates the church. – FONT. Octagonal, C15, the usual pattern with rosettes. – SCREEN. Simple Perp, narrow lights with cusped tracery heads. Very different from the wealth of Devon and Norfolk. – PULPIT. 1628. Pokerwork patterns.

The centre of Bury is a cross-roads. The best cottage, FOGDENS, is in the lane running N from it, a good example of the Kentish type of timber-framing with oversailing wings and a recessed centre. Sandstone infilling, whitewashed.

W of the cross-roads, BURY HOUSE, in accurate and unremarkable Tudor of 1910. Galsworthy died here. Next to it is the POST OFFICE, on which some C19 monumental mason went quite crazy. Everything from lions' paws to men smoking pipes.

BYWORTH

9020

A hamlet in romantic hilly country a mile SE of Petworth. The best COTTAGES are next to one another at a bend in the road – both of *c.*1600, both with regular timber-framing and a continuous first-floor overhang. They are Nos 373 and 374 (Leconfield estate numbering), and look as though they were built by the same man at the same time.

CAKEHAM MANOR HOUSE *see* WEST WITTERING

CALCETTO PRIORY *see* ARUNDEL, p. 94

CASTLE GORING

1000

1½ m. N of Goring, beside A27

An astonishing and unknown house, though it is only fifty yards

from one of the busiest roads in South-East England. It was
designed by *Biagio Rebecca c.* 1790 for Sir Bysshe Shelley, the
poet's grandfather. The design was probably a collaboration
and reflects the equivocal taste of the 1790s as well as anywhere in the country. The entrance side is Gothick, flint and
stone, with a symmetrical three-towered centre and lower
wings, that on the l. like a college chapel, that on the r. like a
castle keep. The details themselves are unexpected so early,
including dogtooth and chevron ornament, and accurate
mouldings. But if the details are accurate, they are mixed in
a bizarre way so that there are chevrons on Perp doorways
and orders of dogtooth around Perp windows.

That is not the only bizarre thing at Castle Goring. Immediately through the archways between centre and wings, the
style becomes Graeco-Palladian, the mixture used by architects such as Henry Holland and Bonomi. Even the materials
change completely, to expensive white brick and white stonework with a beautiful purple tinge to it. There is no doubt
that the whole house was built at one time, and there could
not be a more telling illustration of the exact moment at which
architecture became an affair of styles. Rebecca's classical was
far better than his Gothic, a little hard and heartless, but firm
and powerful, and inventive within the limitations of the style.
Five-bay centre with three-bay pediment and Ionic pilasters,
first-rate *Coade* stone decorations between them in high relief.
The base an eloquent ramped entrance worthy of France,
with Grecian ironwork and Greek Doric columns underneath
the first floor in a 1:2:2:1 rhythm. The classical backs of the
Gothick wings, set far back, are given pairs of Ionic columns
in antis on corner quadrants.

The inside is just as surprising. A baronial door in the
middle of the Gothick front leads immediately into a central
circular hall with a large glass dome and a spiral staircase
winding up from the centre to a circular balcony. Behind this,
blind arcading as Dance might have done it, effective and
powerful. Beyond, on the first floor, a severely decorated
classical suite, the centre room with pairs of Corinthian
columns framing the doorcases and *Coade* stone reliefs over;
the ground-floor room underneath this has free-standing Greek
Doric columns all round the walls, an enchanting effect.

The final refinement of sensibility – and how Horace Walpole would have loved it – can be seen in the main corridors.
The corridor flanking the classical rooms is classical also, and

ends in elegant ovals framed in parabolic arches. Turn back
towards the castellated entrance down either arm, and the
ceiling changes without batting an eyelid into an elegant
Gothick rib-vault. By the deepest standard, all this was fiddling
whilst Blake's Albion was beginning to burn; but what a
splendidly sophisticated and self-aware end to an age!

CHANCTONBURY RING see WASHINGTON

CHARLTON

1 m. E of Singleton

8010

A beautiful downland site in the valley N of Goodwood Racecourse. No church, and no central group or open space, but
an informal meander of flint cottages along a quadrilateral of
tiny lanes which does just as well. At the s end is FOX HALL,
which must be one of *Lord Burlington*'s* least-known buildings. It was built in 1730 as a hunting lodge to Goodwood, in
connexion with the famous Charlton Hunt. Plain, one bay
and three storeys, the outside with a hint of its designer in
the finely detailed window surrounds, one rusticated and one
pedimented. Inside, ground and top floors are plain, but the
first floor has Palladian details out of all proportion to the size
of the house. Tall cubical room with gilded ceiling and overmantel; lower bed-recess off to the E with an arched entrance.
Everything strict and a little thin.

CHESTHAM PARK see HENFIELD

CHICHESTER

8000

* According to Elwes, 1879. But is it in fact by *Morris*, who was then
doing work at Chichester? Certainly the detail is far better than the Chichester Council House.

ROMAN TOWN

The site appears to have been occupied almost immediately after
the Roman conquest, but remained an open settlement until
the end of the c2, when a bank faced with flint and mortar
and a ditch were constructed around the town. In the late
c3 the wall was further strengthened by bastions, of which
sixteen are traceable (the best face Westgate Fields), placed at
regular intervals along its length. The city was of polygonal
plan, the walls enclosing an area of approximately 100 acres.
Entrances occurred at the four cardinal points: these were connected by two main streets which crossed at the centre of the city
where the Cross now stands. Few Roman buildings have been
discovered in recent times, much having been obliterated during
the construction of the modern town. Excavations in the
garden of East Pallant House revealed portions of a tessellated
corridor and a well which may represent the remains of a
small fulling mill. The Roman occupation was overlain by the
remains of a SAXON HUT of wattle and daub. Excavations in
Chapel Street and North Street suggest a pre-Roman Belgic
settlement overlain by a courtyard villa with tessellated pavement.

CATHEDRAL

INTRODUCTION

The story of the cathedral can start almost anywhere in South-
West Sussex. Chichester from the Selsey peninsula is like
Chartres from the Beauce: no other English cathedral, not
even Lincoln, exerts such a continuous presence on the flat
surrounding countryside, and it is the continuity which is the
important thing; the spire becomes as invariable and natural
as the sky and sun. What Chichester has in addition, on any
kind of clear day – and there are a lot of clear days in Sussex –
is the gently rising backcloth of the South Downs two or three
miles away, so that God, man, and nature always seem to be
in equilibrium. And from anywhere on those slopes, behind
Goodwood or on Bow Hill, the effect is unforgettable: the
plain like a sea, tipped with a glitter or a shimmer which
really is the sea, punctuated only by one slim spire. Nothing
of the same height must ever be built near Chichester: spire
and countryside form an equation or a symbol experienced by
millions of people every year, which cannot be given a value
purely in terms of landscape or architecture.

Closer to, the famous view of the cathedral seen across fields 5 from the by-pass to the SW cannot be matched in England. And this can still just be carried through on foot over the railway, to the walls of the Close, still in rough pasture (or in reverse, a walk of two hundred yards out of the busy South Street leads to fields from which, turning round suddenly, the image of the cathedral almost knocks the viewer over). But in 1960, after a long struggle, the Westgate Fields were designated for a ring road and two schools. However well designed and landscaped, the old essence will have gone. It is up to the twentieth century to construct something just as exciting, and it will have its work cut out.

In the near views, the whole proportions, medium-long and medium-low, building up to the central spire, seem directed to make a single point like an outstretched hand. The W towers do not interfere (though they would if Pearson's scheme for reconstructing them had materialized) and the detached bell-tower, the only one remaining in an English cathedral, can hardly be seen from this side. It is the same mass as Salisbury, and it seems as single-minded as Salisbury.

Yet in temperament, Chichester and Salisbury are exactly opposite. Salisbury's single-mindedness is the result of one ruthless design, Chichester's the result of repeated piecemeal accommodations and repairs and additions. A history of English medieval architecture could be written without mentioning any single part of Chichester, yet as a whole, as the most typical English cathedral, it could never be left out. Nothing to excess, a bit of this and a bit of that, tolerance without servility, have over the centuries produced an effect as penetrating as Ely but in a completely different way. Without any doubt it is one of the most lovable English cathedrals: this is partly the architecture, partly the way in which city and church flow together easily, partly the way in which the church authorities make you free of the cloisters and passages without harangue or stuffiness. It is a well-worn, well-loved, comfortable fireside chair of a cathedral – St Francis, not St Bernard: St Augustine of Hippo, not St Augustine of Canterbury.

HISTORICAL SUMMARY

Chichester, like Norwich, was the result of the Norman centralization of sees. It had been founded at Selsey, and was moved in about 1080 (also perhaps because of erosion there) and established on a site which already contained a Saxon church of St Peter (liturgically this became incorporated in the N transept and was not given a separate building until 1850, *see* p. 171). Bishop Ralph de Luffa succeeded to the see in 1091 and built the church 'a novo', as William of Malmesbury writes. There was a dedication in 1108, and building continued throughout the C12, retarded by a fire in 1114. Bishop Seffrid consecrated it in 1184. In spite of additions, this forms the whole structure of the present church, except for the E end – i.e. eight-bay nave, transepts each with an E chapel, crossing, and three bays of the choir. Luffa's church had an ambulatory and probably radiating chapels, and apparently just before the great fire of 20 October 1187 this had been extended eastwards to form the first three bays of the Lady Chapel.

After the fire, Seffrid II rebuilt rapidly and could reconsecrate in 1199. He and his successors used and sometimes ornamented the earlier work, providing a new clerestory and quadripartite vaults throughout. At the same time the chapels in the transepts, which had been apsidal, were enlarged and squared off. The ambulatory was replaced by a new retrochoir of two bays with E chapels l. and r. of the Lady Chapel. Work went on well into the C13. A royal licence to the then bishop to carry Purbeck marble by sea was granted in 1206. A storm in 1210 wrecked two towers, probably the S tower of the W front and the central tower. A statute of 1232 speaks of the church as 'needing manifold repair', Bishop Nevill, who died in 1244, left 130 marks to the building, and Bishop de Wych – i.e. St Richard – £40 in 1253. Nothing big was done after that date for some time. Then the Lady Chapel was lengthened by Bishop Gilbert (1288–1304) 'a fundamentis', the S transept was remodelled and given its big S window by Bishop Langton (1305–37), the cloisters were built c.1400, the detached belltower added c.1375–1430, the spire added some time in the C15. The NW tower, which had still been engraved by Hollar, was called ruinous in 1658 and was replaced in 1901 by *J. L. Pearson*: the central tower telescoped in a spectacular way in 1861 and was reconstructed in replica by *Sir Gilbert Scott* and *Slater*. The main C19 restoration, which was mild, was carried out by *R. C. Carpenter* and *Joseph Butler* in the 1840s and 1850s.

The original building material is almost entirely a greenish tinged limestone from Quarr Abbey in the Isle of Wight. The late C12 and C13 work used Caen stone.

AESTHETIC SUMMARY

In spirit Chichester is a Romanesque building from end to end. Even the outside, with its big central tower – which is after all almost exactly the size and shape of Norwich – has preserved the measured, leisurely bay-to-bay rhythm of the original C12 design. The existence after the fire of 1187 of a recently completed shell must have been a strong inducement to continue the rhythm, but only if the builders were already temperamentally prepared for it. Only this can explain why, when the Lady Chapel was extended, a hundred years later, the designer maintained the rhythm of the heavy late C12 corbel table and completely defeated the original purpose of his bigger windows. Adapt and re-use, rather than sweep away and rebuild, has been the cathedral's leitmotif.

So, inside, the space is still basically Bishop Luffa's of c.1091–1108. His design was straightforward, with no mannerisms and no *terribilità*, paying for its balance and reasonableness with a lack of intensity: good committee-man's Romanesque. The bay-unit, with arcade, gallery, and clerestory* of almost equal height, was used again and again in Norman England, and achieved for example at Norwich and Ely a much greater power than it does here. But in relating it there is a missing building which ought to be given a bigger place in the history of English architecture. In realizing that the best Norman buildings were built in England, not France, we may have over-reached commonsense. The natural source of Norman ideas immediately after the Conquest was William the Conqueror's capital of Caen, particularly as so much building stone was imported from there; and it certainly seems fair to look to the Abbaye aux Hommes, built in 1066–86, as the father of the family of designs like Chichester. If engravings are compared, the proportions are identical, and the only big difference in the Chichester scheme is that the gallery is subdivided.

Luffa's design, without being austere, had hardly any ornament. It must indeed have looked bleak and officially impersonal to the designers of the late C12, because that is the

---

* Which nowhere survives unaltered, due to the fire.

only way to explain the extraordinary things that happened to it after the fire of 1187. Though they maintained the Roman- esque space unimpaired (the quadripartite vault with which they replaced the original flat wooden ceilings is barely pointed, and the clerestory is just a paraphrase of the standard Norman pattern of one big and two small openings), they embroidered the Norman design delicately and liberally, add- ing Purbeck marble shafts and string-courses, quickening the rhythm without altering the basic design. Medieval architects faced with conversion or addition were usually more bold (Gloucester and Winchester) and occasionally more discreet (Yevele at Westminster Abbey). An equivalent operation today would be to slow up the rhythm of a Victorian building by taking off some of the ornament. It is no recipe for distinction, and whilst Chichester nave is friendlier for it, the remodelling has no more basic force than the original design.

The two-bay eastward extension of the choir is a different matter altogether. The Norman rhythm and proportions are kept, but within that framework everything is new – though gentle even here; round arches in the arcade, round arches enclosing pointed ones in the gallery. The design is returned around the E end, where the gallery shrinks to a wall-passage with a sliding rhythm, and this makes a splendid enclosed box in which the proportions are impeccable – no upward eager Gothic thrust but an exact balance, very typical of Chi- chester, between round arch and pointed arch – a dynamic living balance, where Luffa's High Romanesque was static and dead; the difference if you like between a good committee and a bad one. The thick expressive sculpture here must be later; yet again, a wish to quicken the rhythm, and yet again, addition instead of rebuilding. The middle piers, composed of a central core and four shafts, are a classic solution to the problem of expressing the different loads that have to be borne (main vault, aisle vault, main walls, subsidiary arcade mouldings). They are inspired by the work of 1175–84 at Canterbury, and a chain of a sort can be made out from Can- terbury to Chichester via New Shoreham.

The next part of the story at Chichester is purely English: three porches, using the fully developed E.E. style to do one of its favourite jobs, the single sharply defined bay. St Richard's Porch, now the entrance from the cloisters, is a classic example, in both design and carving: yet it must also be a hybrid, compounded of c.1200 and c.1240. And there the story peters out abruptly. The Dec style, in the Lady Chapel, was completely alien to Sussex, and only with the straightforward Early Perp cloisters was there again a consonance between the inherent virtues of a style and the temperament of the designers who were using it.

EXTERIOR

This description starts with Luffa's work, i.e. at the crossing, transepts, and W part of the choir, then works continuously westwards to the W end. Thereafter it returns to the post-fire parts of the choir and works E; then the bell-tower. St Richard's Porch appears here (p. 148), the rest of the cloisters are on p. 161.

Bishop Luffa would probably recognize his cathedral today, because of the continuity of proportions and spaces. But externally there are not many details to be picked up. As usual, they are around the CHANCEL, the TRANSEPTS, and the CROSSING – the evidence complicated little by *Scott & Slater*'s rebuilding after the crossing tower fell. Their work is an accurate copy, and the join of old and new stonework is quite clear. Luffa's style was astonishingly consistent from the chancel to the NW tower, and astonishingly plain: his masons cannot have got much fun out of their work. He used a standard type of window that recurs throughout the building: a big opening with jamb shafts and cushion capitals, the arch with a thick roll-moulding and an outer label of two rows of billet ornament. This can only be seen easily in one place – the W side of the N transept.* In spite of the plainness and blandness it makes a surprisingly rich unit. Here also is the best glimpse of what the outer walls looked like, with massive clasping buttresses, themselves given nook-shafts, and a low string-course made up of chains of billets. Above the ground-floor windows followed small round-headed windows to light the gallery, but these are to be seen better in another place. A little higher up is a slight recession in the wall which probably marks the position of the original roof. The heavy corbel-table above with its multiple repeated trefoiled heads between

* The less easy places are N transept E chapel ground floor for one in the chancel aisle, upper floor (library) for another, Vergers' Vestry for one S transept E wall window, S aisle E bay for two blocked ones, N aisle W bay inside for another blocked one. Incidentally there is also a small Norman doorway preserved. It is now inside the Sacristy (i.e. Song School).

the corbels is probably late C13.* The earlier corbel-table can be seen on the S choir aisle, ornamented with grotesque heads which are now badly weathered.‡ Here are also three blocked windows of the gallery. Their details cannot be seen, but evidence in less obvious places shows that they had a plain single-step moulding.§ Immediately E of the easternmost of the three blocked windows the walling can be seen to turn inwards slightly. From this Willis deduced that Luffa's E end was an apse with ambulatory and from the asymmetrical spacing of this third window that it took into consideration a radiating chapel.** The clerestory windows of the Norman chancel are intact, again with shaft and billet in the hood-mould. Otherwise there is more C12 evidence in the transepts, especially the stump of a very broad centre buttress in the N transept N wall and clerestory windows like those of the chancel in the W and E walls of the S transept. Evidence of the apsidal chapels in the transepts are traces of the arch of an upper floor and the roof-line on the S side, an actual fragment of the curve of the apse on the N side (visible from the library, i.e. the upper storey of the C13 E chapel of the N transept).

Later work must start with the CROSSING TOWER, which, as has been said already, is now a replica of 1861–6. It is a comfortable, unaspiring design: big twin bell-openings consisting of two lights enclosing a trefoil with blind arcading below and a heavy corbel-table above – so heavy that it is almost blind arcading also. The battlements and squat polygonal embattled pinnacles and the spire above are probably C15, the latter a fine, light design that does more for the distant views of Chichester than anything else. Octagonal, with two bands of panelling, approximately one-third and two-thirds of the way up. At the base, four free-standing octagonal spirelets with firm, rich details in the diagonals between spire and pinnacles. The whole will stand a long and close look, yet its great virtue is that it never asserts itself.

* Willis suggests that its purpose was to raise the wooden roof off the stone vaults, which allowed no room for tie-beams.

‡ They are very like the heads in the corbel-table of the S transept of Winchester Cathedral, carved c.1110. A closer view of the corbel-table can be obtained on the N side inside the library, i.e. the upper floor of the N transept E chapel.

§ One of the N chancel aisle visible on the library floor of the N transept E chapel, one of the N aisle visible plainly from outside in the first bay W of the transept.

** It sounds convincing, but it ought to be said that trial digging has not shown a sign of any.

The SOUTH TRANSEPT is surrounded by the cloister, an extremely unusual thing, an irregular cloister and, in fact, not a normal cloister at all. The main feature in the transept is the big S window put in by Bishop Langton, say about 1330, and heavily restored. It is an unsympathetic and wiry design, even discounting the restoration. The overall flickering effect is killed by the big spherical triangle in the head. Seven lights, formed into 3–1–3 sub-heads under the spherical triangle; all filled with reticulated tracery and cusped and foiled dagger-shapes. Plenty of technique but no understanding of the style. Above, in the gable, a small rose-window filled with equally clever and equally inorganic shapes, and between them a corbel-table, recut in 1932, including recognizable heads of King George V and Lloyd George.

On the E side of the transept is St Pantaleon's Chapel, re-built in the C13, now the canons' vestry. Simple E.E. detail with E window of three stepped lancet lights under a round-headed arch. On the W side is the externally three-storeyed-looking sacristy, now Song School and Chapter Room, an impressive hybrid. The two lower stages are C13, with narrow lancet windows, more vigorous than most C13 details in the cathedral, to the S as well as the W, the latter visible in the cloister. It must have been built after St Richard's Porch because it incorporates a buttress from it in its W wall. The difference in the masonry (seen inside the cloister) is unmis-takable (Willis). The top stage is Late Perp, clipped and effective. It has to the S two segment-headed windows of three lights without any mouldings at all.

The NORTH TRANSEPT is less complicated. It also has a show end window, Perp and assigned without documentary authority to Bishop William Rede (1368–85), spurred on per-haps by its equivalent on the S side. It has seven lights and shows an uneasy compromise between Dec forms and the newly arrived straight lines of the Perp style. The lights are grouped 2–3–2, the outer pairs with steep heads, the inner trio meeting the apex of the arch in a flattened head containing an octofoil which ruins the overall pattern, bathos where there should have been climax. Above this a repaired C13 corbel-table, above again a C19 gable and rose-window. Both E and W sides have clerestory windows typical of the E.E. repair and enlargement – pointed arches with obtuse heads, jamb shafts with stiff foliage capitals, the proportions almost exactly the same as Luffa's windows. The same windows recur in the

Library, i.e. the upper floor of the E chapel off this transept, on the site of the Norman transeptal chapel, making an impressive two-storey composition at the E end. Below, a lancet on either side of a buttress. The buttress projects upwards and makes a stepped triplet out of the lancets in the upper storey: but it is not set centrally, so that one is at a loss to know whether any deliberate effect was intended. Perhaps it was an emergency repair. To the N the E chapel has two Perp four-light windows, later evidently than the great N window.

Now for the NAVE. Starting on the s side, the bays w of the crossing are partly obscured by the former sacristy (p. 135), but on the N the first bay is the best place to get the feel of Luffa's scheme. The clerestory window is a C13 repair, but the gallery window is authentic, with its single-step moulding exactly as in the chancel (*see* above). Below it, the main window is later C12, and pointed. But it has an outer label of billet ornament, like the Romanesque windows, and the capitals to the shafts are stunted and uneasy. It is obviously an earlier stage than most of the E.E. work at Chichester. The question is – something which will recur inside – whether in fact it was part of a remodelling which started before the fire of 1187.

Westwards of this the outer aisle begins: one bay with two lancets, above them, in plain plate tracery, a quatrefoil, and above this, in the bit of wall left, a tiny sexfoil. Then four bays of *c.*1270* whose windows now make an impressive show, especially by comparison with the Dec work at Chichester; three bays under two large circles under a smaller one. In fact, the shafts and arches are authentic, but the tracery is an early C19 repair (by *Carpenter*, 1847) which repeated the original design but added the foiling inside the circles. The tracery is all of the bar, not plate, kind, and this appeared first at Westminster Abbey in 1245, but at e.g. Salisbury only about 1270. The pattern of the three unfoiled circles exists identical at Grantham and there must be as late as *c.*1280. The s aisle consists of St Richard's Porch (*see* p. 148) and four bays almost identical with the earlier bay on the N side, but for reasons of Victorian imitation not of original contemporaneity. Fragments of string-courses show that both aisles originally had a gable over each bay, as many Continental churches still do; the buttresses between the bays are capped with heavy octagonal

* A chantry of two altars was founded in 1269.

turrets, those on the N side just a little later and more ornate than those on the s.

Above, the clerestory is Luffa from end to end, with his un-varying big round-arched windows. In the C13 flying but-tresses were added for the new vault, one tier visible, another, on the s side only, below the roof of the aisle gallery. In the C14 the nave roof was heightened, like all others, to prevent the load bearing directly on the stone vault, and here a func-tional makeshift led to one of the oddest features of Chichester, a second corbel-table on the N side, about 3 ft below the normal position. The reason for this is that the clerestory walls had gradually sagged towards the s so that the N wall was concave and the s wall convex. To keep the parapets straight the con-cavity had to be reduced, and a single corbel-table was not sufficient, so that a second had to be used. It runs westward from the central tower for five bays and then dies into the wall.* On the s side a simple set-back of the masonry was sufficient.

With that, except for the porches (see p. 148), we are at the WEST END. And a very typical English west end it is too, an unreflecting stopping-up of the nave space which is neither a showpiece in its own right nor a crisp expression of the nave and aisles behind. There is plenty of compensation at Chi-chester in the overwhelming sense of mass of the whole cathe-dral enduring through all the alterations and restorations; but that need not have inhibited a more eloquent design. It is very English, too, in its patchwork. Luffa's front clearly had two W towers. The top of the SW tower was blown down by a storm in 1210 and replaced by an E.E. design; the NW tower fell down in the C17 (see p. 130) and was not replaced until 1901, when J. L. Pearson designed and his son executed a near-copy of the others.‡ But even so, Luffa's buttresses pop up everywhere, and the s face of the SW tower is one of the best places to see his style close to – or rather, the style he bequeathed to his successors, assuming that the W front was one of the last parts to be finished. Three storeys survive, two with the familiar windows, the ground floor with a blocked doorway which represents the limit that C12 Chichester per-mitted itself in the way of ornamentation. Two orders of zig-

---

* To reappear inside, as can be seen up in the nave gallery. So there was a double sag, convex and concave.

‡ He included funny openings high up on the SW buttress. Did he have any evidence for them from C17 engravings? If so, they were the only bits of Chichester to reflect the extraordinary Late Norman details at Climping.

zag are separated by a thin rope-like moulding decorated with
chevrons. It does not represent much slackening of the reins.
The only similar work is the doorway in Canon Lane and,
near Chichester, at Tortington. The C13 re-working began
with a single lancet and went on to the fine deep paired bell-
openings, each of three orders with jamb shafts, carrying on a
way of designing that is as common in Normandy as in
England. The heavy parapet brings things back firmly to this
side of the Channel, however. The part between the towers
was almost rebuilt then or a little later; above the porch (*see*
p. 149) there is a three-bay arcade, in the gable are two lancets
on a diapered background; between them the main W window, Early Dec in style, is *Carpenter*'s, of 1849, replacing
C17 and C18 repairs.

That completes the nave and aisles, except for the three
porches, on which *see* p. 148. To follow in detail what went
on in the E parts after 1180 the story must be taken up again at
the third bay of the CHOIR. Here, according to Willis, the
Norman ambulatory had started. In its stead, after the fire,
the choir was lengthened by two bays, the change being reflected only in the shape of the clerestory windows, round to
pointed, and the shafts and capitals, not in any alteration of
the proportions. The flying buttresses, one tier only, as it is
everywhere except on the S aisle length, are massive, as they
must be, being as early as they are. They are, of course, a
reflection of Canterbury, which can boast flying buttresses
hardly, if at all, later than the earliest in France. Those at
Chichester are very like the later examples at Boxgrove. The E
ending is a group of the high choir, the partly older Lady
Chapel (*see* below) sticking out far eastward, and the two short
flanking E chapels finishing the chancel aisles. This arrangement occurs at about the same time – earlier? later? – in
Bishop de Lucy's work at Winchester, and he was bishop
from 1189 to 1204. The E wall of the high choir has a group
of three widely spaced stepped lancets and above it a big rose-
window of the later C13, terribly renewed. The pattern is that
of six circles surrounding a seventh, i.e. exactly the pattern of
the E window of the Angel Choir at Lincoln, which was completed in 1280. The Chichester rose is flanked by a pair of
turrets of utterly un-Gothic solidity which effectively anchor
down the eastern mass (and are reinforced by another pair of
C19 turrets lower down flanking the ends of the aisles). Both
are octagonal, and both are renewed: the NE has shafts sup-

porting a flat lintel, looking as much C19 as C13: the SE is later and has trefoiled heads between the shafts. The choir aisles have an assortment of C13 to C15 windows. One of these deserves a moment's attention. It has five lights and the intersecting tracery typical of about 1300. But the mullions are not medieval, thin square piers set diagonally, and so this is perhaps a replacement of after the siege of 1643. On the N side are two Perp windows, similar to those of the N transept E chapel. One more puzzle occurs at the NE corner, that is outside St John's Chapel. Here the main window is of *c*.1180, but above it is a small round-headed light which should belong to the early C12.* If the original choir aisles in fact continued in an ambulatory, why was such an insignificant detail moved to the new alignment or imitated? The E walls of both N and S chapels have small octofoiled openings, again probably of the later C13, high up in the gable.

The LADY CHAPEL, to the E of this, is no kind of culmina- 27a tion. At best, it provides one more stepped stage to articulate the long spread-out volume. Four bays are visible outside; the first two were in fact built in the later C12 as we shall see, and as the flat Norman buttresses suggest, but the details are otherwise all of *c*.1290–1300, identical in N and S walls, distressingly mechanical in design and distressingly casual in arrangement – the windows are rarely fixed centrally in the bays and do not match each other in size. It looks as though window designs were ordered blindfold and the masonry then bodged to fit. Historically the windows have all the same some importance. They are typical of the most progressive work of the last decade of the century and can, as we have seen, be firmly dated to before 1304. Bay 2 was the first to get its windows, which are a little bigger and just a little more straightlaced than bays 1, 3, and 4, which are almost identical. The basic pattern is three stepped lights roughly dividing the window into a grid with trefoil and quatrefoil shapes in the tracery heads – a scheme which has neither the flow of mature Dec tracery nor the vigorous pattern of Perp windows. In bay 2 the trefoils and quatrefoils are enclosed in circles, in the others they are unleashed; the E window has exactly the same scheme as the later bays, but extended to five lights.

The last part of the outside is the detached BELL TOWER which in fact is what most people notice first at Chichester.

* Though it has a chamfered surround, while the Early Norman ones had a single step.

Such bell towers were not as unusual as it must seem to us today. We know of their existence, as substantial as at Chichester, at Westminster Abbey, Salisbury, Norwich, Worcester, St Augustine Canterbury, at Tewkesbury and at Romsey. The Chichester bell tower stands a few feet N of the W end of the nave, and was probably built to house the bells as a result of some subsidence or movement in the central tower. It is a lumpish, unlovable building – nothing like the splendid, much slimmer bell tower at Evesham, for example – but if it had been any taller it would have had a disastrous effect on the proportions of the whole cathedral. As the only remaining example close to a cathedral it is a precious relic, but one can see Wyatt's point of view when he removed the Salisbury one. Money was left for the Chichester campanile in 1375, the early C15, and 1436, and this may correspond to the two stages: the lower heavy and blank, with small windows of typical late C14 design and big setback buttresses,* the upper a squat, thinner octagonal lantern with octagonal corner pinnacles, and bell-openings which are equally typical of the years around 1440. They make a disproportionate match. Was any sort of spire intended on top, or should the lantern have been taller? Something like the relative proportions of Boston Stump would have been very different.

INTERIOR

On going in by the W door, the immediate impression, just like the outside, is that this is still entirely a Romanesque church, comfortably spread out under its quadripartite vault, easygoing and balanced and very English. The second impression is of the admirable balance of spatial tensions created by replacing the Arundel Screen (see p. 154). The choir is neither shut in nor opened out, but a mixture of both. Through the openings the eye sees the bottom of the reredos, above the screen the eye sees the lancets at the E end of the retrochoir, and the screen loft performs a beautiful conjuring trick by obscuring the top of the reredos and hence the fact that it is not in the same plane as the lancets but two bays to the W of it. The architectural details have very little to do with the space, something which could not possibly be said of Gloucester or Wells. Space filters away benignly forwards and side-

* But the small W doorway with its continuous mouldings is clearly of the early C14 at the latest and must either be re-set, or else it proves that the tower was started much earlier.

ways without compelling or coercing (and therefore, perhaps inevitably, without drama or rapture). Only the retrochoir would fix itself in the memory so strongly as to force a second visit, yet after two dozen visits there are a multitude of tiny, friendly sensations which add up in the end to something memorable. In its even temperament it is the perfect Protestant and Anglican cathedral, built four hundred years before there was a Church of England.

A detailed look ought to start in the CHANCEL; for cathedrals were as a rule built from E to W, and of Bishop Luffa's E end further E we know no details. The Norman chancel has a three-storeyed elevation, arcade, gallery, and clerestory, and it had no doubt an open timber roof or a wooden ceiling. To study the details it is not advisable to look too closely at the W bay; for this is pretty completely a replacement of after the fall of the crossing tower in 1861. As for the other bays, of the arcade enough remains for us to visualize its late C11 sturdiness. The piers probably had demi-shafts towards the chancel, mast-like as in the Winchester transepts or at Ely. They have been replaced, but the thick demi-shafts to the arch openings are there, with heavy single-scallop capitals, and towards the aisle a strong nook-shaft which originally had its companion towards the chancel. To the aisle was another demi-shaft whose stump exists still. It must have been for a transverse arch. The arcade arches have two slight chamfers to the chancel, one to the aisle. The gallery has survived unchanged. A twin opening for each bay, low and broad, the responds with high, coarse capitals with vestigial volutes and elementary leaves, the sort of thing which is emphatically late C11 and not C12 in style. The thick mid-shafts have two-scallop capitals, the super-arches two strong rolls to the nave, and the tympana lozenge slabs of alternatingly grey and brown stone, again an Early Norman motif.* Transverse arches were thrown across the gallery.‡ Of the Norman clerestory only the windows are preserved and low arches at r. angles to the wall which belong to the wall passage, now E.E. They prove, however, that the Norman clerestory also had such a wall passage, and that it had the stepped tripartite arrangement

* Cf. e.g. Westminster Abbey (*The Buildings of England: London*, I, 2nd ed., pp. 434 and 439).

‡ It is mysterious that the W bay of the E.E. retrochoir on the N side has part of a Norman arch above the E.E. arch, higher than the other gallery arches. Was this the start of a different system for the ambulatory gallery?

which exists at Winchester and Ely and which one would have expected anyway.

The E.E. adjustments after the fire of 1187 are telling. Willis has shown most ingeniously why they are most extensive in the clerestory, less so on the ground level, and absent in the gallery. In a fire the roof will produce the worst heat. So the top storey will go most thoroughly. Then the timbers crash to the ground and damage the arcade. The gallery is less in danger. At Chichester what was done is this. The subsidiary order of the main arcade which faced inwards was replaced by detached Purbeck marble shafts and capitals* (leaf crocket capitals typical of all the Purbeck work at Chichester), the arch-moulding of this order delicately elaborated, and the clerestory rebuilt in an E.E. transcription of the Norman three-part division, one big and two small. Here the side arches are pointed, the central arch still round (perhaps because it had to incorporate the existing windows), and the supports between made up of three clustered Purbeck shafts. The vault above is quadripartite with carved bosses at the intersections,‡ and in general the ribs are slim and have the section of rolls, keeled and unkeeled and hollow.§ The vaulting cells or webs are plastered, but on the evidence of the exposed ones in the nave and the N porch it can be assumed that they were filled in the French (and Canterbury) not the English way, that is by cutting the stones of the courses of infilling so that they met at the crown or apex in a straight, not a saw-tooth joint. The vaulting shafts are triple, one round, two keeled, running up to the same kind of Purbeck capital poised half-way between crocket and stiff-leaf. The aisle vaults and shafts repeat this pattern on a smaller scale, the N aisle distinctly earlier than the S (*see* p. 150). These aisles can of course not really be seen independent of the new retrochoir of after the fire and its aisles and E chapels, but there is good reason why these parts should be treated later.

So we move on to the TRANSEPTS first and again the Norman work there. It is of that Early Norman plainness and severity, as it is in the transepts of so many cathedrals. Each has two bays, each had a two-storey apsidal E chapel, later extended, and plain W walls. The galleries from nave and

* Also linking bay to bay with a Purbeck marble string-course.

‡ One boss has an angel holding the arms of St Richard – a Perp replacement, it seems.

§ For more on this *see* p. 150.

chancel ended in heavy two-light openings, all four renewed, again because of the fall of the spire. The apsidal chapels each had an unmoulded round opening to both storeys of two orders, much more severe than the other Norman work in the cathedral. It survives in the N transept. In the S transept it had from the beginning a slight chamfer towards the chapel, and the face towards the transept was redone with a very modest kind of embellishment – a roll-moulding on the soffit, supported by corbels carved with primitive leaves – which may even have been part of the remodelling begun just before the fire of 1187. Both the upper openings of the chapels were redone E.E. The W wall of the N transept has two impressively severe Norman windows at ground level. Above, the details of clerestory and vault are those of the chancel. The only things to notice specially are that the outer bays have a five-part vault, with a rib of different section running from the intersection of the outer wall. This may have been an alteration done in the C14 when the big N and S transept windows were put in.* Also, the ribs in the S transept have dogtooth ornament on the soffit (cf. Boxgrove and Aldingbourne) and are hence probably slightly later than the other vaults in the cathedral.

The various spaces opening off the transepts had better be described here, although they break the general historical flow. The two apsidal chapels were both given square ends in the late C12 or early C13. That on the S (St Pantaleon) has a quadripartite vault, that on the N (Chapel of the Four Virgins) was enlarged to the S to give a two-naved room with the extension much narrower than the original chapel. It is squeezed in against the choir aisle – part of one blocked Norman window has already been noticed – and hence has awkwardly stilted vault-ribs. The new vault in the original chapel has some but not all of its ribs given zigzag ornament in a puzzling way. Was this, one could speculate, something which was in progress before the fire, was it re-used material, was it conservatism, or were the various ornaments more interchangeable in time than we like to think? Such zigzag does not occur anywhere else, but it does occur in the work of 1175–84 at Canterbury, and this essentially was the most go-ahead work of that moment in England. The foliage capi-

* The surround of the great S window has shafts with capitals carrying sparse leaves, abaci carrying fleurons, and a hood-mould supported on large heads.

tals and responds which support the ribs with the zigzag are
indeed not specially early.

On the w side of the s transept is the SACRISTY, now SONG
SCHOOL. This has already been noticed (p. 135) as being
quite different from other E.E. parts in the cathedral, and the
inside is just as individual; a sober, effective two-bay room
with a five- – not six- – part vault, all the ribs single-chamfered,
resting on corbels with rich, yet flattish stiff-leaf foliage,
among the richest in the cathedral (cf. p. 151). The upper
storey, now the Chapter Room, is C15.

To come back to the CROSSING, or to Scott's reconstruction
of it, Luffa's firm, impersonal scheme becomes much more
evident. One major unmoulded order and two minor roll-
mouldings, corresponding to one major half-column and two
minor shafts, careful and ordered. The E arch has the major
moulding elaborated with rolls and its column subdivided
into two demi-columns with a cable moulding in between,
sharing the same scalloped capital. The roll-mouldings on E
and W arches are decorated with cable ornament, and the E
arch in addition has the sides of the orders decorated with
chip-carved St Andrew's crosses. That is all; and the replica
of the quadripartite C13 vault above is just as plain. Whether
these Norman details are pre-1108 or post-1108 is anybody's
guess.

From catching the rhythm here, it is easy to move on to the
19 NAVE. Nothing essential distinguishes it from the chancel.
The system is the same, the changes concern only details, but
these details do give an indication of historical sequence. The
first bay must again be discarded as of Scott's making. Part
of the original Norman arcade arch, differing in size from
Scott's, is exposed on the N side. Where the original work of
the nave is not exactly like that of the chancel is in these
minor ways: The thick demi-shafts to the arcade openings
have two-scallop capitals like the gallery, not the arcade in
the chancel.* Also, to the aisle, the arcade arches have a thick
roll instead of the slight chamfer. On the gallery the responds
have no longer the primitive volute capitals. The capitals now
have one or two scallops.

More changes from the fifth bay onwards show that here
really a revised plan must have been followed. The piers are
now a bit thinner, the arches a bit wider, as Willis has spotted
(God bless him). The transverse arches to the aisles – so their

* One-scallop just one N and one S respond in different situations.

plinths, if nothing else, show – had twin demi-shafts instead of single demi-shafts. This arrangement was then carried on with the arches between aisle and W tower bays. Incidentally there are two more details which may be of significance. In the W bay of the N aisle by the entrance from the E.E. N porch is a trace of what looks like the usual Norman wall-arcading. Was there more of this? And in the W bay of the S aisle in the angle between the arch to the tower just referred to and the arcade arch is an extra angle-shaft. Its function must have been the support of a vault. Were the Norman aisles then vaulted, perhaps from the start? We cannot say, but there would be nothing surprising in it, as the aisles of Winchester and Ely were also vaulted – groin-vaulted of course – before 1100. Then, in the gallery, also from the fifth bay, the decoration of the tympana changes from the flat slabs to motifs in relief: fish-scales, studs, diamonds.

Curiously enough small changes were made again when the E.E. work reached the nave after the fire. Here the Purbeck shafts of the arcades acquire shaft-rings, from the W respond of the fourth bay onwards. In the clerestory, right from the crossing, the clusters of Purbeck shafts are replaced by taller single shafts (cf. the retrochoir, p. 147). The wall arches show some of the odd faults so frequent in medieval work and so naïvely corrected.

The last bay of the nave connects with the TOWERS. The system of elevation still remains the same, but the gallery arch now has three rolls towards the nave instead of two. As for the E.E. contribution, the most interesting detail is that on the intermediate shafts of the group of lancets in the W wall the arches start with a fat, shapeless stump of an upright roll, out of which the finer mouldings then develop. The base of the SW tower, which was presumably less affected by the fire, is as completely Norman as anything at Chichester, with one tall and wide blank arch and to S, W, and E a billet string-course. Pearson copied and matched up for his reconstruction job on the NW tower.

In the AISLES the C13 work is almost exactly what it had been in the chancel aisles, bafflingly so; for even the capitals of the wall-shafts and the bosses are unchanged and that means as early as any of the post-fire renewal. This even applies – yet more bafflingly – to the entrance arches into the outer chapel at the E end of the N aisle (in spite of the plate tracery of the window) and the two two-bay outer chapels of the s aisle. The capitals are different here from any of the others, but undeniably early: high, crude crocket capitals of the most primitive kind (in stone). Yet on the s side these arches interrupt the string-course of the aisle wall, i.e. are not contemporary with it.

The two two-bay s chapels incidentally were originally separated from one another by a solid wall but later thrown into one to make an outer aisle, with a crude pointed arch (which in a village church would be dated c.1200, another puzzle) and have now been separated again. The transverse arches in each chapel have the same mouldings as those opening from the nave, but the capitals are obviously late, with the same luxuriant elaboration of a basically crocketed shape as in St Richard's Porch (see p. 151). The vaults are quadripartite, as everywhere, and they slope up to the windows to allow these a larger size. The E wall of St Clement's Chapel (the easternmost) keeps a noble REREDOS of two pointed arches flanking one wider trefoiled arch and two quatrefoils over, with new statues inserted. In the arch once dividing the w from the E chapel one jamb shaft, fairly high up, tells of the former existence of another REREDOS. In the outer N aisle the easternmost bay was originally an isolated chapel, i.e. had a solid w wall. On the w another REREDOS just like that of the SE chapel. The remaining four bays – the Chapels of St Theobald and St Anne – were added in 1269 (as said before) and how this by subtler, more complex mouldings of the arches. The bosses on the other hand are of the simplest and must be re-used. The vaults again slope up to the windows. The E chapel of the two, i.e. where there was the solid wall mentioned before, had yet another REREDOS, and the lowish screen wall once separating the two chapels one more. Again it is the outer shafts which are preserved.

Now back to the E end, beyond the choir, to the retrochoir and Lady Chapel. The two-bay RETROCHOIR is the aesthetic and spatial climax of the cathedral, the exact point of balance, perhaps in the whole of England, between Romanesque and Gothic, the point where stylistic transition and national temperament were exactly in step. The designer had to keep the Romanesque proportions and bay width to within a few feet (in fact the gallery is a little shallower, the arcade a little deeper). Many big churches tried this and failed – e.g. Romsey. But here, pointed and round arches are harmonized exactly. The arcade has to be round-arched, the gallery has

two pointed arches under a round arch. The returned E end
has one wide, slightly pointed arch and above it, to connect
the N with the S gallery, a narrow wall passage. To the chancel
there are here also paired two-light openings, but immediately
behind them appears a wall arcade which is given a sliding
rhythm compared with the main arches. The clerestory has
the same tripartite rhythm as the adjoining chancel, except
that the intermediate Purbeck shafts are much taller and
hence the outer little arches are vastly stilted on their outer
sides. In each part of the design, curves and points answer
each other, all in the comfortable overall volume which is still
Romanesque. It is like a medieval debate made visible. The
details generally are the same as in the other E.E. parts of the
cathedral – complicated moulded arches with flat grooved
soffits, crocket capitals interspersed with stiffly formal leaf
patterns, sometimes bending a little, but never submitting
like the capitals in a cathedral like Wells. There are two exceptions: one is the sculpture, which is a problem on its own and
will be discussed presently; the other is the design of the
intermediate piers. These are both mighty and brilliant, consisting of a big central Purbeck shaft surrounded by four
smaller free-standing Purbeck shafts, corresponding (in a way
which would have delighted the logicians of the Île de France)
to the main load of the walls and the subsidiary loads de-
livered by the inner orders of the arches, the nave vault, and
the aisle vault. The idea is inspired by Canterbury, but not
expressed so elegantly or concisely, even to the point of varying the depth of capital according to the width of the column:
a misunderstanding of this principle may explain the occasional
stunted or squashed-up capitals found at Chichester.*

What sets the seal on this harmonization of diverse elements
is the sculpture and decoration in the gallery stage, and this is
probably the biggest single puzzle at Chichester. It consists of
spirited figures in the spandrels of each two-light opening,
small in size but large in scale, and a good deal more foliage
and even chains of monsters around the arches at the E end,
forming complete openwork bands inside the main arch
mouldings. All this is lush, curly, vivid, naturalistic, impossible
to reconcile with c.1200, easy to reconcile with the second

---

* The abacus of the pier follows the division of core and shafts, and that
has led to an awkward junction with the arch mouldings. In the diagonals
there was not enough space for them to land safely on the abacus. Deft little
stiff-leaf sprays of stone are introduced to mediate.

third of the century, especially the figures. These deserve extra study. In the N and S bays they are small, in moderate relief, and set in fancy foiled shapes of ever varied detail, including pointed foils. In the E bays instead they come boldly forward out of their trefoils. In the N and S bays they are two angels and two and one seated figures. Much is C19 renewal, but what is original has draperies clearly in the French style of 1230–40 (i.e. like the end of the Chartres workshop and the Villard-de-Honnecourt-like parts of Rheims). Only the one seated king has been given a Romanesque head. Now these draperies and also the foiled shapes and the openwork stiff-leaf band confirm a date after 1240. So it must have been inserted; a brilliant job both technically and aesthetically, for it catches the earlier rhythms exactly.

Only a few words are necessary on the aisles and chapels of the retrochoir. The aisles are just a continuation of the chancel aisles, except that the bosses in the S aisle are lusher, bigger, and later than those further W and in the N aisle. That also applies to the boss in the S chapel. Both chapels are of an awkward internal shape, due to the strange discrepancy between their responds. Those on the S in the N chapel and on the N in the S chapel are a flat projecting piece of wall with a row of three detached Purbeck shafts in front. Was the intention to do the same on the facing sides? Anyway, it was not done. In the S aisle the Perp doorway into the E walk of the cloister. It has the arms of William of Wykeham and can be dated c.1400.

After this, only the porches and the Lady Chapel are left. There are three PORCHES: at the W end, at the W end of the N aisle, and half-way along the S aisle, forming one entrance from the cloister. They are all E.E., and all of the same basic pattern – a portal, preceded by a single quadripartite-vaulted bay and with the entrance subdivided into two bays by a central column. But within this framework, they are absorbingly different in detail and in quality. The earliest of them, St Richard's Porch in the S aisle, is easily the best, up to the level of units like the N porch at Christchurch or the W porch at Lichfield, a way of designing in which England excelled. But it is itself a composite design, and the parts are not easily dated. The vault is early E.E. on the strength of the mouldings of the ribs and the corbels on which they rest, especially the two heads. But the capitals of the S entrance are lush stiff-leaf, and the unequal quatrefoil above the *trumeau* and the thick crude foliage corbel underneath it must all be of c.1230–40 at the earliest. The statue of St Richard which it now carries is by *Hems* of Exeter, 1894, and does no violence to its surroundings. Inside these is a small wall arcade of four bays in the same style (what for?), then the inner doorway, which is in the usual Sussex C13 style, well done: two orders of shafts with moulded capitals, circular abaci, and an inner order of dogtooth ornament.

The N porch has the same character as this inner doorway, but is skimped where the other was ample – especially in the (re-used?) cramped crocket capitals. The inner doorway has one roll on shafts and one continuous chamfer, the outer arches have two complicated roll-mouldings on shafts with dogtooth ornament on both the extrados and the soffit of the arches. Again blank arcading was started on one side and not continued. Outside on the l. is a steep gabled niche, above head height, of c. 1260.

Finally the W porch. Here the outer arches are a disappointment; for the tympanum and *trumeau* are almost all redone. The inner doorway has three orders of shafts with late-C13-looking moulded capitals and arches starting just like those of the lancets above, in the W wall of the nave, with a bit of an extremely fat roll for each order and then developing finer mouldings out of them (or alternatively the finer mouldings dying into the fat stumps). The shafts of the W doorway are Purbeck marble which has weathered a deep brown to give an almost Northants striped effect. The sides of the porch have three blank arches each side with pointed-trefoiled heads and in the spandrels above them rounded quatrefoils, two complete and, l. and r., one half each – a curious, somewhat heavy, but quite forceful motif.* Both have been cut into for tomb recesses, no longer identifiable – a gabled tomb of c.1300 on the S, a square-headed tomb of the C15 on the N.

So, in conclusion, the LADY CHAPEL of c.1300. It can only be a disappointment. Even for the best of designers it would have presented a problem – how to make a long, low building more striking than the taller and richer main parts of the cathedral. Extreme structural ingenuity and ornamental virtuosity is needed, and it is sadly lacking here. The first two bays must antedate the fire of 1187, and certainly the S capital to the first bay is more archaic than any other late C12 detail

* It can be compared to the treatment of the N and S walls of the Winchester Lady Chapel at a moment after Bishop de Lucy's death.

at Chichester, being still in effect a Norman scallop capital with the mouldings made lighter (it occurs also in the crossing tower at Boxgrove). The remainder is hoist with the low late C12 ridge-line and can find no better solution than to multiply the intermediate ribs and ram the large windows into spaces that are really too small for them, producing ungainly stilted rere-arches. The best details are probably the flickering, bossy capitals of windows, vaulting-shafts, PISCINA, and SEDILIA. Perhaps this is an inevitable price to pay for the classical balance of the rest of Chichester. In turbulent times, nothing-to-excess often produces the best results; when the artistic pressure slackens, it may easily degenerate into dullness.

One longish POSTSCRIPT may be of use. It cannot have been easy, in the whole of this account, to separate in one's mind the Norman work from the E.E. work, and, while the Norman work is all of a piece, the E.E. work differs in its details so much that it should perhaps be summed up once more and a chronological order be attempted, even if not achieved. Willis, than whom no one ever could observe and interpret details better, says that the phases are 'much alike in style' and Walter Godfrey in the VCH that it is 'not easy to place the exact sequence'.

At least one knows where to start: in the W bays of the Lady Chapel; for here one capital is still entirely Late Norman. Another marks the beginning of the leaf development, two tiers of small, close, bud-like leaves, not yet stiff-leaf. The vault on the other hand has close, flat, small stiff-leaf bosses. So the first question is: Was the vaulting done before or immediately after the fire? In any case it is the earliest rib-vault in the cathedral. Transverse arches and ribs have profiles which do not exactly repeat anywhere, but the character and the proportions remain standard throughout the work.

An example is the vaulting shafts. They are triple, two round and one keeled. Go further W and, in the variation of all three keeled, this continues in the chancel chapels, chancel aisles, the high parts of retrochoir and chancel, the transepts (in the N again exactly like the Lady Chapel) and even the nave. Then there are the bosses. Flat, small stiff-leaf bosses also continue more or less unchanged from the chancel chapels (N only – see below), to the aisles of the retrochoir (N only, see below), the chancel aisles, and the nave aisles. These bosses go well with the small, close stiff-leaf capitals of the vaulting-shafts in the aisle walls, again of identical type in the aisles from E to W.* So it looks as if the repair after the fire began with the aisles and their vaulting, not an unreasonable idea, if one thought straight away, as a fire insurance, of future high vaults for chancel and nave. Such vaults would need support against their thrust. Flying buttresses on the Canterbury example were decided on, and so they needed new buttresses and the vaulting (or perhaps re-vaulting; *see* p. 145) of the aisles would be the first stage in the realization of the programme.

The one exception to the small, close bosses is the SE chapel and the aisle bays S of the retrochoir. They are rich, larger, much looser, and more rhythmically composed. In this they tally with the bosses of the high vaults of retrochoir, choir, and nave, bosses which for obvious reasons must have been set up much later. Now this freedom in the treatment of stiff-leaf also applies to the gallery of the retrochoir, of which all the details have been discussed on p. 146. So here work took longest, up to *c*.1230–40, as we have seen – an understandable thing, as after a fire one would repair existing parts first, replace completely later.

Other parts of the cathedral which show evidence of one kind or another of this late date are the following: first the entrance to St Richard's Porch (but the vault inside, i.e. the porch itself, is earlier), see the corbel under the statue of St Richard with several not strictly separated tiers of stiff-leaf, and see the irregular elongated quatrefoil for the statue. The parallel to this would be the odd foiled shapes of the N and S gallery arcades of the retrochoir. The closest parallel to the lush corbel is the yet lusher corbels in the Bishop's Chapel (but the chapel itself could be earlier and indeed of before 1204 – *see* p. 163) and among capitals in the cathedral those of the Sacristy (i.e. Song School), which we know were a later addition to the E.E. work on the aisles and also to St Richard's Porch itself. A further parallel to the quatrefoil of St Richard is the elongated pointed quatrefoil of the entrance to the W porch flanked by two round quatrefoils. The inner arcading of this porch, also with pointed trefoils side by side with round quatrefoils, can be compared to the reredoses in the NE aisle chapel and the SE aisle chapel. The former has plate tracery, i.e. a stage after the untraceried windows everywhere

* The small bosses are also used in the outer N chapels of 1269, but must be re-used.

else in the cathedral (except for the bar tracery of the other,
later, N chapels).

However, there is a catch here. The NE aisle chapel and the
S aisle chapels have capitals in the responds towards the aisles
which, while they cut through their E.E. motifs (string-
courses), are of the crudest crocket type, tall and inelegant.
Crocket capitals otherwise were specially liked by the Purbeck
marblers, and wherever they were busy for the cathedral, they
used them, either as crockets proper or as leaf crockets, i.e.
crockets with stiff-leaf characteristics.

Chichester is not a place to see stiff-leaf in its most luxuriant 'wind-swept' varieties, the varieties of say Wells about
1230–40. The freest stiff-leaf at Chichester is again in the
entrance to St Richard's Porch and again in the chapels along
the S aisle (the transverse arches). Otherwise not much can be
made chronologically of the capitals, except that it can be
stated that moulded capitals come late in the story. This does
not apply without reservation; for the Purbeck shafts of the
transverse arches in the chancel aisles and nave aisles have
moulded capitals. Otherwise they were used in the arches to
the N chapels and in the N chapels, i.e. c.1269, in the W porch
throughout, in the doorway inside St Richard's Porch, where
they have dogtooth, and in the arches from aisles and chancel
aisles to transepts (mostly of 1861, but there was enough
evidence), which were clearly a later embellishment.

Dogtooth has just been mentioned, and this is also a sign of
late date at Chichester. The earliest probably is in the vault
of the S transept (cf. the small, close bosses – and cf. Boxgrove). Those in the E bay of the retrochoir are bigger and
later. Another late occurrence is the rose window in the E
gable. Yet others, perhaps in date between S transept and
retrochoir, are in the N porch entrance and the E windows of
the N transept E chapel.

The profiles of ribs and transverse arches help little. They
are thin and have fine mouldings everywhere in the cathedral,
and the roll, the keeled roll, the filleted roll, the spur, the
small hollow seem to have been used *ad libitum*. To give one
example, the same transverse arches are found in the chancel
aisles, the high vaults of retrochoir and chancel, the N transept
and the chapel E of it. On the other hand the ribs of the chancel
aisles start with a profile slightly different from that adopted
in their more westerly parts, and this second profile is then
carried on in the nave aisles, the E chapel of the N aisle, the S

chapels, and even the w porch. The only fairly convincing criterion is that ribs with more than three principal members are late: four in the nave,* five in the Bishop's Chapel and the N chapels.

If one tries in conclusion to link early and late with actual dates, 1187 stands at the beginning, 1269 at the end. In between dates could only be gained from comparisons.

FURNISHINGS

These start at the NW corner and travel round the church anti-clockwise – i.e.

    N aisle
    N transept and crossing
    N choir aisle and choir
    Retrochoir
    Lady Chapel
    s choir aisle
    s transept
    s aisle

Chichester is in fact meagre in its furnishings, and it is not easy to see why. It was not by any means a poor diocese, and it has never been sacked or drastically restored. Monuments are few and small, especially after the C16, which is true of Sussex as a whole. Most of the Victorian stained glass has now gone and not all of what remains is mentioned: the replacement of the 1940s and early 1950s is certainly not worth mentioning either.

NW TOWER. MONUMENTS. A kind of Sailors' Corner, hence several late C18 reliefs under inscriptions: Lt Pigot Alms † 1782 by *Harris*, Sir George Murray † 1819 by *Joseph Kendrick*, Capt. Thomas Allen † 1781 also by *Harris*. All pleasant and none remarkable.

N AISLE AND OUTER AISLE. Second (first outer) bay. MONUMENTS. Joseph Baker † 1789 by *Hickey*. Female leaning on a pedestal with portrait medallion; urn on top, but still in the Rococo tradition. – A really terrible *Flaxman* to Vice-Admiral Frankland † 1823 (female in profile, heavily draped and looking up sentimentally). – William Huskisson † 1833 by *Carew* (see Petworth). He was M.P. for Chichester and a leading light in the Reform Bill movement. He 'relinquished this station when yielding to a sense of publick duty' – that is,

* But four also in the s porch, where the corbels prove an early date.

he was run over by a railway train. In spite of this, he is still shown in Roman dress, a life-size standing figure with a noble face.

Third bay. MONUMENTS. Richard Fitzalan, 14th or 15th Earl, † 1376 or 1397 and wife. Stiff conventional figures but the hands touchingly joined. What went on in the minds of the designers as they made their hundreds of standard effigies? – Rev. Thomas Ball, erected 1819. *Flaxman* again, but better, with a design as flowing and melting as those of his friend Blake but without any of Blake's force. Mourning lady, comforting angel: more lines curved down than up.

Between fifth and sixth bays. MONUMENT. Edmund Woods † 1833. Standing monument, all white. Standing female by a plinth, soulless and with illiterate inscriptions. By *J. E. Carew*.

Sixth bay. MONUMENTS. Presumed Maude, Countess of Arundel, † 1270, but must be of *c.* 1300 or a little later. Badly worn, but a fine, taut figure, all the rhythms caught and contained. All the subsidiary carving is done with meaning, not mechanically. Tomb-chest with quatrefoils alternately filled with standing figures and shields against a leaf background. The leaves cannot be earlier than 1300.

Seventh bay. Here, across the nave, stretches the ARUNDEL SCREEN, taken out in 1859, stored under the bell-tower, and put back in 1960. From neglecting it, appreciation has now almost swung too far the other way, and it is floodlit and set off at the expense of the more important spaces around. John Arundel was bishop from 1458 to 1477. His screen is an odd mixture of spatial lightness and decorative heaviness: the three arched openings, two wide and one narrow, promise well with their multiple continuous mouldings, but are defeated by the heavy lierne-vault supporting the loft with its repeating pattern of ogee-headed niches. The mixture is typically English – France or Germany would not have been so undecided. The bosses of the vault are carved with foliage and with vivid human and animal faces. This is very English too.

N TRANSEPT. PAINTING. One of the pair of immense wooden panels done by *Lambert Bernard* c.1520 (the other is in the s transept, p. 159). This one has the bishops from St Wilfrid to Sherbourne, all in roundels, all apparently drawn from the same model, and as uniform as the heads in a pack of cigarette cards. Restored by *Tremaine* in the C18; jolly but nothing more. – MONUMENTS. Several medium-size classical monuments, of which there are as few in Chichester as in

Sussex as a whole.– Bishop Grove † 1696. Two cherubs holding the mitre and a proud well-carved bust above. – Bishop King † 1669, surely commemorated by an C18 monument. No figures, cold urn at the top. – Bishop Carlton † 1685. Two more cherubs hold the mitre against an obelisk. Coy looks from both: they seem to have had the Baroque equivalent of a perm. – Eliza, Huskisson's widow, † 1856, by *John Gibson*. From the inscription, Gibson's grief was personal as well as professional, yet the angel and supplicant are fearfully void of feeling. Flaxman's influence had succeeded only too well.

CHAPEL off N transept. A small cathedral museum. *Inter alia*, some chests, the capstone of the old spire, an astonishing triangular Spanish(?) C17(?) chair, much more comfortable than it looks, a Spanish C16 processional cross, a cope of 1956 by *John Piper*, unexpected and welcome, and a good deal of plate, mostly C19.

N CHOIR AISLE. MONUMENTS. Two shoddy C16 tomb recesses with the brass effigies gone, the type of many Purbeck and Petworth marble monuments: a tomb-chest and a back panel for brasses, flanked by solid side walls and with, at the top, a flat arch or a lintel on curved pieces connecting with the side walls; top cresting.

CHOIR AND CROSSING. WOODWORK. Mostly neo-Gothic, spiky or weak. Reredos by *Somers Clarke*, 1910, bishop's throne by *Slater & Carpenter* after 1861, organ case by *Dr Hill*. The iron spiral staircase behind, in the N transept, is far better. The STALLS and MISERICORDS are a different matter, though the stalls are so badly wrought about that they look purely Victorian. Of *c*.1330, a repeating design of ogee arches on thin detached shafts with new panelling on the backs, nothing notable. The more ornate canopied stalls at the W end are modern. The misericords are vivid enough and varied enough (e.g. man with viol, monsters, lions, fox and goose) but not up to the standard of Ludlow or Higham Ferrers. – CHANDELIERS. Two of brass, two tiers, given in 1752. – MONUMENT. Bishop Story † 1503, N side. Stiff alabaster effigy on a panelled tomb-chest. No special effort extended by the shop-workers. Canopy modern.

RETROCHOIR, N AISLE and NE CHAPEL. CHEST. About 8 ft 6 in. long, with C13 ironwork. – MONUMENTS. Mrs Margaret Miller † 1701 (chapel). A good straightforward mason's monument; architectural frame with open scrolly

pediment and mourning cherubs on either side. – Sarah Peckham † 1784 by *Harris*. Elegant shape, elegant use of marble,
but fatally lackadaisical mourning woman juxta urn. – Bishop
Otter † 1840, by *Joseph Towne*, 1844. Not a bad bust, no
attempt at any deep interpretation, but not putting a false
gloss on things either. This is provided immediately by the
terrible monument next door by *John Tweed* (NT) to Bishop
Wilberforce † 1907.

RETROCHOIR. STAINED GLASS. E windows by *Kempe*,
and deeper and richer than he usually is. – MONUMENTS.
Two plain tomb-chests to Bishops Day † 1557 and Barlow
† 1568; not a sign of the Renaissance, or of anything else.

LADY CHAPEL. IRONWORK. Entrance gates, originally in
the Arundel Screen. A thin, nervous pattern of quatrefoils,
thickened and repeated *ad nauseam* in C19 and C20 gates in
the cathedral. The original is surprisingly wispy and appealing.* – WALL PAINTING. The second bay of the vault is
decorated with a pretty foliage pattern, like that at Boxgrove.
It is early C16, by *Lambert Bernard*, the only surviving part
of a much larger scheme. – STAINED GLASS. A complete Victorian set which does not stand a close look but which makes
an effective colour-pattern out of the space, taken all together.
Dark colours: reds, browns, and blues. The E window is the
best. All this is by *Clayton & Bell*, and carefully designed to
fit in with the general internal refitting of 1870–2 by *Slater &
Carpenter* (NT). – MONUMENTS. Early C14 tomb recess on
the S side. In it two coffin-lids of early bishops. The same
type is represented better preserved in the coffin-lid on the S
side which belonged to the monument of Bishop Luffa, the
cathedral builder, † 1123 – see the inscription on the W side.
The lid has a flat-topped hipped roof and carved on it, as
effectively as if it were a trade mark, are a crozier and mitre.

RETROCHOIR, S AISLE and SE CHAPEL. STAINED GLASS,
in the chapel, by Kempe (date of death 1894), and terrible.
But under it a new altar, candlesticks, and altarpiece which at
last (1961) show that C20 religious art is a living thing. Altar
by *Robert Potter*, tall candlesticks flanking it‡ by *Geoffrey
Clarke*, the painting (Noli me tangere) by *Graham Sutherland*.
If it seems, as it is, too self-conscious, that is largely the fault
of the inertia that has sat on the Church of England for a

---

* Only the opening parts are old. The rest is a replica of the original,
which is in the Victoria and Albert Museum.
‡ And the communion rail.

century, and still does in places less enlightened than Chichester. – MONUMENTS. Mrs Frances Waddington † 1728. Plain architectural frame, all idea of the Baroque gone already. – Rev. G. P. Farhill † 1790 (chapel). *Harris* of London again. The usual mourner by an urn. His mourners really do not inspire confidence. – Also a thumping great C14 GARGOYLE which puts the later sculptural inanities to shame, used as a collecting box.

CHOIR, S AISLE. SCULPTURE. Two famous Romanesque [14] panels, the most memorable things in the cathedral. They were found re-used as building stones behind the choir stalls in 1829, and were almost certainly part of a C12 choir screen which was known to have existed here. The stone comes from Purbeck (limestone, not marble); the reliefs show Christ coming to the House of Mary of Bethany and the Raising of Lazarus. For a long time they were thought to date from *c.*1000, and it is hardly surprising, because the architecture looks Carolingian, the impassioned awkwardness of the figures and the empathy between them seems nowhere near the sculptural order and emotional calmness of most later Romanesque sculpture. Yet Dr Zarnecki and others have proved beyond doubt that the panels must date from *c.*1125–50 and that their details depend on such things as the St Alban's Psalter (now at Hildesheim) of *c.*1120 and German ivories of *c.*1130. If this is true, then the gestures and proportions of German Romanesque – already more personal than France – were perhaps refracted by a sculptor who was still thinking in Anglo-Saxon terms. It would be a fair parallel to the case of mid-C12 sculptures like those at Kilpeck, which undoubtedly depend on Poitou and Saintonge but which were carried out by a designer working in the old style and end up looking more like Viking ornament. That is the old spirit using new techniques, but how it managed to survive for almost a century in an area like Sussex is a mystery. Of all the parts of Britain, it would have been most open to Norman–French influence.

The panels are wonderfully preserved: all that is missing is the coloured inlay that would have been set in the eyes, and even here the present empty deep sockets seem to add to the depth of expression. To assess them is not easy or simple. The sculptor was obviously impatient of details, and there is no point in trying to compare the quality of parts, such as folds of drapery around knees, with the first-rate pieces of orthodox Romanesque sculpture of the time (best represented in England by the porch at Malmesbury Abbey). The designer's care and love was all for the heads, for the relationship between heads and for the shades of feeling expressed in the faces. Beside this, the rest becomes irrelevant. In the first panel, Christ and the disciples are approaching the house – a house which looks like a Carolingian folly, a crazy and rustic Pierrefonds. Under the porch are Mary and Martha, in frozen dumb supplication. Christ's face is as preoccupied as that of a surgeon before the operation gathering up strength in himself; hurrying on to the door, already working out technical details. Two of his disciples are compassionate but composed, the third frankly distraught, even to the straining cords in the neck.

In the second panel are recognizably the same characters, like a still from the first and last acts of a play (Dr Zarnecki suggests that in fact the sculptor was influenced by the plays). But the work is completed, and Christ stands fulfilled and almost exhausted, raising up the still immobile Lazarus. His feeling is all outwards, now, where it was self-contained before, which is a miracle of expressiveness. And what adds understanding and wisdom to expressiveness is the treatment of the other actors. There is no simple relief, but a medley of different emotions, just as there would be after a miracle. Mary and Martha, their faces as agonized as Grunewald would have made them, are torn between continuing grief, newly-awakened hope, and simple amazement. Lazarus himself is still: he cannot think and feel yet. The two disciples who raise him are compassionate but do not understand; to the two little lay figures underneath who have brought the coffin it is all in a day's work. And, in the top right-hand corner, two more disciples (one of them was the distraught person in the first panel) are almost troubled, seeing further than the first pair, to what must now inevitably follow in persecution and crucifixion.* – MONUMENTS. Bishop Sherbourne † 1536. Between the two panels. In such a situation, what on earth can be said about it? Bishop Sherbourne was an astute, politically-minded bishop, a type which does not seem to die out. He was instrumental in arranging the marriage of Henry VIII and Catherine of Aragon, and fixing up missions to Rome. He 'steered a prudent course at the Refor-

---

* The two reliefs were, according to Dr Zarnecki's convincing suggestion, part of a choir screen, not in the sense of a rood screen, but of German *Chorschranken*. Parts of a third relief are exhibited in the Library.

mation and was made one of the Commissioners on church property'. His tomb, quite simply, looks like it. Stiff, elaborate effigy in a panelled tomb recess of odd shape, with sides. Two angels hold up the mitre, two more gaze down, all could have been carved out of cheese. There is no hint of Renaissance detail, which is especially odd for a county whose tombs have so much of it. Perhaps it was made long before Sherbourne's death – another politic move. Restored in 1847. – Dean Hook † 1875, by *Sir George Gilbert Scott*. This is, surprisingly, almost the best monument in the cathedral. Simple tomb-chest without figures, ornamented with different marbles used richly, soberly, and discriminatingly, far removed from mechanical piety. The colours are deep red, olive green, olive grey, and black, with a little inlaid mosaic. One of the best things about it is that, like a Victorian drawing-room, it could belong to no other time.

SOUTH TRANSEPT. STAINED GLASS. The huge s window entirely filled with glass of 1877. Bright colours and weak faces. 'One member of the chapter talked over the other members, having been himself talked over by a relative who drew the design for the glass' (Evidence to Cathedrals Commission, 1885).* – WOODWORK. Tall C15 cupboard with a slit for coins. Presumably it contained relics. The ogee-headed top is authentic but does not look it; the whole object is neither better nor worse than if it had been built in 1875. Willis, with his usual prescience, called it a 'machine'. – PAINTING. Large early C16 wood panels by *Bernard*, companions to his Bishops in the N transept. Medallion heads of kings of England from William the Conqueror, with two bigger scenes above: Caedwalla granting the see of Selsey to St Wilfrid, and Henry VIII confirming to Sherbourne the royal protection of Chichester. This last is an engaging diplomatic myth: oh, shrewd trimmer Sherbourne! The style (which of course may have been altered in the C18 restoration by *Tremaine*) is already platitudinous, company board-room painting. It could have slipped imperceptibly into an R.A. exhibition of the mid 1840s. – MONUMENTS. Sacellum between transept and crossing, i.e. a three-bay stone screen which was perhaps the original pulpitum, before the Arundel Screen was put up. Taken down in 1860, replaced in 1904. It was originally put up by Bishop Stratford (1337–62) and encloses what is sup-

* It is supposed to be designed by one *C. Parrish* and made by *Maréchal* f Metz (NT).

posed to be his tomb, a weathered effigy, more than life-size, in a style which has blossomed into humane naturalism – a few years snatched between stylization and mechanical mass production. So the bishop is a real person, and the dog at his feet is prepared to bark. The tomb-chest is modern. Also under the canopy a brass to Dean Burgon † 1888, by *C. E. Kempe*, surprisingly honest and vivid, and a tablet by his partner *W. E. Tower* to Kempe himself, who † 1907, also vivid and unaffected. The screen is of the same family as the choir stalls (i.e. Dec work put up far away from the mainsprings of the Dec style), but much better done – the pinnacles are new but must represent what was there before. Canopy of three ogee arches, given especial bite by the double curve put in them close to the piers. The bosses thus provided have vivid grotesque carvings, human and animal. Inside, a firm but delicate quadripartite vault, showing where the sympathies of the designer really lay. In many ways Sussex jumped straight from E.E. to Perp. – Bishop Langton † 1337. A terribly weathered effigy which must originally have been very fine, under a fat ogee canopy which tries and fails to be sensuous and opulent. – Two bad tomb recesses of *c.*1500, the same style as those in the N choir aisle (p. 155). – J. Abel Smith, erected 1848, by *Edward Richardson*, under a C19 canopy like Langton's.

NAVE. S AISLE and CHAPELS. Seventh bay. Spiral STAIRCASE entrance to the top of the Arundel Screen, 1960. Like the other new things in the cathedral, it is fresh and modern, with steps cantilevered from a steel stem. By *Robert Potter*.

Sixth bay. Traces of another 'marble' MONUMENT of the recess type.

Between fifth and fourth bays. A small early NICHE of *c.*1535 or so, square-headed, with tiny crude putti and arabesques mixed with the Gothic detail – the only sign of the Renaissance in the whole cathedral.

Fourth bay. MONUMENT. Bishop Dunford † 1895, by *Bodley & Garner*. Effigy, canopy, applied piety. Stone dead.

Third bay (chapel). Two sad *Flaxman* MONUMENTS: Francis Dear and his wife Bridget, erected 1802, and Sarah Udny † 1811 – 'Udny! How few thy excellence transcend' and so on, in both verse and stone. But Agnes Cromwell † 1797, also by *Flaxman*, has hopes of nobler things in its freeflowing design, which is again a faint echo of Blake.

SW TOWER (Baptistery). The FONT is trying to be bold and

Romanesque and ends up worse than the most soulless of Victorian fittings. Erected in 1894 (NT). – Behind it in a niche on the s wall PAINTING by *Hans Feibusch*, 1951. What can be said ? More modern in style than most English paintings of this date and position, yet nowhere near a truly C20 religious expression. – Painting also on the w wall: 'The Tribute Money', by *Ribera*, or said to be. There are indeed Riberesque gleams on furrowed brows, but all the name-giving in the world cannot produce art. – Finally, a small set of joke MONUMENTS to take away in the memory: Ernest Udny † 1808 by *Henry Westmacott* (Sir Richard's brother), Jane Smith † 1780 and William Collins † 1759, deep in the New Testament, both carved by *Flaxman* in the 1790s. Judgement would not be so harsh were it not for the great feeling faces of the Lazarus panels a few yards away.

Before leaving, a look at the WEST WINDOW is equally worthwhile, in the same justifiably misanthropic way. It was done by *Wailes* in 1848, using a newly invented rolled-glass technique which 'reproduced the unequal surface of medieval glass'. Faites vos jeux.

PLATE. Two C13 Chalices and Patens, both from graves of bishops.

PRECINCTS

Chichester close is half-way between the miniature towns of Norwich and Salisbury and the traffic-laden fragments at Gloucester and Lincoln. It is small and grew up casually (as the cathedral was never monastic, there was no need for a formal precinct), but it is free of through traffic, it is a good mixture of public and private space, and it has an enchanting plan, contained within the s w segment of the city walls, which also includes the big private gardens of the Bishop's Palace, Chantry, and Deanery. The spine is a cul-de-sac called Canon Lane, leading from South Street to the Palace grounds, but in the easy-going and civilized Chichester way it can also be reached through the cloister and down an alley. The cloister itself, a short cut between West Street and South Street, is almost a public space. Apart from the cloisters and palace the precinct's charm is townscape, not architecture. The minutiae can be followed in the VCH and other places; a lazy walk round will satisfy all but the rabidly antiquarian.

CLOISTERS. The cloisters at Chichester are unusual (unique ?)

in English cathedrals for not being fitted into the angle
between nave and transept. Instead, they span the s transept,
with one entrance into the nave (St Richard's Porch) and the
other into the retrochoir. The reason is typical of Chichester,
where everything is accommodating and nothing is imposed.
The cloisters were apparently built new in c.1400 (perhaps as
a consequence of the rebuilding and enlargement of the
accommodation for the vicars?) and had to fit St Richard's
Porch, a graveyard on the s side called Paradise, and the line
of existing buildings on the s side which in fact became the s
wall of the cloister. The only encroachment was that in the
sw corner the cloisters bit ten feet into the w front of St
Faith's Chapel. But even here, the upper part was kept in its
old place with its w lancet still in position. The s walk is now
part of the cathedral, a short cut for the town, and a front
door to two or three houses. Everything flows together, as it
should.

The design is just as reasonable and unpretentious. It is
supposed to date from c.1400 because of William of Wykeham's arms over the NE door (the then Dean was a Wykehamist). If so, he was a Wykehamist in his architecture as
well as his politics, for the cloister is firmly in the court style
of Wykeham's architect William Wynford. Large-scale, bold,
and as understanding and as extrovert as Chaucer. Tall and
wide four-light windows, the lights forming two sub-windows,
and panel tracery. The roof is a subtle but unfussy timber
construction, where almost every other cathedral in England
would have had vaulting. Barn and church were always close
together in Sussex. A simple trussed rafter roof is given great
elegance by a system of braces forming four-centred arches.
In the E walk, which was perhaps built first, there is also a
moulded beam along the ridge of the four-centred arches. It
is a wonderful relief after the overloaded decoration of so
much Perp architecture. Good simple doorway of c.1400 into
the retrochoir in exactly the same spirit, square-headed, with
bold deep carving of tracery and shields (William of Wykeham's arms – see above) in the spandrels. Where the bottom
of St Faith's Chapel was taken out (i.e. at the SE corner) it was
patched up again with wooden panelling and a wooden door
as nice a surprise as a friendly hello on a formal occasion.

The s walk includes the front of the C13 HOUSE OF ROYAL
CHAPLAINS, which is better described here than with the
rest of the precinct. One blocked lancet remains, but like the

rest of these buildings at Chichester there is not much to follow up inside. Also there is an elaborately carved doorway of c.1500. This is a replica (the original is in the wall at the end of the garden, i.e. backs on to Canon Lane), but above is a weathered but well carved panel with Henry VII's arms above and a group of the Virgin and two kneeling figures below. This is the earliest surviving example of the many similar groups to be seen in C16 Sussex monuments, and it is worth looking at. If it were complete, it might be up to the standard of Westminster or Windsor. – MONUMENTS. A lot of C18 and early C19 tablets, and an earlier one to Percival Smalpage † 1595, with a frontal bust.

BISHOP'S PALACE. SW of the cathedral, approached from Canon Lane through a bulky early C14 GATEHOUSE, designed, like the later bell-tower, much more for use than for ornament. Two entrance archways, one big and one small, plainly double-chamfered, with a pair of windows above, two cusped ogee-headed lights under square heads. Springers of a former vault inside. The palace itself is now a rambling comfortable half-H shape, with its general character that of medieval flint walls overlaid by a straightforward remodelling in brick in 1725–7. The simple but rich staircase belongs to this. The back and sides are even more of a brick and flint jumble. In fact, of course, the story is more complicated.

The palace was affected by the fire in 1187 and must have been rebuilt soon afterwards. Seffrid II is recorded as rebuilding his apartments and he died in 1204. This work may comprise the present chapel and a two-storeyed hall linked by a single-storey vestibule, and forming approximately the central bar of the half-H. In the later remodellings the vestibule was made the same height as the other parts and all the original details of the hall disappeared (except for the original E gable, which is hidden under the present roof). The kitchens formed the E wing, built probably in the C13, and the long plain range further S, which joins up with the gatehouse, is C15 or C16. The other wing is probably C15, given a wholesale remodelling by Bishop Sherbourne early in the C16. The other notable addition is a vestibule in the W angle of the courtyard which must be part of a remodelling of c.1800. The four significant parts (chapel, kitchen, Sherbourne Wing, and vestibule) are described in that order.

CHAPEL. The N and E sides of the bishop's chapel are easily seen from the W front of the cathedral. The entrance is in the sw corner of the close, diagonally across from the sw tower. From the outside all that can be seen is the remodelling of the windows by Bishop Langton, c.1320, and this has the same limpness as the other Dec parts of the cathedral. Three windows on the N side with curvilinear tracery, E window with reticulated tracery. But the E wall outside gives a clue to the real character with the remains of three blocked c13 lancets. In fact, inside, everything is c13 and as good as anything at Chichester. The style is almost the same as St Richard's Porch, and presents the same sort of puzzles, that is of early-looking and late-looking E.E. details achieving complete homogeneity. The structure must be of c.1200 or very soon after, and a grand design it is, with a two-bay sexpartite vault with clunch filling to the cells and carved bosses. The vault-ribs are very similar to those of St Richard's Porch, and have the soffits ornamented with two small parallel rolls. The surviving windows are obtusely pointed,* with the same feeling and detail as the other post-fire work at Chichester (e.g. jamb shafts with crocket capitals); the s doorway is actually round-headed with two orders of complex roll mouldings and pairs of jamb shafts. Their crocket capitals have gone luxurious, as they so often do at Chichester. If only the E end had survived to make the spatial unit complete. The happiest thing is the way the chapel has already managed to avoid the academism and closed perfection of almost any Early Gothic vault in France. It is utterly fresh, where France in its details had already set hard.

So far, so good. The trouble is that the vault rests on big conical corbels, and these have gorgeous and generous foliage carving on them – the effect given in other circumstances by a firm full-bodied woman. One of them is almost identical with the corbel supporting St Richard, in the porch; others have the same intensification and elaboration of crocket capitals as the outer arch of the porch. All are stilted and never move around the corbel or intertwine; all in their surface richness would look more at home in Exeter than Chichester. So the same alternative remains. Either they are the work of a remarkable sculptor of c.1200 who short-circuited a hundred years of development, or they were carved much later; and, after all, there is plenty of additive sculpture at Chichester, e.g. in the retrochoir. But there the change of style is unmis-

* Four blocked on the s side, one open on the N, visible only from the garden.

takable; here there is enough continuity to make the improbable a possibility. – SCREEN. Early C14, the same type as survives in a few Sussex churches (e.g. West Thorney), but better. Narrow bays with the heads made up of a set of oculi. Simple and effective. – STATUE. Of St John, W end, affecting, compassionate figure with the head over-scale to the body – the same concern for feelings rather than abstract patterns as the Lazarus panels. The wooden statue must be South German, of the early C14 and part of a Crucifixion. – WALL PAINTINGS. Famous roundel on the N wall of c. 1250, small in size but not in effect. It looks exactly like a manuscript illustration done large, with the same glittering innocence, and the same rich materials (gold, silver, and lapis lazuli) – the first known example of their use on a wall painting. The subject is the Virgin and Child, with a censing angel on either side. Again, like the Lazarus panels, everything is concentrated on the empathy between the faces, and this carries the design along with it. – Also, on the W wall, Ascension by *Hans Feibusch*, 1953.

KITCHEN. The walls are straightforward enough, 34 ft square, built of flint rubble. But the roof deserves a place among the best English kitchens, which is to say among the oddest Gothic constructions put up anywhere. An empirical problem like this (a big room needing a central flue in the roof) always seems to have brought out the best in English ingenuity. This roof is wood, not stone, unlike Glastonbury. 28 The lantern – only sealed up in the C20, and worth re-opening – stands on four big posts. And these are caught on audacious two-way hammerbeams cantilevered out from the walls, so that each corner consists of a three-way openwork frame. The mechanics of thrust have rarely been better expressed anywhere: walls and roof stop being things to which decoration, however moving, is applied, but are emotive things in themselves, from their own nature. Plenty of cross-bracing, as well there might be. The roof is a good deal like that of St Mary's Hospital (*see* p. 174), which is of c.1300; yet hammerbeams are not supposed to occur as early as that. But engineering ingenuity takes little account of dates and style, and does what it can; and if the walls are C13, which they are supposed to be, what use are they without the roof, or something like it?

SHERBOURNE WING. The interest here is in the ground-floor room, which the bishop made into a very comfy parlour. He knew what was what in this world, at any rate. A long, fairly low room with a ceiling divided into squares by the deeply moulded beams and painted by *Lambert Bernard* with heraldic devices, datable 1524–35. The three-light windows have ample segmental splays, panelled in stone. Rich and jolly, like many a bishop's parlour since. Yet the early Middle Ages could do this and be spiritual too – spiritual *through* the body. This is not.

VESTIBULE. A brilliant design, small in dimensions but huge in scale. It might be the entrance to an enormous country house. It has been attributed to *Wyatt*, and it certainly has the mastery which he could produce at his best. Three bays, two on tunnel-vaults, the third a glass dome on pendentives. Plaster plaques in the various pedimental spaces, an elegant crisp cornice below. Psychologically, this passage makes you feel twelve feet tall, and does it without the overt tricks that Soane would have used. The need for this kind of expertise is more urgent than ever today. So many ceremonial entrances merely contrive, after enormous effort, to make you feel half size.

Good GARDENS, in Repton's taste. Mr Hay in 1804 described them by a beautiful example of damning with faint praise: 'at the same time, that is in the year 1725 or 1726, the gardens belonging to the bishop were modelled anew and laid out in a plan of great beauty and elegance; in which condition they remained till the time of the present bishop: whether they are improved by the late changes made in them I reckon not myself competent to determine.'

For the rest, the easiest point to start is the SE corner of the cloisters. This has already been noticed as part of the C13 ST FAITH'S CHAPEL, and standing in the quadrangle a single blocked lancet can be seen above the cloister roof; this is the top of the original W wall whose bottom was cut away to build the cloister. At the same time the W door was moved to the S side. The chapel continued E to take in both St Faith's House and the courtyard beyond it. The house was converted out of part of the chapel in the C16. The front is now Victorian, and nothing remains inside. E of this is a simple early C18 house, No. 2 ST FAITH'S, and then the long range of the VICARS HALL and PARLOUR. This is of flint, built above a late C12 vaulted undercroft of simple, impressive proportions, now The Crypt Coffee House, entered from South Street. Three by two bays, thick chamfered ribs, circular abaci and piers, blocked round-headed windows in the N wall. This is probably the former Gilden Hall, given to the cathedral in 1394 for the use of the Vicars. The building above has several square-headed cusped two-light windows, more like 1360 than 1390, and a kingpost roof. Elaborate lavatory on the N side with a big bowl under an ogee-headed niche. On the s side a small square projecting bay served as the pulpit. The E part, nearest South Street, was the Vicar's Parlour.

This takes you into South Street. It is easiest now to go down it for a few yards and then turn r. back into the precinct under CANON GATE, a simple Late Perp gatehouse largely reconstructed in 1894 by *Ewan Christian*. It has double-chamfered pedestrian and carriage entrances just like the gatehouse of the Bishop's Palace, which one sees now in the distance. Immediately inside it on the r. is the VICARS CLOSE, which was a long, narrow lane of C15 houses on the same pattern as the more famous example at Wells. In 1825 the eastern range was turned back to front, to become shops facing South Street, and in 1831 the gatehouse on Canon Lane was demolished. So most of the effect is gone and what remains is one long range, mostly refronted in the C18, facing a wall and footpath. The footpath then goes via the former Dark Cloister to a gateway into the SE corner of the cloisters. The doorway here is the original W door of St Faith's Chapel mentioned earlier.

Back to Canon Lane. On the l., set back, the CHANTRY, which is basically an early C13 building consisting of a two-storey chapel, nearest to the road, and a hall behind it. The present entrance is under the chapel through a two-bay quadripartite vaulted passage like the simpler vaults in the cathedral. This leads to the screens passage of the hall. In addition, there are a pair of lancets in the E wall of the chapel, and another (blocked) in the W wall. But everything else has disappeared or been concealed in later rebuildings and refurnishings. More medieval details were brought in *c*.1840. On the garden front is a two-storey bay window from Halnaker (*see* p. 178, below); in the N wall of the chapel, and the most prominent thing in the view from the street, is a four-bay late C14 window (square-headed, cusped lights: the stonework below it is modern). This is supposed to be from Halnaker too, but is a century earlier than the other imported bits in Chichester.

Now, on the r., is a picturesque small building, partly half-timbered, with a crowstepped brick N gable. On the l. a RESIDENTIARY which again has routine medieval work smothered under piecemeal additions. C16 bargeboard on the

E gable of the front to Canon Lane. Beyond on this side the big Georgian DEANERY, cheerfully rustic as the early C18 often was in Sussex. Built in 1725. Three-bay front, smallish windows in a big expanse of brickwork, the sort of style which architects like the Bastards of Blandford did much better. Nice staircase with twisted balusters inside.

Finally, on this side, another RESIDENTIARY, a gross rebuilding of 1871 keeping a mid C12 doorway, terribly renewed, facing Canon Lane. One order of zigzag enclosing balls, a mannerism which turns up occasionally in West Sussex. Jamb shafts, scallop capitals, outer label with zigzag as well. The doorway may be *ex situ*.

This brings the walker to the gatehouse into the Bishop's Palace (*see* p. 163). Back a little way, and turn N up an alley, nicely walled, called ST RICHARD'S WALK. On its l. the old TREASURY, rebuilt in 1835 by Canon Wagner to be a miniature of his new vicarage at Brighton. St Richard's Walk leads back into the SW corner of the cloister, and the shape of the lane can sum up the whole close – sunny, comfortable, not too narrow, ecclesiastical traffic route and townspeople's short cut at the same time. On the r. just before the cloister, No. 1 looks C18. In fact it was the House of Wiccamical Prebendaries and has the usual disguised medieval structure. The cellars form an undercroft 35 ft long which is vaulted in an irregular way. It is probably C14. Bigger hall, above, but only the dimensions can be traced.

CHURCHES

ALL SAINTS IN THE PALLANT, West Pallant. As simple as a barn. Single unaisled space, all C13, with lancets in N and S sides. Renewed triplet at the E end with Purbeck nook-shafts and moulded rere-arches inside. Friars or Cistercians could not have been sparser. – PLATE. Cup, 1731; Patens, 1731 and 1733; Flagon, 1747. All in the bank.

ALL SAINTS, Portfield. 1869. Perhaps by *Woodyer*. Tall and apsed, dominated by the stalky rood screen inside. Surrounded by a queer landscape; instead of Victorian terraces, there are gravel pits, the city cemetery and the jagged buildings that go with it (1858).

ST ANDREW OXMARKET, behind East Street. One of Chichester's redundant churches. It must be preserved, not for its intrinsic merits but because of the fantastic site. The only access to it is from East Street via a U-shaped alley which looks as though it leads nowhere – the ends of it are between Nos 20 and 21, and next to No. 27. Just behind the shops, and completely hidden from the street, is the simple demure roughcast church. Even the City of London can hardly match this, and more should be made of it – not by opening out but by heightening the surprise and seclusion.

The church itself is exactly like one of the smaller buildings in the surrounding villages. Single room, basically c13, with inserted c14 and c15 windows. Victorianized bell-turret. Two small early c16 MONUMENTS built into the outside walls, terribly weathered. – MONUMENT inside. John Cawley † after 1660. Po-faced frontal bust, elaborate surround. Still effectively Jacobean.

ST BARTHOLOMEW, Mount Lane, off Westgate. By *G. Draper*. Built in 1832, but still purely classical: it could easily be mistaken for a mid Georgian church. Very simple, round-arched windows in the sides, three-bay front with a composition of niches and roundels and a small pediment over the central bay. The front ashlar sandstone, the sides of local grey stone, galleted (*see* Sennicotts). Chancel of 1929*; a small W tower was taken down then. Completely plain inside. The original church on the site was destroyed in 1642; it was dedicated to St Sepulchre and was circular.

ST GEORGE, Cleveland Road. By *J. E. K. & J. P. Cutts*, 1901. A good example of an underrated type, the working-class late c19 chapel built after the passion for antiquarian reproduction had blown over. All brick, exposed inside. Single space, clerestoried and aisled without a break, like a Cistercian church. Six bays to the nave, three to the chancel. Honest and thoughtful.

GREYFRIARS, Priory Park. A very noble fragment, the choir of the church built soon after the Friary was refounded on this site in 1269. Probably complete by 1282. Built at the exact time when the friars' need of simplicity and strength in design was matched by the local c13 style with its austere working-out of a few strong ideas. So the friars' church has a classically simple repertoire. Tall, long, and aisleless, five windows in each side with two uncusped lights and a quatrefoil in bar tracery. The E window has five tall lancets in a stepped arrangement under one arch, not too steep. In this place almost anywhere else in 1270 would have experimented with some kind

* By Eric Gill's brother, *Macdonald* (NT).

of tracery pattern. Nothing else remains: two blocked door-ways on the N side seem to have led to the cloister, the chancel arch is blocked. Mr Steer suggests that there never was a nave, because no mention was made of it at the Suppression and no foundations can be traced. Around, perambulators, bowling greens, privet hedges, all accentuating the sharp honesty rather than spoiling it. Inside, a C15 wagon roof coming low over the tallest E lancet (the outer lancets were slightly shortened and received their cusps then. The old heads can be traced outside). Straightforward PISCINA, SEDILIA, and tomb recess. The chancel arch unbends just a little more, with a triple-chamfered arch resting on clustered shafts. The philosophy of 'less is more' is usually invoked nowadays to cover up poverty of invention; but it really works here. Each tiny chamfer and stretch of plain wall tells, in this utterly disciplined architecture. Discipline here is not restraint, but control of white-hot passion; all the forms are charged up.

ST JOHN, St John's Street. Neither beautiful nor lovable, but almost unique in its unaltered extreme Low Church plan. Built in 1812–13 by *James Elmes*,* father of the more famous Harvey Lonsdale Elmes and editor of *Metropolitan Improvements*. Almost indistinguishable from an expensive Non-conformist chapel. Elongated octagon of white brick, the front given a little trim around the windows, and a prepos-terous miniature of the Choragic Monument on top. The in-side has as its focal point a huge free-standing three-decker pulpit, and a gallery supported on thin iron columns which runs round all four sides. On the E side, the organ stands on it. The altar has dwindled to a kind of kitchen table. This kind of layout existed originally in other Late Georgian churches, but how this example survived the Cambridge Camden Society, the *Ecclesiologist*, and the Oxford Movement is a mystery. The pulpit is circular, on a spiral fluted stem, and towers over everything. Alas, no spatial imagination or sensibility to accompany this extraordinary plan. – PLATE. Two s.-g. Cups, 1813; Flagon, 1815.

ST MARY, Wyke Road. The old village church of Rumbolds-wyke which has got caught up in the C20 spread of Chi-chester. C11 two-cell church, recognizable by the high narrow proportions and the heavy chancel arch inside. No ornament at all, unmoulded arch, plain imposts. The windows un-

---

* Supervised, as Elmes was ill, by the young *George Haviland*, who after-wards became famous as a prison designer in America.

usually deep C13 lancets, and an odd C13 S doorway with a continuous roll-moulding round it. N aisle 1866. The outside effect Victorian, the inside still unpretentious and genuine, largely due to a good recent restoration. – PLATE. Cup, 1758.

ST OLAVE (former), North Street, see p. 179.

ST PANCRAS, Eastgate Square. A demure Gothick church of 1750 by *William Ride* 'to a plan already made', as rustic and unfanciful as the Palladian houses in Chichester. Flint, pointed windows, oblong belfry. Terribly treated in 1868 by *G. M. Hills*, with a new aisle and the inside completely re-done. – PAINTED GLASS. Simple armorial glass done after the church was built, by *Tremaine* (see p. 154). – PLATE. Cup and Paten, 1750.

ST PAUL, St Paul's Road, see p. 178.

ST PETER THE GREAT, West Street. A beautifully precise and sensitive church by *R. C. Carpenter*, 1848–52, an effect quite different from any other Gothic Revival architect's at that time.* Nave and chancel with long S aisle to the street, and small N aisle, all ashlar limestone, Curvilinear style. The proportion of window to wall on the street front and the careful but not lifeless details are a joy to look at. The only word for it is elegance, something normally noticeably absent from the 1850s.‡ Tall interior, big windows, big careful four-shaft arcades, rather like a Bodley church of 1880 or 1890; and not insipid – its flavour, although delicate, is persistent and definite. Nearly all of the STAINED GLASS was blown out in the war, a great pity, because it was not meant to be seen bare. Perhaps some unwanted C19 windows from elsewhere could be moved in. Some of the corbels wear C19 dress. – FONT. Octagonal, C15, the Arundel type with two trefoiled panels per side.

ST RICHARD (R.C.), Market Avenue. By *Tomei & Maxwell*, 1958. Well intentioned, and modern, but very depressing. T-shaped; exposed reinforced concrete Portal frames span the crossing diagonally.

PROVIDENCE CHAPEL, Chapel Street, see p. 178.

WESLEYAN CHAPEL, Southgate. 1876 by *Lander*. Not very easy to describe. It is as if Greek Thomson had got very drunk when visiting the Île de France. Gable flanked by stumpy

---

* The church cost £5650, i.e. only the price of a medium-sized Commissioners' church (NT).

‡ W porch 1881 by *Dunn & Hansom*, on the site of Carpenter's projected W tower (NT).

towers, giving this part of Chichester quite a surprise. Very rude things happen to the string-courses.

PUBLIC BUILDINGS

CASTLE, see p. 180.

COUNTY HALL, West Street. Behind Westgate House. By *C. G. Stillman*, 1936: well-mannered, carefully detailed Neo-Georgian like so much C20 building in Chichester. It is difficult to upbraid a building which has been dovetailed so deftly and unostentatiously into the pattern of the town. Eleven-bay centre with big central doorcase: projecting wings to l. and r. with links over arched vehicle entrances. Startling view of the cathedral from the forecourt, where it appears as if the bell tower is wearing the spire of the central tower.

COUNCIL HOUSE, North Street. Built in 1731–3 by *Roger Morris*, Burlington's disciple. Burlington himself made designs for the Council House, now at the R.I.B.A. library and Chatsworth, but although they may have provided some of the details they could not supply the spirit. This is the perfect example of Palladian ideas applied by a man who did not know what on earth to do with them. The building is jolly and friendly, but could have been done just as well by the local bricklayer. Five bays, brick and stone: the ground floor arcaded,* the first floor having four more columns, i.e. three bays in the centre supporting a lintel and a lion; the outer bays contain niches, and above them the ends of a pediment which, if prolonged, would meet at the lion's head. This is the Baroque open pediment given a new twist with a vengeance! Kent himself would have been hard put to regularize such a composition; Morris simply makes a joke of it. Yet if the Baroque had not been killed off by a kind of puritanism, it could have done something marvellous with just these elements. The Council Chamber has simple Palladian details; behind it are plain brick ASSEMBLY ROOMS built in 1781–3 and designed by *Wyatt*. They must have been a casual hour's work: nothing outside, a few niches over fireplaces inside. What a pity. The vestibule contains a display of Corporation PLATE, and this includes a C17 Mace with a gloriously curly and extrovert head that can only date from after 1660.

GREYFRIARS (Council Offices), see p. 180.

---

* Underneath the arcade is re-set a C2 Roman dedication stone to Neptune and Minerva, dug up on the site in 1723.

COUNTY COURT, Southgate, *see* p. 184.

POST OFFICE, *see* p. 176.

BISHOP OTTER MEMORIAL COLLEGE, College Lane. The original buildings are sober neo-Tudor, by *J. Butler*, 1849–50, typically honest and unselfconscious. Several C20 additions of no account, but the large extensions of 1961 by *Bridgwater & Shepheard* are a different matter. Steep gabled cruciform chapel,* the least effective part, with the N and S gables all glass, but first-rate classrooms and hall to W and S of it, forming a small courtyard which has been paved with brick. The sensitivity in the roof-lines and enclosure of space is outstanding, and the style, using red brick and white window frames, has no mannerisms.

PREBENDAL SCHOOL, West Street. Front of 1830, flint and stucco Gothic, older parts at the back, including blocked C13 E and S windows. It was probably the hall residence of one of the cathedral canons. The school was founded in 1497 by Bishop Story.

ST MARY'S HOSPITAL. Medieval hospitals attempted to cure body and soul in one building; the wards were put within sight of the chapel, either by placing it at the centre of a cross-shape, like the Savoy Hospital in London, or by making a two-part building, rather like a church, where the 'chancel' is the chapel and the 'nave' is the hospital ward. That is the plan at the most famous surviving hospital, at Beaune, and also here at St Mary's. It would be unique in Britain in any case as the only surviving example which is still lived in. What makes it probably unique in the world is that the former ward spaces were divided in the C17 not into cubicles, like the Heiligengeist Hospital at Lübeck, but into self-contained flats. The result is like seeing a set of almshouses contained in the aisles of a church: and it is also one of those places, becoming too rare in Britain, where the historical pattern is still being lived instead of being relegated to the antiquarians.

St Mary's Hospital was probably founded originally in 1158 and has always been administered by the Dean and Chapter. The Grey Friars, who had previously occupied the site, moved to Priory Park in 1269, and the hospital was confirmed on its new site by Edward I in 1285. A footpath across the site was stopped up in 1290, and this probably marks the beginning of work on the main buildings. Architectural details would

* Sculpture by *Geoffrey Clarke* in the W gable, and a superb TAPESTRY on the altar by *Jean Lurçat* (NT).

give the same date of *c*.1290–1300, which is just before the
Lady Chapel of the cathedral. The range of low buildings
facing the street was rebuilt in 1905 and is nicely unpretentious.

The main building looks exactly like a big towerless church.
It used to be bigger still, for the 'nave' has been shortened by
one bay. It originally extended as far as the present entrance
gate. It is an aisled hall, with flint walls and timber framing,
carrying an enormous tiled roof sweeping down from 42 ft at
the ridge to 7 ft at the eaves, now broken into by the C17 brick
chimneys. The original windows were tiny single lights, and
one of them remains on the s side. The chapel carries just the
same detail as the chancel of a biggish church would. It is
approximately the same size and proportions as the remaining
part of Greyfriars (*see* p. 169) and the difference in tracery
between them is very typical of 1290 as against 1270. The
shapes have become less grand, more complicated, and suffer
from the same kind of inorganic design as the early Dec work
in the cathedral. Renewed generally, but the patterns authentic: two-light windows in N and S walls enclosing quatrefoils
and cinquefoils. Reconstructed E window of five cusped lights
supporting a circle containing eight smaller quatrefoils and a
complex central shape – tracery which has ceased to have
Geometrical assurance and has not acquired Decorated
sinuousness.

The first impression inside is one of the most surprising in
England. The eye takes in the basic plan but sees the 'nave'
as being supported by the quartet of huge brick chimneys
added in 1680. These are in fact quite independent of the
timber frame. When they are seen to be flues, the viewer is
faced with the odder proposition that the low partitions in the
aisles actually conceal tiny houses. There are seven of these
(originally eight, one now converted to a bathroom), each with
bedroom, sitting room, and gas stove. The mighty timberwork
only shows itself on a closer look. It is built up like a tithe
barn, with a kingpost and trussed-rafter roof supported on
huge posts with a good deal of additional cross-bracing to the
tie-beams and purlins. Four bays remain, approximately 45 ft
wide and 20 ft long. Tall and elegant 'chancel arch', the
responds with clustered shafts typical of the late C13. Typical
also the triple SEDILIA, with renewed C19 heads, and
especially the PISCINA, in much more authentic condition,
also with a crocketed and finialled head and with brilliantly

carved label-stops. – SCREEN. Also of *c.*1290 and one of the best of its date in the country, with a wonderfully resilient and springy rhythm. Seven bays, each with a steep straight-sided gable, stalky and crocketed, enclosing a quatrefoil in a circle. Underneath this two ogee-headed sub-lights, themselves splitting into two. So there is a vivacious up and down contest of various curved forms as well as the overall side-to-side pattern. Heavy top beam, with what looks like C17 ornament on its underside. – MISERICORDS. Set of twenty-four, of the same date as the screen, and a good deal better than the slightly later set in the cathedral. Vividly characterized figures, including a harpy and a merman. Knobbly foliage everywhere, poised brilliantly on the edge of complete naturalism.

ST RICHARD'S HOSPITAL, Spitalfield Lane. Built in 1937–9 by *C. G. Stillman*. Straightforward brick, uninviting but honest, like his other buildings in Chichester.

ROYAL WEST SUSSEX HOSPITAL, Broyle Road. Georgian, but ignoble. Built in 1828 by *George Draper*, plus repeated additions: a long heavy stucco front weakly accented in the centre and near the ends. 2-2-4-3-4-2-2 bays, and as dull as that sounds.

MARKET HOUSE, North Street, *see* p. 179.

MARKET CROSS. Built in 1501 by Bishop Story, and originally[34a] the focus of a market place. Encroachment has produced its present status of a first-rate traffic block, and it would probably improve the townscape as well as the traffic if some kind of square could again be made around it. A luxuriant, almost Cotswold design, not at all like Sussex. Did Story have a West Country prototype in mind? And is the anachronistic spread-out complexity due to an earlier prototype or is it an inevitable consequence of the shape? Friendly, but rather a weak design because the ornamental details are mostly speaking an up-and-down language whilst the forms are sinuous and ogee. Octagonal, with a big round central column like a chapter house. Each corner accented with a big buttress and finial; from it eight ogee ribs run back to the centre to make an openwork crown. Small octagonal lantern at the top, altered in 1746. Each side has the familiar Perp ornamental system of an ogee arch set against vertical panelling. Above this a canopied niche on four sides; a big clock face in an ogee frame on the other four. Complicated vault inside, with sixteen ribs radiating from the central pier to an (octagonal) ridge rib. From the ridge eight ribs run down to the corners, eight to the mid-sides. Each bay also has two more ribs running diagonally from the corners to the ridge. Quite a setting for cabbages. On the E face, a very mannered but brilliant bronze statue of Charles I,* set up after the Restoration, a kind of lightning sketch which gets to the same conclusion as Van Dyck's slow-growing sequence of portraits.

RAILWAY STATION, Southgate, *see* p. 185.

PERAMBULATIONS

(A) *West Street and North-West Quadrant*

WEST STREET starts with a bang: on the l. the cathedral close to the road behind an avenue of lime trees, on the r. the handsome coaching-inn ranges of the DOLPHIN & ANCHOR, C18 and early C19, grandly done up in black and white. Continuing on this side the POST OFFICE of 1937, by *D. N. Dyke* of the *Ministry of Works*, doing one kind of best to keep in the Chichester tradition; red and grey bricks, early C18 style. Then St Peter's church (*see* p. 171), and Nos 22–24, a delightful trio. No. 22 has an early C19 stucco front, a familiar type but beautifully elegant, four bays and three storeys, shallow segmental blind arches on the ground floor, plain lintels over the first-floor windows. It seems to stray over as a coach entrance into one bay of the next house, which is otherwise mid C18 brick with splendidly curly rainwater head. No. 24 is a grey and red brick builder's front of perhaps 1770. The S side has been meanwhile going along in a comfortable C18 way, plus the front of the Prebendal School (*see* p. 173). The next building is again on the N side, WESTGATE HOUSE of 1696, attributed to *Wren* but in fact in a style which is a product of the generation before his, the City of London master-builders of the mid C17. Still half-H shaped, with shallow projecting

* It has been attributed to *Fanelli*.

wings, 2–3–2 bays, heavy eaves cornice, mullion-and-transom cross windows. Ornament on the central bay: doorcase with open pediment and pilasters with blocked rustication, window above with volutes at the sides, crowded pediment above that. Conservatism is in fact a lot of its charm and transforms it from being a naïve attempt to emulate Wren into being a rich style in its own right. Plain sides and backside. Behind it is the COUNTY HALL (*see* p. 172), fitted in with extreme care for the pattern of the town, approached by entrances on either side of Westgate House each with a pair of gatepiers. The l. hand set is original C17, the other a C20 copy: square piers with an urn on top and a pineapple on top of the urn.

Opposite, on the S side, No. 46 is that unusual thing, an early C19 house with a Dutch gable; then both sides turn cosy and cottagey, and the street becomes WESTGATE, with the good things on the S side: MARRIOTT HOUSE,* mid C18, with a pedimented centre, and its stables with a much smaller pedimented centre, No. 15, big blank late C18, and so on. The street has become curved by now, with a pretty two-storey range of cottages on the N side, and this has an enchanting effect on walking back towards the centre, with the cathedral towers playing hide and seek over the roof-line. To the S MOUNT LANE leads down to St Bartholomew's church (*see* p. 169) and then on to the Westgate Fields. On the r. hand side of this, two flat-roofed BUNGALOWS by *Powell & Moya*, 1949, one of the first of their type to be built in Britain. Simple roughcast walls, cheap but not mean: the rather unpromising recipe, which has produced some awfully crude buildings masquerading as modern architecture, is handled here carefully and sensitively.

Westgate continues with one last terrace of C18 houses (Nos 27–39, S side), and then becomes suburban. About ¼ m. further E, on the N side, is ST BARTHOLOMEW'S VICARAGE, *c.*1880, perhaps by *Ernest Newton* (NT), in a blocky neo-Queen-Anne style which is honest and impressive. Five-bay two-storey front, segment-headed windows: three-storey part at the back.

NORTH-WEST QUADRANT. This is the least interesting of the quadrants. Inside the walls a few old cottages, but mostly cleared for car parks and fussy recent flats (TOWER CLOSE). So at the moment in untidy transition. More housing back in

* The Theological College. Additions are planned for a site between Marriott House and St Bartholomew's church. Architects: *Ahrend, Burton & Koralek.* Very chunky.

the centre would be ideal; and failing that, a connected and landscaped system of car parks – i.e. a lot of trees which by accident have cars around their roots. Only three things need to be picked up: the splendid way in which the humble, slightly curved terraces of TOWER STREET frame the cathedral; PROVIDENCE CHAPEL of 1809 at the top end of Chapel Street, 'poor but honest' in the sense of the Victorian song, with its original fittings inside; and THE GRANGE, an odd Early Victorian house NE of the County Hall in Tower Street. It combines all sorts of convincing Late Gothic features in a convincingly asymmetrical way, and looks as though it could have been the house of an antiquary. The convincing features are in fact genuinely Tudor, from Halnaker House: two-bay windows and an oriel window on the N side, all from the S wall of the hall range there, and another window on the S side. Fragments and fireplaces inside too. The character is the nervous, showy Perp of Henry VII's Chapel, without any hint of Renaissance detail. Neglected at the moment (1963); it might almost now be better to return the Halnaker fragments to the ruins there.

The WALLS themselves are over 15 ft high on this side, and from them are views of the long back gardens of the houses in ORCHARD STREET, beyond. Most of these are comfortable, humble, early C19 terraces, part of a suburb called SOMERS-TOWN. Much of it (e.g. High Street and George Street) is about to be pulled down. If this is supposed to be 'slum clearance', in a city as completely unslummy as Chichester, it seems ridiculous. This area needed piecemeal recondition-ing, not demolition. Its unpretentious virtues are worth a look while they stand. With it goes a really horrible lancet Gothic church (ST PAUL, St Paul's Road, by *J. Butler*, 1836) and a much better VICARAGE, not built as such, at the corner of George Street. This is still classical, a good punchy design of flint and stock-brick which would have done well as an early railway station.

Beyond this to the N and W, C20 suburbs, private and council-built. Here outer Chichester looks like outer Manchester. Even in the air view published in the VCH (1935) the fields still began immediately outside the walls.

(B) *North Street and North-East Quadrant*

NORTH STREET is the perfect street for an English country town – firm but not rigid, mostly Georgian but of all heights and shapes, curved enough to prevent monotony, straight enough to give a direction. It starts, not at the cross, but a few feet to the E, so that the crossroads is slightly staggered. So, like Chester, unlike Gloucester, the street views are closed and the centre of the town is established. The only thing it has to fear now is too much mock-Georgian uniformity (see East Street, p. 181), but after a period, approximately 1925–55, when the street was almost sterilized, a deeper understanding of its needs seems to be on the way. Nothing outré or avant-garde is required, just the same cheerful up-and-downness that it has always had.

In fact, few of the individual buildings are worth an individual look. Starting from the Cross and working N, the first thing is the MARKET HOUSE, by *Nash*, built in 1807 (E side). It superseded the Market Cross, and at first looks like Nash designing in a thick, uncharacteristic neo-classical way. In fact, the top storey is a clever addition of 1900. Without this, the design becomes much more Nash-like – a hexastyle Doric portico *in antis* between two arched entrances, with the city arms on the parapet. He could never really gear himself down enough to make this kind of building look more than a frag-ment of some vast scenographic scheme.

Immediately N, on the E side, is the former church of ST OLAVE, now an S.P.C.K. bookshop, sandwiched in between buildings in a friendly way. The street gable shows a reticulated C14 window; in fact the nave walls are probably Early Norman and the chancel is C13, but terribly restored. The best detail is a C14 PISCINA, ogee-headed, now on the N side of the former nave, with all the humanity that is missing from the Dec parts of the cathedral. – MONUMENT. Martha Dear † 1807, by *Henry Westmacott*, moved here from St Martin's. Much better than his monument in the cathedral: decently carved mourner above, quite an original tablet below.

N of this again the Council House (see p. 172); only beyond this do the individual domestic buildings in North Street become worth recording. First, on the W side, Messrs PURCHASE, C18, with a cantilevered first-floor bay window and elegant Adamesque doorcase underneath. Then the site of the old but unremarkable church of ST PETER, demolished in 1957 (E side). Back on the W, No. 40 is a firm early C19 design, the same character as St Paul's vicarage (see p. 178). Four bays, classical flint and stock brick. No. 43 has another cantilevered bay window, this time Gothick, above a Composite doorcase, both perhaps additions at different times in the C18 to a house of *c.*1700.

Thereafter, the interest is on the E side, beginning with GREY-FRIARS (Council Offices), which is plain C18 outside and has a small but very ornate early C18 staircase inside, in a tiny well. Carved tread-ends, and effective rhythm of three balusters per tread – one plain, one barley-sugar, one carved with a crisp spiral moulding. Beyond this the SHIP HOTEL seems to be plain late C18 brickwork, but conceals a remarkable staircase which would not be out of place in the West End. It has a light cast-iron balustrade and climbs around a square well through two storeys. One corner is rounded off and given niches, and the first-floor landing, which is L-shaped (i.e. takes up two sides of the square), has an ornate four-bay arcade with palm-leaf capitals and honeysuckle ornament on the soffits. Above, the ceiling height is much lower, accentuating the upward perspective. It is difficult to suggest a designer; the gusto of the ornament may point to a local man, but it has a beautifully sure spatial touch. Beyond this ARMY HOUSE, an elegant early C19 stucco front with Doric columns *in antis.* Then comes the line of the walls, with a good deal of demolition around, and then (in NORTHGATE) some attempt to provide a formal introduction to the town, with plain and heavy C18 brick houses.

From North Street, LION LANE runs E. Curved, elegant, with its cottages still intact, and No. 6 something rather more. It leads to ST MARTINS STREET and SQUARE, a tiny delightful space. To the S it is menaced by the car parks which, however necessary and however tidy, are a curse in a close-built city like Chichester. The 'square', really just a widening of the road, is made up of the long low front of St Mary's Hospital (*see* p. 173) and two bluff mid C18 houses in échelon, Nos 20 and 21. Almost identical, except that No. 21 has ogee attic windows. To complete the square No. 1 faces S, brick with stone quoins, and Nos 2–3 face E, stuccoed. All the buildings are pleasant, none of them remarkable; but together they make up a very remarkable space. It is as wayward and deceptively casual as one of the little scenographic squares in Rome. St Martin's Square runs N past No. 8, another four-square C18 house in slightly earlier style, to PRIORY PARK. This contains the chancel of Greyfriars church (*see* p. 169) and the low MOTTE of Chichester Castle, all wound round with paths and privet. The park boundary is formed by a complete segment of the walls, and they can be followed round to Priory Road. Here is FRIARS GATE, another mid C18 house surely by the same mason as Nos 20–21 St Martins Street. Three-bay pedimented centre and a refreshing air of sublime unconcern with Lord Burlington's niceties. From here down LITTLE LONDON, with a variety of C18 cottages in good condition, and then back to the walls via EAST ROW to see how well the uncomplicated industry of country towns (corn mills, in this case) can fit in next to housing.

Beyond the walls, North Street becomes BROYLE ROAD. On the r. at the s end CAWLEY'S ALMHOUSES, a humble E-shaped brick block of 1625, the centre crowstepped, the wings with small mullioned windows, the bigger projecting ends added in 1753 when it became the city workhouse. The founder, William Cawley, was M.P. for Chichester and a regicide. He had to leave the country and died at Vevey in Switzerland. The centre contains the chapel, simple and lovable, with an ornamented reading desk dated 1626 and other woodwork which is still more than half Gothic.

Beyond this on the r. is Oaklands Park with the FESTIVAL THEATRE, by *Powell & Moya*, 1961–2. Hexagonal, with an Elizabethan open stage and the shape of the auditorium vividly expressed outside. Everything is cantilevered from a compact centre. It might have been a vehicle for self-advertisement, but Powell & Moya are not like that. The reinforced-concrete detailing is sober, noble, and dignified, with a presence far beyond the actual size.

Then, on the l., we come to the Royal West Sussex Hospital (*see* p. 175). N again is a late Victorian suburb called SUMMERS-DALE; beyond that C20 houses in leafy grounds. On the main road (Lavant Road) is TUDOR HOUSE, an extravagance of 1926 by *H. Osborne*. Half-timbering and twisted chimneys done with enormous gusto, and the proportions as sensitive as Voysey in their funny way. Further E, in THE DRIVE, CARRICK, a pleasant modern bungalow by *J. Paterson*, 1961.

Back between here and the town centre Bishop Otter College (p. 173) and St Richard's Hospital (p. 175).

(c) *East Street and South-East Quadrant*

EAST STREET is almost straight, directly on the axis of the Market Cross. Until recently it looked as though it would become that melancholy but very English thing, a town stree which has more mock Georgian buildings than real ones.

Recent building at the W end has helped to alter that and to
bring back the kind of honest mixture which is what such
streets always were. Especially happy, unassertive yet convincingly modern, is LENNARDS, on the corner of East and
North Streets, by *Sir Hugh Casson*, 1961. Otherwise, there is
just enough to make a pleasant walk. Starting from the Cross,
the OLDE PUNCH HOUSE (S side) has a good C18 shop
window, used as an off-licence. The structure itself is late C16
and simple panelling and a ceiling of this date remain inside.
Then, opposite, the NATIONAL PROVINCIAL BANK is
swagger neo-Georgian of 1929 by *F. C. R. Palmer*. It probably
started the trend to conformity, but did so with much more
panache and expertise than its successors. The bad new
BARCLAYS BANK is by *Green, Lloyd & Son* and *Stanley
Roth*, 1961-3. On the S side, the GRANADA cinema is the
former Corn Exchange of 1832 by *John Elliott*, a local man.
Six-column Greek Doric portico and pediment spanning
the pavement: a sound, unexciting civic building. Back
on the N side again, Nos 45–46 is the only authentic
Georgian piece in a whole stretch of reproduction: a plain,
heavily pilastered early C18 house. The numbering suggests
what is unusual about it – that it is a very early semi-
detached house, with a semi-detached porch on Doric columns
to match. The street ends at EASTGATE SQUARE, an ungainly roundabout with St Pancras church on the N side (*see*
p. 171) and a late C18 pair of houses on the S (Nos 20–21),
where Keats began to write the *Eve of St Agnes*. Beyond this,
The Hornet goes E to Bognor, with nothing special to see:
ST PANCRAS goes NE to Arundel and Petworth, with LION
HOUSE a good way out along it on the N side, a plain, decent
three-storey building dated 1783. Oddly, it was not then out
in the country; old terraces stretch a good half-mile beyond
Eastgate Square, showing that this was an early faubourg or
piece of ribbon development.

SOUTH-EAST QUADRANT. This is the most rewarding sector
of Chichester, containing the Pallant, which is a kind of
village-inside-the-city. It can be reached in a few yards from
East or South Streets. It is a wonderful area to have so close
to the city centre, and it is beautifully kept up. But around
and beyond, it needs terraces of cottages (either old or Span)
instead of a chain of car parks, however carefully they are
treated.

The best way to start is from East Street down NORTH PAL-

LANT, with, straightaway, a good late C18 house with a handsome Ionic doorcase. North Pallant is close-built, without gaps, full of pleasant inflections, the sort of thing that every English urban street ought to be. On the l. No. 5, five bays and three storeys in a chequer pattern of red and grey brick. Mid C18, the top storey probably c.1820. Then No. 7, also c.1820 but smooth and stuccoed. Opposite, No. 8 is plain, tall, late C18. Then back again on the E side is PALLANT HOUSE, built c.1712 by Henry Peckham, called also Dodo House from the comic stone birds on top of the gatepiers.* This is Chichester's most ambitious Georgian house: seven bays wide, the centre brought forward and quoined. All brick, with very narrow tall windows, typical of masons' work for a few years around 1710. Masons' touches also in the keystones to the windows, which have frilly edges and carry brick badges. Fragile early C18 ironwork in front, and a grand doorcase with Corinthian pilasters. But it is oversize for the rest of the front, pointing the fact that Pallant House is an assemblage of handsome individual units, not an organized design. Inside, more handsome craftsman's units: a staircase with twisted balusters and carved sides to the treads, and another Corinthian doorcase on the first-floor landing.

Here is the central cross-roads of the PALLANT. Its plan is a microcosm of the city plan, with North, East, South, and West Pallant. It is a wonderful example of companionable formality, full of dignity yet never overbearing. Slight variations in the street widths and angles mean also that what is in fact a kind of gridiron never reads as such. The easiest way to walk it is to see West and South Pallants by going down and back and leave along East Pallant. WEST PALLANT is only a short stretch, with the cathedral spire grandly in the middle of the view. On the N side No. 5, of c.1770, in the same style as St Martin's Square; on the S side No. 12 is huge and blank early C18, No. 10 (PALLANT COURT) is just as blank but almost a century later, with Greek Doric porch *in antis*. SOUTH PALLANT is a simple business of cottages and then CAWLEY ABBEY just inside the walls, a rambling building with an early C18 core.

EAST PALLANT is also short but very grand, starting with No. 6, plain early C18, then No. 5, of c.1760, very plain and dignified, with an unusual three-part Ionic doorcase (Venetian window and Doric porch on the S side, facing the garden). No. 4 is

* They are bad shots at ostriches, the Peckham crest.

smaller, stuccoed; an early C18 house with a very delicate late C18 doorcase. Beyond this the scale turns to cottages; at the corner of Baffin's Lane is BAFFIN'S HALL, a plain Presbyterian chapel of 1721, now a furniture store. Then St John's church (p. 170) and bigger houses again in ST JOHN'S STREET: Nos 11–14, a three-storey stock-brick terrace, early C19 and very seasidey, and opposite No. 9, a pretty flint and stucco Tudor cottage, equally seasidey. After this the WALLS, ever-present but unobtrusive; low here, higher further W in the stretch leading past Cawley Abbey to the end of South Pallant. Nothing to see beyond the walls except the two churches of St Mary (p. 171) and St George (p. 169).

(D) *South Street and South-East Quadrant*

Busy and mixed up, with a quick turnover of property, leading from the Cross to the railway station. Starting from the Cross, SOUTH STREET is pleasant and blessedly free from gentility, but nothing to notice until quite a long way down. (On the r. first Vicars Hall, *see* p. 166, then Canon Gate, *see* p. 167.) First on the E side, the Chippendale delicacy of the doorcase of RICHMOND HOUSE, No. 47, which must be *c*.1770. Then three good buildings close together. First, the REGNUM CLUB, which looks like a heavy Wren-style house redecorated in the early C19. Recessed centre filled in with two storeys of thin Doric columns *in antis*, windows given thin ironwork detail – a nice compound of lightness and heaviness. The historical diagnosis confirmed by the staircase, early C18, with three balusters to a tread, each different, and thicker Corinthian columns for the newel posts.

Next door, No. 44 is a very individual and delicate building of *c*.1820. It looks like the impact of the seaside style on a local builder. Galletted flint and brick, delicately painted; central first-floor bow window not quite in the middle of the façade, which is rather unnerving. Next to it again is the former THEATRE, built in 1792, now used as a furniture store with a modern shopfront. Here the W side chimes in for the first time with Nos 37–38 of *c*.1800, stuccoed, with two ground-floor bow windows.

The continuation is SOUTHGATE, with the Wesleyan Chapel (p. 171) as a shake-down, then the COUNTY COURT, by *C. G. Stillman*, 1940, sober and symmetrical brickwork, almost shapeless. It may look very timid now, but the freedom from pilasters and pediments was quite rare at that time in civic buildings away from London. Its quiet virtues of proportion and lack of fuss grow on repeated visits. A similar number of visits to the RAILWAY STATION, opposite, may produce exasperation at the smothering of so many good intentions in a welter of badly related materials and clichés. Rebuilt in 1961 by *B.R. Southern Division*. Inside, a pleasant-shaped concourse again spoilt by fragments of half a dozen architectural languages. With so many nondescript stations in Sussex, it is a pity that this replaced one of the few worthwhile ones, a sober classical building.

Beyond the station the former CANAL BASIN, opened in 1824; still with water in it, and up to now a wasted asset, surrounded by careless building or no building at all. Further s in STOCK-BRIDGE ROAD is STOCKBRIDGE HOUSE, a handsome, simple, five-bay front with one figure of the date – 1699 – on each of the four ground-floor keystones. The building contract has survived; the builder was actually a carpenter, *John Lilliott*, who agreed to provide 'a handsome cornish under the roof'. That is exactly what he did.

The rest of the quadrant is taken up by the cathedral precinct (*see* p. 161) and by the doomed WESTGATE FIELDS. While they remain, a walk down a footpath starting in South Street opposite the old theatre can give one of the most piercing townscape experiences in England. In a few yards, you are in open rough fields beside a stream with the cathedral towering above the best-preserved section of the city walls. The ring road and the schools, however well they are landscaped, will taste like American bottled beer after Draught Bass.

CHICHESTER DYKES, 2 m. N. An elaborate series of earthworks to the N and E of the town, good stretches being visible in the grounds of Lavant House and Oakwood House. The bank and ditch now appear as a series of disjointed earthworks, but these unfortified areas were probably defended naturally by dense woodlands. Excavation has shown that the ditch is of V-section and some 9 ft deep. Pottery associated with the Dykes suggests a date *c.*50 B.C. The defences were probably built by the Belgae against the people of the Downs to the N.

CHIDHAM

7000

A cul-de-sac s of the Portsmouth–Chichester road near Bosham, on a tongue of land with an inlet of Chichester Harbour on either side of it. Completely unspoilt, one of the nicest of the West

Sussex coastal villages: completely wayward too – no formal group, just barns, cottages and the bell-gable of the church.

ST MARY. Could be in no other county but Sussex. Effectively all plain C13; nave, chancel, and short N aisle. A good deal of this was due to the restoration of 1864, but simply done, not affecting the general impression, and that is typically Sussex too. Only the Street-like W bellcote seems too assertive. Lancets throughout (the E end and the S nave windows new), except for a two-light C14 window in the aisle. The inside effect simple, pure, not hard; plain double-chamfered chancel arch, two-bay early C14 aisle with double-chamfered arches, octagonal piers and capitals. The bellcote outside is supported by two thick clasping stone buttresses. – FONT. Round bowl flowing into a chamfered square base. Impossible to date; the VCH says c.1660. – PLATE. Cup and Paten, 1704. – MONU-MENTS. Two good cartouches in the chancel, obviously by the same person, to Henry Bickley † 1707 and George Meggott † 1708. Strictly symmetrical, composition of cherubs' heads, skulls, and heavy drapery, still really in the style of c.1660, as the strapwork surrounds to the inscriptions show.

Immediately N of the church the MANOR HOUSE, with a plain five-bay C18 front and a Jacobean core inside.

MIDDLETON HOUSE, ¾ m. NE. Handsome plain farmhouse dated 1759, a type fairly common near the Selsey peninsula. Five bays, two storeys, with a big pattern-book Tuscan Doric doorcase. Grey and red brick, the red brick made up in vertical bands joining the windows.

CHITHURST

Church and farms on the bank of the Rother halfway between Midhurst and Petersfield – lush and intricate in spring, like a Pre-Raphaelite picture. The view from the W door of the church is disturbingly verdant and English, like an over-vivid dream.

CHURCH. The walls all C11 – poverty or remoteness have kept the original dimensions intact without any kind of addition. It was mentioned as an *ecclesiola* in Domesday, and that is exactly what it has remained. Norman, not Saxon, see the herringbone masonry on the N side, the proportions (tall and narrow, but not quite as tall as they would have been before the Conquest), and the plain details – one window on the N side, plain un-moulded chancel arch on plain imposts. All that the subsequent centuries added, mostly c.1300, was more light: cusped lancet in the N wall, E window of two cusped lights, then a little later the window in the s wall near the W end of two cusped lancets with a quatrefoil above. When the C19 copied this immediately to the E, they could not resist adding slightly more intricate mouldings.

CHITHURST ABBEY. Immediately W of the church; the old manor house (never an abbey), a good late medieval yeoman's house. T-shaped, with the stem of the T roughcast,* with overhanging first floor, probably C15; the cross-piece is a taller C16 block of stone with several original windows, mullioned and transomed under hood-moulds. Nicely unrestored.

HILL-FORT, in HAMMER WOOD. An Iron Age promontory fort enclosing an area of 17 acres; it consists of two widely spaced ramparts and ditches and portions of a third rampart cutting off the end of the spur. The sides of the scarps are also fortified. The inner rampart has a stone facing – the outer is unrevetted. The defences are broken by a single oblique entrance on the N. Excavations produced pottery of degenerate Iron Age A type, but it is not definitely associated with the fortifications.

CHRISTS HOSPITAL

1020

1½ m. SW of Horsham

Christs Hospital was founded by Edward VI in 1553 on the site of Greyfriars, Newgate Street, in the City of London. Like Charterhouse it moved out in the C19, and the result is more like a small town than a school, housing 840 boys. The designs are by *Sir Aston Webb*, begun in 1893, finished by 1902. The plan is ingenious and the dimensions huge, but the details are so utterly uninspired that it can only be a vast disappointment. The centre is a big oblong quad. At the N end the Dining Hall, placed laterally, at the s end the Big School (i.e. the school hall), end on to the quad and connected by bridges to side buildings. The W and E sides of the quad are colonnaded. Behind the W colonnade the hall, behind the E colonnade the chapel.‡ Entry into the quad through two gatehouses – transplanted from London: by *John Shaw*, 1829 – E and W near the Dining Hall, linked with the colonnades so that the quad makes a complete enclosure, a spatial idea which is worth remembering. The details of the buildings are alas not worth remember-

* In the C18 this was pargetted.

‡ This has a PULPIT, possibly late C17, and a series of PAINTINGS by *Sir Frank Brangwyn*.

ing. Aston Webb was working with a weak mixture of Gothic and Elizabethan, and applied a fatally low creative voltage to it. A few ornamental bits were also re-used from the C17 buildings. These include, on the N front of Big School, Charles II, after 1676, and Sir John Moore, by *Grinling Gibbons*, c.1695; on the S front Edward VI, 1682.* In the centre a fountain with Edward VII in lead on top. Below, against the high pedestal, the demure figures of four Bluecoat Boys, Coleridge, Lamb, Middleton, and Maire, in scholars' dress (which is still used). They are by *Woolner*, 1875, sentimental, but genuinely sweet, not cloying. It would be nice to know what Coleridge and Middleton, at least, thought of their schooldays: and also what the masters thought of C. and M. All of a piece with the architectural detail, a rare thing in C19 sculpture. It is this harmony between what is said and the way it is said that makes it so successful

L. and r. of the Dining Hall, eight H-shaped blocks containing boarding houses, an interminable vista. Behind it a high WATER TOWER, Aston Webbed, which is the most prominent thing in distant views and makes the whole group look unbearably institutional. To the N, farm and estate buildings, and to the NW the RAILWAY STATION, which is actually a better building than the Hospital itself. It was built in 1899 and must be one of the best examples in southern England of an unaltered Late Victorian railway building – most of them have had to be enlarged to cope with increased suburban traffic. A small junction, hence an improbably big station for the leafy surroundings. Polychrome brick buildings, huge wooden platform roofs on steel girders, with a taut and suave loping rhythm on the bargeboards – no longer the frilly detail taken over from books of Picturesque cottages. Platforms 4 and 5, serving the branch line to Guildford, are enchantingly set at an angle to the rest. A later southern equivalent of Ambergate in Derbyshire. It is worth preserving entire.

61a

CHURCH NORTON see SELSEY

CISSBURY see FINDON

0000

CLAPHAM

A pleasant, unremarkable village on the slopes of the Downs

---

* I am grateful to Mr A. E. Allison, Clerk of Christ's Hospital, for information on these.

NW of Worthing. Many of the houses are new, and the manner in which they have been fitted in is admirable in its quiet way. CLAPHAM FARM, next to the church, is an attractive mixture, the oldest part regular timber-framing, probably of *c.*1600, with massive crow-stepped chimneybreasts.

ST MARY. Humble village E.E. and Perp, the restoration (by *Scott*, 1873) doing much less harm than more serious-minded attempts would have done. Originally a Norman nave; one blocked splay remains above the N arcade. The bones of the church effectively C13, however: lancet chancel, N and S arcades, and attached NW tower. The N arcade earlier than the S, with circular abaci and stylized wind-blown foliage capitals. The S arcade is the standard Sussex C13 style. Various two-light Perp windows, nicely moulded. – MONUMENTS. Brass to John Shelley † 1526 and wife. Big effigies, as the C16 goes, 3 ft high, but as naïve as the angels on a rustic C18 tombstone, without any compensating freshness. – Other later C16 Shelley brasses on the S chancel wall. – Sir William Shelley † 1548, a tomb recess (N wall of chancel). Another example of the local school of carvers adapting Renaissance motifs, here in the most childlike way, along with the familiar vine-trail. Everybody kneeling: Sir John with seven sons, his wife Alice with seven daughters. Poor Alice! Like the brass, no charm to compensate for the roughness.

CLIMPING

Across the mouth of the Arun from Littlehampton, forming the only unbuilt piece of coastline between Selsey and Brighton, and with such a sweeping wind-blown beauty that the meanness and selfishness of the bungalows everywhere else seems all the worse. One wayward leafy street, quite unspoilt, running down to the sea. The church is further N in a scrappy landscape which does the C20 no credit: a disused naval airfield now converted to be an open prison.

ST MARY. 'Climping for perfection' runs part of a saying about Sussex churches, and in this local pride does not exaggerate: for exactness of proportion and for lack of later alteration, Climping is as good a village church of *c.*1220* as any in the country. The only detail that does not come from the C13 is the lower parts of the tower, and in fact Climping is better known for this than for the later work: an extreme example of

* Probably built under John de Clymping, later Bishop of Chichester.

Latest Norman ornamental wildness, *c*.1170 at the earliest.
The tower is attached to the s transept with broad, flat buttresses and a broader stair-turret. Up the centre of each side
another flat buttress, and in it, at first-floor level, a wrought-
about window which seems to be unique in England: a perceptibly pointed lancet with its own thick surround inset into the
buttress and almost obscured by a continuous thick zigzag
moulding, deeply undercut, made up from the buttress itself.
The effect, of wilfully burrowing into the very solid forms of
the buttress, or of windows seen in effect behind a kind of stone
curtain, is extraordinary. It is mannered and extrovert at the
same time, and this is Sussex's own felicity. The same spirit
produced the doorway on the w side of the tower: an outer
order with roll moulding under a dogtooth label, an astounding parody of jamb shafts where each stone of the shaft is a
chevron (this has, in effect, produced a Baroque barley-sugar
column four hundred years early, and in fact may have sprung
from an identical impulse, to liven up the existing established
style). Inside this an order of the very typical kind where two
sets of zigzags at 90 degrees to one another meet at the edge
and thus create a continuous diamond pattern. It runs uninterrupted from base to base. Finally, the inner order is plain
with a trefoil head. On either side plain narrow niches and
above them a tiny roundel (l.) and lozenge (r.). The top of the
tower was finished with simple E.E. detail and parapet on corbels. Inside, the arch to the s transept is pointed, unchamfered,
of two orders with segmental rather than semicircular jambs
and imposts. It must be E.E. also.

The church that was added to this is in complete contrast –
yet, as at Burpham and elsewhere in Sussex, the late c12 and
early c13 make a very good match. It is in the severest kind of
lancet style, depending entirely on proportion outside, consisting of nave, s aisle under lean-to, chancel, and transepts. All
the windows are lancets, those in the chancel a little earlier
with a shallow roll-moulding around them, the remainder completely plain. The effect of each lancet and each detail of roof
pitch and relation seems to have been calculated to the centi-
metre: the NW side, where the tower is out of sight, is like a
textbook of proportion.

This level of achievement is kept up in the inside space, an
even rarer gift. The rhythm of chancel and transept arches is
echoed unerringly in the smaller arch between aisle and transept and is caught up and elaborated in the rhythm of the plain

window splays, then underlined in the simple shafted treatment given to the triple lancets at the E end; the asymmetry of the S aisle is exactly balanced, in spatial weight, by the deep splays on the N side. It is without exaggeration, divine harmony made visible in masonry, a harmony which only that particular moment of the C13 could have expressed. Window rere-arches are plain except in the chancel, where the E window has framing of moulded arches on shafts with the stiffest of stiff-leaf capitals and a pair of blank quatrefoils in the spandrels; the other chancel windows have a simple roll moulding. The variations in the arches also show a slow evolution from E to W, though all are in the same framework of complex moulded arches and plain abstract abaci. The chancel arch has two orders, tiny quarter jamb shafts at the angles, flat grooved soffit and thick corbels as imposts – a rigid, square-cut style. The N transept arch is a little softer, with chamfers replacing the shafts, the soffit rounded and moulded, the imposts less bulky; and the S transept arch and the arcade are well into the familiar serviceable Sussex C13 style: round abaci, round piers, subtly moulded arches of two orders. No structural alteration after the mid C13.

FURNISHINGS. PISCINA and AUMBRY. C13, in the chancel: simple trefoil heads to go with the church. – FONT. Standard Perp, octagonal bowl ornamented with quatrefoils. – Several plain BENCH ENDS: two trefoil-headed lights flanked by buttresses. – PULPIT. Stone, severe Perp which is an admirable match for the architecture: nothing twisty or intricate, just bold, deeply cut panels with cinquefoil heads. – CHEST. Late C13, and delightful: delicate frilly pattern of pointed-trefoiled arcading flanked by two complicated rosette designs like rose windows – very different from the usual rough job. – PLATE. Chalice and Paten, 1661.

Immediately S of the church, the PARSONAGE of c.1833 by W. F. Pocock, with a gimcrack stucco Gothick front. To the S again, beyond the A259, several nice flint cottages and barns, especially BROOKPITS, a good example of an early C17 yeoman's house: flint with brick dressings, two-storeyed central gabled porch, and several of the original mullioned brick windows.

The part on the coast is called ATHERINGTON, and here there is a good set of thatched flint BARNS. Just W of this is Bailiffscourt (see p. 97).

½ m. SE, near the sea, is one of the squat octagonal WINDMILLS which are still fairly common in Sussex. Weatherboarded, sweeps complete, probably c.1800.

9010 ## COATES

Most places called Coates (i.e. shelters) are small and remote. This one, lost in the beautiful heath country SE of Petworth, is no exception. But even so, the tiny group of cottages near the church contains a good weatherboarded BARN and a good small C17 MANOR HOUSE, with stone mullioned windows and a small central gable. Three bays, three- and four-light windows, brick dressings subtly used, i.e. less unselfconscious than it appears.

ST AGATHA. An enchanting sight from the S, backed by trees, for all the world like a toy. Nave, chancel, and spiky bell-turret of 1907, all tiny. The outside too harshly repointed, the inside still humble and sweet. The whole of the walling probably Norman, although only one tiny window remains, on the S side. The remainder lancets in deep splays, the E end with two, not three. Big Norman chancel arch, completely plain, plastered walls and ceiling. – PLATE. Cup and Paten, 1568.

COATES HOUSE, ½ m. W. Quite a big Gothick house, well and truly stuccoed and castellated. Squat central tower, a pair of taller and narrower towers at the S end, lower bits to the N.

8010 ## COCKING

Cheerful roadside village of brick, flint, and clunch on the Midhurst to Chichester road just below the Downs. The road goes over at 350 ft in one of the few gaps in the hills. Mostly owned by the Cowdray estate, recognizable by the yellow paintwork of the cottages. Probably because of this it is very unspoilt for a main-road village, without being at all 'preserved': this and the materials make it look very like the Pas de Calais.

CHURCH. Humble C14 tower, roughcast, with a pyramidal cap: the rest from the outside looks all C19 (N aisle 1865, the remainder refaced, though keeping C14 windows in the S aisle and chancel). The E window is a replica of 1896: the original is now in the rectory garden – a familiar resting place for the surplus from heavy restorations. Inside, there is more left. It was originally one of the small two-chambered C11 churches so typical of West Sussex. The low unmoulded chancel arch remains, and so do one window in the spandrel of the S arcade and traces of two more in the chancel. Crude C14 S arcade: double-chamfered arches on octagonal pier and abacus. –

FONT. Plain, C12, but the bowl curved, not cylindrical. – WALL PAINTING. In the splay of the C11 window, S arcade; Angel appearing to the Shepherds, probably C13. – MONUMENT. Ogee-headed C14 recess in the chancel, carved in clunch with some of the boldness and vitality of the larger one at Bepton (*see* p. 101).

MANOR HOUSE, immediately W of the church. Medieval fragments – jambs and parts of lintels – in a house externally now all C18 and C19.

COLDHARBOUR *see* WISBOROUGH GREEN

COLDWALTHAM

0010

Straggling main-road village near the Downs S W of Pulborough. Some good bulky thatched cottages, flint and half-timber, but no group; the same thing at WATERSFIELD, ½ m. beyond, on the way to Arundel.

ST GILES. As good as rebuilt in 1871, except for the belfry, in a decent village-church style. The S arcade was kept; rough late C13 work with arches dying away into the imposts. The belfry is bulky Norman, plain and almost unbuttressed, with a tower arch of *c.*1200. It has a handsome top with a short half-timbered stage under a pyramidal cap that seems to have come straight from the Welsh border. Is it original? – STAINED GLASS. Early *Kempe* windows of 1877–8 in S and N aisles. – PLATE. Chalice, 1549.

COMPTON

7010

In the middle of the Downs near the Hampshire border, S of Harting: bigger than most downland villages, and showing very well the West Sussex ability to create a memorable place with only hints and fragments of a formal group. Compton is built round the meeting place of three roads, with a tiny square, a big tree, the village store, and the pub. One road winds uphill to the church: the other two form a right-angle bend in the road from Emsworth to Harting. Cottages flint and brick, tiled: none remarkable individually, all delightful collectively.

ST MARY. Flint; mostly built in 1849, but done in a decent, humble village style which does not outface its surroundings. Pretty timber bell-turret with a shingled spire. More left inside than outside. The best part is the blocked N arcade: round-headed, with the remains of one good waterleaf capital,

7—S.

late C12. The chancel arch very soon after, pointed and single-chamfered, with plain imposts; C13 arcade, lengthened and partly renewed, of the usual type (double-chamfered arches, round and octagonal piers and abaci). – TAPESTRY. Foliage, animals, and birds: fresh, not whimsy, done from a design supplied by Debenham & Freebody in 1918. s aisle. – PLATE. Chalice; Paten, given 1716; Paten; Paten, given 1769. – MONUMENT. Tablet to Sarah Phipps † 1793: urn, etc. Bigger than usual but very dull.

NEOLITHIC LONG BARROW, on TELEGRAPH HILL. A magnificent long barrow, 210 ft long and some 60 ft wide at its broad end; the side ditches are clearly visible.

COOLHURST
1020

1½ m. SE of Horsham

By *P. F. Robinson*, 1833–5. Neo-Elizabethan, the half-way stage between the Regency and Victorian seriousness. Here the detail has gone serious but the massing, and particularly the placing in the landscape, is still Picturesque. Moderate size, cemented, pathetically little feeling. Cross-shaped lodge to the W, a little more fun.

COOMBES
1000

Farms, Dutch barns, and tiny church folded into the side of the Adur valley between Steyning and Shoreham, directly opposite the cement works (p. 287).

CHURCH. Lovable and unrestored. Unbroken roof-line outside, ending in a tile-hung bell-turret and let so far into the hillside that the sill of the W window is only a few inches off the ground. Simple two-cell building inside, with a low, plain chancel arch. This and the nave Early Norman (one window on the N side, several more blocked). Chancel of *c.*1200 (see the priest's doorway), with two bigger Perp windows on the s side, in Winchester style (*see* p. 29). E window humble C16, W window humble 1724 – so the church is real century-by-century accretion of piety. The C19 mercifully left it alone. – WALL PAINTINGS. Discovered in 1949, and then properly treated and preserved by *E. Clive Rouse*. No touched up Tristram faces here. Originally a complete set, rather like Hardham and of the same school. The date can hardly be later than *c.*1100, and that alone is memorable. What can be made out is the Visitation over the s door, a Nativity series on the N wall, and Christ in Majesty

over the chancel arch, with, lower down to the l., Christ delivering the keys to St Peter and the book to St Paul. On the soffit
of the chancel arch, a crouching man with a strained face,
mouth wide open, carrying the arch. He is of the type of
Italian caryatid sculpture from the C11 onwards. It is a brilliantly vivid and dramatic figure, and so are the fragments of
other figures that can be made out. What a pity more of it is
not left.* – PLATE. Cup and Paten, 1588.

COPSALE see NUTHURST

COWDRAY HOUSE

½ m. NE of Midhurst

8020

Cowdray took sixty years to build, under three owners, but its
ruins are an absolutely consistent epitome of Tudor architecture at its plainest and most sober, very English in its under-
statement, its dignity and concern for volumes and solidity.
The chain runs, parallel with more ornamented buildings,
from Cowdray to Loseley, Lacock, and Hardwick, to Inigo
Jones and May and Wren and then to the Palladians, independent of style: it is a perennial English trait.

Cowdray was begun by Sir David Owen, Owen Glendower's
son, who inherited it in 1492. He built the E range, including
hall and chapel and kitchen tower, which survive, and perhaps
the N and W ranges as far as the gatehouse, which have disappeared. He died in 1535 and lived at Cowdray to his death,
although the estate had been bought by Sir William Fitzwilliam in 1529 and although he had been granted a licence to
crenellate in 1533. In 1535 Fitzwilliam seems to have moved
in. He was much liked by Henry VIII and was made Earl of
Southampton in 1537 and Lord Keeper of the Privy Seal in
1539. He added the gatehouse and the hexagonal tower in the
NW corner and built the hall porch. He died in 1542, and his
half-brother, Sir Anthony Browne, took over. He also was a
favourite of Henry VIII. He had been granted Battle Abbey in
1538 and converted it into his house. He also held Easebourne
Priory, Bayham Abbey, Waverley Abbey in Surrey and St
Mary Overy Nunnery in London – a dissolution profiteer
indeed. As for court appointments, he was made Master of the
Horse in 1539. He died in 1548. He must have added the huge
bay window N of the hall and the room S of the gatehouse,

* The W wall of the chancel also has a band of key-ornament.

unless he only remodelled these. The C17 and C18 decorated
the inside but left the outside alone, and the fire of 1793, which
left the buildings roofless, ensured freedom from C19 interference. The fire occurred eight days before the last of the family
was killed in a very Byronic way whilst trying to shoot the
Rhine Falls. All this fulfilled a curse.

36b   What the visitor coming from Midhurst sees first is the
gatehouse, but the core of the house is the hall range behind it
on the other side of a courtyard 125 by 100 ft. The HALL has
three Perp windows, high up, each of three lights with cusped
heads and a transom, a huge plain square-sided projecting bay
on the l. of c.1545 and the porch on the r. of c.1535. The bay is
entirely divided into mullion and transom panels, sixty altogether, that is five transoms and nine mullions, and matches
the earlier work perfectly, a true case of a later addition really
being the completion needed by the original work. The only
difference, and a difference telling of the way Perp developed
into Elizabethan, is that Owen's work has all its arches cusped,
Browne's uncusped. The bluntness of this is the sign of another
age.* The two buttresses to the hall were given splendid poly-
hedron finials, another comment of 1545 on 1500. The PORCH
has a four-centred doorway, with Henry VIII's arms above it
in a small-scale Renaissance frame, one of the few mean
touches in the whole building, although the pilasters in purely
Florentine or François-Premier style are very pretty close to.
Inside, the porch has a fan-vault decorated in a very low relief
with an astonishing mixture of Gothic and Renaissance detail
typical of c.1535–40 – and which is light enough and facile
enough to look late C18. We are lucky that this taste did not
spread to the outside of the building. All the main lines of the
vault are Gothic, but the ribs carry a variety of Renaissance
floral scrolls. In between them are badges referring to the birth
of Edward VI and Lord Southampton's appointment as Lord
High Admiral – both events which occurred in 1537.

The porch led as usual to the screens passage, and the three
doors are still present on the right-hand side giving access to
the buttery and pantry l. and r. and the kitchen in the middle.
The HALL is bare and roofless now: it had a grand steep-
pitched hammerbeam roof, rather like Hampton Court. Behind the hall to the E lies the CHAPEL, an extremely unusual
arrangement at a time when ranges two rooms deep hardly
existed. The chapel has a three-sided apse with large windows,

        * But the panelled jambs and soffet inside are cusped.

still Perp with cusped lights, i.e. Owen's rather than later work.
It also is roofless, with pathetic calcined fragments of early
C18 stucco and statues still adhering to the wall. The ornament
is unmistakably *Régence* and very French in style. The altarpiece was by *Amigoni*, who was in England in 1729-36. Next
to the chapel to the N was the GRAND STAIRCASE, replacing
whatever the C16 had been satisfied with, with windows which
may be of 1690 or of 1720. The staircase was painted by
Pellegrini, who was in England from 1708 to 1713 and again in
1719. S of the hall a passage between buttery and pantry ran
into a small irregular kitchen yard, and S of this is the KIT-
CHEN, a large hexagonal room forming the SE corner of the
house. It has large fireplaces inside and chimneys ending in
turrets – a romantic accent in this important corner.

   N from the hall there are two Elizabethan canted bays with
big bald mullion-and-transom windows, and then the hexagonal NE TOWER, too far decayed for the design to be followed
except for a splendid set of chimneystacks. Although hexagonal
too, it is visually not a companion piece to the kitchen. It is
rib-vaulted below and had a room above with, to the NW, one
large window still recognizable by its panelled soffit, similar to
that of the great hall bay. Of the N range there are only low
walls (brick, incidentally: most of the house was faced with
stone on a brick core), but they show two deep canted bays,
facing N and S, and the southern one towards the courtyard
placed pretty exactly centrally. The Long Gallery was in this
range, and these two bays must have been a splendid climax.
The S bay incidentally had to its side two attachments, one of
them a spiral staircase, and the three together gave a double-
canted group such as the age of Henry VIII liked. In the W
range the GATEHOUSE was obviously intended to be the centre
of a symmetrical composition like that at Titchfield in Hampshire, built at almost the same time in exactly the same spirit.
The r. half is complete, the l. half was probably never entirely
finished. The gatehouse is relatively tall and narrow, not
spread-out like Titchfield, and indeed makes better sense as a
foil to broad plain wings than as an independent design. Three
storeys between polygonal battlemented turrets;* four-centred doorway on the ground floor, with the Montague arms
above. Sir Anthony Browne had been made Viscount Montague in 1554 and entertained Queen Elizabeth I at Cowdray

* The gunports make it fairly clear that this gatehouse was still intended
 serve a military purpose when needed.

in 1591. That may date the Elizabethan remodellings. The Montagues then stayed in possession to the fateful year 1793. The first floor has a classical window of c.1700, one of the few later alterations. To the r. is a two-storey link, with simple two-light windows widely spaced, then the sw corner tower, three storeys with a polygonal bay running the full height and the windows about as large as they could be. They are mullioned and transomed on the ground floor but have Sir Anthony Browne's uncusped arched lights on the upper floor.*

The condition and surroundings of Cowdray are delightful, like everything administered by the Cowdray Estate: rough grass, no mown lawns or notices and little huts, an object lesson to the Ministry of Works. s of the main block are cottages forming a courtyard with a nice half-timbered GRANARY on staddlestones; N of it is a small octagonal late C16 CONDUIT HOUSE. The park was landscaped by *Capability Brown*.

COWDRAY HOUSE. The present building is 1 m. E of the ruins, a jolly Victorian affair of turrets, gables, tile-hanging, and a short stone tower, all refreshingly unpompous.

COWFOLD

2020

Half-way between Horsham and the Downs. The centre of Cowfold is really memorable. The cottages all turn inwards towards the churchyard, with road access only at the back, and the result is incredibly picturesque. Soft, gentle, the buildings and planting almost indivisible, yet never false. A real picture-book group, and worth all the praise it gets. Humble houses, brick, tile, and weatherboard (and also one bit of Victorian stucco which makes a good foil). A lot of the effect is given by the long weatherboarded workshop at the W end with its strips of windows, and this must be kept. In the event, it is just as well that the houses face s for across the road to the N is a new (1959) estate of detached houses. Cosy designs, with a lot of trees kept, but ruined at the moment by one simple thing – a brash wire fence along the road edge. Perhaps creeper will cover it, in time: but why on earth was a hedge not grown from the start, in such pretty surroundings?

ST PETER. An anthology of sturdy Wealden details. The solidity and lack of fuss is a great relief after other parts of the country E.E. lancets on the N side of the chancel, also, blocked, on the s side of the chancel, with three double-splayed lancets, a loca

* Mostly of the restoration by *Sir William St John Hope*, but not all.

mannerism; Perp elsewhere, as adaptable and effective as anywhere in England. The thick, dependable W tower is particularly happy. Taller stair-turret in the NW corner, like the
Thames Valley, but everything much firmer. Immensely
solid corbels supporting the tower arch, inside. Horsham slate
roofs all through. Inside, four-bay S arcade and arch between
chancel and S chapel both Late Perp – see the four-centred
arches; money was left for it in 1530. The windows here have
three lights straight-headed outside but a segmental head to the
splay. Chancel arch C19; on its r. a very crude bit of Perp
canopy-work. Originally a statue of the Virgin stood here. –
FONT. Unremarkable Perp, but can be dated exactly, at 1481. It
cost seven and fivepence. – STAINED GLASS. Tiny Crucifixion,
C14 or C15, in one of the chancel lancets. – By *Kempe*, 1894, a
S aisle window. – MONUMENTS. Brass to Thomas Nelond,
twenty-sixth prior of St Pancras at Lewes, † 1433, nave floor. A
mighty effigy, but alas kept locked. The prior himself big
in scale (5 ft 10 in. long) but unremarkable; the canopy is
enchanting, with the Virgin and Child in a gable above, the
gable flanked by St Pancras and St Thomas. Beautifully preserved. – Several stately C18 tablets and cartouches.

Obviously plenty of pretty cottages in Cowfold, but nothing
special. The best building in the centre is in fact the group of
the VILLAGE HALL and LIBRARY, by *Wheeler & Godman* of
Horsham, 1896. Happily and freely grouped, with a big gable
for the hall and curly roof-line for the library. Would that modern architecture had some of the same gaiety; in fact, would
that it had any sense of humour at all.

Several worthwhile buildings W of the village. First is CAPON'S
FARM, on the S side of A272. This is historically one of the
best medieval cottages in Sussex, and has been thoroughly
dissected recently.* It is a very pretty building as well. All
timber-framed: the oldest part was a two-bay hall, the NE part
of the present house. This may be as early as *c*.1300. The overhanging wing to the W is C15 and was the solar. The SE wing,
now refronted in brick, is another timber-framed addition
(late C16?) which may have been brought from somewhere
else. A pair of weatherboarded BARNS on the roadside which
Mr Mason says correspond to the C14 and C15 building periods in the house. The E barn is the older.

Beyond, also on the main road, is THE CLOCK HOUSE, by
Barry Parker, Unwin's partner, built in 1913–14. Absolutely

* Mason, *S.A.C.*, XCV, 1957.

Cowfold, brass to Prior Thomas Nelond † 1433

complete example of the last few years before the Great War, the edge of the abyss. Big half-timbered house, nearly symmetrical, softly and carefully done; farm buildings, lodges, cottages (one of them built as a chauffeur's cottage, a sign of the times), and the fanciful Clock House itself – was this the water tower? As sensitive and quietly individual as the Hampstead Garden Suburb buildings.

½ m. to the N is IVORYS, in a completely different style but just as sensitive. By *Walter Brierley* of York (also a builder of Garden Suburbs, by a coincidence), 1921. Neo-Georgian of the Lutyens sort, but better done: more feeling and less complacency. The main front faces s and has seven bays on the first floor, nine bays on the ground floor, which is unnerving and endearing.

CRABTREE see LOWER BEEDING

CRAWLEY

2030

Crawley was designated a New Town in 1947. It had less than 10,000 inhabitants then (with Ifield and Three Bridges). Growth was slow at first, then it accelerated. Now (1963) the population is nearing 60,000, and administratively the New Town status has been replaced by that of a normal Urban District. The area covers several parishes, including Ifield to the w and Lowfield Heath to the N, in Surrey. The London–Brighton road (A23) ran right along the High Street; now a by-pass has taken it. Before reaching Crawley, it passes the Gatwick airport. So that is the up-to-date boundary of the New Town. In all other directions building tapers off into the countryside.

It was a good idea to make the existing High Street the spine of the new development, place the town centre immediately to its side and make it essentially pedestrian. Yet, for the visual well-being of the High Street, things have not worked out so well – as we shall see presently.

The New Town consists of the centre and the following neighbourhoods more or less clockwise from the N: Northgate, Lowfield Heath, Three Bridges, Pound Hill, Southgate, Tilgate, West Green, Gossops Green, Ifield, Langley Green. They will be discussed in that order, each complete with churches and public buildings.

The master-plan was made by *Anthony Minoprio*. Chief Architect was first *A. G. Sheppard Fidler* and is now *H. S. Howgrave-Graham*.

THE CENTRE

St John Baptist. A large church lying back to the E from the High Street, as it ought to be, but now – owing to New Town calamities – having the main East Grinstead road immediately to its S and one of the car parks serving the shopping centre to its E. Only the nave S wall is medieval. The rest is all of 1807 (W tower) and 1879–80 (N aisle and general restoration by *Woodyer*). Against the W side of the big tower three primitive carvings of frontal figures, late medieval probably and evidently not *in situ*. Inside, the most attractive piece is the nave roof – C15, with tie-beams and wind-braces. Otherwise it all looks dully Victorian. – PULPIT. Formerly dated 1627. Panels with flat ornamental carving. – COMMUNION RAIL. Late C17; with twisted balusters. – STAINED GLASS. N aisle N and chancel E by *John Davies* of Shrewsbury (TK). – PLATE. Chalice, 1579; Paten, 1722. – BRASS. Effigy of a Lady, c.1500, 18 in. long.

St Francis and St Anthony (R.C.), Three Bridges Road. By *Goodhart-Rendel*, 1958–9. Large, of brick, a composition of oddly assembled parts. Low, with a shallow tunnel-vault which runs over aisle-passages and nave. Raised crossing.

Town Hall, The Boulevard. 1961. Town Hall, Police Station, and Court House and College of Further Education are meant to form a Civic Centre, but they are too loosely grouped to come off as such. The Town Hall is by *Sir John Brown & Henson*.

Police Station and Court House, Exchange Road. 1960–3. By the county architect's department (*F. R. Steele*, county architect). A satisfying group of blocks of equal height, the Court House treated a little more formally and having for the Court Room a circular attachment.

College of Further Education, College Road. 1956–8. Also by *F. R. Steele*'s department. A curtain-walled slab with a somewhat mannered porch.

Perambulation. However well conceived the idea of an old High Street in juxtaposition with the new shopping centre was, in the end the HIGH STREET was badly mauled by it, i.e. by traffic and parking mainly. One can only just recognize how nice the street must once have been with the one row of trees closer to the houses of the E than the W side. The best houses are on the E side. Starting from the church and working N there is first the ANCIENT PRIOR'S CAFÉ (why prior?), timber-framed, of the C15, a hall-house originally, with the wings slightly projecting and with oversailing gables. Then, opposite, the GEORGE HOTEL, originally three parts, the oldest being the northern part. Much is of course renovation. The gallows sign replaces one shown in Rowlandson's print of 1789. Again on the E side the BREWERY SHADES, at the corner where steps lead into the new shopping precinct. We shall be ready for it presently. The nucleus of the Brewery Shades is a hall-house of the C15. In the main N–S range a mighty cambered tie-beam and a kingpost. Then, on to the N, the PUNCH BOWL, a low, timber-framed early C15 house, of the hall-house type. Inside, a cambered tie-beam and king-post. Across the Boulevard finally THE TREE, the former Manor House, now externally nearly all C18 and later, but comprising a hall-house of c.1500. Stone chimneybreast to the s. The hall-range runs N and is higher than the better-preserved solar range running E. The latter has original roof trusses with cambered tie-beams and kingposts.

One can enter the TOWN CENTRE from here by car. The street is called THE BOULEVARD. On the l. is CROWN BUILDING, containing government offices, five storeys high, and then the POST OFFICE. Both are by the *Ministry of Works*. Opposite it is shopping terraces all along. To the E the Civic Centre (*see* above) follows. To the s of The Boulevard most of the streets are for pedestrians only, and one must have been there on a Saturday afternoon when it is swarming with people to see the point of it all. The architecture of THE BROADWAY, QUEEN'S SQUARE, QUEENSWAY, and THE MARTLETS is not of the kind to be recorded individually. The streets run in a rectangular grid. The buildings are modern, run-of-the-mill, mostly curtain-walled and only rarely four, mostly three, storeys high. They are, however, not standardized or com-posed uniformly, which helps. Is it to be forgiven if one singles out only one item, and that Victorian, the BAND-STAND in Queen's Square which comes from the Gatwick Racecourse?

Outside this centre proper in STATION WAY, a new office building of the WESTMINSTER BANK, four-storeyed, of brick with long window bands. 1961 by *T. P. Bennett & Son*.

THE NEIGHBOURHOODS*

The new housing is mostly in long terraces of cottages, almost

* They are as follows: West Green 1950–2, Northgate 1951–3, Three Bridges 1952–4, Langley Green 1953–4, Pound Hill 1954–5, Ifield 1955–6, Southgate 1956–7, Tilgate 1956–8, Gossops Green 1960–1, Furnace Green, begun 1962.

exclusively two storeys high. They are, where possible, not straight but curved, and occasionally staggered. Brick of divers colours is used, brown, reddish, yellow, and also whitewash. Variety of details is sought, but cannot lead very far. Old trees are carefully preserved, sometimes whole rows of them. Yet uniformity cannot be avoided, even if it is a friendly, cosy, reassuring uniformity with nothing regimented about it. The neighbourhood centres suffer from the same New Town shortcoming. What is needed is every time almost identical: a row of shops, a pub, a church or chapel. Efforts are made to group and detail them differently: e.g. the shops at Langley Green are L-shaped and exceptionally sensitive, at Southgate they have an arcade, and so on. The pubs differ in architectural quality. One may single out the WHITE KNIGHT (Pound Hill) by *Musman & Couzens*, 1957–8. Then the churches and chapels. There are many of them, but they are without exception so far either entirely uneventful or more often mannered and contorted, with odd spikes and curvy roofs.

Finally there are the SCHOOLS. There are plenty of them, necessitated by the exceptionally high number of school children in so young a community as a New Town is. Here again it is not necessary to mention more than a few, say the group of three w of Tilgate of which the THOMAS BENNETT SCHOOL is specially good (1959–61 by the county architect *F. R. Steele*). Other buildings and points will be taken individually.

NORTHGATE. To the N of this is the INDUSTRIAL ESTATE. Again no single factory calls for comment, except perhaps the tallest building, that of BUILDING AND ENGINEERING HOLIDAY MANAGEMENT, 1959 etc. by *Eric Firmin & Partners*, because it provides at ground level and on the top uncommonly many gimmicks. Much better SILENTBLOC by *J. M. Austin-Smith & Partners*, 1954–5, Newton Road.

LOWFIELD HEATH

Administratively in Surrey,* but the parish belonging to Crawley. Lowfield Heath immediately adjoins Gatwick Airport.

ST MICHAEL. By *Burges*, 1867. Of small regular yellow sandstone, in the C13 style with a SW tower carrying a pyramid spire. Round the w rose window outside figure sculpture, as also on the corbels of the w gallery inside. The chancel E windows are a group of two short lancets with a rose over, and

* And described also in *The Buildings of England: Surrey*

it is typical of Burges how he thickens the shafts inside to short, stumpy columns and the roll mouldings out of all the expectable. Just such stumpy columns in pairs carry the chancel arch. They are placed high up on corbels. – WEST DOOR. With spiky ornamental ironwork.

THREE BRIDGES

ST RICHARD OF CHICHESTER. By *N. F. Cachemaille-Day & Partners*. Consecrated 1954. Brick. Nave and square, raised sanctuary with round lantern. The altar stands in the middle of the sanctuary. Segmental portico to the sanctuary. Behind it, at r. angles to the sanctuary and capable of opening on to it, the church hall.

SOUTHGATE

ST MARY. By *Braddock & Martin-Smith*. Consecrated 1958. Church and hall are designed so that the latter can be used as an extension. Both buildings are included under one sweeping roof, and the walls step outward to a kind of transept. Flèche above the sanctuary, which is in a central position. The E wall consists of decorated concrete slabs pierced with small pieces of blue glass. The roof inside is one shallow tunnel-vault placed transversely from W to E.

TILGATE

For the SCHOOLS, *see* above. Opposite their playing fields, across the A23, is BROADFIELD, a white early C19 house with bows, and nicely modernized. Veranda on columns to the lake.

WEST GREEN

West Green had some Victorian and later pre-New Town development in its s parts, and N of the church there are even a few villagey cottages left.

ST PETER. 1892–3 by *W. Hilton Nash*. With lancet and bellcote. Spacious inside.

HOSPITAL, West Green Drive. By *Yorke, Rosenberg & Mardall* (with *R. Mellor*), 1960–2. Easily the best building in Crawley up to date. A black-steel, white-tile and glass slab of three and four storeys, severe and clean. The windowless walls of sang-de-bœuf glazed bricks. The frame is reinforced concrete. This is only the first stage of a much bigger development.

GOSSOPS GREEN

At the SE corner just by the roundabout on the by-pass is an old farmhouse: LITTLE BUCKSWOOD FARM, picturesque, timber-framed, with a conspicuous chimneystack.

ST ALBAN. By *T. F. Ford*, 1961–2. Not a match architecturally of the excellent shopping arcade next door.

IFIELD

Ifield Street, at the N end of Rusper Road, the approach to the church, is a small tile-hung cul-de-sac, pretty, though without much character, like the villages over the Surrey border. The PLOUGH INN only is specially nice.

ST MARGARET. Entirely roughcast, which in this case increases the homogeneity and heavy Wealden effect. Wide nave, narrow aisles, narrow clerestory, short chancel, W tower with shingled broach spire. So everything hunched and bunched and consistent. The W tower had better be dealt with before it perplexes too far. It was built in 1883, which accounts for the odd and very effective details – triple W lancets and a double tower arch, inside. The character of the rest is all simple early C14, dominated by the wide nave with its vast kingpost roof. But the chancel masonry is C13 (lancets), and there are lancets at the W ends of both aisles. Surely the C13 nave cannot have been as wide as this? If not, what happened? Were they reset? N arcade very typical early C14 – octagonal piers, double-chamfered arches, with squinches above the abaci, arch mouldings dying away into the responds at either end without capitals. The S arcade is simpler and probably slightly later: octagonal piers and abaci, double-chamfered arches. The chancel arch has typical but different and more complex C14 mouldings too. Clerestory windows mostly single trefoiled-cusped lights, other windows C14 (cusped square-headed, two- and three-light) and also Perp. – FONT. Late C12, Sussex marble. Plain square bowl, but first-rate composition of stem and four shafts with something like waterleaf capitals holding the bowl. – WOODWORK. Lectern built up of wild C17 ornamental bits – a barbaric *ensemble*, full of fire and life, especially the caryatids on the stem. – Various small ornamental pieces in the tower, brought from St Margaret, Westminster. Late C17. Crown, lions, and cartouche. – PLATE. Elizabethan Chalice; Paten, 1572. – MONUMENTS. Two C14 effigies, obviously by the same

designer, supposed to be Sir John de Ifelde *c.*1340 and Lady 26a
Margaret de Ifelde who died in 1347. Life-size recumbent 26b
figures, feet on lions, heads supported by angels, but far above
the usual standard, even in their present weathered state.
Delicate and precise modelling, both figures given an inimi-
table sideways sway. They are worth a special visit. The
knight is very similar to John of Eltham † 1337 in Westminster
Abbey. – Rev. S. J. Lewin † 1842. Polychrome tablet in pure
C18 style, except that the details are thicker. – Nicholas
Spencer † 1783. The same applies here. Both monuments are
signed *T. Marsh* sculp., *L. B. Lamb* inv. Surely that must be
E. B. Lamb, one of the oddest of Victorian architects. If so,
we have here another unexpected turn of his mind.

CHURCH COTTAGE, the first school of Ifield. 1843, Gothic.

FRIENDS' MEETING HOUSE, Langley Lane. A lovable ashlar-
built cottage dated 1676 with two half-hipped gables and
mildly classical quoins to the angles and the doorcase. Very
simple interior, truly religious, as the old meeting houses
always are.

New-Town Ifield has a lot of detached and semi-detached
houses instead of terraces, not a visual asset, especially in the
case of the steep-pitched roof of whole groups of cottages.
They lie close to the IFIELD MILL at the s end of Rusper
Road. Tall three-storeyed weatherboarded building near the
mill-pond. (The water-wheel is preserved. MHLG)

N of Ifield Drive, really at LANGLEY GREEN, EWHURST
PLACE, quite a big moated house of *c.*1600. A long timber-
framed range runs E–W. Picturesque, but heavily restored.

DAWES FARM *see* FERNHURST

DEAN HOUSE *see* TILLINGTON

DEDISHAM *see* SLINFOLD

DELL QUAY *see* APPLEDRAM

DENNE PARK
1 m. s of Horsham

1020

What remains of the C17 Denne Park is a four-storey stone
tower, dated 1605, in the NE corner, and the E front, never
designed as a composition, with three gables and a random
arrangement of windows. All the rest is now an accurate match-
up of 1870, including the main W front, replacing an C18

building. The old work is almost indistinguishable from the Cotswold style and is well done, e.g. the elegant mouldings of the window reveals. Mullion-and-transom windows, tower with gables and pyramid finials – a gentle, civilized style not at all concerned with display. (Inside the tower, a simple Jacobean staircase.)

DIDLING

8010

Under the Downs SW of Midhurst, with flint and brick farms and barns, quite unspoilt, in their familiar position on the first knoll N of the hills.

ST ANDREW. By itself ¼ m. to the S on the actual slope of the Downs themselves, a grand situation counterpointed very movingly by the humble sincerity of the building. Simple C13 un-aisled nave and chancel in one room, as many Sussex churches are, but quite unrestored: alterations have been additions-in-harmony, not sweepings-away. Most windows lancets (the E wall has two like e.g. Tangmere instead of the usual three, re-used when the wall itself was rebuilt in brick, probably c.1800); two lancets on the S side have pointed-trefoiled heads and must be c.1300. The inside furnishings a model of simple piety, medieval pews and Victorian oil lamps coexisting in perfect amity. – BENCHES. Village woodwork which could be C13 or C15, more effective than many more elaborate productions. Very heavy ends, quite plain, with two knobs. – COMMUNION RAIL. Jacobean, and as simple as the pews. Turned balusters below a kind of frieze made up of a repeated pattern of semicircles. – FONT. Crude tub font, probably C12, but not smoothed down as so many Sussex examples have been.

BARROW, on Didling Hill. The barrow, which is 18 ft in diameter and 2 ft high, has an unusual feature: it stands within a square ditch with a single entrance on the middle of the E side.

DONNINGTON

8000

A straggle of cottages on the road from Chichester to Selsey, not yet spoilt by housing from either place. Due S of Chichester; hence the full length of the cathedral is seen backed by Downs, a magnificent sight.

HOLY TRINITY. The bones all early C13, without any earlier evidence. Four-bay nave and aisles, chancel and C19 chapel. Restored by *Frederick Etchells* after a bad fire in 1939, hence a

swept-clean impression. The best part as usual is the E end:
triple lancets with continuous mouldings in the rere-arches
and a triple hood-mould as well. Trefoil-headed PISCINA, and
three plain lancets in N and S walls. The re-tooled arcades have
alternate circular and octagonal piers and, oddly enough,
rather mean, misshapen proportions. In the C16 a plain tower
was built rather crudely in the SW corner of the nave, apparently because the churchyard wall was too close to the W end to
permit any extension. – FONT. Decent, by *Etchells*. – PLATE.
Large Paten of *c.*1500 with depressed sexfoil centre enclosing
a Vernicle. – MONUMENTS. John Page † 1779. Grandly classical sarcophagus, well carved. Detached Ionic columns at the
corners, oak and palm branches crossed in the frieze, an urn
on top. No figure carving and unsigned; an elegant if rather
cold talent. – Two unnamed Crosbie busts of *c.*1840, quite
delightful. Contemporary dress, including bushy side whis-
kers, and all the humanity and interest that is lacking in the
official monuments of the time. Whom by?

One COTTAGE in the main street with an elegant segmental bay
of *c.*1830. It looks like the same subtle hand as No. 44 South
Street, Chichester. Galleted flint.

CHURCH FARM, S of the church. A five-bay brick front of 1677,
with semicircular pediment over the entrance. Two storeys
plus hipped dormers, the window surrounds carried between
the floors in strips of brickwork. Yet still a ferociously notched
string-course between the storeys. It marks nicely the transition
between village-Artisan-Mannerism and village-Baroque.

DRAGONS see WOODMANCOTE

DUNCTON

Near the Downs on the main road S of Petworth, and sandwiched
between two parks (Burton and East Lavington), so that it has
not got much character of its own. With such a splendid south-
ward view, perhaps it does not need any.

HOLY TRINITY. Built in 1866; Dec style. Aisleless, with an
attached S tower. The outside has attractively spiky trimmings
such as the roof-ridge and the tiled cap to the tower: the inside is completely blank. – PLATE. Cup, 1568.

ST ANTONY AND ST GEORGE (R.C.). By *G. Blount*, 1866.
Stone-built, apsed, C13 style: fussily attractive details such as
the bellcote.

DURFOLD see ROGATE

DURRINGTON see WORTHING, p. 392

see WORTHING, p. 392

8090

EARNLEY

On the w side of the Selsey peninsula, and only half a mile inland from the unlovely coastal bungalows at Bracklesham, yet still unspoilt. A few cottages sheltering among trees – needed in this exposed site – and the church well placed on a triangular island in the middle.

CHURCH. Simple unaisled nave with bell-turret and chancel, very bare inside. c13 nave, early c14 chancel with two-light E window. A good pointer to the remoteness of Selsey before the c19. – ALTAR TABLE. A bulky chest, hard to date, perhaps c.1840.* The strong and unaffected Gothic design is worth a look.

MARSH FARM, ½ m. s. Almost on the beach. Good set of barns, flint and thatch, in an L-shape with the different roof-levels making a fine composition. Conservation of their present materials would be worth a special effort, and may soon be necessary.

WINDMILL, ¾ m. N, at Somerley. Good, with octagonal tarred weatherboarded body and sweeps and turning gear complete. Bulbous ogee top with a circular finial – something a good deal more than a utilitarian convenience for grinding corn.

9000

EARTHAM

Quiet and unspoilt small village, flint and brick, in lovely country on the s slopes of the Downs NE of Chichester. The old slow rhythms of change still operate here, something which can today only be due to strenuous conservation.

ST MARGARET. A terrible restoration in 1869 has left the outside all new. But much more character inside, like a lot of Sussex village churches. Massive and interesting Norman chancel arch; two unchamfered orders, the inner resting on demi-shafts and volute capitals, carved roughly but powerfully with a face and a rabbit. The VCH calls this c12; the effect is still c11 or even pre-Conquest. The openings on either side of it are c19. Completely plain Norman w doorway, and a two-bay early c13 arcade (rough single-chamfered arches, standard piers and abaci). – ORGAN CASE. Prettily neo-Gothic. How-

* Indeed hard to date. It turns out that it was supplied in 1930.

ever, its date is not the 1820 that it looks but 1945, by *Lawrence Turner*. – PLATE. Cup and Paten, 1568; Paten, 1723. – MONU-MENT. Thomas Hayley † 1800 aged twenty, by *Flaxman*. Small, in the weak style of his Chichester monuments, with an angel (full face) holding a quill pen and a wreath. Hayley was a pupil of Flaxman's and the son of the poet, who wrote the long, florid inscription.

EARTHAM HOUSE. This belonged to Hayley (*see* also Felpham, p. 218). The present house is by *Lutyens*, 1905, simple and symmetrical, in William and Mary style, roughcast. Brilliance of either the New Delhi or the Tigbourne kind is a long way away. N of the house a small late C18 ORANGERY, a pretty composition of brick with rock-work window surrounds.

EASEBOURNE

8020

Almost entirely a Cowdray Estate village, hence very spick-and-span, with the Cowdray deep yellow paint everywhere. Mostly sandstone and half-timber, with a good sprinkling of C19 estate cottages. The best pair SYCAMORE COTTAGE in Easebourne Lane, with a close-timbered C16 gable, and C.378–380 (Cowdray Estate numbers) next door to it. From near the church HIGH STREET goes N with attractive cottages for nearly a mile, many of them the soft Sussex equivalent of the Midlands' Georgian box – hipped tiled roof, sandstone with brick dressings. Further N again Bexley Hill, with a superb view visible on two legs but not four wheels.

ST MARY. A priory church, though neglect and then catastrophic restoration makes this hard to believe now. Almost everything is 1876 at its hardest and worst, by *A. W. Blomfield*. He spared only the plain unbuttressed late C12 tower with humble details – single bell-openings, single-chamfered tower arch without imposts – and one and a half bays of the arcade. This is late C12 too, double-chamfered, but the octagonal capital and the respond are scalloped. They do not look re-used and may be anachronism or conservatism. When the priory (*see* below) took over part of the nave and the chancel of this church, a new wider N aisle was built, indeed as wide as the nave. The N wall is now also all Blomfield, but the tomb recess (*see* below) and the rere-arch of one lancet establish the later C13 date. The S wall is actually C11, with herringbone masonry, though hideously vamped up. There is also a blocked Norman doorway. – FONT. Square bowl of Purbeck marble with unornamented blind arcading. Late C12. – MONUMENTS (the Cowdray monuments, all brought from Midhurst). Sir David Owen † 1535. In a C13 recess, N side of nave. Alabaster, ordered forty years before his death, and well above the average of late medieval alabaster shopwork: instead of contorting the material into a poor imitation of marble, the translucence and mobility is mirrored to some extent in the flowing lines, especially around the head. – First Viscount Montague † 1592, of Cowdray House between Midhurst and Easebourne, and family. By *Richard Stevens* of Southwark. Disarranged in the move from Midhurst church, and the reconstruction has made nonsense of the design. As it stands it is just a standard late C16 production, but originally it must have been more. Kneeling figure of Lord Montague above, two wives, recumbent, below, children lower still, to l. and r. Originally Lord Montague knelt above and between his wives, with the corners of the monument punctuated by obelisks, quite a different thing.* – William Poyntz † 1840, by the Italian *Raffaele Monti*, made in 1848 (Monti fled to England after serving in the Risorgimento) and Elizabeth Poyntz † 1830 by *Chantrey*, made in 1838. Two seated figures, facing each other, in similar niches and identical surrounds. Monti's figure is mildly theatrical, Chantrey's is chaste: neither shows very much feeling.

EASEBOURNE PRIORY of Augustinian Canonesses, founded before 1238, is now a house attached to the s side of the church. It represents part of two sides of the conventual buildings around the cloister, made up into a very English medley of medieval, C17, and C18 detail. The establishment, very strangely, never built its own church, and the canonesses were ready to put up with half the nave and the chancel of the parish church, building solid walls to the w part of the nave and the new N aisle. The main front of the present house faces E, but the building is best understood by going into the former cloister, accessible from a door in the s side of the church. The best feature is visible straightaway: three bays of arcading representing the entrance to the chapter house, admirably detailed in the impersonal E.E. style of South East England – the style of Salisbury or Chichester choir. Arches of complicated section built up of successive roll-mouldings and deep hollows, resting on very short piers and responds made up on a circular core hollowed out in the four main directions to set in four

---

* Especially as the same mason made a fine job of exactly this design for one of the Wriothesley monuments at Titchfield in Hampshire.

detached Purbeck shafts. It is beautifully done, architectural decoration at its most abstract. By the details of the arch mouldings it may be as late as c.1270, a time when most parts of the country were turning to lusher, more sinuous forms.

This E range as well as the chapter house contained the warming house on the ground floor to the S and the dormitory over the whole length on the first floor. Several altered C14 or C15 windows remain, and the original tie-beam roof. The S range is much plainer and seems to have been cellarage underneath with the refectory above, originally reached from the cloister by a doorway, now blocked. The W window of this has intersecting tracery of three lights, c.1300; the S side – i.e. away from the cloister – has three two-light windows with Y-tracery set in chamfered surrounds, an impressive effect out of all proportion to the simple means used. C17 queen-post roof inside.

Finally, the present entrance front, the E side of the E range. This is a picturesque ramble; three-gabled centre brought forward, corresponding to the E end of the chapter house: in the range on the r. an early C17 door, in the range on the l. a two-light square-headed C15 window.

EAST ASHLING see ASHLING

EAST DEAN
Near Chichester

9010

N of Goodwood, in the sequestered, handsome valley of the Lavant, which here runs E–W under the scarp of the South Downs. The village with its quiet cottages fits exactly into the shape of the valley floor, which can hardly be said of the pylon line near by. Flint with a little half-timber, in one long straggly street. At the corner of the lane to the church, a COTTAGE with blocked mullioned windows immediately under the (later) half-hipped gables.

ALL SAINTS. Long and grey like an oversize cottage. The restoration of 1870 renewed and hardened the details but kept the proportions. Cruciform, with a central tower, basically C12, with twin bell-openings on two sides – the plain chamfered crossing arches have been altered. Completed probably in the C13. Two blocked C13 arches on the N side of the nave show that there was an aisle originally. Most windows new, but in the E sides of the transepts are a pair of c.1300 (N) and c.1340 (S) which make an interesting comparison. Easily the best part is the s doorway, a grand, simple design of c.1200 with two orders of roll-mouldings and pairs of jamb shafts to go with them. Simple, direct capitals on the way to becoming crockets. – FONT. Octagonal and completely plain. But the base looks just like a large upturned capital with multiple trumpet scallops. And that, surely, is what it was – not re-used from the church, but brought in by the C12 as their equivalent of Government surplus. – PLATE. Chalice and Paten, 1810.

9000   EASTERGATE

Like Barnham, a long straggling main street on the Chichester-Littlehampton road, with church and manor farm on a secluded site s of it. The main street, with a big tree used as a traffic island, is more attractive than most in the area: WESTERGATE, ½ m. sw, is a more familiar loose mixture of flint cottages and modern buildings without any focus.

ST GEORGE. Nave, chancel, and frilly C19 bell-turret, but too heavily restored to be attractive. The walling probably entirely Norman – see the herringbone masonry on the s side of the chancel, and a narrow primitive window on the N side. Later windows, more or less renewed: C14 in the nave, three-light C15 at the E end, three-light C15 at the W end – built with a bequest of 1534, and already with simple arched and uncusped heads. – PLATE. Cup, 1568; Paten, 1798. – STAINED GLASS. Medieval armorial glass, s side of nave, Fitzalan quartered with de Warenne, datable c.1360.

MANOR FARM, next to the church, is one of the best farmhouses in this part of Sussex. Big, regular timber-framed house of c.1600, unrestored, half-H-shaped, with hipped roofs. At the back half-timbered granary on staddlestones of the same date, and a big later flint and brick barn. The farmyard enclosure is like a miniature village green.

EASTERS FARM see SOUTHWATER

EAST HARTING see HARTING

EAST LAVANT see LAVANT

9010   EAST LAVINGTON

Cottages straggling along the lane leading to church and house, on the foothills of the Downs s of Petworth, which are here mag-

nificently wooded. Only a few feet above the Weald, but enough
to give fine views N.

ST PETER. Simple village–E.E., but so cruelly restored by
Street that it is difficult to sort out old and new. The most
authentic part seems to be the lean-to N aisle and arcade, with
narrow lancets, the arcade double-chamfered on octagonal
piers and abaci, the inner chamfer continuing in the respond
with its own shaft and abacus, as at Ferring. The similar chancel arch looks trustworthy also. Street would have done better
to rebuild the lot, having gone so far; his own lancet work is
characterless. – FONT. Fearful mock-Norman.

LAVINGTON PARK. The entrance from the main road is impressive: curved walls of flint and stone leading to a pair of
identical lodges, each with an Ionic portico with the details
apparently just going debased. They are not, as they look, of
c.1840, but 1903 by *Detmar Blow*. After this, the house is
rather a comedown. The centre part, when it can be deciphered, is a five-bay house built in 1790–4 by *James Lewis*, whose
best known work was the second Bedlam, now the Imperial
War Museum. This must have been the *beau ideal* of one kind
of late C18 person with its deliberately cultivated understate-
ment, cool stock bricks, and cool absence of ornament. Only a
chaste intermittent balustrade is permitted. This is almost
invisible (ivy on the S side, a vast early C20 porch on the N) and
the two flanking wings, which look authentic, are in fact a
clever match by Blow. Slight projections with porticoes on the
S side, deep projections with suave curved Venetian windows
on the N side.

The STABLES to the W also by Blow; a grandiose quadrangle
with cupola and pair of neo-Baroque arches.

EAST MARDEN see THE MARDENS

EAST PRESTON

Between Worthing and Littlehampton: a few old cottages near
the church, fairly well-to-do surburbia between church and sea.
Increase in income does not, alas, mean increase in architectural
quality, though it does mean more trees.

ST MARY THE VIRGIN. A simple story, too common along the
Sussex coast, of a C19 aisle being added so heartlessly as to
make one side and the interior look hard and characterless.
The N side, outside, is much better. Nave originally late C12,

shown by the mutilated – almost unrecognizable – N door. Chancel C13, the E end with three windows set wide apart and quite circumstantially framed inside by moulded rere-arches and marble shafts with stiff-leaf capitals, the arches, as so often in Sussex, only just pointed. The windows either C13 lancets or simple two-light Perp; simple Perp W tower – which had a spire until 1951 – whose dignified sandstone tower arch with continuous mouldings is the best thing in the church. Aisle 1869, by *Sir George Gilbert Scott*.

East Preston has some flint cottages and the familiar shopping parades: at the S end, two small blocks of flats called FORBAN COURT are a model of how all the C20 building could have looked if it had been done carefully and sensitively. Two blocks at right angles, brick with a little tile-hanging – quite modern, yet not at all aggressive; by *J. D. Forbes-Nixon*, 1958. Further E on the coast is ANGMERING-ON-SEA, a warren of private estates; at the extreme E end SEA LANE HOUSE by *F. R. S. Yorke & Marcel Breuer*, 1937. Both architects have since become famous, Yorke as head of one of the best large architectural firms in Britain, Breuer largely as a house-designer in America. Both, probably, were not in sympathy with the bare, sweeping international style of the 1930s, hence this Angmering house is not as successful as a Connell, Ward & Lucas house would have been: it wears its white paint a bit shamefacedly. T-shaped, with one very long wing forming the stem of the T, open underneath, with the main living rooms above. (The shape was dictated by the building line and by the wish to give as many of the first-floor rooms as possible a view of the sea.)

EAST WITTERING

Near the W end of the Selsey peninsula: bungalows, chalets, and caravans near the beach, in an untidy half-grown-up state, and the church by itself half a mile inland – the same relative position as at Earnley, further E.

THE ASSUMPTION. Aisleless nave and chancel, thoroughly re-done in 1875. The nave walls C12, the chancel arch simple C13. The restorers spared a good Norman S doorway, bold and large-scale, with a single order of chevrons resting on jamb shafts with scalloped capitals. Each voussoir carries eight chevrons and ends in a lobe. By the shallowness of the carving it looks fairly early C12, and it has an impressive coherence and

sureness of touch; Cathedral Norman scaled down, as it were.
– PLATE. Cup and Paten, 1613.

EAST WORTHING *see* WORTHING, p. 387

EBERNOE

9020

3 m. N of Petworth

An improbable, enchanted place in the middle of the Weald with
an air of never having been touched by the twentieth century.
It has a tiny box-of-bricks chapel (HOLY TRINITY) by
Habershon & Brock, 1867, and a handsome plain late C18
house (EBERNOE HOUSE), simply five bays and three storeys
of brickwork with a pedimented doorcase.

EDBURTON

2010

Church and tiny village under one of the most sheer and spectacular bits of the whole Downs escarpment, W of Devils Dyke.
The hills might as well be five thousand feet high, instead of five
hundred. Framed magnificently and perhaps consciously in the
porch of

ST ANDREW, which is one more Sussex case of a sober and
simple C13 rebuilding. No aisles, lancets throughout; dated by
Walter Godfrey late in the century, which would make the style
distinctly conservative. But the N chapel was founded as a
chantry in 1320, and the details here (trefoiled lancet and a
two-light trefoiled window) are also fifty years later than one
would expect them to be. Happy county, to stay in its old ways
without affectation. Chancel arch and trefoiled PISCINA seem a
little more 'modern'. The tower arch is Perp, the E window is
C19 Perp. The restoration (in 1878) was a little too harsh; the
detail remained, the atmosphere evaporated. – FONT. Small,
circular, leaden. Decorated with scrolls in very low relief, and
also trefoil-headed arcades, hence probably early C13. Dainty
but not outstanding. – PULPIT. Naïve Jacobean, or rather
Laudian, like the COMMUNION RAIL.

EGDEAN

9020

¾ m. NW of Fittleworth

No village, just an isolated church with a glorious view S towards
the Downs.

ST BARTHOLOMEW. Built in 1622, obliterated in the C19 restoration. The S doorway remains, with a brick four-centred

arch and spindly hood-mould, to show that it must have been
built in the same idiom as the early C17 manor houses around
Petworth. Plain brick chancel arch inside. – COMMUNION
RAIL. Sturdy early C17, the top still trying to wear battlements. – The plain octagonal FONT looks early C17 too.

ELSTED

On a foothill of the Downs W of Harting: flint, clunch, brick
dressings, and tile, more compact than most of the villages under
the Downs. It is one of the cases where a few new houses very
carefully designed and sited could give the village a splendid
shape.

ST PAUL. A case of all's well that ends well: a series of mis-
fortunes in the last century have ended up with an attractive
little building which is not what it seems at first glance. When
the Victorian church was built at Treyford (p. 355), Elsted
church was left to moulder. A tree collapsed on the nave roof
in 1893 and only the chancel remained usable. But the Victorian church at Treyford became unsafe in its turn and was
pulled down, and Elsted was rehabilitated and given a new
nave (1951) under the auspices of the S.P.A.B. by *J. E. M.
Macgregor*. This has preserved all the old work without copying
it.

The old nave was C11, more likely Norman than Saxon,
built up entirely of herringbone walling, one of the best examples in the county: it remains in part of the W wall, the E wall,
and the whole of the N wall, impressive from outside. In the
C12 the chancel arch and two arches on the N side were let into
this: unmoulded and semicircular, with plain abaci. The chancel is simple C13, heavily restored, with two E lancets, like
Didling. The new nave has round arches, clerestory, a lean-to
aisle that is actually a vestry shut off from the church, and a
frankly C20 hexagonal W window. In its care yet freedom from
compromise it is nicely in the original spirit of 'anti-scrape'.
Of the cottages in the village the most interesting is almost the
smallest, No. 4 in the main street. Clunch walls and thatched
roof, providing the same essentials of shelter as a cabin in
the Scottish Highlands.

FELPHAM

Immediately E of Bognor. William Hayley, the poet and biographer, lived here and brought down Blake for four years. Here Blake had his set-to with an *agent-provocateur* soldier, turning him out of his garden with apocalyptic language. He wrote of Felpham:

> Away to sweet Felpham for heaven is there:
> The Ladder of Angels descends through the air
> On the turrett its spiral does softly descend
> Through the village it winds, at my cot it does end.

The centre of the village is still to some extent a matter of flint walls, flint cottages, and trees, and Blake's cot is still there, but he would have had other words for most of the rest of the parish.

ST MARY. Slow-growth medieval church which has suffered a good deal in the C19. Originally an aisleless C12 nave, with the original eaves level visible inside just above the arcades. N arcade *c.*1200 – round piers, square abaci, plain arches barely chamfered; s arcade mid C13 with the usual double-chamfered arches. Clerestory C13, comparatively rare in Sussex, with trefoil-headed windows on the N side. Chancel built after 1345 by Shaftesbury Abbey, and quite a noble design, though terribly renewed: very tall two-light windows on N and s sides, particularly effective outside, and a three-light E window with prickly curvilinear tracery. Chancel arch with mouldings dying into the imposts. Finally, the C15 alterations: decent w tower of the Arundel–Pulborough type, with renewed bell-chamber of two lights under a segmental head, the tower arch with imposts prolonged the whole width of the wall. At the same time the s aisle was raised, with new windows. All this is in quite an intricate chequer pattern of flint and local brown sandstone which today looks rather strange, for the sandstone has weathered far more than the flint, which is now noticeably proud of the surface. – FONT. Sussex marble, square bowl, crude round-headed arcading; *c.*1200. – CHEST. C13, like Climping but much plainer. – PLATE. s–g. Chalice and Cover, 1580. – MONUMENT. William Hayley † 1820. Quite plain, with a long inscription.

Hayley's house is THE TURRET, E of the church, built by him *c.*1800 in pasteboard stucco Tudor; Blake's, a little further s in BLAKE'S LANE, is a nice unrestored thatched flint cottage. The pair make an apt comment on their owners.

Immediately s of the church, CHURCH COTTAGE has a joke of a porch (early C19?) with bulbous and uneven flint columns supporting it.

8020

FERNHURST

Stone and tile-hung village near the Surrey border, under the s slopes of Blackdown. The best part is a small triangular green E of the church, with one side almost open like so many of these Sussex greens, pretty cottages, and the plain stone early C18 front of THE WHITE HOUSE.

ST MARGARET. All but rebuilt in the C19. S aisle 1859,* tower and spire and general restoration by *Salvin*, 1881, one of his last jobs, decent and responsible but deadly dull. It was originally C12: two windows and a buttress remain on the N side. – PLATE. Chalice, 1590.

Salvin lived at Fernhurst, and his house, HAWKSFOLD, is ¼ m. W of the main crossroads. It is rather a surprise, comfortably tile-hung and hipped-roofed, not at all violent. It was built in 1878.

DAWES FARM, 1 m. S on the A286, near Henley. The best of the farms near Fernhurst: Burgate stone block with broad-eaved hipped roof. Some hood-moulds and mullions, probably C16, but the effect all a rustic C17. Good barns, weatherboard and stone, big hipped roofs making a splendid composition of planes at 45 degrees.

0000

FERRING

On the coast W of Worthing, the usual case of a flint village swallowed up in seaside housing. Church Lane preserves the fragments; there is nothing to be said of – or for – the C20 building here.

ST ANDREW. Roughcast outside, with a little tile-hung bell-turret, a pleasant change from the hardened flint churches hereabouts. The inside too, though restored, keeps happy proportions, and a lot of soft village character. Much of the walling doubtless Norman. But most of what remains is C13, and probably *c.*1250: lancets in the chancel, and the fragments of shafted and arcaded rere-arches in the E end, the dimensions almost identical with Preston, brutally cut into by a three-light Perp window. Mid C13 S arcade of four bays, simple but smartly turned out: double-chamfered arches, circular piers and abaci, the W respond ending in half-octagonal capitals and a shaft, a neat example of architectural syntax. The transverse wall midway along the aisle is presumably a buttress: it contains a trefoil-headed stoup of *c.*1300. Weird PISCINA in the

* By *Woodyer* (NT).

chancel with projecting square bowl and nailhead ornament. Part-C13 and part-modern. – PLATE. Cup and Cover, 1631. – MONUMENTS. Thomas Olliver † 1782. A very endearing example of a rustic mason's tablet. Architectural frame, combining Corinthian pilasters, Adam swags, naturalistic roses, and – still – memento mori such as skeletons and hourglasses. – Thomas Richardson † 1797. The same size but quite different character: coloured marble and repeated urns. Elegant, but much less touching as a memorial.

FIELD PLACE
1 m. SW of Warnham

1030

The original parts are humble and stone-built, probably C15. These are now the kitchens forming three sides of a courtyard. No original detail remains. In the late C17 a taller block was added to close the fourth side. It probably dates from 1678, a typical local equivalent of Wren. Two storeys, heavy eaves cornice and heavier Horsham slate roof facing w. Half-H-shaped also, with a small central pediment. Now stuccoed, except for a brick cornice between the storeys. A loggia between the wings, with cast-iron columns and curious Egyptian lotus capitals. This is supposed to have been done in 1846, but looks earlier. On the N side a matching bay was added in 1931 (by *R. W. Symonds*) incorporating a shell-hood door from Ipswich. Across the garden, good early C18 GATES brought from a house in Chiswick Mall.

Plain interiors, except for the Dining Room with pretty doorcases and overmantel of 1752, and a robust, simple late C17 staircase. The screen in front of it, with its delicate Corinthian columns, is more likely to be C17 than 1752. House and gardens are beautifully kept; this unlikely setting was Shelley's birthplace, in 1792 – the Shelleys had been Sussex landowners for generations. He returned in 1815, when his grandfather died, after he had been estranged from his father, and was refused admission. So Sir Bysshe Shelley's will was being read inside, whilst the poet was reading Milton's Comus outside. Sir Bysshe was the builder of Castle Goring (*see* p. 125).

FINDON

1000

N of Worthing, the first village out on the main London road. Almost linked to Worthing by solid building which is euphem-

istically called 'Findon Valley', but the village centre itself still
keeps a precarious identity, which steadily decreases as each new
house is built. Sometimes they are carefully done and keep the
high flint walls which are the essence of the place. The tiny
centre, called THE SQUARE, is still close-built with plain C18
flint and stucco fronts and could be very impressive indeed.
Church and Findon Place are by themselves on the other side of
the by-pass with a good view E to Chanctonbury.

ST JOHN THE BAPTIST. An odd, lovable sight from the approach lane, with one enormous nave gable above two E gables,
and a shingled broach-spire behind that. All flint, even to a
chimney which sprouts out of the nave at the NE corner. The
interior view is even odder. What has happened, very roughly,
is that to an C11 or C12 cruciform church was added first one
of the familiar lean-to N aisles and then a much bigger C13 N
aisle, as wide as the nave, with its own N chancel chapel. So
far, so good. But some eccentric, probably in the C15, chose to
roof over nave and aisle in a single span, resting his king-posts
on top of the masonry above the arcade. The effect is of a
single-span roof, and hence a single space, with an arcade
galumphing down the middle of it. *Sir G. G. Scott*, who restored it in 1867, and thereby thoroughly confused the evidence, called it 'almost unique', as well he might. (*See* also
Ashurst p. 96.) The architectural details to be recorded are
very humble except for a puzzling big blocked round-headed
arch in the E wall of the S transept, perceptibly horseshoe-
shaped, the label made up of a kind of pointed billet ornament.
Was it the old chancel arch, or was it the entrance to an apsidal
chapel? It, like Sompting, encloses a small round carved stone
with floral patterns on it: what on earth was it? A boss? But
closing what vault? Pointed unchamfered arches, late C12, in
arcade and between nave and S transept. The arcade piers
round, but still with square abaci. Tower early C13, with lancet
openings and a plain, slightly chamfered tower arch. Chancel
arch mid C13, keeled responds, double-chamfered arch. Arch
at the E end of the N aisle probably later C13, with mouldings
dying away into the imposts. One good Perp window at the
SW corner of the nave, the inside mouldings worth a special
look. Scott did for most of the rest. The nave roof has kingposts, tie-beams, and a kind of double queenpost spanning
between tie-beam and rafters, leaning outwards at about 20
degrees. – SCREEN. C13, and hence a rarity. Hard and stalky,
heavily restored, almost exactly what Scott would have put up

himself. Tall pointed lights enclosing trefoils, shafts with three shaft-rings and octagonal capitals. The date must be near 1300. – FONT. The old font is in the N aisle, very battered. The replacement probably *Scott*'s. Purbeck marble, beautifully moulded and detailed, yet purely C19 in spirit. – PLATE. Chalice, 1618.

FINDON PLACE. Built in the early C18 and enlarged after 1786. The front must date from then: five bays of stock brick, gone bright green. Pediment over the centre three, split to allow room for the central round-headed window. Heavy porch with Tuscan pilasters. Not a sympathetic design: thin, more like East Anglia than Sussex. Early Soane houses look pretty much like this. On the r. of the front a one-storey attachment with a tripartite arched window and two oval windows over.

MUNTHAM COURT, ¾ m. NW. By *Woodyer*, after 1850. Demolished 1960–1. His style was neo-Jacobean, and the entrance lodge on the main road must be his.

FLINT MINES. There is a small group of mine shafts on a hill ¾ m. to the w. Near the top of the fill of one of the disused shafts was found a cremation accompanied by a beaker and two flint axes. Traces of the flint-knapping floors, where the raw material of the mines was worked into tools, have been located in the area of the shafts.

CISSBURY. The Iron Age HILL-FORT, 1 m. E of Findon, is of elongated oval plan, defended by a great rampart and external ditch with a smaller counterscarp bank outside the ditch. There are two original entrances on the s and SE. The gap in the ramparts on the NW side is modern.

In Roman times the interior of the fort came under the plough, and LYNCHETS can still be traced in the SE area of the fort. The small ENCLOSURES near the ramparts on the NW and SE sides are to be associated with this phase of occupation.

Finally, in the last years of the Roman occupation, the fort was hastily re-fortified with a turf bank built on to the Iron Age rampart, which must by then have been considerably weathered, while the SE entrance was widened. These precautions are probably to be associated with the threat of Saxon raids.

At the w end of the ramparts of the hill-fort and extending beyond the fortifications are a large number of shafts of FLINT MINES, represented by slight hollows and low mounds of waste material from the galleries. The seams of superior flint in this area lie at a depth of over 40 ft, and to work these deposits, vertical shafts were sunk to the level of the seams; at this point galleries radiated in all directions from the central shaft. Finds from the galleries and the neighbouring flint-knapping areas suggest that the mines were in use in Early Neolithic times.

8000 ## FISHBOURNE

Old Fishbourne is a pleasant but rather battered street of cottages along A27 with its heavy traffic; New Fishbourne is $\frac{1}{2}$ m. E, at the w end of the Chichester By-Pass, with church and manor house by themselves within sight of it.

ST PETER AND ST MARY. Attractive at first glance, but in fact almost all indifferent C19, rebuilt first in 1821 by *George Draper* (e.g. stuccoed N porch) and then in 1847 (nave and s aisle). The chancel contains one C13 lancet.

Immediately s of the church, the MANOR HOUSE in plain brickwork, dated 1687.

s of the main road at the extreme N end of Chichester harbour, a white-painted three-storey block of FLATS, simple and modern, by *R. L. Reynish*, 1958.

See p. 691 ROMAN VILLA. The site, which is currently being excavated (1964), lies at the head of the E arm of Fishbourne Creek, just N of the main Chichester–Portsmouth road. Work so far has revealed three principal building phases. The first phase, shortly after the Claudian invasion of A.D. 43, is represented by the post-holes of timber buildings, including a granary. In the last quarter of the C1 a more substantial structure of green-sand blocks was erected on the site to the N of the earlier timber buildings. The villa is arranged around an open court and consists of an E and a N wing. A number of the rooms in the latter wing had mosaic floors; most bore geometric patterns, but one consisted of a naturalistic, polychrome design incorporating floral motifs, dolphins, fish, and vases (this mosaic is now in Chichester museum). The villa was remodelled in the C2, the principal alteration in the E wing being the construction of a bath building. In the late C3 and early C4 occupation continued in the shell of the C1 building, and there appears to have been considerable stone robbing of the earlier structures.

FISHERSTREET *see* SHILLINGLEE PARK

0010 ## FITTLEWORTH

A collection of small groups which together make up quite a big village between Petworth and Pulborough. Occasional views southwards through the trees to the Downs, four miles away.

St Mary. Plain E.E. tower with stumpy broach-spire, plain bold E.E. lancet chancel, large scale and nobly detailed. A triplet in the E wall. Between the tower and the chancel, the C19 saw fit to insert a very horrible nave and aisles, 1871 by *Woodyer*, who should have known better. The internal effect is especially sad. The old nave had a timber frame. – FONT. Octagonal, with rosettes, but C14 rather than C15. – ROYAL ARMS. George III, painted. – PLATE. Cup, 1580; Paten, by *J. E. Couchman*, 1670.

At the N end there is a good group of cottages in UPPER STREET, around a bend in the main road. Sandstone, carstone, and timber-framing. S of this LOWER STREET runs down to the river, at first with indifferent and largely Victorian cottages, but then with Nos 1–6, a fine group slightly raised above the road. Quite humble cottages, C18 and early C19, in brick and carstone (dark brown irregular rubble), but a wonderful rhythmic rise and fall of roof-lines which the most self-conscious Picturesque designer could not have improved on. A little further S another good group around the tile-hung SWAN INN, with an inn sign spanning the road. Up a lane W from here THE GRANGE, a five-bay house of *c.*1700, altered, with a shell-hood doorcase.

LITTLE BOGNOR, ¾ m. NE, is an idyllic hamlet of stone cottages in surroundings as remote and beautiful as the loneliest parts of the Dordogne.

FORD   9000

Farms and barns on the W side of the Arun looking across at the red roofs of Littlehampton. The nearer view is the accumulated buildings of Ford airfield, now an open prison. They include decent modern BARRACKS designed by *R. E. Rossell* (Ministry of Works) in 1956.

St Andrew. One of Sussex's prettiest churches; a lovable 6a unrestored exterior, nave and chancel, brick porch and white-painted bellcote in a small churchyard almost surrounded by large trees. Humble village interior. The framework C11, more likely Norman than Saxon, with two tiny windows in the N side of the nave. Two larger windows also, still Norman, an unusual form of addition; chancel arch Norman, a plain arch and imposts carrying a repeated crude star-shaped ornament, partly renewed, which looks very like the ancestor of dog-

8—s.

tooth. The chancel N and S windows have round heads but pointed rere-arches and it would be unwise to date them more accurately than the C12. The most remarkable is an unmistakable Norman 'low-side'. E window Dec, three lights with reticulation, w window a typical Early Perp type, of two lights with a quatrefoil above, and a nice comparison in the straightening out of forms. Elegant S porch of 1637, brick, with a Dutch gable, the style of Barnham Manor House. – FONTS. A rough square bowl, Saxon or Norman. But a tiny pottery font of the early C19 is hidden away behind the chancel arch. It looks just like a comfit box. – SCULPTURE. In the vestry, above the doorway to the church, a piece of Anglo-Saxon interlace. – PLATE. Cup and Cover, 1567; Paten and Flagon, 1694. – HARMONIUM. Not usually mentioned in *The Buildings of England*. This one, however, defies omission. Splendidly gross and bulgy, *c.*1870, and made, like so many harmoniums, in America. It came via Lyon & Hall of Brighton and Hove, but it was designed by the *Chicago Cottage Organ Company*. – WALL PAINTINGS. Several, C15, very faded now; Last Judgement over the chancel arch, Agony in the Garden in a splay on the S side of the nave.

PLACE FARM. L-shaped brick house, much altered but with tell-tale signs that it was originally a mid to late C17 house of 'City of London' or 'Artisan' type: bracketed cornice, chimneys decorated with blind arcading, and remains of thick brick surrounds to the first-floor windows.

FOREST SIDE *see* STANSTED

FUNTINGTON

Unaffected flint and brick cottages NW of Chichester where the Downs slide into the Sussex plain. Modern building has just been kept decent.

ST MARY. Visually nearly all of 1859, in one of those senseless restorations which took away all charm and did not give back any character. From the look of the E window the culprit was Teulon. Four-bay C13 N nave arcade, retooled, of the usual type; s arcade C19. N and S chancel chapels originally late C13 to C14, given preposterous arcades to the chancel. Simple C15 W tower, nibbled at, with two diagonal buttresses and square-headed bell-openings. Tower arch with two chamfered orders and irregular semi-hexagonal imposts and jambs. – PLATE. Cup and Cover, 1637; Almsdish, 1785. – MONUMENT. Fragments of C15 panelling from a tomb-chest built into the S porch: again what one would expect from Teulon.

ADSDEAN, ¾ m. NW. Simple gabled Tudor house of c.1850, but delightful S addition by *Norman Shaw*, 1877, a two-storey wing with big white-painted polygonal bow window, the end gable made into a composition with the chimney in his very best manner. Flint and stone, hence no chance to be heavy-handed; instead there is freshness and sensitivity.

FURNACE GREEN see CRAWLEY, p. 203n

FYNING see ROGATE

GARLANDS see RUDGWICK

GASKYNS see SLINFOLD

GOFF'S FARM see NORTH CHAPEL

GOODWOOD   8000

House, grounds, and racecourse cover an area of several square miles on the southern slopes of the Downs NE of Chichester. Surroundings and estates splendidly kept: in fact there is more interest in the grounds than in the house itself.

GOODWOOD. Only 150 ft up, yet with a beautifully managed view S across the coastal plain. (There are a lot of managed vistas at Goodwood: e.g. the avenue cut through woodland SW of the house to give a view of the cathedral spire.) It is one of *James Wyatt*'s most puzzling designs, built in c.1790–1800 at a time when his own taste was turning finally from classical to Gothic. Perhaps he was subdued by his client, the Duke of Richmond, perhaps he was out of sympathy with the style: at any rate it is one of his very few dull designs, whether classical or Gothic.

He incorporated the existing small house of 1720, and this can be seen at the NW end: a plain brick building with skimped stone dressings, the N front of seven bays with a central pediment. This had been enlarged c.1760 by *Sir William Chambers*, and the centre of the present S front is probably his rather than Wyatt's: five bays with a three-bay pediment, plain and correct. Then came Wyatt. His intention seems to have been an irregular octagon around an open courtyard with circular corner turrets and saucer domes, a grandiose neo-classical idea which could only have looked impressive from the air. Only three sides were completed, and so the house comes to an ignominious end to the NE. Flint and stone, a low-toned combination forced on Wyatt by the Duke, two storeys with three-storey turrets. The s front has a stone centre, as mentioned, the sw front a two-storey hexastyle portico – Greek Doric below, Ionic above – the E front simply has the centre three bays brought forward slightly.

Nor are the interiors much more noteworthy. In the 1720 house is the LONG HALL with simple screens of Ionic columns at either end. In this part also the TAPESTRY ROOM, the most attractive in the house, with a Wyatt ceiling still in the Adam-esque manner that made him famous, done with an unerring decorative touch, handling a difficult and sugary colour scheme – pink, green, and gold – perfectly. In the room a very fine fireplace by *Bacon**★ done in the true neo-classical way without a hint of false sentiment or of academic frigidity. Two half-nude figures, male and female, hold aside draperies which form the base of a large mirror – the dictatorship of having an architectural frame for a fireplace finally broken. On the hearth in front, *Anne Seymour Damer*'s enchanting sculpture of two entwined dogs, one plain and one very shaggy. Horace Walpole thought so highly of her that he left Strawberry Hill to her when he died.

Most of the other rooms are plain; the entrance hall has a screen of marble columns set too close together (six plus two half-columns, altogether) and the LIBRARY, the most ornate room in the house, if all by Wyatt, is a sad example of how limp he could be. (It might be a remodelling of a Chambers room.) Ceiling a geometrical pattern of crosses and octagons with weak paintings by *Riley*, frieze a jaded design of swags, dado painted in grisaille, by *Biagio Rebecca*, and much better. The staircase, in an irregular polygonal well, dates from 1904.

GROUNDS. Immediately to the sw are the STABLES, built by *Sir William Chambers* in 1757–63 and more impressive than the house. They show Chambers at his very best, building coolly and academically, but with absolute control and extreme delicacy. Everything is firm and calculated to a hairsbreadth. A quadrangle as big as the house, built of beautifully knapped flints with stone dressings, the sides pedimented, the entrance front fourteen bays wide with a central triumphal arch, the differences in scale beautifully managed. The arch is grandly coffered, framed by pairs of Doric columns, surmounted by a superb frieze of flagons and rams'-heads; above the cornice

★ Made in 1777. So Wyatt must have begun by remodelling ten years before he went on to rebuild.

the attic is plain except for two sculptured garlands. Hardly anyone in the C18 could have done as well.

w of this COTTAGES probably by *Wyatt*, rather a different thing: L-shaped and Gothick, with pointed and quatrefoil windows, jolly but no more. To the N of the house, on a hillside with a magnificent view to the SW over Chichester, is CARNE'S SEAT. This was built in 1743 by *Roger Morris*, and is in fact a more elaborate edition of his Council House in Chichester. Alas, it is not really more accomplished, without either Burlington's certainty of purpose or Kent's decorative charm. The real trouble is that the ornamental part (a three-bay pedimented projection over an open rusticated ground floor) is far too small in scale for the pyramid-roofed box behind. In the hillside N of this is a SHELL HOUSE which from photographs is quite clearly one of the best in the country, completely decorated in shell patterns of incredible delicacy (Adam delicacy before Adam) by the second Duchess and her daughters in the 1740s. Most of the shells were collected in the West Indies by naval officers. The colour scheme is made up of pinks, whites, mauves, and blues. It is not now open to the public.

Finally, a complete set of lodges and outbuildings designed by *Wyatt* in the late C18. They start with the KENNELS of 1787, now the Golf-Club house, beside the road to the racecourse. These are actually Wyatt's best building at Goodwood, crisp and elegant, with a subtle polychrome of flint and yellow bricks that must have appealed to the cool late C18. Eleven bays (1-3-3-1), the end bays pedimented, the centre taller with a separate roof: arcaded ground floor and tiny upper windows. The design is Palladian, but given a new energy and urgency.

The other Wyatt buildings are very much of a piece: beautifully built in flint, crisply detailed and rather bloodless. They include VALDOE LODGES, to the S, and KENNELS LODGES, to the N of the kennels, an ORANGERY immediately N of the house, and, more ambitious, with a centre-and-wings composition, MOLECOMB, the Dower House, 1 m. to the NW.

RACECOURSE, 1½ m. N, 600 ft up on top of the Downs. Laid out in 1802, and without any doubt the most beautifully sited racecourse in the country, as much a triumph of Picturesque landscaping as any Repton park. The course is a horseshoe along the top of a deep wooded combe in the downs, with views N right through the escarpment, a rare thing, to the

country N of Midhurst. The Grandstand of 1904 is a jolly
Edwardian building by *A. J. Henderson* of Esher, like an enlarged Oxford college barge, which is exactly what is needed
here.*

THE TRUNDLE, 1½ m. SE of West Dean, overlooking the
Racecourse. This hill-fort is of octagonal plan, defended by a
massive bank and ditch with a lesser counterscarp bank outside the ditch. There are two original entrances on the SE and
SW. Excavation in the area of the SE gate shows a complicated
series of structural alterations. The entrance at the SE consists
of a long passage formed by the inturning of the ramparts at
this point. The first gate structure, contemporary with the
construction of the rampart, *c.* 250 B.C., consisted of a double
gate set in the middle of this entrance passage and abutting
on a central post-hole. This structure was later dismantled
and two gates were set up, one behind the other, in the manner
of a medieval barbican. Finally, shortly before the abandonment of the site this too was dismantled, and work was begun
on a double-entranced gateway once more, although this time
set at the inner end of the entrance passageway. This structure
was never finished, however, and the site was abandoned in
the C1 B.C.

Within, and partly overlain by, the ramparts of the hill-fort
lies the site of a NEOLITHIC CAUSEWAYED CAMP. The
earthwork consists of three roughly circular, concentric banks
and ditches, the innermost enclosing an area of 3 acres. It is
this innermost ring which is most readily observable by the
casual visitor, with its bank standing to a height of almost 7 ft
on the N. The interrupted or causewayed ditches of the
intermediate ring can be traced as slight depressions, particularly on the S, and a portion of the outermost ditch can still
be seen on the N, outside the ramparts of the Iron Age hill-
fort. From the ditches of the camp came sherds of Windmill
Hill pottery, animal bones, principally ox, and a variety of
flint and bone leather-working tools.

GOOSEHILL CAMP *see* WEST DEAN

1000

GORING-BY-SEA

W of West Worthing, with all that this implies; a few trees, a
multitude of little houses, the older buildings lying around like
flotsam.

* To be replaced. The new designs will have a job to catch the atmosphere
as well as this.

ST MARY. Rebuilt in 1837 by *Decimus Burton*, but as disappointingly limp as his other Gothic churches. Nobody would guess
who the architect was. Inside, he kept the old arcades, re-
tooled, and they and the thin plaster details make a pretty,
uncomplicated match: late C12 with scalloped capitals and
pointed single-chamfered arches. – WALL PAINTING, over
the chancel arch. Christ in Glory, by *Hans Feibusch*, 1954. A
good deal better than the customary C20 English idea of
church decoration: a swirling, baroque design well fitted to
the wall space. – MONUMENTS. Bad brass, probably to the
Coke family, probably *c.*1490. Man and wife, effigies 26 in.
high. – Susan Cook, undated. It looks *c.*1740, but she died in
1707. Plain frame but a lively Cheere-ish bust, full of feminin-
ity. – Isabella Lyon † 1836. Carved by *Chantrey*, 1841, but a
terrible comedown; an offhand medallion in a Greek frame,
homely face in funny hat. Yet, probably, it is the Chantrey
which is the more 'true to life' of the two.

GOSSOPS GREEN *see* CRAWLEY, p. 206

GRAFFHAM   *9010*

In lovely country SE of Midhurst: one cul-de-sac winding street,
with no formal plan but very great charm, ending at the church,
which is within a few yards of the great hanging woods of the
slopes of the Downs. The cottages combine about half a dozen
different materials: brick, flint, clunch, timber-framing, and a
little sandstone.

ST GILES. All but rebuilt in 1874–87 by *G. E. Street* or his firm
as a Wilberforce memorial. Crisp E.E. style in flint, hard but
not harsh, and better than the average Street village church.
Nave and aisles, chancel, N transept, tower with shingled
spire. What was kept was, outside, the W door, unexpectedly
delicate and intricate E.E. (especially by contrast with Street),
and, inside, the nave arcades. These, partly renewed, are very
familiar local late C12: circular piers, scalloped capitals, some
of them oddly irregular, square abaci and single-chamfered
pointed arches. – DOOR to vestry with complicated C15 key
incorporating tiny heads of a king and a lady; inside the vestry
an elegant mid C13 PISCINA.

Just S of the church is the W LODGE to Lavington Park (*see* East
Lavington), *c.*1840, stuccoed and over-equipped with detail in
a typical 1840 way: portico and pediment, four Ionic columns
with four Ionic pilasters behind them.

WOODSIDE, ½ m. N, beside the road to Selham. Built by *Halsey Ricardo* in 1905 for himself. We have been used, in the last thirty years, to architects building into their own houses all that they want to say but cannot persuade their clients to accept. The situation in 1900 must have been the other way round: here there is none of the faience of houses like that in Addison Road, Kensington, but a simple, dignified house in Voysey style. Three storeys, roughcast, with gables and green shutters, otherwise plain. Inside, fireplaces by *de Morgan* and a beam with moulded plaster decoration by *Ernest Gimson*.

BARROWS. On Graffham Down are a number of Early Bronze Age bowl barrows, including one magnificent example some 15 ft high.

0010   GREATHAM

Church and manor house by themselves beside the Arun near Pulborough. The MANOR HOUSE has a gabled s front with an armorial panel dated 1672; the rustication around the windows must be a good deal later.

The CHURCH is delightful, a single room with a bell-turret hung with slates. Rubble ironstone walls, no restoration, and a wonderful texture. Most of the windows lancets (two in the E end) but the walls probably C12. Rustic C17 COMMUNION RAIL with the top still trying to be crenellated, and two-decker early C19 Gothic PULPIT. Nothing much has changed here in the last century.

HUMPHREYS. On the lane to Amberley: a good bulky C17 cottage in attractive materials – ironstone, with brick window dressings and red tiles, sweeping down over lean-to additions at either end.

GRITTENHAM FARM *see* TILLINGTON

9000   HALNAKER
                    4 m. NE of Chichester

Pleasant straggle of houses along the Chichester to Petworth road. The ruins of the house are ½ m. N of the road in the garden of Little Halnaker.

HALNAKER HOUSE. Halnaker and Cowdray have a remarkably similar history. Both were medieval houses given a wholesale remodelling in the C16 by owners who used up-to-date Renaissance ornament. Both became ruined about 1800. But where Cowdray still impresses as architecture, too much has gone at Halnaker to make it more than a pretty, picturesque group of walls. (This is not only the fault of the weather. Details were transplanted wholesale to Chichester, see p. 178, above.) It is a pity, for the complete Halnaker would have been very impressive.

It was begun by the de Haye family, the founders of Box-grove Priory. The site faces s at the exact point where the Downs begin to rise out of the coastal plain, and consists of an irregular retaining wall enclosing separate hall and chapel ranges. Closed at the s end by a nearly symmetrical c14 gate-house and wings, achieving a semi-fortified, semi-regular effect which suited both the political climate and the visual inclinations of the c14. Halnaker was the type of Stokesay, not Bodiam. The hall range became the Tudor house and then received multiple additions, mainly by Lord de la Warr (of the Renaissance chantry at Boxgrove and the Renaissance tombs at Broadwater). It became redundant when Goodwood was built.

The hall keeps plain c14 inner and outer doors to the porch: foundation and walling can be matched with the late c18 drawing by Grimm. A big range which has completely dis-appeared ran s from this to link up with the chapel. Most of the chapel walls remain and show it to have been c13. Two squat lancets are left in the s side, the bases of three more in the E wall. The gatehouse has a hefty sandstone doorway with segmental lintels; the rest of the walling is knapped flint (i.e. made into a regular pattern of squares), common in East Anglia but rare in Sussex. It is flanked by curious turrets which begin as buttresses with broader octagonal tops. Dr Bromet in 1840 talked about tall arched recesses in them, making the buttresses into flying buttresses, but this is impossible to reconcile with the bonding of the stonework as it is at present.

The present HALNAKER HOUSE is by Lutyens, 1938, late and sober, almost dowdy, with a heavy hipped roof. Half-H-shaped front facing s. Neo-Georgian, of course.

The house immediately N of the ruins is LITTLE HALNAKER, built in 1961 and still classical, but nicely done. Largely designed by the owner, Margery McGrath.

HALNAKER MILL, 1 m. NE, a splendid hilltop site. Built c. 1750, restored in 1934 and 1955, a squat brick tower mill keep-ing sweeps and fantail. Rustic and crude compared with the elegance of later windmills, which were really as much a product of the Industrial Revolution as cotton mills or ware-houses.

HAMMER WOOD *see* CHITHURST

0010

HARDHAM

A hamlet near the Arun s of Pulborough. The main road is literally a few feet away, and this effect (a winding lane separated from fast traffic by a thick hedge) is exciting. Unexpectedly, it intensifies the village character. The cottages mostly stone and half-timber with tile roofs. The best is YEW TREE COTTAGE, E of the church.

ST BOTOLPH. Very typical of West Sussex: a complete primitive CII church. Two rooms only, tiny windows high up in nave and chancel, plain unmoulded chancel arch on plain imposts. The later centuries only added a minimum of windows – lancets in the nave, and simple E and S windows in the chancel, late C13 and early C14 respectively.* The Victorians added the bell-turret and the porch, a little too fussily. The outside is whitewashed all over and looks very attractive. Simple king-post roofs, probably early.

The fame of Hardham is its WALL PAINTINGS. They form a complete covering to both nave and chancel and were apparently covered up by the C13 and not discovered until 1866. With Copford in Essex they represent one of the very few cases where one can guess at the total appearance of a painted C12 church. Alas, it is still a guess, because so much has faded at Hardham that except in one or two places there is not much more than a confused blur of red and yellow ochre, atmospheric and attractive in itself but not at all what the designers intended. How much of this has gone since 1866 (i.e. because of inadequate preservation) it is impossible to say. The alternative at that time would have been touching up and repainting, and we should not have enjoyed that either. The cycle dates from *c.*1120–40 and is supposed to have been done under the Priory of St Pancras at Lewes. It is in two tiers. According to Professor Tristram the designs may come from manuscripts such as the Cædmon MS. of *c.*1000, originally at Canterbury, now in the Bodleian. The subjects are best described wall by wall. Only those on the front and back of the chancel arch can give anything but archaeological enjoyment.

Nave.

   W wall: Torments of the Damned

   N wall: Nativity scenes above, scenes of St George below –

* Plus a pronounced blocked squint, visible outside, in the SW corner of the chancel.

the earliest known representation in Britain. On the left, St George either slaying the dragon or victorious at Antioch (1098). C11 window splay painted also.

s wall: Nativity scenes above, unidentifiable below.

E wall: The best in the church. Badly preserved below (the painting on the r. seems to be the Baptism), but still clear above, around the head of the chancel arch (originally the voussoirs and soffit were painted also: this was cleared away in 1862 to 'expose the stonework'). On the l. Christ with the Doctors, above the arch censing angels, on the r., well preserved, the Annunciation and Visitation. Red and yellow, with the haloes delicate light green. Even here, detailed expressions have gone. The best part is the wonderfully vigorous body and wing of the right-hand angel: on the r. a text preserved in the frieze: VIRGO SALUTATUR STERILIS FECUNDA PROBATUR.

Chancel.

N wall: Elders and Apostles above, Betrayal and Last Supper (?) below.

E wall: Christ in Glory and Entombment.

s wall: More Elders and Apostles above, lower tier uncertain.

w wall: Eve milking a cow on the r. of the chancel arch, and the Temptation on the l. Violent elongated figures of Adam and Eve, as distorted as a Russian ikon. Serpent in its tree on the r., rather faint. The diagrammatic sketching in of belly and buttocks here is brilliant.

Other fittings: WOODWORK. Plain, straight-topped, C15 BENCH ENDS in the nave. – COMMUNION RAIL, Laudian in type but with a date 1720. – FONT. Octagonal, Perp, quite plain.

HARDHAM PRIORY, ½ m. SW. A beautiful site on the very edge of the Arun water-meadows. Hardham was a small house of Augustinian canons, founded after 1248, dissolved in 1534 after having been out of repair for half a century. What remains now is the walls of the REFECTORY, made into a very picturesque farmhouse (formerly on the s side of the cloister), and the roofless CHAPTER HOUSE, which was, as usual, on the E side. The site has never been excavated. The farmhouse was burnt in 1912, exposing good C14 wall paintings which have now disappeared, and only a vaulted undercroft remains: six bays, groin-vaulted, central arcade with round piers and round abaci. Also at the SE end, fragments of walling which perhaps formed part of the warming room. What is left of the chapter house is much more worthwhile. It must have been a beautiful building, and even in ruins shows the enormous difference between Gothic detail and Gothic detail used selectively and imaginatively. The difference between good and bad is sharper in medieval architecture than anywhere else (if we are prepared to recognize it and not accept C13 or C15 building blindly), because there are no false issues to cloud it, such as accurate reproduction of antique examples. The chapter house is oblong, with three lancets in the E end and one blocked lancet in the projecting part of the N and S walls. It was originally vaulted, and fragments of shafts and springing remain. The N and S lancets have nook-shafts and moulded rere-arches: the E lancets have a continuous moulding for each rere-arch, and this is surrounded by another moulding resting on shafts with capitals; a delicate, intelligible, elegant scheme. The best part is the tripartite arched W entrance. The combination of discrimination and force here would be a model to most C13 cathedrals. Arches of equal height, the central opening slightly wider, the side openings filled with two sub-arches under a quatrefoil, increasing the contrast in size. The details are brilliant: the main arches rest on marble shafts with round abaci and oddly stilted foliage capitals. They could almost be crocket capitals of c.1180 except that the ends curl over with a breathtaking live submission. Yet it must be c.1250 at least.* There is none of the joyous looseness of C13 stiff-leaf carving here, perhaps something to do with the control used in the rest of the design. On either side of the door, four detached shafts round a central stem – the Chichester retrochoir motif. The sub-arches have circular abaci but plain capitals. The most eloquent feature is the use made of dogtooth carving – a silly name, especially here where it is obvious that the four-lobed ornament is intended to be a simplified leaf or flower pattern. It is used on the outer label and on the soffits of the arches: the outer label has exquisitely calculated stops of stylized foliage – again, more stilted than one would expect from the date.

HARROW HILL see ANGMERING

HARTING

On the Hampshire border at the foot of the Downs, near Petersfield. The main village with the church is at South Harting,

* This is the pattern of St Richard's Porch and the Bishop's Palace Chapel at Chichester.

and, appropriately, looks more like Hants (Hambledon or the Meons) than Sussex – demure brick and clunch cottages, winding up to the church which deftly dominates, as it should do, by its cruciform shape and by being at an angle to the street. The street seen the other way is elegant too, winding down to a pair of road junctions, each accented by similar-looking C18 cottages painted buff.

East Harting is a random collection of cottages of all dates around a pair of lanes forming an oval; West Harting is a straggle of cottages that looks purely Hampshire.

ST MARY AND ST GABRIEL. Big church dominating the village: nave and aisles without clerestory, transepts and chancel, central tower and broach-spire. The effect a comfortable, heavy early C14, complicated inside by a big repair after a fire in 1576. The nave walls, by their combined height and narrowness, could be pre-Conquest, but nothing can be proved. The earliest visible work is the original E arch of the crossing tower, obviously quite elaborate, with an outer order of dogtooth, but obscured by the lower supporting arch put in in 1576. The rest followed at various dates in the early C14: nave arcades, surprisingly rough, with only slightly chamfered unmoulded arches on octagonal piers which run into them without capitals: monstrously big stop-chamfers effect the join at the corners. The E bay of the nave is lower to give support for the tower and may be of 1576. The transepts, which are the most impressive part outside, are more typically Dec: the N transept slightly earlier, with a three-light N window the tracery of which is made up of two trefoils and a spherical triangle, and with nook-shafts, the S transept (and chancel) later and leaner, with cusped Y- and intersecting tracery. The boldly E.E. E end is of 1858, the Caryll Chapel S of the chancel was built in 1610 and is now ruined. The fire of 1576 meant new tower arches and responds which were carried out in a bluff minimum Gothic which combines with the nave to make the overall effect ungraciously heavy, but it also provided a complete set of new ROOFS that is an anthology of Elizabethan carpentry. Nave and transepts are straightforward jobs as they might have been in barns, with kingpost and trussed rafters respectively. The chancel, however, has been treated more elaborately. Tie-beams with wall posts, ornamented pendants to the wall posts and three pendants on the beams themselves. Collar-beams above, linked to the main beams by three turned carved balusters: a very nice balance between sturdiness and decoration, and a very rare example in church buildings. – WOODWORK. Spiral staircase to the tower, 1852:* the Victorians at their most ingenious, and hence most truly Gothic. – FONT. Rough square arcaded C13 bowl, Purbeck marble, but the COVER is elegantly Jacobean, a central spike and four scrolly brackets. – PLATE. Paten, 1638(?); Chalice, 1675. – STATUE (S transept). Virgin, late C13. Is it Spanish? – MONUMENTS. Medieval fragment in chancel – head and shoulders of effigy, probably C13. Terribly weathered, but originally a fine monument. – In the chancel, on the S side, a very plain Elizabethan tomb recess. On the surround only the most elementary geometrical shapes. – Cowper and Coles families, S transept. Three effigies of c.1600, apparently rearranged when the inscription was put up in 1795. Male and female figures semi-recumbent on their sides; male figure above, kneeling. All the effigies stiff, effective only from their accidental juxtaposition. – Sir Richard Caryll † 1616. Badly weathered recumbent stone figure, S transept. – Sir Henry Fetherstonhaugh † 1846, by *Westmacott Jun.*, chancel. Female figure, blasted tree, Landseer-like dog. The carving still crisp, the effect a little touching perhaps because of its absurdity. – In the churchyard, WAR MEMORIAL by *Eric Gill*, a tall, well-outlined cross and relief carvings at the foot, and a lot of good late C18 headstones, especially SW of the church. May they never be set out in rows or as pavements. – Outside the churchyard the village STOCKS.

Many nice minor buildings in the main part of the village, but the only building worth special notice is the VILLAGE SCHOOLS, 1866, a copybook example with its careful near-symmetry and spiky bargeboarded gables. With so many now being closed down or enlarged, the complete ensemble like this may become quite a rarity.

The best cottages are S of the church, almost out in the country: first BEACON COTTAGE and DOWNSEDGE, thatched early C17 twins with regular timber-framing and brick infill. Then No. 6 THE STREET, the same date and type but more picturesque, with a couple of curved braces on the upper floor and the roof carried down almost to the ground over a wooden lean-to.

S of East Harting, on the slopes of the Downs, is a good modern HOUSE by *Geoffrey Challen* of Challen & Floyd, 1959, fitting perfectly into the landscape without any concessions to period

* Made by a local carpenter (Rodney Hubbuck).

design at all. Half-H-shaped; two-storeyed part on the l. clad
mainly with wood and with a monopitch roof matching the
slope of the hillside; single-storeyed part on the r., glass and
sandstone. It is much more a house to be lived in than an
exposition of some architectural theory – and hence of course
is much better architecture too.

(A good new COUNCIL ESTATE is projected in TIPPER LANE,
by a local firm, *Peter MacIver & Associates* of Petersfield.
Information from Mr Hubbuck.)

HEATHLANDS FARM *see* MIDHURST

HENFIELD 2010

A cheerful big village N of the Downs, about midway between
Horsham and Brighton. So big, and so straggling, especially to
the w, that it would be worth converting into a small town. The
expansion will come naturally anyway; if it were directed it
could be given point and elegance. One bright main street exactly
half-way towards being a town, like Storrington. The church is
away from the road to the w, and there is a good network of
leafy suburban footpaths in the area s of it.

ST PETER. A Perp tower like a keep, as grim as it would be in
Northumberland; from outside all the rest is 1870 by *Slater
& Carpenter*. Flinty and spindly, aisles and two-bay outer
aisles. Much more of an effect inside because in fact the nave
walls were kept with their four-bay C13 arcades. Usual style,
usual wide Sussex roof. The C15 N chancel chapel remains
too, but very much hedged around. Impressive five-light (N)
and four-light (E) windows, in completely different styles. –
STAINED GLASS. Lancet by *Lowndes & Drury*, 1901, almost
Art Nouveau, inscribed 'She hath done what she could' (s
chancel chapel). More life than the various *Kempe* windows,
e.g. the E window, of 1875, and aisle windows of 1905. –
PLATE. Salver, 1704; Flagon, 1732; Chalice, 1733; two Patens
and Almsdish, 1753.

Many pleasant buildings in Henfield, few notable. The best
cottages are at the SE end, where there is a green on either side
of the Brighton road. On the N edge, two groups: one with
the thatched LAVENDER COTTAGE, the other L-shaped
brick and flint (ANTS MANOR) and very pretty indeed. It
would take a dour academic not to be charmed by it, or by
Sussex generally.

More cottages near the church, and further w a pleasant C of E
SCHOOL, 1962. Further out, CHESTHAM PARK, 1 m. N,

is a plain Grecian house with big eaves and Doric porch. The MHLG attributes it to *Amon Henry Wilds*.

STREATHAM MANOR, 1¼ m. SE. The original main manor house of Henfield, by itself on a lonely site beside the Adur and the railway. It was already deserted in Elizabeth's time. Later, a farmhouse was made out of one wing of the larger composition. Tile-hung at the front, close-timbered at the back.

HEYSHOTT

8010

Under a majestic stretch of the Downs SE of Midhurst, its plan about as easygoing as can be imagined – a long shaggy green running N–S, which gathers itself into a winding village street which is more than half fields at the S end, including, happily, UPPER COMMON, a nice modern house opposite the village pub, by *Douglas Clayton*. Flint and brick, and a little more half-timber than these villages usually have. The whole place is so much more harmonious, yet with so much less strain, than the average village in, say, Surrey. *The Buildings of England* does not concern itself much with landscape, but AMBERSHAM COMMON, 1 m. NE, has got to be mentioned: a heath 200 ft high, with views to the Downs and N to the Midhurst hills that make up a quintessence of different types of scenery in a small distance probably unequalled in Britain.

ST JAMES. Humble C13 flint building with C19 enlargements done humbly – rebuilt chancel and new N aisle – so that it is still all of a piece. C13 arcade, double-chamfered arches on circular piers and abaci, two windows (W and S side of nave) which are probably late C14, two lights with a sexfoil above, representing a straightening out of one of the commonest Dec forms, and a surprisingly elaborate Perp S window which, although it is in the rebuilt chancel, must surely represent the original: three lights splitting to six, all under a segmental head. This type is commoner in East Anglia than in Sussex. Like so many of the West Sussex churches, decent without being memorable. – FONT. Seems to have been C13; on a stem and four shafts; cut down and mutilated. – C17 FONT COVER similar to that at Harting. – ROYAL ARMS. Painted, C18, over the S door. Very fey lion.

HOYLE FARM, 1 m. NE. The original parts C16, with small mullioned windows and hood-moulds.

BARROWS. There are some ten bowl barrows scattered over the down. They range between 30 and 60 ft in diameter and 1 and

5 ft in height. Most have depressions at their centres suggesting that they have been opened, but there is no record of this work.

HIGHDOWN

HIGHDOWN TOWER. Free Tudor house with a squat stuccoed central tower and lower flint wings. The core *c.*1820, the present appearance *c.*1900, and nicely fitted on to its hill-side, like a Voysey house.

HIGHDOWN HILL. There is a HILL-FORT here of univallate construction and rectangular plan with a second bank and ditch on the s side. The ramparts are cut by entrances on the s and E sides. The hill was first fortified in Iron Age A times, when the rectangular work was constructed. The rampart was separated from the steep-sided, flat-bottomed ditch by a berm and was revetted on its outer face with a flint and chalk wall. A row of timber uprights supported the inner face of the rampart. Reconstruction of this first fort was carried out by Iron Age A folk when the ditch was re-cut and became V-shaped in section, the slope of the rampart now beginning on the inner edge of the ditch. At the time of the Iron Age B invasions this remodelled ditch had again silted up and was in part re-cut once more. The date of the second bank and ditch on the s side is uncertain but they may be the work of these new immigrants.

The site was reoccupied at the end of the C3 or early C4 A.D., when a square wooden HUT was constructed immediately within the ramparts.

Inside the rampart of the hill-fort lies a SAXON CEMETERY. Both inhumations and cremations in urns were discovered. In addition to spearheads and knives of iron there were a number of objects of Late Roman manufacture, and four glass drinking horns. The most interesting of these glass vessels was a pedestalled flask, possibly of eastern Mediterranean manufacture, with a frieze of hare and hounds on the globular body and an inscription in Greek characters on the neck.

ROMAN BUILDINGS. Half-way down the slope of the hill on the W side is a small bath house, consisting of an apsidal cold bath and a similarly shaped hot room with large rectangular hot bath. Red tesserae were found on the floor of the latter room, along with fragments of window glass and red wall plaster. The pottery indicates a date for the building in the early C2; it appears to have continued in use until the late C3.

HOLLYCOMBE *see* LINCH

2030

HOLMBUSH
Half-way between Horsham and Crawley

Very typical Gothick house of the 1820s – actually 1823 – by *Francis Edwards*, who designed the Lion Brewery from which the lion outside Waterloo Station comes. Like most Gothick houses, it sits beautifully in its landscape, a wooded hillside with a big view N across the Surrey Weald. Also like most Gothick houses, it is depressingly limp close to. L-shaped, battlemented: two-storeyed with a big square three-storeyed tower at the corner. All Tudor except for a plain classical doorcase midway along the N front. Seen from the main road below, as it would seem in one of the innumerable books of country seats, it deceives the casual traveller perfectly.

1030

HORSHAM

An exasperating, traffic-laden, half-realized town. It has always been the centre of the western Weald, with the nearest towns fifteen miles away, yet it never acquired a big central space or any impressive civic buildings. Petworth, with a tenth of the population, has more of an urban air. Traffic winds through it, and parked cars flood over pretty streets much too small in scale to take them. Removal of the through traffic and perhaps a big multi-storey car park would make it a very different place. The main E–W street has its middle section made pedestrian, which is a welcome relief, and the idea could be extended. The best parts are S of this, the backwater of Causeway leading down to the church, a perfect example of quietness in the midst of bustle. Beyond the church, straightaway, is open country; and one of Horsham's best attributes is the amount of worth-while open space in and around the town. But most of the main streets, especially around Carfax, are disjointed and gap-toothed, grown up too suddenly and genteelly.

St Mary. At the S end of Causeway, heavy and towny, with the shingled spire managing to get into most of the town views in spite of being low-lying. The earliest parts are severe C12 – the NW corner of the nave, with one window and a plain doorway of two orders, and the base of the tower, with a similar doorway, a bit like Wisborough Green. The tower arch is now off centre – does this mean a nave originally wider than the present one? The bell-openings in the tower have details of *c.*1300.

In 1231 the advowson of St Mary passed to Rusper Priory. They must have rebuilt straightaway, and this is what makes Horsham impressive, or would do if there had been fewer alterations. The plan was classically simple: wide five-bay plain nave, round piers and abaci, double-chamfered arches, lancet clerestory (chamfered reveals outside). The three-bay chancel continued in the same style but must have been built much later in the C13, a medieval case of keeping in keeping. Piers and abaci have gone octagonal, and more significantly, the outer reveals of the clerestory lancets have been given two hollow chamfers, beautifully crisp. The best part is now the E end flanked by octagonal turrets with spirelets and triangular crockets round the base. The strong striding rhythm can still be followed through outside and dominates the inside, especially as there is no chancel arch. Was there one originally? A C13-looking wall shaft runs up here to clerestory level, but the piers themselves have been altered in the C14. Chantry chapel N of the N aisle founded in 1307, with cusped lancets and also two-light windows (the arcade joining it to the church is C19). Chantry chapel S of the S aisle founded in 1447, with three-light windows under segmental heads. Two-storey sacristy at the NE corner late C15 or C16, all three E windows Perp. The huge main window, an impressive design with seven lights of panel tracery – two threes gathered into sub-arches, the seventh running straight from top to bottom – is an authentic replica of 1865. 1865 also, by *Teulon*, the outer S aisle with its fussy gables. So the grand original design is well and truly wrought around. – STAINED GLASS. A complete C19 set, something which does not help the medieval effect. Most of the artists are known, so a list may help, though not much of it is worth attention. Main E window by *O'Connor*, S aisle E window by *Wailes*. Windows in the SE chantry by *Clayton & Bell*. Window in the outer S aisle by *Kempe*, easily recognizable. The only memorable glass is by *Heaton & Co.*: w end outer S aisle, w lancet in S aisle, w end N aisle. Violent colours, browns and purples, a real attempt to make the whole window speak as a pattern of glass, and, especially in the first of these, vivid and passionate design, almost Pre-Raphaelite. – MONUMENTS. Thomas Clark, early C15. Headless Priest. What is left is 2 ft 6 in long. Chancel. – Engaging naïve C15 brass to a Lady, S chancel aisle. Unnamed, 18 in. long. – Sir Thomas de Braose † 1395. Life-size stone effigy in armour, a stock, stiff figure. – Thomas Hoo † 1485. Canopied altar

tomb with much more life in the carving than usual. Canopy
on triangular arches, fan-vaults and pendants inside. How
much of this is late C16? – the enchanting carving in the
frieze of an angel playing the lute must surely be. – Elisabeth
Delves † 1654. By *Edward Marshall*, for a long time attributed
to Fanelli. Marshall was the sculptor who carried through
Stone's ideas to the next generation. This is therefore a well
carved figure on a restrained classical tomb-chest. He lacked
Stone's imagination, and so the carving inspires respect but
no more. Full-size recumbent figure, expressionless features,
unpleasantly shiny marble. – C18 tablets shoved under the
tower. One is by *Westmacott Jun*. There was also apparently
one to Mrs Duncomb † 1705 by *James Hardy*. Is it in the
ringing chamber?

ST MARK, North Street. Originally 1840 by *W. Moseley*. Nothing of this is left (except perhaps the nave roof), and the
character is all that of the 1870 rebuilding by *Habershon &
Brock*. A very personal, effective, purely C19 character it is
too, as uninhibited as Burges would have been. w front with
two wild gables and a tall SW tower and octagonal spire.
Everything rock-faced, including the bottom stage of the
spire; all the detail small-scale yet forceful. The transition
from tower to spire is pure fun, as it might have been in the
C13. Inside, tall polished granite piers, tall aisles, and tie-beam
aisle roofs with details worthy of H. H. Richardson. It is a
relief in South East England to come across something so
unaffectedly of its time without any worries about what the
Ecclesiologist might say. Chancel extended 1888, when the
STAINED GLASS was put in the E window, by *Mayer* of
Munich. – SCREEN. Hard and spiky, catching the mood of the
church exactly.

TOWN HALL, Market Square. Built by the Duke of Norfolk in
1812, rebuilt except for the façade in 1888. The sort of design
which made some sweeping architectural change in the C19
inevitable – as deeply sunk in eclecticism as the wildest parts of
the nineteen-twenties. Central crowstepped gable, octagonal
corner turrets, three panels containing well-carved arms (a
judicious each-way bet: Royal, Duke of Norfolk's, Civic). On
the ground floor arcading whose genesis was the neo-classical
design of someone like Mylne but which has gone Norman
for novelty's sake. The cushion capitals on the doorcase have
gone even further and are decorated with ivy leaves. Even
with all this, the design is a very pleasant thing to have in a

town: its townscape value in blocking off the Causeway beyond is enormous.

Horsham, like Oxford, has a CARFAX, that is a crossroads. Horsham's has mysteriously grown to be a horseshoe-shaped street, a sort of market place, which is now crammed with street furniture (including a nice BANDSTAND of 1892) and has traffic snaking through it in all directions. It could be made nice. Mostly a depressing jumble of buildings, but they include the big WESTMINSTER BANK of 1897, by *Frederick Wheeler*, the architect of the later and better bank at Petworth, RICHMOND TERRACE of *c.*1840 with sinister Doric doorcases, and one sweet Regency villa (No. 13 in the NW corner) with Ionic pilasters.

PERAMBULATIONS

(A) *North of Carfax*

NORTH STREET starts at the NE corner. In it first a pre-war ODEON with something very phallic in front, then St Mark's church (*see* p. 244). Further out it becomes quite a good attempt at a boulevard, with indifferent modern offices on the E side and the wall of HORSHAM PARK (now U.D.C. offices) on the W. This has a blunt take-it-or-leave-it E front, Wren style, locally done. Nine bays, central pediment, central doorcase just as Wren used at Winslow, Bucks, banded rustication, not quoins, and segment-headed windows, dour concessions to the English Baroque. The date *c.*1720; the plainer garden front, also pedimented, is about twenty years later. On the other side of North Street is NORTH CHAPEL, quite a complex C16 farmhouse later made into cottages. L-shaped, with a two-storey gabled porch and an oriel window to the l. of it. Timber-framing widely spaced but very irregular – there seems to have been no incentive, even on this scale, to make up ornamental patterns. Opposite, two smaller pretty cottages giving an illusory air of a village green, dispelled by the roundabout and the really horrible front (1938) of the STATION opposite.

These cottages continue round to the l. in HURST ROAD, an extraordinary enclave like a C16 garden suburb which ought to be kept if possible, though the pressure to build there must be strong. The best is PORCH HOUSE, stone-built and early C17 with mullioned windows. Further along COLLYERS SCHOOL, founded in 1532, moved out here from Denne Road in 1892. Neither the C19 buildings (*Arthur Vernon*) nor the 1961 additions (*Godman & Kay*) are much fun. Hurst Road joins NORTH PARADE. From here back into town first past modern flats, a hopeful sign reflecting the relative nearness of London, and then SPRINGFIELD PARK, a late C18 house built in exactly the same dour spirit as Horsham Park but seventy years later. Nine bays, three storeys, pediments, utterly plain. Back to Carfax via LONDON ROAD. Here some old cottages and one villa (No. 63) of *c*.1820. Three bays with the outer bays just perceptibly curved, an extraordinarily subtle effect. Then the stucco BRUNSWICK TERRACE, which must by its name be of *c*.1820 too. Stepped uphill, an effect which the designer chose to ignore when he equipped it with pilasters. The effects are extraordinary, with no two houses the same. They culminate in No. 55, where a pilaster sits firmly on the lintel of a doorcase which has for jambs Doric half-columns with a pronounced taper. Was this man a joker, or one for whom nothing would ever come right? Further along Nos. 27–29 is a bit later (*c*.1835) and has its architectural ideas much better organized. This is quite early for a semi-detached house out of London. Opposite, OLD HOUSE is C18 with double bow front, and No. 18, almost in Carfax, has flimsy neo-Tudor detail on its stucco front. The great trouble with all these N parts of Horsham is their disconnectedness – bits of this, bits of that – and the through traffic which roars through them.

Further out, N of Hurst Road, beyond the railway, the CIBA LABORATORIES. The older parts of 1939 by *O'Donaghue & Halfhide*, with a squat tower, rather monstrous. Newer, lower parts at the back by *E. D. Jefferiss Mathews*, 1958, rather nice.

1 m. out NE along Crawley Road is FOREST HOSPITAL, the old Workhouse, 1838, Late Classical. Pedimented centre, lower wings concealed by single-storey links. Dull.

(B) *Main Street from E to W*

Out along the Brighton road, occasional cottages and C19 suburbia for about a mile but nothing special. Central Horsham starts with EAST STREET. At the corner of DENNE ROAD No. 3 with one close-timbered gable. The tiny MARKET SQUARE opens out here; on the l. entirely filled by the front of the Town Hall (*see* p. 244), which blocks the view to the secluded Causeway. Then comes MIDDLE STREET, the short pedestrian section, like a sigh of relief. Alleys run off it N and s and create a town within a town. On the corner of Middle Street and Carfax a new building, which is, mercifully, modern and unaffected. In WEST STREET nothing except at the far end, with the former CORN EXCHANGE, now attached to the Black Horse Hotel, firmly and powerfully Italianate. By *Edward Burstow*, 1866. From the w end of West Street, WORTHING ROAD runs s down to the Arun. Good COTTAGES on the w side, together with the plain cottage-like UNITARIAN CHURCH (1721) and FRIENDS MEETING HOUSE (1834). The weatherboarded cottage downhill from the Meeting House is especially nice. At the bottom of the hill the motor showroom of WALTER A. WOOD. This was built in 1955 by *Louis Erdi* (who has designed many of Britain's motels) and is worth a special visit to see how ideas which elsewhere become weary clichés can be used freshly and enjoyably. One big shed with monopitch roof. The front all glass, displaying tractors, framed by walls of rubble limestone, canted forward. Elegant and decorative; alas, for every architect like Mr Erdi, there are ninety-nine of the other sort. And, in fact, his later offices for W. A. Wood in BISHOPRIC, on the way to Guildford, are not nearly so good.

(c) *Causeway*

This is the hidden, secluded part of Horsham, completely screened from the shops, leading down to the church. As an anthology of cosy Wealden buildings it would be hard to beat. Funnel-shaped, planted with lime trees in 1940 to replace an avenue which became diseased. These are already delightfully leafy. It begins on the l. with the HORSHAM MUSEUM, a big half-timbered house, *c*.1600 by the details in the gables. All plastered, a rarity (and something of a relief) in Sussex, with double gable and double overhang. Handsome. Opposite this the MANOR HOUSE, a design of 1704 by *Nathaniel Tredgold*, as blank as the other Georgian houses in Horsham. Seven bays, three storeys, a pediment, and quoins. Nice stables on the garden side.

On the l. No. 12 is an old cottage light-heartedly done up about 1870. Beside it, a narrow passage called MORTHS GARDENS gives a glimpse of astonishing garden structures like small signal boxes, put up at the same time. Beyond that two very pretty early C19 cottages, one of them (REGENCY COTTAGE) with an ordinary brick front transformed by being built on a very slight segmental curve.

Back in Causeway, the l. side continues very nobly with a stucco brick C18 group, Nos 13–17, all two-storey, nothing jarring yet nothing subservient. Meanwhile the other side has begun to do exactly the same thing in slightly earlier tile-hung terms with Nos 29–31. This part ends on the l. with Nos 19–20, weatherboarded fronts on a half-timbered building with the same sort of gable pendant as the Horsham Museum. A break, then the street reaches the churchyard gates with the apposition, appropriately enough, of a plain C18 brick house and a very pretty asymmetrical plastered cottage (FLAGSTONES), dated 1615. Beyond, to the E of the churchyard, are the depressingly genteel rebuilt ST MARY'S ALMSHOUSES of 1955 by *Denman & Son* and then the former Collyer's School, now a PRIMARY SCHOOL. The buildings, small but vivacious, were by *George Smith*, 1840, and look exactly like a Jacobean railway station.

CHESWORTH. By itself among meadows, ½ m. SE of the church. The house itself is a soigné Tudor brown study with old materials and ornamental gardens to match. Well done. It incorporates one wing of the late medieval house on the site, which was built by the Dukes of Norfolk and in which Catherine Howard spent her wild adolescence. When the fourth Duke was executed in 1572 for plotting for Mary Queen of Scots the house was forfeited to the Crown, and decayed. What is left is rather puzzling. It surely cannot have been a chapel, as it is reputed to be. E wall with one three-light and a chimneybreast, W wall with one wide single light and two bays containing blocked openings which must also have been three-light windows. Octagonal buttresses at the SW and SE corners. First-rate brick details, where they survive – e.g. the spandrels of the big windows and a cable moulding in the smaller one. All entirely Gothic, and hence probably C15, not C16.

PARTHINGS, 1 m. SW, beside the railway, on a cul-de-sac off the road to Christ's Hospital. C15 farmhouse. Close timbering with overhanging first floor and Horsham slate roof. Impressive and unrestored.

HOUGHTON

One long downhill street in a lovely position at the N end of the Arun gap, looking across the water meadows to Bury and Amberley. Although there is no group, the village has a lot of good simple cottages of all dates, probably because it has been an estate village, and is worth a special visit because of this.

ST NICHOLAS. Almost rebuilt in 1857, but done in such an unaffected style that it has far more character than most restorations. Architect unknown. It is astonishing how late into the C19 the local men in Sussex maintained their common sense. All lancets (is the E window, with its group of three, original?), big spaces, big beam-like kingpost roof. As a genuinely unsophisticated Victorian village interior it is well worth a look; even that least sympathetic of Victorian materials, pitch-pine, looks pleasant and natural in the pews and roof here. The S doorway, with a subtle stop-chamfer, looks original C13 also. – FONT. Gargantuan and octagonal, C15 style but thickened up immensely. So is it late C16 or C17?

The sequence of cottages starts at the uphill end (W) with the GEORGE AND DRAGON, timber-framed with flint infilling. Opposite is HOUGHTON HOUSE, plain L-shaped mid C18, and then, on the N side again, a handsome pair of estate cottages (Nos 16 and 17), dated 1846, with wavy bargeboards. On the same side, at the corner of the lane to Bury, OLD FARMHOUSE, bulky and thatched. One half flint (with timbers painted on!) and the other half-timber with an overhang.

Opposite this a cul-de-sac lane runs down to the best cottages in Houghton: first a good BARN, then Nos 26 and 28, both thatched, with various combinations of flint and half-timber due to piecemeal rebuilding; and No. 20, one of the best in Sussex. Regular timber frame with flint panels and original casement windows. It looks early C17 and is a worthy companion to the more famous earlier cottage at Bignor.

Finally, just W of the church, HOUGHTON PLACE looks entirely C18 and C19 outside but keeps a late medieval roof of tie-beams and kingposts.

HOYLE FARM see HEYSHOTT

HUNSTON

Immediately S of Chichester; fertile flat fields and too much untidy building. Church and manor house are by themselves.

ST LEDGER (i.e. St Leodegar, a C7 bishop of Autun). There are very few Sussex churches for which absolutely nothing can be said. Alas, this is one of them. By *A. W. Blomfield*, 1885.

MANOR HOUSE, opposite the church. A long plain front (nine
bays) of c.1670, stone with brick dressings.

KIPSON BANK, ½ m. SW. Nice pattern book Palladian farmhouse, three bays and two storeys.

IFIELD see CRAWLEY, p. 206

8020

IPING

W of Midhurst, in the Rother valley. Old cottages, church, mill,
and five-arch bridge in the familiar Rother style, but they never
come together to form a group like Chithurst or Stedham.
Perhaps the mill is responsible, with its disparate buildings and
large floral gardens.

ST MARY. 1840 by *Thomas Greenshields*, but rebuilt except for
the tower in 1886 by *Loftus Brock*. A heavy, naïve sandstone
building: not a lot to be said for it. – PLATE. Set, 1568 and
1635. – MONUMENT. Peter Bettesworth † 1725. Nice crisp
late C18 tablet. Unsigned.

ITCHENOR see WEST ITCHENOR

1020

ITCHINGFIELD

SW of Horsham, near the strange prickly skyline of Christ's
Hospital. The land near the church has a panoramic view N to
the Surrey hills, unexpected in this close, lush landscape. Only
a few cottages by the church – another unusual thing for a
village near Horsham; the rest scattered about in hamlets like
Barns Green, to the S.

ST NICHOLAS. At first sight more Essex than Sussex, with its
timber belfry. Up to 1865, when *Scott* added an aisle, this
must have been an impressively sheer building. The N side
still is, with tall walls and nothing but Norman windows. It
formed a single rectangular space without a chancel arch, an
unexpected plan. The chancel was rebuilt in 1713, which may
explain it: but the C12 windows were re-used, and they are
larger than the westernmost window in the nave. So perhaps
there was a C12 eastward extension of an early Norman apsed
room like North Marden. C12 windows on the S side of the
chancel too, the westernmost made into a 'low-side' by the
odd expedient of popping a two-light C14 window under it.*

---

* On the N side, a complete Norman AUMBRY with unmoulded arch and
plain abaci.

The w window is also Dec, and now faces into the belfry. Scott transferred one good C15 window to his new aisle. The belfry itself has lean-to aisles to N and S but not to the W. When it was built in the C15 there was no existing tower and it was simply butted against the old W front. Shingles above, massive vertical weatherboarding below. It is built up, as usual, on four posts with diagonal bracing between them. – PLATE. Patens, 1678 and 1719; Flagon, 1748.

Sequestered leafy churchyard, and in it the PRIEST'S HOUSE, a rare and lovable survival. Tiny half-timbered building tucked under a tree, looking quite unrestored and just like a toy. It was probably used as a temporary lodging for a travelling priest (from Sele Priory). The oldest (E) part is C15, the rest is probably of c.1600, when it became an almshouse. Just N of Barns Green, which is largely Victorian, SANDHILLS, a good C16 building, formerly a farm, half-timbered with random framing. In the hamlet itself, a completely unspoilt village pub, the QUEEN'S HEAD, and BENNETTS, a timber-framed house which has a lovable mixture of frilly dormers and brick-nogging in diagonal patterns added in the C19. The big house here is MUNTHAM, a perfunctory neo-Tudor design by *J. P. St Aubyn*, 1887. Not worth a look, perhaps; yet in everything but the details it could be by Norman Shaw. Nearly symmetrical, very carefully proportioned and grouped. Further E, beside the railway, SHARPENHURST FARM, the old frame faced this time with brick and weatherboarding.

IVORYS *see* COWFOLD

KING EDWARD VII SANATORIUM
2 m. NW of Midhurst

8020

By *Adams, Holden & Pearson*, that is probably by the young *Charles Holden*, 1903–6; immense but not at all crushing; certainly one of the best buildings of its date in the country. The main building faces S on the crest of a ridge and a mixture of gabled Free Tudor and artless classical motifs has been used on a fifty-three bay façade so that it always seems friendly and humane. The whole group is a model of how to build very large institutions – something we have not yet learnt. Wings canted slightly to catch the sun: at the W end is the CHAPEL, a very carefully thought out building. It is L-shaped with the altar diagonally set in the angle of the L (one nave for men, one for women) – in effect two churches with one altar.

The inner sides of the L face SE, are almost completely glazed (open, originally) and have loggias. The style again is a mixture of Tudor and round arches. – WOODWORK (pulpits, altar) by *C. R. Ashbee*'s Guild. – CHANDELIER in front of the altar, big, with very delicate ironwork, typical of 1900, Art Nouveau in effect but not in style.

2000   KINGSTON BUCI

Between Shoreham and Portslade, an area that has lost all its old patterns and is waiting, unhappily, for new ones. Church and house are still by themselves among a few fields. Buci probably means *beau site*: it has also, naturally, been corrupted to -by-Sea. On the sea, or rather opposite the mouth of the Adur, there are hard-bitten cottages, a lot of coal on the quayside, and a pretty, small stone LIGHTHOUSE built in 1846.

ST JULIAN. Pleasant and unremarkable outside, but a lovely interior, thanks to the tall and narrow N aisle, lit only by a W lancet, and the big C18 pulpit, placed exactly at the point where it is most dramatic and effective. This is really the principle of landscape gardening taken inside. But even without this, very few parish churches have such unerring proportions and relationship of parts. Three-cell building, the middle part a tower without transepts. All the details now C13 or later, but the plan is obviously older. The nave walls C11 and probably pre-Conquest by the proportions. The E parts rebuilt in the C13, and the tower given a serene, powerful vault with moulded ribs, resting on clustered shafts with round abaci – not at all a village effect. E and W tower arches have three chamfered orders, and the inner faces are cut away to allow the vault ribs to reach their springing. The big and beautifully proportioned arches of the N aisle are C13 too. Standard Sussex style, very assured, e.g. the bases and the stop-chamfers. Two bays. Lancets and simple Perp windows; E window modern. – WOODWORK. First and foremost the PULPIT. Two-decker, classical sounding-board, but the rest made up with re-used linenfold panels. – Two medieval BENCH ENDS, BOX PEWS, and also a rarity, a SINGING DESK (N aisle). It looks Jacobean. – SCREEN. Dec, with a wing motif of hanging ogees, but very restored. – PLATE. Cup and Paten, Flemish (?), C16 (?). – MONUMENT. Lewknor tomb and Easter Sepulchre, in the usual place on the N side of the chancel. Late Perp; canopied top adequately done, an ogee against vertical panelling, small groups of the Resurrection, Pietà, and Trinity, too badly defaced to guess their quality.

KIPSON BANK *see* HUNSTON

KIRDFORD

0020

A gracious place, with almost the air of a small town, in the middle of the Weald NE of Petworth. The centre of the village is a small oblong green, not much more than a wide street, with the church at the S end. What makes it special is the grave formality of the row of big horse-chestnut trees up the centre. The effect is of a French *place* done in purely English terms.

ST JOHN THE BAPTIST. Admirably solid and straightforward, an epitome of Wealden building. All Burgate stone with Horsham slate roof. Originally C12 nave and chancel; the blocked S doorway remains, heavy and impressive. Two orders with cushion capitals, the same character as Ewhurst in Surrey. The C13 added a big and long N aisle with standard three-bay arcade: the E window of the aisle is Dec. Thereafter, straightforward C15 alterations – good windows in aisle and chancel and a very odd sacristy to the N of it with a heavy lean-to roof. It has a tunnel-vault inside with thick chamfered ribs. The W tower is C15 too, the heavy details fitting the materials perfectly. Angle buttresses, three-order tower arch without capitals, three-light W window below, segment-headed openings above which have lost their tracery, giving an effect of *c.*1700. The mouldings show them to be Perp, of the same type as the tower of Arundel church: in fact the advowson belonged to Arundel College after 1376. Wooden W porch, a charming mixture of medieval and Elizabethan details. The C19 dealt fairly lightly with Kirdford: new windows on the S side of the nave, and a new chancel arch, C13 in style, which looks like a replica. – FONT. Plain and octagonal. The odd thing is the date: 1620. – BENCHES. N aisle. A very simple set, probably C16. – COMMUNION RAIL. Late C17. – PLATE. Cup, 1601; Cup and Paten, 1622. – STAINED GLASS. Medieval glass, a little of it coloured, in one of the lancets of the N aisle. It came from local furnaces: Kirdford, like Chiddingfold in Surrey, was a glass-making centre.

Good cottages in the main street, brick, tile-hung, and occasionally stone built. The FORESTERS ARMS, a little further W, is a delightful example of unconscious grouping. With tile-hung parts from the C16 to the C19. May it never be modernized, or even smartened up in the prevailing architectural fashion.

BARKFOLD HOUSE, ¾ m. E. Originally a small stone-built C17 house. The early C19 added or converted a big three-storey porch with crowstepped top and windows generally, the late C19 added two-storey wings.

Good cottages at BALLS CROSS, 1½ m. W, and something more in LANGHURST FARM – a long, low, stone-built front of c.1600 with small mullioned windows and the air of immense solidity which fascinated Voysey three centuries later.

KNEPP CASTLE
Between Shipley and West Grinstead

1020

Built by *Nash* in 1809, immediately after West Grinstead Park (*see* p. 371), but surprisingly different. Stucco, not stone, and much more flamboyant. Symmetrical entrance front with four turrets, and big circular tower housing the staircase in the middle of the rear elevation. Ancillary towers of various sizes and shapes quickly dispel any feeling of regimentation. The really delightful thing about Knepp is the plan, which combines inside this apparently careless exterior a beautifully related sequence of rooms. Hexagonal vestibule, with a passage leading off l. to the Gun Room. Octagonal hall with circular staircase beyond, octagonal salon, rectangular library with a disarming window-niche formed inside one of the turrets. So all the apparently silly details were made to serve a useful purpose.

Knepp was burnt out in 1904. The details were reproduced exactly, a remarkable thing to do at that time. Except for one or two fireplaces, they are simple lightweight Gothick, similar to West Grinstead – pretty Gothick friezes to all the main rooms, each with a different pattern.* The most impressive thing is the stairwell and staircase, which is circular and entirely cantilevered. Cast-iron handrail. Big three-dimensional Gothic window half-way up. In one room complete panelling and chimneypiece, dated 1655, in others fine late C18 chimneypieces. They were all brought in, the chimneypieces after the fire from Irish Georgian houses. Also after the fire the splendid mid C19 chandelier from Dorchester House, London, was bought for Knepp Castle. Complete

* One is four-light church windows with cusped interlacing tracery, a motif of which 1800 was very fond.

set of OUTBUILDINGS and kitchen gardens, and splendid Picturesque landscaping in the park. A big lake, the former hammer pond, runs N and S near the house.

KNEPP CASTLE RUIN, by the Worthing Road, ¾ m. SE of the house. Fragment of a Norman keep. Small motte with one fragment of masonry on it, 30 ft high, containing two round-headed windows. Built by the de Braose family, probably in the C11.

LACKENHURST see SHIPLEY

LANCING
1000

NE of Worthing on the edge of the Downs. The village street is by-passed by the main road (A27) and keeps some of the old character, flint walls and cottages, without any noteworthy buildings. But new building is all round it – for a mile S, as far as the sea, and, especially bad, a valley of pre-war bungalows between Lancing and Sompting which is often quoted as a copy-book example of how to spoil the landscape. Postwar planning can and has prevented anything as cruel as this going up since.

ST JAMES THE LESS. Typically Sussex, closely massed and withdrawn. Flint and roughcast. Low crossing tower, lean-to aisles, narrow clerestory originally without windows. Spatially it is in fact a coherent design of c.1300, more impressive inside than outside, with satisfying proportions of wide nave and narrow aisles, and of the rhythm of the tower arches.

The detailed sequence of events is much harder to describe; the reconstruction evidently took about fifty years and was piecemeal, in spite of today's overriding impression of cohesion. If only a similar rebuilding of 1910–60 was as harmonious! Extreme E and W ends in fact retain C12 masonry, including part of a billet frieze near the E window. Reconstruction also accounts for the position of the other C12 detail at Lancing, an impressive doorway which now serves as the outer door to the S porch. It is of the type which occurs occasionally all over England which has purely Gothic mouldings* but a round arch. In this case it is probably due to Chichester. Jamb shafts, and capitals carved with stiff foliage. Its date must be very near 1200. The chancel seems to have been reconstructed first, with two- and three-light windows and also trefoiled lancets in blind arcading. Then came tower, nave, and aisles: octagonal piers and abaci, double-chamfered

* Inner order chamfered, outer order a deeply undercut roll.

arches. On the N, S, and W sides of the tower the mouldings
die away into the imposts. But some kind of buttressing seems
to have been needed, probably whilst an existing tower was
being replaced, and this explains the pair of blind arches at
the E ends of the aisles (which continue for an extra bay to
surround the tower). Good kingpost nave roof. Aisle windows
square-headed, of two lights: Perp windows N and S of the
tower, which was lowered in 1618. All windows harshly
renewed, some of them quite recently. – Ogee-headed
RECESS in the N side of the chancel. Big-scale, thickly carved.
– FONT. Square C12 bowl, very narrow, divided into square
panels. – STAINED GLASS. Three Pre-Raphaelite windows of
1866 (N side of chancel, E end S aisle, SE window S aisle).
Bright colours, languid faces: not great but characteristic.
Who did them? – PLATE. Cup, 1685.

SECONDARY SCHOOL, at the corner of A27 and Upper
Boundstone Lane. Built in 1960–1 by the *County Architect's
Department*. Three-storey classroom block plus workshops,
etc. Curtain walling and cedar boarding. Decent and careful,
but without the refinement of the Bognor Regis Grammar
School.

LANCING COLLEGE.* High up on a beautiful exposed site above
the Adur, some atonement for the many heaps of ugliness
which the C19 unloaded blindly on to the English landscape.
The huge chapel is what everyone will remember, but the
school buildings are just as good in their quieter way. Halfway
up the drive, chapel and quadrangle suddenly compose so
perfectly that the elusive dream of the Gothic Revival suddenly seems to be a possibility. This is nearer to Pugin's
vision than any of his own buildings.

The college was founded in 1848 by Nathaniel Woodard,
who was then curate of New Shoreham. His aim was a
comprehensive and classless federation of schools, 'the union
of classes by a common system of education'; by the time of
his death in 1891 there were fifteen of them (including
Ardingly, p. 398, and Hurstpierpoint, p. 542). There are now
twenty, independent of the State system yet without the
covert exclusiveness of the public schools, fulfilling a need as
urgent now as it ever was in the C19. Woodard was lucky in
his architect: *R. C. Carpenter*, whom he had met whilst
working at Bethnal Green, was almost the only person in

* Mr Nicholas Taylor has supplied a considerable amount of information
on the college.

England who could design Gothic buildings with the right
mixture of competence, sincerity, and common sense. Pugin
and Butterfield would have been too fanatical, the rank-and-
file would not have cared enough. Because Carpenter initiated no twist of style and produced no decorative fireworks,
he is passed over too often, yet he more than anybody else
could have made the Gothic Revival work. His death at forty-
three was as great a loss as Pugin's.

Carpenter's first designs were dated 1848. Building began
in 1854, Carpenter died in 1855, the pupils moved in in 1858.
Work continued under Carpenter's partner *William Slater*,
then under his son *R. H. Carpenter*, always a little fussier and
more mechanical than his father. The chapel, by R. H.
Carpenter, was begun in 1868 and got to its present state in
1911. All the work was done by direct labour, all the stone
quarried in the college quarry at Scaynes Hill, near Haywards
Heath, by one family.

The lower quadrangle shows Carpenter's quiet virtues 54b
to perfection. Three storeys, restrained stone dressings, plenty
of plain flintwork between. A cloister runs round three sides,
the arch in each bay given a cinquefoil head. The N and S sides
have even parapets, the W side, the library and former chapel,
has gables*. Restrained and contemplative, but immensely
strong. The S front, facing towards the sea, has the same soft-
spoken power applied to an asymmetrical elevation. The
court is not quite closed: on the l. the headmaster's house (the
free-standing block in front of this is a very good match by
the then headmaster, Dr *Blakiston*, and his clerk of works,
1930), on the r. the pricklier, more cerebral, and more commonplace dining hall. The outward view is an amazing hybrid of
Downs, ribbon development, Portslade power station, New
Shoreham with its church looking like a stray from Flanders.
The foreground is a busy civil airfield. It must be a wonderfully varied and exciting mixture to grow up with.

Beyond, in the upper quadrangle, the S and E sides are mostly
by Carpenter & Slater, the N side, with the ugly School Hall,
mostly by R. H. Carpenter. It was completed in 1913 with
the W side (Gibbs' House) by *Maxwell Ayrton*. The style is
decent neo-Gothic and very near Carpenter's, but with all
the conviction gone. Later Ayrton tower block and classroom
block to the N (1930). If additions are ever thought of, they

* It is spoilt by the central clock gable, added in 1906 by an old boy, *P. A.
Robson.*

9—s.

must clearly be in a modern style as adaptable and humane as the original. Formalistic fiddling and flashy brutalities would be put to shame here.

54a   Finally, the CHAPEL. This represents a triumph of Woodard's will-power. It is built over a mixture of flint and clay, which means that the foundations have to be taken down sixty feet to the chalk; and there was no real building fund. It was built by his third son, Billy, and Woodard rushed ahead work on the apse to the full height before he died so that there should be no possibility of cutting down the design. Billy Woodard carried on early in the C20, adding the vault himself without professional help. 'There was a time', says the guide, 'when the vault was complete but two of the buttresses were missing. Professional architects were shocked at the risk, but Billy was in no hurry.' And in fact the dimensions are huge. The present incomplete length is 145 ft, the internal height 94 ft – only Westminster Abbey, York Minster, and Liverpool Cathedral are higher. Carpenter designed a huge N tower which was luckily not built, for it would have wrecked the sheer soaring composition. Work has now started (1962) on the remaining bay of the nave, which is to a sober Gothic design by *Dykes Bower*. W of this there is to be a narthex.

The outside is magnificent, with the imitative detail carried off by the total romantic effect, a Gothic chapel as Turner might have imagined it in paint or Mendelssohn might have personified it in music. But inside, doubts creep in slowly and unwillingly. The detail is C13 French, the proportions late C15 French; tall arcades, tiny triforium, huge clerestory in the apse. The triforium is glazed too, increasing the sense of height – the effect like Flamboyant churches such as St Nicholas de Port near Nancy. But really, this is the same family as buildings like the Catholic church at Arundel (*see* p. 90), even though it is so much more wholehearted and effective here. Instead of building a school and thinking in Gothic, as R. C. Carpenter did, it starts out by wanting to build a *Gothic* school chapel. So all the details come unnatural, and there is an immense gulf between this and a late church by J. L. Pearson, which is a close parallel in style, space, and religious intent. It is the whole nineteenth-century tragedy that good intentions and architectural talent are useless unless they are tuned in to the right wavelength.

Nine bays plus the apse; crypt underneath with impressive

octagonal chapel at the E end. On the S side, war memorial
cloister by *Temple Moore*, 1921–7, his sober spatial sure-
footedness lost in the need for elaborate detail. Inside, two
chantries by him near the ends of the aisles, equally elaborate
and mechanical. The S one contains a lifeless effigy of Woodard
by *P. Bryant Baker*, 1915, and a reredos by *Comper*. – STALLS.
Canopies from Eton College Chapel. By *Sir George Gilbert
Scott*, 1851, carved by *William Thompson* of *Rattee & Kett*,
good proportions due to whatever medieval prototype was
selected (Nantwich?), but grudgingly mechanical. – STATUE.
St Nicholas (S aisle), C17 Flemish; probably from Aerschot.
– LECTERN. By *Bainbridge Reynolds*, c.1900. Heavy, clumsy
style, not at all *Art Nouveau*. – STAINED GLASS. E window of
the S aisle by *Comper*, and as limp as his glass design usually
is. – PAINTINGS. Woodcut Stations of the Cross by *Brangwyn*
to his usual standard, and one much better painting of the
Crucifixion (S aisle) by *Christopher Shepherd*, a haunting
composition of greys. Mr Shepherd did it in 1961 when he
was seventeen and still at the college. Also several copies of
old masters and originals by *Alonso Cano* and *Gaspar de Crayer*.
– CANDLESTICKS. Two, C18 copies of a pair by the C16 artist
Annibale Fontana in the Certosa at Pavia. – TAPESTRIES.
Three, behind the high altar, designed by *Lady Chilston* and
woven at Merton Abbey in 1933. Huge – the biggest in England until the new tapestries at Coventry – but hopelessly weak.
– PLATE. Two processional Crosses; the larger South German,
the smaller C17 Sienese and as naïve as if it had been
made in Herefordshire. – Two CRUCIFIXES. That in the
Lady Chapel (N aisle) is C17 South German and ordinary;
that on the high altar is of c.1490, from Toledo, and worth a
special look. Intense, frilly design, the same forceful all-over
covering of surfaces as Spanish Late Gothic architecture.
But it is not decoration for its own sake; it is a burningly fierce
religious expression too. The matching base and candlesticks
are by *Bainbridge Reynolds*.

LANGLEY GREEN *see* CRAWLEY, p. 207

LAVANT

8000

A group of villages immediately N of Chichester on the edge of
the Downs. West Lavant has no church and is a collection of

farms; Mid Lavant is on the main Chichester–Midhurst road, spoilt by heavy traffic and oddly straggling and boring. East Lavant, the best of the three, is ½ m. E beside the river Lavant. All share splendid views N to the Downs.

St NICHOLAS, Mid Lavant. Terribly renewed and swept clean. Originally C12 nave, with one small window in the S side; originally C13 chancel with some of the usual plain lancets. N aisle 1844. Awful C19 triple chancel arch. The restoration which took away all the character also, for good measure, made the church's one notable possession quite inaccessible. This is a MONUMENT by *Bushnell* to Dame Mary May † 1681, with 'life size recumbent effigy, apparently pockmarked as in life,' said Dallaway; 'capricious, but the portrait exact and the execution good'. This was walled up under the floor. The man responsible for all this seems to have been *Woodyer*. – PLATE. Paten, given 1686; Chalice 1686 (?).

St MARY, East Lavant. As at Mid Lavant, an appalling restoration (of 1863 by *G. M. Hills*); but here some interest in the original work as well. Attractive from a distance because of the very plain brick tower of 1671 on the S side of the nave, the windows at last round-headed. Close up, the fussy C19 limestone windows are all too evident. C12 nave – the W doorway remains, probably *c*.1140–50, and not even renewed. It has two orders of zigzag at ninety degrees to one another, separated by a roll-moulding and jamb shafts with scallop capitals. Inside, two-bay C13 arcade, double-chamfered, of the elegant type which has the inner order continued at the responds as a shaft (cf. Ferring). All the rest is 1863. – WOODWORK. Five STALLS with MISERICORDS in the chancel, standard work. – STAINED GLASS. S side of chancel, by *Kempe*, 1883, before he went green. – RECESS under the tower, moved from the chancel. Damaged cinquefoil arch, crocketed straight-sided canopy over it, flanked by ornate pinnacles, one a restoration. Early C14, the same general type as Bepton, but not so vital. – PLATE. Chalice and Paten, inscribed 1618.

At West Lavant a big plain brick FARMHOUSE dated 1711: in Mid Lavant nothing special except THE SMALL HOUSE on the W of the main road by *E. S. Prior*, 1912, L-shaped, flint and brick and not very attractive or imaginative, although the combination of E gable and chimney is nice. East Lavant is largely mid C19 estate cottages but also, up the hill, flint and half-timber. The biggest house in the village is MEADE HOUSE, the former rectory, flint and stone neo-Tudor of 1834.

LEE FARM see STOPHAM

LICKFOLD see LURGASHALL and WIGGONHOLT

LINCH

8020

A set of scattered hamlets NW of Midhurst, much more remote than one would expect, in splendid jagged hilly heathland. One of the hamlets, REDFORD, could easily be in Monmouthshire with its cottages thrown against a bracken hillside. The church is N of this, at WOODMANSGREEN.

ST LUKE. Originally a small church of 1705, but nothing of that is to be seen now except the S door, still Gothic: the rest all smothered in very unpleasant alterations of 1886 by *Lacy W. Ridge*. – STAINED GLASS. Two small panels, probably German and probably C15, of the Descent from the Cross and the Ascension.

WOODMANSGREEN FARM, next to the church. Late C16 farmhouse, keeping one mullioned window in the E gable. More impressive is the complete quadrangle of tiled sandstone barns just S of it, some of them clearly as late as the C19, making a composition of hipped roofs which would have defeated Lutyens. Inside the quad, an octagonal dung-pit with open sides, *c.*1870.

HOLLYCOMBE, 1 m. NW of Woodmansgreen near the Hampshire border. A small house in very friendly free Tudor of *c.*1900. Lovely situation, perched in a small col between hills with views both N and S. The S front long and low, two-storeyed, with a loggia, the N front with a gable and a square-topped tower. Although the details belong to the C16, this has all the informality, serviceability, and most of the freshness of a Voysey house. It is really astonishingly appropriate, and without any applied mannerisms. The original house here was a thatched *cottage orné* by Nash.

LINCHMERE

8030

The north-westernmost village in Sussex, just over the border from Haslemere – but very different from Surrey's houses in pinewoods and cosiness. Rough rural group high up in lumpish hills – a tiny green with a few farms around and the church at the S end, overlooking a steep valley.

ST PETER. A small hill-chapel, enlarged out of all recognition: inner aisle 1856 by *W. Woodyer*, outer aisle (timber arcade) 1906 by *P. M. Johnston*. Old work now on the S and E sides: Norman nave with round-headed W door, blocked window now re-set between nave and aisle. Eastward extension in the C13 with several lancets and the best part of the church – an E window of *c*.1260, simply two lights under a circle, plate tracery. At the W end two tall slim columns supporting a slim stone bell-turret. A sundial on the turret is dated 1654 and is probably the date of the whole thing. – PLATE. Chalice, 1538. – ORGAN CASE. 1953, by Capt. *Schweder*, incorporating C17 cherubs. – SCULPTURE. Italian relief of the Seven Deadly Sins, *c*.1300, brought from France.

LITTLE BOGNOR see FITTLEWORTH

LITTLEHAMPTON

Littlehampton is pleasant but exasperatingly disjointed. The old town is on the E bank of the Arun a little way up from the mouth, a familiar small-scale affair of hard-bitten flint cottages running E from the river to the church, like Shoreham or Newhaven. The seaside fever hit Littlehampton in the early 1800s and a few terraces were erected by themselves near the sea $\frac{1}{2}$ m. to the SE. The two parts were only linked up by building in the late C19, and the expansion has meant that the close-built character of the old part has almost disappeared. So the final result is a rather bewildering mixture of Old Hastings and Bournemouth.

ST MARY THE VIRGIN. 1826 by *G. Draper*, but completely recast in 1934 by *Randoll Blacking* in the eerie disembodied Gothic of the very end of the Gothic Revival. Brick outside, cemented walls inside, everything light and papery. Yet Blacking clearly had a sound spatial sense, and, like Comper, a sound sense of how to make religious spaces (they are not always the same thing), so that the result is far more of a church than most religious buildings of the 1930s – or the 1960s. Galleried aisled nave, transepts and short chancel, apse with its own westward arch. Most of the fittings – pulpit, rood screen – are in C17 classical style, which is also how Comper would have done it: the way they are related to the complicated space gives one a lot of respect for the designer.

ST CATHERINE (R.C.), Beach Road. Violently mid-Victorian: the presbytery has wooden tracery in its dormers. Mostly 1864 by one of the *Hadfields*.

CONVENT OF THE HOLY FAMILY, Norfolk Road. Good new school extensions, in a deceptively simple style, stone-faced, by *H. Bingham Towner*, 1960. Yet the same firm at the same time is putting up awful neo-Gothic churches (*see* Billingshurst). How odd.

The old town is quickly seen and in fact has very little to offer: one plain late C18 terrace in SURREY STREET near the river and the boat yards, a few cottages at the W end of CHURCH STREET, at the other end of the curving but banal High Street. One of them, VINE COTTAGE, is dated 1727; another, FUCHSIA COTTAGE, is a pretty piece of 1840 seaside Gothic on a tiny scale.

The sea front is ½ m. away to the SE, and was built from the farther or E end, nearest to Rustington. The stages can almost be followed year by year. The first part is NORFOLK PLACE, which was intended to be a square but fizzled out with plain buildings and backyards; then SOUTH TERRACE, beginning with Nos 1–18, mostly *c*.1800–10, three storeys with wooden balconies, brick or stucco, by various hands – a poor relation of Brighton, but equally agreeable in its unpretentious way. It may even be possible to discern the actual piecemeal order of building, always extending further W – e.g. Nos 3–10 by one builder, Nos 11–12 by another, then Nos 13–15 carrying on again with the first design. Further W Nos 30–38 later, *c*.1830, in a miniature Belgravia style with sweeping curved bow fronts, severe and heavy at the same time, then finally, with Nos 39–47, comes the full mid-Victorian dowdiness of heavy thick window surrounds and a fussy roofline.

Further N, TODDINGTON FARM beyond the railway is basically a C17 building with brick stepped gables exactly as though it were in Norfolk, and, beside A259 on the way to Rustington, the recent GLASSHOUSE CROPS RESEARCH INSTITUTE has two-storey offices, ancillary buildings, and cottages all neatly and humanely designed by the *Ministry of Works*. For all its semi-industrial appearance it is settling into the landscape far better than any kind of applied picturesqueness.

LITTLE THAKEHAM *see* THAKEHAM

LODSWORTH
9020

Half-way between Midhurst and Petworth, in some of the loveliest and best kept countryside in England. Lodsworth itself is not quite up to the standard of its neighbours, Lurgashall and Tillington, though it would be noteworthy anywhere else. One long narrow village street running downhill to the church:

one centre at a T-junction with a big tree in it, beside the pub, then a downhill stretch with cottages on one side and a wall on the other to another T-junction where a cul-de-sac runs down to the church.

ST PETER. A magnificent situation, looking E across a wooded valley. The building, alas, is almost all bad C19: neo-Norman in the S transept (1840), spindly Gothic elsewhere. The old nave walls remain behind the new aisles, and from the look of the NW corner they seem to be of the usual Sussex C11 pattern, high and unaisled. The W tower was spared (in fact, it is the opposite of the rest and is under-restored), unbuttressed, c.1300, with a weathered W door with jamb shafts and cramped pointed head. Depressing inside. – PLATE. Set, 1567–8.

Most of Lodsworth's old cottages are pretty, but the most notable pair of buildings are later and stand next to one another where the lane runs down to the church. On the left is DOWER HOUSE, a dignified, close-mouthed building of 1728, three storeys and five bays with segment-headed surrounds to the windows, all in ashlar, the style pretty much that of Petworth. On the right is GREAT HOUSE, the late C18 equivalent, now with a pretty fanlight over the door and a pair of pretty two-storeyed wooden bow windows painted white.

MANOR HOUSE. S of the church, and from outside an apparently uninteresting stuccoed cottage. In fact the walls are substantially those of a C13 house. It was an oblong running E–W; additions and partitions have made it almost impossible to decipher, but it seems always to have been two-storeyed, the entrance represented by the present porch of the S side. Upstairs the hall must have been quite big and has an impressive plain C13 fireplace now split between two rooms. The E wall was apparently rebuilt c.1290 and the shape of the big E window of the hall remains, though blocked, visible from outside. Inside, one room has the bases of complex jambs and jamb shafts (the head of the arch with its capitals is now in the attic).

LORDINGTON see RACTON

2020

LOWER BEEDING

SE of Horsham, on the edge of the unusual landscape of St Leonard's Forest, half park and half heath. Upper Beeding is a good ten miles away (see p. 360). Scattered cottages along an A-road.

HOLY TRINITY. Built in 1840 by *H. J. Underwood* as a copy of Littlemore near Oxford, enlarged in 1864 by *Habershon*. Quiet outside, rather like Salvin; wilder inside because Habershon's arcades have coupled marble columns.

HAMMER POND, 1 m. N. A beautiful site. The old furnace pond 2b is now quiet and serene, and the former forge is now a guest house. A delightful building: small, recessed centre. Brick and green-painted weatherboarding, cared for but completely unspoilt.

At CRABTREE, 1 m. S, a very pretty farm group (PARK GATE) beside the A-road. Stone and half-timbered centre, tile-hung wings, making an L with its black weatherboarded barn. Worth any amount of pickled antiquity.

SOUTH LODGE, also at Crabtree. Some lodge! In fact a long, quiet Victorian Tudor house, beautifully sited. By *F. D. Godman*, 1883.

LOWFIELD HEATH see CRAWLEY, p. 204

LOXWOOD 0030

On the Surrey border W of Horsham. Leafy, with pleasant tile-hung cottages, but no pattern. The centre is a T-junction with an oddly urban row of shops and an oddly urban pond. Across the road from the pond a good unrestored COTTAGE, with splendidly unplanned half-timber work and a Horsham slate roof.

ST JOHN THE BAPTIST. Horrible fiddly neo-Perp of 1898 by *Roland Plumbe*. Medieval BENCHES in the aisle, the same type as Dunsfold over the Surrey border, with the ends carried up into unequal projections with knobs on them.

LUMLEY SEAT see STANSTED

LURGASHALL 9020

A glorious village NW of Petworth, under the E slopes of Blackdown, a sloping triangular green with a big tree at the top end and most of the houses along the lowest side. Like many Sussex greens, it is even now only half filled up with houses. The variety of shapes and angles of the buildings on the SE side are equal to the highest level of asymmetrical design, and it really matters very little whether they were achieved accidentally or subconsciously. Mostly stone, but the proportion of tile-hanging shows the nearness to Surrey.

ST LAURENCE. What attracts straightaway is the simple C16
lean-to timber gallery built on to the S wall of the nave. It seems
to have been used as a meeting place after Mass and later
became the village school. A similar but later gallery existed at
Fernhurst up to the C19. Behind it the tall, wide, unaisled nave
is C11, with a flat buttress remaining on both N and S sides.
The chancel C13, repaired in 1731 and then renewed in the
mid C19, including the elegant E wall, which one would not
have credited the Victorians to have thought of unaided: two
lancets wide apart, with marble nook-shafts, and a bracket
surmounted by a quatrefoil between them. The way the lobes
of the quatrefoil are deliberately made unequal is worth a
special look. Tower Perp, perhaps C14, attached to the SE corner of the nave, a position similar to that at Tillington. Sturdy
and unbuttressed, the openings two-light and square-headed
in deep, well-managed reveals. It had a spire, recently taken
down. – FONT. Dated 1661, and quite extraordinary. Square,
with slightly projecting top and base, covered entirely in lumpy
rustication. Very effective, but a formidable thing to be bap-
tized in. – PLATE. Chalice and Paten, 1563; Paten 1729;
Flagon, 1743. – MONUMENT. William Yaldwyn † 1728. A
grand city-mason's Baroque tablet, as good as it could be.
Architectural frame with open scrolled pediment and an urn
between, thick festoons of flowers spilling down on to the pediment. Beautifully designed, even to making the inscription
plate slightly curved, to fill out the volume.
The RECTORY, SW of the church, was originally a Tudor house,
but is now effectively all C19, the additions as sober and sensible as though Voysey had done them. By *William White*,
1854.
1 m. SW is LICKFOLD, only a hamlet but with a better selection
of old and picturesque cottages than many small towns. There
are several good regular timber-framed cottages, late C16 or
C17: the best is at the W corner of the tiny triangular green.
At the SE corner is LICKFOLD COTTAGE, a weird early C18
mason's front, jumbled and crowded with detail. Seven bays
and two storeys plus a pedimented parapet (!). All windows
have heavy panels above them, some window spaces have been
blocked and the blocked areas tile-hung, an unnerving sight.
As well as all this there are odd small square and rectangular
panels.
A little further S another FARMHOUSE, just SE of the tin chapel,
with a splendid build-up of roof-lines. T-shaped, the stem

tile-hung, the cross piece rubble stonework, a little higher and built up in two stages. This gives three sets of gables, and as each is hipped a magnificently chunky outline results. The older parts look C17.

LYMINSTER

Near the River Arun N of Littlehampton. More a collection of houses behind flint walls than a village – most of the coast villages must have looked like this before the C20. The church is by itself further W on a bare site with a splendid view across water meadows to Arundel's exciting, un-English skyline.

ST MARY MAGDALENE. From the N a typical Sussex picture, with huge roof sweeping down over nave and aisle to within a few feet of the ground, and a general impression of C13 solidity. This is not the whole story, as can be guessed at the NE corner of the nave and seen clearly on the S side: the bones of Lyminster church are a big aisleless Saxon nave and chancel, tall and narrow as they always were – and this also is typically Sussex.

The church was part of the Benedictine nunnery of Lyminster: the unmistakable Saxon remains are the main walling of both nave and chancel, and hence the whole proportions of the interior, high, narrow, and majestic. The walls are 20 ft high, and only 2 ft 6 in. thick: the chancel arch is the same height and only 8 ft 2 in. wide – plain and unmoulded with plain abaci. (It has another set of plain abaci about 5 ft lower which match the late C12 arcade; if they are genuine, it suggests rather amusingly that the Normans were quite nonplussed with the strange proportions that they found.) A blocked arch in the S wall of the nave has the same very plain character and the head of a window appears in one spandrel of the arcade. This is Transitional, c.1160–70, the same general character as Rustington: pointed unmoulded arches, plain responds, two scallop capitals and one capital with a very early form of stiff-leaf carving at each corner. The aisle roof is part of a most complicated piece of timber-framing independent of the arcade, which seems like an emergency repair, perhaps late medieval: something similar occurs in the same circumstances at Chobham in Surrey. The W doorway, now inside the tower, is early C12, of two plain orders; the tower base C13, plain with angle buttresses: several C13 lancets, and a big sexfoil window in the middle of the S side of the nave (why?). Perp E window and tower top. – Trefoil PISCINA, N aisle, late C13. – MONUMENT.

Tablet to William French † 1836, by *J. M. Carew* of Brighton.
Angel and medallion as they would have been in 1800, but a
lot more extraneous detail.

9010

MADEHURST

Not a village, just a scattered handful of C19 estate cottages, two
of them flanking the church formally. But the setting is magnificent – a wooded valley in the Downs N W of Arundel. A cul-de-
sac, hence quiet and remote.

ST MARY MAGDALEN. All but rebuilt in 1864 by *T. G. Jackson*,
a sober flint job. The plain late C12 W doorway and one Dec
window in the nave remain from the old building. Mildly
outré details inside – the window splays in the aisle, the red
marble FONT. The old FONT, small and octagonal, looks early
C19. – STAINED GLASS. The glass by *Burne-Jones* was destroyed in 1944 when a flying bomb landed near the church.
Only the small tracery lights remain. – PLATE. Chalice and
Paten, 1568.

DALE PARK. Demolished in 1959. It was a plain and ugly house
by *Bonomi*, 1784.

MALTMAYES see WARNHAM

MAPLEHURST see NUTHURST

MAPSON'S FARM see SIDLESHAM

THE MARDENS

One parish, three tiny churches in the remotest part of the South
Downs, near the Hampshire border s of Harting. Scenery majestic and utterly unspoilt. East Marden has a minute centre: North
and Up Marden are just farms with a church, West Marden is a
larger hamlet without one. Portsmouth, incredibly, is only fifteen miles away from these lost places: it might as well be a hundred and fifty.

8010

NORTH MARDEN

ST MARY. Almost invisible among trees and beyond a farmyard,
on the E side of a valley which looks across at Uppark. The
simplest kind of Norman building, more common on the Continent than in England: a single apsed room quite without

additions, a good measure of the remoteness.* The only original window is high up in the W gable, but the others are all in the style of plain C12 openings and hence keep the primitive effect. The spacing around the E end is original. S doorway of *c.*1130–40; one order of zigzags with the inner edge of each chevron enclosing a ball-shape. Trefoiled C13 PISCINA in the apse. – ROYAL ARMS. George III. Only 8 in. across and made of iron.

EAST MARDEN 8010

Tiny, charming flint and tile village in a cup-shaped hollow, plain farms, cottages (one dated 1728), and church around a thatched well-head.

ST PETER. Apparently all plainest C13, though it could have been a C12 plan like North Marden given a C13 chancel. One room, no aisles and no chancel arch; triple lancet in the E end, other original lancets in N and S walls. This kind of simple interior depends on texture and gentle compounding of centuries; and at East Marden this has been swept away – not violently, but enough to leave it characterless. – FONT. Goblet shaped, i.e. plain circular cup-shape on a tapering slightly concave stem: probably late C12, and a nice piece of abstract geometry. – PLATE. Chalice, Elizabethan.

WEST MARDEN 7010

No church, but actually the biggest of the Mardens, 1 m. S of Compton. Pretty collection of flint cottages straggling up a hillside to the l. of the road from Chichester to Harting.

UP MARDEN 7010

Church and farm only, the remotest place on the Downs, 500 ft up on top of the ridge N of Stoughton. Although the surroundings are demurely leafy and rural, it is surprisingly inaccessible. The church itself, approached through a farmyard, is quite invisible from the road.

ST MICHAEL. One of the loveliest interiors in England. Atmosphere is perhaps something which ought not to have much to do with *The Buildings of England*, but at Up Marden the atmosphere is as tangible as any moulding, the slow, loving, gentle accretion century by century until it is something as

* According to Mr Rodney Hubbuck, one of only four single-cell apsida churches in England. The others are Nately Scures, Hants, Winterbourne Tomson, Dorset, and Little Tey, Essex.

organic as any of the South Downs views around it. It must not be seen in antiquarian terms or even as an interesting specimen of an unrestored church but as a visible loving testimony of the faith of successive generations. It is incredibly moving whether one is Anglican or not, whether one is religious or not. Clear glass and white or cream plaster, brick floors, plastered wagon roofs, candelabra all askew, lupins on the altar at Whitsun. It is little used, but it and the unmown churchyard are the very reverse of neglected or desecrated.

Up Marden is all c13, without a window altered: big single, simple dignified lancets, the rustic equivalent of a church like Climping. Unaisled nave and chancel, plain later c13 tower with a weatherboarded bell-chamber, lancets throughout, the E window with three grouped under a rere-arch. Trefoil-headed PISCINA. The triangular chancel arch is not, as it looks, Saxon, but an emergency c16 repair to the c13 arch which can be seen above it.* – PULPIT. Stone, Victorian, with ogee-panelled sides, but fits in perfectly. – PLATE. Chalice and Paten, 1724.

MARSH FARM see EARNLEY

8000

MERSTON

A tiny village SE of Chichester, on a loop between two main roads. Still surprisingly remote. Pleasant little street of farms and Victorian estate cottages. The church is futher S.

ST GILES. A delightful situation, among big trees with a little house like a gatehouse at the entrance to the churchyard. A disarming building, mostly roughcast, with N aisle roof that swoops down to within a few feet of the ground, leaving the N side windowless. c13 nave and chancel, as usual, with lancets (the E window is c19). The four-bay arcade is dated c14 by the VCH on the strength of the bases of the piers, but it also looks c13; standard details of abaci and arches. Perp W window, trefoil-headed PISCINA. Simple village effect.

9000

MIDDLETON

On the coast E of Bognor Regis. The surprising thing is, even now, the cornfields in among the bungalows. They cannot be due to remain very long.

* It could conceivably be Saxon work reused: the VCH suggests that it might have come from the former church at West Marden.

ST NICHOLAS. Tiny lancet chapel, built by *John Elliott* in 1849 after the old church had been swept out to sea by erosion, like Dunwich. Bellcote supported touchingly and naïvely on free-standing shafts, rather as the original early C13 builders might have done it. The w doorway is also hard to tell from original work. – PLATE. S.–g. Chalice and Paten, 1576.

MIDDLETON HOUSE *see* CHIDHAM

MIDHURST

8020

To the main-road traveller, Midhurst, like Petworth, is a bewildering series of acute ninety-degree bends combined with an inexplicable cottagey cosiness in the buildings, so different from the open market-places of Hampshire. Few towns are more deceptive, few towns withhold themselves so firmly until the traveller gets out of his car and on to his feet: few towns in particular have a more exciting relationship with the surrounding countryside. Almost all of this must in fact be due to the careful eye kept on the town by the owners of Cowdray.

ST MARY MAGDALENE AND ST DENYS. A disappointment, after the part it plays in Midhurst's townscape: there has been too much restoration (by *Lacy W. Ridge*, 1882), and the Cowdray monuments have been removed to Easebourne. The old parts are all on the s side: the base of the tower is early C13 (one tower arch, two windows). In the C16 a new nave was built N of the old, and the present s nave and chancel arcades as well as the tower top are C16, in rather sloppy Perp: octagonal piers and abaci, double-chamfered arches with the step between the chamfers stopped short of the abaci, appearing as a deep groove. All the rest is 1882 or later. – ROYAL ARMS. Flamboyantly painted Queen Anne. – PLATE. Flagon, 1736; Almsdish, 1804.

HOLY MARY (R.C.), Bepton Road. 1957 by *Guy Morgan & Partners*. The church is modern, and very dignified and successful outside: all sandstone, a shape like a segment of a circle, with the point rounded off to make the apse and the w front the circumference, divided into seven parts by vertical stone fins; six of these parts are glazed, forming the only lighting for the church, which consequently becomes one big trapezoidal room lit from behind. Unfortunately this takes away any directional emphasis, needed perhaps more in a Roman Catholic church than any other: the effect is very light and humane, but rather bewildering as the eye travels uninter-

ruptedly from side to side through the altar. However, it is
so much better and more responsible than most church building in England today that one feels that criticism is a bit churl-
ish. To be completed with a detached bell-tower and with
Madonna and Child over the central door. – SCULPTURE.
Christ on the Cross, behind the altar, by *Michael Clark*.

PERAMBULATION. The walk starts at the S end, where Midhurst begins, as all towns should, direct from the country.
SOUTH STREET runs uphill from a pond, and the first view
gives some idea of the subtlety and intricacy of the whole town:
the road splitting around a half-timbered building with the r.
branch leading past the church with a hint of a small square
on the right-hand side. A little further, and the l. branch
reveals itself as making a dog leg around a strategically placed
pub with, again, the hint of another open space beyond where
the branches reunite. Already, the town is beginning to look
like a bit of the Art of Fugue.

Then the buildings start: mostly stuccoed on the r., the SPREAD
EAGLE on the l., with a gruff seven-bay front of *c.*1700, brick
with heavy stone window surrounds, then a gabled and half-
timbered part, with overhanging first floor, probably quite
early C16. The stables carry a naïve pedimented tablet dated
1650. This brings one up to the C16 OLD MARKET HOUSE,
timber-framed with brick infilling and restored. The ground
floor was originally open. All the time the interplay of buildings and spaces, especially the church tower and the roof-
lines, has been flickering and changing so quickly that it defies
description. Meanwhile on the other side what is called
MARKET PLACE starts as a lane, turns sharply ninety degrees,
and becomes the open space in front of the church. At the
angle two admirable C18 fronts, just right for their station in
life: BIERTON HOUSE, three bays and two storeys, and GATE
HOUSE, five bays and three storeys. Both use red and grey
bricks, Gate House making the red bricks into vertical strips
between the windows. Both *c.*1750, both perhaps by the same
person. Around the corner, one end of the churchyard with a
lane running off beyond it: on the r. ST ANN'S HILL which
ends straightaway in the country, then becoming a magnificent
footpath walk to Cowdray House. Most of it is taken up by a
large block of Cowdray ESTATE COTTAGES, by *E. C. Lee*,
in tile-hung Norman Shaw style, or more accurately Philip
Webb style, well and freely grouped. The extreme care taken
with the corner is especially worth notice.

In the MARKET SQUARE itself, an indifferent MARKET HALL originally of 1552, and an odd building on the s side, a seven-bay pilastered C18 front, stone and brick, with alterations in the rather slapdash taste of the 1830s: knobs on the skyline, strapwork and floral panels let into older surrounds in the attic. The N side is the church; the W side is the side of the SWAN INN, the strategically placed pub mentioned earlier, and the over-restored half-timber front, c.1600, of the NATIONAL PROVINCIAL BANK. Then beyond, a r. turn brings in CHURCH HILL, the second open space of this part of Midhurst. This time it is triangular, the W side cottagey except for EAGLE HOUSE, plain late C18, the E side an impressive run of two-storeyed C18 houses N from the church, the whole much more than the sum of the parts.

The street becomes a funnel and takes a sharp bend to the l.; meanwhile yet another delightful loop, SHEEP LANE, curves off from the r. back to the churchyard. At the bend, a splendid ramble of timbered and tile-hung C17 cottages including the COUNTY LIBRARY; around the corner, KNOCKHUNDRED ROW runs downhill into the wide NORTH STREET, which on a quick visit is all that there seems to be of Midhurst. Not very much here: on the W side the R.D.C. OFFICES, in a mid C18 house with first-floor Venetian windows, vainly trying to be assimilated into the composition, then the old building of the GRAMMAR SCHOOL, mostly c.1800, sandstone with pretty Gothick sashes and battlements, the centre a mid C17 brick shaped gable. N of this in the playground a SCHOOL inscribed 'Schola Grammaticalis' and dated 1821, which is quite a personable neo-classical design, with broad eaves and restrained pilasters and window surrounds, nothing overstated. Opposite, early C18 entrance gates on the main axis of Cowdray, dramatically appearing across fields. To the N, again fields and the river Rother almost immediately, with, set back on the W side, the SECONDARY MODERN SCHOOL, 1949–51 by *F. R. Steele*, the county architect. Long low brick blocks, modern but still rather institutional and impersonal, typical of the 1940s, but nicely sited under a wooded hill. Two-storeyed classrooms on the r.; school hall and single-storeyed class-rooms on the l.

Back now to the junction of North Street and Knockhundred Row. S of this several lanes run S with nice cottages: DUCK LANE, RUMBOLDS HILL, with the plain Gothic former R.C. CHURCH by *C. A. Buckler*, 1869, neatly tucked into the street

line, and especially WOOL LANE, which has several C16
buildings with overhangs. Further S and nearly back to the
Market Place, WEST STREET has a timber-framed house with
a date 1650 in a moulded plaster panel.

HEATHLANDS FARM, 1½ m. SW, half-way to Bepton. Good late
C17 builder's front in grey and red bricks, the ground-floor
windows with elliptical brick arches above, surely here a continuation of the imported Dutch trick of shouldered lintels.

MID LAVANT see LAVANT

8020

MILLAND

In the extreme NW of the county, on the Hants border near Lip-
hook. Scattered groups of cottages rather than a village, with
the churches by themselves further NW, only a few yards away
from the Portsmouth Road yet completely remote. MILLAND
PLACE was large and gabled, c.1600: it was burnt down in
this century and only some C18 gatepiers remain.

ST LUKE. 1878. A nasty, fussy job, with aisles, clerestory, and
big W tower with stair-turret. Behind it, the OLD CHURCH
makes a very telling contrast between true piety and C19
religious advertisement. It is a single chamber with a bellcote,
very humble and very similar to an unrestored chapel in Wales
or Lancashire. The simple requirements of remote areas, such
as this was, all tended to be the same. Square windows without
tracery, impossible to date, probably C16 or C17. Early C19 N
transept, in the same style; the whole church roughcast. Inside, a few BOX PEWS and a plain C18 PULPIT. The church
is in bad condition at the moment: it ought to be made weather-
tight, at least, both because it is a rarity in the South of
England and because the inside keeps its moving simplicity –
so hard to achieve consciously – in spite of the rubbish and
bird-droppings.

8010

MONKTON HOUSE
3 m. NW of Singleton

A small house by *Lutyens*, 1903, as a kind of retreat house to
West Dean Park, in an extraordinary situation. It lies by itself
just under the crest of the Downs, approached only from the
S by a two-mile drive through sinister woodland. This site,
which called for a miniature Castle Drogo, was in fact given a
weakly genteel neo-Georgian brick box. Fortunately, this has
been well and truly submerged in an extraordinary redecora-

tion: the whole house painted green, bronze imitation palm trees introduced as columns, painted drapery decoration around windows, Art-Nouveau-like chimneystacks.

MUNDHAM

8000

Between Chichester and Bognor: North and South, both straggling villages without a central group, typical of the coastal plain. North Mundham is overbuilt and untidy, though with pretty cottages to the E at Runcton; but South Mundham, being in a cul-de-sac, is one of the best places to catch the feel of the Selsey peninsula – rich cornfields, winding lanes, and always the Downs filling the whole northern horizon, with Chichester Cathedral like a pointer in front of them.

ST STEPHEN, North Mundham. Bigger than the run of churches near Selsey: four-bay nave and aisles. Everything but the tower re-tooled or rebuilt in 1883 by *A. W. Blomfield*, who put in one of his fussy iron CHANCEL SCREENS. The original framework was C13, and of this the arcades remain, more or less, in the familiar style – double-chamfered arches, circular piers and abaci. The S arcade has one of its chamfers hollow and must be a little later than the N; also one of the abaci of the N arcade is cruder and earlier than the rest: one of the multitude of unsolved little puzzles in parish churches. Both arcades have elegant moulded bases with spurs. The tower is interesting, and another of these little puzzles. It is also nice to look at, especially after the fearful texture of the rest. Stone with two diagonal buttresses. C13 W doorway, a Perp window immediately above it, and fine-drawn trefoil-headed bell-openings that look *c.*1300, in oblong recesses. Tower arch without capitals but with an odd groove in it. The VCH say C16, with inserted material. But there is nothing to rule out a C14 date. – PLATE. Cup and Paten Cover, 1568; Almsplate, 1751. – SCULPTURE. On the E jamb of the S porch: small group, badly weathered, which seems to have been one of the local late medieval monuments with kneeling figures on either side of a religious symbol. Believed to commemorate someone who † 1497.

SOUTH MUNDHAM HOUSE. Delightful front dated 1671, the very end of Artisan Mannerism, here compounded quite happily with the plainer brickwork of the late C17. Seven bays facing E, with semicircular Dutch gables over the outer two bays at each end, and a pointed Dutch gable on the N end as well. Plain brick string-courses, semicircular pediment over the entrance. An almost perfect marriage of plainness and ornament.

BOWLEY FARM, ½ m. SE of South Mundham. Plain, seven-bay C17 front to a rubble house, the walling probably medieval.

MUNTHAM COURT see FINDON

NALDRETT HOUSE see RUDGWICK

NEALS FARM see ALDWICK

NEWBUILDINGS PLACE see SHIPLEY

NEW PLACE see PULBOROUGH

NEW PLACE FARM see ANGMERING

NEW SHOREHAM

2000

One of those funny places which have always been important but (except for the church) have nothing to show for it. Perhaps it was all comings-and-goings. Shoreham has always been a busy port, especially after the Adur silted up in the Late Middle Ages and ships could no longer get as far as Bramber. It was a busy shipbuilding town in the C18 and has gradually attracted more coastal traffic since the building of the basin to the E (i.e. at Portslade) in 1854. Now, because of its lower overheads, it is taking trade away from the Port of London. Yet nothing later than 1250 in Shoreham is worth more than a quick look. Inigo Jones was M.P. here, in 1620.

ST MARY DE HAURA (i.e. de Havre). Gaunt and bleached above the cottages of the little town in a way that looks more Flemish than English. From outside it could be a twin of Boxgrove: Norman central tower and transepts, E.E. choir, ruined nave. Yet it was never monastic, and the nave was ruined, as far as we can tell, in the C17, either by a French raid in 1628 or in the Civil War. The question put in such rolling terms by Professor Freeman in 1880 has never been answered: 'Why should they go and build them a parish church absolutely without a fellow in England? It is not merely the size, one might easily find a fellow for that, but the type and character, so wholly of the kind which one is used to find only in Conventual and the greatest Collegiate churches.'

The church, like Old Shoreham, was given by the de Braose

family to the monastery of St Florent at Saumur, on the Loire.
The first mention of the church is in a confirmatory deed of
1103, when Philip de Braose returned from the First Crusade.
The earliest parts are all of a piece and look *c*.1130: what is
left of the nave, the transepts, and the lower stage of the tower.
This church had an apsidal E end (traced in 1915) and transeptal E chapels which had steep pitched roofs whose weather-
marks can still be seen. The C19 assumed these to be apsidal
in the same way as Chichester Cathedral: excavation in 1950
showed longer stretches of square-ended wall running E which
might themselves have had apses at the ends. So what in fact
happened?

About 1170 this E end was replaced by a much grander
scheme. It has five bays and is aisled and square-ended, and it is
this which makes New Shoreham worth a special visit. Although
it was completed in several stages, somebody – probably the
original designer – had caught exactly the moment of change
which the C19 hazily but justly described as 'Transitional'.
For 'Gothic' did not succeed 'Romanesque' in a simple way;
it merged and blended and superseded in a hundred different
ways. In the end, more probably depended on human temperament than anything else. At Canterbury and in the Île de
France it drove ahead, sure of itself: it was a mission. But to
other people it dropped in from outside, as today Communism
might do on a new African republic. Sometimes this resulted
in a bizarre set of experiments and combinations – the whole
history of the transition in the West of England is like this.
And, just occasionally, the new style of pointed arches and
pointed rib-vaults reached someone who used a rich Late
Romanesque style and who saw the possibilities of harmonization, not supersession. One of these designers worked at
New Shoreham – another, perhaps, at Walsoken in Norfolk.
The effect is a high-powered, inventive raciness, the formal
old zigzags given a terrific head of steam. And although in fact
the choir of New Shoreham has half a dozen mini-styles in it,
this effect forces its way through independent of details.

EXTERIOR. The choir immediately looks like Boxgrove
because of the big solid flying buttresses, two on each side.
These were added to support the vault after the aisle walls had
been built, as the joins in the stonework show. How soon they
were added, we shall have to see. They are crowned by the
plainest square pinnacles with the plainest square spirelets.
The clerestory has some plain lancets, the aisles have C19

Norman windows replacing Perp ones. The E end, though restored, has the same panache as the inside. Only the NE window is original. The lower stage has three round-headed arches, shafted, in deep niches, a very different effect from the usual stamping out of windows in a sheer bare wall. Above, the later designer caught the spirit with three tall lancets, given copious mouldings and shafts, above a band of quatrefoils. In the gable there is a wheel window with new tracery, flanked by sunk, pointed quatrefoils.

The Norman work, in the W parts, is as blandly official as Chichester but with a bit more force. Clerestory windows with jamb shafts, huge round nave piers with scallop capitals. Apart from shapeless lumps of flint at the W end, only one bay survives, patched up in the early C18. There were originally six. A later Norman doorway was reset here. It has an order of beakheads, an unusual thing in Sussex, and it has a pointed arch, presumably done in the repairs (like the W tower arch at Broadwater). Badly weathered. The transepts have their upper windows, two to each side, again shafted, and to the S there is in addition in the gable a triplet of arches. The tower is a noble composite, and, like other Norman buildings in Sussex, leaves a lingering feeling that a duplicate will turn up somewhere in Northern France. Two stages, the lower obviously *c.*1130, with two-light openings each with a central shaft, in a shafted round-headed outer arch. But the upper stage has two taller three-light openings, and the outer arch is pointed. Either the whole of this is late C12, or – more likely – it was remodelled and lightened then. Certainly the pointed arches give just the right amount of uplift.

INTERIOR. The early parts are seen first. Three of the tower arches may in fact be the oldest parts of Shoreham. They have three plain arch orders, big, delicately carved capitals like those at Old Shoreham, mostly with scallops in various forms but also with interlaced leaf trails and one with fighting winged beasts. The W tower arch has similar capitals but is much taller, and the arch orders are given several roll-mouldings, like the blocked arches of the surviving nave bay. The middle order also has a weird design in which a wide merlon with a V-shaped trough in the middle is always followed by the same shape upside down. The effect is literally as though stones from two arches had been shuffled together. Is it inventiveness, or just a mistake in the order to the mason's yard? The transepts, as outside, are firm and grand. The upper storeys are

16b

complete, with two windows to the sides and two to the ends, all shafted. Roll-mouldings in the N, a good deal of zigzag as well in the S.

But everything at New Shoreham leads in fact to the CHOIR. Five bays, a quadripartite vault,* a bewildering variety of details, and a wonderful light but rich consistence, due no doubt to one man. But who was he? The story is as intricate as can be, and the following is no more than a suggestion as to what might have happened. For a final explanation of this story of one man of genius and much muddle one has to wait for the completion and publication of Professor Bony's research. That the story starts about 1180, however, and that it starts with the outer walls of the aisles is pretty certain. They were no doubt built while the Norman E end still stood intact. They have round-headed blank arcading, two wide bays to each bay of the nave, and the arches are decorated with purely Norman motifs, individual chevrons projecting to a roll-moulding (beakheads stylized out of existence) and affronted simple leaf scrolls. And among the capitals also there are scallops, waterleaf, volutes; and many others – N more than S – are on their way to becoming stiff-leaf; hence the proposed date. Each two arches are separated from the next by a vaulting shaft, triple, without keeling. These presuppose the intention of vaulting, and the vault is definitely E.E. There are two possibilities. Either there was first a stronger single shaft and this was carved into when the vault was conceived, or the aisles correspond in their historical situation exactly to the W parts of the Lady Chapel at Chichester (of before 1187, one assumes) with the same vaulting shafts (except that the middle one is keeled) and a mixture of Late Norman and Early E.E. leaf capitals. After that stage came the great man of Shoreham. He designed the N arcade. This consists of piers alternatingly 17b round and octagonal, and that indicates at once that he came from Canterbury, where William of Sens had given his piers these shapes in 1175–80. But the Shoreham capitals are different, not the French feathery and antiquish foliage, but stiff-leaf in two tiers, lively, though keeping fairly closely to the bell. The arches are finely moulded, with only one keeled order, and the outer order has still among more developed ones Late Norman leaves much like the affronted ones in the aisles. Did he intend the high vaults? It has been argued that he did not, because

* The second bay has weird bracing ribs of a different section. These look first-aid.

otherwise he would have started vaulting shafts on the abaci of
his piers, as William of Sens had done. There is no certainty in
this. What can be assumed is that next, after the N piers, either
the S piers were tackled or the N aisle was vaulted. The latter
order is perhaps preferable. These vaults are certainly Early
E.E. Transverse arches and ribs are almost identical with the
work after the fire, i.e. after 1187, at Chichester, and the leaf
bosses are small and close, as in the Chichester chancel aisles
and aisles.

The S arcade must be the consequence of a change in the
direction of the masons' lodge. Or else one would not have
tolerated such lop-sidedness. Yet the date cannot be long after
the N arcade. Now the piers have a compound shape, unhappy
in the absence of clear demarcations between the attached
shafts. They run or undulate into each other.* Only the E
responds have entirely separate shafts, and they are the same
N and S.‡ The ground stage of the E wall of the chancel with
its thin shafted round arches may belong to the first or second
master. Neither would have minded round next to pointed
arches. They had not minded that at Canterbury nor at Chichester. The vaulting was done by this second master in conformity with the N aisle. The next question is when the flying
buttresses were added, i.e. first the massive buttresses against
which they carry the thrust. That they are an addition to the
flat buttresses of c.1180 can be seen at once. There is no know-
ing the moment. It depends on the first and second masters'
indications on what was to be done higher up in the nave.
What is, however, evident is that at the stage we have reached,
a phase of great muddle started, illustrated painfully in the
gallery. Here not only N is different from S, but all is different
from bay to bay too. Where is one to start? The W end of the
N side, it may be proposed. Here each bay has a twin opening
in an unfortunate alternating rhythm of a shaft in front of the
mid-shaft starting from the foot and a mid-shaft starting on
abacus level. None of these carry anything. The first mid-shaft
consists of four detached shafts, the second is round, the third
concave-sided octagonal. These are Chichester ideas – carica-

* The arch mouldings are much more similar to those of the N, but there
is more keeling.
‡ The leaves of the responds are freer than those of the N side, but similar
to those of the S. Is then the NE respond already a deviation from the Canterbury man's plan? The last two transverse arches in the N aisle differ from
all others (by a chamfered middle member).

tured. Then they went on on the s side, with only one opening per bay oddly widening for the plain round-headed mid-wall centre first into a pointed arch and then into a shafted label. In two bays these shafts are not of the full height, but stand on corbels of a cornucopia or candle-bracket shape which was going to be repeated in other places as well. Now for the vaulting of the chancel. On the N side the triple vaulting shafts stand on candle-brackets (perhaps preceding the ones just mentioned). On the s side they form part of the pier design, i.e. start from the ground. From this it has been assumed, as has been said before, that the N arcade master did not intend a high vault. Now these vaulting shafts on the s side are not identical throughout. The first two from the w have a break at the sill level of the gallery and then continue with new bases, i.e. the upper part is just like the vaulting shafts on the N side. So perhaps more of these had already been made when the new design of the s piers was initiated. Only after the s gallery was complete was the N gallery finished. The two E bays have a different design: single openings with pointed trefoiled heads; and the corbels for the vaulting shafts have stiff-leaf of a type most closely matched at Chichester after 1230 (Sacristy, Bishop's Chapel). The clerestory is virtually the same throughout with only very small differences between N and s. The capitals of all the vaulting shafts on which the vault rests are less developed than these two, and the vault in the details of its thin transverse arches and ribs is most similar to the N transept vault at Chichester. Transverse arches and ribs incidentally have the same profile, which is a rare thing. The triplet of lancets in the E wall above the round-headed arches is a noble composition. Finally the arches from the chancel aisles to the transepts. Where is their place chronologically? With the N arcade? It may seem so, but one would hardly have destroyed the Norman E end and opened up from the transepts to the *novum opus* before it was in a presentable state. None of the few and small later medieval additions needs mentioning here.

Incredibly few FURNISHINGS. FONT. Late Norman. Shallow square bowl, each side with a different ornamental pattern, on a stem and four shafts too big for it. A more elaborate example of a common Sussex type. – PLATE. Pewter Flagon, 1639; pewter Paten, *c.*1639. – MONUMENTS. Brasses 3 ft high (s aisle). Man and wife, mid C15, standard. – Several tablets of *c.*1800 (N transept); nothing remarkable.

Shoreham has the High Street parallel to the river, then a set of lanes and flint walls running N and E to the church. They keep a pleasant, intimate scale but are in a chaotic state, part preserved, part rebuilt, part empty. A really sensitive comprehensive plan could make something very impressive out of them. In the High Street the TOWN HALL, converted in 1886 from *Sydney Smirke*'s Custom House of 1830. Thick classical design, stuccoed. (Inside, early C17 overmantel taken from the Fountain Inn.) On the other side of the street, the engaging chequerboard front of the MARLIPINS. This always seems to have been a two-storeyed store (perhaps originally the de Braose Custom House). One C12 window on the E side, low down, but the front itself, with simple and restored two-light windows, is C14. Across the harbour a bungalow town, destroyed in the war to prevent it being used as a beach-head, rebuilt since 1950 by the County Council. Again, it could have been made into a marvellous place without heavy-handed direction, but the opportunity has been lost.

The original BRIDGE across the Adur was by *W. Tierney Clark*, 1832; elegant, like his bridge at Marlow. But it was replaced in the 1920s by what passed for engineering design then.

Pleasant seaside cottages further E, at the end of NEW ROAD, especially one with a veranda and chubby pilasters on the first floor (Nos 55–57). Finally, on the road N to Old Shoreham, the crazy entrance to the former SWISS GARDENS, opened in 1838.

HILL FORT. The site's history begins with the construction of a small rectangular bank and ditch enclosure of 1½ acres, broken by two entrances – the bank can still be traced as a slightly raised feature. This construction was later enclosed with a stouter bank and ditch of roughly circular plan with inturned entrances on the N and S. Both structures appear to have been erected in the C3 B.C.

E of the fort was a ROMAN SETTLEMENT. The site is now marked by a series of slight depressions indicating the presence of foundations of wattle and daub huts. Incorporated in the settlement, which covers almost an acre, were two drying kilns. The banks of CELTIC FIELDS which surround both fort and settlement probably date from the period of the latter.

NORE FOLLY *see* SLINDON

NORTH BERSTED *see* BERSTED

NORTH CHAPEL

9020

On the Guildford to Petworth road near the Surrey border, on the dividing line between the hilly and flat Weald, neatly demonstrated by the mixture of sandstone, brick, and tile-hanging in the cottages. Small square green as one incident in a good curving hilly street, rather like Chiddingfold, the nearest Surrey village. Splendid views w to the side of Blackdown.

ST JOHN BAPTIST. Unbuttressed early C19 stone tower, the rest rebuilt by *Salvin* in 1877 and terribly characterless. – FONT. Sussex marble, dated 1662 and rather weird. A plain square bowl on square stem with pilaster strips, like a parody or reminiscence of a C13 font. – PLATE. Flagon, 1729; Paten, 1732.

GOFF'S FARM, ½ m. s. Typical bulky Wealden farmhouse, with small two-storeyed porch. Stone-built, dated 1657.

NORTHGATE see CRAWLEY, p. 204

NORTH MARDEN see MARDEN

NORTH MUNDHAM see MUNDHAM

NORTH STOKE

0010

Above a loop of the Arun at the N end of the Arun gap, hence with splendid views in every direction. A tiny, trim hamlet of flint and brick, with more slate than thatch, approached by a dead-end road from Houghton, or, better, by footpath from South Stoke across the river, which combines several quite different kinds of scenery in a mile's walk.

CHURCH. Unrestored* and delightful, outside and in. Cruciform and aisleless, with a small timber bell-turret astonishingly situated astride the ridge of the N transept: the inside a wonderful atmospheric blend of white, yellow, and faded red, lit by clear glass. The nave is Norman, wide and tall, one window remaining high up on both N and s sides. The chancel is E.E., probably mid C13, with lancets in N and s sides, modern E end of three lancets under a rere-arch. To l. and r. of this are two image-brackets supported on charming foliage corbels which might come from the minor parts of Chichester Cathedral: one is stiff-leaf, wind-blown, the other a lusher, more complicated tangle of leaves that is looking forward to the end of the century. The undersides are carved with tiny expressive faces. PISCINA and SEDILIA of the dame date, made into one com-

6b

25a

* At the time of writing.

position cleverly adjusted for the different levels in the chancel.

Next come the transepts, *c.*1290, with a fine variety of window design: N and S windows geometrical, two round-headed lights under a quatrefoiled circle. E window of the N transept three pointed lights under a cinquefoiled circle with in addition cross-pieces from sides to centre that look as though they want to be the beginning of an ogee. The E window of the S transept more normal, with three-light intersecting tracery. Opposite it, in the W wall of this transept, is a recess formed by two tall blank arches joined in a corbel of an animal's head, in its way as lovable as the foliage in the chancel. Finally, in what looks like early C14 work, the complex chancel arch on octagonal responds, made into a composition with niches on either side – and, yet again, the human mason's touch: a hand as a corbel between the arch and the left-hand niche. In some ways this little church can teach more about the medieval spirit of working than a cathedral. – FONT. Bulbous and circular, without ornament. It looks like a tub font given a little more elegance – i.e. perhaps of *c.*1200. – WALL PAINTING. Above the chancel arch, medieval stencil-like floral patterns. – STAINED GLASS. Coronation of the Virgin, E window. Only tiny, but beautifully drawn. By the swaying gestures it looks early C14. – A second fragment of the same representation and date, yet smaller, in the S transept E window. – PLATE. Cup and Paten, 1568.

MANOR FARM, N of the church. Rebuilt in 1819 with a severe and elegant front in that most astringent of combinations, squared flint and white brick. Five bays, the centre bay with small pediment and a doorway with fluted Roman Doric columns *in antis*, the ground-floor windows in arched recesses.

NORTON *see* ALDINGBOURNE

NUTBOURNE *see* SOUTHBOURNE

1020

NUTHURST

Only four miles from Horsham, but remote, rolling Weald, thickly wooded. Nuthurst itself is simply a church and some pretty terraces of cottages.

ST ANDREW. Terribly restored. It seems, orginally, to have been a Dec building with wide aisleless nave and chancel. The character of this is still suggested, but no more, by the paired cusped lancets in the nave and the three-light E window with

reticulated tracery. Double-chamfered chancel arch, the
mouldings dying into the imposts. A redecoration in 1951 by
H. S. Goodhart-Rendel and *Thomas Derrick* did what it could.
The best part is the convinced and outré vestry of 1907 on the
N side, which is almost Art Nouveau. – STAINED GLASS. Old
bits in the tracery lights of the E window: Christ in Majesty and
censing angels.

At Nuthurst the best thing is the terrace of cottages N of the
church with the village pub in it; some brick, some half-timber. 1 m. S is MAPLEHURST, with BROOK FARM, a good,
small C16 timber-framed house. Horsham slate roof and good
tile-and-weatherboard barns.

At COPSALE, 1½ m. SW, is COPSALE FARM, a picturesque C16
farm. Half-timbered building almost all refaced bit by bit with
brick and tiles.

SEDGEWICK PARK, ½ m. W. The house is sober neo-Tudor.
In the park to the W of the house the site of SEDGEWICK
CASTLE. Overgrown, with only a few lumps of masonry standing and those few hard to find. Licence to crenellate (on an
existing site) was given in 1258. It was excavated in 1923 and
revealed a keep and curtain walls – i.e. a plan as up-to-date as
the Welsh castles.

NYETIMBER BARTON *see* PAGHAM

OKEHURST *see* BILLINGSHURST

OLD ERRINGHAM *see* OLD SHOREHAM

OLD SHOREHAM   2000

A few old cottages around the church, where the Brighton-
Portsmouth road crosses the Adur by an archaic-looking timber
BRIDGE of 1781, shortly to be replaced. Joined to New Shoreham by continuous building, but quite distinct in spirit. Fine
view of Lancing College across the estuary.

ST NICHOLAS. At a distance, a solid, sturdy mid-Norman
church which on a close look is obviously a good deal more
Norman than it was in 1800. It looks very like an important
village church in Normandy, and this may be no accident, for
it was given by William de Braose along with Bramber to
Saumur Abbey in 1075. The W part of the N wall of the nave
is actually Saxon, with a tall blocked doorway on the N side.
Baldwin Brown assigns a date before 900 to it, regards it as

part of a tower-nave, and draws attention to the thickness of the wall, the lack of alignment with the wall further E, and the stripwork of the doorway. The Normans added the rest of the nave, a central tower, an apsidal chancel, and transepts with E chapels. The remaining details are all of c.1140. What can be trusted is a blocked doorway in the N side of the nave, the doorway in the S transept, and the tower and tower arches. The tower outside has a bell-stage made up of three arches, one open with twin sub-arches, the others closed, a type which was very common in Normandy. Above, a pair of circles or œils-de-bœuf giving the tower the same scheme as East Meon in Hampshire, but not the same richness or quite the same quality. The effect of Old Shoreham is the effect of the Romanesque parts of Chichester, even though the details are very different; that is, of something a little parsimonious. The next generation in Sussex resolved this very well, at Broadwater, Climping, and New Shoreham. But a comparison with exactly the same stage of Romanesque in Norfolk (at Norwich Cathedral or Hales and Heckingham and Wroxham) shows what happens when style and expression are exactly matched. Here the details would like to turn Late Norman and the vocabulary was not yet invented. This is true especially of the tower arches, all to the same basic pattern. Responds with three demi-shafts, the middle one much thicker. Capitals of two to four scallops with and without decoration. Arches of a plain soffit and two rolls l. and r., broad labels with zigzag, billet, etc. This decoration appears on the show-sides only, i.e. on the W side of the W and E arches and on the crossing side of the transept arches. Within this framework a lot of variations in detail and quality, with some beautiful vignettes, e.g. the magnificently crisp capital on the N side of the arch to the nave and the spiral fluting on the roll-moulding here. Many human vignettes as well, like the faces on the S transept arch, and especially the faces used as stops to the outer labels. Those on the N transept arch have an elongated, very French look. These labels are actually the most interesting parts of the arches and include shells and rosettes as well as the more familiar billet ornament. Billet ornament is what helps to suggest that the TIE-BEAM at the E end of the nave is Norman also (? the old rood beam). If so, it is of the greatest rarity. The doorway in the transept has the same character, with an odd inner order made up of a repeated T-shape. The capitals here look earlier. In the C14 the chancel was lengthened and given a square

E end. The same happened to the chapel off the N transept,
which later became ruined (blocked arch and PISCINA on the
outside wall of the chancel). Dec tomb recess in the S wall of
the chancel. The chapel off the S transept has disappeared
entirely.

All the rest is restoration, and there is a lot of it. The work
was done in 1839–40 by *J. M. Neale** with *J. C. Buckler* for the
chancel. It included every window except the low-side in the
chancel – the pseudo-Norman funnies in the transept ends were
copied from Climping and replaced plain lancets in the same
position – and a new E arch in the N transept copied from the
nave and perhaps incorporating some old fragments. The
cumulative effect inside is depressing. – WOODWORK. Elegantly moulded carved tie-beam in the chancel, ornamented
with dogtooth, *c.*1300. Original colouring. – SCREEN. Very
restored, but of the same date. Gawky trefoiled heads to narrow lights, rather a mean design. – PLATE. Paten, 1721;
Chalice and Paten, 1785. – MONUMENTS. William Monk
† 1714. Jolly rustic tablet, half-way to Palladianism. – Two
Grecian monuments in the churchyard, surrounded by hefty
ironwork. The smaller is over a vault on the N side of the chancel, signed by *Croggan*, 1828. Delicate sarcophagus on a stepped plinth, in *Coade* stone (Croggan became head of the Coade
firm in 1813), charmingly carved with naturalistic flowers.
The only inscriptions are FUERUNT to the W and FUERUNT to
the E. – The other monument, S of the S transept, is much more
strictly Grecian, commemorating Colvill Bridger † 1797 and
his descendants. Impressive heavy build-up of masses to a
plain sarcophagus. Inscriptions on huge stone slabs which form
the shoulders of the composition, flanked by down-turned
torches. Far above the standard job.

1 m. N is OLD ERRINGHAM, half-way up the Adur gap, with a
barn converted from a small C13 building, probably the chancel of a chapel. One lancet on the S side, two in the E wall. A
little further N again, the impressive machinery of the CEMENT
WORKS, spanning the road, which may in time be as highly
prized as we now value mills and railway buildings. We will
never much enjoy the siting, which spoils the whole Adur gap.

BUCKINGHAM HOUSE, ½ m. NE. Nervous, mannered early C19
house by *J. B. Rebecca*. Henry Holland's style gone acid.
Straw-coloured brick, bow window on the S side and project-

* The rather classical nave windows were done before Neale arrived on
the scene – he hated them (NT).

ing centre to the E flanked by giant Corinthian columns. Surrounded by villas, but being preserved as a semi-ruin.

9000   OVING

In the flat arable land E of Chichester, on the s side of Tangmere airfield. A small straggling village built round a quadrilateral of lanes, with quite a large council estate which would have made an impressive place out of Oving, if the houses had been fitted in one by one instead of being stuck out together at one end.

ST ANDREW. Complete unaltered E.E. plan, complete even for Sussex, of aisleless nave and chancel, transepts, and w tower with shingled broach-spire. Nearly all the windows and the bell-openings are lancets with stepped reveals outside.* Apart from its tower, it would be almost indistinguishable from a medieval tithe barn; unhappily, the C19 touches inside have made the barnlike interior merely hard and empty. New E window; wide C13 chancel arch, the arches to the transepts C14. The showpiece at Oving is the N doorway, in a simple but very sophisticated style. Two orders with shafts and complicated mouldings including a slight upward prolongation of the shape of the shaft, into which the arch mouldings die away. Abaci with a tiny band of nailhead ornament, familiar in Lincolnshire or Yorkshire but very rare in the South, and a label with elegantly carved foliage stops. Although in effect this is all E.E., an elaboration of the style of 1200, it must date from well into the second half of the C13. – ARCHITECTURAL FRAGMENTS. In the N transept w wall some pieces of Norman zigzag. – STAINED GLASS. E window. By *Powell*'s, *c*.1880. Unmistakably influenced by Morris, yet unmistakably not his, but Powell's. Was it designed by Holiday ? – s transept lancets by *Kempe*, 1901. Small-scale and pretty, above his average for that date: the ground cornflower blue instead of the usual sickly green. Madonna and Child, and angels carrying frilly texts.

Opposite the church, flint and stucco ALMSHOUSES and SCHOOL by *John Elliott*, 1839, quite a period piece. They were illustrated in Loudon's *Encyclopaedia*.

At SHOPWYKE, ½ m. NW, two worthwhile houses: SHOPWYKE HALL, a sturdy five-bay brick house with a Doric doorcase, dated 1720, and WESTBOURNE PARK, formerly Shopwyke House, an unexpectedly restrained and handsome classical

* Several of them new, but this was undoubtedly the original appearance.

house of 1841, still effectively Georgian, with an enormous four-bay Ionic porte-cochère dwarfing the windows around it.

PAGHAM   8090

On the coast between Bognor Regis and Selsey, largely a half-built bungalow town whose only hope is to become completely built up and achieve some kind of urban character of its own. The church and a few cottages are ½ m. w on a cul-de-sac and keep the old character remarkably well.

St Thomas à Becket. Bigger-than-usual Selsey church, with aisles, long transepts, and a NW tower. In the chancel some C11 herringbone masonry, but mostly c.1200, with a weird restoration of 1837 by *John Elliott* which tinkered with the architecture but was surprisingly responsive to the spirit of the building. Plain lancets outside, with small two-light clerestory windows of the C14 or C15; the bell-opening is C19 and so is the intriguing w wall, with an unconvincing rose-window above a very convincing wall arcade. The inside, ceiled and plastered, has outstandingly happy and comfortable proportions in spite of the fact that chancel and transept arches are all new. Both three-bay arcades original, the arches unchamfered but with complicated keeled roll-mouldings. Chronologically the story started by the tower. This has a Norman w window which can be trusted, and so it is not surprising that the arch to the nave, i.e. the w arch of the N arcade, has scalloped capitals. Then the N arcade was continued to the E. Round pier, but shafted responds with small stiff-leaf capitals. The s arcade is plainer, just three bays with round piers. Transepts with grandly plain lancets in the Sussex way, largely rebuilt, the E end just a little more ornate, three lancets stepped and shafted, the rere-arches shafted too, with dogtooth ornament on the arches. – Stained glass. E end, a bright show, partly C16 Flemish from a church in Rouen, partly armorial by *William Miller* in 1837. The C16 pieces represent the Adoration of the Child, the Adoration of the Magi, and the Presentation in the Temple. – Poor painted glass in one s aisle window. – Plate. Cup and Cover, 1568.

Nyetimber Barton, ½ m. NE. In a hamlet with several old cottages and, potentially, a nice shape. Remains of an early medieval house, terribly obscured and added to. It seems to have consisted of two separate blocks, chapel and hall, at r. angles to one another, now joined to make one house. Of the hall only walling and one blocked arched opening in the s

10—s.

gable remain: the herringbone masonry shows that it is probably of the C11. Of the chapel only the E part remains, clearly
C13, with lancets in the sides and a group of three plain lancets
in the E end, just like a small Sussex parish church. Inside,
plain trefoil-headed PISCINA.

PARHAM

oo10

1½ m. E of Amberley

Tudor house in a Tudor landscape, a 'chase' of big trees and
bracken which was accentuated instead of being smoothed
down by the C18 landscaping. It faces the bare Downs, and the
contrast makes up an equation or a signature which operates on
many levels at the same time – visual, geological, historical.
The house seems far more a flourish to the signature than an
architect's design imposed on the landscape. This is what Repton understood and tried to practise when he suited his houses
to his parks and not vice versa.

38a   The house itself is straightforward and sober, without a hint
of Elizabethan extravagance, one of a group which includes
Loseley and Baynards Park in Surrey, Wiston and Danny in
Sussex. It looks much more Tudor now than it did in 1800, due
to the C20 restoration of *Victor Heal*; but it has been done
with a genuinely humble wish to re-create the C16 pattern and
with understanding too: so the eye takes it in and accepts it.
Originally, Parham was a grange of Westminster Abbey, and
big fireplaces with four-centred arches in the NW corner are
thought to be part of the original kitchens. The new house can
be dated exactly, for the foundation stone was laid in January
1577 by a two-year-old boy – for luck, just as John Thorpe
laid the foundation stone of Kirby Hall in 1570. This date is
fifteen years later than Loseley, and in the interval the outside
appearance has become more regular, though the style has
stayed exactly the same – the same, also, as Lacock in *c.*1550.
Unlike Wollaton, built at the same time, probably nobody
thought of this for display or as a design – which is not to say
that their subconscious did not do it for them. Here, the hall
was always entered from the centre of the S front, unlike the
asymmetrical porch at Loseley. Everything else developed
around this. Façade on the E-plan with the projections in the
re-entrant angles, and everything gabled, the Elizabethan love
of picturesque regularity. Big grid of mullioned windows
lighting the hall; no ornament at all except a delicate frieze.
These windows are original; everything else with mullions is

C20, replacing Early Georgian windows which survive to the r. of the porch. The doorcase itself has been kept. This (from heraldic evidence) must be after 1705, and is a fine bit of braggadocio. Pilasters, and probing, nervous achievement above which is very much like the stonework at Petworth. The façade of Parham faces S – which is very unusual. The N and E fronts are irregular jumbles, the W front could be called a regular jumble, with windows arranged without any intention of being seen as a design, but symmetrical *malgré lui*.

Inside, the main room is the GREAT HALL. It is still entered via a passage and screen, but above, instead of a gallery, is the steward's room. He could look into the hall through two wooden mullioned windows – wooden, because the wall above the screen is timber-framed. The big windows and the S view take the hall out of straightforward architectural space into an older and deeper set of rhythms. The windows are three, closely set, each of three lights with three transoms. The bay window has two plus six lights and also its three transoms. The W side of the bay window does not project, as it is placed in one of the re-entrant angles. So the doorway into the parlour is here.* Ceiling with pendants and elaborate, sinuous pattern of thin ribs, much of which may have been done or re-done in 1832. The screen is undoubtedly original, and with its pilasters and rich, crisp, small-scale ornament is a good example of a style which we undervalue by tracing all the motifs by repeated comparisons with France or Italy. A late C16 Italian would not necessarily have been better or worse, only different.

The only other notable C16 room is the LONG (158 ft) GALLERY, at the top of the house. This has simple panelling with Ionic pilasters, and is high enough to have bay windows with views on both sides, an effect quite different from Blickling or Hardwick. The poor roof is C19, and was originally coved. The idea of such a gallery is a microcosm of the kind of life desired by the builders of Parham – and undoubtedly, unlike Blenheim or Holkham, the pattern of life came before the architectural pattern. The up-and-down walk provided the regularity, the side-to-side views and the ability to stop provided the freedom. Shakespeare kept the same balance between fate and free-will.

The other rooms are simple: the main staircase behind the high-table end of the hall rising round a solid square core of

* Above it an inner window, of mullion and transom cross – a very odd arrangement.

masonry, a plain but elegant late C18 SALOON, and the GREAT CHAMBER and the room beneath it (in the W wing) recreated in the C20 with appealing plasterwork done without moulds by *Esmond Burton*.*

The STABLE BLOCK to the N was built in 1778 and must have been made more Tudor in the C19, perhaps by *Salvin* in the 1830s.

Plain late C18 LODGES at the W entrance, and a demure classical farmhouse (SPRINGHEAD) to the S, dated 1811. Black brick, Brighton style, with stock-brick dressings.

ST PETER. On the lawn S of the house. All remodelled *c*.1820, and as complete and attractive inside as Stansted (p. 335). The S chancel chapel was kept as built in 1545, and in fact most of the walls must be medieval as well – e.g. the blocked two-bay arcade on the N side. The bottom of the tower is Perp, the top an innocent and very early kind of neo-Norman which is in the same style as the early C19 alterations at Arundel. The inside is all unspoilt Gothick, done at a level where it was more than an artificial change of style. Box pews, pulpit, fretwork screen, coved ceiling to the nave, pretty panelled plaster vaults to the chancel and N transept, which was the squire's pew (with a fireplace) and to the parson's pew opposite. – FONT. Lead, mid C14, and very rare. Thin circular bowl which as its decoration has nothing but strips of inscription, horizontal and vertical, repeating 'IHS Nazar' and the arms of Andrew Peverel, Knight of the Shire in 1351.

PARKMINSTER *see* ST HUGH'S MONASTERY

PARKSTREET FARM *see* SLINFOLD

PARTHINGS *see* HORSHAM, p. 248

1010

PARTRIDGE GREEN

The centre of population for West Grinstead. By the railway, mostly C19, mostly agricultural, with the same careless unself-

---

* Exhibited at Parham is a Roman LEAD CISTERN with raised decoration including the Chi-Rho monogram, found at Lickfold near the Roman villa (see p. 378). Eight of these are known over the country, though only two of them bear the Christian monogram. Their wide distribution makes it difficult to suppose that they could have been fonts, and Professor Ian Richmond's opinion, which he kindly communicated in a letter, is that they might be vats connected with beer brewing.

conscious throwing down of houses and sheds as Tiverton Junction in Devon or Craven Arms in Shropshire.

ST MICHAEL. Simple flint village church, 1890.* Most other counties would have had it much fussier. The inside unexpectedly is exposed brick, and dignified. – STAINED GLASS in the E window by *Kempe*, also 1890.

PATCHING

On the S slopes of the Downs NW of Worthing. A pleasant scrappy village street with a few old flint and thatch cottages. What it needs to give it shape is consolidating and perhaps enlarging – new building, but new building done in the right way, not the casual insertion of bungalows, which is what often passes for village infill in Sussex.

ST JOHN. Entirely C13 as only Sussex can be, plain and barn-like, accentuated by a bad restoration in 1888. Lancets throughout: aisleless nave and chancel, attached N tower. This has the look of being an earlier position; for because of it the nave is pushed S so that it is not quite in line with the chancel. E end with two E.E. lancets and trefoil PISCINA with good stiff-leaf capitals. Nave roof exactly like a barn, with tie-beams, king-posts, two-way struts, and trussed rafters. Many Sussex churches keep their original C13 roofs but this seems especially typical. The tower is the best part: unbuttressed, with a delicate bell-stage of two coupled lancets, a continuation in E.E. terms of the more familiar Norman bell-openings. The shingled spire is C19. Tower arches good too: to E and W as well as to the nave (i.e. this must almost certainly have been originally a crossing tower). E and W arches of two orders, the inner chamfered and shafted: the S arch has in addition a roll-moulding and jamb shafts on the S side. – FONT. Standard C15; octagonal, with quatrefoil panels with rosettes. – PULPIT. C19, incorporating good early C16 arabesque panels, delicately carved without a hint of Gothic survival. Where do they come from?

FLINT MINES. On a spur on S of BLACKPATCH HILL are a group of Neolithic mines represented by slight hollows and mounds – the filled-in shafts and waste material of the mines. Over 100 shafts have been located, all sunk to a depth of 10–11 ft to work a buried flint seam. These mines appear to have been worked both in Early Neolithic times by people of

* By *Sir Arthur Blomfield?*

the Windmill Hill Culture and by Late Neolithic Beaker groups.

9020

PETWORTH

Few English towns can catch the heart now from outside: too much has been added around them too recently and without enough love. But Petworth still can, though it can only be seen at a distance, from the South Downs or its foothills. Petworth is on the sandstone ridge which answers the Downs about four miles to the N, and the slope is shallow enough to show the town as though it were on a tilted plate. Around it green fields on both sides, the big house on the left, the rose-red church tower in the middle – an image of urbanity without poverty.

Petworth, inside, is just like Midhurst to the casual visitor – a bewildering series of ninety-degree bends. But once out of the car, a miniature city unfolds, and one which must have a by-pass before the weight of traffic forces demolitions and widenings.

It has one odd, un-English quality. The big house is close to the town and its outbuildings and high walls come right down to the centre, producing the pattern of sharp turns and blind corners. Cirencester is the only English equivalent, though there are many more in France. What Petworth shows more than anything else is Sharawaggi, or the lion and lamb lying down together: good buildings of all dates mixing perfectly at least up to 1920. What it now needs is a few really good but unequivocally modern buildings.

St Mary. Rebuilding and renewing have made the church an exasperating puzzle, and one that there is not really much value in deciphering. The one splendid thing about it, from a distance or close to, is the SE tower (cf. Tillington and Lurgashall), stone below, rose-red brick above, the picture of unrestored mellow age, more like Flanders than England. Its true history is rather different. The base is indeed medieval (? Perp), but Sir Charles Barry added the top stage and a rather monstrous spindly spire, all stuccoed, in 1827.* The spire proved to be too spindly and was taken down in 1947, the stucco was then stripped from the tower, leaving an agreeable stucco clock face and a comely design of vertical panelling in brick and stone. Finally, in 1953 the tower top was finished off with a simple brick parapet and pyramidal cap (by Seely & Paget; NT). This kind of piecemeal addition must have been

* According to Mr Rodney Hubbuck, originally designed for St Peter Brighton.

exactly how the great Continental belfries got to their present state.

Otherwise, there are only medieval odds and ends. The chancel is C13, with windows of c.1260 in the S wall, two lights under a roundel. The N arcade is C14, although piers and capitals are quite new, in a thick impressive style – complex mouldings dying into the uprights above the capitals. The Perp windows of the N chancel chapel, though completely renewed, seem to have authentic patterns – five-light panel tracery, like the E parts of Arundel. The thick arches between this chapel and the transept and chancel are difficult to date. The details look C13 but they could equally be off-hand Perp work. Bad restoration by *Barry* in 1827, mostly replaced by a general prettifying, including the S arcade by that odd firm *Kempe & Tower* in 1903. Tower did the structural alterations, Kempe the decoration, and it is easiest to group them here; plaster nave ceiling, pretty but vapid neo-Gothic ORGAN CASE, downright bad REREDOS and ROOD SCREEN, and of course STAINED GLASS, e.g. the E window. It all has a depressing air of somehow having been ordered from a catalogue. The odd plaster decoration on the outside of the chancel looks like Kempe & Tower also. – AUMBRY. Tiny Netherlandish or French panel with the Virgin and Child and two angels as applied relief figures in bronze or brass, no more than 2 in. high. Early C16, an exquisitely delicate piece, brought here in the C20. – FONT. Under the tower. Octagonal with quatrefoil panels, but from the shape of the quatrefoils probably Dec, not Perp. – ROYAL ARMS (N aisle). Coade stone, signed *Coade & Sealy*, 1812, and undoubtedly ordered from a catalogue. – STAINED GLASS. Roundel above chancel arch: strident German glass of c.1840, gold, green, and purple. Still, a relief after Kempe's weak piety. – SCULPTURE. Virgin and Child by *Flaxman*, oval relief under the tower, moved from behind the high altar. Small, dainty, and Wedgwood-like, beautifully carved but conveying no effect whatsoever of being a Virgin and Child. – PLATE. Cup and Cover, Elizabethan; Cup and Cover, 1628; Flagon, 1640; Paten, 1665; Almsdish, 1665.

MONUMENTS. A lot, though none first-class, best described topographically. Start in the N chancel chapel, as the only medieval monuments are there: a mutilated C16 recess and Sir John Dawtrey † 1542 and his wife, now naïvely but appropriately repainted. Small stiff kneeling figures compositionally

derived from brasses against the back walls of such recesses –
a relatively early example – in a recess which is mostly
mechanical Gothic (e.g. the loveless carving of the vine trail),
but with a knowledge of some of the apparatus of the pudgy
Renaissance cherubs. Sussex has a lot of these c16 monuments
and there is not much to be said for most of them. – In the
chancel, several plain c18 tablets and also John Wickins † 1783
and his wife Philadelphia, a very early *Flaxman* – so early in
fact that it is still really a Rococo cherub, though put in an
original and disturbing composition: the cherub has become
an angel, opening a book and floating on clouds. The carving
nothing special. – Also in the chancel, Rear Admiral Richard
Willis † 1829, by *Carew*, decent and straightforward, with a
stern medallion. – In the nave: I. H. Robinson † 1871 by
Catherine A. Fellows, an adequate, benign bust. – John Johnson † 1831, seated; low relief. By *Carew*. – John Peachey † 1693
a cartouche that looks as though it could be by Gibbons or
Selden, though not very good. – Under the tower, collective
monument to the Percy family, erected 1837, by *Carew*, signed
'Proh Pudor Academiae non Academicus'. Mourning figure
full face, full size, carrying a cross: decent, but no more. –
In the N aisle, George, 3rd Earl of Egremont, † 1837, by *Baily*
Seated figure, full size, lifelike. Again, nothing more than
decent; compare the similar figure of Wilberforce in West
minster Abbey, in a similar position, carved at the same time
   Good set of c18 GRAVESTONES in the churchyard, most o
them badly weathered.

SACRED HEART (R.C.), Angel Street. By *F. A. Walters*, 1896
   Curvilinear, with an apse and attached s tower with an up
   roariously tall thin copper spike on top. The outside merel
   busy; the inside correct and elegantly proportioned, in
   Bodley way, though without much life. The apse is particu
   larly well thought out.

TOWN HALL. Built by the Earl of Egremont in 1793, henc
   probably designed by the estate surveyor of the time. A decen
   dour stone building, not adding much to the town. Thre
   plain façades, the fourth, to the E, with a three-bay pedimen
   Seven bays altogether, the ground-floor windows round
   arched, the first-floor windows oblong under blind arcadin
   and crude pilasters. But, attached to the N wall is an earlie
   BUST of William III that is one of the best pieces of Baroqu
   sculpture in England. The King's proud patrician face turr
   r. with a breath-catching yearning expression; a swaggerin

asymmetric wig hangs down over one shoulder, his torso rises
out of a froth of draperies dancing diagonally around the bust.
Form and expression are magnificently the same thing: the
sort of person portrayed and the way the drapery is disposed
are indivisible. Who can have done it? Perhaps, as Dr Whinney
suggests, *Honoré Pelle;* or perhaps *Prost* of Dijon, who did the
trophies on the main gate to the house (*see* p. 306).

WALKS

The centre of Petworth is the MARKET PLACE, tiny, insulated
from the park wall by buildings. From it streets run waywardly
N, E, and S; the way to the W is blocked by Petworth House. It is
almost filled by the town hall, and this is a pity, because Petworth has no other central space. But the buildings around it
show immediately and perfectly the lion lying down with the
lamb. The N side has a big but very good WESTMINSTER
BANK of 1901 by *Frederick Wheeler*, a delightful example of
what Edwardian Baroque can mean if it is handled freshly.
Four bays, the two end bays framed by giant Ionic columns
holding up split pediments, the centre bays lower with windows in complicated segment-headed recesses making a virile
counterpoint.

On the E side, the sequence is worth listing building by building:
EAGER BROS, decent stock brick of *c.*1860, then a four-bay
mid C18 ashlar front, almost covered in an arabesque of thick
wistaria projecting several feet over the pavement, a wonderful marriage of vegetable and mineral. It looks, especially in
perspective, just like an old English sheepdog. Then comes
AUSTIN & CO., mid C18 stone and brick, with a hipped roof,
then one bay of 1883 with a shaped gable painted maroon, and
finally BOWYERS, a demure C18 builder's front with split
pediment. And all that jars in this catholic collection is the
too-genteel shopfront of Austin's. On the S side, cottages; on
the W side the SOUTHDOWN offices, a plain pattern-book
Palladian house, all the better for being painted black and
white, then, set back, the SWAN HOTEL of 1899, big and tile-
hung, yet a perfect fit.

The Swan Hotel is in SADDLERS ROW, and this leads to the
first longer walk, out to the S. At the corner THE CORNER
SHOP, an attractive unplanned half-timbered building, with
one of its rear gables improbably shortened by one-third.
Then l. into POUND STREET. The E side is cottages, the W
side a continuation of the park wall. Bigger things only where

the Midhurst road turns off to the r., a handsome pair of plain
c18 houses which are a subtle contrast in style: YORK
COTTAGE stone-faced with a bracketed doorcase, perhaps
c.1750 (and again, with an air of the North of England about
it) and NEWLANDS, firmly in the home counties: big blank
five bays and three storeys, with a Tuscan Doric porch, c.1790.
s of this one seems to be straightaway in the country, or in
Petworth's gentle equivalent of a suburb. But ¼ m. along the
road is the tiny GASWORKS with its toy gasholder and a stone
entrance flamboyantly carved with the date – 1836: one last
gesture of civic consciousness by Petworth's admirable land-
lords.

Back now to the Market Square again. There are two alternative
roads to the E, and the walk goes out along one and back along
the other. The s continuation of the E side of the Market
Square is called GOLDEN SQUARE. In it, immediately,
AVENINGS, a handsome plain house of c.1770. Brick, seven
bays with a three-bay pediment and Doric porch, but quoined,
i.e. a generation earlier than Newlands. Opposite, and an improbable, perfect match like a marriage of opposite tempera-
ments, a CONGREGATIONAL CHURCH of c.1850 with asymmetrical turret and wooden spire. The road bends l. and
becomes HIGH STREET, a grand name for a charming street
of domestic cottages. Nothing special until MIDDLE STREET
comes in on the l., with a good terrace of tile-hung COTTAGES
on the corner. Opposite them FAIRFIELD COTTAGE, c16
half-timber with diagonal braces and overhanging first floor,
and its neighbour, a much bigger plastered gable with all its
present detail c.1850. Then c17 and c18 cottages, all part of
the Leconfield estate, recognizable by the brown paintwork:
the effect of a town whose ordinary back streets like this are
kept up is very striking in these days of pointless slum clearance and council neglect. Sandwiched in between them on the
r. is STONE HOUSE, a perfect little late c18 front. Three bays
and two storeys only, with Ionic doorcase and fanlight, but
very elegant. Its studied reticence is a living definition of
Style. Probably c.1770. Early c19 cottages and workshop
behind, entered through an equally elegant and reticent iron
arch. The conjunction is just about a textbook of architectural
manners – a far cry from the 'good manners' of the Neo-
Georgians. On the other side, the more robust taste of the
mid c19 can be seen in COTTAGES 328A–L, a long terrace
with heavy chimneys, segment-headed windows, coupled

bargeboarded porches. The details are almost those of the 1720s. On the opposite side, set back, the POLICE STATION of 1835, a quoined classical block done without much fire. It was formerly the warden's office of the prison, which replaced a *Wyatt* prison of 1785 (itself replacing an earlier one stigmatized by Howard). This is the edge of the town, with, straightaway, a magnificent view of the Downs and the rolling country leading to them. On the w side of the road NEW GROVE, originally the Leconfield Estate Agent's house, quite clearly an applied C18 refronting of earlier parts. Stone, L-shaped, the end of the projecting arm given a pediment and Venetian windows, robustly detailed and *c.*1740, the windows on the sides of this wing still with stone surrounds and keystones. The other part plainer and slightly earlier. The total effect greater than this bald account indicates. Beyond again SOANES FARM, a nice simple C17 stone house, empty at the time of writing. Three bays, mullioned and hood-moulded windows, probably quite late in the C17.

From here, ANGEL STREET can be reached by a footpath. The way back into town is past the Roman Catholic church (*see* p. 295) and a charming set of cottages including the ANGEL HOTEL, stucco and tile-hung, taking up the curve of the road beautifully. The rest of Angel Street is minor but nice (e.g. the mid C19 lettering on OLGER'S, the grocers) and leads back to the Market Square, accompanied by too much through traffic. But on the r. EAST STREET has the most ambitious house in Petworth: DAINTREY HOUSE, mid C18, a chequerboard of grey and red brick. Seven bays, with quoins and heavy window surrounds, the top storey with its small pediment probably thirty years later. It looks more like Chichester than the elegant suavity of most Petworth C18 buildings and it is not an outstanding design, but the ironwork of the garden railing in front is magnificent. Probably *c.*1800, a pattern of horizontal ellipses between thicker uprights with tiny urns on top. This is first-rate art, not merely clever craftsmanship, in the way it quickens the rhythm and performs a kind of fan dance in front of the staid house. The inspiration, really, is the same wholehearted understanding of Industrial Revolution forms in all their applications that produced Wedgwood china and the early iron bridges. East Street continues N with THE LEADS, a plain mid C18 front with a rich doorcase with Composite and Doric columns side by side, a strange sight. Then, on the l., DENMAN'S, probably the best half-timber house in Petworth, close-studded front with overhang and moulded bressumer, and brick nogging. A little restored but still impressive. Opposite this a nest of very Petworth-like buildings forming the GIRLS SCHOOL: two jolly tile-hung houses of c.1880, a plain red-brick building behind and a pedimented stock-brick building of 1819, badly converted which was a Unitarian chapel. One more plain brick C18 house, THE INSTITUTE, and the walker is opposite the church, part of the third route.

For this, back to the Market Square again (Petworth is so attractive that repeated re-tracings are a pleasure rather than an imposition). This time the exit is at the NE corner, up LOMBARD STREET. This is a delight: narrow, curving, sett paved, with the church tower appearing at the end in half a dozen combinations. A stuccoed front faces into the Market Square, and the road shifts round it. Simple brick and stone cottages not needing special description, but a superb total effect, one of the best picturesque streets in a county that is full of them. The reverse sequence, opening into the square is admirable too.

At the N end, opposite the church, TUDOR HOUSE, in fact dated 1629, in the happy Sussex style: mullioned and transomed windows, gables with ball finials. Part stone, part stucco, more than part restored. At the top turn r. (with a glance l. at the forbidding backside – Gilpin in 1780 called it the back-front-of-Petworth House) and begin NORTH STREET. At the junction with East Street a plain C18 house (THE SURGERY) and a very strange LAMP STANDARD in the middle of the road. It has a Gothic stone plinth and an extraordinary prickly iron superstructure. The intention seems Art Nouveau, but the detail is a cross between Gothic and sweet-pea tendrils: in fact it was put up in 1851, and the designer was *Sir Charles Barry*. As a curiosity it should most certainly be preserved.

Then into North Street proper. On the l., again, the park wall or Park Offices. On the r., the best set of buildings in Petworth: first NORTH HOUSE, plain late C18 brick, very similar to Newlands, with a Doric porch and a good iron lampholder above. Then cottages stepped downhill, interrupted charmingly by PREYSTE HOUSE, early C19 stucco painted green and maroon. After that, two fine C17 buildings next to one another, SOMERSET HOSPITAL and SOMERSET LODGE, now in good condition after a period of disrepair. The hospital is an early C17 house converted to almshouses in 1746: not quite the usual Petworth style – brick and stone, two big bow windows, and a taller three-storeyed brick centre, almost a tower, ending in strange flattened gabling, more odd than attractive. Somerset Lodge is smaller but a beauty, the nicest house in Petworth (it was nearly demolished recently). Stone-built, dated 1653, a front as elegant and as conservative as Dean House at Tillington was of 1613. Yet again a North Country effect. Three bays, three storeys, three shaped gables carrying three ball finials, the centre gable projecting deeply. It is almost a nursery rhyme description and it is really a nursery rhyme house. Mullion-and-transom windows, string-courses, admirable proportions. If it were not dated, all the details would delude the topographer into an assured *c.*1620. In particular – and this is very odd for the Home Counties – there is no hint of Artisan Mannerism. From here a long ribbon of cottages runs N for half a mile or more right out into the country, which appears enchantingly in the gaps between them. Among them the stucco Tudor THOMPSONS HOSPITAL, founded 1618, the present front mid C19, and a good half-timbered COTTAGE end on to the road just N of it.

PETWORTH HOUSE. One spirit runs through all of the Petworth estate, whether inside or outside the park wall: proud and patrician, scorning false ostentation but not afraid of extreme richness when richness is needed. In the house and surrounding grounds, superbly kept, the impression is overwhelming and ennobling. Some parks are no more than the sum of the objects inside them: Petworth is so much more that it is possible to come out of a walk in the park feeling that it represents a quite different order of environment, an order that can transfer its values to the views like a physical essence. It may be an illusion, but it is far more real than much C20 so-called reality.

Petworth was a Percy castle, enlarged from an existing manor house after licence to crenellate was granted in 1309. More remains of the C13 house than one expects: the walls of the chapel, and also, at r. angles to and SW of the chapel, the undercroft of the hall, with thick plain piers without capitals and a thick plain groin vault without ribs. In the late C16 the 8th and 9th Earls of Northumberland enlarged the house, and gave it a famous stable court, but nothing is left of this; it was all removed in the wholesale rebuilding of 1688–96 by Charles, 6th Duke of Somerset, who married a Percy heiress in 1682.

43b   The house he built consisted really of a magnificent w front, with the back and sides left very much to themselves. The main rooms were decorated then, the staircase hall painted after a fire in 1714, a famous sculpture gallery added to the N end *c*.1780, by the cultured and humane 3rd Earl of Egremont, and some of the interiors and the s front rearranged by *Salvin* in 1869–72. The stables and outbuildings of various dates in the C18 and C19 are all plain, decent, and almost featureless.

The 6th Duke of Somerset's one magnificent front has puzzled scholars ever since. It has clearly French elements, but was it done by a Frenchman? The C18 believed that *Pierre Puget* designed it, by association with the Mr Pouget who rebuilt Montague House in London for the 6th Duke after a fire in 1686. *Daniel Marot* has also been suggested (by Mr Christopher Hussey), and more recently the idea has been put forward that the designer was an Englishman interpreting French ideas (Sir Anthony Blunt). Payments were certainly made for measuring work done by Mr Scarbrow in 1690, and he is probably the John Scarborough who was then Wren's clerk of works at Greenwich. On the other hand it would have been fairly easy for a Frenchman to have left a design to be worked out by the masons, and the way the rooms are arranged along one long *enfilade* goes to support this. Scarborough himself seems to have been no more than a measuring clerk – he did the same at St Paul's and Hampton Court.

One thing must always be remembered when looking at Petworth – that it originally had a dome of some kind. It appears in 1690 as a 'circular roof'. If it was a dome proper, one should remember that Wren had just two years before designed a dome for his Grand Front of Hampton Court, never built. Whatever the circular roof, the front of Petworth immediately makes much more sense, the reticence is justified, and it becomes one of the finest C17 compositions in England. Without it, all that can be seen above the parapet, rather oddly, is the very top of the church tower. When Barry's spire was in position it must have looked extremely puzzling. The front is far better than photographs can show or than has generally been allowed (the nadir of appreciation was the late C19. Elwes in 1879 says 'A long monotonous façade ... without even a pediment or portico to give relief to the eye or dignity to the building', whilst even Soane had a monstrous proposal to face it with stucco).

The design, twenty-one bays long (3–6–3–6–3) is based on the tension between the overpoweringly horizontal proportions (it is only two and a half storeys high) and the tightly organized vertical strips made up of the windows in the wings and the spaces between them. The three-bay centre is uniform, to anchor the composition (and of course the dome would have reinforced this), and the articulation of the parts of the front is done with a magnificently rich yet subtle polychrome – which is what photographs cannot show. Two stones, were used, the familiar white Portland stone for the dressings and local green sandstone for most of the walls. The whole of the centre, the cornice and all the window frames are Portland stone, and so are the vertical strips made up of windows and wall in the wings. All the windows have deep concave reveals, and the vertical panels are effected simply by continuing the recession of the reveal downward between the windows and then placing ornaments in the ready-made recesses – two busts and a central eagle between ground and first floor, pairs of consoles and a central trophy between first floor and cornice. The centre, distinguished by banded rustication, is unified as a little three-bay façade of its own: blind balustrade shafts and linked ovals between ground and first floor, brackets above. The whole thing is done with an exact calculation of means, yet without any meanness of spirit, that is very rare in English architecture, which tends to be all emotion or no emotion, rarely controlled and refined emotion. Often Vanbrugh and often Wren, but not so often the balance of feeling and intellect: and Petworth, to say it once more, is this kind of balance, not just twenty-one bays of platitude. The carving on the front is superb, as it is throughout the house: the mason may have been *Samuel Fulkes*, who worked on St Paul's.*

The other fronts are almost unplanned. On the N side everything is confused by the plain late C18 sculpture gallery; above it are straightforward windows with stone surrounds and keystones which occur in several places around Petworth (and also, in one place, the odd sight of star-shaped rustication

---

* The scores between French and English elements are as follows. English the length, the even lowness, the use of smooth ashlar facing, French the banded rustication of the centre, the central doorway with its straight entablature on strong brackets and the coupled brackets with the rich and close carving between. These three motifs together give the centre an unmistakable French character, but it is a French set-piece in an English façade. The motifs of the angle pavilions are far less French.

around the head of a niche). The E side is a medley of C18
windows, pairs of buttresses (of what date?) and the big E
window of the chapel in a deep recess. The S side is plain and
dignified, six bays wide, in the style of the quieter stretches
of the main front. It was rebuilt by *Salvin* in 1869–72, who at
the same time designed the entrance arch attached to the E
side, a composition of niches and coupled columns, showing
its date by flabby proportions – the niches e.g. are far too
small. Finally, to l. and r. of the main front are ornate mid
C19 iron gates copied from one of the designs at Hampton
Court.

The INTERIORS are described in the order in which they
are normally shown. The visitor starts in the middle of the E
front. The first room with anything to notice is the SQUARE
DINING ROOM, redecorated in the early C19 with *Jonathan
Ritson* as carver. His work is evident in the elegant pelmets
and in the fireplace. From here into the MARBLE HALL, the
original entrance hall, in spite of its name dominated by
Selden's wood-carving. The style is the grand and not very
personal Baroque typical of the late C17 in England and not
much altered throughout the C18 (Palladianism was a matter,
often, of façades. Inside, things could go how they pleased).
The Marble Hall has very strict, sparing architectural decoration – plain bolection mouldings for the fireplaces, but large,
reredos-like overmantels with broken pediments, plain niches
but scrolly surrounds for statues,* and a splendid overscale
cornice with a plain flat plaster ceiling immediately above
it. The cornice is deliberately more than life-size, to overcome
the effect of height, a trick which the C18 forgot in its search
for correctness. Superbly carved bulls and unicorns on the
pediments. The carving as a whole is drumming on the surface
of the material, and is as vivid in its way as C13 stiff-leaf
foliage. From here the visitor moves l. through the Beauty
Room, with another panel by *Selden* over the door, to the
GRAND STAIRCASE. This is a disappointment, for the banisters (and the enormous window on the E side) are obviously
C19, presumably *Salvin*'s, and overshadow the C18 painted
decoration, showing Elizabeth, Duchess of Somerset, and in-

* Collected statues are outside *The Buildings of England*. But it goes hard
not to mention the splendid Roman statue of the C1 in the niche to the r. of
the door, or the C4 B.C. Greek head of Aphrodite (which has been attributed
to Praxiteles) in the Beauty Room next door, or the collection in the Sculpture
Gallery, ranging from a sombre woman of the C2 or C3 B.C. to *Rossi*'s alarming and still half Roman 'British Pugilist' of the early C19.

cidents from the Prometheus–Pandora myths. Therefore, a deal of goddesses and architectural framing. Handsome and four-square, without any real attempt at *trompe l'œil* – and without that, the C20 visitor is embarrassed. What is he supposed to do, believe that this stiff yet naturalistic decoration is three-dimensional? He cannot accept it as a kind of visual shorthand, as he could at Ravenna. The date *c*.1720, after the fire, the painter – on the unauthenticated statement of Horace Walpole – was *Laguerre*.

From here the visitor retraces his steps. Further s are the private rooms, not normally shown to the public. They include the White and Gold Room with sparing Rococo plasterwork of *c*.1760, not at all Adamesque, and the private dining room with clever early C19 carving by *Ritson* in Grinling Gibbons style. Beyond, on the other side of the Marble Hall, the Little Dining Room, again with a plain ceiling and also with a plain coving, but again a frieze as sumptuously embellished as possible, the stucco being *à jour* to a marvellous degree. The Little Dining Room is followed by what is accurately and understandably called the GRINLING GIBBONS ROOM. *Gibbons* worked on this in 1692, and the carvings are probably 42a the most technically astounding he ever did. They make a vast cornucopia of naturalistic carving, in his favourite lime-wood, arranged to frame the C16 and C17 portraits; a mixture of fruit, flowers, fish, cherubs' heads, musical instruments, an amphora, and a fiasco, plenty of birds, done in the round with a miraculously light and lively touch. Most brilliant of all, perhaps, the intricate cyphers, completely detached from the wall. This vast rediscovery of the beauty of the physical world for its own sake – innocently, as though Gibbons were still in the Garden of Eden – is typical of England after the Restoration. Paradoxically, the extreme virtuosity defeats the effect of the room as a whole. It is not unified, like the Double Cube Room at Wilton, because the eye travels enthralled from one superb festoon to the next. The cornice by its style is by *Selden*, the carving in the cove is early C19 by *Ritson*.

From here the way is through the TURNER ROOM, with a fireplace whose bolection moulding is nobly underlined by stylized leaves, into the plain late C18 SCULPTURE GALLERY, simply an unemphatic north-lit space for an astonishing variety of paintings and sculpture; now that the collection at Ince Blundell has been broken up the only English equivalent

42c   is at Newby, in the West Riding. From here into the CHAPEL, where the C13 and C17 mix without any compromise yet without one obliterating the other. The chapel must have been a lavish building, and happily its main motif is intact – a grandly scaled wall arcade framing two-light windows in the sides with unencircled trefoils above. Three-light window at the E end (the tracery is all new (i.e. of c.1800?) but must have been something similar, though no doubt with three motifs in the tracery instead of one). The arches have multiple mouldings, and rest on Sussex marble shafts and circular abaci – these shafts are not nook-shafts, but are placed on the wall between successive splays – i.e. the intention is not to accentuate the windows but to quicken and bind the room into a single space. The splays in fact have their own continuous roll-mouldings, as has each light. The date must be c.1260–70, a good example of how the abstract and purely architectural C13 style in Sussex kept its vitality almost to the end of the century. Above the arcade is a C17 ceiling, below it is C17 woodwork; so the effect, odd and nice, is of an E.E. sandwich. The chapel was refitted in 1690–2: the painter was 'Mr Tourner', the carver was Selden, and the whole is one of the best late C17 chapel interiors we have left. The decoration includes painted spandrels to the wall arcade* and painting on the (blocked) windows on the N side, a tunnel-vaulted plaster ceiling, sparse contemporary heraldic painted glass attributed to John Oliver, surveyor and architect in the City of London, and a splendid W gallery with a kind of painted proscenium arch above it of imaginary drapery part painted and part carved, with a virile pair of angels supporting arms and crown. But the best part of the chapel is the WOODWORK – splendidly designed as well as splendidly carved. A grave repeating pattern of wall panelling accentuates the C13 arcade: an urn and canopy in front of each wall-shaft, a cherub's head and wings under a pediment in the stretches between. The reredos has a semicircular pediment and heavy festoons – this is Selden imitating Gibbons – and the altar rails have a thick pattern of balusters and festoons which make them seem almost solid. It is the cherubs' heads that are the finest thing of all, and which eventually make Selden a greater artist even

* The first and last spandrel has an angel. Can this have been inspired by the C13 angels in the spandrels of the transept at Westminster Abbey, after all the great national monument of the style of the chapel? Wren appreciated the Abbey, why not Mr Tourner?

than Gibbons. Each one is different, each one a roaring can-
tankerous epitome of babyhood – real little people, not decoration. One or two would get their way by stealth, rather than
frontal attacks, and the quintet on the reredos, appropriately,
look as good as gold. There is nothing quite like this anywhere else: yet Selden was simply an estate servant and as far
as we know never worked outside Petworth. The final touch
in this enchanting room is a neo-classical stove, tucked into
the wainscot.

The GROUNDS are as fine as the house. They were landscaped in the late 1750s by *Capability Brown* and are now at
full maturity, a beautiful example of carefully calculated informality, with clumps and vistas and a long serpentine lake
running N–S. Immediately N of the house, and a splendid foil,
are the thickly wooded Pleasure Gardens. In them first a neat
TEMPLE, Roman Doric, and then a ROTUNDA, ten Ionic
columns supporting an entablature, now without a roof,
though one was clearly intended.

Finally, the tangle of OFFICES and STABLES, which is all
the motorist sees of Petworth House and which give it the
uncomfortable air of turning its back on the town. Most of
the buildings are plain C19 and require no comment: the two
things that do can both be seen from the main road and form
one of Petworth's sharp right-angle bends. One is a dourly elegant late C18 LODGE with a central pediment and a swag on a
white stone panel beneath it, a fine contrast with the yellow
sandstone walls. The other is the main GATE, two C18 piers
surmounted by macabre trophies, beautifully carved – armour
and helmets without any men inside them, the helmet
supported on a thing like a tree trunk, done in a dashing
wafery style, very eerie and very un-English. These are by
V. Prost of Dijon.

PLAISTOW

Remote village in the Weald, N of Petworth, still keeping a good
deal of its original character of a clearing in the woods. Pretty
brick and tile-hung cottages; the centre by the church is a T-
junction. The green a little way E has hardly any houses around
it.

HOLY TRINITY. Decent stone lancet chapel by *J. Butler* of
Chichester, 1851. The old church was half-timbered.

PLAISTOW PLACE. C16 half-timbered house in authentic con-

dition, with plastered walls and a complex pattern of roof
gables. One polygonal bay with mullion-and-transom stone
windows on both floors. With so many such houses over-
restored, this is worth a special look. On a small hill with a
twenty-mile view s across the Weald to the Downs.

QUENNELLS, ¼ m. E, on the Loxwood road. Regular timber-
framed house with an overhang and quite a complex moulded
bressumer (i.e. the horizontal beam covering the ends of the
floor joists at the overhang). The date is presumably C16: the
bressumer looks earlier, the timber-framing looks later.

POLING

A cul-de-sac N of Littlehampton, and a good place to see what
the Sussex coastal plain was like before the C20 got there: flint
walls, thatched flint and brick cottages, informal grouping. Long
may it remain so: the horizon s and w is already urbanized. For
about twenty years it was overshadowed by a set of enormous
radar towers, removed in 1958.

ST NICHOLAS. A simple addition of medieval parts very typical
of Sussex, mellow and gentle. Plain Saxon nave with one
double-splayed window high up on the N side. The wooden
shutter was found in position and is preserved below. Two-
bay s arcade of c.1300, pointed chamfered arches, plain responds, circular pier with octagonal abacus, perhaps altered.
The chancel was rebuilt c.1380 and the remaining detail is
all unaffected Perp: windows generally square-headed of one
and two lights, and the C15 tower, similar to East Preston,
with angle buttresses, small square-headed bell-openings, and
a tower arch of two chamfered continuous orders. E window
1830, the plain tie-beams of the roof ornamented with six
ornate carved bosses given at the same time by the Duke of
Norfolk, presumably from Arundel church. – SCREEN. Simple
wooden base with small square openings with quatrefoil
tracery. Above, battlemented ROOD BEAM, perhaps from
Bargham Chapel. It makes a simple and moving composition
with the tie-beam above. – FONT. Saxon? Crude bowl, circular at the top, tapering at the bottom. – PLATE. Chalice,
1567–8. – BRASS. Walter Davy, vicar in the mid C15, demi-
figure 20 in. high. Simple bold lines, and surprisingly good
and expressive for a C15 brass.

W of the church, good simple BARN and COTTAGES, flint with
brick dressings, thatched: to the N more cottages and PECK-

HAMS, a little more ambitious, with C18 brick and flint re-facing concealing a half-timbered house.

½ m. N again, at Poling Corner, is FAIRPLACE FARM, or St John's Priory, incorporating a Commandery of Knights Hospitallers of St John of Jerusalem, founded in the C12. The present house has six bays under a hipped roof: two bays in brick of c.1830, the other four in flint representing the original hall and chapel. One small lancet on the S side and one on the N; pointed door with label on the S side which looks c.1300, blocked window in the E wall which looks as if it has been Dec or Perp rather than E. E. Inside, small C15 square-headed PISCINA. Kingpost and tie-beam roof.

POUND HILL see CRAWLEY, p. 204

PRINSTED see SOUTHBOURNE

PULBOROUGH

0010

A puzzling place, undecided whether to be village, town, or suburb. As an important crossroads (London–Chichester and Winchester–Brighton), it is a natural town site. But it has not grown up so, and most of the building of the last fifty years has been suburban. One long road running W–E under a small escarpment, parallel with the Arun, with two or three miniature centres. The church and most of the older houses are a little further N along the top of the hill. This is potentially an exciting plan (a parallel High and Low Pulborough) and should be exploited. Stone, brick, and both yellow sandstone and dark brown carstone.

ST MARY. Mostly simple, good Perp. Although not large or showy, it is admirably done (as most Perp work is in Sussex) and is more worth a visit than many larger buildings in other counties. Clerestoried nave, aisles, and tower which can be dated fairly accurately around 1420–30. Money was left for the tower in 1404, for the church as a whole in 1422. The tower is in the same style as Arundel or Kirdford, with two-light bell-openings under segmental heads, angle buttresses, and a bold square stair-turret at the NE corner. The clerestory uses those same two-light windows but the aisles have 'Winchester' windows – two main lights subdividing into four in the tracery under a segmental arch and label, as in Winchester nave. Inside, the tower arch has three continuous chamfers, but the four-bay nave arcades have four attached shafts and four hollows in the diagonals and double-chamfered arches. So perhaps different masons were used (if the tower is c.1410 and the nave c.1430, that would be understandable). Both parts share simple, strong lines, good proportions, and excellent use of the porous texture of the sandstone. Good kingpost roof and good Perp N porch. For the tower a vault was projected, but given up.

The E parts at Pulborough are in fact earlier. Lancet chancel, quite late in the C13, the E end with a triplet gathered under one rere-arch with mouldings and nook-shafts.* N chancel chapel C13 too, with two-bay arcade of the usual style between it and the chancel. The chancel arch is similar. One early C14 window re-used at the E end of the S aisle. – FONT. Purbeck marble. C12 square arcaded bowl. – PLATE. Cup and Cover, 1587.–MONUMENTS. Brass to Thomas Harlyng † 1423, rector of Pulborough. Effigy 4 ft high, complete with canopy but weary (N aisle). – Two C15 brasses (S aisle) † 1452 and 1478. 3-ft and 18-in. effigies, hack work. – Rough Perp tomb-chest, N chancel chapel. The inscription is later. – Rev. Harvey Spragg † 1796. Decent Adamesque tablet. – William Hammond † 1895, by *John Gibson* of Rome. It must have been carved much earlier, for Gibson died in 1866. Sick man in chair, consoling woman, children and angel, all in low relief. Pathetically empty of feeling, pathetically full of sentimentality, the feeling that one ought to feel.

Good simple LYCHGATE outside, wood with a Horsham slate roof.

The centre of Pulborough is now down by the Arun. Here a BRIDGE, by-passed, which looks exactly like a simpler edition of Stopham Bridge but in fact dates from 1787. Beside it a decent new pub, THE SWAN, detailed if anything with too much care (i.e. not pubby enough), by *E. Whittaker*, 1961. To the W a soigné WESTMINSTER BANK by *Frederick Wheeler*, 1914 (cf. Horsham and Petworth), to the E a long street of cottages. The best are the partly tile-hung ODDFELLOWS ARMS and No. 77, half-timbered with a recessed centre. Above, on the ridge, good simple SCHOOLS of 1859. Who did them?

NW of the church, over the railway, is OLD PLACE. Here the house has been completely altered, but the former barn, now

* The PISCINA is late C13, the ogee-headed SEDILIA C14 (or, by the blandness of the detail, even C15. An ogee arch here was almost inevitable to get the priest's head in).

also a house, contains a bewildering unrelated variety of C15
or C16 details. Most of them must be re-set. Single and two-
light windows under hood-moulds, and towards the N end a
combination of a large and small arch, almost round-headed,
under thickly carved hood-moulds. This looks C16 and may
have been the original wagon entrance.

NEW PLACE, ½ m. NE, also beside the railway. Moderate-sized
stone farmhouse, s front with several mullioned windows and
a big brick chimneystack at the W end. This also has a mullioned window in it, high up. What can it have lit?

TOAT MONUMENT, 1½ m. N, on top of a knoll in lovely countryside. Spindly octagonal tower with battlements built in 1827.
It looks as though it ought to ventilate a railway tunnel.

BEEDINGS, 1½ m. NE, on a dramatic ridge-top site. Battlemented, with corner towers. Deliberately grim and unaccom-
modating, with a force which is rare in C19 houses. Unfortunately, the architecture does not match the intentions.

RACTON

No village: scattered houses in the tiny Ems valley NE of Emsworth just at the point where it enters the Downs proper.

CHURCH. Humble C13 and C15, externally; largely roughcast,
concealing the fact that the nave walling is C12, the chancel,
probably, a C13 addition. Just a shade too restored to be
really attractive. Surprisingly heavy Perp E window, renewed
but apparently on the old lines. The inside pleasant because
it keeps a tympanum above the tie-beam marking the division
between nave and chancel – big ROYAL ARMS with frilly wood
tracery on either side, probably all C18. – PLATE. Elizabethan
Cup; Paten, 1691; Flagon, 1716. – MONUMENTS. Hugh
Gounter(?), c.1520. Showy canopied table tomb of the same
general family as the de la Warr chantry at Boxgrove. Canopy
with four-centred arch, a thin band of vine-trail ornament, a
thick band above that with two panels bearing half-Renais-
sance ornament – the Gounter arms flanked by swans in one
case, by crude putti in the other. More putti round the corner.
Above that again, thistly cresting of fleur-de-lis and anthemion – a nice, spirited, extrovert performance. The surprising
part is the bas-relief under the arch. Husband, sons, and wife
and daughters form a kneeling pattern facing one another, as
usual, but in between them a figure of the risen Christ which
looks much earlier than the C16, although they make a very

good match. If it is re-used,* it seems to show unexpected piety which is matched by other C16 carvings in Sussex and which makes sense of the ornamental display around. Many tombs of this date had eschewed religious symbolism altogether. – Sir George Gounter † 1624 and wife. Kneeling figures under a canopy. Justice and Charity above. Standard quality, nicely coloured. – Sir Charles Nicoll † 1733. First-rate bust in elaborate architectural frame, all completely in the newly arrived Palladian style. White and black marble, pedimented frame with volute scrolls at the sides. The bust, in contemporary dress, has a noble expressionless face, the clothes arranged loosely and asymmetrically around the throat with a panache worthy of Rysbrack at his best. These three tombs, close together, make a rewarding comparison.

Nice thatched timber-framed COTTAGE immediately SW of the church. Regular spacing, presumably C17.

LORDINGTON, ½ m. N. L-shaped house with its detail mostly plain C18. This represents, as it often does, the ground plan of half of a Tudor building. Inside, parts of a C17 staircase, badly re-set in the late C19: heraldic beasts, as at Hatfield, and panels combining swags and strapwork (mostly re-set upside down!) in a way which must date it c.1630–40.

In the gardens, two pairs of fine and very unusual C17 GATEPIERS: cylindrical, not rectangular, with bold circular mouldings above ending in balls.

RACTON TOWER, ½ m. W. An isolated site in a grove of trees with a wide view S – mock sinister rather than truly sinister, which is appropriate. Built in 1772 by *Theodosius Keene*, a very typical C18 folly, rather like a foreshortened joke edition of Beaumaris. Triangular base with short sides and round tower at each corner, each originally surmounted by a smaller round tower: much taller round tower in the centre. Brick core with flint skin, most of which has fallen off; like most follies, better from a distance.

REDFORD see LINCH

REDLANDS FARM see WEST ITCHENOR

RIVER HOUSE see TILLINGTON

* It certainly was not added later, see the way the banner coming from the staff is taken up on the separate slab of the man and sons.

ROFFEY

A suburb of Horsham on the road to Crawley. Largely Victorian terraces, with bigger houses beyond, out in the country.

ALL SAINTS. By *A. W. Blomfield*, 1878. Hard and soulless, though impressively proportioned inside. SE tower, surprisingly big.

ROFFEY PARK. Enormous lumbering house of *c.*1870, stone below, half-timber above, tile-hanging in the gables. Put in because it is so typical, and because of its undeniable picturesqueness at a distance.

ROGATE

On the Hampshire border near Petersfield, in the valley separating the South Downs from the hilly heathlands of the 'Midhurst country' to the N. Bigger and more compact than most of the Rother villages, with a nice group of church, unfenced churchyard, and surrounding cottages at the main crossroads – when it can be seen for the traffic. Yellow sandstone and tile roofs.

ST BARTHOLOMEW. An odd kind of restoration (*J. W. Penfold*, 1875) which has made the outside look quite new, yet kept most of the old features inside. Chancel, aisled nave, and shingled bell-turret with western lean-to all included under the nave roof – bulky, picturesque, and a nice focus for the village. The arcades have circular piers and square abaci with chamfered corners; one arch on the N side is round-headed, the others are later, a typically thick C13 style, commoner in the South Midlands than in Sussex: double-chamfered, slightly pointed, with the arches dying into the continuation of the pier before they reach the abacus, giving the effect of squinches. Scattered C13 to C14 details elsewhere: mutilated SEDILIA and chancel arch C13, arch to N chancel chapel C14, with continuous mouldings.* The interesting thing at Rogate is the massive framing for the bell-turret: four big corner posts, but the framing built up with diagonal braces on N and S sides only, with a series of arches spanning across between them, rather like Thursley in Surrey. The effect is much more deliberate and less of a carpenter's job than most English timber-framed belfries. – MONUMENT. Thomas Ridge † 1828. The usual mourning woman, but crisply carved, without sentimentality.

* The old Dec E window apparently had an ogee top – see drawing formerly in tower.

s of the village, BRIDGE over the Rother, the same humble
character as the others between here and Midhurst. Four
round-headed arches with cutwaters: two are C16 or C17,
two are C18, and given the extra touch of formality that the
C18 relished by a pair of keystones.

No cottages worth especial notice in the village. ½ m. E is
FYNING, a separate hamlet of its own, with FYNING
HOUSE, plain C18, the main front stuccoed, of seven bays
with a pediment. Across the road, good BARNS, the best and
biggest of them tarred weatherboard on a sandstone base and
entirely thatched – even to the separate-topped roof over the
wagon entrance.

DURFOLD, 1½ m. W. Founded as an Abbey of Premonstratensian Canons before 1161. What was left of this was removed
in 1784, when the present plain farmhouse was built, except
for fragments of capitals and arches built into the garden
wall. Good BARN, tarred weatherboard and tile. Just E of this,
DURFOLD BRIDGE is probably the nicest and least altered of
the Rother Valley bridges: four round-headed arches and
cutwaters, a comfortable warm-textured jogtrot from bank to
bank.

Of the other hamlets near Rogate, BORDEN, 1½ m. NE, is worth
a special visit, not for any individual building, but for the
way that quite ordinary cottages are made into a memorable
place by respecting the site – high up in a tiny wooded valley.
The individuality is quite unsuspected on the map and is a
perfect example of the way in which the Midhurst country
can produce effects in a small distance without any corresponding sense of being small-scale.

0030

RUDGWICK

In thick Wealden country NW of Horsham, the church on a hilltop only a few yards from the Surrey border. No definite shape,
but a good group of tile-hung cottages in front of the church,
screening it from the road, and a sober, plain early C18 house
(COUSENS) immediately to the N.

HOLY TRINITY. Effectively all of the early C14, quite a rarity
in this part of the country. From the proportions, the s nave
wall is probably Norman, and the heavy tower with its shingled
cap is early C13, but the building was completely re-done in
the early C14 with a big new N aisle and probably a new chancel. The inside effect is wide, high, and surprisingly spacious.

The designer had a fondness for tall two-light windows,
delicately moulded, with an absorbing variety of Geometrical
tracery in the heads: trefoils, spherical triangles, and in one
case (N aisle) 'Kentish' tracery, i.e. with a downward-pointing
cusp going against the upward flow. Well carved small heads
as label-stops in the N aisle. New E window, but a handsome
moulded rere-arch with nook-shafts. The C14 arcade is just
as full of quiet individuality; octagonal piers and abaci, and a
most complicated arch section using both concave and convex
mouldings, absolutely characteristic of its date. Tower arch
with mouldings fading into the imposts. Dec PISCINA and
AUMBRY too. – FONT. Sussex marble, late C12, square bowl
with a shallow pattern of round-headed arcading, and an
elegant moulded base. Very much restored. – PLATE. Cup
and Paten, Elizabethan.

NALDRETT HOUSE, I m. S, on a cul-de-sac off the road from
Bucks Green to Billingshurst. Delightful C18 farmhouse, not
too common in Sussex: three bays and two storeys, with big
windows set wide apart, and a door with a big fanlight. Brick
with stone quoins.

GARLANDS, 1½ m. S, near The Haven. Handsome early C17
farm, big enough to have a developed half-H plan with gabled
wings. The top half is tile-hung and the bottom courses
project slightly (to throw off the rain) and give a slight overhang, which is coved. Does all this conceal the more familiar
half-timbering and a more definite overhang? The same
effect done very prettily at REDHOUSE FARM at BUCKS
GREEN, I m. N; with quite a circumstantial late C17 front
and shell-hood doorcase. The older half-timbering shows at
the back.

RUMBOLDSWYKE see CHICHESTER, p. 170

see CHICHESTER, p. 170

RUSPER

Unspoilt village in unspoilt country N of Horsham. Central
triangular space, with pleasant cottages around, half-timber and
tile-hung. On the Surrey border and very like a good Surrey
village.

ST MARY MAGDALENE. Hefty, impressive Perp tower, possibly C16 incorporating C13 fragments, with big buttresses and
big square stair-turret at one corner – the Thames Valley
type done with more force. Local Weald stone. The top 10 ft
and the W window are in fact C19, done in 1855 when the

rest of the church was rebuilt, flavourless and spindly. –
ROYAL ARMS of George I. – Handsome CANDELABRUM in
the nave, given in 1770. Another in the s aisle is supposedly
medieval. – BRASSES, in the chancel. Thomas Challoner †
1532 and his wife are the usual C16 hack work; John de
Kyggesfold, c.1370, is much better. Demi-figures in civilian
dress, 11 in. high. Sensitivity and even humour in the simple
drawing of the man's face. The inscription is Norman French,
not Latin.

Rusper had a Benedictine nunnery, but the last fragments were
demolished in 1781. The present house there (THE NUNNERY)
is C19. Near the entrance to it is OLD PARK FARM, the best
of Rusper's cottages, tile-hung and half-timbered with a
picturesque small gable in front. Probably C16, empty at the
time of writing.

RUSTINGTON

On the coast E of Littlehampton, hence a predictable pattern – a
few flint walls and flint cottages, and a great many small modern
houses. It could, still, be very individual and attractive, and
in purely C20 suburban terms.

ST PETER AND ST PAUL. The w tower is the best part: late
C12, nicely unrestored, with twin round-headed bell-openings
and a central octagonal shaft under a pointed arch with nook-
shafts: a good direct piece of village building, exactly Transitional. In the rest, although nothing has been violently
altered, the village simplicity has gone in repeated small
hardenings and furbishings. Tower arch late C12, pointed and
unchamfered on scalloped responds; s arcade of the same date,
a rough little anthology of the Transitional details that Sussex
is so rich in: arches only just pointed, unchamfered and unmoulded, two capitals with waterleaf, one a combination of
waterleaf and scalloping, square abaci and alternately round
and octagonal piers. Chancel and N transept C13 in the usual
plain lancet style, the E end with a composition of a triplet
under a rere-arch with a single lancet above. The arch from
the transept to the N aisle is C13 too, but the N arcade itself
is C14 and rather a surprise: two big arches with complex
mouldings dying into piers without capitals. Are the quatrefoil clerestory windows C14 also? – MONUMENT. Very
battered small C16 monument in the N transept. Enough
remains to pose a small enigma but not to solve it: kneeling
figures under a roughly classical arch, but in the centre also

Christ on the Cross – not at all a usual combination. It looks about 1550, and what is left seems to have a lot more feeling than the usual productions of that date.

Nice flint cottages w of the church, in The Street; to the s in Sea Lane first HOBBS FARM, date 1690, then KNIGHTS-CROFT, a decent house in Norman Shaw's tile-hung style – and in fact by *Norman Shaw*, 1879.

In Worthing Road, N of the church, RUSTINGTON HOUSE, a bald stock-brick Tudor house of *c*.1880, not original in itself but providing a basis on which the architects of 1900 could build original things. E of this THE ANCHORAGE, a very piquant small house in Norman Shaw style. L-shaped, tile-hung, with a tower in the angle of the L sporting both dormers and a cupola. A good example of how serviceable and effective the style could be. Is it by *Shaw* himself ?*

RUSTINGTON CONVALESCENT HOME. On the sea front: a dashing free-Wren design of 1897 by *F. Wheeler*, done with enough panache to give it a life of its own – a very good seaside building. The main block with hipped roof and dormers and a central tower; a gabled projection on the l. with a polygonal bay opening out from the corner of it.

ST HUGH'S MONASTERY (PARKMINSTER)
1 m. s of Cowfold

2020

The tall steeple is a puzzle on the skyline to travellers in the Weald. The near surroundings are very secluded, so the mystery remains. This is a Charterhouse, or Carthusian monastery, the only one in England. It was built all at one go in 1875–83, and the architect was French, M. *Norman* of Calais. The plan is magnificent and can only be properly seen from the air: an outer courtyard leading to the chapel, and an enormous cloister behind, one of the biggest in the world (377 by 440 ft), with the separate cells of the monks opening on to it. The outward-facing walls are entirely blank, a reflec-tion of the rigorous, contemplative discipline. Alas, the design does not keep up this standard. Imported bodily from across the Channel, it represents the French Gothic Revival at its weakest and harshest. The impression of being in the outskirts of somewhere like Béthune or Arras is overwhelming. Chapel tall, apsed and unaisled; screen painted by *Sublet* of Lyons.

* Demolished 1962 to make an industrial estate, at a time when new bungalows were going up in Rustington by the dozen. It's a funny world.

2030

ST LEONARDS' PARK

2 m. E of Horsham

The noteworthy bits all *c*.1840, still classical – e.g. the third storey with pediment, and the porte-cochère. But underneath this the centre seems late C18. Was it the house known as St Leonard's Lodge and designed by *John Johnson*?

SANDS FARM *see* WARNHAM

SEDGEWICK PARK *see* NUTHURST

SELE PRIORY *see* UPPER BEEDING

9020

SELHAM

Near the Rother E of Midhurst, in lovely rich scenery, an intimate mixture of meadow and heathland. No centre, just scattered houses, stone, brick, and tile-hanging.

St JAMES. The outside tells a typical Sussex story: nave and chancel only, tall and narrow, clearly C11 at the latest. The proportions are noble, but restoration has given too many fussy details – bellcote, w wall, the whole s side with a lean-to aisle hidden from the road, most of the windows. The question is whether Selham is pre- or post-Conquest, and it sets quite a puzzle. The proportions and thinness of the walls are Saxon, but it has herringbone walling and there are regular quoins, not long-and-short work; the N doorway, unmoulded with plain imposts, has impressive Saxon proportions, narrow and tall (the imposts are 6 ft up), but the arch has a rubble core. Perhaps the answer, as in many parts of England, is the Saxo-Norman overlap, i.e. a mason working in the Saxon manner after the Conquest. However, the remarkable part of Selham, which does nothing to help solve this problem, is the
12a,   chancel arch. It is narrow but not abnormally tall, and its arch
b&c   has a rubble core and a roll-moulding on the W side, and looks Norman. The abaci, capitals, and jambs are another matter. They consist of attached columns, above which are capitals, above which are abaci, and then imposts, quite different in character. One base is quite civilized Norman, the other has three rolls of diminishing size. One capital is of a crude Composite order; the other, vividly carved, has interlaced snakes and a beast-head in the Viking tradition. Above this on the abacus is Saxon interlace on the l., stylized foliage on the r. The entirely independent imposts have a Norman

moulding and foliage on the l., a long Saxon coil and a beast-head on the r. The whole thing is rough but marvellously spirited and worth any amount of official carving, Romanesque or otherwise. Clearly these things are not all of the same kind. Could not this be a case of the overlap being extended exceptionally long? Could not Saxon pieces have been used by a mason of 1130–40 who then himself provided for the missing parts his Norman formulae and carved the capitals in his style, in itself inspired by Viking traditions?

The arch between nave and rebuilt s chapel is wide, double-chamfered, probably C13. – FONT. Tub font, curved sides, no stem. – PLATE. Chalice and Paten, 1568.

SELSEY

8090

Somehow very English, in the inconsequential way it has muddled through with its topography. Like Dunwich, it was originally an important town in Saxon England which has been affected by coastal erosion; like Dunwich, it still looks as though half of it is missing. It was the see of a Saxon bishop. The see moved to Chichester only in 1075. Since Domesday about half a mile has been eroded from Selsey Bill, and therefore the legend of a 'cathedral under the sea' is almost certainly true. The village developed about half a mile inland from the Bill, with its church a mile further NE at CHURCH NORTON. In the early C19 it began to expand, moved the nave arcades into a new church in the village, and left the chancel by itself in the old churchyard. Then the C20 came, fairly cheerful, with its bungalows and caravans. So today's Selsey is one main street still with a good many small old cottages in it, which runs straight on to the sea and stops abruptly without pier or esplanade. Church Norton to the NE is still rural and isolated, and is worth a special effort to preserve its sequestered leafiness, a rare thing on the Sussex coast. Even a few more houses would spoil it.

ST PETER, Selsey. By *J. P. St Aubyn*, 1865, cosy and spiky like a Surrey village church. It incorporates the arcades from the old church, which consist of three bays of *c.*1180 (circular piers and abaci, single-chamfered arches, the E responds with scalloped capitals) and one of *c.*1230 with standard details. The difference in spirit is greater than the bare description suggests. – FONT. Of *c.*1100, square bowl with plain round-headed arcading on the stem and four shafts. – PLATE. Chalice and Paten, 1568 (?); Paten, 1688; Paten, 1714.

OLD CHURCH, Church Norton. The chancel of the original
church, in a delightfully secluded position. Almost on the
shingle beach, looking across to Bognor Regis and its monster
gasworks. Simple C13 with lancets in both N and S sides, and
a three-light Perp E window. – MONUMENT. John Lewis and
his wife Agnes † 1537. One of the local variety of C16 tombs
combining kneeling figures with purely Gothic and purely
religious subjects. Here the central panel, probably a Trinity
or Crucifixion, has gone, but there are naïve little reliefs on
either side of St George and the Martyrdom of St Agnes.
Roughly carved but touching.

WINDMILL, W of Selsey village. A simple brick tower mill in
good condition with its sweeps complete.

SENNICOTTS

Not a village, but an area of small parks and farms immediately
NW of Chichester. Sequestered.

ST MARY. 1829, perhaps by *Draper*. By itself in the woods, a
sweet example of unselfconscious local C19 Gothic before
the Gothic Revival took hold of it. One room, quite plain
inside, small battlemented tower, crowstepped E and W ends.
Built of grey stone, galletted, i.e. with multiple tiny chips
fixed in the mortar joints.

OAKWOOD HOUSE. Plain stuccoed box of 1809–12: perhaps by
James Elmes, who exhibited a design for it in 1811. Porte-
cochère on the W side, curved bow window to the E. Several
other similar houses around, e.g. SENNICOTTS and NORTH
LANDS.

SHERMANBURY

N of Henfield, in a part of the Weald that is pretty well urbanized.
Ribbon development along the A-road, but the church and plain
late C18 Shermanbury Place are by themselves in parkland to
the E.

ST GILES. Makes a pretty group with the house, with its timber
bell-turret and spike. Difficult to sort out. Aisleless, the walls
medieval, but restored in 1710 when the nave was extended
and again in 1885. The inside character is now a rather weird
mixture of the two, with box pews (still with the farm names
on them like West Grinstead) but also a curly timber chancel
arch. Windows C19. – FONT. Probably c.1300. It is a job to
be sure about the patterns. – STAINED GLASS by *Kempe* in

the E end, as frilly as the chancel arch. – ROYAL ARMS.
Queen Anne's, put in at the C18 restoration.
In the park to the NW, EWHURST MANOR, itself C16 brick and
half-timber, keeps a small stone gatehouse on its lawn from
an earlier house. Perhaps c.1300; featureless.

SHILLINGLEE PARK

9030

2 m. w of Plaistow

An C18 house of two dates, burnt out during the Second World
War. The shell is kept in good condition. The main front
faces s and was built in 1776–8, a standard Palladian composition of seven bays and two storeys with a pedimented centre
and pediments over the ground-floor windows. Brick with
stone dressings, a type which was put up all over the country,
though not very often in Sussex. Behind this – the house is
T-shaped – is another pedimented front, also of seven bays,
which makes a nice comparison in style. It was built in 1735
by *Thomas Steel Jun.* of Chichester, and it represents a country
mason's experience of the exact moment of transition from
Baroque to Palladian. This is Baroque in intention, Palladian
in detail. Two storeys and an attic, all windows slightly
segment-headed, rusticated lunette in the pediment, doorway with Gibbs rustication. The design is very like Milford
House, Surrey. Here 1735 is vital and gauche, 1775 is anaemic
and correct.

In the park to the s a DEER TOWER, squat and stuccoed,
late C18, with four corner turrets; the pedimented pair of
LODGES on the main road at FISHERSTREET, 1 m. SW, must
also be connected with Shillinglee. They would be part of the
1735 rebuilding.

SHIPLEY

1020

s of Horsham, in a part of the Weald where the whole countryside looks like a tidy landscaped park. More open than the
landscape further N and W, with continuous views of the Downs.
No village centre; scattered cottages near the church, which is
on a cul-de-sac beside the tiny river Adur.

ST MARY. A N aisle and vestry of 1893 (by *J. L. Pearson*) have
slightly impaired a most impressive Early Norman building.
The s side is quite untouched and should be looked at first, 15a
where the huge scale and the plan will be apparent straight
away: unaisled nave, central tower without transepts, unaisled
11—S.

chancel. A central tower without transepts was fairly common
in Norman parish churches (cf. Albury, Surrey, or South
Lopham, Norfolk), especially early ones. This is indeed early
in style, for the big windows are still double-splayed, and the
plain two-order S doorway still has tall, narrow Saxon proportions. Yet, in fact, it seems to have been built as late as
c.1125 by the Knights Templars to serve a preceptory which
they established here; if true, it must be one of the latest and
oddest examples of Saxo-Norman overlap in the country.
Mighty unbuttressed central tower with big plain bell-openings and square stair-turret on the N side. No break between
it and the nave S wall, not even quoins. Mighty effect inside
too, with huge tower arches and short chancel. The W arch
is much thicker than the E, and both carry similarly unusual
ornament, made up of a roll-moulding interrupted by chevrons
and bands as though it were being held on to the stonework.
The chevrons are actually very odd. They are triangles lapping
into the roll, very much like beakheads converted into something purely geometrical. If this derivation is accepted, then
c.1125 is an early date. In the W arch this motif forms a
second order on the soffit (which is 8 ft thick) and rests on
three-scallop capitals and well-carved grinning heads. Below
the heads plain doors: on the N to the stair-turret, on the S,
rather oddly, to the outside. The E arch is thinner and plainer,
the moulding starting about 4 ft off the ground and continuing
round the arch, interrupted only by plain abaci. In both
arches, the ornament is the merest surface decoration compared with the huge areas of plain masonry. Very few later
additions: good late C12 W doorway, arch decorated with zigzag
ornament, jamb shafts, and two beautifully carved capitals,
the r. waterleaf, the l. a form of Corinthian. They are as good
as those done by the Templars in Sompting church, which
was attached to Shipley. Simple W window of c.1300. At the
same time the plain tower arch and the W doorway were made
pointed from being no doubt round. Three-light Perp chancel
E window, effective plain timber S porch probably C16. The
former N porch is re-erected as a shed in the churchyard, E
15b   of the chancel. – RELIQUARY. In a niche, N side of chancel.
A marvellous thing: a wooden box 8 in. long, covered with
copper and Limoges-enamelled with Saints, Crucifixion, etc.,
all the heads in low relief. Gold, dark and light blue, the whole
of Romanesque childlike formality in a tiny space. It is of
the C13. – PLATE. Almsdish, C17; Cup, 1713; Paten, 1731.

– STAINED GLASS. Several windows by *Kempe*. Only the E
window worth a look: enthroned Madonna, in blues and
yellows and greys, not the usual greens. Tiny scale but very
pretty. Inserted in 1893. – MONUMENT. Sir Thomas Caryll
† 1616 and wife. Absolutely standard big alabaster monument.
Recumbent life-size figures, daughters underneath, architectural background.

KINGS MILL, W of the church. A splendid smock mill in 8b
splendid condition. Low octagonal brick base, then a gallery
and tall octagonal weatherboarded top with pointed cap,
all freshly painted white. Sweeps and fantail complete, and
hence the effect of the horizontal weatherboarding versus the
similarly spaced lines of the sweeps at various angles and, in
sunlight, the patterns made by the sweeps on the smock. It
must be early C19.

S of the church, across the stream, CHURCH FARM SOUTH is
good unspoilt C17. Brick base, weatherboarded centre, tile-
hung wings, mellow tile roof half-hipped at either end – a
fine study in texture.

On the S side of A272, just E of the intersection with B2224,
are two BARNS, all by themselves in a field. Natural weatherboard, half-hipped tile roofs, and more to tell about the design
and apposition of forms than most town centres. The un-
treated wood makes them look, improbably enough, like
Kentucky or Missouri.

N of the village, several isolated farms, seeming almost as remote
now as they must have been in the C16. LACKENHURST is a
good big half-timbered farm probably of *c.*1600; TRAWLER'S
is smaller but much odder. It is almost a Tea-Pot Hall, i.e.
shaped like a triangular wedge of cake with flat front and back
and enormous steep pitched roof going down close to the
ground. Front and back are now tile-hung.

NEWBUILDINGS PLACE, near Trawler's, 1½ m. N of Shipley
church. A late Artisan Mannerist house, something which is
commoner in Surrey or Kent than Sussex. Here it is late
enough for the shaped gables to be the only thing which mark
it out from the ordinary. Dated 1683. Two parallel ranges,
with shaped end-gables and a sober handsome front facing E:
five bays, two storeys, with projecting central bay given shaped
gables, still in the Jacobean way. Stone with brick quoins: no
fancy window trim as there would have been earlier in the
century. The windows themselves are still mullioned and
transomed. Solid chimneystacks with blind arcading.

SHOPWYKE see OVING

SHOREHAM see OLD SHOREHAM and
NEW SHOREHAM

SHRIPNEY see BERSTED

8020

SHULBREDE PRIORY
½ m. s of Linchmere

An Augustinian priory, founded c.1200. The plan has been
recovered and shows an aisled church with three-bay nave
and chancel and central tower – quite circumstantial for a
house with only a prior and five canons. The remains are the
buildings in the s w corner of the cloister – prior's lodging and
undercroft (buttery), and part of the refectory – made into a
house which remained a farm until 1902 and hence escaped
the killing kindness of the c19. The result, which Lutyens
rather slightingly called 'Mary Ann all round', is delightful
outside and in, and is not reproducible by any artificial means
whatsoever, though Lutyens himself tried hard enough in
his early days. The undercroft has a rough vault – groin, not
rib, which is unusual, and rough responds – and must date
from c.1200; the central pillar, Purbeck marble with a circular
Sussex marble abacus, is later (mid c13). The refectory was
originally one hall, now divided into two floors. The most
tangible monastic evidence is the lavatorium, on the outside
N wall of the refectory, and it makes one regret the absence
of the rest very much: three trefoiled arches, beautifully done,
outlined by one thin groove – maximum effect with minimum
display. It again is mid c13.

In the mid c16 a partition was put up in the middle of the
prior's lodging, probably for structural reasons. It was
decorated with paintings, faded now, which are Shulbrede's
best-known feature: ladies in Elizabethan costume, the
animals celebrating the Nativity in a typically late medieval
way (Cock: Christus natus est; Duck: Quando Quando;
Raven: in hac nocte; Bull: Ubi Ubi; Lamb: in Bethlehem).
The central panel was repainted later with the arms of
James I.

8090

SIDLESHAM

Half a dozen hamlets of all dates, midway between Chichester
and Selsey. Thatched flint cottages near the church, and a very

pretty group 1 m. s on a creek of Pagham Harbour, like a miniature Bosham. The main street is mostly Victorian, mixed up with the inter-war mansard roofs of one of the Land Settlement Association's sites.

ST MARY. Built of (local?) rubble stone, not flint, and as big and barnlike as a Romney Marsh church. Noble proportions inside, helped rather than hindered by the violent pulling-about it received some time before 1700 which left it as a T-shaped building of aisled nave and transepts and without a chancel. As usual, the bones are early C13: pairs of tall lancets in the transepts and standard three-bay nave arcades, quite high. Unusually the transepts had two-bay E aisles, now blocked: the details of the arch in the N transept must make it a little earlier than the nave. Narrow lean-to aisles with traces of the original windows but now windows which look early C19. The aisles mercifully have kept their C19 dormer windows: clear glass throughout. The attractively decayed W tower is probably C16, with brick dressings for the simple two-light bell-openings and what looks like re-used earlier details also. – FONT. C13, with square bowl on central stem and four shafts. Out of the ordinary in that it is decorated with stylized rosettes. Badly weathered. – RAILING in the N transept, for a former monument presumably. C18?

MAPSON'S FARM, ¾ m. w of the church. A handsome and very solid farmhouse, dated 1796. Three storeys, three bays, the windows still with the proportions of the early C18, and plenty of brickwork between. Good tarred weatherboarded and thatched barns.

SINCLAIRS COTTAGE see SOUTHWATER

SINGLETON

8010

Sober, beautifully kept village on the main road between Chichester and Midhurst, at the point where the Lavant valley turns E. The simple flint houses around a tangle of lanes have nothing worth special notice and no special group; yet Singleton is extraordinarily satisfying to walk round.

ST JOHN EVANGELIST. The tower Saxon, or Saxo-Norman, with double-splayed windows low down on three sides. One angle of dressed stone preserved inside the N aisle, and a triangle-headed opening high up above the tower arch, inside. The arch itself is c.1200. The extraordinarily tall nave walls, without clerestory, must be CII too. But all the other details are now late medieval, and a good example of how impressive these could be in Sussex, even on such a simple scale. Chancel arch and three-bay arcades, the standard E.E. pattern given more sharpness and complexity by hollow chamfers. The VCH, on the strength of the form of the bases, suggests a reconstruction in the C15 and goes even further (the whole N arcade C15 work), which is not convincing. N porch C15, originally perhaps two-storeyed, with different but equally thoughtful and direct mouldings. Windows two-light, c.1400, and three-light, probably C16. The offhandedness and neglect in detail of so many smaller churches in the Midlands and East Anglia is quite absent here. – STAINED GLASS. In the window high up above the chancel arch. It is an attractive jumble, well put together to look like saints under canopies. – WEST GALLERY. Complicated and attractive arrangement around a central post, probably C18. – BENCH ENDS. Simple, with straight tops; C15. – PLATE. Paten, 1683; Cup, 1707. – MONUMENTS. Two terribly mutilated C15 or C16 tombs near the altar, one still with its canopy. The usual standard. – Thomas Johnson † 1744. A famous huntsman of the Charlton Hunt. Plain tablet but endearing inscriptions. The official eulogy ends 'erected . . . as a reward to the deceased and an incitement to the living', which sounds like a rap over the knuckles for his successor. And underneath is the rhyme:

Here JOHNSON lies. What Hunter can deny
Old, honest TOM the Tribute of a Sigh
Deaf is that ear, which caught the op'ning Sound
Dumb is that Tongue, which chear'd the Hills around
Unpleasing Truth – Death hunts us from our Birth
In view; and Men, like Foxes, take to Earth.

SLINDON

9000

A good flint and brick village on the S slopes of the Downs between Chichester and Arundel. Only 200 ft up, yet a prodigious view S over the plain as far as the coast. Built around a quadrilateral of lanes, with the focus in the NW corner, above the church, with a tiny handsome open space where three roads meet and a big tree in the middle of it. Quite unspoilt.

ST MARY. Shockingly restored outside (in 1866) by *T. G. Jackson*, who was usually quite sensitive. Perhaps he was young and coltish. His is the tower-top, the aisles which embrace it, the E window, and the chancel arch. Quite a lot more remains inside. Aisleless C11 nave walls with one window on the N side preserved. The S side broken through with two arches in the late C12 (two slight chamfers, jamb shafts with scallop capitals for the inner order). The N side broken through with one arch for a chapel a little later: similar work, but the inner order has two rolls instead of chamfers, and there are corbels instead of shafts. The chancel was extended in the C13 (one delicate blocked lancet on the S side and several later lancets). Finally, some time after 1300 the long-suffering nave walls were extended to the W by another bay to give the effect of arcades. All three arches are double-chamfered, with mouldings dying into the imposts. The lengthening was probably connected with the decision to build the W tower. Dates are all very hazy. The wall at the W end of the S aisle and what looks like a buttress in the SW vestry seem to indicate that a SW tower was planned just before the W tower was begun. – FONT. C13 square bowl on stem and four columns. – BENCHES. Crude poppy-heads, W end of S aisle. – PAINTING. Some ashlaring of the late C12 or C13 and a frieze by the E respond of the S aisle. – STAINED GLASS. Small scenes in the chancel, designed by *T. G. Jackson*, made by *Powell's*. – MONUMENT. Probably Sir Anthony St Leger † 1539. The only wooden effigy in Sussex, 5 ft long, in armour, the head turned slightly to one side and admirably modelled, alert and inquiring and individual. Worth any number of mechanical effigies. The rest of the tomb has vanished. – Edward Long † 1813. By *Sir Richard Westmacott*. He was Chief Justice of the Admiralty Court of Jamaica. So there is a young woman, a very tender figure, seated under a palm-tree.

ST RICHARD (R.C.). Spindly and harsh, by *C. A. Buckler*, 1865. But inside a tiny MONUMENT by *Bertel Thorwaldsen*, the famous Danish sculptor, one of three in England. It commemorates Antony, Earl of Newburgh, † 1814. Kneeling woman and disconsolate standing angel on either side of a column. The idea is thus nothing out of the ordinary, but the detailed execution – of hair and toes and drapery – is brilliant. However sentimental the attitudes, the figures have great sculptural force: but they could easily be overlooked on a first visit.

SLINDON HOUSE. Originally a palace of the Archbishops of Canterbury. From this the stump of a TOWER remains, attached to the kitchen garden, part stone and part flint. No medieval detail, Gothick battlements.

The house itself was rebuilt by the Kempe family, about 1560. Ostensibly, quite a bit remains of it. But this is not what it seems. The building was so gratuitously messed about by *Mervyn Macartney* in 1921 that the result is worse than a complete rebuilding. All of flint.

The s front has six plain c18 bays between a pair of octagonal turrets with lead caps. These were circular before Macartney appeared. He also added a storey to the basically c16 w front and tampered with the windows on the r. of the door and in the polygonal bay on the l. The character is flint with stone dressings, mullion-and-transom windows of varying sizes and heights, and that is about all that can be said.* Inside, an early c18 screen and a pair of late c17 doorcases were kept, but most of the early c19 decoration was removed, and 'more appropriate plenishings substituted'.

The c18 STABLES to the w of the house were demolished after a fire in 1960.

NORE FOLLY. On a hill ½ m. NW of the village. One arch consisting, apparently, of a summer house joined to a column. Built for shooting-luncheons.

Voysey designed a cottage for a client at Slindon Common. It looks as though it could be the building in the angle formed by A29 and B2132; nothing special.

₁₀₃₀   SLINFOLD

w of Horsham: leafy Weald, slightly rolling and beautifully cared for. Caring has not impaired the character as it sometimes does: the old cottages are preserved but not made artificially quaint, a new estate on the road w of the village has been admirably landscaped, and the best individual house in the centre is in fact modern. Sussex is a better place to see this happy marriage of old and new than anywhere else in England.

ST PETER. By *Benjamin Ferrey*, 1861. Proud and uncompromising but not unsympathetic. Burgate stone. Late c13 style, with a tall tower and broach-spire towering above the cosy village street. Steep-pitched roofs, accentuating the contrast with the humble old churches around. What appeals most is its integrity: this is not a mechanical job as a Scott building might have been, but a deliberate, individual design. Details

* *Country Life*, vol. 50, p. 880, charts the melancholy transition.

like the way the bell-openings incorporate the clock are beautifully managed. The inside is big and the arcade capitals are enormous, but it is, inevitably, rather empty. – PLATE. Cup and Paten, 1618: Flagon, 1626; Almsdish, 1697; Paten, 1748. – MONUMENTS. Unknown female figure with a wimple, perhaps of c.1300 and perhaps a Tregoz. Life-size, stone: badly weathered but was originally good, by what remains of the dress folds. – Several C18 tablets stored under the tower.

The centre of Slinfold is a short, leafy street which runs up to the church. At its s end BRICKWOOD, by *C. Wycliffe Noble*, a paradigm of how to fit a completely modern house into a pretty old village. Single-storeyed and (monopitch) two-storeyed parts, tied in with the garage by a loggia to form an L-shape. Weatherboarding and old red bricks. It is now (1961) two years old: in terms of mellowness it might well be two hundred.

After this auspicious beginning, everthing else in Slindon is mellow too. Going towards the church, LITTLE HAMMERS on the l. is half-timbered, then on the other side the street widens slightly to make a tiny formal gesture: two late C18 cottages at r. angles, one of them the POST OFFICE, with trees in front. Rustic Doric porch with the columns wide apart and segmental lintel: a trick repeated on several other cottages in the village. More good cottages N of the church (C16, tile-hung) on the road to the W, and an impressive C16 half-timbered range further W again at Park Street on the main A29 road. This is PARKSTREET FARM, and was originally a pub. In the other direction, GASKYNS, ½ m. SE of the village, is a biggish yeoman's farm, restored. Mostly wide timbering of c.1600 but a little close timbering in the NE corner.

SLINFOLD MANOR, 1½ m. s, beside A264. Grim cemented late C18 house. Three-storeyed centre, two-storeyed wings, Ionic porch off-centre.

DEDISHAM, 1 m. NE. One long range, brick and tile-hung with a Horsham slate roof. The details C17 or modern, but it has the look of being one wing of a larger house, perhaps C16. Licence to crenellate was given in 1271, and a house on the site was sacked by Waller in 1643.

SOKENHOLES FARM *see* TILLINGTON

SOMERLEY *see* EARNLEY

SOMERSTOWN *see* CHICHESTER, p. 178

SOMPTING

NE of Worthing, almost joined to it by building. The village street, s of the A27 road, still keeps a good deal of its brick and flint character, whilst the church and Sompting Abbots, a few yards N of it, are already on the slopes of splendid rolling downland. The church looks marvellous from the main road to the w.

10a ST MARY. A famous Saxon tower, the only one in the country with a gabled pyramidal cap,* the sort of thing which is called a 'Rhenish helm', because many German and most Rhenish Romanesque towers are equipped with it. The connexions of Sompting are with Germany rather than northern France, and it is in fact probably fifty years older than most Saxon work in Sussex, i.e. about 1000. It is an elegant, almost dainty design which is a long way removed from the crudities of a tower like Earls Barton and which makes one wish that more like it had survived. After the standardization of so much Norman building it seems immediately fresh and alert. Tall and unbuttressed, with pilaster strips at each corner and attached semicircular strips on the mid-walls running up to the apexes of the gables on which the shingled 'helm' sits. These carry rough capitals (volutes and rows of small primitive leaves) below the bell-openings and may have had another set at the top. The bell-openings themselves are small and delicate; pairs of triangle-headed lights on the E and W sides, pairs of two-light round-headed openings on the N and S with the familiar mid-wall shaft. They have lobed foliage terminations not easy to see from the ground. The tower arch is complete, too, roughly carved but not barbarous. The inner order is semicircular and rests on shafts with crude leaf capitals, the outer is plain and has pairs of strong upright leaf scrolls with pomegranates in their centres – a hint almost at Ionic capitals. It is somehow incredibly moving, this fumbling recognition of the classical past which was already so many centuries ago. It may be childlike, but it is the same family as the children in Blake's Songs of Innocence. The arch itself is markedly off-centre, perhaps explained by the tower being the main porch and possessing an altar of its own on the NW side.

The other Saxon fragments at Sompting ought to be collected here. They consist of a number of pieces of SCULPTURE.

---

* St Benet's, at Cambridge, had one until the beginning of last century.

On the N side of the nave two stones with interlaced ornament, used as the back of an early C13 Christ in Majesty which is an impressive bit of sculpture in its own right. The Signs of the Evangelists and two rosettes surround the almond-shaped halo. – In the chancel, five lengths of ornament which were presumably part of a frieze and are remarkably delicate. Their feathery leaves and intertwined stalks are quite irregular. Two of them form the triangular head to a PISCINA. On the E wall of the chancel, an arch surrounded by looped foliage, not *in situ*. Finally, in the S transept, a figure of an abbot with crozier under arcading, with the same crude effectiveness as the tower arch.

The next stage at Sompting is a plain blocked early C12 doorway on the N side of the nave. However, later in the C12 the church was rebuilt after having been granted to the Templars in 1184. They produced a very odd plan. They kept the Saxon nave proportions, without aisles, and continued them through to the E end without a chancel arch. But on the N side they provided a transept with a two-bay eastern aisle, to accommodate two chapels, and this aisle is given an accomplished quadripartite rib-vault with plainly roll-moulded ribs and very small bosses. These rest on shafts at the NE and SE corners and on a big grotesque head in the middle of the E wall. The arcade itself has a round pier and semicircular responds with many-scalloped capitals, square abaci, and pointed unchamfered arches. The scallops are of the concave, trumpet variety and the leaves in one of the bosses are on the point of turning into stiff-leaf. So the date must be about 1180–90. On the S side of the nave the Templars put up something even odder: a complete little building for their own use. Apparently, it was originally quite separate from the rest of the church – the arch opening into the nave, and converting it into a S transept, is Victorian. It is also built at a level about 2 ft 6 in. lower than the church. The attachment is square, and has a S door, long and austere, with a round-headed arch with a roll-moulding and hollows on shafts with multi-scallop capitals, and it has a tiny circumstantial sanctuary, square-ended, and only half a bay deep. This also is rib-vaulted, the ribs ending on shafts with waterleaf capitals – another proof of *c*.1180 or so. The capitals return along the E wall as a string-course. Framing it, a bold, proud round-headed arch: two unchamfered orders, the outer with jamb shafts and the most resilient kind of foliage capitals, very crisply carved and nearly Corin-

SOMPTING · SOUTHBOURNE

thian. This must surely have a foreign connexion: but what is is? Tiny round-headed PISCINA on the S side.

In 1306 the Templars were expelled. At Sompting they were replaced by the Knights Hospitallers, who built the extension on the NW side of the nave which is now in ruins. It had openings into it both from the tower and the nave, and still keeps a trefoil-headed PISCINA, now on the outer N wall of the nave. Most windows in the church are Perp in the usual large-scale Sussex way: square-headed in the nave, pointed in the chancel. – PLATE. Cup, 1572; Server, 1699; Flagon, 1713. – SCULPTURE. Female head in a wimple, N transept. Defaced but clearly good. Early C14. – MONUMENTS. Richard Burre † 1527. Tomb recess, N side of chancel. Quatrefoils on the chest, cresting above it, thickly and mechanically done. – Several tablets of c.1800, N transept. One of them is signed by *King of Bath* (to John Crofts † 1771), but is no better than the others.

SOMPTING ABBOTS, E of the church. By *P. C. Hardwick*, 1856, Tudor, flint with a few brick panels and very spiky indeed. Taller tower at the back, with ornamental ironwork on top. Very much of a period piece.

LATE BRONZE AGE AND IRON AGE SETTLEMENT, 1 m. NE of Cissbury hill-fort. The Late Bronze Age settlement consists of a number of wattle and daub huts whose foundations can still be traced as slight ridges on the spur of PARK BROW. The Iron Age settlement, consisting of two huts and a number of storage pits, lies to the NE. In addition to pottery, loom-weights, and spindle-whorls, a fine finger ring of silver was found in one of the pits; this can be dated c.325–250 B.C.

SOUTH BERSTED see BERSTED

SOUTHBOURNE

7000

Between Emsworth and Chichester on the main A27 road, which is in effect built up for ten miles. No character along the road but a surprising amount off it to the S, where lanes run down to Chichester Harbour.

ST JOHN. 1876 by *T. Chatfield Clark*; bad.

To the E is NUTBOURNE, with a good C16 COTTAGE on a lane S of the main road: timber-framing and brick-nogging, herringbone pattern, with an overhanging upper storey. Just S is one of the best BARNS in West Sussex: simple, but a grand size and scale, low brick and stone walls (sandstone, not clunch,

which is unexpected) and enormous thatched roof. One
thatched cross-gable.
To the w is PRINSTED, around a Y of lanes running down to a
tiny mooring. It is a very pleasant surprise, because it contains
some of the prettiest cottages on the Sussex coast. Nothing
grand, but unbelievably leafy. At the centre of the Y a pair of
thatched cottages forming a tiny square; up the l. branch two
almost identical regularly framed timber cottages with flint
infilling and overhanging first floor, probably C17: WEST
COTTAGE and LITTLE ORCHARD. The whole place is like a
travel agent's poster, without any selfconsciousness.

SOUTHGATE see CRAWLEY, p. 205

SOUTH HARTING see HARTING

SOUTH MUNDHAM see MUNDHAM

SOUTH STOKE

0010

A handful of flint and brick cottages in the Arun gap N of
Arundel, at the end of an enchanting two-mile cul-de-sac road
which takes in about half a dozen changes of scenery – parkland,
riverside, chalk cutting, open downland. The surroundings
are superb; little affected by the electric railway, rather more
affected by a badly sited electricity grid line.

ST LEONARD. Like so many Sussex churches, this is in essence
the original C11 building. Wide, tall, unaisled nave and chancel, with a completely plain S doorway and blocked N doorway
to go with it. No other Norman details, and much of the rest
unnecessarily hardened in the C19; the inside impression is
just bare and swept clean. Windows mostly C13 lancets, E
window and chancel arch new. The best part is actually the W
end, which the C13 made into a simple but effective composition: one lancet either side of a very thin tower hardly taller
than the gable, now with a frilly C19 cap to it. (The tower
itself may be pre-E.E.) Inside, the tower is open to the nave
with a very tall, narrow double-chamfered arch, making a
pattern with the splays on either side, whose effect is out of all
proportion to the means used. The same hand detectable in
the simple C13 S porch, with chamfered transverse stone ribs.

SOUTHWATER

1020

Hamlet S of Horsham, where the Worthing road crosses a branch railway line. This and a brickworks have made it into a small village of the sort which can be expanded fairly happily. In fact, the new building here, both council and private, is surprisingly good.

HOLY INNOCENTS. Small decent chapel of 1850, by J. P. Harrison. Quiet curvilinear style. Nicely suited to a village church.

SINCLAIRS COTTAGE, ½ m. W, near the railway. Unrestored and attractive C16 half-timber. L-shaped.

STAKERS FARM, ¾ m. E, lost in the Weald on a dead-end. Good unrestored early farm, probably C15. Plastered and tile-hung now, very picturesquely, but underneath a 'hall house' with a kingpost roof.

EASTERS FARM, ¼ m. N of Stakers. A delightful mixture of a C16 brick and half-timber farm given a weatherboarded front, probably c.1800.

2000   SOUTHWICK

Between Shoreham and Portslade. A bit of everything and not quite anything – a long green, rows of suburban houses old and new, the chimneys of Portslade power station, the Downs on the skyline to the N. The *genius loci* seems to have gone on strike, or to have been locked out. Around the green only No. 49 is worth a look, handsome hard-bitten early C18. L-shaped, flint with brick dressings, very taciturn – as the Sussex coast was until the C19. The church is further W.

ST MICHAEL. As disparate as the village. The part worth seeing is the tower. This had to be taken down in 1941 because of bomb damage; admirably rebuilt in 1949 by J. L. Denman, who then added vestries on either side. The base of the tower is supposed to be Saxon, but most of it is C12 and C13, obviously under Shoreham influence. Tower arch with one tubular moulding and coy volutes which recur in the S chancel arcade. The W door, entirely new, uses the arcading motif of the New Shoreham aisles: above it paired wide round-headed arches, above that much narrower and taller lancets and a shingled broach-spire, perhaps done after the church was given to the Templars in 1225. This simple and sturdy solidity is what makes the tower impressive. C13 lancets in the chancel, but terribly restored. The nave and aisles are a loveless cover for pew-space put up in 1835 by *John Garrett*. Round-headed arcades, lancet windows, equally unhappy in either style. – SCREEN. C14. Painfully thin detail, narrow bays. At the E end of the S aisle. – PLATE. Chalice and Paten, 1632. – MONUMENTS. Several C18 tablets and a good cartouche to Elizabeth Gray † 1745 in the chancel.

ROMAN VILLA, ¼ m. N of the railway station. The site was excavated in the C19 and in 1931. It consists of a N range of buildings surrounded by corridors attached to a further rectangular corridored block enclosing a courtyard 65 ft square. The E corridor of this courtyard was interrupted at its centre by a large building with an apsidal E end. The walls of this building, which was probably a cold bath, were elaborately decorated with painted wall plaster. Coins and Samian ware suggest an occupation from the late C1 to the mid C4.

SPARR FARM see WISBOROUGH GREEN

STAKERS FARM see SOUTHWATER

STANSTED

On the Hampshire border N of Emsworth, mostly park and woodland (Stansted Forest), just S of the Downs, and remarkably unspoilt, considering the nearness of Portsmouth and its satellites. House and chapel are at the S end; the church and a few remote-seeming cottages make up FOREST SIDE, 1 m. to the N.

CHRISTCHURCH, Forest Side. Built in 1856, architect unknown (it could have been Teulon). One group with SCHOOLS: flint chapel, rather outré, with a very successful E end, two lancets under a pear-drop-shaped light with flickering tracery and good bright STAINED GLASS.

CHAPEL. Disarming. Built in 1812–15 around fragments of the original late C15 house, SW of the present house and beside a large walled garden with good C17 urns. The W front and most of the two-storeyed S porch are Tudor brickwork with simple details. The rest is brick Gothick, with big windows with wooden intersecting tracery, decent outside and quite delightful inside. The W gallery is supported on four shafts forming a low lobby to nave and aisles of the same height. The nave is groin-vaulted and painted white, with pretty, sparing stucco floral decoration, the chancel purest fantasy – a tiny hall-church with very thin columns, rib-vaulted, the E end with a spiky reredos and then a seven-light segment-headed window filled with PAINTED GLASS: entirely in Jewish Old Testament symbolism because the then owner, Lewis Way,

devoted his money to the conversion of the Jews.* Greys and
yellows, the chancel itself red, dark blue, and gold: one of the
nicest pieces of Gothick decoration anywhere, not trying to be
anything more than a bit of fun. It is actually a match of c19
and c20, for the colouring is due to the good restoration of
1926 for the 9th Earl of Bessborough by *H. S. Goodhart-
Rendel*; there was another restoration by him in 1947 after
bomb damage. Keats attended the consecration in 1819. He
found it 'not amusing', but the armorial glass in the nave
found its way into *The Eve of St Agnes*, the E window into
The Eve of St Mark. – FONT. Grey marble: enormous, like a
Roman bath. – All the WOODWORK Gothick and nicely frilly,
especially the eagle LECTERN.

STANSTED HOUSE. The original building was a royal hunting
lodge and then belonged to the Fitzalans, and what remains of
it is incorporated in the chapel. In 1686 this was replaced by a
house ¼ m. to the NE designed by *Talman*, very similar to
Uppark (*see* p. 358). This was recased and wings were added
by *Wyatt* in 1786; this in turn was burnt out in 1900 and
rebuilt by *Sir Reginald Blomfield* in neo-Wren style. So the
present house consists of the main block of the early 1900s
and a lower late c18 part to the N. Blomfield's rebuilding was
accurate, convincing at a distance, just a little harsh and heavy
close to: his interiors, especially the staircase, are meticulous –
and, of course, rather lifeless. But in terms of its own forms it
was an honest job. The lower N wing is a little complicated.
The centre is a pedimented five-bay block in white brick and
stone, decent Late Georgian, which is presumably Wyatt's.
But it has been wrought around by heavier early c19 additions
that may be due to *Thomas Hopper*, who worked here: archways flanked by pairs of columns, and a cupola which is incredibly be-columned and over-elaborated, like Soane at his
worst.

To the W two LODGES. Both look as if they had similarly
been given more ostentatious detail *c.*1820: the N lodge has a
portico, the S lodge has attached columns. A lodge identical
with this at the W end of the park at Rowland's Castle, in
Hampshire.

Splendid GROUNDS, splendidly maintained: to the W one
of the best avenues in England, laid out in the early c18,
replanted in 1820, 1½ m. long, of beech trees. When Defoe

* And attempted to persuade the Holy Alliance to encourage Jews to buy
land in Palestine.

visited the house in 1724 he said 'through the west opening (in the woods) which is from the front of the house, they sit in the dining room and see the town and harbour of Portsmouth, the ships at Spithead, and also at St Helen's'. To the E a smaller avenue of Canadian maples was planted in 1956, at a time when few landowners were prepared to plant anything. (In the park 1 m. E is LUMLEY SEAT, an C18 temple. It had a rotunda, destroyed in the war, but the pedimented Ionic façade remains.)

STEDHAM
8020

In the Rother valley w of Midhurst: bigger and more sprawling than most of the Rother villages, with one long brick and sandstone street running down to the river, and the church and Hall off to one side.

ST JAMES. Very plain unbuttressed tower of 1673, still more Gothic than anything else. All the rest serious and decent lancet Gothic by *J. Butler* of Chichester, 1850; no spikiness at all. One Norman-looking window high up at the E end of the N aisle is probably transplanted from the old church. – MONUMENT. Rev. Thomas Wrench † 1778. Crisp Adamesque tablet by *Charles Harris* of London.

STEDHAM HALL, N of the church. A little old C17 work swamped in a great deal of C20 rebuilding, as in so many Surrey houses. The result is still picturesque: stone ground floor, half-timbered first floor, two big projecting gables. All effectively of 1919, by *John Malcom*. A formidable fairy-castle effect from the river side, which is really the spiritual descendant of houses like Wispers (*see* p. 381).

BRIDGE. One of the Rother Valley series, in this case probably C17. Six low arches.

STEYNING
1010

A pretty, small-scale place just N of the Downs, which like so many others in Sussex is half-way between a large village and a small town. Enough pleasant things and enough connexion between them to make a good walk.

ST ANDREW. Late Norman, virile and inventive; certainly the best in Sussex, and among the best in the whole country. The church was founded in the C8 by St Cuthman, and given c.1047 by Edward the Confessor to Fécamp – another example of the connexions between Sussex and Normandy before the

Conquest. By 1086, when the grant was confirmed by William, it had become collegiate; it was relinquished in 1415 and granted to Sion Abbey in 1461. The choir, transepts, and central tower were taken down after 1577 and the present w tower was built instead.* The chancel was patched up then, and totally and grossly altered in 1863 by *G. M. Hills*.

18   What remains is the w tower arch, and four bays of the nave (originally probably five or six).‡ The tower arch, the companion arches to the aisles, and the E nave responds are *c*.1100; the rest is about fifty years later and could be as late as 1170–80. The spirit underlying the two parts is identical, high and rich and purely Romanesque; only the ornamental details change. It is a far cry in quality both from the weary repetition of motifs that went on for the best part of a century at Chichester, and from the slack, confused detail of the late C12 in the West of England. Here, the vocabulary fits exactly what has to be said. This is rare enough to make Steyning worth a special visit – it is not just any old Late Norman nave, of which England has plenty, but a very good one.

The early arches all have multiple orders and roll-mouldings, each order with separate shafts and capitals. It looks as though the s aisle arch was built first – it has more roll-mouldings – then the N aisle arch and the main arch, which both carry shallow zigzag ornament (*c*.1120). Scallop and volute capitals, debased Corinthian (N aisle) and an extraordinary set of three on the s arch, s side: cushion capitals completely covered with a writhing flow of interlace and lions addorsed, or rather bottom to bottom. Underneath, wrapped around the pier, and in the same style, two men grasping tree stems. The spirit is exactly the same as in the Celtic initials, the Viking ship prows, the jambs at Kilpeck – a general northern convoluted subtlety. The style is at the exact moment when it had left off its original semi-pagan inspiration and was adapting itself naïvely and touchingly to more regular Continental influences.

Then the late C12 designer took over. The detail becomes a little more free from E to W, as might be expected, but not much: this, far more than most Norman buildings, is a single design. It is a magnificent design too, quite apart from the

* The date-plate 1684 on the tower, however, cannot refer to the building. It is certainly too late.

‡ The w responds are clearly not responds, but piers disappearing into the tower walls. On the s side there is part of the hood-mould of the next arch.

wonderful gusto of the detail. Big cylindrical piers and abaci, three-order arches (two major and one minor). Above, clerestory windows in deep reveals prolonged downwards to a string-course just above the arcade; the space between windows split into panels of exactly the right size by queer vertical demi-shafts let into the wall and by a firm, almost classical horizontal prolongation of the clerestory abaci. Nothing fumbled, nothing misshapen, and a great rhythmic richness of multiple orders and thick walls. The ornament is a joy. Mercifully, it defeats detailed description: most arches have some variation on chevrons at ninety degrees to one another (one arch has chevrons at forty-five degrees as well). The westernmost arch on the s side has the whole soffit scalloped, something which occurs again at Winchfield in Hampshire. Smaller mouldings are often keeled. The capitals have scallops or formalized foliage, no two alike: there is an exquisite label with grotesque heads for label-stops and a regular pattern of delicate rosettes (they even occur enlarged in the spandrels on the N side with almost a classical, Wyatt effect). On the s side the label in the clerestory has dogtooth ornament. Clearly, the designer was having more and more fun as he travelled w. What were his destroyed bays like ? Outside, the N clerestory has plain two-order arches and may be a repair, but the s side has a lovely way of combining the familiar motif of two orders with nook-shafts that says straightaway that something out of the ordinary can be expected. A look at the windows of the clerestory at Chichester in almost the same style can tell more about the difference between the good and the moderate than most textbooks.* As a final flourish, the s doorway simply has chevrons lapping around a roll-moulding from floor to floor,‡ and from the porch frames the arcades perfectly. One C12 window and a mysterious shaft (which, if it is a jamb shaft, means a window at a different level) remain in the N aisle; otherwise the openings are either Perp, with deep reveals outside, or utilitarian C16. The W tower is bulky and uncommunicative, simply a good place to hang some bells: the same C16 character as Westbourne or Micheldever in Hampshire but gone dour. Chequer pattern of stone and flint. The tower arch is 1885 and looks preposterous, next to the C12 grandness.

* One window (SW) has waterleaf – which helps to date the second campaign.

‡ The idea used later and differently in the aisles at New Shoreham. It also occurs in a doorway at Arundel. It is, as it were, beakheads made abstract.

FURNISHINGS. FONT. Square C12 bowl of Sussex marble, carved with a thin zigzag pattern. Stem and shafts later, but not much. The shafts have good capitals. – ROYAL ARMS of 1703, S aisle, along with the Mace and Staff of the Borough (two M.P.s until 1832, like Bramber). Both c.1685, good and circumstantial. – DOOR. The S door has some original ironwork. – PLATE. Cup and Paten, 1676; Flagon, 1740. – (MONUMENT. In the churchyard a headstone of 1791 (Daniel Easton) with the Resurrection taking place in a churchyard with typical Sussex monuments.)

The heart of the town is the HIGH STREET, which curves gently up and through the middle. There is no formal centre, which is typical of Sussex. It begins from the W with a sharp bend; on the r., Nos 1–3 MOUSE LANE, the old poorhouse, a good C15 timber-framed cottage, with recessed centre. Unrestored. Then there are some plain C18 terraces (Nos 91 etc.), then a pair of C15 houses, one each side of the street, both with long overhanging first floors, both close-timbered (No. 90 and No. 65). Next is the OLD MARKET HOUSE, with a comfy tile-hung front and a little clock-turret, the exact mood of these cosy half-towns. This begins the centre of Steyning, which goes a little more formal with Georgian houses like the CHEQUER INN and LLOYDS BANK. Just beyond, Church Lane leads off to the N and will be described in a moment. Opposite this STONE HOUSE, the old gaol, with a flint base and a close-timbered overhanging gable impressively high up. Then, on the way out to Bramber, two more C18 houses: No. 17, probably c.1750 and rather blank, and CHARLTON HOUSE, built a generation earlier, with a little more going on, including a robust Doric doorcase. The best part is the late C18 ironwork in front.

CHURCH STREET begins with a bang on the S side: a set of plastered and gabled C16 and C17 houses as good as any in the county. They have just the right sort of variation within a common rhythm, and they have not been over-restored. The temptation, here, must have been strong. The sequence starts with Nos 3–5, with overhanging wings and a recessed centre, part of which has been waywardly filled in. Then CHATFIELD, probably C15, with a plastered overhang, running into the long range of the GRAMMAR SCHOOL, founded in 1614. Here the centre is a brick porch with C19 top, but the wings are converted from the C15 buildings of a hall of the Fraternity of the Holy Trinity. These have a first-floor overhang, now

tile-hung, quite without windows, something which adds a lot
to the rhythms of the street. The gables above, with their
ornamental timber-framing, must be c.1600.

Beyond this, HOLLAND COTTAGE, another C15 house with an
overhang. This time the close timbering is exposed. After this
the s side becomes less spectacular but no less pretty, and
interest moves over to the N:* first the sweetly shaggy SAXON
COTTAGE, thatched and timber-framed, and then an opening-
out, almost a small green, which makes a fine end to the street.
Two plain C17 brick cottages frame the bigger and grander
CHANTRY HOUSE, one of the best C18 town houses in this
part of Sussex. Five bays, segmental windows, delicately cut
brick cornice. Probably c.1740. It succeeds very well by not
trying to do too much, and relying on the pattern of grey and
vermilion bricks.

Beyond this is the church, and N of it the handsome C18 brick
front of the VICARAGE. A little way beyond again, there is a
good railway WAREHOUSE of c.1860 in the station yard. Still
Georgian in proportions and delicacy. The station building
with its tricoloured brick is a rather different thing.

WAPPINGTHORN, 1½ m. N. The old parts on the N front dated
1609. Brick, with a huge stone-mullioned window running up
to the roof with four tiers of six lights. This is completely built
around with neo-Tudor additions of 1928 by *Maxwell Ayrton*.
Of the same time the WATER TOWER to the N and the fine,
complex set of farm buildings to the E, which are a clever free
variation on vernacular themes, very typical of the 1920s.
Vaughan Williams did the same thing in music. The tower has
a summer house on top.

STOKE DOWN *see* STOUGHTON

STOPHAM

Church and a few cottages on a hilly cul-de-sac NW of Pulborough. Beautiful countryside and beautiful views from it.

ST MARY. A good place to see what the first few years after the
Conquest meant in church architecture. Impressive very early
Norman nave and chancel, tall and narrow, keeping a blocked
window (N side of chancel) and two massive doorways. These
are to a huge scale (12 ft high), but narrow, obviously C11
rather than C12. Both have one thick roll-moulding, the N
doorway (which now opens into the vestry) with cushion capi-

* A simple conservative staircase of c.1660 in the NORFOLK ARMS.

tals, the s doorway with odd capitals made up of three rings, one above the other. This is Saxon rather than Norman. Plain chancel arch, with imposts and one roll, and plain unmoulded arch beyond it, which suggests that the present good Perp E window (three lights, square-headed) replaced a Norman apse. In it armorial STAINED GLASS dated 1638. Apart from new windows, hardly anything else has been done at Stopham, and the heavy, very solid space is still overpowering. To the N of the chancel arch a reredos recess with a stop-chamfer, probably of c.1200. The simple w tower with its pyramidal cap was rebuilt c.1600 by the look of the details. – FONT. Perp; quatrefoils, octagonal, standard. – STAINED GLASS (N side of nave). Kneeling figures, Elizabethan or Jacobean, signed by one *Roelant*. An inscription on it commemorates Brian de Stopham † 1273; he is in medieval dress, the other figure in that of c.1600. So was it made as an unusual kind of retrospective monument? Much restored in 1853. – PLATE. Elizabethan Cup and Cover. – BRASSES. Three pairs of C15 effigies on the nave floor, all with effigies about 3 ft tall: John Barttelot † 1428 John † 1453, and Richard † 1462. All stiff and unremarkable, but some parts restored in the late C17. The difference in technique is rather fun. – Richard Bartelot † 1614, with his wives. Well engraved but expressionless. Chancel floor.

STOPHAM MANOR HOUSE, immediately N of the church. A splendid stone-built farmhouse, quite unrestored. The front is E-shaped with hipped roofs. Some of the windows C18 and some mullioned. The back is a delightful asymmetrical composition of gables, with many small mullioned windows. It looks like a C16 or even C15 house gently refurbished in the C17. In fact the glass of 1638 in the E window of the church is supposed to come from this house when it was partly dismantled.

STOPHAM HOUSE, ½ m. S, near the bridge. An old house rebuilt in 1787 and then much added to in 1842 and 1865. The later additions are weak Tudor; from the earlier house the W front remains (two storeys, two bow windows) and part of the E front, with a plain pedimented three-storey centre. The doorcase wandered from the E to the W front in the C19. Plain unremarkable work, in ashlar sandstone, pretty much the style of the Petworth Market Hall.

33 STOPHAM BRIDGE. An idyllic spot, with what is easily the best of the medieval bridges in Sussex. Rebuilt in stone in 1423. The raised centre arch dates from 1822, the others are original – six low, obtusely pointed arches with blunt cutwaters be-

tween. The rhythm of arch and cutwater, and of the overall line of the bridge, from bank to bank, could hardly be improved upon. As a Grade 1 building (in the grading system of the MHLG) it is presumably sacrosanct. But what will happen to the setting if road widening forces another bridge within a few yards of it?

LEE FARM, ½ m. SW. Half-timbered house with stone roof and good barns. Stone mullioned windows on the S side, which faces a spectacular view of the Downs. Dated on the walls either 1492 or, more likely, 1592.

STORRINGTON

0010

A big, untidy village which, like Pulborough a few miles away, is halfway towards being a town. The transition is not much fun to look at, though potentially the shapes and spaces are good.

ST MARY THE VIRGIN. Impressive stepping of gables from the N, but a closer look shows the hand of 1876 all too clearly. The original church is the present N aisle, with the usual tall thin wall to the nave, probably C11. The details in this part simple C13. Good Perp arcade (now the N arcade of the church), which from its size belonged to an aisle which became the most important part of the church.* Double-chamfered arches, piers made up of four attached shafts, elegant and effective. The part beyond was rebuilt in 1750 (the simple W tower remains from this; the builder was *John Battcock*) and then again in 1876, when another aisle was added with a matching arcade. – PLATE. Cup and Paten, 1686. – MONUMENTS. Sir Henry Bradford † 1816, slackly military, and Major Hugh Falconar † 1827, mourning women as usual, both by *Sir Richard Westmacott*.

Very little to see in the village: perhaps the plain C18 MULBERRY HOUSE (Barclays Bank) in The Square, and one or two cottages in CHURCH LANE. Also in Church Lane, at the corner of Brown's Lane, an intriguing big DOORWAY in a garden wall. The style a mixture of Moorish and Renaissance, very delicately done – a kind of Walter Pater or Henry James doorway. It looks as though it came out of an International Exposition.

Beyond the church to the S, ST JOSEPH'S CONVENT, an agglomeration of buildings of the last hundred years which is as picturesque as many Tudor houses.

* This must originally have been done in the C13, for there is an early C13 arch between the N aisle and the present chancel. The slightly later arch opposite this is the old chancel arch, re-set.

STOUGHTON

Brick and flint farms in a fine large-scale downland valley NW o
Chichester. Like so many of the downland villages, althoug
there is no formal grouping of buildings it stays in the memor
through a looser map-like arrangement in the surroundin
countryside. BOW HILL to the SE of Stoughton has some of th
best scenery in the whole of the Downs.

Another nice group of cottages, without a church, at WALDER
TON, I m. SW.

ST MARY. On the hillside just N of the village: plain outsid
and impressively rich inside. Stuccoed nave, but tell-tale pro
portions, wide and high (25 ft high, the walls only 28 in. thick)
In fact this is a complete late C11 church, cruciform and aisle
less, in what is usually called the Saxo-Norman overlap. Th
s transept was made into a tower in the C14, the window
generally were remodelled in the late C12 and C13. What i
left from the C11 is chiefly the grand chancel arch, large-scal
and assured, setting the rhythm for the whole interior. It ha
triple shafts with roll-mouldings, the same basic pattern a
Bosham (see p. 111) but done in purely Norman terms.*]
makes a nice comparison, and they are really far more alik
than Stoughton is to a Late Norman arch. Capitals on th
smaller shafts plain, on the larger carved with a very crud
adaptation of the Corinthian order, typical of the C11. On th
N side it seems perversely to be given the form of a hangin
cloth. A double-splayed w window in each transept, the
single-splayed round-headed windows in the s transept, an
windows of the same form in the nave: they all seem in fact t
be late C12. Similar windows in the chancel, with more elabora
tion: rere-arches with shafts and mouldings, circular aba
and shaft-rings – altogether a rather odd method of C13 er
largement. The E window is complete, the N and s window
have had their heads barbarously cut off short above the abac
A little earlier than these the two arches opening into th
transepts, probably c.1200: two orders, hollow chamfer on th
outer, complicated three-part roll-moulding forming the inne
order. Shafts with palm-leaf capitals to the inner order only
The same character in a pair of doorways, one in the s side o
the chancel, one at the w end of the nave: double-chamfere
surrounds, the hood-moulds turning ninety degrees and be

* It might still, of course, be 'pre-Conquest', as Norman influence w
already strong in Sussex before 1066.

coming the imposts – an individual, economical style. The N transept has a typical mid C13 PISCINA – pointed-trefoil head, continuous order of dogtooth ornament, under a label with two cheerful heads as stops. Simple late C14 tower top with pyramidal cap; when it was added a plain wooden framework was fitted inside the s transept to support it. Brick C17 porch, altered. – FONT. C12, square, partly re-cut. On one side scrolls arranged in a tree-of-life fashion. Purbeck marble. – REREDOS. Copybook Victorian, by *Ewan Christian*.

WATERGATE HOUSE, 1 m. N of Walderton. Rebuilt by *Soane* and again in 1882: now demolished. The pretty small lodge on the main road to the sw may be Soane's. Flint, with Ionic portico of four columns.

NEOLITHIC LONG BARROWS. On Stoughton Down are two fine long barrows, 200 yards apart, both standing to a height of over 5 ft and with clearly visible flanking ditches.

FLINT MINES. ½ m. NE of the village, on STOKE DOWN and E of Bow Hill barrow cemetery, is the supposed site of a group of Neolithic flint mines. These are recognizable only as a line of shallow depressions; three of them, however, have been excavated and shown to be up to 12 ft in diameter and 15 ft in depth, with rudimentary galleries. They contained antler and flint tools, a shoulder-blade shovel, and a grain rubber.

BARROW CEMETERY, on BOW HILL, w of the flint mines. The group consists of two very fine bowl barrows on the NE, both over 100 ft in diameter and 12 ft high; and two smaller bowl barrows, 10 ft high, lying to the s w and forming a linear cemetery with the bell barrows. ssw of this group is an isolated twin bell barrow consisting of two mounds 60 ft in diameter and 6 ft high surrounded by a single, oval ditch. From one of the bowl barrows came a cremation accompanied by a whetstone.

STREATHAM MANOR *see* HENFIELD

STROOD PARK 1030

1½ m. sw of Warnham

An Elizabethan house remodelled in the late C18. The front now has two inner polygonal bays with mullioned windows and two outer semicircular bays with big Georgian windows, quite elegant. The back is all plain Georgian, and so are the stables, with a sturdy neo-classical composition of open and blind arches under a cupola.

0010

SULLINGTON

A memorable place E of Storrington. Church and farm on the foothills of the Downs with big views both ways. Cul-de-sac lane which ends up in the farmyard, passing a good big BARN, tarred weatherboard and tile, which has a date 1685 on one of its timbers. Really fine interior, one of the best in Sussex, with aisles and braced tie-beam roof. Worth a special look.

ST MARY. Like a farm building itself, in a churchyard full of enormous yew trees. Stumpy tower, nave and chancel – the nave by its high, narrow proportions immediately shows that it is Saxon, but all the details are later. One C12 window on the N side of the chancel. Tower and chancel arches early C13 (some of the tower walling looks much earlier, and the W doorway was early C12 but has been terribly restored), two-bay N arcade, probably late C13. The W respond is earlier and the inner order of the arch performs a complicated and elegant stop-chamfer to fit it. In fact all the appearances seem to suggest that this inner order was actually added later, for the outer order is plain and of different stonework. Would such a thing be practicable? Reticulated E window, worth a look for its subtlety by comparison with the hundreds of Victorian copies. – FONT. Perp, with quatrefoils. – PLATE. Chalice and Paten, 1672. – MONUMENT. C13 Knight in chain mail, lifesize. Terribly mutilated; the details that remain are first-class.

SUMMERSDALE *see* CHICHESTER, p. 181

9010

SUTTON

Near the Downs S of Petworth. One long straggling village street which has no pattern but is almost an anthology of Sussex building materials: sandstone, brick, half-timber, clunch, flint. One of the cottages on the E side has a big white curved rear addition, made by *Basil Ward* of Connell, Ward & Lucas in 1938. The result is surprising but successful.

ST JOHN. Bigger than most churches around Petworth. Nave originally C11, shown by the herringbone masonry on the N side of the nave. Late C12 aisle of two bays, or rather two and a quarter, for at the E end there is a plain narrow arch where one would expect a respond. The similar effect at the W end is C19. Big and stately, though plain: circular piers, arches with a barely perceptible chamfer, and waterleaf capitals. The tower looks *c.*1300, plain and bulky, with a single-light trefoil-headed bell-opening and tower arch, without capitals. The chancel is Dec and surprisingly showy for a Sussex village: the tracery is renewed, but accurately so, and consists of two lights and a cusped quatrefoil in the sides, three lights under a circle made up of quatrefoils at the E end. PISCINA and elegant triple SEDILIA with well-managed mouldings: clearly this was out of the ordinary. The shallow N transept is Dec too, and was heightened later. Finally, one simple but splendidly detailed three-light Perp window in the N side of the nave: square-headed, with a mastery of bold mouldings that the Victorians never achieved. – The SCREEN by *Woodyer*, of Butterfieldian hardness, was removed between galley and page proof. – PLATE. Chalice and Paten Cover, 1568; Flagon, 1673; Paten, 1679.

OLD RECTORY. Originally built *c.*1330, at the same time as the chancel of the church. The shape of this building, which was a hall house, remains, but it has been altered so often that nothing is now visible. The outside was completely refaced in the C19.

TANGMERE   9000

E of Chichester, in the coastal plain. It is a famous R.A.F. station; the way to the church is past the Officers Mess, and the church itself is only a few yards from the runway: yet it is still a pleasant place.

ST ANDREW. Very simple decent village building: nave, chancel, and bell-turret carried, unusually for Sussex, on a complete timber frame inside the nave, with four posts and diagonal cross-bracing. The nave is simple C12 with windows on N and S sides,* the chancel simple C13, with two very large wide E lancets. The chancel arch C13 with scalloped imposts, like Oving. – FONT. Plain tub font, not retooled. – SCULPTURE. The head of one of the Norman S nave windows is a carved stone. It is crude, puzzling, and badly weathered, and may represent a beheading. It has the look of being a re-used Saxon fragment.

A good set of flint and tile BARNS immediately S of the church, probably C19.

TELEGRAPH HILL *see* COMPTON

---

* Two on each side, probably the complete original scheme.

TERWICK

1 m. E of Rogate

No village, just scattered farms and a church.

St Peter, beautifully sited s of the Petersfield to Midhurs
road: alone in the fields, with a foreground of hilly meadow
and a background of the South Downs at their most majestic
Simple C12 nave and chancel, with too much restoration to
live up to the expectations aroused by the setting. Plain restored C12 w door and window above; the chancel arch has
the same character but is modern. The other windows either
lancets (C13 and C19) or Perp. Decent and unaffected, yet
somehow there is all the difference between this and a church
like Didling: here the C19 additions were backward-looking
and selfconscious, and this is fatal to a village church. – FONT.
Plain C12 font, the familiar pattern of tapering bowl on circular base, but less restored than most. – PLATE. Chalice,
1588; Paten Cover, 1569; Paten, 1712.

Opposite the w door, head of a medieval CROSS, completely
plain and oddly moving.

THAKEHAM

E of Pulborough and N of the Downs, in fairly quiet Wealden
country. The village, strung out along one street, is quiet and
rather flavourless, until the corner with the church, which makes
a good group with the regular timber-framing of CHURCH
HOUSE. A few feet higher, from the churchyard itself, the view
changes dramatically to include the whole sweep of the Downs.

St Mary. The nave is Norman, but that can only be seen in
one window on the N side. All the rest is another bold, simple
C13 rebuilding, chancel and transepts added to the old unaisled nave, impressively articulate in the stepped roof-lines,
severe lancets and groups of lancets. What looks so homo-
geneous from the outside must in fact have taken about fifty
years, for none of the internal details agree. The chancel arch
and N transept arch are probably c.1200. Both slightly chamfered, the transept arch, renewed, with three chamfers.
Walter Godfrey suggests that this was a N tower, possibly
with an E apse; for there is a blocked arch there, filled with a
later window. Details of chancel and transept are early C13;
odd lancets, the three at the E end gathered together under a
shafted rere-arch. The s transept must be appreciably later in
the C13 by the hollow chamfers on the splays, and the arch

here may be C14. The parallel slight differences in the PIS-CINA in chancel and transept are worth a look too. The sturdy W tower is late Perp, the simple details as well carved as usual, trim square-headed belfry lights, tower arch without abaci. Late Perp also the timber S porch. – FONT. Perp, more elaborate than the Sussex average. Narrow octagonal bowl with each side different; coved stem and panelled base. Delicate and individual. – PAINTINGS. Two copies, and one original, a well-composed Assumption of the Virgin by *Sebastiano Ricci*. Tiepolo's way of design, but a generation earlier, hence darker. – PLATE. Chalice, Paten on foot, Dish, and Flagon, all inscribed 1763. – MONUMENTS. Five to the Apsley family, all C16. Two poor small brasses † 1514 and † 1515, then life-size incised slab to John † 1527. Unusual, but the quality no better (S side of chancel). – Finally, two Renaissance tombs, William † 1582 (N transept), with a big architectural frame, crisply carved and quite individual, and John † 1587, more conventional, with a smaller frame and inscription above a tomb-chest decorated with strapwork. – Odd gauche tablet to Edward Apsley † 1651 (or 1654 – the correction is made in the stone itself) with lion's feet and disembodied arms holding wreaths.

LITTLE THAKEHAM, ¾ m. S. One of *Lutyens*'s best houses. 1902–3, just when his style was changing from Tudor to Georgian. Still fresh, and on a lovely site, with the long view N over a steep valley instead of S to the Downs, as expected. The outside is all Tudor, but both fronts are now strictly symmetrical (at Tigbourne, three years before, the entrance front had been symmetrical, the garden front random). Centre-and-wings compositions: on the entrance side the sides stronger because of the tall chimneystacks running up the gabled wings; on the garden side the centre wins, because of 6 ob a big polygonal bay window. Its mullions and transoms and those of the other windows are not period at all, they are completely flat and flush. But the movement of Tigbourne has gone completely, replaced by an unforced repose which is many times better than what Lutyens was going to do in his later and more laborious classical houses. The material is local sandstone which has weathered so well (or so badly) that large parts, e.g. the N doorway and the big N chimneybreasts, look as if they were three hundred years old.

Immediately inside, a long transverse corridor, a favourite Lutyens device, concealment where the visitor looks for exposition. It is partnered on the first floor by a splendid extravagance with the dimensions of a long gallery. The main living room is beyond, reached by one of three mighty, classical doorways, in their scale a preparation for what is to follow. The living room has the plan and placing of an Elizabethan hall, entered through a 'screens passage'. Above it is a gallery reached by the main staircase of the house, a plan Norman Shaw had used earlier (at The Hallams near Bramley, Surrey, for example). But what is purely Lutyens is the way he has made the two bays of the screens passage into a Piranesian fragment, something left over from an abandoned Gonzaga palace. Straight lintels, ponderous keystones, and the same deeply disturbing effect as in its Mantuan prototypes. This is a complete understanding of classical design rather as Hawksmoor understood it, and something very different from applying styles. Perhaps it was impossible to expect Lutyens to stay at this pitch of creative interpretation for long. What a brilliant young man he was, and how thoroughly and wilfully he burnt himself out. Plenty of the humorous and loving touches which make a good Lutyens house a joy to walk around – a mini-balcony above the fireplace in the hall, a children's window in the nursery low enough down for small children, a nanny's window from the nursery anteroom into the hall to see where the children would be expected to come down, huge inglenooks in the main rooms at the SE and SW corners, designed down to the fire-grates. Even the exposed ends of the landing floor joists are coffered so that the eye is not jolted when coming downstairs.

The garden begins formal but grassy and leads out through a long pergola into an orchard and paddock which match the formality and grassiness at one remove, a gentle but powerful transition.

THREE BRIDGES see CRAWLEY, p. 205

TILGATE see CRAWLEY, p. 205

9020

TILLINGTON

A Petworth estate village, just w of the park, hence impeccably maintained. Built mostly on a ridge just above the Petworth to Midhurst road, with superb views across to one of the best stretches of the Downs. The surrounding countryside is some of the finest in Sussex, and to partner it Tillington and its hamlets seem to have an inexhaustible stock of good small houses and farms.

ALL HALLOWS. Improbable at a distance, because of the tower with its Scots Crown, at the E end of the S aisle. This was built in 1807, presumably to be an eyecatcher for Petworth. The effect does not work now, but did in the early C19, as the Turner landscapes at Petworth show. Robustly and incorrectly Gothick, with heavily emphasized string-courses, quatrefoils, and plain pointed bell-openings – still purely C18 in effect. It would be nice to know the designer: a splendidly unfounded tradition has ascribed it to *Turner*, who was trained as an architect. The core of Tillington is medieval, though this can only be guessed on the outside by the masonry of the S aisle, only 9 ft high under its lean-to roof: the rest is all over-cosy late C19 work, with tiled dormers. But inside the complete spatial vessel of arcades and chancel arch is preserved, and impressively blunt and urgent it is too. The W respond of the S arcade is still Norman, with scalloped capital: otherwise the three-bay arcades are *c.*1200, thickly carved in the coarse-textured sandstone: two orders with slight chamfer, octagonal abaci, round piers, and very effective and resilient crocketed capitals which are roughly carved but throbbing with life – not the usual Sussex style at all. Chancel arch C13 and less remarkable, with semi-octagonal responds on brackets: the arch from the chancel to the tower in the same style. The E arch of the S aisle plain without imposts. – STAINED GLASS. Roundel in the W wall, looking like *Burne-Jones*. – MONUMENTS. William Mitford † 1777. Chaste and strict architectural frame in four different colours of marble. By *A. Outridge* of Petersfield, a nice local talent. – James Clarke † 1834, the very end of the tradition, with a lifelike medallion in a thick frame. By *Carew*.

The best house in the village is on the lane running W from the church: Nos 534–536 (estate numbering), former MANOR HOUSE, a stone-built house of *c.*1600 with a half-timbered extension further W. One big gable and smaller two-storeyed porch: windows with brick mullions and hood-moulds, a local habit. Probably the same mason as Dean House (*see* below). On the main road to the S TILLINGTON HOUSE, with a plain C18 front. Further E estate ALMSHOUSES of 1840 and a pair of LODGES to Petworth Park of *c.* 1860 in what looks like *Salvin*'s best style, thick, almost French and almost Baroque.

A good deal of Petworth estate building N of the church too; e.g. the SCHOOLS, of 1835, with symmetrical Tudor windows under classical eaves, and, opposite, a sensitive VILLAGE HALL by *Brian O'Rorke*, 1958. Behind this another entrance to the park, this time battlemented, c.1800. The whole village is a model of conservation without selfconsciousness.

½ m. to the N, on top of the ridge, is UPPERTON, which is just about a perfect example of an unspoilt hamlet, stone-built, warm tile roofs, tremendous view s. Built around an L-bend in the road, the cottages pleasant individually and magnificent collectively. N of this again is the MONUMENT, just inside the park wall, a tall, plain Gothick folly of c.1800, stone built, with an even taller stair-turret on one side of it. What it looks like more than anything else is the engine-house to a C19 waterworks; this was presumably not the intention.

S of the village, between the road and the river Rother, several good farms and an idyllic landscape. ½ m. due s is SOKEN-HOLES FARM, a stone-built early C17 cottage given a de-lightfully circumstantial touch in the shape of a pilastered pedimented doorway, much bigger than anything else on the façade, of 1665.

1½ m. W, nearer Lodsworth than Tillington, is GRITTENHAM FARM, mostly C17 with some mullioned windows, but more notable for the magnificent complex groups it makes with its cottages and barns, a town in miniature.

DEAN HOUSE, ¾ m. W. Delightful symmetrical small manor house of 1613. Two big gables with smaller projecting two-storeyed gabled porch, four-light mullion-and-transom windows, rubble stone walling. Four-centred entrance arch with the date above in cut brick. The proportions exceptionally happy, even in such a felicitous field as this, a matter of having plenty of plain wall space around the windows. It is all the better for the complete absence of Jacobean frills and knobs.

PITSHILL, 1 m. NW. Fine-drawn late C18 house. The limestone is almost white, and has taken on the same ethereal pinkish tinge as some Dorset houses. The situation is magnificent even for the surroundings of Petworth; for it has a belvedere site looking N to Blackdown and s to the Downs. Rather oddly, the house does not make full use of it; the main front faces E, looking directly into some trees, and although the valley to the s is beautifully landscaped in an C18 way, it is immediately outshone by the superlative natural landscape beyond. One can see, here, what Uvedale Price and the other protagonists

Blackdown, view across the Weald to the Downs

(a) South Heighton (E), Heighton Hill

(b) Lower Beeding, hammer pond

2

(a) Rye (E), Mermaid Street

(b) Hove (E), air view

Petworth, Lombard Street

Chichester Cathedral from Westgate Fields

(a) Ford, church, eleventh and twelfth centuries

(b) North Stoke, church, thirteenth and fourteenth centuries

Up Marden, church, thirteenth century

(a) Clayton (E). Jack (*right*), b. 1876, and Jill, b. 1821

(b) Shipley, Kings Mill, early nineteenth century

8

Pevensey Castle (E), Roman and c.1100

9

(b) Bosham, church, chancel arch, Anglo-Saxon

(a) Sompting, church, tower c.1000

(a) *left*. Bishopstone (E), church, coffin-lid, twelfth century. (b) *above*. Worth (E), church, window in the north aisle, Anglo-Saxon. (c) *right*. Lewes (E), St John Baptist, Southover, tomb slab to Gundrada de Warenne, later twelfth century

(a) (b) and (c) Selham, church, chancel arch and capitals, twelfth century (?)

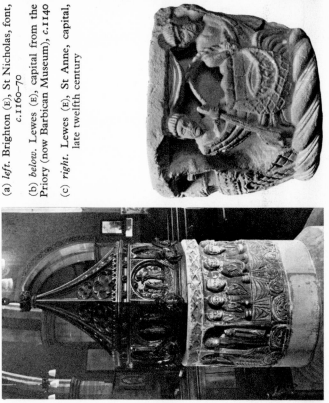

(a) *left*. Brighton (E), St Nicholas, font, c.1160–70

(b) *below*. Lewes (E), capital from the Priory (now Barbican Museum), c.1140

(c) *right*. Lewes (E), St Anne, capital, late twelfth century

Chichester Cathedral, panel with the Raising of Lazarus, *c.*1125–50

(a) Shipley, church, *c.*1125 (?)

(b) Shipley, church, reliquary, thirteenth century

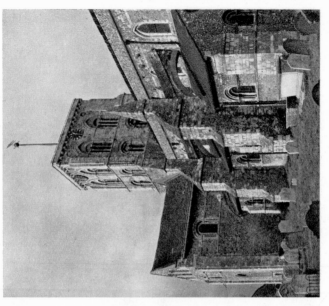

(a) Old Shoreham, church, crossing tower c.1140

(b) New Shoreham, church, crossing tower c.1130 and late twelfth century

(b) New Shoreham, church, north arcade, c.1200

(a) Climping, church, west doorway, c.1170 (?)

17

Steyning, church, nave *c.*1170 (?)

Chichester Cathedral, nave, begun after 1091, altered after 1187

Chichester Cathedral, retrochoir, after 1187

Boxgrove Priory, *c.*1220

Climping, church, c.1220

(a) Boxgrove Priory, *c.*1170 and *c.*1220

(b) Hardham Priory, chapter house entrance, thirteenth century

23

Battle Abbey (E), dormitory, thirteenth century

(a) North Stoke, church, corbel, thirteenth century

(b) Winchelsea (E), Salutation Inn, cellar, c.1300

(a) Crawley, Ifield church, monument to Sir John de Ifelde, *c.*1340

(b) Crawley, Ifield church, monument to Lady Margaret de Ifelde †1347

(a) Chichester Cathedral, Lady Chapel, *c.*1300

(b) Arundel, St Nicholas, begun after 1380

Chichester, Bishop's Palace, kitchen roof, thirteenth century (?)

(a) East Grinstead (E), Cromwell House, fifteenth century (?)

(b) Rye (E), Old Hospital, fifteenth and sixteenth centuries

29

Battle Abbey (E), gatehouse, licensed 1338

(a) Amberley Castle, gatehouse, *c.*1380

(b) Bodiam Castle (E), licensed 1385

(a) Mayfield (E), Convent of the Holy Child Jesus, chapel (formerly hall of Archbishops' Palace), fourteenth century

(b) Appledram, Rymans, after 1410

Stopham, bridge, 1423

(a) Chichester, Market Cross, 1501

(b) Arundel, St Nicholas, pulpit, Perpendicular

(a) Arundel, St Nicholas, chantry and tomb of the 9th Earl of Arundel †1487

(b) Boxgrove Priory, chantry of Lord de la Warr †1526

(a) Herstmonceux Castle (E), licensed 1440

(b) Cowdray House, *c.*1495–*c.*1540

(a) Camber Castle (E), 1511–14 (?) and 1539–43

(b) Camber Castle (E), 1511–14 (?) and 1539–43

(a) Parham, begun 1577

(b) Hassocks (E), Danny Park, east front, c.1582–93
(*Copyright Country Life*)

(a) Chiddingly (E), church, monument to Sir John Jefferay †1578

(b) Barnham, Barnham Court, c.1640

Rye (E), Peacock's School, 1636

Petworth, Somerset Lodge, 1653

(a) Petworth House, Grinling Gibbons Room, carving by Gibbons, 1692

(b) Maresfield (E), cast-iron tomb slab to Robert Brooks †1667

(c) Petworth House, chapel, c.1260–70 and 1690–2

(a) Uppark, by William Talman, c.1685–90

(b) Petworth House, west front, 1688–96

(b) Ashburnham (E), church, monument to William Ashburnham †1675, by John Bushnell

(a) Withyham (E), church, monument to Thomas Sackville †1677, by C. G. Cibber

(a) Petworth, Town Hall, bust of William III

(b) Eastbourne (B), Compton Place, plasterwork in the State Bedroom with portrait of Colen Campbell, by Charles Stanley, 1728

45

Castle Goring, by Biagio Rebecca, c.1790, entrance front

Castle Goring, by Biagio Rebecca, c.1790, garden front

(a) Bognor Regis, The Dome, *c.*1787

(b) Brighton (E), Pavilion, by John Nash, 1815–22

Brighton (E), Pavilion, by John Nash, 1815–22, Music Room,
decorated by Crace & Sons

(a) Hove (E), Brunswick Terrace, by Amon Wilds & Busby, 1825–7

(b) Hastings (E), Pelham Crescent, by Joseph Kay, 1824–8

Hove (E), Brunswick Square, by Amon Wilds & Busby, 1825–7

(a) Hove (E), St Andrew, Waterloo Road,
by Sir Charles Barry, 1827–8

(b) Brighton (E), St Peter, by Sir Charles Barry,
1824–8

Brighton (E), St John Baptist, relief of the Baptism of Christ, by J. E. Carew, 1835

(a) Lancing College, chapel, by R. H. Carpenter, begun 1868

(b) Lancing College, lower quadrangle, by R. C. Carpenter, begun 1854

East Grinstead (E), St Margaret's Convent, by G. E. Street,
chapel, 1879–83

Petworth, North
Street and East
Street, lamp
standard by Sir
Charles Barry, 1851

(a) West Lavington, church, by William Butterfield, 1850

(b) Brighton (E), St Michael, stained glass, by Morris & Co., c.1862–5

Groombridge (E), Glen Andred, by R. Norman Shaw, 1867

East Grinstead (E), Standen, by Philip Webb, 1891-4 (Copyright Country Life)

(a) East Grinstead (E), Standen, by Philip Webb, 1891–4

(b) Thakeham, Little Thakeham, by Sir Edwin Lutyens, 1902–3

(a) Christ's Hospital, railway station, 1899

(b) Worth Priory (E), Paddockhurst, frieze by Walter Crane, 1897

(a) Bailiffscourt, by Amyas Phillips, 1935

(b) Bexhill (E), De la Warr Pavilion, by Erich Mendelsohn
& Serge Chermayeff, 1933–6

Peacehaven (E), air view

Falmer (E), University of Sussex, by Sir Basil Spence, begun 1960

of romantic landscaping were getting at with their dislike of landscape gardening in Capability Brown's sense.

The E front was designed by *John Upton*, the Petworth estate surveyor, in 1760. It is a good deal more than estate surveyor's architecture, and in fact better than the Earl of Egremont's London architect (Matthew Brettingham) could do in his London house, now the Naval and Military Club. Not original, but very personal and tense, something not usually found in Late Palladian houses. Seven bays and three storeys, the centre three bays pedimented, the pediment filled with a lunette and plumes. No proper doorcase, only a curved pediment on console brackets. Odd, elegantly carved incised panels, rather like the wall panels in a drawing room, in lieu of pilasters. The W and N sides are plain additions of the 1790s.

RIVER HOUSE, 1½ m. W, in another hamlet with several cottages which in a less fecund part of the country would merit special notice. Obviously by the same mason as Dean House, two big gables and a two-storeyed gabled porch, the same style of windows but not the same strict symmetry. It has, however, been restored – not gently, but with sophistication – to the point where it is indistinguishable from a Lutyens house. This does not make it unattractive, only different. The face-lift was given in 1934.

TOAT MONUMENT *see* PULBOROUGH

TORTINGTON

Hamlet of farms near the Arun SW of Arundel, really still representing the old C12 group. The church is barely visible behind a farmyard.

ST THOMAS. Small, with a nice white-painted bell-turret, similar to Ford, but not quite so pretty, due to restoration; the inside nicer than the outside. The bones are all C12, and nothing has been substantially altered since. Round-headed windows, big as Norman windows go, in deep splays. The S doorway is Late Norman, but a whole generation before Climping, say *c*.1140. The ornament here is rich, but is always keeping inside the established pattern, not trying to break it; by comparison with Climping it seems distinctly inhibited. Two orders of zigzag ornament, the outer order with a motif like a bunch of grapes in each angle (*see* also Buncton, p. 120), the label with a repeated star-pattern;

12—S.

jamb shafts and capitals with rough chevron decoration. Inside, the chancel arch is of about the same date, but uses a different vocabulary. Two orders, the inner one plain, the outer with jamb shafts and renewed capitals, the arch covered with a fearsome collection of that most puzzling of Late Norman ornaments, the beakhead. This is the only Sussex example apart from New Shoreham, and here the faces, although they exhibit an admirable range of expression, are too small and too close together to give the usual fine barbaric effect. Is it, in fact, *in situ*? s aisle early C13, in the usual style: double-chamfered arches, round abacus, semi-octagonal responds. Abacus and responds have been painted grey: is this original, and was it a humble attempt to emulate the Purbeck polychrome of Salisbury or Chichester? It was later blocked, and re-opened in the C19. – FONT. C12, naïve and disarming. Circular bowl with arcading, but every other bay has a pendant with motifs like Greek honeysuckle patterns instead of a pier, and a scallop capital. – PULPIT. Humble Jacobean, with a little ornament around the top. Stands on legs, not a stem. – STAINED GLASS. E window probably by *Willement*.

TORTINGTON PRIORY. A house of Augustinian Canons, founded before 1180. What remains now forms the s face of a barn at PRIORY FARM, ½ m. N of the church. This seems to have been the N wall of the nave and includes two delicate mid C13 wall-shafts and the stump of the vaulting above them. Either shaft supports a circular abacus and is made up of three smaller shafts. Traces of windows are visible to the r. of the r.-hand shaft. It must have been a very elegant building.

TRAWLER'S *see* SHIPLEY

TREYFORD

N of the Downs, midway between Midhurst and Harting. Scattered cottages, clunch and flint, more coherent seen above from the Downs than actually walking about the village. Treyford has a fine exercise in the eerie in its two churches, or rather lack of two churches.

OLD CHURCH (ST MARY). Above the roadside near the Manor House. E and W walls remain, and most of the s wall; it was the customary unaisled C13 building, with one lancet in the W wall and quite an impressive E triplet, plain but well-proportioned. Both church and tiny churchyard are a nearly impenetrable thicket of elder and sycamore trees and are sinisterly claustrophobic. The old church was deserted when a large new church of ST PETER (the 'cathedral of the Downs'!) was built in 1849 to the NW, designed by *Ferrey*. This was blown up in 1951, leaving a big burial ground, more overtly melancholy, full of evergreen trees. So now Treyford has two churchyards and no church.*

MANOR HOUSE. A striking front of *c.*1690–1710, unusual for Sussex and a little un-English. Five bays and two tall storeys, clunch with brick dressings, the brickwork continued vertically between the windows to make continuous strips from ground to eaves. The central bay has a doorcase with semicircular pediment under a window framed by scrolled volutes, all in brick, and the wayward proportions of these make it likely that this is a local craftsman's job. The idea of lacing the elevation with vertical strips – used around Hanover Square in London, and much more often in C18 France and Belgium – probably comes from the end bays of Petworth House.

COTTAGE, E of the Manor House. Thatched, with simple brick hood-moulds to simple mullioned windows. Dated 1638.

BARROWS, ¾ m. S of the village. A cemetery of five huge bell barrows, arranged linearly. The barrows vary from 6 to 15 ft in height. Two produced unaccompanied cremations.

TROTTON

In a bend of the Rother between Petersfield and Midhurst, with one of the best of the Rother BRIDGES: five round-headed arches with cutwaters, probably early C15. Each of the Rother villages has its own particular picturesqueness, and in Trotton's case it is the view of church and Trotton Place across the fields to the E, with medieval gable and Georgian brickwork in a purely English counterpoint.

ST GEORGE. Oblong E.E. tower, very dour, with the bell stage indicated only by single lancets. All the rest is *c.*1300, bare and simple, without any hint of Dec richness. One single wide space of four bays, the windows two-light with quatrefoil above (i.e. no real difference from the earliest type of Geometrical tracery), the rere-arches moulded and given hood-moulds. Only the E window is Victorian. The effect is plain and dignified outside, but bafflingly blank inside. This is due

---

* This church was intended to serve Didling, Elsted, and Treyford: in its place Didling has remained unrestored and Elsted recently repaired after being ruinous.

to the total absence of a chancel arch. Perhaps with a rood
screen and other medieval fittings it made more sense.
Original roof consisting of tie-beams and arched braces rising
to a collar, the sides given purlins and wind-braces like a
welsh roof. – COMMUNION RAIL. C17; a pretty conceit.
Every second baluster does not reach the full height and is
embraced by an arch thrown from one to the other of its
neighbours. – WALL PAINTING. Last Judgement, covering
the W wall in the same way as at Chaldon in Surrey. Christ at
the top, Moses below; on the l., Carnal Man naked surrounded
by the Seven Deadly Sins, on the r., Spiritual Man clothed
and the Seven Works of Mercy. Dated c.1380 by Professor
Tristram. All in the familiar red monochrome, a nice picture
book but not very much more. Appropriately, the Seven
Deadly Sins have decayed much faster than the rest. –
PLATE. Flagon, 1615; Cup and Paten, 1719.

MONUMENTS. Margaret, Lady Camoys, † 1310, the oldest
existing female brass. Nave floor. Severe full-face, life-size,
with the same control over flowing line as is possessed by C13
sculpture. Headdress and the dog and feet are subordinated
to the whole composition without ceasing to be likenesses.
Indents for ornate canopy and also for nine shields in the
figure itself. – Thomas Lord Camoys † 1419 and wife, brasses
on tomb-chest with sides ornamented by shields and quatrefoils. Centre of chancel. One of the biggest and most ornate
and best preserved brasses in England. Figures nearly 5 ft tall
with joined hands under a double ogee canopy, itself surmounted by shields and battlemented cresting. The figures
are blank and limp compared with the earlier brass, but seen
inside this rich frilly canopy this becomes much more com-
prehensible, for one sets off the other. Particularly majestic
seen from the E, in perspective. – Three other table tombs
without inscriptions: S side of nave (C15), SE corner of chancel
(plain and pilastered, to Anthony Forster † 1643), and NE
corner of chancel (probably to Sir Roger Lewknor † c.1478).
This is individual and elegant, within the crushing limitations
of the type: repeated tall narrow niches on the sides, with
the edge of the slab delightfully carved with swags.

TROTTON PLACE. C16 core, but both the main elevations now
plain mid C18, five bays with the central bay brought forward
and plain stone surrounds to the windows.

UP MARDEN see THE MARDENS

Trotton, brass to Thomas Lord Camoys † 1419 and wife

7010

UPPARK

Up indeed, at the top of a valley within a mile of the crest of the Downs, near Harting. Oddly enough, the view from the house is wide rather than deep, taking in nearly 180 degrees of the lower Downs and stretching as far as the Isle of Wight.

Uppark was built *c.*1685–90 by *William Talman*, and its three main fronts have not been altered since. It is a copybook example of the Wren-style country house, moderate-sized brick with stone dressings, comfortable to look at and live in. In fact its parentage is Dutch, and it was brought to England after the Restoration by men like Hugh May; Talman may have been May's pupil.

The design has to be judged by the very highest standards, and by these it is good but not quite first class. The main
43a   front faces s, its homeliness poignantly emphasized by the rough grass which covers the original formal terraces. It has nine bays, the centre quoined and pedimented, and the basic trouble is that these bays are a little too crowded, and their ornament a little parsimonious. It is essential that in a house depending on proportion, the proportion is exact, and if the ornament is going to be spare, it must be free from meanness. A look at the almost identical centre of Tadworth House, Surrey, will bring out clearly the difference between the good and the excellent. Mid c18 arms in the pediment; below, the first-floor window is flanked by pinched scrolls and swags of fruit, the ground floor has a doorcase with open scrolled pediment supported on rich Corinthian demi-columns and between them a lintel packed with curly carving. Plain wings, again with slight but important defects in the proportion: bays three and seven have their windows too near the quoined centre, e.g. The w front is seven bays wide and plain, with markedly different spacing from the s front, which does not help; the E front is identical except for a plain doorcase with segmental pediment resting on brackets, of the type used by Wren at Winslow, Buckinghamshire.

The E façade was originally the entrance and was approached via two two-storeyed offices. This was all changed after 1746, when the estate passed to the Fetherstonhaugh family: the lodges were demolished and a matching pair of offices built to l. and r. of the house on the N side. They are plain Palladian with a three-bay pedimented centre and might well be by *Paine* (who built the Fetherstonhaugh town house in Whitehall, now Dover House). The entrance was then moved to the N side, and was elaborated with a Tuscan screen by *Humphry Repton* in 1812 (presumably designed by one of his sons, giving their customary 'assistance in the architectural department'). Nothing has been altered since.

The description of the inside is in the order that the rooms are shown to visitors. In general, the interiors are mostly of 1750–70. The tour starts down an elegant Repton corridor via an octagonal vestibule, subtle and simple, into the STAIRCASE HALL. This is in the space between the former projecting wings on the N side and was apparently filled in *c.*1750, though the staircase itself is undoubtedly late C17 with two twisted balusters to each tread, rising around three sides of the well to the landing. Customary Venetian window half-way up; this and the mildly Rococo plaster ceiling look *c.*1750. Unsatisfactory proportions, which is understandable if the staircase was moved: wide treads in a narrow well, giving a crowded effect. Several busts by *John Cheere*, 1759. Next come three rooms across the front of the house exhibiting progressively later stages of mid C18 decoration. First is the DRAWING ROOM, with another Rococo ceiling and original wallpaper and mirrors (the fireplace looks earlier and might be late C17; it is heavily carved with garlands of flowers and fruit). Then the SALOON, the principal room of the house (the roof had to be raised to get it in, and this can be clearly seen from outside, the first-storey floors starting part way up the window). This is a perfect example of the impact of Adam ideas on a fundamentally Palladian designer (unknown: possibly Henry Keene, possibly Paine). The elegant forms are reproduced, but have become slightly straightened out and mixed with the half French ornament of Sir William Chambers. Splendid detailed carving and single ornaments, but not a splendid room as a whole, because the Adam spatial sense is absent too. Ceiling with big central coffered oval, the remainder cut into panels decorated with dainty swags: beautiful wall garlands in which swags disappear and reappear behind trails of foliage, and splendid doorcases, the central door with Corinthian columns and a frieze of swags and *œils-de-boeuf*, the side doors with astylar jambs ornamented near the top with volutes which, at a second look, turn out to be snakes. The bookcases are by *Repton* and are beautifully fitted in; the fireplaces, strictly classical, are by *Thomas Carter Jun.* Frontal termini caryatids l. and r. with the staid faces of Homer and Virgil and two noble young Romans. Next is the

LITTLE SALOON, with a similar ceiling of oddly inelegant shape (the main motif is a Maltese cross with concave sides) but incorporating low-relief medallions also. The doorcases, by comparison with the Saloon, are just a little lighter and crisper. Then the plain Stone Hall, the former entrance hall, and then the DINING ROOM, the only C17 interior to survive, and one with a more sure decorative sense than the C18 showed at Uppark. Plain sides, plain ceiling, but the ends grandly equipped with pilasters framing alcoves, into which Repton ingeniously fitted mirrors. Early C19 black busts, and also black reliefs of animals done by *E. Garrard*, making a nice counterpoint to the white and gold of the architecture. Beyond, visitors go out via an oval Service Room of Repton's with a weird STAINED GLASS window of 1813 by *W. Doyle*, incorporating figures drawn from the Elgin Marbles by *G. S. Repton*. The intention was to illuminate it from outside for dramatic effect.*

In the grounds to the E, VANDALIAN TOWER by *Henry Keene*, 1774; only portions of the ground floor now remain.

H. G. Wells spent part of his boyhood at Uppark, where his mother was housekeeper, and livened things up there considerably.

1010   UPPER BEEDING

Opposite Bramber, at the N end of the Adur gap. One narrow street of cottages along the main road, and very depressing sporadic C20 housing N of it, up to the church. It can only benefit now from further building up, though not much can be said for the present standard. The most interesting house is not one of the old buildings but a terrifying house called THE TOWERS, now a convent, on the road to Henfield. Built c.1880; quadrangular with four corner towers, bleak and forbidding. With less medieval detail it could have been very impressive. Is it connected with Beedings near Pulborough?

ST PETER. William de Braose founded the Benedictine priory of Sele here in 1075 from Saumur, on a site immediately to the N, now occupied by a bow-fronted Georgian house. The present church seems to have been the priory church, with

---

* The complete survival, untouched, of the C18 wall fabrics and curtains is due to the extraordinary history of the house in the C19. Sir Harry Fetherstonhaugh married his dairymaid in 1825. She survived him until 1875, and her sister until 1895. They preserved the atmosphere and fittings of the C18 until the C20. This was the *ménage* H. G. Wells knew (NT).

the monks using the chancel and the parishioners the nave.
It was never a lavish building and was cruelly treated in the
C19, so that the result is hard and unattractive. The old parts
are mostly c.1300. Plain W tower, off-centre, with single bell-
openings and queer (altered ?) tower arch with undersize inner
order which actually looks early C13. Wide nave with renewed
lancets in the N side, the easternmost a pair with foliage
carving inside on the spandrel between them. The S aisle is
C19; is the chancel arch also ? It has brilliantly carved foliage
capitals, vibrantly and intensely alive. The remarkable thing
is the fragment of arcading and doorway built into the S side of
the small C16 stone chancel. Two lights, and the stump of a
third, with a frenzy of deeply cut small-scale mouldings.
Circular abaci, clustered shafts, and round-headed arches
which must surely have been trefoiled originally. Late C13. –
PLATE. Paten, 1669; Paten, 1794.

UPPERTON see TILLINGTON

UP WALTHAM

9010

A wonderful group in a downland valley between Petworth and
Chichester. From the S, church, farm, and barns look like a
monogram in flint.

ST MARY THE VIRGIN. Untouched and lovable. Nave and
   apse, with bellcote, the original C12 church for an area whose
   population can hardly have gone up since then. C14 windows
   in the apse and W end, C13 chancel arch. Simple and humble
   inside, with kingposts, which must represent the original patterns (could radio-carbon tell whether they are also the original
   timbers ?). The only obviously C12 detail left is the enchanting
   PISCINA, which is simply an elegant volute capital with the
   top hollowed out. It is carved on all four sides and looks too
   ornate to have been something preserved when e.g. the chancel
   arch was widened. So was it in fact bought from a Romanesque
   mason's yard to add a tiny touch of richness to such a remote
   building ? – CHANDELIERS. A complete set, preserved unself-
   consciously here because the church is still lit by candles. –
   PLATE. Cup and Paten, 1675.

BARROWS, on WALTHAM DOWN. A small linear cemetery
   running NW–SE and consisting of four bowl barrows and a fine
   bell barrow, 10 ft high at the SE end. There is no record of the
   excavation of this group, although all appear to be disturbed.

9000

WALBERTON

One cheerful long street in the flat land E of Chichester. Old flint and brick. More than its share of new buildings. The best part is the quiet corner by the church and Walberton House.

ST MARY. A mulish restoration in 1903 by *Richard Creed* led directly to the setting up of Diocesan Advisory Committees, which helped the rest of the country. Laudable, but small comfort here at Walberton. Lean-to aisles and no clerestory, sweeping nave roof, bell-turret on modern timber framing – a common type near Chichester and comely enough even after restoration. The original nave was probably pre-Conquest. The W wall showed this much more clearly before 1903, when brick quoins and a Saxon gable-cross disappeared. It was cut through piecemeal in the C12 with unmoulded round-headed arches of the same type but bewilderingly different widths and heights. C13 chancel with the usual comfortable proportions and lancet windows; lancets in the sides of the C13 N porch too. – FONT. Tub-shaped, crude but powerful. Quite plain, probably the best of the group.

WALBERTON HOUSE. Simple, elegant house by *Smirke*, 1803, beautifully maintained. White stucco, plain S front of seven bays with a svelte Doric loggia along the whole length. Smirke shows up much better here than when he was trying to be more demonstrably Greek. Ample plain stairwell with the staircase climbing round the wall.

WALDERTON see STOUGHTON

WALTHAM DOWN see UP WALTHAM

WAPPINGTHORN see STEYNING

WARMINGHURST

1010

One of Sussex's proud surprises. Church and farmhouse only, in the otherwise unexciting Weald country E of Storrington. On a knoll with a splendid view S to Chanctonbury Ring, and in the other direction, a charming vignette of Thakeham church, which is half a mile by footpath across the fields and three miles by road. A noble, remote site.

HOLY SEPULCHRE. A noble, remote church too. It remained unrestored until 1959, when the job was beautifully done by *Denman & Son*. The architectural history is simple: long E.E. single space, lancets in the sides, and a roundel in the W wall, with a three-light window of c.1300, the head made up of quatrefoils already unencircled but not yet cusped. Blocked brick s porch, small N vestry in Survival Gothic, tile-hung bell-turret, and fine mellow texture. The inside is magical: like Up Marden, far more than a matter of being unrestored. The roof is single-framed, with only a few tie-beams and all the rhythmical advantages which the single-frame roof can possess. The lack of structural division between nave and chancel was remedied c.1700 by a wooden screen, three arched openings below and tympanum above carrying splendid painted ROYAL ARMS of Queen Anne. Around the arms proper wide-stretched purple drapery like a royal robe. Complete set of C18 BOX PEWS, and three-decker PULPIT. Natural wood, clear glass, uneven floor, and especially, the tall E window appearing behind the low screen, which is beautifully managed. Not a place to forget easily. – Late C17 COMMUNION RAILS with twisted balusters, C18 FONT with bulgy stem, scrolly iron BRACKET to pull up the font cover. – PLATE. Set, 1713. – MONUMENTS. Rough small C16 brass to Edward Shelley † 1554 and wife in a Perp niche. Kneeling figures, which formerly had the Trinity above, in the C16 Sussex way. – Two good big early C18 tablets in City of London style: Elizabeth Benet † 1727 by *Stanton & Horsnaile*, entirely architectural except for one putto head at the bottom, and John Riches † 1718, unsigned, with three putto heads above the inscription.

WARNHAM

1030

NW of Horsham, near the Surrey border, in unspoilt leafy country which is in fact a triumph of careful preservation. No centre, but carefully tended groups, almost an estate village, especially s of the church, with a lot of bulky late C19 building.

ST MARGARET. The outside effectively Victorian (*A. W. Blomfield*, 1885) except for the N aisle, which is Late Dec, and the plain SE tower, which must date from well into the C16, shown by the diagrammatic detail in the spandrels of the doorway. The chapel, E of the tower, is C16 too (money left in 1524), though terribly restored. Inside, the N arcade goes with the aisle (octagonal piers and abaci, double-chamfered arches). Blomfield was not a good architect, and he does not show up well here. – FONT. Late C12, square bowl with plain arcading. – MONUMENTS. Sir John Caryll † 1613. Kneeling figures, sons and daughters below. – Matthew Napper † 1801. Urn and inscription, still purely C18 in spirit; and in the naïve skull and leaves in the predella, older than that. Hence a local job – by *Page* of Horsham. Affectionately done.

Several good groups of cottages. The best N of the church, on the E side of SCHOOL LANE, which is a potted history of the English small house. Five or six buildings, the materials including weatherboard, roughcast, brick, tile-hanging, and half-timber: five or six dates, from the C16 (gabled and roughcast) to the C17 to 1752 (grey and red brick in patterns and a dainty dentilled cornice), to the early C19. Immediately N of this, good asymmetrical Victorian SCHOOLS, 1878 by *A. W. Blomfield*.

SANDS FARM, ½ m. NW. Good C15 timber-framed farmhouse. The front faces W and has the familiar Wealden pattern – overhanging first-floor wings, recessed centre. Impressive close timbering, except at the S end, which has been largely redone in brick. Unrestored compared with similar buildings like OLD MANOR, a little further E.

WARNHAM COURT. The original parts decent neo-Elizabethan of 1828, perhaps by *P. F. Robinson*. They must include the tower with its pretty, wayward details. Big additions of 1866 by *A. W. Blomfield*, and many more just recently. The LODGES to the SE at a sharp bend in A24 are pretty neo-Elizabethan too, done by *Arthur Blomfield*, his son, in 1889.

WARNHAM LODGE, ¾ m. NW. Mostly demolished 1961. It was a heavily picturesque house of 1894 by *Batterbury & Huxley*, the firm which laid out so much of Hampstead. It looks thirty years earlier. Lodges and a tall water tower (with a spire and dormers) remain. Immediately N of this is MALTMAYES, a C16 timber-framed house with recessed centre, the effect spoilt by the rock-faced infilling, sandstone and flint, which must be Victorian.

FIELD PLACE, *see* p. 221.

WARNINGCAMP *see* BURPHAM

WASHINGTON

Immediately under the Downs, on the main London–Worthing road. One lane of cottages runs W to the church, rather disjointed and scrappy. The interesting thing is the variety of building materials at the exact meeting point of Downs and Weald. It includes two sorts of sandstone (green Burgate and dark brown) and clunch as well as flint and brick.

ST MARY. Rebuilt in 1867 by *Gordon Hills*, except for the tower and the N arcade. Hard and unlovable, but the inside with its rich, self-assured mouldings and stencilling* has some High Victorian vigour of its own. The tower is Late Perp, its simple bell-openings filled with stone tracery, apparently original, which gives it a Wiltshire look. The tower arch is unusual: two chamfered orders, the inner given half-columns, the outer quarter-columns. The arches and responds of the arcade are rough work of *c.*1200: the intervening circular piers and abaci were made more polite in the C13. – PLATE. Paten, 1727.

CHANCTONBURY RING. An Iron Age HILL-FORT, 1 m. SE of the church. It consists of a small enclosure of 3½ acres defended by a low bank and ditch; these are best preserved on the SW, where the single entrance occurs.

Within the fort are the remains of two ROMAN BUILDINGS, one of which is a Romano-Celtic temple consisting of a square *cella* surrounded by a veranda. The site appears to have been occupied by the Romans in the late C3 and C4 A.D.

The DEW-POND within the fort is a C19 construction.

WATERGATE HOUSE *see* STOUGHTON

WATERSFIELD *see* COLDWALTHAM

WEST ASHLING *see* ASHLING

WESTBOURNE

7000

On the Hampshire border N of Emsworth: a quiet place now, but with an air of a small town, not a village. This is no accident: it was the old centre for the district and had a market until the C18, rather like tiny Hampshire towns such as Botley and Wickham. The whole of the area N of the church was probably the original market-place, now encroached on by later islands of buildings.

ST JOHN THE BAPTIST. Biggish church with nave and aisles, visually all Perp, hence unusual in Sussex: the outside effect late C14, the inside and tower early C16. Older walling in several places (see the VCH), but only manifest in the blocked lancets of the E window. Unlike most Sussex churches, it has had a really unpleasant restoration.‡

* By *Heaton & Butler*, 1880. All under pink paint now. A pity.

‡ Carried out *c.*1865 to the designs of the vicar, the Rev. *John Hanson Sperling*, an Ecclesiologist who later joined Rome (NT).

Effectively, the outside is all of *c*.1390. Influences in Perpendicular architecture are often hard to trace, but most of the windows at Westbourne are unmistakably 'Winchester windows', i.e. of the same type that Wynford used when remodelling the nave of Winchester Cathedral. They have two main lights, splitting up into four smaller lights, segmental heads, and hood-moulds which come a long way down the jambs. At Winchester they seem to have been used to fit the space available in the Norman nave, and then became a style in their own right: they are surprisingly effective. The design was copied in the C19 windows, but original and imitation are easily separated. The E window (renewed) is a more familiar late C14 type, three lights with panel tracery under a pointed arch.

The second building period was the early C16, and is also typical of Winchester building (it was done by the Earls of Arundel) when it can be seen underneath Victorian stupidity. Boldly, they rebuilt the tower inside the existing walls of the church, open to the nave on three sides,* with continuous chamfered mouldings. The same form was used for the chancel arch; the three-bay arcades have very tall piers, octagonal abaci, and single-chamfered four-centred arches. It is all bluff, rather impatient Gothic, but big-scale and sure of itself, refreshing after the normal Perp interior which carried on an earlier multiplicity of mouldings without understanding the reason for them. Outside, the tower has a two-light bell-opening, square-headed, filled with stone tracery (cf. Micheldever, Hants) and then a big shingled spire behind battlements, replacing a Gothick one by *Henry Keene*. In the chancel, nice PISCINA of *c*.1400: ogee flanked by quatrefoils under a square-headed label. – PLATE. Chalice, *c*.1390, Sienese, given in the C19; Set, 1717. – MONUMENTS. Tablets to Henry Barwell † 1785 and Richard Barwell † 1804, both by *Nollekens*. Really deplorable workmanship, showing the basically rotten state of the profession then: a C17 sculptor would never have been so slapdash over any job, however small.

Westbourne is a satisfying place to walk through, because of the intricacies and angles of the various islands of buildings and the way in which they all lead back unobtrusively to the tower and spire of the church. N of the church there is a roughly triangular place called THE SQUARE: the prettiest street in Westbourne is NE of this off Foxbury Lane (where there is

* In the s aisle, jamb and beginnings of an arch: this may have been the original position of the tower.

MILE END HOUSE, C18 with a Doric porch). It leads to Southbourne and has a wall on one side and a pretty sequence of thatched half-timbered and C18 brick cottages on the other.

WEST BURTON

1 m. W of Bury

Built round a quadrilateral of lanes, like Bignor, the next village; also like Bignor, no village group, but fine views of the Downs escarpment. No church.

COKE'S HOUSE. Impressively solid late C16 stone house, set above the road and approached by steps to a charming Jacobean doorway in the garden wall, crowned by a pediment plus pedestals and balls. One long range not broken up by gables, with mullion-and-transom windows of various sizes; more like the North of England. Ornament only on the porch, which has a shaped gable and cornice supported on brackets. Porch dated 1610, and garden gate probably of this date also; the house is of c.1580. Inside, one room has a thickly moulded plaster frieze of fruit and flowers.

WEST CHILTINGTON

In intricate Weald country E of Pulborough. Two parts, both pleasant, a close-built village around a cross-roads with a street leading down to the church, and a Common a mile to the S which is largely a leafy C20 suburb. Occasional views to the Downs, which are here about three miles to the S.

ST MARY. Attractive and unrestored, as so many of the churches in this part of West Sussex are. Nave and chancel, rubble stonework, lean-to aisles to both, and a big central shingled bell-turret and spire, a very happy, unexpected effect, like a French village church. The woodwork of this is dated 1602, but the idea may be older, for the chancel arch wall is thickened by 5 ft to support it and the arch itself has two unmoulded orders, of c.1200. Nave and chancel walls are probably C11; an aisle was already needed by the late C12, of three bays with scallop capitals (a nice variety of patterns, no two the same) and unmoulded pointed arches. The W window of the aisle is still round-headed. Fantastically long squint to the chancel through the E respond of the aisle and the thickened chancel wall. Big early C12 N doorway, terribly renewed in the C19. Jamb shafts, one order of zigzag, one roll-moulding. The arch between chancel and aisle is C13, and so is the E window (three

lancets under a rere-arch). Most of the later windows are C14.
The s chancel chapel is C13, and the arch between aisle and
chapel was probably opened up then. – WALL PAINTINGS.
There are a lot. They are of two dates, according to Professor
Tristram. C12 work over and around the arch at the end of the
s aisle, which was originally blocked: Majesty and Angels and
four apostles, red and ochre. Mid C13 scheme on both sides of
the nave. Trefoiled arches enclosing Passion scenes (s) and
scenes from the life of the Virgin (N), some of the figures still
clear enough to be eloquent. In addition, geometrical decoration around the arcade, C13 and C14, and a figure of Christ
in a splay of the N nave window. The ensemble can still give a
ghostly echo of the original effect. – PULPIT. Sober and handsome. Octagonal, tall linenfold panels with a little Jacobean
decoration above them. – PLATE. Chalice and Paten, 1568.

The cottages in Church Street make a pleasant group, unexpected in this countryside of deep lanes and isolated farms, but
they are not remarkable in themselves. Green Burgate stone,
not the dark brown ironstone used at Pulborough.

½ m. to the W, a smock WINDMILL of c.1800. Big weatherboarded octagonal body, heavy cap, two sweeps remaining.
On the other side of the road, FRIAR'S HOUSE is a pleasant
C17 small house. Mullioned windows and a shell-hood doorway, added later or imported.

WEST DEAN
By Chichester

Largely a matter of secluded flint cottages on a lane parallel to
the Chichester to Midhurst road. Nice situation but not much of
a group. The church and house are just N of this, surrounded by
high flint walls. The best COTTAGE is immediately E of the
village pub (No. 105): C17, timber-framed, thatched, and quite
unrestored, e.g. the windowless back elevation.

St ANDREW. Largely rebuilt, very simply and sensitively, by
Frederick Etchells, after a bad fire in 1934. The happy inside
effect, with its decent FITTINGS and unmoulded crossing
arches, is now all C20 and is worth a good look for its care over
details. But what the fire left was conserved: the nave walls in
fact are pre-Conquest, with a blocked doorway of unmistakable proportions on the N side, extremely tall and narrow –
9 ft high, 32 in. wide. The E end with its triple lancets is C13;
most of the nave windows are C18, big with segmental heads,

and must have been put in at the time of the W tower of 1727, which still has a Gothic outline but uses the same sort of openings. The transepts are late C18 Gothick, vaulted in plaster, and one with a small vaulted altar recess. – STAINED GLASS. C20 E window by *Armitage* of *Powell's*, above average, like the rest of the fittings. – MONUMENTS. Sir Richard Lewknor † 1616 and his sons, damaged and calcined in the fire. What is left is two big kneeling effigies under round arches; by the style and quality of carving it looks as if it was not done until c.1640. – William Dodge James † 1912, by *Sir W. Goscombe John*. Recumbent bronze effigy; hand on breast, and lifeless.

WEST DEAN PARK. A limp Gothick house, all flint, by *James Wyatt*, 1804, no better than Goodwood on the other side of the hill. Only the N part remains as Wyatt left it: the rest was made considerably less limp by *George & Peto* in 1893. Still flint and stone, but a big porte-cochère with a tower on top of it in Arts-and-Crafts Gothic just like an advanced Methodist church. (Sumptuous late C19 interiors. MHLG)

GOOSEHILL CAMP, 2 m. W. The site, which is partially obscured by a stand of yew trees, consists of two concentric banks and ditches enclosing a roughly oval area of 4½ acres on the E slope of BOW HILL. Traces of a counterscarp bank are visible, associated with the inner ring, which is broken by entrances on the W and SE. Excavation has revealed the ditches to be of V-section and some 5 ft deep. The site is datable to the late C3 B.C.

The indefensible nature of this earthwork suggests that it may have been used as a cattle-rearing enclosure rather than a fortress.

WESTERGATE see EASTERGATE

WEST GREEN see CRAWLEY, p. 205

WEST GRINSTEAD

Half-way between Horsham and the Downs, at a point where the Weald has opened out and also become more park-like, with trim hedges rather than copses. The Burrells with their pair of Nash houses and the attendant landscaping have given it a character unlike anywhere else in Sussex: the Weald has first been tamed, then let back, on a leash as it were, to be wild within limits. No village.

ST GEORGE. Heavy-roofed and shaggy, down beside the Adur.

The strong overall impression could come from nowhere else but the Sussex Weald. Stone-built, rather disappointingly cemented, dominated by the squat C13 tower and its prodigious slated and shingled lid. The N side of the nave is oldest, with herringbone masonry and two tiny windows, one open and one blocked. Probably C11. Next comes the S door, defaced but to a huge scale, like Kirdford, and Ewhurst in Surrey. Scallop capitals to jamb shafts which have disappeared. It had to be re-set when the aisle was built and perhaps received its keeled arch-moulding then. A tower, or at least a S transept, was begun c.1200, with a sturdy low arch towards the nave. The responds go with this, having complex circular abaci. One has the stiffest of stiff-leaf foliage also. The E respond of the arcade is of the same date. But a change of plan made the aisle as wide as the nave and provided much taller E and W arches to the tower – converting this part of the church, as Walter Godfrey remarked, into a complete three-part building with an axial tower. Tower arches and arcade have standard mid C13 Sussex details (circular abaci, double-chamfered arches), and the way in which the abacus mouldings became simplified is worth looking at. The chancel is late C13, with three trefoiled E lancets under a rere-arch. The W windows of nave and aisle have three cinquefoil-headed lancets which must be even later. The part E of the tower was rebuilt as the Halsham Chapel in the middle of the C14, with typically transitional windows. Good three-light C15 windows in the N side of the nave, and delightful wooden C15 N porch, about the best in Sussex, with heavy bargeboards matching the low pitch of the roof perfectly. Plain panelled sides, and a mutilated niche in the gable. Arch between chancel and Halsham Chapel C16, plus PISCINA and battlemented recess on the E wall. Not much architectural effect inside, for all this detail, except in the view E through the tower from the aisle. – STAINED GLASS. C14 fragments, W aisle window. Grisaille, and impressive reds and yellows. – Chancel E window by *Kempe*, 1890. Very pretty intricate green scenes under the main figures – far better than his N window of 1892. Both an interesting comparison with the gritty blues and reds of the chapel E window, which is earlier: 1876. – FONT. Dull C12 arcaded bowl, but a most disarming C14 stem. Square, the sides plain, the corners bevelled off and given a little trefoiled niche and a wild face. – WOODWORK. Plain BENCHES, each place with the name of the owner's farm on the back in elegant early C19 lettering. – PANELLING in the chapel. Renaissance, undoubtedly. But whose Renaissance, and where from? Religious scenes above, profile heads underneath. Forceful and elegant carving. – WALL PAINTING. Bits of a C15 St Christopher, N wall of nave, almost gone. – PLATE. Chalice and Paten, 1722; Paten, 1722(?); Flagon, 1730. – MONUMENTS. Philippa de Strabolgi † 1395. Brass 3 ft long under canopy, firm but expressionless. – Sir Hugh Halsham † 1441 and wife. Brasses 4 ft long under a double canopy. Better because bigger, especially around the eyes and feet, but no more than competent. Almost the same as the C15 brasses at Etchingham (E). – William Powlett † 1746. A big monument by *Rysbrack*, but not one of his best. Favourite composition of husband and wife in Roman dress standing on either side of an urn. With all the sculptural conventions satisfied, there is nothing left over for feeling. – Sir Merrik Burrell † 1787. By *Nathaniel Smith*. Less pretentious and much nicer. Sober inscription, big sympathetic medallion portrait above, a kindly periwigged face full of wrinkles. – Sir William Burrell † 1796. By *Flaxman*, and back to pretensions again. Pretty urn on top of a bloody-minded kind of sarcophagus with little pediments.

OUR LADY AND ST FRANCIS (R.C.). A terribly harsh stone-vaulted building of 1876 by *J. Crawley*. Next to it, the PRIEST'S HOUSE, much more lovable, with a plain C18 front and a finely detailed Ionic porch, up to the best provincial standards. It incorporates an earlier cottage with a secret Roman Catholic chapel used in the C17 by the Carylls of West Grinstead Park. In it were found under the floor in 1925 a pewter travelling CHALICE, of *c*.1450, and one of *c*.1600 which was used surreptitiously by priests in the C17.

WEST GRINSTEAD PARK. Gothick, built by *Nash c*.1806 for the brother of the builder of Knepp Castle half a mile away (*see* p. 254). Big additions in 1866. but not enough to blur the beautiful siting in rolling parkland with a view towards Chanctonbury. That it is almost derelict at the moment does not blur the effect either: Nash in fact would probably have appreciated it. His Gothick houses always look much better in the flesh than in photographs, through sweetness of proportion and the fact that the detail, however flimsy, is never weary or mechanical. L-shaped with a big round tower at the angle, Burgate stone cut and coursed to resemble brick. The 1866 additions chiefly a tall tower to replace Nash's porch, on the l., and a three-bay hall with a steep pitched roof on the r.

Inside, a striking plan: one corridor going back the depth of
the house from the porch. The staircase opens off this behind
three pointed arches. It starts with one arm, returns with two,
all as lightly Gothick as Northanger Abbey. The Drawing
Room, at the back, is simple classical, with a big recess
screened by pairs of columns. The best room is the Dining
Room on the ground floor of the round tower. This is circular
also, and has a tiny delicate vaulted Gothick frieze with some
of the ribs prolonged to make wall-panelling, a brilliant idea.
The pair of simple late classical LODGES ½ m. w on the
main Worthing Road are also probably by *Nash*.

Only a few houses near the parish church, but most of them
worth a look. To the NW GLEBE COTTAGE, a plain C18 brick
front with a modern shell-hood door. To the E GLEBE HOUSE,
the former rectory. Two parallel ranges, the s front now C18
but the N front a dour design of *c*.1600. Brick with wooden
mullions painted white. Three to five lights, no transoms, not
even hood-moulds. Sussex and the North of England are unexpectedly close here. The entrance still off-centre. Across the
Adur, BUTCHERS ROW, a nice collection of cottages of all
dates.

8000

WESTHAMPNETT

A mile out from Chichester along Stane Street, leading straight
to London. The simple cottages have the air of a French faubourg, quite dominated by the city and its cathedral spire.

ST PETER. Quite a complex, interesting church but spoilt by a
restoration of 1867, which added a N aisle, renewed most of the
windows, and replaced a plain C12 arch of Roman brick by a
particularly hearty club or smoking-room Gothic arch. The
brick is still evident on the s side of the chancel, laid herringbone fashion, probably Saxo-Norman overlap, as the one
original window has a pre-Conquest look. Tower at the E end
of the s aisle, quite a usual place for Sussex towers. Late C12,
together with what remains unrestored of the s arcade, plain
and grand, with one-step unchamfered pointed arches, responds and capitals either scalloped or (NW angle of tower)
plain bells, and part of a complex oblong pier made up of a
central core with seven attached shafts – three large and four
a little smaller in the diagonals. It is the same character as
Boxgrove nave (Boxgrove appropriated the church *c*.1180).
The other medieval details worth notice are the present N

aisle w window and the label over the present N door, both
transferred when the aisle was built. They are rather extraordinary: the window has three lights and a semicircular head,
the label has a flabby semicircular roll moulding. The heraldic
details on the label could refer to the union of the Tawke and
Ryman families in the early C16. Both pieces would look much
more at home in a Continental Late Gothic building. – PLATE.
Cup and Cover, 1569; Paten, 1721 or 1723. – STAINED GLASS.
E window by *Clayton & Bell*, 1867, a clever, sinuous design
made up of their astringent reds and blues. – w window evidently by *Powell's*, c.1885. – MONUMENT. Richard Sackville
and wife, c.1535. One of the local school of C16 monuments,
still purely Gothic, which has small kneeling figures either
side of a terribly defaced Trinity.

The big house, WESTHAMPNETT PLACE, was burnt in 1899;
on a loop road w of the church is OLD PLACE FARM, an
altered early C17 house still keeping a pair of shaped gables.

WEST HARTING *see* HARTING

WEST ITCHENOR   7000

On the w side of the Selsey peninsula, with a ferry across to
Bosham. All dinghies and ships' tackle, with one short, nicely
unpretentious street of cottages, mainly C18, running down to
the water's edge. Further s an equally pleasant leafy suburb extends as far as the Wittering road.

ST NICHOLAS. The simplest kind of C13 Sussex church, a
single room without chancel arch, terribly restored inside.
Lancets (three in the E wall) and Late Perp two-light square-
headed windows. The best thing is the shingled bell-turret –
supported on massive buttresses, a good piece of C19 vernacular. – FONT. C13 arcaded bowl on stem and shaft, but octagonal, not square. – PLATE. Chalice, c.1568.

ITCHENOR HOUSE. Built for the 3rd Duke of Richmond in
1787 and hence probably by *Wyatt*, especially as the design is
similar to Molecomb in Goodwood Park. Plain centre block of
three bays and three storeys, with single-storey wings. Nothing
much. It was built as a yachting lodge and also to accommodate the staff of the RACING STABLES. These survive E of the
house, dated 1783, and form a plain hexagonal courtyard with
three of the sides pedimented. Again very much in the style of
the minor buildings at Goodwood.

REDLANDS FARM, ¾ m. s. Bulky farmhouse with half-timbered

c16 centre and brick and flint wings, all under one thatched roof.

WEST LAVANT *see* LAVANT

8020 ## WEST LAVINGTON

Not a village: just a church and a few largish houses tucked away among trees a mile SE of Midhurst, a kind of very gentle, very secluded little suburb.

57a ST MARY MAGDALEN. 1850, by *William Butterfield* for Manning, who was the rector. Butterfield's artistic pattern – like Beethoven, unlike Haydn – was one in which inspiration was everything. Without it, his buildings are worse than dull: with it, they catch alight, ordinary Middle Pointed details smouldering away with an intensity and rigidity which would probably astonish their c13 creators. West Lavington is one of these buildings, built at the same time as All Saints Margaret Street. Nave, aisles without clerestory, deep, tall chancel, very pretty, oddly thin shingled bell-turret – Sussex style, done with complete mastery of all the details, e.g., among many, the hoodmould around the E window, the handling of the roof pitch over the aisles, and the buttresses on the W front, always a favourite trick of Butterfield's. It is all sheer Will, forcing God back into the Gothic Revival by conscious effort. The inside is firm but not so convincing: the intensity has flagged, perhaps from lack of colour. There are normal octagonal piers and normal stiff-leaf capitals. Only the E corbels are monstrously big, as if all the personal mannerism had been forced into one place. The corbels of the chancel arch are a mystery. They are yet bigger, but where those of the arcade are entirely naturalistic, these are firmly and powerfully stylized, as though someone had done them for Lethaby, not for Butterfield. The FITTINGS simple and very sincere: PISCINA and SEDILIA, CHOIR STALLS, and particularly, a low CHANCEL SCREEN of Sussex marble which is incredibly moving, and so natural that it looks as though the stone itself had been metamorphosed into simple Gothic detail.

THE RECTORY is also clearly by Butterfield, simple and honest, far better than average and really not far removed from Voysey. Splendid chimneypots. One unexpected large three-light window with reticulated tracery to insist that this is after all not a commonplace affair. Cobden the Free-Trader is buried in the churchyard.

WEST MARDEN *see* THE MARDENS

WEST STOKE

8000

Church and irregular c18 house only, in very agreeable wooded country NW of Chichester. Surprisingly remote, at the exact point where the Downs meet the plain: the view N is thick woods and bare hillsides, the view s is flat fields and copses. One of the most impressive limbs of the Downs starts just N of West Stoke and runs up into Bow Hill.

ST ANDREW. Lovable plastered flint exterior, visually all the simple lancet E.E. of West Sussex, with a stumpy tower on the s side of the nave, its pyramidal tiled cap lower than the roof ridge. In fact the nave walls are c11, shown inside by a crude round-headed arch now leading into the vestry. Restoration has made the interior less attractive than it ought to be (new chancel arch, e.g.). The c13 details are quite plain except for the s doorway in the tower: two orders, hollow chamfers, attached shaft to carry the inner order. In the chancel, trefoil-headed PISCINA, renewed. – MONUMENT. Adrian Stoughton, erected 1635. Kneeler type, with pair of figures under canopy and children below. Stock carving.

WEST TARRING *see* WORTHING, p. 392

WEST THORNEY

7000

The road to Thorney village is a kind of c20 topographical joke. It lies at the SE corner of Thorney Island, which juts into Chichester Harbour at the extreme w end of Sussex. Almost the whole island was taken over as an R.A.F. station in 1936, so the only access road has to cross the middle of a busy airfield, runways and all. Beyond it, a lot of R.A.F. housing, a few cottages, the church, and a lovely view E across the harbour towards Bosham and Chichester.

ST NICHOLAS. Essentially all late c12–c13, but very eloquent of leaner days since. Several Sussex churches have lost one aisle: Thorney has lost two, probably in 1608, although, with the lancets re-set in the nave walls, it looks completely convincing, especially inside, with long unbroken space, simple triple lancets at the E end, simple tie-beam and kingpost roof. Very like a barn in the best sense, that of humility and honesty. The oldest part is actually at the w end of the chancel, where Norman windows remain on N and s sides. The chancel was extended and the aisles built in the early C13. Windows generally lancets* of various lengths. The s arcade cannot be traced properly,‡ the N remains visible in the wall: circular piers and abaci, obtusely pointed unmoulded arches. On the N side a doorway with dogtooth label, re-set. The attractive low tower is of the same general date, the type of Rustington but about thirty years later. Unbuttressed; bell-chamber with coupled pointed openings under a pointed arch. Simple and village-like, with a short pyramid spire. The tower arch is oddly grand for the rest of the building: two chamfered orders with chamfered imposts and circular shafts. It looks later than the rest. – FONT. Tub-shaped, with crude shallow arcading and chevron carving. Early Norman. – SCREEN. Only a fragment, but very attractive – ogee arches and a continuous band of early C14 oculi with mouchette wheels in a beautiful flowing rhythm, re-set in frankly Victorian framing. Another, simpler band re-set in the screen under the tower. – PULPIT. Excellent modern pulpit by *John Skelton*, 1962, simple, polygonal, tapering, the sides faced with slate slabs. – PLATE. Chalice and Cover, 1568.

N of the church is a moving airmen's graveyard, directly on the axis of Chichester Cathedral. Commonwealth and German airmen lie side by side and make a kind of nonsense fairy story out of recent history.

7090

WEST WITTERING

The Witterings form the w end of the Selsey peninsula. They have polarized rather amusingly into posh and plebeian without any kind of external pressure, and West Wittering is the posh one. Suave houses in moderate gardens with a lot of trees around, instead of bungalows and chalets. The same influence has made a high-class arcadia out of the road leading down to the church – using restored cottages instead of new houses – which is very pretty indeed. It is not in the least rural, but it is a worthwhile landscape in its own right.

ST PETER AND ST PAUL. An awful restoration (*William White*, 1875) has made the outside hard and uninviting, but, as in

* On both N and S sides of the chancel the westernmost window has been converted into a 'low-side' by lengthening downwards, the original sill remaining as a transom.

‡ Especially as a wicked restorer has heightened the one remaining respond to nearly double its length, using original stones.

most churches in Sussex, it conceals worthwhile things. The
N nave wall CII (herringbone masonry); an aisle was thrown
out c.1200 and the four-bay arcade remains, with crude unchamfered pointed arches, alternate round and octagonal piers,
and very odd square capitals. They are badly weathered and
consist of squashed-up bands of stylized foliage, in most cases
with a volute at each corner, a very unusual kind. Chancel and
S chapel are C13 (the beautifully proportioned twin E lancets
are in fact C19 but must represent the original shape). The
two-bay arcade between is quite elaborate: circular pier of
Purbeck marble and complex moulded arches of two orders
with the inner order resting on fluted responds. The feeling of
the work is all C13, yet the arches are still determinedly round.
– STALLS with two MISERICORDS in the chancel. – COM-
MUNION RAIL. C17, the lower part uncommon and pretty. –
MONUMENTS. C13 coffin lid with cross and bishop's pastoral
staff, naïvely elegant (S chancel chapel); and two tomb recesses
with very shallow arches, side by side in the chancel, one
broad, the other narrow, among the best examples of the local
Sussex C16 style. Both are concerned with the same William
Ernley who † 1545.* One is purely Gothic, with a central
relief of the Resurrection, badly defaced (a pity, because what
is left is very spirited), and naïve figures supporting shields,
with the tomb-chest beneath panelled with tracery and saints
in niches. The other has kneeling figures of the deceased on
either side of Christ showing his wounds above, and an
astonishingly naturalistic Annunciation below, both scenes
flanked by Renaissance cherubs carved in the most naïve way.
The flat arch of the recess stands on two pilasters with the
sunk candelabra ornament of the Early Renaissance. But the
pilasters are set diagonally, a Gothic, entirely un-Renaissance
conception. It finds its exact parallel in the de la Warr tomb at
Broadwater, and he died in 1554. Sculpturally these Ernley
tombs are poor (which the de la Warr is not), yet they manage
to be moving in their childlike roughness.

CAKEHAM MANOR HOUSE, 1 m. SE. A palace of the Bishops of
Chichester, now an attractive conglomerate of medieval,
Tudor, and Georgian parts. The oldest is the stone building
on the r. of the present front. This is one bay of an early C13
great hall with undercroft which originally extended to the E
by another three bays, making a building of some size. The

* One is supposed to be William's tomb to his first wife, who died before
1538, the other to be the second wife's tomb to William.

undercroft had a central arcade with normal c13 Sussex
details, supporting a quadripartite vault with thick, cham
fered ribs. Above it was the hall, but nothing of the c13 can
now be picked up here. By 1363 this building was ruined and
roofless; licence to crenellate was granted in 1447 but appar
ently not taken up until the early c16, when the tall brick tower
was built, the most striking feature of Cakeham, at the s w end
of the c13 range. Although the details are plain, the shape
is extremely complex, and surely more than was strictly de
manded by the function. If so, it would be part of a subtlety and
suavity which was very typical of English architecture in the
first half of the c16. The odd thing is that these qualities had
completely disappeared by the time of Wollaton and Hard
wick, as they did to some extent in literature between Wyat
and Marlowe. The tower at Cakeham is an unequal pentagon
with a slightly taller semi-octagonal stair-turret attached to the
fifth side. As a result, the silhouette changes radically from every
point of the compass, an effect which would have delighted
Repton, and one likes to think delighted the c16 Bishops of
Chichester. Some time in the c16 a two-storey range was
attached to the w of this with simple single-light windows
with hood-moulds; and the present house, a plain neat box,
was built on to the front of this in *c.*1800, leaving one bay of
the c16 building visible between it and the tower.

WEST WORTHING *see* WORTHING, p. 389

WIGGONHOLT

A tiny cul-de-sac in the gentle meadow country s of Pulborough
with a lovely view over Amberley Wild Brooks to the Downs
WIGGONHOLT FARM is a plain flint and brick building of 1811
the OLD RECTORY was early c19 Tudor and is now mid-c20
Georgian (by *Christopher Green*, 1959).

CHURCH. Small and sweet, a single room with a shingled bell-
    turret. Most of the windows Perp, and nothing to prove con-
    clusively whether the original walling was c12 or c13. –
    STAINED GLASS. e window by *Powell & Sons*, 1859: central
    medallion of Christ Walking on the Sea which is weirdly
    effective through its colour-scheme: violet, gritty blue, and
    olive-grey. – PLATE. Elizabethan Cup and Paten; Paten, 1662
    Flagon, 1675.
Good farm and barns at LICKFOLD, ¼ m. N.
ROMAN VILLA, ½ m. NE of the church and w of the A283. Por-

tions have recently been revealed by excavation. Five rooms were uncovered, including a bath house with hypocaust and another room containing an altar base arranged around an open court paved with tiles laid out in a herringbone pattern. Three building phases were detected, beginning in the early c2, with a renewal of the floors at the end of the same century. These repairs are of inferior quality, while the final flooring, laid down in the early c4, is a crude layer of tiles and stones with occasional patches of mortar. The courtyard in this period became a dump for kitchen rubbish and broken pottery. Finally, towards the middle of the c4, the villa was destroyed by fire. The destruction may have coincided with the burial of a hoard of 1800 Late Roman coins at Lickfold, a mile distant – both indicative of the unsettled conditions prevailing at this period. For the Lead Cistern found near the villa, *see* Parham, p. 292n.

WINDLESHAM HOUSE
1½ m. s of Washington

By itself in the Downs, a simple, personable house of *c.*1720, spoilt by recent Neo-Georgian additions such as the top storey. Without them, it would be handsome. The main front has nine bays and faces s: segment-headed windows and heavy porch, and quoins – the national Baroque style. The E front was probably two bays wide. The next five may have been added in 1838, when the house was renovated, the remainder are c20 – all in the same style. Houses like this are quite rare in Sussex.

WISBOROUGH GREEN

Green indeed, one of the best in Sussex, in the idyllic countryside, partly hills and partly meadows, between Petworth and Billingshurst. The main part is almost square, and has big trees all round the edge to define it. This is an enchanting effect, because it means that beyond the leafy formal gesture the houses and auxiliary greens can undulate and keep up a perpetual tension between centre and edges. At the SE corner a smaller triangular space, screened from the main green by buildings, leads off uphill to the church, producing another tension: open green and closed green. Cottages in the usual Weald vernacular – brick, half-timber, tile-hanging – with a few weatherboarded terraces as well. None remarkable in themselves, all delightful as components in the ensemble. As a pattern for a 'neighbourhood', with its quota of open space, it is almost ideal.

St Peter ad Vincula. A curious building, spoilt by too much restoration in 1867.* The first impression is entirely heavy and Wealden and C13, with a slender tower carrying a shingled broach-spire, and lancets in the tower, the clerestory, and the aisles. But a closer look, especially at the W front, shows that the tower was built rather brutally over and around an C11 nave which must have been very impressive indeed. It is recognizable at once by the herringbone masonry on the W front (proving incidentally that this side of the tower was simply a heightening of the C11 wall), on the N side, in the SE corner of the nave, and also in the lowest courses of the chancel on the N side. To this C11 building belongs the pair of doorways, N and S, with no imposts at all, let alone any decoration, the round-headed windows (one of them cut into by the tower), and the W doorway with its solid tympanum. This is one puzzle. Why is it set asymmetrically, as if taking the tower into consideration? Perhaps it was re-set when the tower was built. Another puzzle is the thickness of the walls of the W parts of the nave – 4 ft 6 in., which must mean either vaulting or a former tower or tower-like erection, about 35 ft by 30 ft. The nearest parallel is Fingest in Buckinghamshire, where the area is 27 ft square and served as a nave. There the whole tower stands. The type of nave-towers is familiar from Anglo-Saxon churches. This C11 church, about 1200, received two-bay aisles. Round piers, minimum capitals, square abaci, and, on the S side, unmoulded pointed arches. On the N side the arches are a C13 alteration (one slight chamfer, one hollow chamfer). Then the C13. It simply plonked its tower down inside the S half of the W end of the C11 building. That it cannot be later than the early C13 is proved by the flat buttresses without set-offs. The C13 also added the clerestory with its single, widely spaced lancets and also the whole chancel, impressive and large-scale; lancets throughout, the triplet at the E end given continuous mouldings on their rere-arches. The chancel arch with the simplest imposts and one slight chamfer was much widened later (C14), as the wall paintings (*see* below) prove. Two good late medieval porches, the S stone, the N timber-framed with pretty side panels formed of openwork intersecting tracery. Did they originally come from a screen? – PULPIT. Jacobean, panelled, with nice, crisp framing. – BENCHES. Two, in the N porch, plain, with poppy-heads. – WALL PAINTINGS. Recess, S side

* By *Butterfield* (Rodney Hubbuck).

of the chancel, a former reredos to the r. of the chancel arch.
Christ and St James above, Crucifixion below. Crudely
painted, but strong and impressive, and better preserved than
most medieval frescoes in Sussex. The date must be about
1275. – PLATE. Flagon, 1666; Cup, 1720.

ZOAR CHAPEL. On the Petworth road just W of the green: tiny
and cottagey. Built in 1753, enlarged in 1821: the original
date announced on a delightfully lettered sign board over the
gate.

W from Wisborough Green an area of landscape and picturesque
forms hard to match even in Sussex. First comes a good
stone-built neo-Tudor house. Symmetrical entrance front
with porch, symmetrical garden front with loggia, pair of
bulky stone-built gate lodges. Done with a lot of sensibility.
A little beyond this, IDEHURST FARM, early C17. Enchantingly simple, not at all spoilt; stone-built, stone-roofed, four
bays with a two-storeyed porch occupying the second from
the l. Mullion-and-transom windows.

Further S again CRIMBOURNE FARM, big and half-H-shaped,
exhibiting four different building materials as a result of
repeated accretions: brick, stone, half-timber, and tile-hanging. Good barns here, and especially good barns at COLD-
HARBOUR, ½ m. W, in the usual Home Counties style with red
tile roofs and tarred weatherboarded walls. Just beyond Crimbourne on the A272 is BATTLEHURST FARM, partly C15.
Close timbering and an overhang, and yet more good barns,
stone and tarred weatherboarding.

SPARR FARM, 1 m. N. Timber-framed, with the first floor tile-
hung and a pronounced forward sweep to the lowest courses.
Over-restored.

WISPERS
1½ m. N of Stedham

Now ST CUTHMAN'S SCHOOL. By *Norman Shaw*, 1876, before
he started to design in the pretty tile-hung style associated
with him. Not very good, and really hardly distinguishable
from the standard large Victorian house. Stone ground floor,
ornate half-timbering and gables above; limp and mechanical,
without any of the picturesqueness his compositions of the
1870s sometimes have. The best thing is the site – high above
a steep wooded valley with big views S.
To the N of this a first-rate FARM with tiled stone buildings

stepped down the hillside and thatched stone barns stepped down in front of them. The atmosphere more like North Yorkshire or the foothills of Dartmoor than Sussex.

WISTON

Church and house on a lovely site under the Downs near Chanctonbury. The main front faces E, with a gradual slope down to the Adur and the line of the Downs beyond.

St Mary. Terribly treated in 1862 by *G. M. Hills*. Before that it was largely C14. The nave walls assumed to be C13, but they have the high, narrow proportions which in Sussex go with the C11. Simple w tower; E and w windows original, with reticulated tracery. The elegant bases of the arcade look C14 too, but everything else is the blindest kind of mid-Victorian. – SCREEN. Under the tower. Dated 1635, patched up. Thin abstract ornamental patterns. – STAINED GLASS. Two good early C14 shields in the E window. – Chancel N by *Kempe*, c.1881. – PLATE. Cup and Paten, 1726. – MONUMENTS. Brass to Sir John de Brewys † 1426. Effigy 4 ft 10 in. high, and good for the C15. Blank face, but as much invention and fantasy in the details like the helm and the customary lion at the foot as if it had been done a hundred years earlier. – Child under a very rough Perp canopy. – Sir Richard Shirley † 1540 and wives. Mutilated, reassembled, and re-cut so that the composition has lost most of its effect. Kneeling wives, with Sir Richard standing between them full face with his hands up. Simply carved, and touching in a Brueghel way. – Kneeling figures from the monument to Sir Thomas Shirley † 1612, on a window sill. – Sarah Goring, by Mrs *Coade*'s firm, 1798. Very Coadey, with a mourning woman in a frilly Gothic recess. Too sharply carved to be sickly, hence good fun, but a hundred miles from any real apprehension of death.

Wiston Park. Built c.1575 by Sir Thomas Shirley (knighted 1573), rebuilt so much by *Blore* c.1830 that only the main front is original. Blore's work is yellower and twistier, and easy to distinguish. A typical house, but not a great one: as plain as Parham and Danny, except that here the plainness seems to suggest poverty of invention. The front faces E, with deeply recessed centre (the wings are three bays long). In fact there were originally more buildings to the E, including a gatehouse. Wings two-storeyed with shaped gables, the centre

three-storeyed with a flat parapet, which is a mid C18 alteration, and has at its end big scrolls or volutes at r. angles to the
wall. Under it, a shallow attic storey and then the big gridded
windows of the hall, like all the other windows still with
arched lights, a decidedly conservative motif for the 1570s.
The hall is entered at one end, but via a porch which is
central in the façade – i.e. like Parham, but unlike Loseley of
c.1560, where the older and more natural asymmetrical
arrangement was kept. The desire for simple symmetry was
so strong here that windows matching the very big ones of
the hall were provided to the l. of the porch, even though
these parts are two-storeyed, a solution as absurd as anything
the early C20 did and very different from the adaptation to
individual needs of Loseley. So each side has one flush
window of six lights with three transoms, and one bay window
with two plus four plus two and three transoms. The porch
itself is two-storeyed, with classical ideas spread rather thin:
coupled Doric pilasters on the ground floor, coupled fluted
Ionic pilasters above, with panels between carrying patterns
which look as though they had been punched out of leather.
At the top a classical pediment, a motif which the time about
1560–75 seems to have liked better than the later Elizabethan
decades. On top of the pediment a statue of Flora or Abun-
dantia with a cornucopia, uncommonly generous and easy, yet,
it seems, 1575 rather than C18.

Inside, the main room is the GREAT HALL. The S end, now
partitioned off, is galleried. The gallery rests on pillars, and
the screen has become an ornamental wall-covering, rather
than a literal screen between door and hall. Is this original?
If so, it marks one stage in the transition from the medieval
hall where everything happened to the C18 hall where nothing
happened. Spindly double-hammerbeam roof with pendants
and plenty of braces like the Middle Temple Hall in London,
not much fun. More fun in the gay stucco work, including
an eagle in high relief. This is mid C18* and may be to designs
by *Gibbs*, who in fact made designs for rebuilding Wiston.
Also, two niches on the W side, and these are prettily Gothick
in a Batty Langley way. This also could fit Gibbs, who
produced a very early Gothic design at Stowe. Original
decoration otherwise only in the former DINING ROOM,
together with plasterwork in the frieze. Dated 1576, with an
elegant rhythm of tapering Corinthian demi-columns. A good

* At the SE corner of the NE wing at ground level is a date-stone 1747.

deal of Continental woodwork brought in in the C19, including good C18 French panelling in the GALLERY, and both Gothic and Baroque Flemish carving in the LIBRARY. Blore's interiors, like his rebuildings outside, are decent and utterly unimaginative. But built into the outside of the W front is a FIREPLACE which is the most puzzling and interesting thing at Wiston. The style is quite different from the other C16 details, and looks mid C16 and French-inspired. If the date is right, the strapwork is comparatively early.* Three-storeyed, beginning with a delicate acanthus frieze, then a stage with warriors between fluted columns, then another frieze with minutely carved shields, human figures, and animals, then a puzzling concave-sided top which has two sphinxes enclosing tiny reliefs (? of battle scenes) and a top obelisk. Everything is much more refined and small-scale than Elizabethan carving usually is. It ought to be better cared for.

SE of the house, beyond the church, STABLES, contemporary with the house. Mullioned windows, looking just like a grammar school in a small town. To the N, in the grounds of a house called FALCONERS, is a pretty puzzling-looking building which combines stock-brick and tile-hanging. Semicircular, with niches. It was originally the Verderer's Cottage for the house and must also have served as a park ornament, on the principle of two for the price of one.

2010

WOODMANCOTE

1 m. E of Henfield on the Brighton road, in quiet countryside with a faint late C19 suburban air to it. Church by itself in the park of Woodmancote Place; no village.

CHURCH. Quite big, and promising from a distance. But close to, the disastrous restoration of 1868 by *Woodyer* becomes overwhelming. All but rebuilt. The architect kept a PISCINA and the big kingposts in the nave; one wonders why. Expiation, perhaps. What he gave in return was a few skittish details around the vestry on the N side.

DRAGONS, ½ m. E. By *Colin Lucas*, 1936, one of the set of houses by Connell, Ward & Lucas which excited or terrified in the 1930s. An oblong box, set sheer on top of a ridge, with

---

* The size of the fireplace would make it possible for the hall, but a suggestion has been made that it comes from Michelgrove, which was demolished c.1840.

a huge detached chimney at one end. Originally it had white concrete walls which were found to be damp, and Dragons is now weatherboarded. The same thing has happened to a lot of ultra-modern houses of the thirties. A Neo-Georgian house called St George was built near it after the war.

WOODMANSGREEN see LINCH

WOODSIDE see GRAFFHAM

WOOLBEDING   8020

The first village on the Rother w of Midhurst. Just church, house, and farms, delightfully compact from the N. The buildings mostly Burgate stone with brick dressings.

ALL HALLOWS. The unaisled nave clearly Saxon – very tall, thin pilaster strips on both N and S sides. This promises great things, but restoration has removed everything apart from this first striking impression: the chancel is of 1870, the furnishings are ostentatiously Late Gothic Revival. The w tower of 1728 is very plain, in a style that is still basically medieval, with a single tiny bell-opening and eight stumpy pinnacles; possibly the two-light windows in the nave are 1728 also – they were there in 1815. – STAINED GLASS. Continental C16 glass brought from Mottisfont Priory, Hants, in the N chancel window and (better) in the w window, S side of the nave. Scenes from the Passion. – WOODWORK. C18 reredos, now on the S wall of the chancel. – PLATE. Chalice, 1634; Flagon and Paten, c.1700. – MONUMENTS. Rev. Sir Henry Mill † 1782. Nicely carved architectural tablet, probably local. Broken pediment with relief of Charity inside it. – In the churchyard, tempietto to Captain John Dodsworth † 1773: rustic Doric columns and very appealing rustic frieze of military trophies.

WOOLBEDING HALL, just N of the church. A delightful vernacular front of c.1700 with a distinctly French look, due probably to the impeccable formal approach from the road and the shaped sides of the dormers. Five bays and two storeys, the end bays projecting with an Ionic loggia between them. Quite plain, and very much what Wren would have approved of. Far more circumstantial French-looking additions of 1875 on the N side, but not at odds with the house. The interiors mostly plain C18. In the grounds the FOUNTAIN from the courtyard of Cowdray. This was bought by the sixth

Viscount Montague in Italy in the mid C18 and was of course attributed to Cellini. The name now suggested is *Rustici*. The fountain is about 10 ft high and is crowned by an exquisite youthful nude with a trident standing on dolphins. He is always called Neptune, but has anyone ever seen a youthful, beardless Neptune? It is more likely that the statuette (which is only 20 in. in height) represents a triton. It is not at all certain that all parts of the fountain originally belonged together. On the very high quality of the figure there can be no two voices.

WOOLBEDING BRIDGE, ½ m. s. One of the series of Rother valley bridges. Medieval; three arches, two cutwaters.

1000

WORTHING

Worthing is an exasperating town. Put very briefly, it began by imitating Brighton and ended by imitating Bournemouth, and the two seaside traditions have met head-on, without benefit to either. The result is that architecturally it is full of brave beginnings and ignoble endings: socially it seems to have become the most genteel of Sussex resorts without any of Bournemouth's compensations. The thing is summed up by the signs to the public lavatories – itself an English euphemism – which say, coyly, 'Toilets'. Yet at the same time it is both friendly and lively. The chance for a coherent town centre was lost when the gardens between Portland Road and Chapel Road were built over, which was not until the 1870s. Before that, the chapels, public buildings, and terraces were grouped around this big central open space in an impressive way.

ST PAUL, Chapel Road. An ugly tough-minded little building of 1812 by *J. B. Rebecca*, the son of the painter, more in sympathy with the forceful rationality of the original C18 protagonists of the Greek Revival than with the smooth stucco walls of Jane Austen's day. Four-column Greek Doric portico with a dumpy cylindrical cupola riding on the roof behind it, decorated with a bold band of key ornament. The inside, with chancel and hideous roof of 1893, looks even more Nonconformist than it would have done originally. As with Egham church in Surrey, the cantankerousness is not translated into architectural terms.*

CHRIST CHURCH, Grafton Road. Built in 1841, by *John Elliott*. Flint, 'Commissioners' Gothic', and very typical. Mr Good-

* According to Mr Nicholas Taylor, Rebecca's reredos is now in the w gallery.

hart-Rendel said, sadly, 'the roof obviously made by Bryant
and May'.

ST GEORGE, St George's Road, East Worthing. By *George Truefitt*, 1868. Cheaply built but very intelligent and rational, as
Truefitt's buildings often are. One single apsed room, as
spatially open and logical as a Wren church, and without any
of the usual artificial piety of the 1860s. The flat apse has five
tall windows, answered by the flat curve of the spindly rood
screen: the W end has an impressive band of six windows
above the porch. The trouble is that this careful planning has
been given the ugliest and most offhand kind of Middle
Pointed architectural dress, so that the quality remains in
potential.

HOLY TRINITY, Shelley Road. A poor brick building of 1882
by *Coe & Robinson*, containing the cut-down PULPIT from
Broadwater church. This has vestiges of strapwork but also
correctly detailed egg and dart mouldings and must date from
the middle of the C17.

MUNICIPAL OFFICES, Chapel Road. The main buildings
correct and quite lifeless Neo-Georgian with a portico; behind
them an Assembly Hall in a plainer style, like a weak edition
of part of the Stratford Memorial Theatre. The odd thing is
that both were part of the same competition-winning design –
by *C. Cowles-Voysey*, in 1930.

TECHNICAL HIGH SCHOOL. *See* Durrington, p. 392.

Worthing began as a town in 1759, when the first seaside visitor
stayed at a farmhouse. Until then it was simply a seaside
fishing hamlet attached to Broadwater village. George III
promoted it by sending his youngest daughter there in 1798,
and it rapidly began a whole set of speculations on the
Brighton pattern. The earliest ones, rather mauled now, were
simple three-storeyed bow-fronted terraces close to the pier like
BEDFORD ROW* and MONTAGUE PLACE, built in 1802–5.
Also of this date the former THEATRE in ANN STREET, now
a warehouse, the most endearing of Worthing's old buildings,
with an elegant curved parapet, a thin iron portico across the
pavement, and a bust of Shakespeare on the first floor. It was
designed by *Edward Hide* in 1807 and opened with *The
Merchant of Venice*: Mrs Siddons as Portia, the less-known
Mr Siddons as Shylock. Although it closed as a theatre in 1855
it is still in good condition, and a very precious survival. The

* Also in Bedford Row the BEDFORD HALL, with three tall and markedly
Egyptian windows under a pediment. Built in 1839 by *Charles Hide*.

more circumstantial pilastered house next door was built in
1829 as the Worthing Hospital and looks like a design of *A. H.
Wilds*.

The chapel of ease followed in 1812, and STEYNE in 1807–13 –
the name a direct importation from Brighton – a little further
E, a long, blank four-storey terrace of stock-brick houses. E of
Steyne is BEACH HOUSE by *J. B. Rebecca*, 1820, a stuccoed
bow-fronted villa with gardens down to the sea, now interrupted rather weirdly by C20 beach furniture and Peter Pan's
Playground. It was refitted inside in 1920 by *Maxwell Ayrton*,
incorporating a lot of furniture from the sale of Deepdene in
Surrey – i.e. neo-classical pieces of Thomas Hope's. These
were dispersed in the Second World War.

N of this there is just one elegant villa, THE HOLLIES, at the
junction of High Street and Little High Street, built before
1814, stock brick,* with a nice rhythm of blind arches. To the
W there is rather more. In WARWICK STREET one shop with
the typical Grecian show motif of a couple of Ionic columns *in
antis* (No. 7). At the join of Warwick Street and Chapel Road, the
main shopping street, is what is left of the Grecian OLD TOWN
HALL of 1834 by the Town Surveyor, *Ralph Jones*, which used
to have a tower. On the sea front E of the pier is WARNES
HOTEL (formerly York Terrace) of *c*.1825, a heavy design
with heavy ironwork; and to the W and NW are the most spectacular pieces of Georgian Worthing, Liverpool Terrace and
Park Crescent. LIVERPOOL TERRACE was designed by *Henry
Cotton c.*1830 and would be impressive anywhere, a powerfully organized unbroken rhythm of bow fronts accented with
plain ironwork, making a very different effect from the picturesque jostling of most seaside terraces. Just one pair, Nos
11–12, has a porte-cochère and an extra cornice, worn like a
sergeant's stripes, to single it out: otherwise the terrace is
quite plain and allows the rhythm full play. Cotton himself
seems to be unknown. PARK CRESCENT, to the N, is just the
opposite, i.e. the rhythms quite defeated by the ornament. It
was built in 1829 by *A. H. Wilds*, more famous for his work
at Brighton, and conceived in a very ambitious way. A serpentine classical terrace faced thickly planted grounds, in the
manner of Bath, with a couple of cottages ornés embedded in
the trees at the other end. (These were called North and South
Swiss Cottage (!) and now form BEECHWOOD HALL

---

* These stock bricks were local and much admired at the time for their
subtlety and suavity.

HOTEL.) The whole scheme was approached through a triumphal arch, and incidentally must have been right out in the fields for at least twenty years after it was built. Alas, Mr Wilds's architecture was not up to his landscape planning: the triumphal arch is an endearing joke with four big bearded busts as caryatids under the main arch and eight young ladies ditto under the side arches; the Swiss Cottages are bulky and clumsy. The main S-shaped crescent, a set of houses linked by caryatid porches, is terribly overloaded with details of the sort Wilkins used much more sparingly – pilasters with anthemion capitals and so on. It is well worth a visit, but only as a curiosity, and it could have been so much more.

Other buildings are quickly disposed of. The humbler equivalent of Park Crescent is AMBROSE PLACE of *c*.1820, a little further E, whose nice display of carpentry balconies seems absurd until you realize that it originally faced the central space which was so unhappily built on later. The biggest building in Chapel Street is the Neo-Georgian POST OFFICE of 1930 by *D. N. Dyke*. Otherwise, pre-war Worthing can be represented by the pair of blocks of FLATS, BURLINGTON COURT and GLOUCESTER COURT, at the seaside end of King George V Avenue, that is the extreme W end of the Worthing front: they are decent examples by Messrs *Joseph*, 1937, of a modern vernacular that had no time to establish itself before the war: brick with a lot of horizontals in balconies and roof-lines. An equally honest example of 1950 vernacular is CADOGAN COURT, by *Ransford Fletcher & Partners*, 1957, in RICHMOND ROAD, fairly near Park Crescent; the staircases from the upper units come down into an intriguingly complex courtyard.

In Pevensey Road, West Worthing, is PEVENSEY GARDEN, a handsome estate of flats and houses by *James & Bywater*, 1958–60. Two, three, and six storeys, the tall blocks with lifts in effective circular towers of white brick almost detached from the main building. Carefully landscaped, on the pattern of Eric Lyons's Span estates, but with simpler elevations, brown brick with a little weatherboarding. A model of what speculative building could do everywhere if it tried.

WINDMILL, 2¾ m. NW. Post mill complete with the four sails.

WORTHING VILLAGES

Worthing has flooded inland up to the Downs, clean and tidy but utterly amorphous, and has, like Brighton, caught up several old centres.

BROADWATER

1 m. N of Worthing

Broadwater was the original nucleus of Worthing, and the main street still has a village-street air, rather taken aback by the suburban shopping centre it has become. Pleasant cottages N of the church in Broadwater Street East.

CHURCH. The grandly virile bell-openings of the tower promise, rightly, a worthwhile interior: this is part of the series of very late Norman buildings whose richness discovered new forms instead of wearing itself out by repetition. Too much has been restored and repaired at Broadwater to make it of the standard of New Shoreham, or of the C12 parts of Climping, but it is still a good place to go to. It must originally have had nave, chancel, and a central tower between, originally meaning about 1150 or 1160. Whether it also had transepts is doubtful. Evidence in the W and E arches of the tower, the E arch in perfect order, though sagging, the W arch made pointed later. Both have ornament based on the zigzag, with the unusual and exciting effect of zigzags used on the arch soffits. In each element the E arch is more sober, the W arch more frantically seeking to jog the arch into movement. The W arch has small beakheads, but its capitals were obliterated in a late medieval repair; the E arch has C12 foliage, very renewed. In the side walls of the tower, above the later arches to the transepts, are parts of a round arch exposed. Clapham calls them windows, but they are very large for their position, and it is tempting to think of two-storeyed transepts on the pattern of Jumièges. They would also explain why the windows of the transept are small and Norman, and why there is a doorway in the E wall of the transept at just the right upper level. Anyway, the transepts were remodelled, or built, later in the C12, E aisles were projected or built, and the bell-stage of the tower came into being. The bell-stage, with pointed arches with nook-shafts enclosing round arches (two on three sides, three on the fourth), is the most successful part. The N and S tower arches have three-step responds with stop-chamfers and arches of three slight chamfers – late C12, evidently.

The chancel must have come next, but it has been so wrought-about that it can only be thought of as C19. Authentic late C12 string-course, zigzags and pellets still, running right round the chancel; quadripartite vault above, the ribs more richly moulded in the two E than in the two W bays, new windows, and completely new E wall, done in 1857–66.*

Also C13, the familiar plain lancets, and, originally, the four-bay nave and aisles. The arcade piers were given new bases and capitals in the early C15, in straightforward Perp with octagonal abaci; at the same time two-light segmental windows were put into aisles and clerestory – adequate, but no more.‡ The W front is C19.

FURNISHINGS. WOODWORK. Set of six MISERICORDS, very like those at West Tarring. – STAINED GLASS. E window by *Willement*, 1855. Not a good effort. – MONUMENTS. Brass of John Mapilton, rector and chancellor to Joan of Navarre, † 1432 (chancel floor). A good C15 brass, quite a rare thing, with the vivid rhythmic patterns brilliantly rendered. Figure 3 ft high, under a canopy. It is difficult to convey how much more vitality and expressiveness and urgency it presents compared with the ordinary job, particularly as brasses are not a very expressive medium. Worth a special look. – Thomas, 5th Lord de la Warr, † 1524 (N side of chancel). Ambitious three-part canopy, just going Renaissance – e.g. the pendants and the topmost cresting – and one of a series of Sussex C16 tombs. None of the enchanting playfulness of the de la Warr chantry at Boxgrove; instead a strangely impressive thick movement of crocketed ogees and bulbous finials. – Thomas, 6th Lord de la Warr, † 1554. In the thirty years the balance had changed; the Renaissance has arrived. In fact it had arrived in London forty years before and in many places (including Sussex) thirty years before, but has it here? It is true that there are two shields in medallion wreaths, and one pilaster has the typical candelabra motifs, but the others have normal, if rather sparse, Gothic leaf trails, and in any case, can one call a thing a pilaster, if it is set diagonally? Otherwise nearly all the motifs are Gothic. The change lies more in the spacing, the total absence of any crowding, the stress on partitions. The fact that the significance of the monument is still entirely religious is conservative too, and so are the figures of the Virgin and Child and of St George flanking the central space, which was clearly a Christ in Majesty. Although the figures

---

* Very successfully, if only it were not in an old church, with a rich comination of reredos and arcading with marble inlay. Who did it? The *Ecclesiologist* said 'Deplorable caricature / incorrect detail / unsatisfactory design'.

‡ One C13 clerestory window was allowed to remain, a single lancet: SW.

(and the whole tomb) are roughly carved, they have a very moving and truly Gothic directness, the sort of sincere feeling for which one would cheerfully give up any amount of expertise.

DURRINGTON
2 m. NW of Worthing

A confusion of cottages and concrete, but contains the TECHNICAL HIGH SCHOOL, at the corner of The Boulevard and A2032. This was built in 1954 as one of a series of schools designed by the research team of the Ministry of Education (*Stirrat Johnson-Marshall*, assistants *Maurice Lee*, *Mary Crowley*, *J. Kitchin*). It is a model of what devoted attention to detail can do for a familiar building type with familiar and undemonstrative materials. One four-storey block, the rest two- and one-storey, reinforced concrete frame with precast concrete panels, handled subtly and elegantly yet without any applied mannerisms, structural or decorative. The subtle differentiation of beams, columns, and wall panels on the four-storey block for example are a copybook example of what professional expertise ought to be capable of, and so rarely is. The comparison with the more familiar standard can be made directly here, for there is another school immediately to the E.

WEST TARRING
1 m. NW of Worthing

ST ANDREW. A big church for this part of Sussex, but not a very attractive one. It is partly due to the restoration (with a deal of Italian mosaic of 1885), and partly to the mechanical design, seeming to represent the point where the Early Gothic impulse spent itself in Sussex without having led on to anything else. Complete E.E. nave, five bays, lancet aisle and lancet clerestory. Standard piers and arcades, except that there is an outer moulding with foliage label-stops above each abacus. The best detail is a trefoil-headed PISCINA in the S aisle. Tower and chancel are later and may represent Canterbury work, as the church has always been a peculiar of the Archbishop. W window and W door are clearly Perp, two of the bell-openings just as clearly Dec, looking authentic. Shingled spire. The chancel has typical Early Perp two-light windows, but a more elaborate and rather unusual E window, a little like one at Arundel: five lights, two pairs of two, the

centre light running up to the head of the arch and embroidered with sexfoils. – WOODWORK. Six MISERICORDS
in the chancel, Late Gothic, the best pair carved with a
head, the rest with foliage. – Perky Jacobean COMMUNION
RAIL with knobs on. – PLATE. Flagon, 1766; Paten, c.1766.

Tarring has much more of an old centre than the other parts of
outer Worthing. E of the church there is a crossroads and one
complete and very attractive street (HIGH STREET) running
N from it, narrow, with a charmingly varied swaying streetline.
Most of the houses are simple flint or stuccoed cottages, but
Nos 6–10 near the S end is half-timbered, and one of the best
of its type in Sussex: clearly C15, with close-set timbers and
overhang. Three bays, the r. one recessed behind spandrels,
the centre gabled with moulded bargeboards. Carefully restored, with the familiar feeling of only making sense as part
of a whole street, not as a self-contained building.

of the crossroads is the OLD PALACE of the Archbishops of
Canterbury, now the parish hall. It stands in the school yard,
surrounded by the uncomplicated spikiness of the C19 school,
buildings, looking for all the world like their elder brothers
with a kind of natural dignity absent from many more showy
medieval buildings. Flint, T-shaped, with the oldest part
forming the top of the T and running N–S. This is the original
C13 building, and consists of a first-floor room above an undercroft. Shafts and capitals remain inside. In the C14 the hall was
built as the stem of the T – single-storeyed, but almost as
tall – and connected by a staircase in the SE angle to the
original room, which became a solar. Then, c.1400, the whole
building was restyled with very typical Kentish details – deep,
refined two-light windows under segmental heads, divided by
a transom. The present character is entirely Early Perp and
admirably of a piece with the churches of the time: there is no
real substitute for a coherent style underlying every type of
building, however hard a job it may seem to be to attain.

YAPTON   9000

straggling, untidy village in the flat cornfields NW of Littlehampton. Old flint cottages plus piecemeal enlargement that
is really gone on continuously since the early C19 with its neat
stuccoed boxes. The best bits are near the church, away from
the main road. As with most of these Sussex plain villages, it
could be transformed by sensitive expansion.

13*

ST MARY. A complete church of *c.*1180–1220, nicely unsophisticated; with its enormous lean-to roofs and dormer window it is what many West Sussex churches were like before restoration. Inside, especially, a little pattern book of rustic building. The oldest part is the E end of the S aisle, with one Norman window and the original size of the aisle clearly marked in the masonry. Four-bay arcades and SW tower followed in *c.*1180–1200, very similar to Rustington: the tower with two pointed lights and colonnette under a round-headed arch, now happily irregular because of emergency buttressing on the S side; the arcades with chamfered arches just pointed, plain responds, but a variety of capitals which are a charming anthology of the various transitions between waterleaf and stiff-leaf foliage. Some have billet ornament that has turned vegetable, one is a plain capital with one tightly bunched leaf at each corner, the others have quite intricate patterns of naïve foliage in low relief. It is the survival of all the other C12 details that makes Yapton worth a special visit: nave roof with tie-beams and kingposts, aisle roofs swooping down so that the walls are only 5 ft high (the dormers were added in the C17), and one extraordinary detail in the S aisle, two tiny circular windows, only 2 ft off the ground, in what seems to be a desperate attempt to add light to this impressive but dark way of building. The chancel is early C13; double-chamfered chancel arch on fluted corbels, lancet windows. Originally the E end had widely spaced lancets: the present window is of 1902, replacing an C18 one. Simple and pretty W porch, timber-framed with flint infilling, late medieval.

FONT. Early Norman: tub font with crude low relief arcading enclosing Maltese crosses and a band of chevrons round the rim. – PLATE. C17 and C18 Patens; Flagon, 1657; Cup, 1710 – MONUMENTS. Several tablets, including a nice cartouche to John Edmonds † 1687 and a rustic tablet to Stephen Roe † 1766, unexpectedly given a Gothick ogee arch instead of the usual classical frame.

EAST SUSSEX

★

ALBOURNE

2010

ST BARTHOLOMEW. Outside the village but near Albourne
Place. Mainly by *Scott*, 1859. Flint. Front with the nave and
N aisle gables. Bell turret. However, in the chancel S wall a
Norman window, and, inside, the chancel arch with Norman
zigzag, copied by Scott from original parts. In Scott's E wall
is a reredos-like recess which contains Norman imposts to a
former apse (?). – PLATE. Cup and Cover, 1571.
Next to the churchyard a Georgian house of three bays, tile-
hung from top to bottom.
ALBOURNE PLACE. A most interesting mid C17 brick house in
the style christened by Sir John Summerson Artisan Mannerism. The house has tall mullion-and-transom-cross windows
of stone and to the W giant brick pilasters making seven bays.
But to the N and S there is a different rhythm, giant pilasters
set back from the corners, and in the middle two giant
pilasters framing a brick quoin that has strayed into the wrong
position, i.e. alternating narrow and wide raised panels. This
same restless motif is used instead of pilasters on the E side,
even above the lintel of the doorway (which incidentally also
carries a chimneybreast) and in the wing projecting to the E.
Here there are also weird window details. It is all mighty
curious, and more curious than beautiful. Two splendid
original mid C17 doors. Inside, part of the screen, characterized by openwork panels of simple geometrical shapes. The
interior, however, also offers proof that the house was only
refaced. The staircase may (but need not) be earlier than 1650
(square tapered balusters), and one overmantel certainly is.
GALLOPS, on the E side of the village. Timber-framing with
brick nogging; probably Elizabethan. Or is it later, perhaps
as late as 1661, the date on the door? Walter Godfrey thought
so.)

ALCISTON

5000

CHURCH. Nave and chancel and bell-turret, as if it had half-sunk into the roof. The nave is long and the chancel, not at all short, was originally longer – see the position of a jamb of a third, E, lancet window. The windows date the chancel as C13, but there is a small Norman window as well, and the nave NE quoin is Norman too. Nice E.E. N porch entrance, *ex situ*. The roof with tie-beams, kingposts, and raking struts was reconstructed in 1898. – PLATE. Cup, 1661.

COURT HOUSE FARM. To the farm belongs a BARN 170 ft long, i.e. one of the longest in the county. It is aisled and tiled. The bays with the two cart entries have tie-beams and collar-beams, the others very long curved beams right up to the collar-beams, almost like crucks. There is also a ruined medieval DOVECOTE.

ALDRINGTON *see* BRIGHTON, p. 457

ALFRISTON

ST ANDREW. Cruciform, with a tower over the crossing and quite large, of a type one expects to be E.E., yet in this case of the C14 (cf. Poynings) – precisely on the boundary between Dec and Perp. Faced with coursed knapped flint. Some of the windows still purely Dec (two lights), others purely Perp (with panel tracery). Spacious interior. The crossing piers have concave sides and even concave-sided capitals. The arches start out of vertical pieces. Easter Sepulchre with ogee arch, but the SEDILIA and PISCINA very odd indeed and rather perverse. Round arches and ogee gables reaching up through a horizontal top of the whole. – STAINED GLASS. Small figures in the tracery of the N transept N window. – The Jesse Window (S transept) is by *Kempe & Tower*, of after 1912. – (TILES. C13.) – PLATE. Foreign Cup; Cover, given in 1683; Pewter Flagon, 1684; Paten, 1738.

CONGREGATIONAL CHAPEL. 1801. Rendered, with two tiers of windows, the upper ones just arch-shaped. The church stands by a spacious green, and on its other side is the Cuckmere river. To the S, closer yet to the river, the CLERGY HOUSE, a timber-framed and thatched house of the C14, the first building bought by the National Trust (1896) and tactfully restored for them by *Alfred Powell*. Closely set studs and also heavy carved diagonal braces. The hall has one tie-beam and kingpost truss. The solar wing and the service wing project slightly. To the service wing two ogee-headed doorways. The main village street runs S–N, quite some distance from th church. One reaches it up a pedestrian lane past the Congregational church. Not much S of the junction, but to the N a rewarding sequence. First a narrow house of the C15 with closely set studs, then, facing one another, the GEORGE INN, long and low, also C15, also closely studded, and the SHIP INN, one of the best timber-framed houses of East Sussex. Again the close studs, but also brackets to support the first-floor overhang and against them small figures of ecclesiastics. Faces on the bressumers too, and on the sills of the oriels on the first floor more carving. St George and the Dragon on the l. one, two snakes and a Gothic tabernacle on the middle one. Then the street widens into a triangle. On it the MARKET CROSS, i.e. its shaft and knop, but not the cross, and N of it an oak tree. On one side a shop with a handsome late C18 front with two narrow windows.

SAXON CEMETERY. On the summit of a hill to the NW of the village lies a Pagan Saxon mixed cemetery of male and female inhumation burials. In addition to iron knives, spearheads, and shield bosses, the male graves yielded a number of very fine, conical glass drinking horns. C5 pottery and Roman melon beads were found in some graves, and one very fine brooch decorated with a running scroll design, the tendrils being derived from Late Roman motifs.

LONG BARROW, 1 m. W. A fine long barrow, 150 ft long and 60 ft broad at its NE end. The monument still stands to a height of over 8 ft, and the side ditches can still be traced on the ground.

ROUND BARROW. 2 m. W of the church, 40 ft in diameter and 4 ft high. A central depression suggests that it has been opened, but there is no record of this excavation.

ARDINGLY   3020

ST PETER. Outside the village. Low W tower, the doorway C14, the top Late Perp or later. Primitive original wooden staircase in the tower. Simple Dec S aisle and chancel. N aisle by *Carpenter & Ingelow*, 1887. In the chancel on the S side a low-side window with a transom. The S arcade is of two very wide bays and, while the octagonal pier is normal C14, the responds are odd and do not fit. They have at six corners closely attached shafts. Is this C13 work re-used? In the N aisle loose a Norman one-scallop capital. – SCREEN. Perp, very pretty, of close single-light divisions. – COMMUNION RAIL. Of finely twisted

balusters; *c.*1700. – PLATE. Chalice, Paten, and Flagon, 1672;
Almsdish, 1702. – MONUMENTS. Effigy of a Priest, *c.*1330,
not well preserved. It lies in an elementary recess with crude
buttress shafts l. and r. The blank tracery on the buttresses
exhibits a great variety of motifs. – Richard Wakeherst † 1455
and wife. Plain tomb-chest with quatrefoils and on it the
effigies in brass with brass canopies. The effigies are 2 ft long.
– On the chancel floor brasses to Richard Culpeper and his
wife who died in 1504 and to Nicholas Culpeper † 1510 and
wife (née Wakehurst). The figures are 27 in. long. The former
couples had canopies. All these brasses are above the ordinary
in quality and condition. The Wakehursts and then the
Culpepers lived at Wakehurst Place.

WAKEHURST PLACE, 1 m. N. The present S front was originally
the S front of the N range of a courtyard house. Of this only
the stumps of the l. and r. wings remain, giving the house an
E-façade. The rest was demolished in the C17 and in 1845.
The original parts date from 1590 and were built by Sir
Edward Culpeper. The façade is gay and busy with its many
small gables, all with little volutes creeping up and down
them and with plenty of finials. The windows have two transoms on the ground floor, one on the upper floor, and the
lights are still arched – a remarkably conservative feature.
The portal in the middle projection has Tuscan columns, the
window above it Ionic columns and a steep pediment. Inside
the former hall with its thin-ribbed plaster ceiling, a very
sumptuous stone chimneypiece in the library, as usual with
oddly ignorant figurework, an early C18 staircase and much
other woodwork, including parts of the sumptuous original
hall screen now on the staircase landing. The house was much
added to in the 1870s. One addition was a small CHAPEL
(with *Kempe* STAINED GLASS of 1905 and 1907) – another
a room painted by a Japanese artist whom the Mikado had
sent to Paris to study. By the side of the house two fine short
ranges of STABLES with cupolas. The S front is of ashlar stone
with widely spaced segmental windows and has a pediment.
It looks early C18.

(NEWHOUSE FARM, 1 m. NNE of Wakehurst Place. Built in
1848 with materials from Wakehurst Place. Gables with
finials. Windows with mullions and transoms. MHLG)

ARDINGLY COLLEGE. A Woodard school, like Lancing and
Hurstpierpoint. Founded in 1858, begun in 1864, illustrated
in *The Builder* (as a 'Lower Middle-Class School') in 1867,

and opened in 1870. Designed by *Slater & Carpenter*. The buildings are of red brick, in the form of two courtyards, the southern open to the s, the other closed. Good views to the sw and also to the NE. The two s wings date from 1864–70, the N wings from 1880 and 1926–7. In the middle bar between the two courtyards the CHAPEL and the LIBRARY with the low DINING HALL below. The chapel, which was completed in 1883, is tall and ambitious, in a late C13 style, with the brickwork showing inside as well. It has an oblong central tower, large four-light windows, a seven-light window at the E end, and in the two-bay chancel some shafting as a legitimate enrichment. Nothing is as elevating as at Lancing, but it is a noble piece for a school chapel all the same. – STAINED GLASS. E window by *Kempe*, 1912. – The domestic and teaching wings are in a minimum-1300 style, dour and self-denying. The cloister on the s front is an addition of 1892.

ARGOS HILL *see* ROTHERFIELD

ARLINGTON   5000

ST PANCRAS. A flint church. As one looks at it from outside, the nave is Anglo-Saxon. This is recognizable from the blocked s window with its ill-understood Roman voussoir tiles and from the long-and-short quoins NW, SW, and SE. Surprisingly, the N chapel has Norman N windows, i.e. round-headed lancets, to the N and a re-set oculus to the W. The E window however is a Dec insertion (reticulated tracery). The W tower is E.E. It is only a little higher than the nave, so that the shingled broach spire actually starts below the ridge of the nave roof. The chancel E window is early C14, if it is correctly restored. The motif of arches upon arches is a characteristic though not a frequent one. Now the interior. There is indeed the Norman N chapel, though the W arch with a half-dog-tooth motif and two slight chamfers in the pointed arch means that one ought to go to the very end of the C12. In the E wall of the chapel traces of the former round-headed lancets. Of the arch from chapel to chancel only a trace remains. Early in the C14, i.e. at the time of the chapel E window, two higher arches were provided, with typical continuous sunk-quadrant mouldings. One no doubt was for a monument. Hood-mould with good head stops, one still with traces of colour. The chancel arch also bears out the date of the chapel E window. Kingpost roofs. – FONT. Square, Perp, stone with

panelling. – SCREEN. Good imitation, carved at Mayfield. –
WALL PAINTINGS. Faint traces of foliated crosses l. and r.
of the chancel arch, of a St Christopher on the nave N and a
St George on the nave S wall. – PLATE. Pewter Flagon, 1685;
Cup, 1721.

ASHAM HOUSE *see* BEDDINGHAM

ASHBURNHAM

Of Ashburnham Place only a fragment was left standing and is
being adapted. So the church is now far away from a congregation. Yet it is keeping its character and condition admirably.

ST PETER. The W tower is Perp, embattled, and with the
Pelham buckle as label-stops of the doorway. The rest all
looks Perp, but is in fact of 1665. The window tracery is
cusped-intersecting, but under low four-centred arches. Fine
E view of the chancel gable flanked by the gables of the equally
tall N and S chapels. The pre-classical C17 comes out only in
the N porch entrance and N doorway. The interior is wonderfully complete, with panelled wagon roofs. The responds to
the chancel and chapel arches, raised above the family vault,
are convincingly Perp. The original furnishings comprise the
simply panelled PULPIT, the WEST GALLERY on lovably
clumsy Ionic columns, the BOX PEWS, originally higher, the
IRON RAILINGS to the tower, the chancel and the chapels, and
the FONT with a grossly oversized stem and a white marble
bowl and its COVER. Only the tower STAIRCASE, a proper
domestic staircase, and the three-sided COMMUNION RAIL
with its dumb-bell balusters are noticeably later C17. –
REREDOS (former). Painted in 1676, i.e. indeed later. It is a
painted Wrenian reredos with a pediment and Moses and
Aaron l. and r. – ARMOUR. Helms and gauntlets, swords and
spurs. – PLATE. Two Patens on feet, 1665; Cup and Cover,
1665; Paten on foot, 1667; Cup, 1668; two Flagons and an
Almsdish, 1695. – MONUMENTS. Two only in the N chapel,
both large, both standing, both of white and grey marble,
differing in date by only a few years, yet utterly different in
style, marking the change from the Jacobean, i.e. initially
Netherlandish C16, tradition to the Romance Baroque. John
Ashburnham † 1671 (who built the church). Recumbent in
C16 armour between his two wives, one in her shroud, the
other wearing a coronet. Kneeling children against the tomb-
chest, as usual. Two black columns, the inscription plate with

two big garlands. Open curly pediment. – William Ashburnham † 1675 and his wife, the Countess of Marlborough. By 44b
Bushnell. She is seen semi-reclining and trying to look genteel.
He kneels by her in an attitude of conventional but not unconvincing pathos. Background with large drapery canopy.
The Baroque was an effort to a man like Bushnell. He is doing
inadequately what the older sculptor without any ambition
to be modern has done competently. Yet in the history of
English funerary design Bushnell's is as important as Cibber's
at Withyham. In both a new compositional freedom and a
new possibility of inventiveness appear, though it must be
admitted that they had been heralded by Nicholas Stone
earlier in the century. Bushnell had had an Italian training
and Italian experience. This accounts for the attempted
directness in the expression of grief and also for the antique
draperies.

Of the appendages to ASHBURNHAM PLACE the most important
is the STABLES. They must date from *c.*1720–30 and consist of
three separate ranges framing a courtyard. They are of ashlar,
and the l. and r. ranges have a raised centre with low pyramid
roof and a tripartite lunette window. The main, back, range
has five arches for coaches towards the courtyard and a good
front to the gardens with two short towers. For further
appendages *see* Catsfield (p. 468) and Battle (p. 409).

In the village of Ashburnham estate housing and estate building
from the Late Georgian to the Victorian.

ASHCOMBE HOUSE *see* LEWES

ASHDOWN HOUSE *and* ASHDOWN PARK *see*
FOREST ROW

ASHFORD *see* HANDCROSS

ASHURSTWOOD *see* FOREST ROW

BALCOMBE

3030

ST MARY. 1847–50, as a major addition to a modest church the
shadow of which is still the lower w tower with its low, shingled
broach spire and the former nave and chancel to its E. The
Victorians added a new nave and beyond it a N aisle. Lancets
and geometrical tracery. – PLATE. Chalice, Paten, and Flagon,
1733.

RECTORY (former), ⅛ m. SE. An agreeable five-bay brick house of the C18 with hipped roof and pedimented doorway.

BALCOMBE PLACE. Large and Tudor. 1856 by *Henry Clutton*,* with a splendid ballroom (music room) addition and other additions by *G. C. Horsley*, 1899. Free neo-Tudor.

STONE HALL, S of Balcombe Place. A quietly perfect brick house of the late C17, nothing specially inventive yet everything satisfying. Three-bay centre and two-bay wings, hipped roof, doorway with a hood. Stone quoins, the brickwork in red and blue chequer.

KEMP'S HOUSE, 1 m. S. Simpler than Stone Hall, but of the same date and character.

BOWDEN'S FARM, 1¼ m. SSE. Timber-framed. A three-bay hall was added about 1500 as a wing to a C15 four-bay house.

DITTON PLACE, 1½ m. WSW. By *Smith & Brewer*, 1904. Quite a large house in a neo-William and Mary. Brick and stone dressings. The entrance with a semicircular pediment and a semicircular porch. To the garden projecting wings, a colonnade between, and some oval windows above, enriched by garlands. Behind this centre a long, narrow, vaulted hall or gallery with a delightful fireplace, of green marble, quite flat and with a kind of chequer border, very typical of c.1900.

BALCOMBE VIADUCT. One of England's most impressive railway viaducts, 1,475 ft long. Built in 1839–41. It has thirty-seven brick arches, each pier arched at bottom as well as top, and a somewhat classical balustrade.

BALDSLOW

2¾ m. NW of Hastings

BALDSLOW PLACE (Claremont Preparatory School). By *Norman Shaw*, 1878–9. Quite large. Of the type established by Shaw over ten years earlier, i.e. informal and asymmetrical, with half-timbered gables, mullioned and transomed windows, and tile-hanging. The house cost nearly £9,000 to build.

ST MARY'S PLACE, HOLMHURST, The Ridge. In the garden the original statue of Queen Anne by *Francis Bird* from in front of St Paul's Cathedral.

BEAUPORT PARK HOTEL. Neo-Georgian of 1923. In the garden an OBELISK by *Soane*, of c.1790.

BALLCOCKS *see* HORAM

* It cost over £14,000 (G. Spain).

BALNEITH MANOR see BARCOMBE

BALSDEAN see ROTTINGDEAN

BARCOMBE

4010

ST MARY. W tower with shingled broach spire. The tower part
is lower than the nave roof. The church was much restored in
1879–80 (*Luck*), when the S aisle was rebuilt. In fact all the
windows are of that time, except for one C13 lancet on the N
side. The tower doorway and the W doorway are C14 in their
mouldings, and that corresponds to the two-bay S arcade.
The third bay, a transeptal bay, is of the C13. It has a continuous double-chamfer. – (FONT. C14, square, with traceried
sides.) – STAINED GLASS. In a N window Grantham arms,
1657. – The S aisle windows all by *Kempe*, 1882 and 1900. –
PLATE. Cup, 1710; Paten, 1710; Cup, 1739. – MONUMENT.
Susannah Medley † 1730. Large tablet and l. and r. two
abundant caryatid maidens doing their carrying by raised
arms. Quite a personal piece.
SHELLEY'S FOLLY, 1¼ m. NW. Brick, of *c.*1700. Five-bay
front, the windows l. and r. of the centre characteristically
narrow. Three-bay pediment. Hipped roof. Steps up to the
doorway, which has an open segmental pediment. The
windows still wooden mullion-and-transom crosses. The back
of the house has two projections l. and r. of only one middle
bay. On another side a fine cartouche with the Shelley arms.*
BALNEITH MANOR, 2¼ m. NW. Timber-framed, with internal
features of *c.*1500. VCH).

BARTON ST MARY see FOREST ROW

BATEMANS see BURWASH

BATTLE

7010

The name of the little town tells a great deal: that the battle
fought here in 1066 is *the* battle of English history, and that the
town must have been the result of the battle. It was in fact, by
means of the abbey, and the relation between the abbey gatehouse and the market place demonstrates at once that the town
grew out of the abbey, as the abbey had grown out of the battle.

* I have a record from the late *W. E. Tower* saying that he did much of
this house or on this house in 1899.

BATTLE ABBEY. The battle was fought on 14 October. William
vowed the abbey shortly after. The altar was to stand on the
spot where Harold had been killed. In 1076 the church was
sufficiently advanced for the second abbot to be blessed by
the Bishop of Chichester in front of the high altar. In 1094
the church was consecrated in the presence of Rufus. Much
stands of the abbey, but very little of the abbey church,
though its plan is known by excavations. The domestic
premises of the abbey became partly the mansion of Sir
Anthony Browne, Henry VIII's Master of the Horse (cf.
Cowdray House, p. 195), and in 1857 *Henry Clutton* built a
neo-Gothic mansion out of it. This, including the ample
medieval parts used by Browne and by Clutton, is now a
school and not open to visitors.

The description of the abbey might just as well start where
one enters the premises from the town, i.e. with the GATE-
HOUSE. This stands splendidly to the top and is one of the
finest in England. It can be dated by the licence to crenellate
given to Abbot Alan of Ketling in 1338, and its style is indeed
Dec. It succeeds in combining power with the filigree delicacy
of the Dec style. Two tall polygonal turrets flank the main
body. Entry is by a carriage and a pedestrian portal, both
with broad, unmistakably Dec mouldings. Above, a yet more
unmistakably Dec frilly blank frieze of highly cusped ogee
arcading. Then two niches for images, and higher up a two-
light window, again with intricate ogee tracery. The design
repeats to the inside. To the r. of the gatehouse an Early
Norman part with a small window to the outside and a doorway inside, to the l. of the gatehouse a range allegedly built
by Sir Anthony Browne and used as the court house of the
town. It has mullioned and transomed above mullioned
windows. The lights are not arched; so 1548, the date of
Browne's death, seems too early. Beyond this range again a
Norman continuation, see one exposed Early Norman arch
at r. angles to the range. Inside the gatehouse two plus two
quadripartite vaults.

Once through the gatehouse the perambulation gets confused. In front is Clutton's mansion, to the l. are gardens. As
one walks in them, turning SE, one must head for a place
where the undercroft of the E end of the church has been
exposed. It cannot be mistaken, once it has been found.
William's church was only 224 ft long. It had a w front without towers, a nave and aisles of seven bays, a crossing no

doubt with a tower, transepts each with an apsed E chapel, and a chancel with ambulatory and radiating chapels. This chancel was, as was so usual in the Middle Ages, substantially lengthened later (early C14), and the lengthening had its own polygonal apse with ambulatory and five polygonal chapels, the type e.g. of Narbonne Cathedral. It is the undercroft of these that one sees.

To find one's bearings from here one must seek out the one monastic building standing still, the one with the end wall with gable and lancets. This wall is the S wall of the 24 dormitory block which was, as always, the range E of the cloister. One will now also easily recognize the W wall of the cloister – none of the walks proper remain – which is set in the back wall of the house. Of the chapter house, which was apsed, nothing is above ground. The DORMITORY was of course on the upper floor above the whole E range. So what we see is its S two-thirds, and what we enter is its undercroft, subdivided into four parts of which the southernmost, owing to the fall of the ground, is much higher than the others. We enter by a doorway with shafts carrying stiff-leaf capitals. All is indeed E.E. here, but no exact date is recorded. The first room is three-naved, with slim round piers and hollow-chamfered ribs, the second a tunnel-vaulted passage, probably towards the infirmary, the third like the first, only shorter, and then the last, two-naved with tall piers. It has an entrance from the W with two hollow chamfers. These rooms all have windows to the E, the first small, but the last tall lancets, with one transom. This is also the design of the upper windows, i.e. those of the dormitory proper. Their mouldings are one chamfer and one hollow chamfer. The S wall of the range is an exquisite sight with its lancet windows on three levels. To the E of this are the scanty remains of the Norman lavatories, the REREDORTER, i.e. the unrelieved arches of the S wall of the drain.

The S range of the cloister with the REFECTORY has almost entirely gone. Only part of its S wall is outlined in the ground, and S of it the KITCHEN, a cruciform room surrounded by probably lower subsidiary rooms. But what survives of the refectory is the blank arcading of its W wall, amply cusped and late C13 in date. This was inside the refectory. What continues it immediately to the N is the blank arcading of the CLOISTER. The first four bays from the S are E.E., later C13 too, but not quite as late as the refectory. They have the patterns of bar tracery – an octofoiled circle (cf. e.g. the cloisters of Westminster Abbey and Salisbury). The seven bays further N, while preserving the basic elements of the C13, were restored in the Perp style. But a C13 doorway remains in the northernmost bay with most complex small mouldings.

It is difficult to follow matters beyond this point, as all now lies within the house. Behind the cloister wall to the W were, as always in the claustral arrangement, the STOREROOMS. They are here vaulted in two naves and were subdivided into one one-bay and one four-bay room. The piers are round again, but the rib-profile is different. To the W of these storerooms runs a vaulted corridor which would be not at all customary. In fact it was not a corridor, as three bays have arch openings to a former W continuation. N of this group and ending the W range was the PARLOUR, the connexion with the outer world. This also was rib-vaulted, the ribs having a more complex profile. One of the capitals of the wall shafts has coarse diagonal stiff-leaf, the others – like all the other capitals so far – are moulded.

On the upper floor of this range was the ABBOT'S LODGING, and this has to be even more laboriously pieced together to make sense, especially as the abbot's quarters, as was again usual, tended to expand beyond the claustral confines. Here it is better to start from the porch into the mansion. The walls of the porch are E.E., but the doorway is Perp, with traceried spandrels. It leads into *Clutton*'s great hall, but the C15 hall of the abbots too, an addition taking the place of some minor monastic buildings. To this addition also belongs the TOWER which appears to the SW of the end wall of the refectory. In it, on the ground floor a very large fireplace. The enormous fireplace of the hall is of course Clutton's. The other room entirely Clutton's is the LIBRARY, SW of the hall and projecting beyond it. It runs S and takes the place of a C13 passage to the guesthouse (on which *see* below) and of a range of the C16. Immediately N of the hall N wall and porch N wall is the vaulted undercroft of the C13 abbot's hall. The details here are entirely Clutton's except for the genuine jambs of a N window. The NW angle turret of the hall is C16. From this undercroft a doorway leads into the vaulted rooms already discussed.

On the upper floor of the porch is a small room with an ogee-headed, cusped N window, i.e. of the C14. In the E wall is a lancet which proves that something of the C13 was already in the place where the C15 abbot's hall is. Above the storerooms must have been more C14 remodelling, see one tall two-light Dec window in the W wall and traces of another. On the other hand the ABBOT'S CHAPEL, lying above the Parlour, is E.E. In fact it lay on a second floor. We don't know what the floor between served for. What remains of it is the doorway into it – round-headed, as several C13 doorways in the abbey are – and a delightful trefoiled oculus window to its l., allowing a glimpse into this room. Of the chapel itself we have the SEDILIA and a trace of the PISCINA.

Outside this range, looking at this N end, one can indeed see three tiers of windows. Whoever has a chance should visit this particular spot; for here the Norman church can be observed. It continued the E, not the W, wall of the parlour and a stump of the façade wall stands upright with, on an upper level, a jamb-shaft or arcading shaft to the W and a taller one to the E. One can then follow the few remaining courses of the S aisle wall and end this part of the inspection.

That leaves the GUESTHOUSE S of this whole range. It was shorter in the C13 than it is now. The W end with the two prominent polygonal turrets is Tudor. But the C13 work is very remarkable indeed, though we really know only its undercroft, necessary because of the fall of the ground. It is divided by cross-walls into eight compartments of equal width, all tunnel-vaulted and all but one connected by doorways with shouldered lintels *en enfilade*. Each room has a small lancet window to the S. Of the upper windows only the foot of one is recognizable. Up here was the most regular Tudor range, with mullioned and transomed windows, as the Buck engraving still shows.

ST MARY. Immediately N of the abbey, just as the parish church of St Margaret lies just N of Westminster Abbey. It was founded by Abbot Ralph (1107–24) and is a large church and an early church, though Abbot Ralph's time is represented only by one partially blocked arch now visible in the S chapel and once presumably connecting a Norman S transept with the crossing. This Norman church was enlarged (also probably lengthened) towards the end of the C12 by five-bay aisles. Their arcades are uniform, piers as well as abaci round or octagonal, arches pointed with two slight chamfers, capitals with big, plain, flat, stylized leaves. Only the W bay has moulded capitals. The clerestory has small single lancet

windows above the arcade spandrels, not the arches. The
chancel arch is an imitation. A little later the w tower was
added. Externally the w doorway is of about 1200, but all
features above are Perp. The rebuilding of the chancel
followed immediately, see the s lancets. Inside round them
and the former N lancets are big blank arches on strong tall
shafts. The string-course does crazy things, climbing up from
the window sills to the height of the capitals of the shafts.
The s chapel arch, replacing the Norman transept arch, is
c13 too. So is the N chapel w arch, the two E arches being Dec.
Dec also the chapel windows and the s aisle windows. The N
aisle windows and the s porch are Perp. – FONT. Large,
square, Norman, of the Purbeck type, with shallow blank
arches, seven in this case to each side. – FONT COVER. Perp,
simple and pretty. – TILES. Five tiles under the tower in a
case. – STAINED GLASS. In the N aisle bits, also head and
shoulders of an archbishop; C15. – PLATE. Late C15 German
brass Almsdish; very good Cup, 1552; Cup and Paten, 1568;
two Almsdishes, 1695; Flagon, given 1705; Almsdish, 1766. –
MONUMENTS. Brass to Sir John Lowe † 1426. Knight 4 ft 1 in.
long (N chapel). – Brass to William Arnold † 1435, demi-
figure in armour, 13 in. long (now hidden). – Brass to Robert
Clare † 1450, Dean of Battle, a 22 in. figure (chancel floor). –
Monument to Sir Anthony Browne and his wife who died in
1548. Recumbent effigies on a big tomb-chest, she much
smaller than he and hence provided with a canopy. Against
the tomb-chest typical Early Renaissance decoration, i.e.
balusters not columns, wreaths, shell-tops, cherubs, and also
the inscription in Roman lettering, not black letter.

THE TOWN. The Market Place lies right on the doorstep of the
abbey. It is triangular and has one medieval house, the
PILGRIMS' REST, immediately NW of the gatehouse, a C15
hall-house, closely studded outside, with the timber partition
of hall from solar and services and a kingpost truss still
showing and the moulded beams of the ground-floor room to
the r. in fine condition. Otherwise there are just pleasant little
houses in the Market Place, the High Street to its NW,
Mount Street off the High Street, and Upper Lake to the E
of the Market Place. Few need attention individually. In the
HIGH STREET No. 17 is the best house, dated 1700. Five
bays, three storeys, brick, former door-hood on carved
brackets, the window above with an open scrolly pediment,
and a richly carved modillion frieze. The attached No. 18 is

its little brother and has a small doorway also with curved brackets. The GEORGE HOTEL is probably late C18, three widely spaced bays, no mouldings at all. Then No. 27, dated 1688, ashlar, with a string-course of red and black chequer brick. The windows probably still had wooden mullions. In MOUNT STREET the best house is LEWINS CROFT, a sizeable detached house of the C16, timber-framed. Nearer the High Street on the N the ZION CHAPEL of 1820, the front alas cemented. Round-headed windows.

Then into UPPER LAKE and at once, still w of the church, the drive to the DEANERY (the rectors of Battle were called deans). This is a house with a most interesting front, facing the church. It has two rain-water heads dated 1669 and a plaque on an attachment dated 1677. It is of brick, looking older, but has a façade conservative for 1669 but in keeping with others in the county. The front is flat and has two canted bay windows and three widely spaced windows with mullions between. There are two storeys and battlements stepping up above the centre. In the centre is a Victorian porch and attached to this a doorway perfectly classical at first sight: Ionic columns and a pediment. But the capitals have curious small ornamental details, and the frieze is fluted with broad ribbed leaves rising up in places. So 1669 might be an explanation of the mixture. Along Upper Lake again, as in the High Street, hardly a house that would not fit in nicely. A specially attractive group right at the beginning on the s side: a Georgian three-bay three-storey house with two canted bay windows and then a sequence of lower ones.

So on to the STATION by Mr *Trees* of Finsbury Square, architect to the line (*Ill. Lon. News*, 1852). He has here used E.E. windows and even introduced an E.E. chimneypiece in the ticket hall. Bar tracery, shouldered lintel – a job certainly not done solely from a drawing board in Finsbury Square. By the station the METHODIST CHAPEL with pointed windows; 1826.

WINDMILL, by the Whatlington road. A smock-mill with a date 1810, the sails surviving only partially.

HOSPITAL (the former WORKHOUSE), 1¼ m. w. The front an unusual composition. The main block with octagonal centre and three arms lies behind a gatehouse flanked at a distance by short corner ranges. Its style is a minimum Tudor, that is gabled. The material is stone.

BATTLE LODGE to Ashburnham Place (*see* p. 401), another

⅝ m. w. Cruciform and also Tudor, but here handled with a remarkable accuracy and smoothness. It is not romantic any longer, but literate Victorian – yet the date is 1835.

ROMAN BLOOMERY. The fields in the neighbourhood of Crowhurst Park contain large quantities of cinders, and trial excavations in the area have suggested a Roman bloomery in operation in the C1 and early C2.

6030

BAYHAM ABBEY

The most impressive monastic ruin of Sussex. Bayham was Premonstratensian. It had been founded at Otham about 1200 direct from Prémontré,* and moved to Bayham between 1208 and 1211. Much of the church and the buildings round the cloister stands quite high up or is at least recognizable. In addition there is, separate, to the N, the former gatehouse. The whole makes a very picturesque ruin and was as such made use of by *Repton* in 1799–1800.‡

The church is specially interesting in that a first and a second C13 period can be distinguished. The second as usual was a very substantial lengthening of the E end. And whereas usually such enterprises in abbey and cathedral churches ended with the destruction of the old E end, at Bayham it was kept almost entirely, with the curious consequence that the church in the end had two transepts. Perhaps it did not seem quite so curious, because Lewes Priory on the pattern of Cluny also had it, and of course Canterbury Cathedral, where the procedure in the early C12 had been exactly the same as at Bayham.

It will be more convenient to start with the second rather than the first build. The plan consisted of a crossing, transepts, a chancel, two plus two straight-ended chapels, and an apse of three sides of an octagon at the E termination of the chancel. A beech tree now grows dramatically out of the low remains of the E wall. The plan is essentially Cistercian and in fact, except for the apse, like that of the first church at Bayham. It is the type called Bernardian after Bernard of Clairvaux and represented e.g. by Fontenay and Buildwas. The polygonal apse is most unusual in England. The Wells and the Lichfield Lady Chapels are both later; for all the details at Bayham point to a date about 1260 or 1270. In France on

* The only other direct foundation from Prémontré in England is St Radegund's in Kent.

‡ Another report by Repton 1814.

the other hand such Cistercian houses as Obazine and Fontfroide have them. The E parts of Bayham are completely rib-
vaulted, though the vaults mostly stood on shafts starting
not from the ground but from corbels. Those in the chancel
have rich, mature stiff-leaf. Capitals, where they are preserved,
are as a rule decorated also with mature stiff-leaf. The
chancel walls have in addition the odd, almost Gothick, motif
of a large blank sexfoiled circle. The crossing piers had many
detached shafts now missing. The mouldings of the piers
proper are consequently provided with many concavities.
They are particularly pronounced in the abaci. The capitals
are moulded here. From the N transept an arch leads into the
N aisle. As one explores it, it turns out to be not a normal
aisle, and on the S side the evidence is as confused. In any
case, these aisles had solid walls to what seems the nave. In
fact it turns out to be the chancel of the first church and the
aisles turn out to lead into the inner of the pairs of E chapels
of the first transept. On the N side little of this can be seen,
but on the S side it becomes clear, as soon as one takes the
buildings along the E side of the cloister into consideration.
These, which will be described later, belong to the first
campaign too, and if one remembers that cloister E ranges
always ran flush with the transept, one can pinpoint the transept without difficulty. It is the space with a trefoil-headed
recess in the W wall and two small round-headed windows in
the S wall. The traces of the early transept E chapels now fall
into place too, and it is instructive to compare the early C13
moulded capitals with those of the later C13, especially in the
W arch of the later N transept already referred to.

The nave is a more straightforward proposition. It is a
Perp remodelling without aisles. The tall shafts and the out-
lines of the large S windows are there to see, and the plain
C13 wall below. Big buttresses supported the vault, especially
on the S side, where they are so deep that the cloister N walk
leads through them. Access to the cloister from the nave is by
a doorway in the first bay from the W, again with the early
moulded capitals.

As for the ranges round the CLOISTER, the W range lay W
of the church façade, so that the wall which is standing and
runs in line with the façade was its E, not its W wall. The
STOREROOMS were here, and, though the ground has risen a
good deal, traces of the vaulting can still be seen. The ribs
were single-chamfered, a utilitarian form, and the capital is

clearly of the first period. The s range also stands up high, with one complete lancet window. This is in the s, not the N wall, and again the ground has risen, and again vaulting is visible. It was the undercroft of the refectory. The E range of course is more complex. It starts from the N with the SACRISTY, and after that comes the CHAPTER HOUSE. Of this the entrance from the cloister has only the l. jamb of the usual l. window preserved. A doorway and a r. window can be presumed. Then, very prominent, are the two round piers inside the chapter house, originally supporting rib-vaulting. The chapter house projects further E than the rest of the range. Above was the DORMITORY and this, as a piece of E wall and crags of s wall show, stuck out s beyond the refectory walls. The beginning of a staircase up to the dormitory survives in the SE corner of the cloister.*

The GATEHOUSE stands just s of the stream which to its w is dammed into a lake. Above this lake to the N stands the present BAYHAM ABBEY, a Tudor mansion on a hill, actually in Kent. The house is by *David Brandon*, 1870–2. It has a symmetrical grey front with two shaped gables and a lower r. hand attachment. The gatehouse is really part of the picturesque make-believe of the Repton age. It is the real gatehouse, with a segmental arch and a tall, formerly Dec, window over, and with side apartments, but the western one has been provided with two round E.E. piers so as to make a loggia with a view over the lake. Only the Aislabies of Studley Royal had a better ruin than Bayham. Theirs was Fountains Abbey. To the s of the gatehouse was the DOWER HOUSE, two-storeyed, Gothick, castellated and with canted bay windows. It is no longer kept up. It dates from before 1752, the year when Horace Walpole saw it.

BEACHY HEAD

BELLE TOUT LIGHTHOUSE. Disused. By *Stevenson*, 1831. Of Aberdeen granite. The top, which housed the lantern, is missing.

BECKLEY

ALL SAINTS. The w tower was begun in the C11 and completed in the C12. Herringbone masonry below and a wider N window than the upper Norman slit-windows are. The arch

* (C 13 and C 14 TILES at Bayham Abbey are mentioned by the VCH.)

to the nave is not original. Heavy timbers inside to support the upper floor boards. The tower has a shingled broach spire. The arcades inside are of three bays, both before 1300, but different from one another. Octagonal piers, double-chamfered arches. The chancel arch stands on stronger octagonal piers, and one-bay chapels follow. The windows of the N chapel are indeed late C13. The chancel is Dec with reticulated tracery in the E window and an ogee arch to the PISCINA. Timber S porch. Victorian dormers in the nave roof. – FONTS. Fluted oval marble bowl; C18. – Remains of a small fluted Norman bowl. – The tower screen seems made up from a late C17 COMMUNION RAIL; twisted balusters. – PLATE. Set of 1729.

CHURCH HOUSE. Early C18. Red brick, of two storeys. Giant pilasters, off the angles, carrying pieces of entablature. Segment-headed windows, panelled parapet. The middle window has a little decoration. The doorway has fluted Doric pilasters and a frieze. (Inside in the Oak Room an overdoor with strapwork and the date 1626 and an elaborate overmantel with caryatids and arched panels no doubt of the same time. SCM, VIII. The staircase has thin twisted balusters. NBR)

KNELLE DOWER HOUSE, ¼ m. W. C15, close studding and thatch.

HORSEPEN, ¼ m. E, at the road junction. L-shaped, early C16, with the main gable-end closely studded in three tiers.

(GREAT KNELLE, 1½ m. NNE. C18, of five bays, brick, painted. Porch with Doric columns and pediment. MHLG)

BEDDINGHAM

4000

ST ANDREW. Of the Norman church there is no more than a fragment of a N window and re-set pieces in the S aisle W wall and the tower. The arcades, i.e. the aisles, were made about 1200. They differ considerably. The S arcade has round piers and square abaci, undecorated capitals, but heads or *cul-de-lampe* supports at the corners and unmoulded sharply pointed arches, the N arcade round abaci and pointed arches with a slight chamfer. Dec clerestory windows (ogee cinquefoils), Dec chancel E window (cf. West Firle) but trefoil-headed lancets otherwise in the chancel. Perp W tower of flint and stone in an irregular chequer. The tower was called 'intended' in 1540, 'in progress' in 1557–9. The bell-openings are indeed more Elizabethan than Henry VIII. – PAINTING. Red scrolls of the C13 and a restored figure in one arch of the S arcade. – PLATE. Elizabethan Cup.

COBBE PLACE, ¼ m. s. Timber-framed and Elizabethan or Jacobean. A symmetrical composition, which is unusual for timber-framed houses. Two identical wings with pendants and finials to the gables and a recessed centre. This was remodelled c.1840.

ASHAM HOUSE, 1¼ m. ssw. Early C19. Pretty three-bay front of two storeys with one-bay, one-storey attachments l. and r. All the windows of two lights and Gothick.

THE CABURN. An Iron Age HILL-FORT, ½ m. NW of the church. The earliest occupation on the hilltop is an Iron Age A unfortified settlement. The first defences, consisting of the small rampart, now little more than 1 ft in height, and its accompanying ditch were built c.100 B.C. These defences enclose an area of 3½ acres and are broken by a single, simple entrance on the NE. Associated with this structure are a large number of grain storage pits within the enclosure. Shortly before the Roman invasion the enormous outer bank and ditch were constructed, presumably as a reaction against the Roman threat. The inner and outer faces of this rampart were revetted with timber uprights, further strengthened by horizontal beams running through the thickness of the bank. Associated with this phase of construction are the elaborate outworks around the old entrance on the NE.

LATE BRONZE AGE SETTLEMENT, 1 m. W of the church, or ITFORD HILL. The settlement consists of eleven small embanked enclosures, each containing a circular hut. The settlement is approached by a sunken way on the w.

The FIELD SYSTEM S of the settlement is possibly Roman.

BENTLEY WOOD see HALLAND

BERWICK

5000

CHURCH. W tower with shingled broach spire. Nave and chancel windows and other details, as far as they can be trusted, late C13 to C15. But the church has suffered much at the hands of the restorer of 1856. The N arcade he put in is quite illiterate and clumsy on top. So is the chancel arch. The s arcade is original. The chancel windows have rere-arches in the form of shouldered lintels, a late C13 feature (cf. the Rectory, Westdean). – PLATE. Cup, 1630; Paten, 1753. The MONUMENT in the chancel on the N side with a big bold, rather bleak Dec canopy. – MONUMENT to John Nutt † 1656. With two frontal busts in oval recesses and garland

over. Flat, fat faces. – What makes the church worth
a visit is the WALL PAINTINGS, done for Bishop Bell of
Chichester by *Duncan Grant, Vanessa Bell,* and *Quentin Bell*
in 1942–3.* It was a noble effort on the part of the bishop‡ –
art in wartime and modern art in a church, yet if one
remembers Duncan Grant and Vanessa Bell in their prime,
how sad does it seem now, so conventional, so sentimental.
By far the best is Duncan Grant's Crucifixion and Christ in
Glory.

BEST BEECH see WADHURST

BEVINGFORD see BUXTED

BEXHILL

7000

Bexhill, like Eastbourne, has an old centre away from the sea
and the seaside development as an independent enterprise of the
lords of the manor, in this case the Earls de la Warr. And, as at
Eastbourne, the old and the new have grown together. But
whereas Eastbourne as a resort started about 1850, Bexhill
started about 1880.

OLD BEXHILL

ST PETER, the parish church of the old village, now in Church
Street. Externally all smooth, of the various restorations,
except for a few untouched details and patches, but internally
rewarding. The W tower, which is low and embattled, has to
the N and S simple Norman arches. Did they lead into W bays
of aisles ? The E arch is pointed and has a slight chamfer, i.e.
seems to date from the late C12. By that time the Norman
nave certainly had aisles. They were of two bays. The N
arcade has decorated round scallop capitals and round arches
with a slight chamfer, say 1180, the S arcade capitals have
plain upright stylized leaves instead. A third bay was added
in the C13, the arches pointed and with two hollow chamfers.
The SE respond is Perp. Yet another N bay is Perp, but this
clearly was once a chancel chapel. The two-bay S addition is
of 1878, as is the chancel. – PAINTING. In the chancel the

* By Vanessa Bell Annunciation and Nativity, by Quentin Bell the altar
painting, the roundels on the E side of the screen (Sacraments) and the E
side of the chancel arch, by Duncan Grant its w side and the w wall; also
the w side of the screen.

‡ And Sir Charles Reilly, Sir Kenneth Clark, and Mr Etchells, who all
helped to make the realization of the plan possible.

wall-painting and pretty ceiling decoration are by *W. G. Rich*, 1893. – The large wall-painting of four saints in a neo-Quattrocento style is by *Alan Sorrell*, 1951. – STAINED GLASS. In a N window whole figures and fragments of the C15. The window was removed to Strawberry Hill in 1774, a present of Lord Ashburnham to Horace Walpole, and returned in the C20. – PLATE. Paten and Flagon, 1723; Cup and Paten, 1775. – MONUMENT. Small coped Anglo-Saxon coffin-lid; very fine and well preserved. Close interlace etc.

Close to the church a few old houses. The principal one is the MANOR HOUSE, SE of the church. This is irregular and not very promising from the street. But on the E side of the N wing is a buttress and an ogee-trefoiled window, i.e. evidence of the C14. In CHURCH STREET itself weatherboarded cottages along the curve of the street. At the junction of Church Street, more or less opposite the Manor House, a Georgian house with a doorway with pilasters and pediment.

VICTORIAN AND AFTER

CHURCHES

Not one of them is anything outstanding. A list must be enough and need not include all.

ALL SAINTS, Sidley. 1909 by *Streatfield*, chancel and tower 1927–9 by *G. E. S. Streatfield*.

ST AUGUSTINE, Cooden Drive. 1934 by *W. H. Randoll Blacking*, completed 1960–3 by *H. Hubbard Ford*. A free Gothic, with window tracery decidedly C17 Gothic (cf. e.g. the Oriel College Chapel, Oxford). The figure of St Augustine above the entrance by *John Skelton*.

ST BARNABAS, Sea Road. 1891 by *Sir A. Blomfield*. The aisles built only in 1908–9. Flint with a W flèche, the details of *c.*1300. Inside brick piers and brick facing. The S chapel by *Leslie Moore*, 1939.

OUR LADY OF THE ROSARY (R.C.), Southlands Road. By *A. F. Watson*, 1954–5.

ST MARK, Little Common. A composite story. The lancet nave of 1842, the chancel and S aisle by *Woodyer*, 1857, the recent N aisle by *Duncan Wylson*, 1962. Did Woodyer provide the round arcade piers with the arches dying into them?

ST MARY MAGDALENE (R.C.), Sea Road. Stone. 1907 by *Arthur Young* (GR). With an embattled central tower; well placed.

ST MICHAEL, Glassonbury Drive. 1929 by *John B. Mendham*. Brick, with SW porch tower ending quite prettily with some tile-hanging and a pyramid roof.

ST STEPHEN, Woodsgate Park. 1898–1900 by *Henry Ward*. Brick inside and out. SW tower Perp, but the rest lancets and Y-tracery. Apse at the E end.

PUBLIC AND OTHER BUILDINGS

TOWN HALL. 1893–5 by *Henry Ward*. Modest. Brick and stone, symmetrical.

CHURCH OF ENGLAND PRIMARY SCHOOL, Buckhurst Road. By *Hilton & J. M. Wright*, 1955–6.

NAZARETH HOUSE, Royston Gardens. By *Leonard Stokes*, 1893–4. Red brick and stone bands. The façade of eleven bays with a hipped roof. Stokes's typical broad ground-floor arches are prominent. Two low towers at the back. A building of much character.

DE LA WARR PAVILION. 1933–6 by *Erich Mendelsohn & 62b Chermayeff*. Mendelsohn's *magnum opus* during the short time that he lived in England, and although the concrete looks grey (at the time of writing) and creepers climb up the wall which was meant to have the *signet* or badge of the pavilion, it has aged very well. Its clean long lines towards the sea leading to the ample glazed staircase projection in which the staircase effortlessly performs its spiral, and the contrasting block shapes towards the road are as effective as they were thirty years ago. It was a bold move of an enlightened client to commission such a building.

The pavilion is the centre of Bexhill's modest seafront development, but it does not seem to belong, or did not, until in the very last years tall blocks of flats have begun to appear – three to the E of the Sackville Hotel, others further W. The SACKVILLE HOTEL, now closed, is the prototype of the Bexhill style, the style of the 1880s, in a manner indebted to Sir Ernest George, i.e. with Dutch gables or, in the case of the hotel, gables with white bargeboards. This characterizes the terraces of hotels and boarding houses, and there is nothing else to be said.

BUCKHOLT FARM, 1¾ m. NE. The façade is of 1670 and typical of the date, i.e. symmetrical, with mullioned windows and a gabled porch. The symmetry incidentally is still not without qualifications: three-light windows to the l., two-light to the r. The house is of brick and only three bays wide.

14—S.

4000

BISHOPSTONE

Off the mouth of the Ouse, in a slight hollow of the Downs, with beech screens.

ST ANDREW. The church is historically so interesting that it deserves to be described in chronological order. The story starts with a building of the early c8 of which the whole s *porticus*, i.e. side chamber (not porch; it had no entrance),* the sw quoin of the nave, and two single-splayed w windows, now inside the tower, remain. The angles with long-and-short work. Then the Norman additions and adaptation, a w tower and, because it must have taken away the Saxon w doorway, a s portal into the *porticus*, a chancel space, as though for a central tower, a square altar space, and a N aisle. They must be taken in order. The tower has to the w a round window, twin bell-openings with middle shaft and a corbel table with heads, monsters, etc. The arch to the nave with an angle roll moulding. The s doorway has one order of colonnettes with decorated scallop capitals and an arch with zigzag. In the gable above it a SUNDIAL inscribed EADRIC. This is supposed to be Saxon. The doorway from *porticus* to church, round-headed and completely unmoulded, is not in the centre and might well be Saxon too. The chancel space has along its N and s walls two blank arches each. One capital is of the decorated scallop kind, as in the doorway. The arches have to the E zigzag and to the w a plain roll moulding. To the E two round windows high up. To the E and W the chancel is connected with the church by ornate arches. That to the w oddly enough is an E.E. re-doing. Stiff-leaf capitals and fine mouldings. That to the E is triple-shafted and Norman. Multi-scalloped capitals. But the arch is pointed and moulded and has a hood-mould of dogtooth, i.e. must have been re-modelled E.E. Finally the altar space. Here the E angles have triple shafts high up, meant for vaulting. The present rib-vault is of 1849, when some more Normanizing took place too. The shafts have waterleaf capitals, a Late Norman motif, which is curious. In the gable of the altar space another round window. As for the aisle, it simply has very small Norman windows. That, however, is curious too; for the N arcade is of *c.*1200. Two bays, round pier, round abacus, pointed arches with two slight chamfers. Is it not more likely then that the

---

* Inside the *porticus* a very pretty Perp recess with ogee arch and fleuron framing.

N windows were re-used? Altogether the church remains
puzzling in its chronology. – ARCHITECTURAL FRAGMENTS.
Some Norman ones in the porch. – PLATE. Cup and Paten,
1568. – MONUMENT. Fine, small C12 coffin-lid with a shaft 11a
on which three roundels in rope mouldings. Inside them a
cross, the lamb and cross, and two birds drinking from an
urn.

BLACKHAM
⅔ m. N of Withyham

5030

ALL SAINTS, by the railway. By *L. W. Ridge*, 1902. Small,
with lancet windows and a polygonal bell turret half poised
on a w buttress.

(SALEHURST FARM, ¼ m. SW. Mid C16. One gable with
moulded bargeboards and pendant. VCH)

BLACKLANDS *see* HASTINGS, p. 520

BLETCHINGLY *see* ROTHERFIELD

BODIAM

7020

ST GILES. Away from the village and in trees. Oblong Perp w
tower with beacon stair-turret. E.E. chancel with lancets.
But in fact the top of the w tower, the chancel E window, all
aisle windows, and much more is by *R. C. Carpenter*, who
restored the church in 1845–56. Original a lancet at the w
end of the s aisle, most of the tower, some of the E.E. evidence
of the chancel, and the chancel arch. – PLATE. Cup and Paten
on foot, 1724; Almsdish, 1761. – (MONUMENT. Very fragmentary, but originally excellent brass to a Knight, mid C14.)

BODIAM CASTLE. Bodiam is the ideal picture of the powerful, 31b
wholly planned castle, as against the multiform, grown castle
– i.e. it has an architectural impact, not a picturesque one. Its
type is one of the early C13, created in the France of Philip
Augustus and developed concurrently in the Southern Italy
of the Hohenstaufen. England took it over at Harlech, i.e. in
an Edwardian castle of about 1285. Bodiam is exactly a
hundred years later. Sir Edward Dalyngrydge was granted
licence to crenellate, i.e. to build a castle, in 1385. No wonder,
as the French had burnt Rye in 1377 and Winchelsea in 1380.
Sir Edward became Keeper of the Tower shortly after and

died about 1395. In 1919 Lord Curzon of Kedleston had the
castle restored excellently.

Bodiam is a perfect square with mighty round angle towers
placed in a perfect moat, bridged originally on the exact N
and S sides. In the exact middle of three sides is a square
projection, in that of the fourth, the N side, is the main
entrance. It is preceded by a GATEHOUSE of which only a
fragment stands. However, one can recognize the portcullis
groove and the springing of vaulting. Attached remains a
tiny room vaulted by a tunnel-vault with transverse arches.
The entrance proper is guarded by two towers projecting in
two steps. They are machicolated and have loopholes. The
centre between them has no machicolations, because the giant
four-centred arch above the entrance has slots taking the place
of the machicoulis. The entrance itself has a four-centred
arch too, with a higher four-centred blank arch and a rectangular frame above with three shields. The windows on this
side and most of the other windows are single-light, single-
chamfered lancets, a hundred years out of date. One of the
few larger windows, the E window of the chapel in the E front
of the castle, is just as out of date. It is of three stepped lancet
lights under one arch. Otherwise there is only one two-light
window. This is on the N front, has trefoiled lights and a
transom, and belongs to the hall.

As one enters the castle, the GATEHOUSE is found to be
vaulted in two bays, the bays divided by a portcullis. Only
the vault of the second bay is preserved. It is a tierceron-star
and has holes in the bosses and the wall-half-bosses – an
ominous detail. Chambers to the l. and r., both with base-
ments. The COURTYARD of the castle makes one significant
fact patent at once. This was not, like e.g. Harlech, a wall
with permanent or temporary buildings leaning against it
but a regular four-range house with an inner courtyard, even
if a heavily fortified house.* The four ranges are of two
storeys with three-storeyed towers. The principal features
are the CHAPEL in the E range whose window has already
been mentioned. To its S is a small VESTRY with an ORATORY
over. A two-light window connects the chapel with this. The
oratory was no doubt accessible from the main upper rooms,
for the hall is in the E half of the S range. Its high-table end
was to the E, and from it a suite of rooms between hall and

* The same is true of Bolton Castle in Yorkshire, where licence to
crenellate was obtained in 1379.

chapel was reached and another by means of a staircase
which must be assumed between s and E ranges, the upper
suite ending in the oratory already mentioned. The oratory
indicates that this was the owner's private suite. But what
was the purpose of the suite below? The HALL is 46 by 24 ft.
To the s it has at the high-table end the two-light window
referred to above. The entrance, at the screens end, is of two
continuous chamfers. The three usual doorways from the
screens passage to buttery, kitchen, and pantry are preserved.
They also have continuous double-chamfers. What is unusual
is the continuation of the screens passage to the s by a porch,
i.e. straight to the postern-gate – not a militarily ideal arrangement. The porch has another tierceron-star vault, again with
the ominous holes in the bosses. It can still be seen that the
portcullis was operated from the room above. Next to this is
a garderobe. The KITCHEN lay in the sw corner. It has
two enormous fireplaces. Two-light windows with transoms
to the courtyard. Under one of them is a doorway direct from
the courtyard to the kitchen. In the sw tower a big tank. In
the w range a second kitchen with fireplaces along the N and
s walls. Above the gateway in the N range is on the first and
second floors a complete apartment of six rooms. On the
second floor the passage from the spiral stair to the rooms is
rib-vaulted with foliage bosses.

(GUINNESS HOP FARM. Cattle Unit by *John Voelcker*, 1963.
The unit is for 162 animals. Precast concrete cantilever
frame.)

BOLEBROOKE see HARTFIELD

BOLNEY

ST MARY MAGDALENE. Norman nave and chancel, see the s
doorway with early-looking reeded bands round the arch and
hood-mould, and see two chancel windows. The chancel E
window is of *c.*1300 (Y-tracery and an oculus in the gable).
w tower dated in accounts 1536–8. The w doorway with its
nicely carved spandrels suits that date. But are not the heavy
conical pinnacles C17? N aisle of 1853 with crazy-paving wall
surface and crude plate tracery. – PLATE. Cup, 1567; two
Patens on feet, 1725. – MONUMENT. Tablet to Cap. A. H.
Huth † 1915, a neo-late-C17 piece.
The village is one narrow street, nice in scale, below the church,
but continues to the N as council housing.

WYKEHURST. 1872–4 by *E. M. Barry* for Henry Huth. Decaying at the time of writing. A French-château type of mansion with turrets and conical roofs and a polygonal 'chapel' (i.e. staircase) window. The entrance side is asymmetrical, the garden side is essentially symmetrical and very lavish. From the 280-ft terrace beautiful view to the South Downs. The house was centrally heated.

GARSTON'S FARM, ½ m. SW. C15 and C16. The C16 part has a jutting gable on carved brackets and with carved bargeboards.

BACON'S FARM, ⅝ m. W. C15, timber-framed, much restored and enlarged. On the N side a bay window.

HOMEWOOD HOUSE, 1 m. W. Probably late C14, though the exterior would not let one expect that. The plan consisted of a two-bay hall, a two-storey service end, and two two-storeyed solar bays (W end). The service and solar bays have a single aisle, but the hall truss is constructed to span nave and aisle space without an intermediate support. The system is the same as at Dunsters Mill House, Ticehurst.

DAWE'S FARM, 1¼ m. SW. Fine timber-framed C16 house, L-shaped with a three-storey stair-tower in the angle and to its l. a chimneybreast with a stepped brick gable.

YE OLDE TUDOR HOUSE, ¾ m. N, on the A23. Timber-framed, C15 and C16, with three gables to the W, two of them on the slightly projecting wings. The centre is the C15 part.

BORDE HILL see CUCKFIELD

BOREHAM STREET see HERSTMONCEUX

BOWDEN'S FARM see BALCOMBE

BRAMBLETYE see FOREST ROW

BREDE

ST GEORGE. A Perp church, as one looks round it, with a lowish W tower with beacon turret and generally large windows. But there is a small lancet in the W wall of the N aisle, and that aisle is narrow. So earlier things are to come. In fact, as one enters, one notices even a pre-lancet past. The W bay of the S arcade has a Norman impost which suggests a Norman SW tower. The Norman church which had this was then, about 1200 or a little later, given a S aisle of two bays (round piers, arches of one chamfer and one slight chamfer).

The N aisle received its form about 1300: three bays, standard elements. In the C14 the Norman chancel was extended by N and S chapels of one bay. The piece of wall now standing between these and the arcade further W represents the Norman chancel arch. Then a new Perp chancel was built, and finally, apparently about 1537, this was given a S chapel (*see* below). Its arch to the chancel is round, the capitals of the responds have floral decoration, and the E respond in addition a coat of arms with supporters. The E window has most uncommon tracery. This must on heraldic evidence belong to the period *c.*1537 and is French Flamboyant in derivation. – FONT. Perp, octagonal, with plain arched panels alternating with shields. – SCREEN. To the S chapel from the N, on the way out from Perp, i.e. with mullions and no arches or tracery. – POOR BOX. Dated 1687, yet entirely pre-classical. – CHEST. Dated 1633. With religious scenes on front, sides, and top. Scandinavian. – ARCHITECTURAL FRAGMENT. A bracket in the S aisle, with dogtooth. – SCULPTURE. Virgin and Child by *Clare Sheridan* (*see* below). In memory of her son who died in 1937. – PAINTINGS. Stations of the Cross by *W. T. Monnington.* – STAINED GLASS. Some medieval glass in the window above the porch. Some later glass in the S chapel E window. – MONUMENTS. Robert Oxenbregg † 1482 and wife. Brasses, his reduced to one leg and two feet. Length of the figures 27 in. They are now set in the back wall of a tomb recess with the usual projecting tomb-chest and the usual flat arch, panelled inside, and top cresting. Stone, though the type is more often found in Purbeck or Sussex marble. – Sir Goddard Oxenbridge † 1537, builder probably of the S chapel. Sumptuous tomb-chest with shields. Excellently carved effigy. Low back wall with pilasters and the date 1537. – Mrs Hele † 1829. With a female figure seated on the ground by an urn. By *M. W. Johnson* of London. – The same did the monument to Robert Hele Selby Hele, who died in 1839. Kneeling female figure by an urn.

BREDE PLACE, 1 m. E. A stone-built C15 manor house with mid or late C16 alterations in brick. The W front shows both phases. The C15 house had a hall with the entrance where the C16 brick porch now is, service quarters to the l. which have gone, the chamber with solar over to the r., beyond the polygonal brick extension, and beyond the chapel, the best preserved C15 part, though its windows are re-done. The S wall has a remarkably long three-light window with Perp panel tracery, the other windows are smaller. Attached to the chapel yet further is a vestry and above this the priests' room, accessible originally by a primitive ladder, happily preserved on the central part of a subsidiary staircase. It is simply a post with concave sides and the rungs sticking out l. and r. The chamber and solar have windows of four plus four lights on both floors and to W and E. The middle mullion is given a special concave-sided shaft inside. The lights of the windows are arched, but not cusped, which looks later than the rest of the fenestration. At the back they are in fact set in a brick remodelling with a big stepped gable. Also the panelling of the chamber, preserved perfectly, has pilasters, i.e. a mid or late C16 indication. The house still has parts of its C15 king-post roof. The hall was in the C16 divided into lower and upper floors and given a big fireplace. The main staircase is Elizabethan and takes up the E part of the chapel. Services in the chapel could be followed not only from the ground floor, where there is indeed a separate doorway into it on the W front, but also, for the family only, from a gallery. The screen of the gallery is in position, though only partly original.* The original chimneys have single octagonal stacks with a top moulding.

6020

BRIGHTLING

St Thomas Becket. Low E.E. W tower, with later battlements. E.E. N chapel. The E window of the chapel however is Dec, with reticulated tracery, as is the chancel E window. Other Dec windows, though the quatrefoiled circles above the S window can hardly be medieval. Would they be C18, Victorianized? The S porch is dated 1749 in figures set in flint; the date is set in a typically Early Gothick quatrefoil. The interior is confusing. The tower and the chancel are in line, but the N arcade is further N than one would expect. Also the arches end to the E in a three-quarter arch. Yet the arcade is C14, while the arcade of the chancel chapel is C13. The nave has an original wagon roof. – PULPIT. Simple, Gothick, and attractive. – WEST GALLERY. On Roman Doric columns; also C18. – On it a Gothick BARREL ORGAN. –

* In the chapel three STALLS with MISERICORDS and some linenfold panelling. – The works of art in the house are no business of *The Buildings of England*, but the carvings of a former owner, *Clare Sheridan*, must at least be mentioned. They include bronze busts of Lenin, Trotsky, Zinoviev, and Kamenev made when Clare Sheridan visited Russia as early as 1920.

MONUMENTS. Brasses to a Civilian and Wife, late C15, 18 in. figures. – Brass to Thomas Pye † 1592 as a child. Kneeling boy and inscriptions, the main one in black letter beginning: O happy child. A scroll on the l.: Dns dedit dns abstulit. A scroll to the r.: Vive pius, moriere pius. And at the top: Pius S. Theologiae Doctor Thomas filio unico immatura morte abrepto moerens posuit. – Cartouches, all enjoyable, dates of death 1690, 1705, 1720. – Dr Primrose Blair † 1819, with a big urn, its handles in the form of snakes. – William Shield † 1829, by *Peter Rouw Jun*. Profile in medallion and a garland over. – John Fuller † 1834, i.e. Mad Jack Fuller. White with an eloquent bust. By *Henry Rouw*. – In the churchyard is Mad Jack Fuller's MAUSOLEUM, a most monumental pyramid. You cannot miss it. It was built by Fuller in 1810, and it is said that he is buried inside, seated, wearing a top-hat and holding a bottle of claret. He was an M.P. and a collector of Turners. He also bought Bodiam Castle, when it was in danger of demolition. For his own buildings, *see* below and Dallington, p. 480. – (Also in the churchyard a headstone with one of *Harmer*'s terracotta plaques. SAC 1962)

BRIGHTLING PARK. The house of the Fullers has recently been reduced in size to a fraction of what it was and in the process has lost its great Rococo saloon.* What remains is the oldest range facing the courtyard. It is of nine bays and two storeys with a panelled parapet. The date 1699 is recorded on rain-water heads. Inside, opposite where the front door used to be, a stucco overmantel of cannon against a landscape, including a Vanbrughian temple.

In the grounds a ROTUNDA with colonnade and dome, outside the estate an OBELISK, 65 ft high, and the OBSERVATORY, one-storeyed, with two-storeyed centre and a lead dome. They are all embellishments of Jack Fuller. *Sir Robert Smirke* designed the observatory and may have been responsible for the others, as he was for part of the demolished ranges of the house.

SOCKNERSH MANOR, 1⅝ m. NE. Timber-framed, with the most happy-go-lucky brick-nogging. Two doorway pediments are supported by man-brackets, one holding a child, and two in chains. They may originally have supported an oversailing bressumer. Early C17. The house in its architecture and its setting is the perfect Christmas card subject.

OLDCASTLE, *see* Dallington, p. 480.

* The chimneypiece is now in Hambro's Bank in Bishopsgate.

14*

BRIGHTON

INTRODUCTION

Brighton was not an important ancient town like Hastings, before it set out on its seaside career. It was a fishing village named Brighthelmstone, and when that was lost to the sea, started on the height of the cliff and developed into a small town. The parish church was outside in an elevated position, just as it still is at Newhaven and as one finds it in the West Country. The area was between West Street, North Street, and East Street. No architecture prior to the C17 survives, nor is any of the C17 or early C18 recognizable externally. So architecturally Brighton is all later C18 and after. The seaside story starts with Dr Russell's *Dissertation concerning the Use of Sea Water in Diseases of the Glands*. This came out in Latin in 1750, in English in 1753. Conveniently, Dr Russell also discovered a chalybeate spring in St Ann's Well Gardens. Visitors began to appear. There must have been quite a number and of a genteel kind, if the Castle Inn could build its ballroom (now St Stephen) in 1766, and the Ship Inn its assembly room in 1767. The Duke of Gloucester came in 1765, the Duke of Cumberland in 1771, 1772, and 1779, and the Prince of Wales in 1783, 1785, 1786. In 1785 he had married Mrs Fitzherbert. *Henry Holland* built him the Marine Pavilion in 1786–7, safely away from the cruel sea. The Royal Crescent, the first architectural composition of houses and the first to face the sea, was built in 1798–1807. Then development set in properly and gathered momentum to a degree unparalleled among English resorts, including even Bath. The Brighton one thinks of is the creation of the 1820s and 1830s. Much of what was done, was done by three architects resident at Brighton: *Amon Wilds* (*c.*1762–1833), *Charles Augustus Busby* (1788–1834), and *Amon Henry Wilds* (born *c.*1790 or later). Busby had been trained in London and had visited America *c.*1815–20 to study gaols. He settled at Brighton in 1822 and formed a partnership with Wilds, who had carried on a builder's business at Lewes before moving to Brighton *c.*1815. The partners were responsible for much of Kemp Town and the Hove development, i.e. the principal sea-front developments. The sea-front faithful users of *The Buildings of England* will have to walk is about four miles long. In the course of the C19 the select Brighton became the people's Brighton, and now on an estimate between May and September three million visitors arrive by rail and between June and August four million by coach. The population was 7,339 in 1801, 65,569 in 1851, 102,320 in 1901, 163,000 in 1961.

But the Brighton for the architectural visitor who may well choose to come out of season is not Regency Brighton only. There is Victorian Brighton as well, and this is no less rewarding, though far less familiar. The principal buildings are churches, and in the centre of the ecclesiastical *fleuraison* stands Father Arthur Wagner (1825–1902), stout, genial, and very rich. He was the son of H. M. Wagner, vicar of Brighton from 1824 to 1870, who built St Paul for his son, and the church was completed in 1848, before the son was actually ordained. Arthur Wagner was a ritualist like John Mason Neale (*see* East Grinstead, p. 493) and was attacked as such, summoned to the Jerusalem Chamber and even beaten up. Nothing could however break his mild determination. For the poor people of the expanding Brighton he built, all out of his own pocket, St Mary Magdalene (1862), now demolished, The Annunciation (1864), the tremendous St Bartholomew (1872–4), the Resurrection (1875), now demolished, and St Martin (1874–5). The latter was built in memory of H. M. Wagner, and Arthur Wagner shared the cost with his family. He commissioned *Bodley* at the start – a good choice – then the local architect, *E. Scott* (for St Bartholomew), and *R. H. Carpenter*, son of the architect of St Paul. St Martin is by *Somers Clarke*. Somers Clarke also built the chancel of St Peter, and *Bodley* had introduced himself to Brighton by St Michael of 1858–61. But the bulk of the church was designed by *Burges* and built posthumously in 1893. *Pearson's* is the superb All Saints of 1890–1 and also St Barnabas. In short, it is evident that Brighton deserves extensive Victorian exploration.

CHURCHES

ST NICHOLAS, the parish church of Brighton. On a hill outside the old town. It is a C14 flint church, but only the low embattled tower can really be called C14. The rest was too severely restored by *Carpenter* in 1853 for the Rev. H. M. Wagner. Five bays, octagonal piers, double-chamfered arches. The clerestory is of 1892. Two-bay s chapel with typical C14 mouldings. The pier has the equally typical four shafts and four hollows. – FONT. The best piece of Norman carving in 13a Sussex. The font is drum-shaped and seems to date from *c.*1160–70. The representations are the Last Supper, very nobly and severely composed, St Nicholas and the Ship, another scene referring to St Nicholas, and the Baptism of Christ, the latter under three narrow arches. Brighton belonged to Lewes Priory, and that may explain the high quality of the workmanship. The style is reminiscent of North Italy (Pontile, Modena). – FONT COVER or WELLINGTON MEMORIAL. By *Carpenter*, and carved by *John Birnie Philip*, 1853. A towering hexagonal piece inspired by the Eleanor Crosses and executed with the highest elaboration. It is now banished into a corner but deserves better treatment. – SCREEN. Said to be partly old. Wide single ogee openings, crocketed. – PAINTING. On W and E walls and otherwise. By *Kempe* to the design of *Somers Clarke*, 1892, and very good it is, with long foliate trails, angels, etc. – STAINED GLASS. Much by *Kempe*. In the s aisle as early as 1878, and with more colour than later, if deep colour. – The rest of what he did is 1879–87, except for the tower window of 1897. – PLATE. Flagon and two Almsdishes, 1823. – MONUMENTS. Frances Crosbie Fairfield † 1830. By *Sir Richard Westmacott*. An angel carries her up. – Lady Westmacott † 1834. Just an antique matronly bust. By her husband. – In the churchyard headstone to Phoebe Hessel † 1821 ('she served for many years as a private Soldier in the 5th Regt of Foot') and to S. Dunn and his wife † 1815 ('she was Peculiarly Distinguished as a bather in this Town nearly 70 Years').*

ALL SAINTS, Eaton Road, the new Hove parish church. A superb building by *Pearson*, 1890–1. Ashlar, with a SW tower left alas a stump. Side view with buttresses and the five-light s transept window. The N transept has three two-light windows and a large rose-window above, the chancel E three windows of two lights. Fine E end flanked by two turrets, but apsed s chapel. The style is that of the C13, the scale inside reminiscent of cathedrals. Piers of clustered shafts carry vaulting shafts, and these carry transverse stone arches. No vault except in the chancel and s chapel. – REREDOS. Sumptuously carved. This also was designed by *Pearson*. His son *F. L. Pearson* designed the ORGAN CASE (1905).

ALL SOULS, Eastern Road. 1834. Heavily classical; rendered. Developed along the street. Into the nave two doorways with Tuscan pilasters and pediments. To the W the main entrance with a turret over. Inside, galleries with thin columns and on thin columns. The chancel and the nave roof (with dormers) by *Edmund Scott*, 1879. – STAINED GLASS. Hol-

* I owe these two gems of inscriptions to Mr Reece Winstone.

beinish, or Swiss c16, in style. By *Kempe*, 1903 and 1906 (cf. Glynde).

St Andrew, Church Road, Hove. The old parish church of Hove was all but rebuilt in 1833–6 by *Basevi*. The church is neo-Norman and uninspired. Coursed flint. w tower with higher stair-turret. The chancel E.E. with lancets, and so is the interior. Round piers, stiff-leaf capitals. Kingpost roof. – STAINED GLASS. The E window by *Wailes*, 1851 (TK). – MONUMENTS. Mrs Yard † 1836. In a medallion an angel carries her heavenwards. – Lt Henry Sandeman † 1852. Baconish in style. Two kneeling female figures with a portrait medallion.

St Andrew, Waterloo Road, Hove. By *Barry*, 1827–8, i.e. 52a only three years after St Peter, but how different in style and learning. Barry here turns to the Italian Renaissance, a style for which he later became as famous as for his Gothic. His inspiration was France, where Quattrocento motifs occur already in Ledoux and Durand. In London the sensation was the Travellers' Club, but that was begun only in 1829. So St Andrew is the first-fruit of this change from Antiquity to the Renaissance which was to have such universal effects. As in the Travellers' (and the Attree Villa, *see* p. 455), Barry takes his cue from the Quattrocento. Later, in the Reform Club, it was to be Cinquecento. The façade of St Andrew is quite modest, of three bays only, and basically on the Georgian scheme with giant pilasters and a square turret on top. But the portal and the bell-openings are without any doubt Quattrocento, and so is the interior, in spite of later alterations. The chancel in its present form is by *Charles Barry Jun.* and dates from 1882. The BALDACCHINO however is by *Blacking* and of 1925. – STAINED GLASS. Good single figures in the side windows, probably of 1869. – (SANCTUARY LAMP. Called c14 and said to come from a French cathedral.) – PLATE. Almsdish, 1755; Two Cups, two Patens, a Paten on foot, and a Flagon, 1828. – MONUMENTS. Lord Charles Henry Somerset † 1831. A female figure with a wreath standing by an urn on a pedestal. – Sir George Dallas † 1833. Mourning woman by an altar. Both evidently by the same sculptor and conceived as companion pieces. The Dallas Monument is signed by *Ternouth*.

Annunciation, Washington Street. Built in 1864, and one of the Wagner churches (*see* p. 427). This one, like Bodley's destroyed St Mary Magdalene of 1862, is a modest church

See
p.
691
for a poor district, not, like St Bartholomew, an overwhelming
church for a poor district. The architect is unknown, and the
front is in fact mean rather than modest. But the interior is
truly modest, with wooden piers and much strutting – almost
like a New Zealand pioneers' church. And it glows with one
gem: *William Morris*'s E window of angels and the Annunciation, by Morris and *Burne-Jones*, 1866.*

ST AUGUSTINE, Stanford Avenue, Preston. 1896 by *G. E.
Streatfield*, the impressive E end of 1913.‡ Red brick, large,
and still unfinished to the w. Perp, with tall windows of two
lights. Perp piers inside too, and brick above. The nave cants
towards the chancel, and the chancel has a proper Gothic
ambulatory. Narrow chancel aisle between the chancel and
the apsed E chapel. Altogether a design of ambition and
personality. – STAINED GLASS. By *Kempe*, 1901 and 1902
(both s aisle).

ST BARNABAS, Sackville Road, Hove. 1882–3 by *Pearson*.
Flint and red brick, with a polygonal apse, transepts, and a
flèche. Grand transept windows with geometrical tracery.
The interior exposed yellow brick. Clerestory with inner
arcading in the chancel. Lady Chapel low, two bays deep and
two bays wide. – REREDOS. By *Bodley* (*& Garner*), 'a signal
example of that master's inability to harmonize his work with
that of other artists' (GR). – PLATE. Later C17 Almsdish.

ST BARTHOLOMEW, Ann Street. This is an unforgettable
experience. As far as East Sussex is concerned it may well be
the most moving of all churches. Yet it is Victorian, and it is
by a local architect, known to very few, *Edmund Scott*. He
did it for Father Wagner. So this tremendous church owes
its existence to an individual's munificence and devotion. The
church was built in 1872–4. It is Gothic, but of no historical
or local class. Plain brick throughout. The view from Ann
Street prepares for the impact to come. An immensely high
wall with nothing to relieve it, until the eye reaches high up
four lancets in a row and a gloriously large rose window.
The side to the w (ritual N) is as plain and relies as unhesi-
tatingly on lancets only. One enters, and there is this nave,
135 ft high, i.e. a good deal higher than Westminster Abbey
and nearly as high as, say, Palma Cathedral, and 58 ft wide.
The roof, a wagon roof with tie-beams, Italian rather than
English, disappears in darkness. There are no aisles. Indeed,

* Information kindly conveyed to me by Mr A. C. Sewter.
‡ *Sir T. G. Jackson* acted as consultant (G. Spain).

as at Albi (of which one may be reminded a little), internal
buttresses, forming very high and very narrow side chapels.
Only above that level is a kind of triforium of three slit lancets
per bay, and then at last follow the wide and tall clerestory
windows. There is no enrichment whatever, no mouldings,
no shafts, no ornamental carving. Scott had intended to continue the present nave into a chancel. Instead of that there
is now a bare E wall, but this and indeed the whole church
has received a decoration not in the initial spirit of Scott, but
of so high a quality as to stand up to it. It was gradually put
in between 1895 and 1910 and was designed by *Henry Wilson*,
Sedding's most brilliant pupil. What there is of metalwork is
purest Arts and Crafts of the very top quality, what there is
of variegated marbles is Byzantine, in the Westminster
Cathedral spirit and distinguished by surfaces and forms as
plain and direct as Scott's. Thus the CIBORIUM e.g. has
square pillars and an arch under a square top with no bases,
capitals, or mouldings.* In front of the ciborium are two
enormous CANDLESTICKS, plain round pillars, but on them
the candle-holders of convoluted metal forms as if they were
of 1960. – The COMMUNION RAIL is Arts and Crafts, brass
and enamel insets. – The LADY ALTAR (of 1902) has a figured
repoussé frontal and a CROSS again of the most resourceful
metalcraft. – The PULPIT and the FONT (of 1906 and 1908)
on the other hand are marble once more, ample and rich,
but plain.

BISHOP HANNINGTON MEMORIAL CHURCH, Holmes
Avenue, Hove. By *Sir E. Maufe*, 1938 etc. Historicism at its
latest and most simplified. Slender Gothic windows and an
Italian attached campanile. Whitewashed interior with steep
unmoulded Gothic arches, especially striking in the low aisle-
passages.

CHAPEL ROYAL, North Street. Built in 1793 and all but rebuilt
in 1882 by *Sir A. Blomfield*. Brick and terracotta, with round-
arched forms and a square corner tower. Inside, the impression is of a Nonconformist chapel. Square with square lantern.
Galleries round three sides with heavy, dark Gothic detail.
Instead of the fourth gallery the altar space.

CHRIST CHURCH, Montpelier Road. 1837-8 by *George Cheeseman*. Gothic, rendered, squeezed in between houses. Low w

* Behind it and to its l. and r. is MOSAIC work by *Hamilton Jackson*,
glittering in the C20 spotlight, but definitely not foreseen by Wilson let
alone Scott.

tower with big, clumsy pinnacles and a recessed spire. Incorrect tracery. Galleries inside, on clustered stone shafts and with clustered iron shafts. The interior was remodelled by *E. Scott* in 1886. This must include the clerestory and the roof.

ST GEORGE'S CHAPEL, St George's Road. 1824–5 by *C. A. Busby* for Kemp. A typical Regency church. Yellow brick, unrelieved, windows in two tiers. Entrance between unfluted Ionic giant columns *in antis*. Square bell turret with cupola. Inside, galleries round three sides on thin columns and with thin columns. Alterations 1890. – PLATE. Two Cups, two Patens on feet, a Flagon, and an Almsdish, 1825.

GOOD SHEPHERD, Dyke Road, Preston. 1921–2 by *E. P. Warren*, continued to the E in 1927. Mixed bricks, simple Gothic with dormers and a SW tower. Low and broad interior with very prettily decorated wagon roofs. Low aisle passages behind short square piers. – ORGAN CASE. By *W. H. R. Blacking*, as are other furnishings.

ST JOHN BAPTIST (R.C.), Bristol Road. 1835. By *William Hallett*(?). Three-bay façade with pediment and giant Corinthian columns *in antis*. The interior re-cast in 1890. –
53   SCULPTURE. Relief of the Baptism of Christ; life-size figures. By *John Edward Carew*, 1835. Remarkably good; in the Baroque tradition, not at all neo-classical. – By the same the MONUMENTS to Mrs Fitzherbert † 1837, a large kneeling figure by a draped table with a bible, and to the Rev. Edward Cullin † 1850, with a profile at the top and palm fronds l. and r. below, and a big cherub's head at the foot (again Baroque, not classical).

ST JOHN EVANGELIST, Carlton Hill. 1840 by *George Cheeseman*, the façade restored by *L. A. Mackintosh*, 1957. A strangely bleak Late Georgian front with a recessed blank centre with giant Doric pilasters. Pedimented small entrances in the outer bays. Big metope frieze, not quite a pediment, and tiny bell-turret. This façade is to the S. But the interior is orientated. So one makes a right-about turn. Galleries on Greek Doric columns. Shallow, lower altar space, nicely decorated. The altar PAINTING Flemish, it seems, and *c.*1650.

ST JOHN AND ST PETER, Preston Road, Preston. Of stone. Long, with a flèche at the E end of the nave. Lancet windows. 1902 by *Sir A. Blomfield & Sons*. – PLATE. Cup and Cover, engraved 1569.

ST JOSEPH (R.C.), Elm Grove. 1866–9 by *W. Kedo Broder*, the E end 1881–3 by *J. S. Hansom*, modifying Broder's design.

The temporary w front by *Walters*, 1900 (GR). The church is in the E.E. style and very high. It was meant to be much longer. What there is, is most ambitious. An E end with a polygonal apse and two side apses, also polygonal, and, as they are of five sides of an octagon, they actually project beyond the transept end walls. The transept is two bays deep and long, i.e. has a tall round pier to divide its width. All details are disappointing.

St Luke, Queen's Park Road. 1881–5 by *Sir Arthur Blomfield*. Flint, E.E., with plate tracery. The sw tower not yet built. Spacious. Not attractive in the details, but curious for one design point. The aisle windows alternate between one tall and two very small, and there is a cross-gable over every tall one. Now the tall ones in the s aisle have small ones opposite in the N and *vice versa*, a disturbing motif.

St Luke, Stanford Road. 1875 by *John Hill*. Poor.

St Mark, Eastern Road. 1849. Terrible stone facing. w tower with recessed spire, lancet windows. Later s addition. Inside, thin cluster piers of iron.

St Martin, Lewes Road. By *Somers Clarke*, 1874–5. Built by Father Wagner in memory of his father (*see* p. 427). Yellow *See* and red brick, big forms, almost ruthless. Long, with a long $^{p.}_{691}$ row of tall clerestory windows, windowless aisles, a w front with large lancets, and no tower yet. Instead a bellcote on the E end of the nave. A wide, high interior with octagonal piers and brick arches. Decorated wagon roof. A wall-passage in front of the clerestory. – Very large REREDOS with paintings in several tiers. Made *c.*1875. By *H. Ellis Wooldridge*, with the carved figures by *Josef Mayer* of Oberammergau. – STAINED GLASS. E windows by *Powell*, designed by *Wooldridge*, 1874. Two small windows (s chapel, s aisle w) by *Powell*, designed by *Holiday*, 1875.

St Mary and St James, St James Street. 1877–9 by *Sir William Emerson*. Red brick, E.E. A tower meant to be built at the NW corner next to the low semicircular baptistery. Transepts; apse at the E end with a narrow ambulatory. The aisles to the streets with cross-gables. Inside, crossing, transepts, and apse are vaulted. – PLATE. Set, given in 1813, and Chalice and Paten, given in 1820. All silver-gilt, and all given by Nathaniel Kemp, uncle of Thomas Read Kemp (*see* p. 449).

St Mary (R.C.), Surrenden Road. 1912 by *Percy Lamb*. In a Gothic of Arts and Crafts licence in the details. The portal in the NW tower seems incomplete.

ST MATTHEW, Sutherland Road. 1881-3 by *John Norton*. Of mass concrete faced with flint outside, brick inside. E.E. On quite a large scale. The tower still incomplete. Wide nave and narrow aisles.

ST MICHAEL, Victoria Road. This church is the outcome of two campaigns. The splendid, soaring nave and N aisle are of 1893, C13 in style and cathedral-like, with a triforium and a clerestory tied together by detached inner arcading which repeats the tracery. Beautiful E end with three stepped two-light windows high up. All this was designed by *Burges* in 1865 and carried out after his death by *Chapple*. It is not like Burges, and may have been modified in execution. The S side of the church is an early work by *Bodley*, 1858-61, with its own S aisle and S chapel, the latter entered under an internal flying buttress. The old part is much humbler than the new, though with the rose-window composition at the W and E ends also not without distinction. The exterior on the other hand is bleak in the old part and in keeping with the old in the later part. Red brick, and stone windows with plate tracery. – In the new part Cosmati-type low SCREENS, marble
57b PULPIT. – In the old, exquisite STAINED GLASS by *William Morris*, i.e. his firm, established in 1861. Bodley was the first ecclesiastical client. The glass here in the older part is of *c.*1862-5. There are the small windows in the S chapel, a delight to see from so close by, and then in the grand W window with, in the rose, the Virgin in the centre and angels in the medallions around. Large figures below. Much brown, yellow, dark green. – PAINTING. *Morris* and *Webb* did the delightful painting of the roof with an all-over pattern. The painting of St Michael and angels in the W tympanum was done by a member of the congregation. – In the N aisle three windows by *Kempe*. – REREDOS in the S nave. An altarpiece with wings, early C16, Antwerp and worthy of being better known. – The big REREDOS in the chancel is by *Romaine*
See *Walker*. – PLATE. Jewelled Chalices, one gold, one silver, by
p. *Burges* and made by *Hardman*, 1861.*
691

ST PATRICK, Cambridge Road, Hove. Begun in 1858 to the design of *H. G. Kendall Jun*. Squeezed in between houses, its side to the street. Rock-faced, with the clerestory windows as dormers and a hammerbeam roof starting between them. – PULPIT. Designed by *Sir G. G. Scott*. Stone, with seated

* The Rev. E. G. Ogden also tells me of a C14 Crucifix, a Flemish C15 Processional Cross, and an Italian C15 Chalice.

figures. – LECTERN. Designed by *Butterfield*. A brass eagle
and, at the foot, St Patrick and three round towers. – STAINED
GLASS. Most of it of *c.*1860–70. – PLATE. Almsdish, *c.*1616–
42.

ST PAUL, West Street. 1846–8 by *R. C. Carpenter*. Built by the
Rev. H. M. Wagner, Vicar of Brighton from 1824 to 1870 and
father of Arthur Wagner. To the street the chancel end and
the tall tower with an octagonal timber bell-stage and spirelet. See p. 691
It was meant to be of stone, but is in its present form also a
beacon in Brighton. The narthex is by *Bodley*, 1874. The long,
plain wooden passage from the street to the church entrance
by Carpenter, but entirely remodelled by *Denman*. The
interior is humble. No fuss, no enrichments. Quatrefoil piers,
double-chamfered arches, bare spandrels. Steep roof, with
high arched braces and wind-braces. – SCREEN. By *Bodley*.
With loft and rood. – PAINTINGS. The retable behind the
altar is by *Burne-Jones*, of 1861, i.e. when Burne-Jones was
still very young. He was recommended by Bodley, who had
been commissioned to design the reredos himself. Annunciation and Adoration of the Magi. One of the Magi is a portrait
of William Morris; Burne-Jones and Swinburne are among
the shepherds. – The retable in the S aisle is Flemish, early
C16. – Wall painting above the chancel arch, by *Bell*, a pupil
of Bodley, the style still reminiscent of Dyce. Recently
restored. – Nice decorative painting of the chancel roof by
Bodley. – STAINED GLASS. Much by *Pugin*, 1848, made by
Hardman, especially the E window, the chancel side windows,
the aisle windows, and the S chapel E window. The colours of
the windows have been 'toned down' later, e.g. by Bodley. –
Also glass by *Kempe*, 1887, in the chapel of the Holy Spirit
and in the narthex. – (PROCESSIONAL CROSS. C15; silvered
brass, said to be Flemish.) – MONUMENT. *William Bainbridge
Reynolds* † 1935 and wife. No doubt by himself. An angel
holding a banner and a coat of arms in coloured enamel.*

ST PETER, Victoria Gardens. 1824–8 by *Sir Charles Barry*. 52b
Won in competition when he was still under thirty. It is a
large church and undoubtedly impressive. It is still entirely
pre-archaeological and remedies this fault by remarkable
inventiveness and boldness. The tower, facing S down to the
Steine and the sea e.g., has in its lower part to S, E, and W giant
recesses with the doorways and main windows set in and

---

* Mr McHardy drew my attention to this plaque.

manages the upper part by setting it back behind four big pinnacles with flying buttresses attached to them. The ashlar work is fine, and there is plenty of Perp decoration. Barry designed a spire in 1841, but this was never built. The side windows are Perp too, and here the Commissioners' conventions are unmistakable. Buttresses with pinnacles. Tall Perp windows of three lights horizontally subdivided – in this case by transoms with panel tracery below to house the galleries which the interior originally possessed. The interior is very high and wide. The piers are thin, and the aisles without their galleries are very high too. Nave and aisles are or rather appear vaulted. The vault is of plaster. At the (ritual) W end the nave is canted towards the tower. Barry's polygonal apse was removed and a much larger chancel was built by *Somers Clarke & Micklethwaite* in 1900–6, an impressive job in itself, though not a happy ending to Barry's church. Eleven-light E window, four-light S chapel windows, three-light clerestory windows. – STAINED GLASS. Much by *Kempe*, e.g. S aisle, 1882, the others 1898–1906. – PLATE. Flagon, 1824; two Cups, two Patens on feet, and four Plates, 1825. – MONUMENTS. Joseph Allen † 1831. Bust and drapery. – Caroline Lancey † 1897, yet still the motif of the angel carrying her heavenward: only now it is done in small detached figures.

ST PETER (R.C.), Portland Road, Hove. 1915 by *Marshall*. Red brick, Early Christian, with a campanile. Basilican interior with Tuscan columns, an apse with marble pilasters, and a tunnel-vault with penetrations.

ST SAVIOUR, Ditchling Road, Preston. Of 1886, by *Scott & Cawthorn*. Flint and brick, the tower to be at the SE corner. Inside, very large REREDOS with the Ascension in life-size figures. The relief is under a gable on grey and pink polished marble shafts, E.E., but the gable motif rather reminiscent of Italy about 1300. The reredos was intended for Chichester Cathedral. It is by *Slater & Carpenter*, of 1870.

ST STEPHEN, Montpelier Place. *See* p. 452.

ST THOMAS, Davigdor Road, Hove. 1913 by *Clayton & Black*. Inconspicuous red-brick exterior. Inside, instead of aisles, internal buttresses with passages through.

HOLY TRINITY, Blatchington Road, Hove. 1862–4 by *James Woodman* (GR). Red brick, with yellow and black bricks. S porch tower, apse; heavy-handed. No special interest inside.

HOLY TRINITY, Ship Street. The façade now Gothic with a thin W (E) tower. But inside still the chapel built by *A. H.*

Wilds for Thomas Read Kemp's own sect in 1817. Oblong with galleries on columns and with columns. Open roof. The chancel with the triplet of round-headed lancets of 1866–70. Its long side externally with blank round-headed arcading.

ST WILFRID, Elm Grove. By *H. S. Goodhart-Rendel*, 1933–4. Red brick, of as original an exterior grouping as is the interior. The climax is a tower with saddleback roof which stands over the chancel space. It has two tall segment-headed windows to N and S (ritually). The altar space is somewhat lower and separated by a lintel, not an arch. At the same level a lintel separates to the W (ritually) the nave from the chancel. The nave has a canted concrete roof, internal buttresses, and very low aisles, differing S from N. All windows are segment-headed. The W end rises by steps to a kind of platform, and added to this is the baptistery, appearing outside as a canted windowless front. The building does not imitate any style of the past, nor indeed the modern style of 1930, as the Continent had developed it. Its originality and resourcefulness are equally remarkable. – PAINTING. The NW chapel was painted by *Hans Feibusch* in 1941.

NONCONFORMIST CHAPELS

BAPTIST CHURCH, Regency Road. 1834. Arched windows on two storeys. Front with unfluted Ionic pilasters. – PULPIT. On a pedestal; in the form of a lyre.

CHRIST CHURCH (UNITARIAN), New Road. 1830 by *A. H. Wilds*. Greek Doric, tetrastyle, stuccoed.

THE DIALS CONGREGATIONAL CHURCH, Dyke Road. 1870 by *T. Simpson* (GS). Auditorium shape with Transitional details, very uncouth and with a Late Romanesque Rhineland tower, 130 ft high.

ELIM FREE CHURCH, Union Street. 1825 by *Amon Wilds Sen.* Very Grecian, especially the door and window surrounds, but with the middle three bays emphasized by Doric pilasters carrying a pediment. Semicircular interior.

FIRST CHURCH OF CHRIST, SCIENTIST, Montpelier Road. A private house of *c*.1850 converted in 1921 by *Clayton & Black*. The giant pilasters and other details of *c*.1850, the rest 1921.

FRIENDS' MEETING HOUSE, Ship Street. 1811. Brick. The centre of three bays with pediment, but the details unmistakably Victorian. There were indeed alterations *c*.1850, and the l. part dates from 1876.

PRESBYTERIAN CHURCH, Queen's Road. 1825. The church
lies far back from the street. This is a remarkably original
version of the universal chapel theme. Four bays, giant
pilasters. Bays one and four have the doorways (with Tuscan
columns) and pediments at the top. In the middle on the
ground floor two basically Venetian windows, but in fact they
are just round-headed and have columns l. and r. which
carry an outer blank arch.

PROVIDENCE CHAPEL, Church Street. 1803. Plain, chequer
brick, with a vestigial pediment.

SALEM CHAPEL, Bond Street. 1861. On the way from the old
Classical to the Italianate.

SYNAGOGUE, Lansdowne Road, Hove. By *Edward Lewis*, 1938.
A remodelling. Small, and a typical piece of the so-called
International Style of the thirties. White, with an asymmetrically placed entrance and an asymmetrically placed
window-band.

UNION CHURCH, Air Street. 1854 by *James & Brown*. Large;
E.E. A restless group, the tower not yet built.

PUBLIC BUILDINGS

ROYAL PAVILION. The Prince of Wales had met Mrs Fitzherbert in 1784 and secretly married her in 1785. She took a
house at Brighton, and he, in 1786, leased from Thomas Read
Kemp Senior a farmhouse facing the Steine. This in 1786–7
he had converted and enlarged into a Marine Pavilion by
Henry Holland, the most refined of architects in London then.
He repeated the farmhouse and connected the two buildings
by a rotunda with two apsidal extensions. To the outside the
rotunda came forward and had a detached colonnade, and
each wing had a pair of shallow bows – parents to many at
Brighton. A shallow dome on the rotunda showed to the outside too. The rotunda had one tall storey, the wings two.
The first addition to this villa came in 1804–8. It was the
Riding House and Stables. They covered an area much
larger than the house and they included a dome very much
larger. The architect was *William Porden*, a pupil of S. P.
Cockerell, then about fifty years of age. Cockerell had begun
a house for his brother in Gloucestershire, Sezincote, about
1805, and this, since his brother had made a good deal of
money in India, was in the Indian style, i.e. a Mahometan-
Indian not a Hindoo-Indian, although the style was later
often called Hindoo. Sir William Chambers in the gardens of

Kew had already had a mosque and an Alhambra as early as
about 1760 side by side with classical temples, a ruin, and a
Chinese pagoda. Those were the years of the most *insouciant*
playing with the forms of other peoples, and by the 1790s
they were on the whole over. Uvedale Price took his Picturesque more seriously, and the Goths their Gothic forms
and Gothic connotations. For Indian forms indeed in those
years more accurate information could not be got. William
Hodges' *Views of India* came out in 1786 and Thomas
and William Daniell's far more attractive *Views of Oriental
Scenery* began to appear in 1795. In fact, on the strength of
his intimate knowledge of India Thomas Daniell himself,
though not an architect, had designed a Warren Hastings
Memorial at Melchet Park in 1802 in the form of a miniature
Indian temple. Porden may well have received his initial idea
from Daniell and not from Sezincote; for he exhibited at the
Royal Academy a 'Design for a Place of Public Entertainment in the style of the Mahometan architecture of Hindo-
stan' as early as 1797.

The prince must have been tickled by this design and
thought that what suited a place of public entertainment
would be eminently suited for one of private entertainment.
He can have had no other reason for the choice than a craving
for novelty, in any case. For in 1802 already he had converted
Holland's chaste and elegant interiors into thorough-going
chinoiserie. What will Brighton, what will the visitors have
thought of it and thought of Porden's Dome? It is one thing
surely to build yourself a house in the style of a country you
have every reason to be partial to, and another to use the
style of any outlying, picturesque country, and it is one thing
to build the unexpected in your own grounds, another to put
it into a town, immediately side by side with normal houses?
Anyway, the Dome built, the Prince was so taken with it that
he began to consider a change for the Pavilion as well.
Humphry Repton, that most reasonable of landscape gardeners,
submitted drawings in 1805 for an Indian Pavilion, and they
were published in 1808. In the event nothing happened for
some years, lack of money being the reason, and when the
conversion and enlargement was finally carried out, the
Prince's favourite architect *John Nash* was chosen. The result
of Nash's work in 1815–22 is the Pavilion as we have it now. 48b

Nash kept the shape of Holland's building entirely and
only threw his fancy dress over it, and he added as outer

pavilions larger rooms than any so far. The fancy dress was, as fancy dress should be, not pedantically correct. Nash was not a scholar, and as one examines the Steine side as well as the entrance side, one is struck by the mixture of motifs and allusions. Basically of course the classical scheme was not given up: central motif, angle motifs, unstressed links between them. But the Prince and Nash could not tolerate anything unstressed, and so in addition to the capital dome and the naughty pagoda roofs of the angle pavilions each of Holland's four shallow bows, two l., two r., received another two domes. The entrance is not symmetrical, owing to the interference of houses on the s side. Its centre here is a deep *porte-cochère*, not an Indian nor a Mahometan motif. And similarly, though the scalloped arches ending in an ogee tip, as Porden had introduced them and Nash taken them over, are Islamic, they are also at once reminiscent of the Gothick. Indeed the most curious of all features is that in places Nash has frankly Gothic friezes of cusped lozenges, a motif familiar from Perp parapets. The domes of course are Indian, the pinnacles are Indian, and the columns starting bulbously and ending in lotus shapes are Indian too. The mixture appears at its gayest from the Steine, piquant, varied, not too big. It needs a high finish, and this after the Second World War it has achieved.

The same applies to the interior. It has recently had much of its original furniture restored, all the original wall decorations are cleaned, much is copied afresh and carefully, and the two principal rooms are used for functions and entertainment. It is ideal for the Brighton of today; for it can be admired by the *cognoscenti* with a *penchant* for Victorian fantasies as much as by the Brighton *hoi polloi*. As a matter of fact it is vulgar – there is no denying it. The colours of the main rooms are rich, the forms heavy, the motifs startling. Such drapes, such pelmets no-one would expect to see before the Victorian Age. At the same time a staggering inventiveness has certainly gone into the furnishing. *Crace & Sons* are the firm which provided it. Take the Music Room. The colour scheme there is lacquer red and gold. The room is oblong, as is its companion, the Banqueting Room, and both consist of a central square with the additions a little lower and under grossly oversized convex (not concave) covings. In the Music Room they represent bamboo roofs and the centre has a dome on a low octagon. The dome is all gold fish-scales and black. The octagon has lunettes with glass painted with much brown and yellow. The same colours are those of the glass of the nine lustres, lit of course by gas. In the lustres above the glass you can spot water lilies and sunflowers. The wall paintings are by Crace's assistant *Lambert* and are of course Chinese, and indeed throughout the Pavilion it is the Chinese taste that re-asserts itself. The Chinese scenes are framed by painted columns with serpents coiling round them, and dragons are in the top corners. The four doorways have gilt columns and Chinese canopies. Big dragons again along the pelmet. Only the chimneypieces, like those in nearly all the rooms, are of the 1860s, a more solid, less convincing replacement. In the Banqueting Hall the dome is round and stands on four shallow glazed segmental lunettes. The wall decoration is Chinese again (by *Robert Jones*), the covings are black and gold with Chinese dragons, and the dome represents the blue sky with clouds – an entirely unoriental idea – and out of the centre lustre grows a glorious and monstrous tobacco plant. The illusion is made complete by four of the leaves being of bronze painted like the others. A silvered dragon below holds the lustre, which cost £5,613 and weighs nearly a ton. That is it: everything impresses by cost and by weight. Subtleties must not be expected, neither intellectual nor aesthetic.

For an entertainment that is fine; for habitation it was bound to fail, and George IV in fact never returned to Brighton after 1822.

Some other features of the Pavilion must be drawn attention to, even if, in the presence of excellent guide books, no room-to-room description is attempted. The Saloon, round with two apses, is in its space still noticeably Holland's. The Corridor, i.e. the gallery that runs through the middle of the house from Banqueting Room to Music Room, has at its two ends staircases, and they are of cast iron entirely, even the steps with pierced risers. The hand-rail has a bamboo pattern. Cast iron again is used in the Kitchen, where the traditional louvre stands on four slender shafts ending in palm fronds. It was one of the first times that iron was used for other than utilitarian purposes. But, while this is a feature pointing forward and while the whole of the interior points forward in style, in the intellectual attitude behind it, it points back into the Rococo. It is this combination of Rococo and Victorian that sends us. We, i.e. those of us who have grown up with the emotional appreciation of the International Style of the 1930s and the more intellectual appreciation of the finesses

of Georgian proportion, details, and craftsmanship, may well
laugh at first, but then a feeling of intoxication will follow.
There is in the end a great release in looking at and walking
about in this folly, and so we stop asking questions.

With all the paraphernalia, i.e. the estate and the other
buildings and all the furnishings, it cost just over half a
million pounds.

The other buildings are these: the KITCHENS to the S,
Doric of all styles and discussed on p. 447, the NORTH GATE,
added in 1832, entirely in the spirit of the Pavilion, NORTH
GATE HOUSE, a perfectly harmless house with a pair of centre
bays which was hindooed-up as naïvely as Horace Walpole
gothicked the toy-house he had bought at Strawberry Hill,
before he got down in earnest to building a Gothic manor,
the SOUTH GATE, added in 1921 in a much more substantial
and correct and less enjoyable Indian, and finally the Dome.

The DOME was, as we have seen, built first. It is Indian
in its details but fails entirely in that lightheartedness or, if
you like, jollity which the Prince must have wished to express
and which Nash succeeded in expressing. It is a big block of
yellow brick, and one never gets over noticing that. Towards
the Pavilion, it is true, the dome dominates and the two wings
have big Indian windows. But towards the sides – and the
building has much depth – it is all just utilitarian, and
towards the N, as street architecture, it is monotonous and
heavy, especially the centre with its two rows of windows, no
more genuinely or playfully Indian than Wilkins's front of
Corpus Christi College at Cambridge is Gothic. The dome as
such was a constructional feat, even though the technique
was taken over from Belanger's Corn Exchange of 1782 in
Paris. The materials are wood and glass, and the diameter is
80 ft. There were originally forty-four stalls around, and on
the gallery were the ostlers' and grooms' quarters. In one of
the wings was the Riding School, 178 ft long, in the other
was meant to be a Tennis Court. In the event the Stables
were extended instead. The Riding School as a room still exists,
the Dome was converted in 1935 into a concert hall.

TOWN HALL, Market Place. 1830–2 by *Thomas Cooper*. The
building is high and not happily placed. It has two fronts, to
N and W. Both have a portico in two orders, Greek Doric
below, Ionic above. A S wing to make the building cruciform
was never built. The main upper windows have pilaster
aedicules. Inside a remarkable staircase arrangement, dating

from 1899. The staircase rises in two stages straight through and then turns l. and r. at the end. The first floor has heavy Ionic columns all along the landing gallery. Beyond the staircase a glazed court with a gallery round and a bridge between the stair part and the court part. Also, the staircase goes up to the second floor, repeating the pattern but this time flying. It is all both intricate and airy. – REGALIA. Mayor's Chain, C17. Presented in 1855.

TOWN HALL, Church Road, Hove. 1882 by *Waterhouse*. Unmistakable: so red, so Gothic, so hard, so imperishable. Brick and terracotta, symmetrical with a middle tower. L. and r. gables and between them and the tower five dormers each side. A characteristic predilection for panels with lozenge or trellis decoration, a Norman and E.E. motif.

MUSEUM AND ART GALLERY. *See* Royal Pavilion.

HOVE MUSEUM (Brooker Hall), New Church Road. 1876. An Italianate villa with asymmetrical tower.

LIBRARY. *See* Royal Pavilion.

BRIGHTON COLLEGE. The original buildings are of 1848 by *G. G. Scott*, flint with stone dressings, symmetrical and joyless, with small Gothic two-light windows and larger ones with geometrical tracery, steep gables and dormers. The Headmaster's House followed in 1854, the Chapel in 1859, the Hall in 1863, all these by *Scott*, and the grand S range in 1886–7 to designs of *Sir T. G. Jackson*. This is of brick and terracotta, also Gothic and more lavishly so, especially in the details of the gateway.

WHITTINGHAME COLLEGE, Surrendon Road, Preston Park. By *Vivien Pilley*, 1936. An excellent job and early for its style and function, at least as far as England is concerned. It is for 100 boarders and cost no more than £16,000. Long, white main block of two storeys, reinforced concrete, with staffroom, common rooms, dining room. Fine spiral staircase in the middle. This leads up to the dormitories. On the N side the separate assembly-hall and gymnasium. Single-storeyed class-rooms project at r. angles to the S front.

COLLEGE OF TECHNOLOGY, Lewes Road. 1962–4 by *P. Billington*, the Borough Engineer, with *Sir Robert Matthew & S. A. W. Johnson-Marshall* as consultants. T-shaped, with a low and a high range. All windows in raised concrete frames.

MUNICIPAL SCHOOL OF ART, the old building in Grand Parade. 1876–7 by *John George Gibbins* (GS). In an Italianate Trecento style. Only five bays, with a round-headed portal

with granite columns and two terracotta reliefs of artistic putti
higher up.

GRAMMAR SCHOOL, Old Shoreham Road. 1911 by *J. B. Russell*.
Neo-Early-Georgian. Red brick. The connexion between
centre and wings by staircase links all with circular windows.

ST MARY'S HALL, Eastern Road. Built as a school in 1836.
Designed by *Basevi*. Symmetrical, Early Tudor, with gables
and mullioned and transomed windows.

BRIGHTON GENERAL HOSPITAL (the former WORKHOUSE),
Elm Grove. 1865–7, by *George Maynard*. (A late date for a
workhouse.) Italianate, four storeys, a long front with a
thoroughly debased turret. Later additions.

ROYAL SUSSEX COUNTY HOSPITAL, Eastern Road. The
original part by *Sir Charles Barry*, 1828. Four storeys;
rendered. Seven bays, pedimented three-bay centre. The
centre is at the end of a vista from the sea-front down Paston
Place. Many additions.

MARKET HALL, opposite the Town Hall. 1900 by *F. J. C. May*,
the Borough Engineer. Terracotta and, even in the lettering,
somewhat like the London underground in the same years.

CORN EXCHANGE. *See* Royal Pavilion.

PALACE PIER. 1898–9. The landward palace with a low glass
dome. Several pagoda roofs around.

PERAMBULATIONS

(A) *The Old Town and the Steine*

This comprises the area between West Street, North Street, East Street, and the sea. The walk starts from the Pavilion, the spiritual centre of Brighton. NORTH STREET is just the shopping street of a town the size of Brighton. The CLARENCE HOTEL on the l. is of eight bays and three and a half storeys, quite plain, with a Tuscan porch, probably in this form of *c.*1820–30 and not Old Town in character. Opposite, the PRUDENTIAL BUILDINGS, red brick with late C17 gables, by *Waterhouse* of course; 1904. Also in North Street the ALLIANCE BUILDING SOCIETY, by *H. S. Goodhart-Rendel*, 1935, a big steel-framed corner block with a circular top at the corner. The framing is rationally exposed. The building dates from the years when Goodhart-Rendel had been unmistakably impressed by the International Modern style. So to the CLOCK TOWER, of 1888, worthless, with granite columns and pediments below, Gothic above, and with portraits of Victoria and Albert, the Prince of Wales and Alexandra. Down WEST STREET again mainly shopping. The MERMAID with lush carving, the details reminiscent of Treadwell & Martin, and one house (No. 77) of two storeys with a pair of shallow bow windows such as we shall see so often. Original cast-iron lamps in front. This is probably early C19. In the streets E of West Street little of note. In SHIP STREET several attractive houses with pairs of bows and early C19 doorcases (Nos 15, 9, 7), and at the end, just before the front, HENEKEY'S, wonderfully phony, even with a portcullis. At the junction with PRINCE ALBERT STREET, next to the Friends' Meeting House, a five-bay brick house of two and a half storeys with a heavy Tuscan porch. Another opposite with a pedimented doorway. This is on a curve, and the curve is continued in a terrace of houses with the shallow bows. The CRICKETERS' ARMS close by (Black Lion Street) has a pair of them too. These old streets are still connected by LANES, that is narrow pedestrian passages. In EAST STREET more bows, and off East Street, close to the front, a little more of note, a shopfront in LITTLE EAST STREET (No. 6) and another in POOL VALLEY (No. 9). The house with this shop is faced with black mathematical tiles and has three canted bay windows above the ground floor. It was built in 1794, i.e. is ancient, as Brighton houses go.

The sea-front of the old town is of course sea-front and not old town. From West Street E there is first the VICTORIA HOTEL, by *Sly*, dated 1882, high and in the style of Sir Ernest George, then the OLD SHIP HOTEL, memorable because of the Assembly Room (now Card Room) behind. This was built in 1767 by *Robert Golden*. It has a handsome shallowly vaulted ceiling with discreet Adamish decoration, looking 1780 rather than 1767. The ballroom is of the same date but far too drastically remodelled. Then the QUEEN'S HOTEL, high, with three pairs of canted bays and giant pilasters whose entablature embraces one pair of bays.

So beyond East Street the PALACE PIER HOTEL with nice Regency balconies, the ADELPHI HOTEL, and the ROYAL ALBION HOTEL. Both originally faced towards the Old Steine (*see* below), the first with four giant pilasters stretching themselves painfully to comprise three storeys, the second now very large, but originally only the NE of what there is now, i.e. four storeys with six giant Corinthian columns in the middle and three plus three giant pilasters l. and r. The pilasters are taken round to the E side as well. In the attic storey windows with blank arches, and in these shells. This is one of the hallmarks of *Amon Henry Wilds*. The hotel then grew in breadth and height. A Greek Doric porch on the W side. The Adelphi Hotel has a porch of heavy Tuscan columns coupled towards the sea. The Royal Albion was built in 1826, partly on the site of Dr Russell's house.

So to the OLD STEINE. This was a common with a stream running down it. In 1793, after the Prince had built his Marine Pavilion, the Steine was improved and the stream put underground. In the centre is a FOUNTAIN by *A. H. Wilds*. It has three intertwined dolphins. Further N is the bronze STATUE of George IV, by *Chantrey*, erected in 1828. Close to the Adelphi Hotel is ROYAL YORK BUILDINGS, the former Royal York Hotel, the first on the new scale. It stands on the site of the C18 manor house of Brighthelmstone and was built in 1819, it is not known by whom. It is also of four storeys and an attic and has a pair of bows and a porch of pairs of Greek Doric columns. The principal mullions of

the windows are prettily reeded. On the w side of the Steine
Nos 44–46 are late c18, three-storeyed only and with canted
bays. Then the finest house in Brighton, MARLBOROUGH
HOUSE, designed in 1786 by *Robert Adam*. This has a nicely
balanced front and a delicately detailed doorway, with Roman
Doric columns and pediments, and one would wish that
Brighton architects had looked at it more closely than at
Nash's terraces. The façade is of five bays and two storeys,
stuccoed. It has pediments l. and r. and windows on the
ground floor under them with the Adam variety of the Venetian type, i.e. like a Venetian window but with a blank band
making the whole into a round-arched feature. Amply spaced
windows between these two and the doorway. The original
interiors have nice ceilings and chimneypieces. The room to
the r. of the entrance has a groin-vault with wreaths playing
round the ridges and segmental lunettes. The back room has
its corners canted, and in these diagonal fan-decoration. The
same in the panelled ceiling, and also Wedgwood-like plaques.
Mrs Fitzherbert's house, now the Y.M.C.A., was built by
Porden in 1804. It is sadly transformed outside, but inside it
has the original staircase, of cast iron, with a cast-iron
balustrade on the model of those in the Royal Pavilion. Fret
patterns.

After that CASTLE SQUARE, named after the Castle Inn (*see*
p. 452), not a castle. No. 5 deserves a look. Off into PALACE
PLACE, with a kitchen attachment to the Pavilion with Doric
pilasters and a pediment. It was built in 1816. Then off, a
little further w, into NEW ROAD, which faces the Pavilion
Gardens. Here again some nice houses, e.g. No. 23, with an
iron veranda with Ionic openwork pilasters, the PARIS
CINEMA, florid Victorian of 1892, and a view at the end
towards the CENTRAL SCHOOL of 1830, stuccoed and
Gothic of three bays only but quite stately.

To the N we do not go into Victoria Gardens yet. The houses
on the E side of the Steine are nearly all of *c.*1800, though
many were refronted in the great twenties. The N half is
called PAVILION PARADE. It is an enjoyable lot, many with
balconies, some with verandas, and most of them with doorways with broken pediments. Nos 3–4 is cobbled and tarred,
a Brighton custom, reminiscent of a more rustic and reasonable past. In the OLD STEINE No. 3, facing s, is a really
unchanged house of *c.*1790, three-storeyed only and cobbled
with brick dressings. No. 26 was refronted by *A. H. Wilds*

and introduces us to the ammonite capitals which he favoured.
The form had been introduced by Dance, and Wilds no doubt
took to it because of his name Amon. He used it for the first
time in Castle Gate, Lewes, before he moved to Brighton.
The house is bow-fronted and has a Greek Doric doorway.

(B) *The Sea-front East of the Old Steine and the area immediately
behind it*

The start is not promising. Off into MANCHESTER STREET for
No. 10, with only three storeys, black mathematical tiles, and
a pair of bows – *c.*1800 (now Golden Girl Café). Off into
CAMELFORD STREET for some real, entirely unselfconscious
cottages. In MARINE PARADE the themes are familiar, bows
and balconies chiefly. Building went on in the twenties. Only
occasionally a feature, successful or more often otherwise,
strikes one as out of the ordinary. Nos 41–43 has bows and
giant pilasters connected by blank arches and coupled doors
with three Doric columns. No. 54 has giant Corinthian
pilasters, No. 70 (CREST HOTEL) is a sub-Norman-Shavian
intrusion by Col. *Edis*, 1879–80, knapped flint, red-brick,
tile-hanging, a gable. Nos 80–83 has the second and third
floors (rather incongruously) tied together by giant pilasters.
Then an earlier interruption, the ROYAL CRESCENT, built
in 1798–1807, the earliest unified composition of Brighton, a
crescent because of Bath and Buxton, and the earliest demonstration of a sympathy with sea and beach. It is a shallow
quadrant, and the houses are faced with black mathematical
tiles. They have four storeys, canted bay windows, first-floor
verandas, and doorways mostly with broken pediments. Nos
102–104 have bows and giant Ionic pilasters squeezed into the
valleys. In BLOOMSBURY PLACE balconies run all along
both sides quite consistently. In MARINE SQUARE on the
other hand all manner of balconies and verandas. One house
even has balconies on three floors. Nos 129–133 is the first
more consistent composition, with giant Corinthian pilasters
as accents; and we are indeed approaching Kemp Town. But
first PORTLAND PLACE, the whole again one composition. It
is by *Busby*, 1824–8. PEARSON HOUSE in St George's Road,
at the end of Portland Place, however, is of a different brand
of classical, no orders, but window pediments. It is in fact a
replacement after a fire of the original grand mansion that
stood here and had a detached giant portico of six Corinthian
columns. At once more away from the front into PASTON

PLACE, to the SASSOON MAUSOLEUM, now the Bombay
Bar. This was built during his lifetime by Sir Albert Sassoon
in 1892, and he was buried in it as was his son. It is a curious
little building, square with a pagoda roof and Indian details,
Royal Pavilion in inspiration, but here used for a serious
purpose and by a man who could claim connexion with
India, which the Regent could not. Anywhere but at Brighton
this mausoleum might have been considered appropriate.

So to the facts about KEMP TOWN. Thomas Read Kemp came
of a Lewes family. His father had been High Sheriff of Sussex
and Member of Parliament for Lewes. He was joint lord of
the manor of Brighton. His son of the same name inherited
the manor, became a dissenting minister in 1816, a Member
of Parliament in 1823, left England in 1837, and died in
1844. He started Kemp Town in 1823, and the scale was
certainly differently from what Brighton had seen until
then. His architects were *Wilds* and *Busby*. Among the builders
was Thomas Cubitt, whose own Brighton house was in
Lewes Crescent. The pattern of the terraces is Regent's Park,
but the details are coarser, the accents nearly always too weak,
and the panache of Regent's Park is lacking. First EASTERN
TERRACE of *c*.1828, one composition, no features.* Then
PERCIVAL TERRACE, all bows and decidedly monotonous,
ten houses, five storeys, and as late as the mid forties. After
that CLARENDON TERRACE, six houses, also broad and yet
a little later. CHICHESTER TERRACE has all deep Greek
Doric porches carrying enclosed verandas. So to LEWES
CRESCENT and SUSSEX SQUARE. Kemp's own house (after
the Folly, *see* p. 452) was No. 22 Sussex Square. The Crescent
and the Square are so large that one cannot read the façades
together (a failing found contemporarily in Belgrave Square
in London). Moreover they never go beyond giant pilasters
to place accents. The landscaping looks wind-swept, as well
it may, but as perhaps it was not meant to. Below, reached by
ramps, at the lower level of the ESPLANADE and neglected
at the time of writing, is the entrance to a TUNNEL, leading
from the beach to the square. It is flanked by cottages, and
the whole has a front with arched entrances and Tuscan
pilasters. At a lower level yet the former READING ROOM
with coupled Tuscan pilasters, the middle ones thinner than
the others. The architect is *H. E. Kendall* and the date
1828–40. Up to the road again and finally ARUNDEL TER-

* In No. 1 a complicated and sumptuous staircase (NBR).

RACE, the only one where giant Corinthian columns appear, and thus a proper building up of effects. Arundel Terrace was built in 1825–8. The total of the terrace is thirty-nine bays, and the accents go from attached columns by way of recessed attached columns to detached columns. After Arundel Terrace Brighton is at an end. One looks out to a dreary institution of 1898 (Maison de Convalescence Française), a large new block of flats, MARINE GATE, and Roedean School.

(c) *The Sea-front West of the Old Town and the areas immediately behind it*

The beginning on this side is desolation. Then at once the two swagger Victorian hotels. The GRAND HOTEL, 1862–4, by *J. Whichcord*, is what was called Italian. Eight storeys with corner eminences and balconies in six tiers. It cost £57,000 to build. The METROPOLE HOTEL, 1888 by *Waterhouse*, on the other hand, is Waterhousish. Red brick and red terracotta. Five storeys and dormers. The porch and the top alterations are of 1961 and by *R. Seifert & Partners.** CANNON PLACE runs up between the two and returns us to the Brighton of the Brighton Age. The best house is Nos 31–32 by *A. H. Wilds*, built as an Assembly Room. The façade has two columns *in antis* with egyptianizing capitals and a pediment. This façade is turned towards St Margaret's Place. On to the N first into RUSSELL SQUARE, with nice Regency verandas, especially on the W and S sides, and then into CLARENCE SQUARE, where Nos 48–49 deserve a look. It is by *Wilds & Busby* of *c.*1825. Two storeys only, one bay each house, three giant fluted Ionic pilasters.

Back to the front, a mixed lot, with ABBOTTS, quite a good recent block of flats, by *Fitzroy Robinson & Partners*, 1961–2. Opposite the WEST PIER of 1863–6, lengthened in 1893. The pretty Rococo piece landward is no doubt of the earlier build. Away from the front again to REGENCY SQUARE, begun in 1818. On the l. at once a nice three-house group, each with two bows. The details are more sparing than is usual at Brighton. The rest of the square is all bows and verandas. The name of the square in the parapet at the far end is not enough of an accent to pull the square together. Then a block of flats of between the wars, architecturally without interest.

* They are now also engaged on the erection at the back of a Conference Hall and flats, i.e. a two-storeyed podium and a 300 ft tower.

Next up PRESTON STREET. No. 5a has a good shop-front
with Corinthian columns. No. 70 is a two-bay cottage with a
bow. The ROYAL SOVEREIGN INN has again a pair of bows.
   Back and at once the BEDFORD HOTEL, opened in 1829.
This was designed by *Thomas Cooper*. It is something special
at Brighton. Five wide bays with a recessed centre. In the
centre four fluted Ionic giant columns. Above two more
storeys with small Grecian motifs. The interior is special too.
Splendid two-storeyed centre hall with Ionic above Tuscan
columns, a glazed dome, and boldly-holed tympana. Staircase
with good cast-iron balustrade. To the w of the hotel Ionic
columns *in antis*, and, recessed, more w but again facing the
sea, a front of six bays with Corinthian giant pilasters. The
range repeats the other side of an opening (BURLEIGH HALL
HOTEL), and turns out to belong to CAVENDISH PLACE,
which carries on with the giant pilasters. Only the end is
different. The HOTEL CURZON is astylar. Six bays, pedimented first-floor windows. After that along the front the
KING'S HOTEL, three houses with porches of coupled Greek
Doric columns. Three bows and giant Corinthian pilasters
awkwardly placed. Next off into ORIENTAL PLACE, part of
an abortive bigger scheme with an Anthaeum or Flower Conservatory as its centre. Oriental Place is a long, symmetrical
composition. It was begun in 1825 and is typical *A. H. Wilds*,
with his ammonite capitals and his shells in blank window
arches. However – the same failing time and again – it is all
too flat to support a length of thirty bays. On into SILLWOOD
PLACE, also by *A. H. Wilds*, and also unified as a composition, again with giant pilasters. At the end a former private
house of four bays and three storeys with canted bays and
balconies running right through on two storeys. The whole
composition is of 1827–8. Next on the front ABINGER HOUSE,
neo-Georgian of 1956, and then into MONTPELIER ROAD.
This is a street of mixed cottages, and no special events. On
reaching WESTERN ROAD, turn r. and take in the GOTHIC
HOUSE (part of Messrs Plummer's; *c.*1822–5) by *A. Wilds &
Busby*, fanciful and irresponsibly Gothic, and the WESTERN
PAVILION, actually in WESTERN TERRACE, *A. H. Wilds*'s
own house of *c.*1827, the Pavilion's baby brother, complete
with dome and Hindoo details. In Western Terrace also the
N side of the end house of Sillwood Place, with giant pilasters
here carrying ammonite capitals. A little to the w and for a
moment down towards the front again a glance at the pairs

of emaciated giant pilasters in the descending row of the E side of HAMPTON PLACE. Then in Montpelier Road higher up Nos 53–56 are of value, again with *A. H. Wilds*'s ammonite pilasters, shell-tops to windows, and little wreaths. Opposite nice two-storeyed semi-detached villas. Higher up still to the l. in MONTPELIER PLACE the former church of ST STEPHEN, now Association for the Dumb. Behind the plain classical façade of presumably 1851, with pilasters, pediment, and cupola, remains what was originally the ballroom of the CASTLE INN, built by *John Crunden* in 1766. George IV bought it in 1821 and converted it into the Royal Chapel of the Pavilion. It was re-erected here in 1850. The ballroom is oblong and has a coved ceiling and arched windows. In the middle of each side is a recessed group of two columns between two pilasters. The pilasters are crisply decorated. The style is classical without anything of the Rococo.

Turn r. instead of l. and you will see in MONTPELIER VILLAS a specially charming series of semi-detached villas, each with a bow-veranda. Yet further N continue in Montpelier Road, and the PARK ROYAL HOTEL will remind you of the fact that you have now reached the 1840s at the earliest; for here is a Jacobean façade with three shaped gables. At the corner of Montpelier Road and TEMPLE GARDENS is the GIRLS' HIGH SCHOOL, including what remains of THE TEMPLE or Kemp's Folly, i.e. his own house, before he moved to Kemp Town. It was built in 1819, and the measurements were taken from Solomon's Temple. It is square and had on the ground floor to all sides colonnading of coupled columns, clearly of Pavilion derivation, though bleaker and carrying normal round arches. It has alas lost its crowning dome and its tall chimneys and with them much of its interest. The gateposts remain in their original state.

N once more, along Denmark Terrace, to MONTPELIER CRESCENT, built in 1843–7, not to one design. Some of the houses and groups of houses have *A. H. Wilds*'s wreaths, some his ammonite capitals. All around here, in CLIFTON HILL, CLIFTON ROAD, etc., one can find nice balconies of about 1830, and *The Builder** reports in 1849 of houses springing up E of Montpelier Crescent. From this expedition one can return via NORFOLK SQUARE with, on the s side, some starved Ionic pilasters, on the W side all bows, and NORFOLK ROAD, where No. 3 has a pair of bows, wreaths,

* So Mr Spain tells me.

and a honeysuckle frieze, and No. 32 at the corner of
WESTERN STREET a nice corner shop-front.

So back at last to the sea-front and back for a moment to BED-
FORD SQUARE of about 1810. This is a square without programme. Nos 27–31 are the best group, with bows and enough
space between them for coupled pilasters. No. 146 KING'S
ROAD has an Ionic colonnade carrying a veranda. The
NORFOLK HOTEL, 1864–5 by *Horatio Goulty*, is in imitation
of E. M. Barry's hotels, i.e. Charing Cross and Cannon Street,
with pavilion roofs. After that the first block of modern flats,
and a good and historically interesting one. It is called
EMBASSY COURT, and was built as early as 1934–5 and by
Wells Coates, fresh from the sensation which his Lawn Road
Flats in London had caused. He uses the same vocabulary
here, concrete-framing, long unbroken bands of concrete
between the windows and as balcony parapets, and the same
bands rising diagonally in tiers to express an outer staircase.
But, well designed in itself or otherwise, a modern block,
twelve storeys high, is a bad neighbour to the Regency, and
it is unfortunate that Wells Coates had to demonstrate his
style in the very place where the Brighton and Hove sea-front
becomes serious neo-classical architecture for the first time.
The development to which we now come belongs to the
years 1825–7, i.e. it follows Kemp Town immediately, and
like Kemp Town is the outcome of a good look at the Regent's
Park terraces. The enterprise was financed by the Rev.
Thomas Street, who owned the Wick Estate (*see* p. 456). The
architects were *A. Wilds & Busby* and mainly *Busby*. The
composition consists of the two terraces called BRUNSWICK
TERRACE and BRUNSWICK SQUARE between. Each of the
terraces is of thirty-nine bays, and the square is very large
too, though not as excessive as Lewes Crescent and Sussex
Square. The square is landscaped too. What distinguishes
the Hove or, as it was originally called, Brunswick Terrace
development from Kemp Town is that here – and Kemp
Town learnt this lesson only at Arundel Terrace – accents
have sufficient strength to articulate long rows of windows.
Both of the ranges of Brunswick Terrace are of three, not
four, storeys and have a centre of ten giant columns, and only
above this an extra storey as an attic instead of a pediment.
The end accents are giant pillar–column–column–pillar and
an attic too, and in between all has giant pilasters. That
gives enough relief – in both senses. The square tries the

same, not so successfully. Every second bow has giant Ionic columns, and every so often a bow-front has no order at all. The N parts of the sides of the square are different and later. But the N side must be original again, with a long row of giant pilasters and alas no accent.

If one continues N, one finds BRUNSWICK PLACE, two long rows of bow windows, completely without interruption, as far as the eye can reach. The same applies to LANSDOWNE PLACE, the next street to the W running up N. Both started about 1830 and took some fifteen or twenty years to complete.*

The next terrace on the front, after Lansdowne Place, can afford only giant pilasters for its thirty bays – a pity – but then follows something monumental again, even if of a different
3b character. It is the corner house to ADELAIDE CRESCENT, facing the sea with a terrace up steps. Eleven bays only, i.e. a mansion rather than a terrace, with a raised pediment. Some windows have pediments, there is a frieze of garlands below the pediment, and the first-floor windows have individual stone (stone-looking) balconies – i.e. away from the Regency to the neo-Renaissance. The top bracketing points in the same direction. The building is by *Decimus Burton* of London and Kemp Town and dates from 1833–4. In fact the bracketing of the eaves shows at once that we are on the way to the Victorian Age. There is no companion piece to this on the W side, and the Crescent itself and PALMEIRA SQUARE,‡ into which it merges by convex curves, are of little architectural merit, though of architectural interest, as they show the transition into the Italianate as clearly as contemporary work on the same scale N and S of Hyde Park in London. According to *The Builder*, Adelaide Crescent was in fact not complete in 1849, and Palmeira Square not yet in existence.§ But it is ST CATHERINE'S TERRACE which finally demonstrates the fall of the Regency; for here (interrupted by THE PRIORY, a recent block of flats) are Jacobean shaped gables, such as we have already seen in Montpelier Road.

* *The Builder* in 1849 says that the W side of Lansdowne Place is now built up (G. Spain).

‡ On the site now occupied by No. 13 PALMEIRA AVENUE was a Bronze Age ROUND BARROW. It covered a burial in a tree-trunk coffin accompanied by a stone battle-axe, bronze dagger with wooden sheath, perforated whetstone, and amber cup. The group belongs to the latter part of the Early Bronze Age Wessex Culture (see *Buildings of England: Wiltshire*) and may be dated *c.*1500–1400 B.C.

§ Information from Mr Spain. Palmeira incidentally refers to Sir Isaac Lion Goldsmid, Baron of Palmeira.

(D) *Outer Brighton*

The only area other than those already perambulated which makes sense, and a specific Brighton sense, is by VICTORIA GARDENS and St Peter's church, a number of terraces to its E, starting from where Pavilion Parade ended, i.e. with the GRAND PARADE. There are again the familiar bows and some mathematical tiles (9-13). No. 18 has two bows, a Greek Doric doorway, and giant pilasters above. That is home ground. Nothing special in Waterloo Place. Then Nos 1-3 RICHMOND TERRACE, yellow brick, stuccoed below, with four bows. Nos 4-6 is by *Amon Wilds Sen.* and of 1818. It is a piece on its own, a little raised by steps, and very prettily handled. Three bays, narrow, wide, narrow; giant Ionic pilasters. The middle entrance under a wide segmental arch. Above a tripartite window and a tripartite segmental lunette. The mullions are reeded as in the Royal York Hotel. The side bays have normal entrances, normal windows, and semicircular lunettes. ST PETER'S PLACE is mixed, again occasionally going to giant pilasters. ST GEORGE'S PLACE again bows and balconies, and finally the N end of this development of the twenties, HANOVER CRESCENT of *c.*1827, by *Wilds Jun.* This is a complete composition of two-storeyed houses carried out quite consistently. The centre piece has giant Corinthian columns and a pediment. Sub-accents with pilasters, including some with ammonite capitals. Onestoreyed lodges with Tuscan columns at the entrances.

From Victoria Gardens to the E an area of slums, demolition, and rebuilding. Round RICHMOND STREET and CARLTON HILL mixed development of high blocks of flats of no distinction and three-storeyed housing (by *P. Billington*). They border on council housing of *c.*1895 (ST JAMES'S AVENUE, BLAKER STREET) in rows of red-brick terraces and occasionally on nice older housing (34-35 MICHELL STREET, a former farmhouse, three bays, cobbles and red brick, doorway with pediment – early C19).

As one carries on to the E, one soon reaches QUEEN'S PARK, laid out by *Barry* in 1829. It was to have villas around, similar to Regents Park and St Leonards, but only one was built, now the XAVERIAN COLLEGE. It was built for Thomas Attree, owner of Marine Square and developer of this new area. The villa is memorable as another Quattrocento design of Barry's, just a little later than the Travellers' Club and indeed similar to it in the central motif of a loggia with three

arches on slender columns. To the l. and r. only one bay,
widely spaced. It must have felt less ponderous to prosperous
people at the time than the accepted classical apparatus, and
is indeed a graceful piece. The TOWER to its W once belonged
to it and was a water tower, though called an observatory. It
has an octagonal base and a rotunda with a domed top. The
base is now lavatories. The SOUTH GATEWAYS to the park
were once Barry's too, but they now look entirely Victorian,
and one has a date 1890 on it. Just inside them the ROYAL
GERMAN SPA, a once pretty little building with a portico of
six fluted Ionic columns towards the park. It was built for
Dr F. A. A. Struve of Dresden for the sale of his artificial
mineral water and is still Messrs Hooper Struve's, who, however, at the time of writing are making a disgraceful mess
of it.

A walk from Victoria Gardens to the W is less profitable. Up
CHURCH STREET first, to pass the former Drill Hall of the
ROYAL SUSSEX REGIMENT, 1889–90 by *E. Scott*, a queer
building, long, with segment-headed windows, and a portal,
as if it stood at Salzburg and dated from the C17. A turn into
QUEEN STREET for the ODDFELLOWS HALL of 1853, a
composition exactly like a Nonconformist chapel. Five bays,
giant pilasters, and entrances in bays one and five. On in
Church Street to St Nicholas, and below it to the S WYKE-
HAM TERRACE of *c.*1830, Gothic, cemented.

Further W, but on its own, and better reached from Lansdowne
Place (if one wants to reach it), the WICK ESTATE. Of the
Furze Hill villa of Decimus Burton there is only one lodge
left. The rest has become flats, and there are good ones
amongst them, especially PARK GATE in Somerhill Road, of
four storeys only. This is by *Eric Lyons*, 1957–9. The WELL
HOUSE in St Ann's Well Gardens, i.e. Dr Russell's Chalybeate Spring, has also been demolished.

Finally to the N from Victoria Gardens, and what for ? A former
CHAPEL in ANN STREET, close to St Bartholomew, dated
'1830, enlarged 1857' (three bays, giant pilasters, one-bay
pediment, Venetian doorway of 1857), and a new flatted
factory in BOSTON STREET, a curtain-walling job by
P. Billington.

NEOLITHIC CAUSEWAYED CAMP, on Brighton Racecourse.
The site consists of four concentric rings of ditches with
internal banks interrupted by numerous causeways. Of the
outermost ring of bank and ditch, which when excavated was

found to be 7 ft deep, only sectors in the N and S can now be traced on the ground. The depth of the ditches decreases towards the centre, the innermost having a depth of only 3 ft. Most of the occupation material from the site, in the form of sherds of Windmill Hill pottery, bone and flint tools for leather working and skinning, animal bones, and fragments of a number of human skulls, came from this latter ditch. Beaker sherds were found in the secondary ditch silting.

HILL-FORT, on HOLLINGBURY HILL, 2¼ m. NNW, between the Ditchling and Lewes roads. The fort is of roughly square, univallate plan, broken by original entrances on the E and W sides. Excavation showed the ditch to be flat-bottomed and almost vertical-sided. The ramparts were revetted with upright timbers and supported by a framework of horizontal beams running through the bank. The E gateway was hung on two massive timber uprights. The fort appears to have been constructed in the middle of the c3 and abandoned in the middle of the c2 B.C.

BRIGHTON VILLAGES

ALDRINGTON   2000
2 m. W

The westward extension of Hove: terraces and cottages from 1850 onwards running back from the sea on a gridiron plan.

ST LEONARD. Tower and S aisle 1878 and decent, by *R. H. Carpenter*, using bits from a ruined medieval church on the same site (the lancet windows, e.g.). Bigger nave clapped on to this in 1936, and very horrible, by *H. M. Milburn Pett*. It looks like the 1870s at their worst. LYCHGATE with a good deal of personality, by *F. A. Crouch*, 1949. The personality can be called Gothic, Gothic Revival, or Gothic Revival Revived, or just English.

HANGLETON   2000
2½ m. NW

The end of Brighton's sprawl. It had better remain so. Church and Downs look across at the sea over a green, well planned in itself but surrounded in the 1950s by as grisly a set of parodies of the English cottage as it would be possible to find.

ST HELEN. Mellow and humble in these desperate surroundings. Flint and tile, tower, nave, and chancel. C13 tower, C11 nave

with herringbone masonry, C14 chancel with trefoiled lancets
and a modern E window. The inside still plastered, with barn
roofs and no chancel arch. Unctuous C19 piety here would
have been unbearable. – PLATE. Cup, 1568; Paten, 1715. –
MONUMENT. C16; person unknown. Tiny kneeling figures in
a big, badly weathered architectural frame.

HANGLETON MANOR. Simple flint manor house. Probably
built *c.*1540, as carved stones from Lewes Priory, demolished
in 1537, were incorporated in it. Two-storey gabled porch,
off centre; big four- and five-light mullioned windows. The
long, low block to the N of it is supposed to be C15, from an
earlier house.

MOULSECOMB

3000

2 m. NNE

Not a village, nor in possession of a church. But MOULSECOMB
PLACE is an early C19 seven-bay house of yellow brick, and
behind it survives the one and only worthwhile timber-
framed cottage of Brighton. The N side has an overhang,
studding, and big curved braces.

PATCHAM

3000

3¼ m. NNW

Though genteel bungalows come right up to the church, there
is still a village feeling about Patcham, with the open Downs
behind and on them the MONUMENT to Hindoos who died at
Brighton in the First World War (by *E. C. Henriques*).

ALL SAINTS. A Norman church, though that can be seen only
inside. Plain chancel arch, with two reredos recesses l. and r.,
according to the VCH 'possibly original'. Also the blocked N
doorway. Externally it is all C13, especially the thin W tower
with small lancets as bell-openings. The N aisle is of 1898. –
PAINTING. Above the chancel arch, all re-drawn, the remains
of a Last Judgement of *c.*1230. Christ enthroned, the rising
of the dead and the weighing of the souls, and the Virgin and
St John. – PLATE. Cup, with Cover engraved 1568; foreign
Paten, engraved 1666. – MONUMENT. Richard Shelley † 1594.
In a fragmentary state. Short tapering pilasters, a coat of arms,
and l. and r. grave-diggers – oddly enough in the nude.

Immediately N of the church the BARN of Court Farmhouse. It
is nearly 250 ft long and dates from the C17 or earlier. Part
flint, part weatherboarding. Across the street the contemporary

DOVECOTE, circular in plan. Along Church Hill and down a
little towards Brighton, near the end of OLD LONDON ROAD,
is SOUTHDOWN HOUSE, a handsome Early Georgian house
of five bays and two storeys, knapped flint and brick. Parapet
with a lozenge pattern. Doorway with Gibbs surround and
pediment.

PATCHAM PLACE. A mid C18 house of seven bays, all faced
with black mathematical tiles. Centre of three bays with
pediment. Even (wooden) quoins to the angles and the angles
of the centre. Doorway with Tuscan columns and a broken
pediment. The E side has two canted bay windows.

WINDMILL, ¾ m. WSW. A tower mill with its sails.

PORTSLADE

2000

3 m. W

Bizarre landscape NW of Brighton and effectively part of it.
Flint cottages and walls around the church give way to a huge
stock-brick FACTORY of 1881 at the crossroads. The housing
up on the Downs, at Mile Oak, is terrible and is still going up.
Yet a big area near the centre of the village is allotments. On
the coast, Portslade-by-Sea is a euphemism for the refinery, the
big Brighton power stations of 1902–6 and 1952 etc., and the
skein of wires running in from the N. Both power stations are
well sited between the basin and the sea, and suddenly the view
looks like Hartlepool or Whitehaven.

ST NICOLAS. Straighforward C12 and C13, with a lot of
enlargement, very much a Sussex average. The S arcade and
its narrow aisle late C12: round piers, scalloped capitals,
obtusely pointed unchamfered arches. The windows were
altered to lancets in the C13. Chancel and plain unbuttressed
tower both C13. Good, simple composition in the E wall:
two big lancets close together with a sexfoil above them. The
same simple effectiveness in the restored SEDILIA. N aisle,
matching but much wider, 1874. Brackenbury Chapel at the
W end 1874, far more ornate than anything else in the church,
and successful out and in. Heavy grief, like a mausoleum. –
PLATE. Cup, 1637; Paten and Almsdish, 1726; Flagon, 1727.

MANOR HOUSE. In the grounds of St Mary's Convent, but
partly built into the churchyard wall – and barbarously
jostled by a utilitarian addition at the end of the church's N
aisle. S and E walls of a C12 house which had a hall on the first
floor, a two-light window, plain and round-headed, in each.

Much more was left as late as 1800, but was pillaged to make up sham ruins a little further up the hill.

Just one elegant seaside villa, THE LODGE, stuccoed and of c.1820, in Larks Road, s of the church.

3000   PRESTON
                              1½ m. N

The village character of Preston is exhausted by church and manor house. All the rest is Brighton. So the churches, other than the parish church, appear as Brighton churches.

ST PETER. Of flint. E.E. Nave and chancel and a thin W tower. Single-lancet bell-openings, larger lancets otherwise, mostly renewed. – WALL PAINTINGS. Substantial remains of the early C14 on the nave E wall and N wall. Before a fire in 1906 there was far more. On the N wall one saw in three tiers the Last Supper, an altar with a chalice, and the Christ Child. Ox and ass on the sides. Above the chancel arch Doubting Thomas, Noli me tangere, and Saints. Below N Martyrdom of Thomas Becket, S St Michael weighing souls.* – PLATE. Cup and Cover, engraved 1569. – MONUMENT. Used as the altar a tomb-chest with shields in closely cusped quatrefoils, either perfectly preserved or sensitively re-cut. Said to be the tomb of Edward Elrington † 1515.

MANOR HOUSE. Built in 1738, but evidently added to later in the C18. Five-bay plus one-bay one-storey wings with segment-arched tripartite windows. Staircase with two balusters to the tread and carved tread-ends.

OLD COTTAGE, South Road, W of Preston Manor. Just one older house, i.e. Georgian, of three bays, flint and brick with a nice doorway.

3000   STANMER

Stanmer is the only one of the Brighton villages that is really a village, and at present it seems more likely that the University of Sussex will swallow it than Brighton. The house of the Earls of Chichester already belongs to the University.

CHURCH. The church lies by the house in the (now public) park. It would make a good university chapel – for the time being. It dates from 1838, is of flint, and has transepts, a thin W tower with recessed spire, and lancet windows. The

* (In the nave is a PAINTING of the Deposition, attributed to *Burne-Jones*.)

mouldings and capitals inside are remarkably correct. If this is not a Victorian remodelling (and there is none recorded), one would like to know the name of the architect. – PLATE. Paten, 1759; Paten, 1762; Chalice, 1816. – MONUMENT. Sir John Pelham † 1580, with wife and son † 1584. Small kneeling figures (from Holy Trinity, Minories, London).

STANMER HOUSE. 1722–7 by *Nicholas Dubois*, translator of Leoni's Palladio edition. Of fine ashlar, with a seven-bay front. Pedimented three-bay projection. Closed-in porch with paired Tuscan pilasters. Entrance hall with bits of garland decoration and busts in them. Big simple fireplace. The former dining room at the S corner has a good plaster ceiling of *c.*1740 and a screen of two Corinthian columns. In another room a fine Adamish ceiling of the late C18. More good chimneypieces. Staircase with thin turned balusters. Behind the house is a C17 WELLHOUSE with its original machinery. In the grounds, S of the car park, a MONUMENT of 1775 to commemorate the father of the then Lady Pelham. It is of *Coade* stone, an urn on a triangular base resting on tortoises (cf. the triangular Coade stone monuments at Brocklesby in Lincolnshire and Mount Edgcumbe in Devon).

WEST BLATCHINGTON
2½ m. WNW

No village left. Only the church and the windmill, both isolated and, as it were, on a platter. The windmill is the more interesting of the two.

ST PETER. 1890, with a large addition of 1961–2. The older part consisted of nave and chancel and a bell-turret. The addition amounts to a new nave and chancel. It is by *J. L. Denman*. Brick and flint. Stepped-up E end, N side cobbled. Inside, transverse arches and a curious clerestory arrangement by which glazed skylights give light to both the new and the old churches.

WINDMILL. This is an eminently curious piece. It rises on or out of an L-shaped barn in which is the machinery driven by the mill. The mill itself is of the smock-type and has its sails. It dates from 1724.

PREHISTORIC AND ROMAN SETTLEMENT. Just N of the church is an area which appears to have been settled from Middle Bronze Age times. Apart from stray finds of a Neolithic flint axe and a barbed and tanged arrowhead of Neolithic/Early Bronze Age form, the first traces of deliberate settlement consist of an oval cooking place containing large quantities of Middle Bronze Age pottery and animal bones, and a portion of a ditch, possibly a field boundary, which produced two bronze palstaves and Middle Bronze Age pottery.

Iron Age A and B settlement is represented by isolated rubbish pits, and to the C1 A.D. belong a complicated series of ditches probably forming field boundaries. Associated with one of these ditches was a small Roman cemetery.

In the C2 A.D. a VILLA, which lay between Amberley Drive and Bramber Avenue, and an oval HUT in Findon Park were constructed. The former, rectangular in plan and measuring 115 ft by 49 ft, was of the basilican type, with two rows of posts running along its length, dividing it into a nave and two aisles. A small offset on the W wall appears to represent the jamb of the main doorway. Corn-drying kilns, of which seven have so far been discovered in the area, were in operation at this time and continued in use for about a century. Towards the end of the C3 occupation of the area appears to have ceased, although there is nothing to suggest the destruction apparent in so many Late Roman sites in Southern Britain.

BUCKHOLT FARM see BEXHILL

BUCKHURST see WITHYHAM

BULVERHYTHE see HASTINGS, p. 529

BURGESS HILL

One shopping street from the station to the church, and seas of houses all around.

ST JOHN. 1861–3 by *T. Talbot Bury*. Big, of brick, with bands of black and yellow bricks. SW steeple. The style is Late Geometrical. Odd clerestory windows: groups of three pointed quatrefoils in a row.

ST ANDREW, on the road to Wivelsfield Station. By *Lacy W. Ridge*, 1907–9 (GR). Red brick, geometrical style, no tower. Very wide aisleless nave and short wide transepts. Low short chancel with shallow panelled vault.

CONGREGATIONAL CHURCH. 1881 by *L. J. Hamilton*, large and still entirely classical in style; surprisingly chaste. Four-column Tuscan portico with pediment.

(ST GEORGE'S RETREAT. 1870)
LITTLE HAMMOND'S FARM, ½ m. SW, on the road to Hassocks.
Small farmhouse, the N side timber-framed, the E side added in
brick in 1566. Black-brick diapers. Only three bays, the middle
one a porch. Lugged gable. The porch pilasters are typical of
the mid C16, no longer 'Early Renaissance' (with sunk panels
containing candelabra and fine foliage), nor yet 'Elizabethan'.
Odd band round the pilasters. Fluted lintel. Little aedicule
above with a shield and the date.

BURWASH   6020

ST BARTHOLOMEW. Norman W tower with twin bell-openings.
The capitals of the shafts have three heavy scallops. It might
be *c*.1100. E.E. chancel, very wide. Lancet windows, including a generously spaced stepped triplet at the E end. E.E. S
arcade of three bays. Round and octagonal piers, double-
chamfered arches. Dec N arcade of four bays. Standard details.
Most of the windows are renewed or new. – FONT. Octagonal,
concave-sided, Perp, with simple motifs, including the Pelham
buckle. – PLATE. Cup and Paten, 1568; Almsdish, 1596;
Cup and Paten on Foot, 1724; Flagon, 1728. – MONUMENTS.
The earliest cast-iron tomb slab in existence; C14, with a small
cross and an Orate inscription for John Colins. – Brass to a
Civilian, *c*.1440, 15 in. figure. – Lively cartouche to John
Caton † 1675. – (John Courtail † 1806. By *Flaxman*. Handsome, with Faith and Hope l. and r. – In the churchyard two
headstones with terracotta plaques by *Harmer*.)
ST JOSEPH (Salesian Novitiate), 1¼ m. NW. By *B. Whelan*, 1887.
An impressive church on account of its consistent vaulting,
marred only by the shortness of the nave. The nave has a
pointed tunnel-vault of brick, the lower transepts have tunnel-
vaults too, with a curious ridge-rib; chancel and apse are
rib-vaulted. The style is E.E. Round the apse a complete wall-
passage with tripartite stepped arcading, as if taken from a
cathedral and placed low. Rich stiff-leaf in the chancel arch
and the corbels of the transept arches.
The HIGH STREET of Burwash ought to be walked to appreciate it. Starting from the church one has first a glimpse of timber-framed cottages below on the l., and then at once RAM-
PYNDENE, the one outstanding house. It was built in 1699
and, being built by a timber merchant, is timber-framed.
That, however, is not visible on the outside. Here we have red
brick with grey headers. Five bays, two storeys, and a hipped

roof. Wooden cross-windows, except above the doorways, where there is still a three-light transomed window. To the l. and r. of the doorway narrow windows, a Queen Anne fashion. The frieze, carried on two opulently carved brackets, runs above them too. Above it and the doorway a hood carved with birds and a cherub's head. The hall has a splendid stucco ceiling with almost detached leaves and flowers. At its far end an elegant staircase with thin turned balusters.

After that nothing eventful, but a pleasant walk. The High Street is not wide, and it undulates gently. The colours are red and white. On the N side, with interruptions, pollarded trees forming a N pedestrians' pavement. Past Rampyndene, a large early C17 timber-framed house with two gables, now tile-hung. Then on the opposite side a wide, symmetrical early C19 house with a Tuscan porch and broad horizontal windows. Further on, on the same side, a row of six cottages, chequer brick below, tile-hung above, and with a big wavy tiled roof. Then the WHITE HOUSE, with a flat hood on heavy, scrolly brackets.

To the E of the Church only GLEBE HOUSE, ½ m. ENE, the former rectory. This has a façade of 1721. Three storeys, five bays. (Good interior. MHLG)

BATEMANS, ¾ m. SW. Kipling's house. It was built, no doubt by an ironmaster, in 1634. The façade was symmetrical (or very nearly), but the r. wing does not exist any longer. The doorway was in the middle in a projecting porch. This is gabled, as is the wing (and was the other). The entrance to the porch is round-arched and decorated. The windows are mullioned and transomed, of five lights on the ground floor (except that the hall window to the l. of the porch has six), four on the first (but the room above the hall has five and the room in the porch three). Gable and porch gable are on kneelers and have ball finials. Inside, doorways with four-centred heads and elementary decoration in the spandrels. Original staircase with turned balusters.

BURWASH COMMON

2¼ m. WSW of Burwash

ST PHILIP. 1867 by *Slater & Carpenter*, a serious job. Nave and low aisles with a row of small lancets, bellcote on the W end of the chancel and polygonal apse. Chancel and apse are vaulted. The aisle arcades have round grey granite piers. The chancel arch with very rich stiff-leaf.

HOLMSHURST, 1 m. N. Brick, dated 1610. Front with two gables and recessed centre. Mullioned and transomed windows, mostly of five lights. Perfectly regular except for the squeezing in of the doorway.

BUXTED

4020

ST MARGARET. Much restored. The W tower C13, and higher up C18. Shingled broach spire. C13 also the four-bay arcades, S before N. The S arcade has round piers with double-chamfered arches, the N arcade alternating octagonal and round ones, and double-hollow-chamfered arches. Their bases and capitals differ, and it seems that the octagonal piers and the arches may be replacements. The chancel is of c.1300, see the renewed E window with cusped intersecting tracery (if the details can be relied on), one N lancet, two S lancets, and the chancel arch. Perp aisle walls and embattled N porch. The clerestory, which is unrestored, seems to be C17. That would go with the canted chancel ceiling, which is of c.1600 and the most attractive feature of the church. Panels with a simple geometrical motif, but a frieze of long branches in vases. And what of the SEDILIA and PISCINA? They cannot be c.1300, nor can they be Victorian. Would they be an example of that crude C17 Gothicism which one meets here and there? The foliage at the foot of the piscina and the cusping of the sedilia are especially telling. – FONT. Of the square Purbeck type on five supports, but the flat blank arches pointed-trefoiled. Is this late C13? – PULPIT. Jacobean, with the usual blank arches in flat carving. – BENCH ENDS. Two with fleur-de-lis poppy-heads. – CHEST. A memorable late C13 piece. The top like the roof of a shrine, its ends like bench ends. Rosettes at the top of the verticals, plain cusped arches along the front panel. The chest is over 3 ft 4 in. high and quite short.* – COMMUNION RAIL. Of strong dumbbell balusters, later C17. – BEADLE'S STAFF. With a little painting. Probably early C19. – STAINED GLASS. S aisle E, by *E. Baillie*, 1853, and of no merit. – PLATE. Chalice, 1733; two Patens, 1752. – MONUMENTS. Brass to Britellus Avenel, rector in the later C14. Ogee cross, at the top of a staff, and in the cross the demi-figure of the rector. – Deonicius Slon † 1485. Demi-figure of another priest, 12 in. long. – George Medley † 1796. Nice tablet by *C. Regnart*, who signs Cleavland Street,

* Mr McHardy in fact queries whether this is a parish chest at all.

Fitzroy Square, London. – Also two very plain tablets by *Sir R. Westmacott*, 1815. – (Basil Ionides (*see* below), † 1950. Noble, oval, white-marble plaque with majestic lettering. G. McHardy)

See p. 691 The WHITE HART, W of the station, is a nice Georgian five-bay job.

BUXTED PLACE. Buxted Place before the fire of 1940 was an Early Georgian house of nine bays and three storeys with a three-bay pediment to the N and S and on both sides in the middle an added one-storey portico of Tuscan columns. The columns are doubled in depth. Now the house has only two storeys and no pediment; but the porticoes are preserved. That on the S side is known to date from 1810 and stands on elegant segmental arches. *Basil Ionides*, who owned the house, restored and remodelled it in a society-Georgian, but with many original C18 features brought in and distributed skilfully. Externally such a feature is the new entrance doorway on the W side, which has a pediment on columns intermittently plain and with stalactite rustication. This comes from West Harling Hall in Norfolk and is Early Georgian. The balustrading of the new W forecourt was salvaged from Chesterfield House, off Park Lane, a house by *Ware*, and other parts of the forecourt come from other houses. The new W entrance hall also is a museum of brought-in pieces: the fireplace from 19 Arlington Street of *c.*1740, the long porcelain cabinet from Basildon near Reading, the doors from *Robert Adam*'s Nos 23–25 Portland Place. The former great hall on the N side was lowered. Here the fireplace comes from Queensberry House, Richmond, the doors from Kensington House, Kensington Gore, but the glorious Rococo stucco-work above the fireplace belongs to the house, though it must be somewhat later than the architecture. The staircase, exceptionally splendid, was originally in No. 30 Old Burlington Street in London and must be of *c.*1725–30. It is extremely chaste and Jonesian. The balusters are strong, not slender. And so it goes on. Dining room with an exquisite, closely decorated chimneypiece from Clumber, Notts., built *c.*1715. Saloon with chimneypieces from Kingston House, plaques from *R. Adam*'s Adelphi, and doors from *Adam*'s 38 Berkeley Square. Library with panelling and chimneypiece from Felix Hall in Essex and overmantel of *c.*1735 from Stowe, Bucks. Drawing room chimneypiece again from Felix Hall and probably designed by *Adam*. More in other rooms.

LODGES etc. by *Basil Ionides*. A fine wide avenue from the
NE, another on the W.

At the entrance to Buxted Place HOG HOUSE, three bays with a
panel of a hog dated 1581. The windows Tudor – and c.1840-
looking.

At Totease, E of the railway, UPPER TOTEASE is a Georgian
three-bay ashlar house of three wide-spaced bays. Quite an
ambitious middle window.

HARROCK HOUSE, ½ m. NNE. Brick. Late C17 with two somewhat projecting wings. Giant pilasters set back from the angles.
The windows of the front are all altered.

(BEVINGFORD, 1½ m. N. C15 hall-house, the S wing gone, the N
wing extended in the early C16 and again in 1606. The hall
part is now tile-hung. VCH)

CADE STREET CHAPEL *see* HEATHFIELD

CAMBER   9010

That is, Camber Sands. For Camber Castle, *see* below.

ST THOMAS. Of brick, with a weatherboarded bell-turret and
dormers in the roof. It looks nice and neat in the mess of bungalows, but, as it was built in 1955–6, it is of course nearly
fifty years behind the times. The predecessor of the church
had been destroyed in the war, in 1944.

CAMBER CASTLE   9010

1¼ m. S of Rye

The series of castles built by Henry VIII against the French 37a
from Kent (Sandgate, Deal, Walmer) to Cornwall (Pendennis, &b
St Mawes) date from c.1540. The *devisor*, i.e. probably designer,
was an Austrian, *Stefan von Haschenperg*, and the designs are
interesting enough. They are, in contrast to earlier castles, all
low, with platforms for mounting cannon. But the aesthetically
remarkable fact is that they all have symmetrical plans with a
preference for patterns of lobes (Walmer four, Deal six). Camber is no exception, although the castle was apparently built
much earlier and only remodelled and enlarged in 1539–43.
The cost of this enlargement was £23,000. The circular centre
tower is ascribed to the years 1511–14, when Sir Edward
Guldeford received over £1,000 for making a tower at Camber. It may even be earlier. The mantle laid round this tower
is a shallow dodecagon with four semicircular projections in the
main directions and a fifth taking the place of the two NW sides

of the dodecagon. This is later. Originally there was here the entrance to the castle. Ashlar on a rubble core. The central tower and the bastions brick-faced inside. The bricks used are yellow. Tunnel-vaulted passages round the central tower and to the four bastions and connecting passages between them. Recent excavations by Mr M. Biddle and Mr H. Colvin have shown that these passages led to stirrup-shaped bastions preceding the present ones by a short time. When the present bastions were built, the stirrup-bastions remained as cavaliers. Low, broad, segment-headed windows with deep splays in the present bastions. The castle was dismantled in 1642. It had become useless anyway, owing to the shifting of the river Rother.

CARTERS CORNER PLACE *see* HELLINGLY

7010   ## CATSFIELD

Two churches, the METHODIST CHURCH the much more ambitious, thanks to its NE steeple, out of all proportion with the church to which it belongs. It is of 1912, but looks Victorian. The architect was *Henry Blackman*.

ST LAURENCE is humble, with a Norman nave (see the wild herringbone laying), a W tower of *c*.1200 (with later shingled broach spire), and an E.E. chancel. The tower has a characteristic W doorway with a broad convex quadrant moulding and a characteristic arch to the nave with a continuous chamfer. To the N of the chancel a later C13 N chapel. The terrible N aisle, very crudely Norman, is by *Carpenter*, one is sorry to report, and dates from 1845. Kingpost roof in the nave. – PLATE. Cup, 1641; Paten and Flagon, 1676. – MONUMENT. John Fuller † 1810, by *Nollekens*. Above the inscription military still-life including oak-leaves.

ASHBURNHAM PLACE LODGE, Stephens Crouch, 1½ m. NW. The Lodge is Tudor (cf. the Battle Lodge), but the GATES themselves, the quadrant walls, and the one-bay pavilions with pyramid roofs are by *Robert Adam*. The design of the gates is of exquisite elegance and economy of ornament, the centre part mostly uprights and only framing ornament, and only in the side parts one longer circular motif each.

DEER PARK COTTAGE, ½ m. NNW of the former. This was the ranger's lodge, and it seems to be mid C17. Symmetrical three-bay front of two storeys with gabled middle porch. Four-light windows l. and r.

TOWER HOUSE, ¾ m. NW of the gates. In an Italianate style with detail as heavy as Cockerell's can be. Asymmetrical, i.e. with a lower attachment. Dated 1836.

CHAILEY

3010

ST PETER. Short C13 tower with shingled broach spire. C13 chancel with widely spaced side lancets. Inside, the N arcade also C13. Round piers and double-chamfered arches. The church was considerably enlarged in 1878–9 by *J. Oldrid Scott*. He added an outer N aisle and a fragmentary S aisle. – STAINED GLASS. Chancel S by *Capronnier*, 1865 and 1871; chancel N *Powell's*, no doubt; 1879, and so much better.
The church faces an unusually pretty green.

CHAILEY MOAT (Old Rectory), ⅛ m. W. Two-storeyed, low, tile-hung above a brick ground floor, hipped roof. C18 five-bay front (Venetian window on the upper floor). The house itself is older and stands in a moat.

ADES, ½ m. E. Georgian, five bays, brick. Built probably before 1728. The deep porch with Tuscan columns and the additions l. and r. of before 1827.

THE HOOKE, ¾ m. SW. Stone. Late C18 N front with two canted bay windows and battlements. The much more thoroughly Gothic S end has been largely demolished. (The centre between these two parts late C17, and a staircase with twisted balusters etc. of that date inside. VCH)

WAPSBOURNE FARMHOUSE, 2½ m. NNE. The house once had a date 1606. Partly timber-framed, partly vitreous brick. Against the N end a two-storeyed bay, mullioned window below, mullion-and-transom window above. Pendant in the E gable.

NORTH COMMON is quite an area apart, very different in character and attraction. The principal attraction is the WIND-MILL, a smock-mill with sails and fan-tail. The mill stands close to the St George's Residential Block of the HERITAGE CRAFTS SCHOOL, built in 1932 to the design of *J. B. S. Comper*. A good composition with two projecting wings, but in the middle the large neo-Perp window of the dining hall. Red brick, a minimum of enrichment, except for the pretty tree above the r. hand archway – but of course in the style of the Hampstead Garden Suburb, i.e. of twenty years earlier. The Heritage Crafts School was started in 1903 as a residential school for crippled children.

ST MARTIN'S CHAPEL, of the School. By *Sir Ninian Comper*.

Dedicated in 1913. Gothic, but in the external outline certainly not a copy of anything. Low embattled W tower, S steeple. The interior undeniably impressive, even if still entirely historical. Wagon roof running through from W to E, blue and gold, and gold above the altar space. Tall Perp windows S and E. On the N side a tall transeptal extension, two bays deep (not long), with a tall round pier. Complete rood screen and rood of course, also by *Comper*, 1927. – STAINED GLASS, sentimental and insipid, and one of Comper's gold and blue altar triptychs, neo-International-Gothic-of-1400.

ST MARY, the church of the North Common. 1876 by *J. Oldrid Scott*, and very good. Sandstone and tiled roofs. With a low central tower with saddleback rook making an effective silhouette. Nave and chancel have lancets. Two transeptal side chapels, internally playing no part. The tower stands inside on two strong transverse arches. – STAINED GLASS. All of one character, probably *Powell's*. Single figures and much transparent glass with ornamental designs.

CHALVINGTON

ST BARTHOLOMEW. Nave with bell-turret and chancel. The bell-turret is weatherboarded and has a shingled broach spire, but the W and E gables of the nave are tile-hung. The nave windows E.E., with simple bar tracery, the chancel windows, if their strange details can be trusted, Dec, i.e. E window with intersecting tracery replaced by a foiled circle at the top (a motif of *c.*1300), but with ogee-headed lights, and the side windows small, of two pointed-trefoiled lights with a straight hood-mould across. The nave roof has low collar-beams on arched braces, the chancel roof is single-framed, except for one tie-beam with a long, thin kingpost. – ARCHITECTURAL FRAGMENTS. Two bits of Norman zigzag above the N doorway, outside. – STAINED GLASS. Small fragments in a nave N window, including a Dec demi-figure. – PLATE. Cup and Cover, 1568; Paten, 1725.

CHAPEL ROW *see* HERSTMONCEUX

CHARLESTON BROW *see* WEST FIRLE

CHARLESTON MANOR *see* WESTDEAN

CHELWOOD GATE *see* FOREST ROW

CHIDDINGLY

CHURCH. Ashlar-faced Perp w tower. Stone spire with polygonal pinnacles. Doorway with the Pelham buckle as its label-
stops. E. E. aisles, see the w lancets and the masonry. The other
windows are Perp. The s transept, i.e. the Jefferay Chapel, has
an Elizabethan E window with transom. The chancel is of
1864. The arcades of three bays are later than the aisle lancets,
probably C14. Kingpost roof. – PULPIT. Later C18, with a
Gothick sounding board terminating in an ogee cap. Rays in
tarsia on the underside. Simple panels on the pulpit itself. –
BOX PEWS. – STAINED GLASS. N aisle E evidently *Powell's*;
c.1877. – PLATE. Cup, 1639; Paten on foot, 1717. – MONU-
MENTS. Sir John Jefferay † 1578, his wife, his daughter Lady   39a
Elizabeth Montagu and son-in-law Sir Edward Montagu.
Alabaster. A big monument filling the s wall of the s transept,
heavy throughout, e.g. without any columns. She is shown recumbent, he lying on his side propped on his elbow behind
and much above her. To the l. and r. standing in niches –
which is very rare indeed before the C17 – the two members
of the younger generation, he in crinkled robes, she in a preposterous costume. A daughter kneeling at the foot of the
monument. – William Jefferay † 1611. Small alabaster tablet
with kneeling couple facing one another. – Margaret Jefferay
† 1618. Small alabaster tablet with two seated allegorical
figures and a skull set into an urn, the recess surrounded by
the inscription: Margarita fui. – John Bromfield † 1735. A
purely architectural tablet, as is typical of the 1730s. – (In the
churchyard headstone to John Bray † 1814 with one of
Harmer's terracotta plaques. SAC 1962)

CHIDDINGLY PLACE. Fragments of the Jefferay mansion indicating a date so early in the reign of Elizabeth I that the fragment gains a great rarity value. What remains is principally
this. In the N front of the farmhouse, to the l. of the pretty Ionic
porch with its frieze like the lintel of a fireplace, two windows
with transoms but depressed-arched lights, i.e. a Henry VIII
type. However, the fluted friezes above them are classical.
Then, round the l. corner (w front), re-set no doubt, the
doorways from the screens passage to the kitchen, buttery, and
pantry, two-centred arches, but in the spandrels classical allegorical figures. This part must have been the centre of the
house. The windows round the r. corner (E front) must be
re-set too. Detached now, but formerly no doubt a wing of the

house, a BARN with several windows and blocked windows and also fireplaces on the former ground and first floors. s of the barn another part, also with blocked windows. At the time when Grimm did his drawings, i.e. in the 1780s, a great deal more survived, including the porch and the hall. They exhibited the interesting mixture which the remaining parts still present.

FARLEY FARMHOUSE, Muddles Green, ½ m. s. Georgian five-bay house with hipped roof.

STONEHILL HOUSE, 1½ m. NE. The perfect timber-framed Sussex house of the C15, extremely well restored in 1912 and 1924. Heavy timbers, much close studding. The wings l. and r. of the central hall with oversailing upper floor on brackets including diagonally set brackets. Curved braces run from the wings along the recessed centre to help to support the eaves, which do not recede. – i.e. the so-called Wealden arrangement. The bay window is an Elizabethan addition, see the transomed window and the concave-sided lozenge bracing.

PEKE'S HOUSE, 1¼ m. SE. The Elizabethan stone porch with frontal termini caryatids with a claw foot and the frieze they carry could well come from a chimneypiece. (Inside the house in a room wall paintings of c.1572, a frieze with flowers and inscriptions still in black letter.)

CHIDDINGLYE see WEST HOATHLY

CLAYTON

2010

A small village below the South Downs with a small church. The village holds in store one overwhelming surprise and two engaging oddities: the entrance to the TUNNEL, 1840, yellow brick, with a pointed arch for the trains to disappear into and 8a castellated turrets, and JACK AND JILL, the two unequal windmills on the height, he a brick tower-mill of 1876, she a wooden post-mill of 1821 with four sails. Jill came from Dyke Road, Brighton, about 1850.

ST JOHN BAPTIST. It is a humble church from outside, nave and chancel and a wooden bell-turret. The masonry looks ancient, and the N doorway seems plainest Norman. Also there are traces of Gothic arches to low transeptal chapels. The chancel is largely of the C19, but the chancel arch is a very powerful C11 piece in the style of Worth. The responds have thick semicircular projections in the intrados and also on the extrados to W and E, i.e. accompanying outer bands of jambs and arch, as it were. Instead of capitals a slab and a chamfer binding the three semicircular projections together. Once one has seen this, is it not likely that the low transeptal chapels were Saxon *porticus* or something on the lines of Worth?

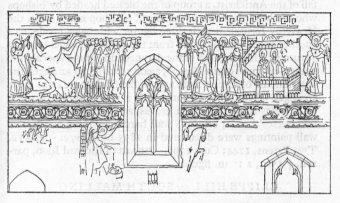

0 1 2 3 4 5 6 7 8 9 10 11 12 13 14 15ft

Clayton church, wall painting on the north wall, *c.*1140.

The chancel arch is enough of a surprise, but the WALL PAINTINGS are unique in England for their extent, preservation, and date. They date from *c.*1140 and must have covered at least nave N, S, and E walls, and probably the W wall as well. They belong to a group with the slightly earlier Hardham in West Sussex and Coombes. Clayton and Hardham both depended during the operative years on Lewes Priory, but the style of the wall paintings is not really Cluniac. Its sources are mixed. Wall paintings in Poitou, Anglo-Saxon early C11 manuscripts, and Sicilian, i.e. Byzantine, mosaics contributed. The figures are extremely long and lean, with heavy, ample garments and exceedingly small heads. They tend to bend and sway, and joints are indicated by whirlpool-like forms. Characteristic also are the strange headgears and the low architectural screens round groups, as though they were play-pens seen from above. What is preserved is the upper tier of stories S, N, and E, and fragments of the lower tier. A broad band of loose scrolls with crockets as leaves divides the two tiers, and above the upper tier is a band of Greek key. The stories are, above the chancel arch. Christ in an almond-shaped glory, the glory supported by angels, and to the l. and r. standing apostles. Below, i.e. to the l. of the chancel arch, Christ delivering the keys to St Peter, to the r. Christ delivering the book to St Paul. Then N wall from w: an angel blowing the trumpet, the fall of the Antichrist, a group of the blessed headed by bishops who are being received by an angel, a bishop and a saint, the Heavenly Jerusalem with three figures with halos inside, and another angel. On the s wall from the w also an angel blowing a trumpet, then a group of the damned, one of the apocalyptic horsemen, more of the blessed, again received by an angel, the Instruments of the Passion, and as the final figure once more an angel. Of the lower tier only little is recognizable: on the N wall bodies rising from their graves, an angel weighing a soul, two horses' heads; on the s wall hardly anything at all. The wall paintings were discovered in 1895 by *Kempe*. – PLATE. Two Patens, 1744; Cup, 1796. – BRASS to Richard Idon, parson, † 1523, a 17 in. figure.

CLIFFE HILL *see* SOUTH MALLING

COBB COURT *see* SELMESTON

4030
COLEMAN'S HATCH
2 m. SE of Forest Row

HOLY TRINITY. 1913 by *Sir A. Blomfield & Sons*. Sandstone, with a sw tower with stone spire. Tracery of *c*.1300. The chancel E gable half-timbered. Spacious interior.

HOLLYHILL. By *J. Oldrid Scott*, 1885. Brick and stone dressings. Symmetrical Jacobean façade.

COLIN GODMANS *see* DANEHILL

COMBE HILL *see* JEVINGTON

3030
COPTHORNE
2 m. NE of Worth

Overbuilt Sussex border village.

ST JOHN EVANGELIST. In Sussex by a few yards. By *Habershon & Brock*, 1877. Quite large, rock-faced, with a NW steeple. Late lancet style, thin but not derivative, the inside unexpectedly wide, and in polychrome brick, also thin, but well proportioned.

NEWLANDS. Also in Sussex by a few yards, on the w side of the
B-road. Built in 1848–9 by *George Smith* for himself. Smith,
who was a dispirited practitioner in several styles (Grecian for
St Albans Town Hall, Tudor for the Whittington Almshouses,
Highgate, Romanesque for London Colney church), preferred
a simple comfortable styleless box for his own house; very wise
of him.

COWBEECH see HERSTMONCEUX

CRABBET PARK see WORTH

CRALLE PLACE see WARBLETON

CRAWLEY DOWN   3030

ALL SAINTS. 1843. The chancel lengthened and a N aisle added
in 1871. s aisle 1888. In the lancet style, with a bellcote, a
lower chancel, and low aisles under separate pent roofs. The
arcade has wide bays and round arches. – STAINED GLASS. In
the s aisle by *Kempe & Tower*, c.1908.*
HEATHERWOOD (formerly Oaklawn). At the corner of the road
to Felbridge. By *Maclaren*; 1871. An irregular façade, brick
with a tile-hung gable and a big chimneybreast right next to
the recessed entrance. Round the corner an odd recessed loggia on the first floor. Note the Arts and Crafts lettering on the
sundial.

CROSS-IN-HAND   5020
2 m. w of Heathfield

ST BARTHOLOMEW. By *St Aubyn*, 1864 (GR). Not small. Below
the road in a romantic dell. Nave and chancel and a little
square bell-turret set diagonally somewhat E of the w gable. –
PLATE. Paten, 1732(?).
WINDMILL. A smock-mill actually at work. It originally stood
at Uckfield.

CROWBOROUGH   5030

ALL SAINTS. Built in 1744 at the expense of Sir Henry Fermor,
and enlarged in 1881–3, at the request of Lord Abergavenny

* Mr McHardy tells me that in the vestry there are two unusually
interesting pieces of late C19 FURNITURE, a bookcase and a mirror. The
Rev. R. J. Blakeway-Phillips adds that they were made in Antwerp.

in a classical style (GR). The classical style, as interpreted by *Whitfield & Thomas*, is a mongrel affair with so-called Venetian tracery in the windows, an apse, and a heavy mid-Victorian Italianate doorway. But the tower below the straight spire is of 1744, as the keyed-in round bell-openings show. Inside, all is of the time of the rebuilding. Aisle arcades with round piers and round arches. The vestry with its entrance dated 1897 is by *M. B. Teulon* (PF).

VICARAGE. The vicarage next door is of 1744 and very fine externally. Like the church, it was built by Sir Henry Fermor, who recorded his name on the doorway. The doorway has a Gibbs surround, typical of the date of the house. The house is ashlar-faced, of five bays and two storeys with a broken three-bay pediment. The central window is round-headed.

Church and vicarage face a triangular green. The main street is away to the N, short and, in spite of its widening, entirely without character. Further on in all directions housing, and mostly houses in their gardens.

WINSCOMBE HOUSE, Deacon Road. By *Baillie Scott*, c.1899. This is one of the major houses by a brilliant and rare architect who vies with Voysey in importance in the field of domestic architecture at the end of the C19. The exterior in fact is not all that different from a Voysey exterior. The garden side is symmetrical, with two gables reaching lower on the outside than the inside. The entrance side is more informal. The long low windows especially are similar to Voysey's, but Baillie Scott's interiors are much more fancifully Arts and Crafts than Voysey's. The present tense is, alas, not appropriate here; for the principal rooms, as they were illustrated at the time,* have been altered considerably or totally.‡

GILHAMS BIRCH, 1¾ m. ESE. By *May*. A comfortable design, symmetrical to both main sides, with big half-hipped roofs.

(ANGROVE HOUSE, ½ m. NW. By *Fairfax B. Wade*, c.1908–9. A large, irregular group with half-timbering.)

(CENTRE FOR ARTHRITICS, 1¼ m. NW. By *James A. Crabtree & Associates*. Still incomplete at the time of writing.)

7010 CROWHURST

ST GEORGE. Perp w tower, not high. The bell-openings two small ogee-headed lights. The w doorway has as its hood-

* *Academy Architecture*, 1900 and 1902.

‡ I judge from illustrations, and may therefore be unjust to certain rooms or features.

mould stops the Pelham buckle. The tracery of the w window takes that form too. The rest of the church by *W. M. Teulon*, with late C13 details and a run-of-the-mill interior. – PLATE. Cup, Paten, and Flagon, 1684.

s of the church an enormous yew-tree, and s of that the ruin of the hall of a late C13 MANOR HOUSE. It was on the upper floor. The E gable stands to full height and had a large window with geometrical tracery. Below on the ground floor two small lancets. There was some continuation of the walling to the NE, and a fragment of the hall N wall is also preserved.

HYE HOUSE, ⅜ m. s. A fine house of brick, dated 1744 but looking rather earlier. Seven bays, two storeys, giant angle pilasters, parapet. To the l. and r. of the (altered) doorway narrow windows. The same above, where the window is round-headed and has brick rustication around. The other windows are segment-headed.

CUCKFIELD

3020

An unspoilt village, so close to the agglomeration of Haywards Heath. It lies up a hill with a winding South and High Streets, in the end, to the N, ascending. There are no special houses. If one starts from the church, the only ones worth mentioning are Nos 28–9, timber-framed, No. 22 with a funny little open scrolly pediment dated 1722, OCKENDEN, lying back to the N and consisting of a minor timber-framed N part and an added stone part of 1608 with mullioned and transomed windows and a gable, then the KING'S HEAD with an Early Victorian Tuscan porch, the recessed OLD VICARAGE, C18, of five bays, THE SANCTUARY with perfect decorated bargeboards of *c*.1500, and, finally, opposite, MARSHALL'S, with a Georgian ashlar front.

HOLY TRINITY. The church has a fine, open view to the s. From below, it stands out by its recessed shingled broach spire and its long, unbroken stone-slate roof in one sweep down over nave and aisle. The w tower is of the C13, apparently of two phases, the top with battlements on a frieze of pointed trefoils. The rest is mostly of about 1330, including the straight-headed windows with ogee lights. *Bodley* restored the church in 1855–6. The s porch (1883) and the N lychgate are by his pupil *C. E. Kempe*, who lived at Lindfield, the N porch (1878) is by *R. H. Carpenter*. Inside, the three w bays of the s aisle arcade belong to the C13 build. Round piers and double-chamfered pointed arches. The N arcade and the fourth bay of the s arcade are c14. Hexagonal piers. c14 also the two-bay arcades into the chancel chapels. The roofs of canted wagon form with tie-beams on traceried spandrels are of the late c15, but charmingly painted in 1886 by *Kempe*. When the big roof was put on in the c15, the quatrefoil clerestory windows of the nave became useless. They were covered up, and rediscovered only in 1925. – SCREEN. Tall, by *Bodley*, 1880. – STAINED GLASS. Much early work by *Kempe*: W 1875, N aisle W 1887, N aisle NW 1889 etc. – W window by *Hardman*, 1858 (TK). – S aisle W three large figures of 1844. – S aisle E by *Ward & Hughes*. – S aisle S *Clayton & Bell* 1869, 1879. – HELM. A Tudor helm high up on the chancel S wall. – Also two BANNER STAVES. – PLATE. Two Chalices, 1636: two Patens, 1682; Paten on foot, 1726. – MONUMENTS. Henry Bowyer † 1589. Brass plate with kneeling figures in stone surround. – Guy Carleton † 1628 and others. Slate plate with curious allegorical devices, justifiably attributed to *Epiphanius Evesham* (cf. his monument at Marsworth, Bucks., of 1618). – Ninian Burrell † 1628. Small kneeling young man; two artless angels hold a curtain open. – Charles Sergison † 1732. By *Thomas Adye*. Seated white figure of Truth holding a mirror and a portrait medallion. She sits on a grey sarcophagus in front of a grey obelisk. – Sir William Burrell † 1797. By *Flaxman*. Nothing special (over the S door). – Mary Sergison † 1804. By *Sir Richard Westmacott*. Grecian woman leaning over an urn (over the N door). – Percy Burrell, by *John Bacon Jun.*, 1810. Percy Burrell fell before Buenos Aires. On the monument he sinks into the arms of a brawny soldier.

Immediately N of the church is the GRAMMAR SCHOOL, a stately six-bay range of two storeys with three-light mullioned and transomed windows, probably Jacobean.

CUCKFIELD HOSPITAL. The former WORKHOUSE. Long brick range, still classical, the centre with a big pediment. By *H. W. Parker*, Assistant Poor Law Commissioner, 1843.

CUCKFIELD PARK. The house of the Bowyers and later the Sergisons. It is approached by a delightful brick gatehouse of the late c16, with four angle turrets. The windows mullioned, also small and round-arched and even medallion-shaped. The façade of the house behind that gatehouse, i.e. the E front, is brick too and Elizabethan too, but rendered and ruthlessly regularized, probably in 1848–51, when the S range was added. The N range however is part of the Elizabethan house, see the fine chimneystacks, some of them twisted. Inside, however,

the rich plaster ceiling with small pendants of the former NE
room, now part of the hall, is original. So is the screen now *ex
situ* in the SE room. This is dated 1581 and has sumptuous
columns and panels. The fireplace is original too. A fireplace
in a room along the S front is dated 1579

(LEGH MANOR, 1¾ m. SW. A gabled house of *c.*1550. Tile-
hung on a brick plinth. The short N wing is of the later C16.
On the N side a five-light transomed window. Entrance hall
and E porch are recent. *Lutyens* did work in the 1920s.)

MOONHILL PLACE, 1¼ m. S. By *Mawson & Horder*, *c.*1898.
Brick and pebbledash with half-timbered gables and a nicely
placed tower with copper cap.

NYMANS, 1 m. SE. This amazingly deceptive evocation of a
major manor house of the C14 to C16 by *Sir Walter Tapper*,
*c.*1925–30, for Col. Messel was mostly burnt after the Second
World War. The splendid gardens remain.

BORDE HILL, 1⅞ m. NE. Much of 1912, but the W front of 1598.
Three gables, a central one-storeyed porch, and mullioned and
transomed windows. (The VCH VII, 1940, reports that the
Drawing Room has an ornate ribbed plaster ceiling extending
into the bay and window soffits. In the SW room a plaster ceiling with flat ribs and a plaster frieze. Also panelling with fluted
pilasters. Overmantel with inlay decoration.) Panelled rooms
also on the upper floor. Stone and wood chimneypieces, two
dated 1601. Altogether a fine interior.

(PILSTYE, 2¾ m. N. Dated 1647. Stone, with mullioned windows.
The third storey is C19. Inside, ornamental plaster ceilings.
MHLG)

DALEHAM *see* FLETCHING

DALLINGTON 6010

ST GILES. Perp W tower, the doorway with leaf spandrels.
Battlements. Short recessed stone spire, a thing rare in Sussex.
The rest 1864 by *Habershon & Brock* (GR). N arcade with big,
coarse leaf capitals. – FONT. Octagonal, Perp, with concave
sides (cf. Burwash) and simple motifs such as shields. –
PLATE. Paten on foot, 1692; Cup and Cover, 1710.

By the church a timber-framed house of the Wealden type, i.e.
with the wings oversailing and straight braces running from
them parallel with the wall of the hall in the middle to help
support the eaves of the roof.

SUGAR LOAF, ¾ m. NE, at Wood's Corner. One of Mad Jack Fuller's follies (*see* Brightling, p. 425). A conical spire to give the illusion from a distance of a church standing where there is none.

(OLDCASTLE. Made from a cottage into a substantial house by *Sir E. Newton* in 1910. A picturesque group of stone, brick and tile-hanging.)

DANEHILL

4020

ALL SAINTS. 1892 by *Bodley & Garner*. Lying broadside, a little elevated above the cross-roads. A substantial, earnest job, conservative for its date, i.e. yet without anything too personal let alone wilful. Dec style. W tower quite powerful, though not high. Serious, solid interior, with the contrast of the mighty tower arches and the thin, inconspicuous aisle piers. Long single-framed roof with round transverse arches. Veranda ROOD SCREEN of 1892 with the ORGAN high on it, reaching to the roof. – RETABLE by *Comper*, the typical gilt triptych, 1936. – All STAINED GLASS by *Kempe*, mostly 1892. – PLATE. Paten, 1635 (?).

COLIN GODMANS, ¾ m. E, quite hidden away. Small square timber-framed house of the C16 and late C17, enclosing a miniature courtyard. Timber-framing on a stone ground floor. Towards the courtyard some C18 brick refacing.

DANNY PARK *see* HASSOCKS

DAWE'S FARM *see* BOLNEY

DENTON

4000

ST LEONARD. Flint. Nave and chancel and weatherboarded bell-turret. Most of the external details are Victorian. E.E., however, the N doorway, a N chancel lancet, and a smaller chancel S lancet originally of the low-side variety. Dec the chancel E window* and the SEDILE and PISCINA, the one with an ogee arch, the other with an ogee-cusped arch and a steep gable. – FONT. Norman, exactly like that of St Anne at Lewes: tub-shaped, with a main motif of basket weaving and narrow bands of pellets and plait above and below. – STAINED GLASS. E window 1897 by *Kempe*.

---

* The Rev. Victor Downs tells me that it was given in 1368 by a Flemish merchant.

w of the church the ruin of a PRIEST'S HOUSE. Plain oblong.
One window with a pointed-trefoiled head is preserved, i.e.
c.1300 or thereabouts.

s of the church the MANOR HOUSE, quite small, with a flint
front with plain, flat red-brick dressings. The house has a date
1724.

At SOUTH HEIGHTON, ¼ m. N, the MANOR FARMHOUSE is
L-shaped, with a late C18 doorway and round the corner black
mathematical tiles.

DITCHLING   3010

ST MARGARET. Ditchling is a cross-shaped village, and the
church lies a little above one of the four streets. It is externally
over-restored, but can be recognized to be essentially of the
C13. In fact the minimum details of the S aisle inside (piers
and pointed arches without any moulding) show that the nave
existed in the C12; for the aisle must have been added about
1200 at the very latest. Otherwise the C13 is almost ubiquitous.
Low crossing tower with a small pointed window to the N,
chancel N lancets, chancel N priest's doorway, with elaborate
mouldings like those of the lancets. In the doorway they actually die into vertical pieces (cf. Chichester W portal). The N
transept was rebuilt in 1863. Inside, the story is more eventful
and also more complicated; for though the S aisle arcade comes
first, the chancel must precede the present crossing. These
parts are all unusually ornate. The chancel windows are all
shafted, and the shafts have stiff-leaf capitals. There are hood-
moulds too with heads as label-stops. To the l. and r. of the E
window are tall blank bays, the l. one with a trefoil arch, the r.
with an ogee replacement arch of the early C14. The replacement may be due to damage done when the S chapel was built.
This has simple Dec windows and a single arch to the chancel
which dies into the imposts. Inside, however, the windows are
shafted just like those of the chancel, which is fairly safe proof
that these parts were re-used from the former S chancel windows. The stiff-leaf in the SE window incidentally is just turning naturalistic, a sign that the E.E. work is late in the century.
Another sign is the crossing; for here a change of plan is unmistakable from the E.E. of the chancel to a time about 1300.
All four arches have strong triple shafts in the responds, but
for the chancel arch they were soon given up and replaced by
fine shafts carrying stiff-leaf capitals. The stiff-leaf continues
on the E responds of the N and S arches, but the W responds of

16—S.

these and the W arch have moulded capitals too fine to be of before 1300. The bases also are post-E.E. – PLATE. Cup and Cover, 1567. – MONUMENT. Henry Poole † 1580. Two-tier tablet with shields in arched panels, of the type so frequent in Elizabethan pulpits, overmantels, and bedsteads.

The village is disappointing. The only major effect is at once made as one leaves the church: ANNE OF CLEVES'S HOUSE, which has nothing to do with her, but is eminently picturesque in a watercolourist's way. Timber-framed with details of the late C16, struts in the panels forming concave-sided lozenges, and also decorated bargeboards. To the l. a projecting wing with a brick front; four-centred arch to the brick doorway. Near by to the W COTTERLINGS, timber-framed but faced with black mathematical tiles, the dressings of red mathematical tiles. Then, as one continues to the E, at the main crossing CROSSWAYS with a Jacobean gable with pendants to the street. Down to the S some minor Georgian, up to the N a much-restored gabled half-timbered house (Barclays Bank) and off into EAST END LANE. Here, a little elevated and set back, the UNITARIAN CHAPEL, built c.1740. Tall wooden cross-windows to the front. Further E PARDONS, with a triangular GAZEBO in the garden, and altogether the nicest corner of Ditchling. EAST END has an odd semicircular flint projection to the front, almost reminiscent of E. S. Prior.

DITTON PLACE see BALCOMBE

DOMONS see NORTHIAM

DUTTON HOMESTALL see FOREST ROW

EADE'S PLACE see FRAMFIELD

4000   EAST BLATCHINGTON

Part of Seaford, with well-to-do houses and – of course – schools. Of the village only the faintest traces up Blatchington Hill.

ST PETER, Belgrave Road. Long nave, by the thickness of the wall in its E parts originally a Norman nave and a Norman central tower. But no Norman evidence is left. The earliest item is the priest's doorway, which is round-headed and has one plain slight chamfer. That looks c.1200. The chancel windows are lancets. SEDILIA and PISCINA are E.E. The latter has a cusped pointed arch, i.e. a late C13 motif. C13 also the w tower. It now carries a shingled broach spire. In the nave s wall recess of two large round-arched openings not considered medieval. – PLATE. Cup and Cover, c.1633.

EASTBOURNE

Eastbourne 'consists of four detached parts, two of which near the sea at the eastern and western extremities of the parish are denominated Senhouses and Meades. The others are South Bourne and East Bourne, about a mile and a half from the sea. Between these last stands Compton Place.' Thus *The Beauties of England and Wales* in 1813. They add that Eastbourne 'has of late years become a fashionable bathing-place'. Grimm in his watercolour of 1785 shows among a few houses along the front one with two bow windows called 'the hotel'. The earliest guide-book dates from 1799, but the main development started only in 1851, on the initiative of the lord of the manor, the seventh Duke of Devonshire, of Compton Place. The parts of Eastbourne have since grown together, and the confines of the town are vastly extended. The population in 1961 was over 60,000. But the parts are still recognizable, and the following description takes them into consideration.

OLD TOWN

ST MARY, Church Street. A large church of flint and stone. Broad, embattled green-sandstone w tower. On the N side of the church a big rood-stair projection. The windows are all renewed. The chief interest of the church is inside. Four-bay arcades of c.1200, the piers alternating between round and octagonal, the capitals of the early E.E. type with one row of small stiff-leaf leaving much of the bell of the capital visible. Pointed arches with hollows and fillets. The chancel aisle arcades and the chancel arch in the same style, but different. The chancel arch is round, a little out of shape now, and has, like the chancel aisles, capitals rather of the leaf crocket type. The arch, again like those of the chancel aisles, has to the w a still decidedly Late Norman outer frieze of crenellation with triangular merlons, like a pulled-out zigzag, one might say. To the E it has a frieze of lobes. This ornamentation may make one inclined to suggest for the chancel a date earlier than the nave, but there cannot be much in it, and the capitals are rather later. So far the aisle arcades have been called four-bay. In fact they have a fifth, w, bay, and this was added later to lengthen the church, at the time when also the tower was begun. Thin mouldings. They and those of the tower arch tell of the early C14. The aisle windows are later, though also C14, see e.g. the polygonal capitals of the shafts which are given to the chapel and most aisle windows inside. A tomb recess in the S chapel. In the chancel another recess, for the Easter Sepulchre, oddly set under the last arcade arch. Ogee arch with blank panelling l. and r. The same, rather coarser, for SEDILIA and PISCINA opposite. That also may be later C14, as is no doubt the canopied recess immediately above the high altar. Behind the E end of the chancel a low E sacristy, a rare thing in this part of England. – FONT. Square, the stem with angle shafts and panelling between; Perp.* – SCREENS. Two C14 screens, both with shafts with rings instead of mullions and both with relatively simple ogee tracery. – ROYAL ARMS. Painted by *Lambert Jun.* of Lewes in 1791, but the frame still Kentian in style and very country-housish looking. – STAINED GLASS. S chapel E. The last work of *Douglas Strachan* (cf. Winchelsea, p. 635). – PLATE. Cup, 1775; two Patens, 1775; Paten, 1775; Flagon, 1775. – MONUMENTS. Katherine Gildredge † 1625. Tablet with columns and open, broken, segmental pediment. Two angels on it. – Henry Lushington † 1763. With a proper, detached bust on a pedestal. The recess is Gothick, i.e. ogee-headed, and the grey back wall is a shield with garlands l. and r.; a handsome piece. – In the churchyard a CROSS brought from St Erth in Cornwall. It is Norman, with a heavy shaft and a wheel-head. The close interlace on the shaft is all defaced.

Immediately N of the church is the OLD PARSONAGE, a C16 house of rubble and flint with two-light and three-light windows, the latter transomed. It contains a hall, and divided from it by timber-framed partitions the service and solar parts. The hall has a very big fireplace in its E wall.

To the E of the church the LAMB INN, timber-framed with original close studding to the W, a dolled-up front, and, in a basement, accessible from the W by a stone doorway, a rib-vaulted undercroft.‡

Opposite this, at the corner of BOROUGH LANE the MANOR HOUSE (now TOWNER ART GALLERY), C18, grey headers and red-brick trim, seven bays to the street, with a re-used Tuscan porch further r. and the main front to the garden, i.e.

* Mr McHardy comments: Exactly like the font at Willingdon.
‡ I know no details; the publican would not allow me access.

the s. Large bay supported on Tuscan columns serving as a porch. Opposite, a C16 timber-framed house with oversailing upper floor and an C18 brick house of five bays, a nice group. Further w, in THE GOFFS, another old house, GILDREDGE MANOR HOUSE or the Old Manor House, noteworthy mainly because another old house inside Eastbourne. In 1957 decorative mural paintings were found here, Early Renaissance in style and rather coarse.

A good deal further N, in PARK LANE, Ratton Farm, or the OLD MANOR HOUSE, L-shaped, cobbled, with a five-bay C18 front, but its windows apparently an Early Victorian remodelling. For the GATE HOUSE, Ratton, *see* Willingdon, p. 630.

COMPTON PLACE

Quite separate from the village the Earl of Wilmington had his mansion. This happily survives. It was Jacobean or earlier and remodelled in 1726–31 by *Colen Campbell*, but the exterior is largely the result of a remodelling of about 1800, see e.g. the stuccoing, the Tuscan four-column porch, and the tripartite windows in the slightly projecting wings, and also, on the garden side, the Tuscan columns attached to the canted middle bay window. By that time the house had passed to the Cavendishes. Lord George Cavendish became Earl of Burlington and his grandson Duke of Devonshire. The house is of moderate size – two storeys and ten bays and the bay window to the garden. Its real date and its real value come out inside. The Hall was allowed to remain in the Jacobean position. Where the screen had been are now two Ionic columns. To the l., at the far end, the Portrait Room, also with Ionic columns, and, with a thick decoration of the walls round the portraits, a little barbaric. Big fireplace. Even richer fireplace in the Library. The Staircase has a laurel string and strong balusters with leaf at their bulbous feet. But the oval dome on Soanian pendentives must be of *c*.1800. On the first floor a gallery runs through from s to N. It is tripartite, divided by fluted pilasters. Above the centre is a square lantern with delightful Rococo stucco. The second staircase again Soanian. The apogee of the house is the State Bedroom with a ceiling gloriously overdecorated in stucco by *Charles Stanley* in 1728. The portrait of Colen Campbell should be noted, an accomplished, lively bust in 45b relief. Nice square, cobbled STABLES with inner courtyard. On two sides archways with pediments.

Hanging on to the estate a few small houses below in MEADS

ROAD, older than the surrounding housing, one five-bay,
Georgian, of cobbles, with a nice doorway, another *c.*1840,
also of cobbles, with *cottage orné* trim. On the other hand,
immediately next to them and close to the house too, JAF-
FRONS COURT, a big block of flats, introducing us to the mid
C20 Eastbourne. But we must first turn to the mid C19 one.

VICTORIAN AND AFTER

CHURCHES

Eastbourne, as against Brighton and Bournemouth, is poor in
worthwhile Victorian churches. In fact there is only one:
Street's St Saviour. For the others even a few data are sometimes
too much.

ALL SAINTS, Carlisle Road and Grange Road. 1878–80 by
T. E. C. Streatfield.

ALL SOULS, Susan's Road. Italian Romanesque, with a detached
campanile. Yellow and red, and, one would assume, the direct
progeny of Wilton and Christ Church, Streatham, i.e. of the
1840s. However it is of 1882, by *Alfred P. Strong* (GR). The
interior basilican, seven bays, columns, an arch to the chancel,
another to the apse. Stone and yellow brick.

CHRIST CHURCH, Seaside. Begun in 1859 by *B. Ferrey*,
chancel 1879 by *Scott & Hyde* (GR). Flint, geometrical tracery,
SW tower with higher stair-turret. Tall apse. The much richer
World War Memorial Chapel is by *G. H. Shackle* and of
1922 etc.

ST JOHN, St John's Road. 1868–9 by *H. Ewan Rumble* (GR). But
of this church only the tower remains, E.E., and now an isolated campanile. The new church by *A. E. Matthew*, 1955–7
The motif of the N baptistery coming out in an ample glazed
curve is similar to Coventry, but was designed before the results of the Coventry competition were published. Low aisle
passages.

OUR LADY OF RANSOM (R.C.), Grange Road. 1901–2 by *F. A.
Walters*. Ashlar, Dec, with NW steeple. No appearance of any
licences yet. Thin Perp piers inside. The E window high up
above the altar.

ST MICHAEL, Willingdon Road. 1910–11 by *G. E. S. Streatfield*
Flint, large, with W tower.

ST PETER, Meads Road. 1894–6 by *H. Currey*. Stone, without a
tower, but impressive by the long row of E.E. arcading high

up containing the aisle windows. Curious only, on the other hand, the low w lobby not running all along the w front. Interior brick-faced. Good group of five stepped E lancets above the altar. – STAINED GLASS. By *Kempe*, 1896–1906.

ST PHILIP, Whitley Road. 1903 by *G. E. Powell*. Long roof, no tower, yellow and red brick, lancets.

ST SAVIOUR, South Street. 1867–8 by *Street*, 'a very noble church', as Goodhart-Rendel said, although the material is red brick. The outline from the w is particularly fine, with the steeple standing only attached to the N aisle at its w end. It has a rich E.E. stone porch and a tall broach spire. The church itself is tall too, nave and aisles and an apse. The windows of late C13 style. Inside, the brick is also showing. The E bay of the arcading is canted towards the apse, and in the apse is thick blank arcading with mosaic figures. The chancel and apse are vaulted, the nave, high up above the clerestory, has an Italian boarded wagon roof. – Round stone PULPIT.

HOLY TRINITY, Trinity Trees. 1837–9 by *Decimus Burton*. Of that date probably the sw tower with double lancets as bell-openings and clumsy big pinnacles. The nave with tripartite E end. The aisles were added in 1855, the E end was lengthened in 1861.

Of the NONCONFORMIST CHAPELS yet less need be said. There are no early ones nor any of the grand mid-Victorian classical ones. The METHODIST CHURCH in Pevensey Road, 1907–8, is entirely churchy, Dec, with a steeple, and not of that particular Nonconformist character which is typical of about 1900, i.e. the often slightly funny type of the free Gothic, Arts and Crafts Gothic, with asymmetries, mostly brick and stone dressings. Examples are the SOUTH STREET CON-GREGATIONAL CHURCH of 1913 by *Henry Wood* and the Seaside Road METHODIST CHURCH of 1913 by *Baines & Son*. Better than the others is ST ANDREW'S PRESBYTERIAN CHURCH in Blackwater Road of 1878 by *F. J. Barker*, a good group, red brick, lancet-Gothic, cruciform, with a flèche.

PUBLIC BUILDINGS

TOWN HALL. 1884–6 by *W. Tadman Foulkes* of Birmingham. Brick and Portland stone. Free Renaissance is probably the term for this mixture of motifs. Tall tower with domed cap not in the middle of the front. Nor are the l. and r. sides treated identically.

CENTRAL LIBRARY AND CORPORATION OFFICES, Grove Road. 1962–4 by *R. Williams* and *H. Connolly* – Borough Surveyor and Deputy Borough Architect. Front with sixteen identical slim vertical openings all the way up. Normal office fenestration behind that front range.

EASTBOURNE COLLEGE is the result of a long development. The oldest buildings are now relatively insignificant. They can be seen from the E: an originally private house of 1835 (upper floor 1888) and to its r. SCHOOL HOUSE of 1870 with its polygonal projection of 1889 and the Chapel of 1874 and (E end) 1889. They are by *Currey* and, needless to say, Gothic. The aisles were only added in 1929. The N projection of School House is of 1902, but to its r. is another range of 1877 (NEW BUILDINGS). Only after 1900 came the idea of developing along a much longer front which was to run N–S. In 1902 *W. Hay Murray* built a new house at the N end of what is now the real façade of the school. It is attached to the range of 1877 and in the Tudor style with mullioned and transomed windows and gables, and he also built in 1909 BIG SCHOOL at the s end of this new future façade. Between the two is the central building, Tudor, with a middle tower and symmetrically arranged gables and oriels. This dates from 1925 and 1930 and is by *G. C. Wilson* (of Bourchier, Tatchell & Galsworthy). By him also the Master's Lodge (1927). Since then a number of additions, easily recognizable (especially where one of them peeps out in the main façade). They are by *Henry Bradford*, 1954 etc.

ALL SAINTS HOSPITAL, King Edward's Parade and Darby Road. 1869, by *Woodyer*. All Gothic, with an apsed chapel.

STATION. Opened 1861. Yellow brick, low and with an inexorable multitude of funny motifs, basically medievalizing but not shunning a French pavilion roof either.

BUILDINGS IN DEVONSHIRE PARK. The park looks very sorry for itself. The THEATRE with two identical Italianate towers is of 1884, i.e. very conservative. The WINTER GARDEN with a low Baroque entrance building was built in 1874–6 and has now been replaced by the CONGRESS THEATRE, by *Bryan and Norman Westwood & Partners*, a large, well composed and well detailed building of 1958–63. Reinforced concrete frame. Facing with greyish-blue brick and white concrete slabs. No gimmicks. The brick reliefs at the back by *Eric Peskett*. The auditorium can seat up to 1,678, but it is adjustable to several seating capacities.

PERAMBULATION
INNER EASTBOURNE

Arriving by train and making for the sea-front one is at once in
the shopping street of a C20 town,* and one has to get near the
sea end of TERMINUS ROAD‡ to find the first unmistakable
terrace of bow-fronted houses, Regency in character, but
Early Victorian in date. That is the basic motif of Eastbourne. Turn at once N (i.e. NE) and you find the most monumental terrace, GRAND PARADE (with the Burlington and
Claremont Hotels), the only one to stand up to Brighton –
forty-five bays, with attached giant columns for the angle
pavilions and the centre, and the centre marked by a pediment.
Only the lack of finesse might allow one to guess the date correctly, i.e. 1851–5. Then, to interrupt that picture of Georgian
dignity maintained, the PIER, 1872, with Concert Hall and
Pavilion of 1888, of a jollity which becomes a pier: domed
glass roofs and the occasional dome proper. More terraces of
bow-fronted houses in CAVENDISH PLACE, again 1851–5.
The QUEEN'S HOTEL, Marine Parade, of 1880, characteristically higher and with Frenchy roofs. After that a few pre-
1850 houses, smaller, also bow-fronted, with iron balconies,
e.g. No. 7 MARINE PARADE and also a few further on. But
interruptions go on, the ALBION HOTEL of 1887, in its
present appearance Georgeish, i.e. Sir Ernest Georgeish, red
brick, with a tower, and even a block of recent ten-storey
flats, METROPOLE COURT, as if one were at Sea Point, Cape
Town. Royal Parade carries on until one reaches the Redoubt.
The REDOUBT is part of the anti-Napoleonic defences of the
S coast. It is a fort consisting of two concentric brick walls.
The inner one is embattled and has a series of arched recesses
for stores. In the centre is an open space. For the Martello
Towers *see* further on, and, if you want to see one, you need
only follow the next part of this perambulation.

Turn S (i.e. SW) from where we started, and you will find a similar
development. Only the start here is the real start of Eastbourne, an early C19 cottage (former Library) with two gables
and attached to it a one-storey wing with a broken pediment
and a cast-iron veranda. Then the CHATSWORTH HOTEL,

* One recent office building deserves a mention. It is MINISTRY OF
TRANSPORT offices and lies in IVY TERRACE. Five storeys. Bands of brick
and bands of glass; curtain wall. By *Jackson & Greenen.*

‡ One more recent townish building in Terminus Road itself, BARCLAYS
BANK, in a strange, a little mannered, a little thin, classicism, Scandinavian
in flavour and of yesteryear, historically speaking. By *H. Hubbard Ford.*

Langham style, i.e. vaguely and rather grimly Gothic. The name of the hotel and that of the Burlington Hotel have already been a reminder that Eastbourne belongs to the Dukes of Devonshire and that the seventh Duke especially helped in developing. His MONUMENT by *Sir W. Goscombe John*, 1901, is in DEVONSHIRE PLACE, seated on a chair that ought to be observed. The houses around are typical Italianate mid-century. The CAVENDISH HOTEL is an intermezzo, after 1870 and before the late 80s, by *Knightley*, more towering than its surroundings and with Frenchy roofs. Look at the tower if you want to see what one means by debased Victorian details. HOWARD SQUARE again with developments of the fifties or more probably the sixties. At the far end new flats, PARK GATES, by *H. Hubbard Ford*, 1957–8. Continuing in GRAND PARADE one is in the sixties, and so goes on to the WISH TOWER. This is one of the Martello Towers of which more is mentioned under Langney (p. 548) and Pevensey (p. 582). The MARTELLO TOWERS were built between 1805 and 1810 by the Royal Engineers as a defence against a Napoleonic invasion. The plans were made by Col. *Twiss* and Capt. *Ford*. The name comes from the Torre della Martella on Corsica which had impressed the English in the campaign of 1794. The towers are circular, of brick, with walls 5 to 6 ft thick and doorways well above ground. After the Wish Tower back to the sixties, along KING EDWARD'S PARADE, interrupted again by new flats (GRAND COURT).

Behind the front it is less easy to link up in a walk. Close to the front at the NE end of PEVENSEY ROAD is LEAF HALL, built as a working men's club in 1864, and illustrated in *The Illustrated London News*. It is by *R. K. Blessley* and a funny little piece. To return to the main theme, at the far end of Devonshire Place, e.g. CORNFIELD TERRACE with giant pilasters is again of the early fifties, TRINITY STREET has detached Early Victorian houses, mostly Italianate. Typical replacements are the long Norman-Shavian terrace in SOUTH STREET, i.e. gables, tile-hanging, white stucco panels of ornament. Their replacement again is either the pretty-pretty flats of three storeys of today or the taller blocks such as have now taken possession by the Winter Gardens.

EAST CHILTINGTON

3010

CHURCH. Norman nave, with one window and both doorways recognizable. C13 W tower, short, with pyramid roof. – PUL

PIT. 1719, plain panels under a stately cornice. – FONT COVER. Nice, simple Jacobean. – (SCULPTURE. Late medieval Crucifix dug up in the churchyard. VCH) – PLATE. Cup, 1662; Paten, 1739.

EASTDEAN

5090

ST SIMON AND ST JUDE. Nave and chancel and a Norman N tower. The tower had an arch to the E, and this was followed originally by an apse. This would make the tower one of those tower-naves which existed in Anglo-Saxon parish churches and of which Barton-on-Humber is the paramount example. To the nave the tower has an arch below a later half-arch. W of the nave a Gothic lengthening of 1885.* Between it and the old nave a wide arch has been thrown across, and on it stands the organ. In the chancel exposed inside two S and two N windows, the latter lancets, the former Norman or lancets with round-headed rere-arches. In the E wall exposed two E.E. shafts with rings, from the shafting of former E windows. Kingpost roof. – FONT. A copy of the Norman type of St Anne Lewes, said to include genuine parts. – PULPIT. 1623. Flat ornamental carving. With back panel and sounding board. – PLATE. Pewter Chalice and Paten, c.1200–50; Cup, 1690; Cup and Paten, 1810.

The village has an attractive triangular Green. The cottages with much flint and brick dressings. Above them appears THE DIPPERAYS, Georgian, red and grey brick with two bow windows, and a doorway with fluted pilasters and a pediment. The side is flint with two Venetian windows. To the NE a GAZEBO, square, with pyramid roof.

EAST GRINSTEAD

5030

The roaring A-road traffic makes one forget that the core of East Grinstead is intimate in scale and shapely, a High Street nicely punctuated by an island and a large, dignified church lying just behind it (to the N) but entirely separated from it.

ST SWITHUN. Dated 1789 over the W doorway to the tower and 1813 higher up the tower. The preceding church had stood on the same site, and its tower had collapsed in 1785. The new church is by *James Wyatt*. The tower was completed after his death by the *Inwood* brothers. The material is local sandstone, yellow to grey and evenly tooled. The large

* And a further lengthening of 1961.

windows, including the bell-openings of the tower, have Perp tracery. Can they be original, or are they a replacement of the time of the restoration by *J. M. Hooker* (1876)? The Y-tracery in the lower tower windows looks much more a late c18 form. The clerestory windows are round. Between the windows regular flat buttresses. Battlements on the aisles and the clerestory. Inside there are five bays with concave-sided octagonal piers. – STAINED GLASS. One N window by *Kempe*, 1900. – PLATE. Chalice, 1618; Paten, 1702; Flagon, 1703; Paten on foot, 1720; Chalice, 1722; Paten, 1819; Paten, 1825. – MONUMENTS. In front of the chancel two cast-iron slabs with clear, solid lettering in lines along, not across the slabs and no other decoration: one of 1570, the other of 1616. – Brasses to two Knights (husbands of Dame Elizabeth Grey † 1505; 20 in. figures) and one Civilian (*c.*1520; 18 in.). – Lord Abergavenny † 1744, a lively tablet. – Gibbs Crawfurd, 1793 by *J. C. F. Rossi*, tablet with two tripods in relief l. and r. of the inscription and, above, an obelisk with an urn in front.

ST MARY, Windmill Lane. 1891–1912, by *W. T. Lowdell*. With a pretty flèche on the long, uninterrupted roof. The former PARISH HALL to its l. with its funny cupola is by *Arnold Mitchell*, 1923.

OUR LADY AND ST PETER, London Road. 1898 by *F. A. Walters*, yet, curiously enough, in a Norman style, even if the interior is more Early Christian in mood. The (ritual) w tower faces the street.

ZION CHAPEL, West Street. 1810. Red brick. The original part with round-headed windows in double recesses. Pediment.

From the church porch a passage leads s into the HIGH STREET just opposite the island which divides it into a normal, if unusually handsome, street to the E, and a wider, market-place-like w part with a s side a little raised and screened by (alas cruelly pollarded) trees. The E part has the principal houses. On the s side a fine sequence of the DORSET ARMS, c18, eight bays, white, DORSET HOUSE, dated 1705 (on a rain-water head), five bays, red brick and taller, then several timber-framed cottages and after a break the two parts of CROMWELL HOUSE, also timber-framed, the first higher and more ambitious than the other. Opposite, lying back from the road and a little elevated, is Sackville College.

SACKVILLE COLLEGE. Founded 1617 by the second Earl of

Dorset. Dated 1619. Stone-built. The façade stretches out long, is of two storeys, and has three gables over centre and end bays. Small one- and two-light windows. A doorway with pilasters leads into the spacious quadrangle. Each side has a mid-accent with gable. That on the r. represents the chapel and hence has a four-light window (with a transom) in which the religious tradition of arched lights is kept (cf. e.g. the contemporary chapel of Hatfield House). Opposite the same motif is repeated without evocative reason. The furnishings of the chapel are Victorian. Good STAINED GLASS in the E window. The centre of the back range has the small entrance to the hall. This has two large three-light windows with two transoms and no arched lights, and this motif is repeated to the l. of the entrance, again without functional justification. In the hall mixed woodwork, evidently brought in. Gallery above the entrance bay. Handsome hammerbeam roof.

The W part of the HIGH STREET is less eventful. The best group lies back, s of the W end: CLARENDON HOUSE, timber-framed with three gables with more adornment than any other at East Grinstead. Late C16, well restored. To its r. STONE HOUSE with a gabled bay of five lights: c.1600.

Much in the near and farther neighbourhood has to be sought out individually as follows.

EAST COURT (Council Offices), College Lane, ¼ m. NE of Sackville College. Simple mid C18, of five by four bays and two and a half storeys. The columnar features are all attractive additions. Good fireplace in the entrance hall.

ST LEONARD'S HOSPITAL, ½ m. SW, originally the Workhouse. By *Peck & Stephens*, 1859. It cost £6,000 and is of brick with, as a recent correspondent aptly writes, 'no definite suggestion of any particular architectural style'.

ST MARGARET'S CONVENT, Moat Road, ⅝ m. NW of the church. The Sisterhood was established in 1855 by John Mason Neale (1818–66), one of the two founders of the Cambridge Camden Society and hence of ecclesiology. In 1846 he became warden of Sackville College. The Sisterhood was started by him at Rotherfield in 1855 and moved to East Grinstead in 1856. He was an ardent ritualist and for that sin was inhibited by the bishop of Chichester. He lived and worked in that plight from 1847 to 1863. In 1851 a mob tried to burn Sackville College. When the inhibition had been removed, building for the Sisterhood started on an ambitious scale. The buildings were begun in 1865 and designed by *G. E. Street*.

Substantial additions were made later. Street first built the
entrance (w) and the N side of the cloister, Gothic, of course,
with an asymmetrical gabled and dormered front. On its r.
the refectory shows its geometrical w window of five lights.
This room, meant as a refectory – see the reading pulpit –
was used as a chapel, before the real chapel was begun. Along
its N side runs a small, low, richly E.E. cloister walk. The E
range of the cloister (St Agnes' School) is of 1874 – an even
front with six tile-hung gables. To its l. and behind (N) a
taller, yet later range of 1907–9 by *A. E. Street*. In the middle
of the cloister a cross on a pillar. The CHAPEL was built in
1879–83. It is as noble externally as it is inside. It is very tall
with long, slender two-light windows in the nave, one-light
windows in the chancel, a long, even tiled toof, and a bold,
slim, and high tower on the S side, crowned by a saddleback
roof such as Street liked. Panelling around the exceedingly
long bell-openings; tracery in the two gables. The interior
has the splendid effect of very tall, yet strong Irish black-
marble columns along, and in front of, the walls of the chancel,
separated from it by a narrow passage and connected with
them by black horizontal pieces at the level of the shaft-rings.
To the E of the E end a low retro-chapel or retrochoir, vaulted
in three by three bays. Small E apse. Street gave the vaulting
and the marble columns as his own contribution. – REREDOS
by *Earp & Hobbs*. – STAINED GLASS by *Bell & Beckham*. –
STALLS with MISERICORDS carved by a Sister around 1900.
– The GUEST HOUSE, SE of the tower, is of 1889 and has a
timber-framed upper floor. This is by *A. E. Street*, but as
originally planned by his father.

To the SW, at the corner of Turner's Hill Road and Coombe
Hill Road, is GREEN HADDON by *Leslie Gooday*, 1961–2.
Brown brick, single-storeyed, roughly L-shaped with two
elongated hexagons connected by a kitchen link. Low-
pitched roofs. The shorter wing has the garage, the larger
living and bedrooms. The best view is from the garden.
Further out is SAINT HILL, of stone, seven bays and two
and a half storeys, with a top balustrade and giant pilasters.
One-storeyed colonnade on the S front. It all looks *c.*1830.

60a ½m. SE of Saint Hill, i.e. 1¾ m. SSW of the church, is STANDEN,
one of *Philip Webb*'s finest houses, a large and late one, built
in 1891–4. It is a wonderfully relaxed design, informally
grouped round the tall tower, with spacious outbuildings
including a gateway and a main range facing S. Webb liked

the use of a variety of traditional materials and also elements of more than one style of the past. So here there are stone, bricks of different colours, pebble-dash, tile-hanging, weather-boarding, and there are, side by side with the weatherboarded gables, and the tall, proud chimneystacks, everywhere seg-ment-headed Georgian windows. The centre of the main s front which is to the l. of the tower is of five bays with five gables. In the middle a stone porch with a far projecting canopy. The way it comes forward is of the same boldness and force as the fireplaces inside. Especially delightful the 59 metal parts of the fireplaces. Much white panelling. Mostly original *Morris* wallpapers.

1½ m. WNW of Saint Hill is FEN PLACE MILL, an extremely picturesque group of miller's house and mill, the former timber-framed, the latter C18 with white weatherboarding and tiled roofs. To the W a large mill-pond.

(½ m. NE of this, i.e. SW of Imberhorne Lane, is TILKHURST FARM, externally Victorian, but internally much of a medi-eval hall-house. Mason)

Now W of East Grinstead, ¾ m. SE of Felbridge on the Surrey border, GULLEGE FARM, a beautiful Jacobean house at the s end of a long lane and with a good view to the s. That front is stone-faced, smooth, with three equal gables and mullioned windows. The other sides show their timber-framing. Good chimneystacks, one of star-shape, the others square, set diagonally.

EAST GULDEFORD 9020

ST MARY. There is a faculty to build the church which dates from 1499, and we know its consecration date: 1505. From this church much of the present brick walling survives and the angel corbels, two large, four smaller, and the panels with the arms of Guldeford. The church must have been re-modelled *c.*1820, *see* the typical early C19 tracery patterns: intersecting and simply two mullions running up into the arch. The interior wide and aisleless now, but formerly with a row of timber-posts. In fact the church is twin-roofed, with hipped roofs, and the bell-turret sunk between the roofs is responsible for the hunchback silhouette of the church, standing out against the flat fen.* – FONT. Of Sussex marble, square, with on two sides the usual flat arches, on the third

* I wish to thank Mr Austin Blomfield for information on East Guldeford.

three rosettes. – PULPIT. Early C19. – BOX PEWS. Early C19.
– PLATE. Cup, 1728.

5010

EAST HOATHLY

CHURCH. Perp w tower with higher stair-turret. w doorway
with shields and leaf in the spandrels. The arms are the
Pelhams', and their buckle badge is used as label-stops. The
rest of 1856. – Inside a Norman PILLAR PISCINA with zigzag on the shaft. – PLATE. Chalice and Paten, 1567. – MONU-
MENTS. Outside, against the s chancel wall, a tablet to
Samuel Atkins † 1742, who was gardener to the Duke of
Newcastle. – John Mittell † 1734. With an urn in front of an
obelisk. By *Edward Pierce* of Deptford; late C18. – E. T.
Kemp † 1859. Killed in the Indian Mutiny. A military still-
life of sabre and shako. By *E. J. Physick*.

BELMONT. Georgian, of three bays, with hipped roof and
Tuscan porch.

THE GATEHOUSE, to the r. of Belmont. Early Victorian, of six
bays and two storeys. Red and white. Porch of two pairs of
columns.

EAST MASCALLS see LINDFIELD

5030

ERIDGE

HOLY TRINITY. 1852–6. Like a school, i.e. with the entrance
leading into the middle of the small nave and a turret over it.
Also straight-headed windows. The interior must be remodelled.

ERIDGE CASTLE unfortunately was demolished in 1938–9. It
was a castellated affair with machicolated turrets, built for the
second Earl of Abergavenny in 1787. The architect, called
Taylor, was an amateur. Murray in 1877 calls it 'in the worst
possible taste'.

All that remains of the Abergavenny activities is picturesque
estate cottages by the church.

7020

ETCHINGHAM

THE ASSUMPTION AND ST NICHOLAS. Sir William de
Echyngham's church; he is buried in its chancel. He died in
1389, and on the brass one reads that he 'fecit istam ecclesiam
de novo re-edificare'. It is indeed a complete C14 job, and still
not Perp in any one motif. We do not know when it was be-

gun, except that it was under construction in 1366 and that there is a record for 1369 about a contract referring to five windows including one of three lights. It is a large and proud church, with a crossing tower in the earlier medieval tradition, also still maintained at Alfriston, and a high nave and chancel. The chancel is longer than the nave, but then Sir William's was a collegiate foundation. The tower is tall and blunt, ending in a parapet, as does the higher stair-turret. The nave is only two bays long, with a remarkably high clerestory. The chancel has high two-light windows with different patterns of flowing tracery, and the E window is of five lights, with flowing tracery more enterprising than is usual in Sussex. The N aisle E window has the charming feature of a segmental head with a band of quatrefoils under it and the arched lights only reaching up to this. The W window of the church is tall and of three lights, with charming tracery too. On the arches of the three lights sit two arch-heads and on this a complete miniature two-light window. The details inside are all standard and all the same. Octagonal aisle piers, crossing arches higher to E and W than to N and S. Ogee-headed SEDILIA and PISCINA. – SCREEN. One tier of pierced panels. The upper parts are missing. The stalls have MISERICORDS with two foxes as preachers, two keys, fishes, two ladies with the quadrangular hair-dress of the moment, etc. – TILES. Original tiles in front of the chancel and in the chancel. – STAINED GLASS. Much in the tracery heads of windows, especially N transept E, with the Signs of the Evangelists and angels in the tracery. – E window by *J. R. Clayton*, 1857 (TK). – S aisle E by *Mayer*, 1883 (TK). – Funeral BANNER and HELM. – PLATE. Paten and Almsdish, 1679. – MONUMENTS. Brass to Sir William de Echyngham, on the chancel floor. The head is missing. The figure is 4 ft 8 in. long. – Also on the chancel floor, Sir William † 1412 with wife and son. The son died in 1444. The figures are under ogee canopies, and they are about 4 ft 3 in. long, father and son identical, except that the father is a little taller. The brass is almost identical with one at West Grinstead. – Elizabeth Echyngham † 1452, brass, 12 in. – Agnes Oxenbridge † 1480, brass, 17 in. (both S aisle). – Thomas Echyngham † 1482, completely plain tomb-chest in the chancel. – John Snepp † 1823. With a profile medallion at the foot. – Henry Corbould † 1844, by *Charles S. Kelsey*. Gothic tablet, also with a profile medallion at the foot.

STATION. 1852 by *W. Trees*. Tudor.

HAREMERE HALL, ½ m. ENE. Large symmetrical Jacobean stone façade with two projecting bays carrying shaped gables. Four-light transomed windows. At the back uneven fenestration and a date stone 1682. This however cannot refer to the front, though it may to the handsome staircase with twisted balusters. Also inside several brought-in Jacobean overmantels.

KITCHINGHAM FARM, 1⅛ m. NNW. Eminently picturesque, with parts with narrowly studded timberwork and tile-hanging over, and other parts with wider and later timbering.

(SWIFTSDEN, formerly Hillside, on the road from Ticehurst to Hurst Green. 1892–3 by *Sir Reginald Blomfield*. Brick and stone dressings. Neo-Georgian, with hipped roof and dormers. Symmetrical front with asymmetrical attachment. The total cost was £2,670.)

7020   EWHURST

ST JAMES. Of the C12 the W tower, see the doorway with a typical quadrant moulding and one order of shafts. They have shaft-rings and capitals with flat stylized leaves. Of the same date the S arcade. Square piers with slight stop-chamfers; unchamfered round arches. The N arcade E respond is the same, but the octagonal arcade piers and double-chamfered arches are of the late C13, as are the W respond with a chubby man holding his ears and the (renewed) bar tracery of the N aisle windows. The spire is shingled and of a sugar-loaf outline, though in fact there is not a curve but a slight break in pitch. Kingpost roof in the nave. – FONT. C13. Shallow square bowl with tapering sides. A kind of flat spur ornament in the spandrels. Round base with spurs. – PLATE. Cup and Paten, 1758. – MONUMENT. Brass to William Crysford † 1520. Civilian, kneeling, 10 in. long. – Exceptionally well planted churchyard.

THE PREACHER'S HOUSE, W of the church. Closely studded ground floor, tile-hung upper floor – an attractive group with the adjoining oasthouses.

8010   FAIRLIGHT

ST ANDREW. 1845 by *T. Little*. E.E., with a tall NW tower with beacon turret. A jagged-looking building, especially from NE and SE. – PLATE. Cup and Cover, 1697. – MONUMENT. W. and E. J. Janson, by *J. S. Westmacott*, 1881 – the end of a family of sculptors. This is indeed an entirely retrospective design. An angel with a scroll, Early Victorian or even Regency in tradition.

FAIRWARP

4020

1¾ m. N of Maresfield

CHRIST CHURCH. 1881 by *Rhode Hawkins*, but decisively enlarged in 1930. The E end has a polygonal apse windowless to the E. The staircase arrangement of the tower is remarkable: two stages of which only the upper is in the usual position. The tall single-lancet bell-openings have blank fancy tracery at the bottom. The floor of the church is paved with travertine. All this is of 1930 and due to the Eckstein family, whose MONUMENTS are in the churchyard. One has at the angle of a stone sarcophagus bronze angels, another is a bronze statue of Hermione Beatrice Eckstein, a young girl, a third is a sarcophagus with panels of cherubs. They are all signed by *Sir William Reid Dick* and dated 1932, 1930, and 1950 respectively.

FALMER

3000

ST LAWRENCE. Crushingly neo-Norman, and this conversion the work of so late a date as *c.*1856 (VCH). The church had been built in 1815, and the N wall still shows some of the simplicity of that building. Flint and red brick dressings. – The WEST GALLERY could be of 1815 too, with its iron columns. – PLATE. Chalice and Paten, 1666; Paten, 1749; Flagon, 1779.

Belonging to COURT FARM HOUSE, next to the church, is an uncommonly long thatched BARN, aisled inside.

UNIVERSITY OF SUSSEX. The university was established in 1958 as the second new university in England (after Keele). The architect appointed was *Sir Basil Spence*. Building started in 1960, and at the time of writing Falmer House, the centre of the social life of staff and students, the Physics Block, and the Boiler House are ready, the Library and a first Hall of Residence (by *H. Hubbard Ford*, not by Sir Basil Spence) under construction. Sir Basil Spence's work is emphatically post-1955 in style, which is the same as saying post-Coventry. Only the S porch of Coventry, a late alteration of the original design, points in the direction of Brighton University. What propelled Sir Basil's style into this new direction is clearly such buildings by Le Corbusier as the Jaoul houses of 1954 and the Law Courts at Chandigarh of 1956, although he himself also

64

referred to the ruin of the Colosseum as a spiritual source. Falmer House possesses indeed something of the awe-inspiring fragmentariness of the ancient ruin. This is due to the bold and wholly successful way in which on all floors the walls of the four ranges round the inner court are in places left entirely open with spaces later perhaps to become rooms but looking as though they once might have been rooms. The *Leitmotifs* of Sir Basil's work at Brighton University are heavy, chunky slabs of concrete and flat-arched concrete vaults. Both, especially the latter, are to be seen everywhere. The Physics Block e.g. is covered entirely by an aqueduct-like row of such segmental vaults. The exposed concrete is contrasted against the red brick walls, faced with stretchers only. Only the sheer outer wall of the staircase has another facing: knapped flint. The ensemble is exciting in the extreme, in fact so high in its emotional pitch that one may be left in doubt whether the social life in the building will live up to so exciting a visual setting. Falmer House is square, with the refectory projecting from the W range to the outside as well as into the courtyard. The main axis of the university runs through the middle of the building from S to N. Physics then lies to the E of the axis, to be continued by Chemistry and Engineering. The Library is to the W of the axis, and the N will be closed by the Arts buildings and the Offices. The halls of residence are much further N. The main axis will no doubt in the end remain strongly marked. But otherwise all is asymmetrical, both in the grouping of the buildings and in Falmer House itself. Here it is especially the alternation of solid and void which seems at first quite arbitrary but turns out to follow rhythms one can react to, rhythms of brick and concrete, volume and space, cubic and arcuated. The skyline is horizontal except for the raised shallow tunnel-vault of the refectory and an odd two-pronged erection above the staircase, again Corbusian in spirit. The Refectory vault is faced with wood-boarding inside. On one long wall large wall painting by *Ivon Hitchens*. The Debating Hall is oblong, but has octagonal seating, reflected in the ceiling with its lantern lighting. The Physics Block is similar in character but has in addition a less convincing rhythm of windows, axial but of various widths, including the functionally dubious slit windows already used by Sir Basil at Queens' College Cambridge and of course also used by many others in recent years. The roof of the Boiler House has projecting concrete fans.

FEN PLACE MILL see EAST GRINSTEAD

FILCHING MANOR see JEVINGTON

FLETCHING

4020

ST MARY AND ST ANDREW. Norman w tower with twin bell-openings and – of course later – shingled broach spire. The arch to the nave is not genuine. The Norman nave can still be seen by two windows now above the s arcade. They are oddly enough on different levels. Early C13 three-bay arcades with round piers and arches with two slight chamfers. C13 also the transepts, see their E lancets. To the N transept a mausoleum was added in the same style in the late C18. This was built by John Baker Holroyd, first Earl of Sheffield (see Sheffield Park, p. 605), to contain his own monument and those of members of his family. Also buried in the mausoleum is Edward Gibbon of the *Decline and Fall*. The very long chancel in the E.E. style dates from *John Oldrid Scott*'s restoration of 1880. The side windows are lancets, but the E window has intersecting tracery, with curious cusping. Good boarded roof of pointed-trefoil section. – PULPIT. Jacobean, with panels of fine, flat arabesques. – ROOD SCREEN. Perp, with the unusual motif of six-light divisions; panel tracery. – SOUTH DOOR. Perp, with tracery. – STAINED GLASS. By *Kempe* chancel s, 1883; s transept, 1893; chancel E, 1898, a specially good example of Kempe's style. – PLATE. Cup, 1632; Flagon, 1740. – Funeral ARMOUR, helms, sword, gloves, and spur in the N transept. – MONUMENTS. Brass to a Knight of the Dalyngrige family, late C14, and his lady, excellent 3 ft 10 in. figures under concave-sided canopies. – Two small, fragmentary late C14 figures from a monument. – Richard Leche † 1596. Standing wall monument. Alabaster. Two recumbent effigies, he on a half-rolled-up mat. Between them lies a skull. The inscription records that she had the monument made 'of her own accorde and heselfe livinge to be pictured lyinge by him'. Two columns and straight top.

The LYCHGATE is by *J. O. Scott*.

To the SE of the church is CHURCH FARM HOUSE, early C18, of pale brown and vitrified black brick chequer, five bays, Tuscan porch with pediment – a handsome house. (At the back close-studded timberwork of the C15. MHLG) To the SW of the church a castellated GATEHOUSE to Sheffield Park (see

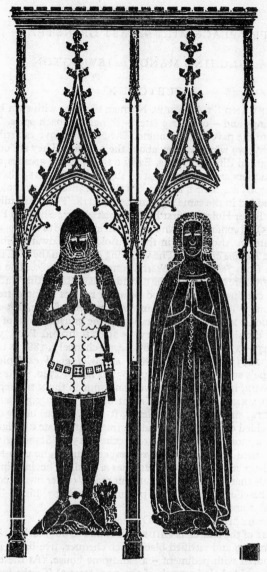

Fletching, brass to a Knight of the Dalyngrige family
and his Lady, late c14

p. 605). Adjoining it w and NW of the church half-timbered
Sheffield estate housing. A little further N CLINTON LODGE,
C18, grey and red chequer brick, five bays, hipped roof, pedi-
mented Roman-Doric porch. Next door ATHERALL'S
FARMHOUSE, the same type but later. Doorway with Greek
key in the frieze.

SHEFFIELD PARK. See p. 605.

(DALEHAM, 1⅛ m. NE. Late C15. Single-bay hall with oriel.
Original closely studded timbering. The service extension is
preserved, the solar extension has disappeared.)

SHEFFIELD ARMS, Sheffield Green. Early C18, of nine bays
with hipped roof and a steep pediment. Nice staircase.

POUND FARMHOUSE, WNW of the Sheffield Arms. L-shaped,
C15 and C16. The closely studded part with the strong posts
belongs to the former, the projecting wing with the gable and
the original mullioned window to the latter.

PILTDOWN, of Piltdown Man memory, is 1½ m. to the SE.

FLIMWELL

7030

ST AUGUSTINE. 1839 by *Decimus Burton*. The chancel 1879,
the spire 1873. Aisleless, with lancet windows and a substantial hammerbeam roof. To the l. and r. of the altar WALL
PAINTINGS in tiles and mosaic. The roof of the chancel with
decorative painting, the walls with stencilled patterns. – PUL-
PIT. Attached to it many disjointed bits of woodwork, C17 and
after.

SEACOX. 1871 by *Slater & Carpenter*. Stone, three-storeyed in
a French château style, the garden side symmetrical with a
large glazed central bow.

ESTATE HOUSING. Steep gabled groups with Gothic windows,
half-timber work and tile-hanging as well.

FOLKINGTON

5000

ST PETER. Flint nave and chancel and weatherboarded bell-
turret. Lancets in nave and chancel. No structural division inside between nave and chancel. Kingpost roof. – FONT. Perp,
octagonal, with panelled stem. – PLATE. Cup, 1718, and
Cover, engraved 1718; Almsdish, 1727; Flagon, 1731. –
MONUMENT. Lady Thomas † 1697. Cartouche with putti. –
Sir William Thomas, *c*.1720, with putti and an urn.

FOLKINGTON MANOR. By *W. J. Donthorne*, 1843. Flint, large,
Tudor, with mullioned and transomed windows and two sym-

metrical principal façades, the one Early the other Late Tudor. The whole is scholarly and unpicturesque.

RECTORY, N of the church. Also probably of the 1840s. Bands of grey and red brick. Asymmetrical façade with one steep and one higher shaped gable – i.e. Jacobean.

WOOTTON PLACE, ¾ m. NNE. Gabled Jacobean front and mid C17 back of brick and flint. To this *Detmar Blow* added in 1915 an excellently imitated mid C17 extension with hipped roof. In an outbuilding a cinquecusped window, in another a statuette of the Virgin defaced and now half-hidden by ivy. (Very pretty Early Georgian staircase with carved tread-ends. It comes from a house in Battersea, London. CL)

FOREST ROW
4030

HOLY TRINITY. 1836 by *William Moseley*. Rather spindly, with a thin W tower and a slimmer recessed shingled spire. Lancet windows and a short chancel. S aisle by *Herbert Green*, 1877–8. Elaborate barn roof inside with pendants. The only remarkable feature is the three W arches, tall, stepped, and in line, built to support the tower. – PLATE. Set, 1835.

CHRIST CHURCH, Ashurstwood, 1 m. NNW. By *Lacy W. Ridge*, 1884. (Inside an early C16 Flemish carved altarpiece. NBR)

VILLAGE HALL. By *Brydon*, 1892. Opposite the church. Small, symmetrical, with tile-hung upper floor and a central porch with lush William-and-Mary decoration. A little lantern with spirelet on top.

BRAMBLETYE, ½ m. NW. The impressive ruin of the house which Sir Henry Compton built in 1631. Still entirely Elizabetho-Jacobean in style. No touch of the Jonesian yet. The symmetrical front of the house is still easily recognized, with its central porch, canted bays l. and r., and towers at the angles. These are of four storeys, and one has still got its ogee cap. The porch also is higher than the house itself, which was two-storeyed with mullioned and transomed windows. It is interesting that the porch, though it has little niches l. and r., has a Gothic rib-vault. The whole front range was standing on a rib-vaulted undercroft too. Access to this was from the side at the foot of one of the towers by a tunnel-vaulted ramp. To the N of the house was a gatehouse. The arch stands, and the lower parts of the two originally domed rooms l. and r.

BRAMBLETYE, 1 m. NW, the new house, in an elevated position. Stone, Tudor. By *Forbes & Tait*, 1919.

BARTON ST MARY, 1¼ m. NW. By *Lutyens*, 1906. Approached by
a tile-hung gatehouse with a roof sloping deep down at the end.
The house itself is in a free Tudor style, roughly symmetrical.
Pebble-dash and brick windows. Many garden ornaments.

(ASHURSTWOOD HOUSE. About 1900; by *McVicar Anderson*.)

(DUTTON HOMESTALL, ⅝ m. N of Ashurstwood church. The
house consists of two parts: Homestall, the original house,
much restored in 1933, and Dutton Hall, transferred at the
same time from Cheshire. Dutton Hall has typically West-
Midlands ornamental timber-framing.)

(GREAT SURRIES, 1¾ m. NE. Of *c*.1565. Timber-framed, with
fine chimneys.)

ASHDOWN HOUSE, 1¼ m. ENE. By *Benjamin Latrobe*, shortly
before 1795, when he emigrated to America. He had been a
pupil of S. P. Cockerell, and Ashdown House and Hammerwood (*see* p. 515) are his two surviving English jobs. Ashdown follows after Hammerwood. It is very perfect indeed, a
prelude to what he was going to do at Philadelphia, Baltimore,
and Washington. The house is only three bays wide, ashlar-
faced, with a middle Ionic portico of four columns, projecting
in a semicircle and corresponding to a semicircular recess behind so that a circular porch results. It has a coffered vault,
and the bases and capitals of the columns are of *Coade* stone.
The windows l. and r. are set in blank arches, and the centre
bay is slightly lower than the side bays. Inside the house, the
principal effect is the staircase, with a thin wrought-iron railing, up to a concave landing from which three tripartite doorways lead l. and r. and centre. They have two columns each
with egyptianizing capitals. Daintily decorated ceiling.
Lutyenesque summer house next to the house.

UPPER PARROCK, 2 m. E. C15 hall-house, the hall no longer
open to the roof. But the kingpost roof remains, with four-
way struts and that of a slightly later cross-wing. The staircase projection is later C16 and has a gable with decorated
bargeboards. The house was an iron master's. The hammer
pond is not far away.

SHALESBROOKE, off Chapel Lane, ¾ m. SE, by the golf course.
By *Mervyn Macartney*, *c*.1900. Stone, Tudor, with gables and
tile-hanging. Asymmetrical composition.

ASHDOWN PARK (CONVENT OF NOTRE DAME), 2 m. SSE.
The core is a mansion of 1867. The additions for the convent
include a large chapel in the Gothic style, built in 1924. Close
to the convent, 2¼ m. SSE, is the disused church of

ST RICHARD DE WYCH, built in 1886. The architect seems unrecorded. It is quite a substantial job, with a crossing tower and an apse, Perp in style. The crossing and apse space is all rib-vaulted, with tiercerons and foliage bosses.

WYCH CROSS PLACE. 1910 by *Edmund Fisher*. On the opposite side of the road from St Richard.

CHELWOOD VACHERY, 1½ m. SE of Wych Cross. A re-created hall-house, originally called TRIMMER'S POND, with the hall space to the roof, the kingpost struts, and the walls separating the hall from the solar and the services wing with a spere truss and an interesting complicated timber construction with big curved braces. The W extension is a little later than the rest, which is assigned to the C15.

SUN HOUSE, Chelwood Gate, ½ m. ESE of the A-road crossing. By *Colin Lucas*, for his grandfather, 1931, i.e. a pioneer piece of the so-called Modern Movement in England. It is yellow, not white, at the time of writing, and it has little of note except its general cubic shape, yet its historic significance remains.

KIDBROOKE PARK. *See* p. 547.

4020   FRAMFIELD

ST THOMAS BECKET. Built largely after a fire of 1509. The W tower rebuilt in 1892 (*B. E. Ferrey*). The arcades, chancel arch, and S chapel arcade all the same. Octagonal piers, double-hollow-chamfered arches. – REREDOS. Alabaster, with figures in the highest relief. By *J. D. Sedding*, 1893, according to Kelly, and in memory of someone who died in December 1891. Sedding himself died in 1891. – STAINED GLASS. Christ and the Children; pretty, in the English wood-engraving way. 1962 by *Jane Ross*. – PLATE. Cup, 1716. – MONUMENTS. Edward Gage † 1595 and family. Brass plaque with a simple stone surround. – Frances Warnet † 1622. In a nice alabaster surround. – Robert Durrant † 1799. Urn in front of an obelisk. By *Parsons* of Lewes. – Sarah Woodward † 1823. By *Sir Richard Westmacott*, a plain tablet with a little Grecian decoration at the top. – (In the churchyard headstone to Ann Leadner † 1825 with a terracotta plaque by *Harmer*. SAC, 1962)

At the approach to the church l. and r. good houses, both timber-framed and both showing it in parts.

FRAMFIELD PLACE. An C18 house externally now much of *c.*1830–40, e.g. with a Greek Doric porch, but the hall inside remodelled by *Norman Shaw* in 1892 and the Drawing Room with its remarkable ceiling of beams set in chequerboard fashion by *Lutyens*.

HIGH CROSS, 1 m. s. By *F. P. Cockerell* (? Kelly: W. Cockerell), *c.*1850–60, red brick, with steep gables and angle buttress shafts, i.e. Early Tudor. Of no architectural consequence.

(HEMPSTEAD FARMSTEAD, 1 m. NW. Timber-framed, C15. Of that time the E wing, partly closely studded, with the original hall and its kingpost roof. MHLG)

(EADE'S PLACE, ¾ m. SSW. On the E side a fine door-hood with flat carving and large carved brackets, dated 1635. MHLG)

FRANT

5030

ST ALBAN. 1819–22 by *John Montier*, W tower, nave, and short chancel. Ashlar, embattled with tall segment-headed windows with a kind of Perp glazing bars, i.e. a tier of slender arched panels and another above arched also at the bottom. The bars are of iron. The porch is embattled too. Only the E window is Victorian. The tall piers inside are again Perp, of a perfectly correct section, but they are of iron too. Depressed arches. The lush leaf capitals including the E corbels with coats of arms as well are remarkable for their date. Mr Montier had a fine antiquarian knowledge. W gallery, also on thin iron shafts. Canted ceiling. – PULPIT and READING DESK, of alabaster, something between Early Christian and Renaissance. Dated 1892. – STAINED GLASS. Some of the C15, including whole figures, in the N and S windows. – PLATE. Flagon, 1766; Font Ewer, 1776; Cup, 1800. – MONUMENTS. (At the W end of the nave three iron slabs, one of them dated 1631.) – Henry Weller † 1720. Tablet with two cherubs' heads below and two cherubs above. – Charles Brown † 1754 and wife † 1789. By *Edward Pierce*. With urn before obelisk. – John By † 1836 and Esther By † 1838, the former with a kneeling woman by a sarcophagus, the latter with a standing woman leaning over a sarcophagus. By *E. Physick* of London. – Third Earl of Abergavenny † 1845. Gothic tablet of bronze.

Opposite the church entrance, at an angle, a terrace of substantial stone cottages with stepped gables.

A short street leads S from the church to the spacious green. On its E side one three-bay ashlar-faced house with angle buttress-shafts and battlements, after the destruction of Eridge Castle and the more recent destruction of SAXONBURY LODGE the one reminder of the second Earl of Abergavenny's taste for Gothick.

On the same side SHERNFIELD PARK, a plain, big, Early Victorian classical job by *Vulliamy*, 1853. The only remarkable thing is the gargantuan central doorway with pilasters and rustication. It reaches up to the second floor of the house.

On the W side FRANT COURT (St Laurence's School), 1912–14 by *Granville S. Streatfield*, brick, with tile-hanging and many gables.

⅜ m. NE ELY GRANGE, by *L. R. Guthrie* (of Wimperis, Simpson & Guthrie), 1932. Chaste neo-Georgian.

FRISTON

5090

ST MARY. Inside the church very odd early traces. A small round-headed window, a doorway to its W, another doorway still usable to the W of that, and another on the N side. The latter two no doubt are Norman. Walter Godfrey's explanation of the situation is that the traces of the other doorway are Saxon and the window belongs to it, so that the church was lengthened by the Norman builders to the W. The church has a tile-hung bell turret and a good kingpost nave roof. The chancel is C14 and has, apart from a reredos recess in the E wall, blank arches in the N and S walls. – STAINED GLASS. In the N chapel by *Margaret Thompson*, 1959. In the not unusual wood-engraving style. – PLATE. Cup and Cover, 1683. – MONUMENTS. Of Selwyns of Friston Place. Thomas † 1539 and wife. Brasses, 15 in. figures. – Sir Thomas † 1613. Excellent standing alabaster monument. Two kneeling figures facing one another across the prayer-desk. Children kneel below, but three babes in swaddling clothes lie on a pillow under the prayer-desk like small French loaves. – Edward † 1704. Also a standing monument. Reredos type, without figures. Segmental pediment, half-pilasters, volutes outside them, and long Latin inscriptions. Not at all provincial either.

FRISTON PLACE. The gabled brick front is early to mid C17. Mullioned and also mullioned and transomed windows. Round the corner some closely studded C15 timberwork is visible. Pretty, though much restored WELLHOUSE in front of the façade. Also a BARN with mullioned windows. (Inside the house, hall with kingpost roof and a room with painted hunting scenes. SCM, X)

FULKING

2010

1¼ m. WSW of Poynings

PERCHING MANOR FARM. Early Georgian five-bay front with

symmetrical windows. No special doorway. Flint and red brick.

CASTLE RINGS, on Edburton Hill. Motte-and-bailey castle with a very small rectangular bailey and a small motte.

GILHAMS BIRCH *see* CROWBOROUGH

GLEN ANDRED *see* GROOMBRIDGE

GLYNDE

4000

GLYNDE PLACE. Fine courtyard house of flint built for William Morley in the 1560s. The w front, originally the entrance side, dates from his time. It carries a date 1569. The front is symmetrical with middle entrance. Three projections carrying gables and two chimneybreasts between. These carry brick stacks. The archway has a four-centred head. The windows are all altered, except the small ones in the gables. Through the archway into the courtyard. Is the porch with its colonnettes really of 1569, and are the mullioned and transomed windows? Opposite, in the E range, was the Great Hall. It is no longer that, as the whole E range has undergone drastic alterations. It was made the entrance range by Bishop Trevor, to whom the house belonged in the 1750s and 60s. To the front (E) three shaped gables, one of them rising above the central porch, and two symmetrically placed bow windows, one of flint, one of brick. What date is all this? Hardly earlier than Jacobean, and moreover it was georgianized in 1755–60 and again tudorized in the C19. The Trevor family had come into Glynde by marriage with the Morleys in the later C17. Bishop Trevor also remodelled the Great Hall. This was done in 1758. The hall has two screens of Tuscan columns. The spacious staircase to the r. with its twisted balusters must be of the late C17.* Above the hall lies the Gallery. This has a chimneypiece of varied marbles which was bought for £143 *c.*1758. Above it sumptuous Gibbonsesque garlands of the 1680s surrounding a bronze relief by *Soldani*. There are three others in the house. A door surround in the gallery, also evidently late C17, has the arms of Bishop Trevor in the open segmental pediment.

The bishop, in connexion with his improvements and the conversion of the E front into the entrance side, had to make a

* Another staircase, in the S range, has vertically symmetrical balusters and looks Elizabethan or Jacobean.

new approach too. This now is s of the house and is formal and monumental. It first goes through the STABLES, built in 1755–60 by *John Morris*, i.e. through a tall and wide archway of red brick with a pediment and a broad wooden cupola over. The stables l. and r. are of flint, knapped on the w. Then follows the house on the l. and the new church on the r., and finally a wall of flint and brick with blank arches and in its middle two mighty GATEPIERS, with lead wyverns by *John Cheere*.*

ST MARY is like a private chapel more than a parish church. It is by *Sir Thomas Robinson*, amateur-Palladian,‡ and was built in 1763–5. It is a small oblong structure of flint with ample stone dressings, e.g. a complete ashlar base. To the w a tall projecting pedimented ashlar porch, an ashlar pediment and bellcote, to the E a Venetian window and also a pediment. Round-headed side windows. Hussey in 1852 calls the church 'in a very bad taste, the style called Grecian'. The interior is perfect, or would be without the screen and the glass. White coved ceiling with a Rococo cartouche, the Venetian window in a frame of rosettes in coffers, BOX PEWS, WEST GALLERY, PULPIT, COMMUNION RAIL – it is all still there. – FONT. A big baluster with round bowl.§ – STAINED GLASS. All by *Kempe*, in the most grossly ill-chosen Holbein style of fat Renaissance decoration: 1894 and 1900 (cf. All Souls Brighton). – In the E, NE, and SE windows many Netherlandish C16 and C17 panels. – PLATE. Cup, 1660; Cup of *c*.1660 on C18 stem; Flagon and two Almsdishes, 1765. – (MONUMENT in the churchyard to Marianne New † 1811 with a terracotta plaque by *Jonathan Harmer*. SAC, 1962)

BARROWS, ¾ m. NW of the church. A group of Bowl barrows, one of which covered a cremation in a collared urn accompanied by beads of faience, shale, amber, and bronze.

GLYNDEBOURNE
1 m. N of Glynde

4010

Glyndebourne means internationally the opera attached to a private house, and for the opera-goer the memory is of a Victorian house plus the opera house with its free semi-period

* £48 5s. was paid for them in 1759.
‡ Or by *Robert Trevor*, the bishop's brother (?), also an amateur architect – *see* his drawings at the RIBA and in the Bodleian. Mr John Harris told me about him and his drawings. But a letter of 1764, mentioned to me by Mr R. F. Dell, seems to imply that Robinson was the designer.
§ £20 was paid for it in 1765.

attachments. It is easily forgotten that this was the house of the Morley family till 1589. In fact the N end of the symmetrical Victorian W wing contains timber-framing inside and to the E back yard and, again inside, mullioned and mullioned and transomed windows. There is also a contemporary overmantel, and of course panelling, including some pre-Elizabethan. Then there is the staircase inside this wing, still with a string, but with the strong balusters of the late C17. Moreover the Library is said to have been two late C17 rooms. The Victorian Tudor is by *Ewan Christian* and dates from 1876. It is dominant in the S apart from the W façade. To this house Mr Christie, early in the 1920s, added, continuing the S range, a long and high Music Room with an organ, a bay window, and a tunnel-vault with Elizabethan plasterwork. The architect was *Edmund Warre*. This room now connects the house with the Opera House.

The OPERA HOUSE was opened in 1934, also to the design of *Warre*. It is of stone and brick chequer, much livelier a surface than the rest. The raised stage part has classical pilasters and an unrelievedly square top. But extending to the S is a group of lower rooms for the artists, in a kind of free Tudor ending in the Green Room with a big oriel window. The materials are brick and stone in irregular chequerwork. It is a curious *ensemble*, and as such perhaps best suited to the informalities of the summer intervals between the acts of the operas.

GRAVETYE MANOR *see* WEST HOATHLY

GREAT DIXTER *see* NORTHIAM

GREAT KNELLE *see* BECKLEY

GREAT MAXFIELD *see* WESTFIELD

GREAT SHOESMITHS *see* WADHURST

GREAT SURRIES *see* FOREST ROW

GREAT WIGSALL *see* SALEHURST

GROOMBRIDGE

The real Groombridge with Groombridge Place is in Kent. The

Sussex Groombridge is New Groombridge, and it has not much shape.

St Thomas. 1883. Perp, with a tile-hung bell-turret. w porch with a lean-to roof. It is not likely that one would guess *Norman Shaw* as its architect.* – STAINED GLASS. By *Kempe*, in the chancel, 1895–9. – The ALTAR CROSS and CANDLESTICKS by *Goodhart-Rendel*. Again one would hardly guess.

58 GLEN ANDRED, ¾ m. SSW. A very important and an enjoyable early house by *Norman Shaw*; dated 1867. Brick, with much tile-hanging. The entrance side in addition three even gables with plaster decoration of an Elizabethan geometrical kind. The porch moreover with a pointed arch. The garden side is quite asymmetrical with, near its centre, a brick chimney running up and, to its r., high under the roof, a tucked-in oriel. Mullioned and transomed windows. High Victorian houses had also been asymmetrical, but what is new in Shaw is the domesticity and informality of his designing, partly to be attributed to the local materials and techniques (such as tile-hanging) he used, partly to inspiration from the much too little-known George Devey. In Shaw's *œuvre* this new character comes out at Glen Andred for the first time. The asymmetries are still a little wild; later, e.g. in Shaw's own house in Hampstead, they will be more controlled. By the side of Glen Andred the rocky glen.

LEYSWOOD, ¼ m. SW of Glen Andred. Also by *Shaw* and also early – 1869, but alas only surviving as a fragment. The disappearance of this most picturesque, even if still a little melodramatic mansion is a shame. The house stood on a wild terrace of natural rocks. What remains is the tower which formed the entrance into the courtyard and a tile-hung range with three dormers to its side. The tower has a correct, historicist pointed archway, but on top, above battlements, a completely asymmetrical roof, more French than English. The tower is of brick, laid incidentally in English bond.

PENN'S ROCKS, Lye Green, 1¾ m. SSW. Up a long drive through a glen and with sandstone rocks just above the house. This is historically memorable as having been William Penn's, and architecturally as possessing a fine S front of *c.*1735–40. Two storeys. Five-bay centre, the doorway with Gibbs surround and pediment, the window above it with pilasters. To

---

* Sutton says in 1902 that *Shaw* also designed the MISSION CHURCH below the present church and school. The date is supposed to be 1872, but may be earlier (letter received from Mrs Skinner, the librarian).

the l. and r. of the front one-bay attachments with arched windows, originally only one storey high and connected by rising double-curves with the centre of the house. Irregular back with much Late Georgian remodelling.

GUESTLING

ST LAURENCE. Small, with tiled roof of a nice geometry. Norman w tower with twin bell-openings. w doorway with one order of shafts with single-scallop capitals and roll-moulding. Flat, clasping stair-turret. The tower arch the size of a doorway is all new. Does it represent reliable evidence? The NW quoin of the original aisleless nave is visible, and next to it the Norman w window of the first aisle. The present arcades are later. The first addition to the Norman church came about 1200. It concerned a two-bay N chapel. Square pier with stop-chamfers. Round arches with two slight chamfers. The N and w windows are lancets. The w entrance to the chapel has thick semicircular responds with early stiff-leaf capitals (one tier of leaves high up the bell). Moulded arch with big zigzag to the w. Fully E.E. chancel, see the SEDILIA. The E window is Victorian, the side windows are Dec. The aisle arcades of two bays are of c.1300, with standard elements. The s chapel goes with them. – STAINED GLASS. Bits in a N aisle window. – PLATE. Cup and Cover, 1685; Flagon, 1719. – MONUMENT. John Cheyney † 1603 and wife. Two of the usual kneelers.

BROOMHAM. By C. F. Callow, c.1925.

GULLEGE FARM see EAST GRINSTEAD

HADLOW DOWN

2¾ m. ENE of Buxted

ST MARK. 1836 by *William Moseley*. How much of this did *G. Fellowes-Prynne* preserve, when he remodelled or rebuilt the church in 1913? By him the thin w tower with thin recessed shingled spire, the spire adorned by dormers. By him the pert bellcote over the chancel w end. And probably by him also the idea of a tripartite arcading at the w and the E ends of the nave, for tower and subsidiary rooms and for chancel and chapels. – PLATE. Paten, 1726; Two Cups, 1794; Flagon, 1795.

HAILSHAM

ST MARY. A Perp church. w tower of flint and stone chequer.

17—S.

Battlements and (later) polygonal pinnacles. Bell-openings of two lights with a transom. The s aisle is of 1870 (*H. E. Rumble*), the clerestory of 1889. Interior unifiedly Perp, with standard arcading. Kingpost roofs. – An ARCHITECTURAL FRAGMENT of the C13, a twin foliage capital, is most probably not from the predecessor of this church but from the cloister of a monastic house (Michelham?). – PLATE. Chalice, 1614; Paten, 1727; Cup, 1732; Flagon and Almsdish, 1807. – MONUMENTS. In the churchyard sw of the church a tomb-chest with terracotta urns by *Harmer* of Heathfield. – Inside a tablet to F. C. Harvey † 1922 by *W. E. Tower* in the style of the late C17.

There is little that needs picking out at Hailsham. From the Market Place Vicarage Road leads to the VICARAGE, the one really worthwhile building, a swagger five-bay house of *c.*1700. Chequered grey and red brick and rubbed brick dressings. Giant pilasters at the angles. Doorway with Ionic pilasters against rustication and with a pediment over a bolection frieze. The middle window on the upper floor has a Gibbs surround all in brick. Pretty staircase with twisted balusters and carved tread ends. Otherwise, go s from the Market Place and have a look at the MANOR HOUSE, early C18, also five bays, but very minor after the Vicarage. The doorway has a straight hood on thickly carved brackets. The parapet curves up at the corners. Dormers too with normal pediments, one with a segmental one. Turn N and you can look behind Nos 25–27 HIGH STREET to see some closely studded timber-framing.

HALLAND

1¼ m. w of East Hoathly

HALLAND PARK FARM, ⅞ m. SE. Here are the remains of the Pelham mansion built in 1595 to replace Laughton Place as the principal house of the family. Of the courtyard house of brick the outer wall remains, but only to a moderate height. Fireplaces inside and chimneybreasts outside are recognizable, and also the walled garden in front. The farmhouse contains one remarkable fragment, some seventy years older than the mansion: parts of an Early Renaissance terracotta frieze, typical in style of *c.*1525. It must have belonged to Laughton (*see* p. 549). Beneath it a frieze with the Pelham buckle. To the SW BARN, said to have been formerly a coach-house. Late C17, brick, of five bays and two storeys with a big hipped roof. The façade is entirely articulated by giant pilaster strips. Cross windows below, mullioned windows above.

BENTLEY WOOD, ⅝ m. wsw. By *Serge Chermayeff*. One of the *incunabula* of the International Modern in England. Plans were made in 1934, and refused by the Rural District Council. A Public Enquiry was held, and the architect and client won. The house was illustrated in 1939. It is an excellent modern composition, nearly entirely glazed to the s and otherwise weatherboarded with unpainted cedar boarding. Some of the setting is no longer in its original state. The Henry Moore figure at the end of a terrace e.g. is gone. There are also other details altered.

HALTON *see* HASTINGS, p. 520

HAMMERWOOD

ST STEPHEN. 1879–80 by *E. P. Loftus Brock*. Nave and chancel, s aisle and se tower with spire. Mildly flowing tracery. And a superb position. – MONUMENT. Anthony Clouston Partridge † 1943. Relief with Elisha and the Shunammite Woman kneeling, the child standing between them. By *Eric Kennington*.

BOWER FARMHOUSE. Large, irregular, timber-framed farmhouse of the c15 to c16. Some of the timberwork closely studded (N side s wing, also N wing). Moulded bressumers on the N and s sides of the s wing. Gables with moulded bargeboards on the s wing (N side) and the N wing. (Inside a fireplace dated 1595 and a staircase with a tree newel-post the whole height of the house. MHLG)

HAMMERWOOD, w of Bower Farmhouse. By *Norman Shaw*, 1872. Attached to a former chapel with imitation Perp e window. The house itself typical Shaw, brick ground floor with blue brick diapering, tile-hung upper floor, big roof with timber-framed dormers. Pronounced overhang to the s. The chapel has a big timber porch.

HAMMERWOOD HOUSE, s of the Farmhouse, at the end of a lane. By the great *Benjamin Latrobe*, c.1793 (cf. Ashdown House, Forest Row), his first independent job. Latrobe emigrated to America in 1795 and there built e.g. the exquisite Baltimore Cathedral. Hammerwood House is of ashlar stone and has, to the s, a five-bay centre with three-bay giant pilasters. Attached to the l. and r. by short links are low angle pavilions with pediments on Doric columns which betray how impressed Latrobe

must have been by the French architects of the Boullée-Ledoux
type. The columns are short and stumpy, taper excessively
and have fluting only right at the top. It is a demonstration of
primeval force.

HAMSEY
4010

ST PETER. Broad, low Perp W tower. Norman nave and chancel.
Preserved one nave S window, one chancel N window, the outline of the nave doorways and the small, plain chancel ones.
The chancel re-done *c*.1300, with a nice three-light E window.
– FONT. Octagonal, Perp, with cusped panels. – STAINED
GLASS. Original bits in a S window. – PLATE. Cup, Flagon,
and Almsdish, 1801. – MONUMENT. Edward Markwick † 1538
(chancel N). Tomb-chest with cusped quatrefoils; recess with
a very flat arch; cresting.

YEOMANS, ¼ m. NW. Dated 1584. Timber-framed with a
porch. Main gable with a pendant. Decorated porch gable.
In the square timber-framing some concave-sided lozenges
and the same motif with spurs.

OLD RECTORY, a little further on, ¾ m. NE of Offham church.
A square three-bay house of the early C19. The motif of the
angle-strips is quite frequent hereabouts.

HANDCROSS
2020

A cheerful village, mostly Victorian, on the Brighton Road S of
Crawley. By-passed in 1959 by a road which has good lines but
is being spoilt by finicky shrub-planting.

ASHFORD, ¾ m. SE, by *Devey*, was demolished recently. The NW
lodge remains, and if this is also Devey's it is a good example
of the kind of design that would develop later into a Voysey
house – the connexion being that Voysey was a pupil of
Devey.

1 m. WNW of Handcross a big, close-timbered hall-house.

(THE HYDE, 1 m. NW of Handcross. In the house some carvings, Flemish or French. Also six Purbeck-marble shafts
taken from the Temple Church in London, when Tite restored
it *c*.1842.)

HANGLETON *see* BRIGHTON, p. 457

HANKHAM *see* WESTHAM

HARTFIELD

4030

ST MARY. The N side has one blocked trefoil-headed lancet, i.e. a late C13 form, but the masonry looks older. The S aisle window and the S arcade are Dec. Octagonal piers and double-chamfered arches. The E bay is large and suggests a transept. Perp W tower with tall shingled broach spire. The nave roof has old tie-beams and kingposts. – FONT. Octagonal, with pointed quatrefoils containing shields. – STAINED GLASS. W window by *Wailes*, 1857. – PLATE. Cup, two Patens on feet, and Flagon, 1713. – MONUMENT. Mrs Maitland † 1823. By *John Cole Jun.* Aedicule with Tuscan columns. – Several other Late Georgian tablets.

THE LYCHGATE, a cottage by the churchyard of which the upper floor extends above the lychgate. A date 1520 is traditionally given to it. Timber-framing with closely set studs and also diagonal braces. The first floor oversails.

The village street is pleasant, though without any special houses.

BOLEBROOKE, 1¼ m. NNW. The substantial fragment of a C16 brick mansion. What remains is first of all the gatehouse with polygonal turrets to the outside, covered with ogee caps. Three-light brick windows. To the inside buttress-shafts instead of turrets. The façade of the house which remains faces E. It is not symmetrical – especially the fenestration is curiously irregular. The front is flat and has four gables with a gap in the middle. In addition there is a taller and wider gable over a r. cross wing flanked by buttress-shafts. – Outbuilding with a brick ground floor and closely studded timber-framing above.

HASSOCKS

3010

No church and no identity.

DANNY PARK, under Wolstonbury Hill. The house has two main fronts, one to the E of *c.*1582–93,* one to the S of 1728.‡ 1582–93 refers to George Goring, later Earl of Norwich, 1728 to Henry Campion. The E front is very monumental, three38b storeys high, of brick with blue brick diapers. E-shape, with wings projecting two bays. They have canted bay windows and so has the recessed centre, two l., two r. of the middle porch. The l. one represents the hall, as is at once visible by – more than anything else – the exceedingly tall windows in the bays. They have three transoms. The other windows are of the

---

* The latter date on a ceiling in the N wing.
‡ Rain-water heads.

normal mullioned and transomed kind, except on the top
floor, where they have mullions only. Dormers over all the bay
windows and the porch. The porch is thinly decorated with
two orders of columns and a meagre pediment. The hall is still
there but in all its decoration altered about 1728. Very simple
large, strictly architectural chimneypiece with open segmental
pediment. The s front is of nine bays with a slight projection
of the middle five bays. Two storeys only. Giant angle pilasters, to the centre two, with stone capitals and bits of entablature, segment-headed windows, parapet – a typical, stately
Early Georgian job. Inside, the main staircase is of 1728 too,
swinging round elegantly, and with two twisted and one
columnar baluster to each tread.

LITTLE COURT, Belmont School Lane, ¾ m. NW of the station.
By *Neville Conder*, 1957–8. A substantial, single-storey house,
well grouped, well placed, and well landscaped around.

HASTINGS

THE OLD TOWN

Medieval Hastings was in possession of a mint already in the C10.
That it was the headquarters of William and the start of the
Conquest need not be said. Little remains of the castle, however. Hastings became the chief of the Cinque Ports in the
C12, but its decline began already in the C13, and both Rye
and Winchelsea were more prosperous as ports. The French
sacked Hastings in 1339 and again in 1377, and the town
never quite recovered. The medieval town lay, and the old
town still lies, in the valley between West Hill, i.e. the castle
hill, and East Hill. It stretches out in a SW to NE direction with
the main streets parallel l. and r. of the Bourne stream and
connected by little more than passages. At the sea end was the
port and is now the fishing harbour. In 1801 Hastings had only
3,175 inhabitants. The seaside development began shortly
after, and St Leonards, which is now administratively and
visually one with Hastings, was a completely separate and
slightly later development. In 1841 Hastings had 12,000 inhabitants, in 1861 23,000. The total is now (1961) over 65,000.

CHURCHES

Hastings in 1291 had seven churches, in 1372 four, in 1801 two.
To these were added first St Mary (1828) as the centre of a sea-
front crescent, then Holy Trinity as a second town church (1851

9). But the rush of new churches came only between 1875 and 1890. During those years eight churches were built, including three by *Sir Arthur Blomfield*, one by *Brooks*, one by *Pearson*, and one – the best in the town – by *Champneys*.

ST CLEMENT, Croft Road. In the middle of the old town, but away from the High Street. Perp, and probably built after the French burning of 1377. SW tower, not tall, of stone and flint chequer, higher stair-turret, battlements, pyramid roof. Four-light W window. The tower arch has bits of leaf attached to some of the capitals, a pretty touch. Tierceron-star vault. Arcades of seven bays, piers of the four-shaft-and-four-hollows moulding, not tall. W niches in those which corresponded to the division of chancel from nave. No structural division exists. – SCREEN. Fragments at the W end of the nave. – PAINTINGS. Moses and Aaron, by *Roger Mortimer*, 1721 (S aisle E). – Also a panel with records of benefactors. At the top putti round a coat of arms. Probably also by *Mortimer*. – CHANDELIERS. Two big brass chandeliers of two tiers, given in 1763. – PLATE. Flagon of 1714 by *Timothy Ley* (cf. All Saints). – MONUMENTS. John Collier † 1760. Handsome architectural tablet with three cherubs' heads at the foot and with garlands.

ALL SAINTS, All Saints Street, at the NE end of the medieval town. Perp, of rubble, and not specially grand or large. Built probably early in the C15, as the church is called new in a will of 1436. W tower, partly of flint and stone chequer with a quatrefoil frieze between doorway and W window. Upper windows with heavy ogee hood-moulds, bell-openings much lighter, tall, of two lights with a transom. Tierceron-star vault inside. The centre ring for the bell-ropes decorated with animals round and round. The inner moulding of the tower arch on short concave-sided shafts. Large aisle and E windows, renewed (by *Butterfield*, 1870). Arcades of four bays, the piers octagonal, the arches moulded and starting from a vertical piece. Dull Perp chancel SEDILIA. – WALL PAINTING above the chancel arch: Doom, with Christ seated on two rainbows, the Punishment of the Damned on the l., the Heavenly Jerusalem on the r. – STAINED GLASS. E window by *Gibbs*, 1861, pictorial. – PLATE. Two Cups, Paten, Flagon, and Almsdish, 1714, by *Ley*. – MONUMENTS. Large incised slab of a Civilian and wife, originally inscribed 1458. The Signs of the Evangelists in the corners. Supposed to be foreign. – Brass to Thomas Goodenough and wife, *c.*1520, 25 in. figures. –

John Edmonds † 1847, by *W. H. Burke & Co.* of London.
With an urn and drapery; pre-Victorian in type.

All the other churches of Hastings and St Leonards belong to
the C19 and C20. They are listed alphabetically, as is always done
in *The Buildings of England*, although it would be more profitable to attempt a chronology starting with St Mary-in-the-
Castle.*

ALL SOULS, Athelstan Road. 1890 by *Sir Arthur Blomfield*. Red
brick; large; no tower. Lancets and plate tracery. Tall clerestory of stepped triplets of lancets. Spacious interior with a
solid open timber roof. A serious town church. – PLATE.
Elizabethan Cup and Cover.

ST ANDREW, Queen's Road. 1869 by *Habershon & Brock*. Thin
square SE tower with a thinner bell-stage and a pyramid spire.
The tower stands close to an apse of three sides of an octagon.

CHRIST CHURCH, Laton Road, Blacklands. 1878–81 by *R. H.
Carpenter*. The lavish chancel decoration is of 1899. It is by
Hardman & Co. (D. J. Powell).

CHRIST CHURCH, London Road, St Leonards. 1875 by *Sir
Arthur Blomfield*. Big, with a long nave and a NW tower
turning octagonal high up. Lancets; five stepped lancets to
the street. Very tall interior.

CHRIST CHURCH, Old London Road. 1878–81 by *Gough*.
Small, with flowing tracery and a very naughty SW turret.
Naturalistic capitals inside, especially notable the chancel
arch with vine trails hanging from the capitals. Also natural-
istic leaves on the roof corbels. – PLATE. Flagon, 1798–9;
Chalice, 1802–3.

CONVENT OF THE CHRIST JESUS, Magdalen Road, St Leonards.
Chapel begun by *A. W. N. Pugin* before 1850. Completed by
E. W. Pugin with some alterations in 1869.

ST CLEMENT, Priory Road, Halton. 1838 by *Thomas Catley*.
Lancets, bellcote, a thinly timbered roof. The chancel is of
1888.

ST ETHELBURGA, Filsham Road. 1929 by *J. B. Mendham*.

FISHERMEN'S CHURCH, Rock a Nore Road (now the FISHER-
MEN'S MUSEUM). 1854. Very plain, with lancets and no
division between nave and chancel.

ST JOHN, Upper Maze Hill. 1881 by *Sir Arthur Blomfield*.
Destroyed in the Second World War except for the SW tower,

* For the churches of villages now part of Hastings see Hollington,
p. 538, and Ore, p. 577.

which is almost entirely octagonal. The rest 1951 by *H. S. Goodhart-Rendel*. Brick, with rich ornament and many mannered details. Inside, a strange bridge across the chancel. – PAINTING. Adoration of the Child, large, by *Ortolano* (cf. Rome, Galleria Doria Pamphili). – STAINED GLASS. All by *Ledger*.

ST LEONARD, the parish church of St Leonards, Marina. 1953–61 by *Sir Giles & Adrian Gilbert Scott*. Gothic, of light brick, facing the sea (not orientated). Tower with high parabolic arch round and above the doorway. The interior also on the same theme of parabolic arches – to the chancel, behind the altar, and also l. and r. towards the side windows.

ST MARY-IN-THE-CASTLE. 1828 by *Joseph Kay*. So called because it is the replacement of the church in the castle (*see* p. 523). To build it, space had to be dug out of the castle rock. The church forms part of the Pelham Crescent composition,₅ₒ♭ and indeed its climax (*see* p. 526). A Louis-Seize façade. Two porches l. and r., insignificant. Portico of four unfluted Ionic columns carrying a pediment. Two columns behind, in the recessed part between the porches. Inside, a more than semi-circular auditorium with gallery. The altar is behind the portico. Light comes in from the top. The altar decoration altered by *H. Weston* and *H. Tickner* in 1893. The conception of the church derives from the Pantheon, perhaps via S. Francesco di Paola in Naples (1817) etc.) or Possagno (1819). – PLATE. Flagon, 1824; Two Cups and two Patens on feet, 1827; Two Almsdishes, 1827.

ST MARY MAGDALEN, St Margaret's Road. 1852 by *F. Marrable*, enlarged in 1872. Dec, with a tall SW tower with beacon turret. The interior not specially interesting.

ST MARY STAR OF THE SEA (R.C.), High Street. 1882 by *Basil Champneys* (GR). Impressive inside and out. Flint. The E end very high because of the fall of the land, and with a round turret with cap between apse and chancel on the N side. Decorated W bellcote. The interior fully vaulted with quadripartite rib-vaults. High clerestory with balcony with wavy tracery. – PAINTINGS. St Matthew and St Mark. Apparently Italian, C17.

ST MATTHEW, St Matthew's Road, Silverhill. 1884 by *Pearson* (GR). Red brick, large, E.E., with transepts and apse, lancets and a flèche. Inside yellow and red brick with blank circular, foiled clerestory windows. The aisles are groin-vaulted in cement, the nave has a big Sussex timber roof with tie-beams

and kingposts. Shafting round the apse windows. The tran
sept end walls differ, as if not built by the same generation:
with very long lancets, s with bar tracery, i.e. 1260 vs. 1230.
serious church, but not inspired, as the best Pearson churche
are.

ST PAUL, Church Road, St Leonards. By *John Newton*, 1868
E.E. With plate tracery, but the NE tower rising next to the
apse with sumptuous bar tracery and shafting to the bell
openings. Brick-faced interior with polished marble columns
The chancel and the apse are rib-vaulted and have polishe
marble shafting with shaft-rings. – Alabaster PULPIT.
REREDOS with the Last Supper in sgraffito. Bands of faienc
tiles l. and r.

ST PETER, Boham's Road. 1885 by *James Brooks*. Red brick
E.E., with lancets and plate tracery. Polygonal NW baptistery
No tower. Brick also the interior. The arcade piers are round
and their capitals a case of true innovation by means of ele
mentary geometry. They are a continuation of the drum shap
of the piers penetrated by truncated pyramids upside down.
The chancel wall is alabaster-faced. – REREDOS with Cruci
fixus fully clothed (the Volto Santo) and two angels. – Ala
baster PULPIT and LECTERN.

ST THOMAS OF CANTERBURY, Magdalene Street. 1889 by
C. A. Buckler. As sparing as a friars' church. Tall, lancets, n
tower.

HOLY TRINITY, Robertson Street, 1851–9 by *Teulon*, and hov
he must have enjoyed the crazy site. A tower was meant to g
on the s porch, which stands at an angle to the church. Ove
the porch in the tympanum a colossal sign of the Trinity
With its N side the church faces Robertson Street with a serie
of cross-gables; it faces towards the Albert Memorial with
polygonal apse. The polygonal vestry was added in 1892. Th
details of the church are in the style of *c*.1300. Wide nave an
s aisle. The shafts for the principal roof-beam stand on bracket
which extend down on to the round piers. Teulon was neve
short of unauthorized motifs. At the E end of the aisle
strange chapel, aisled *en miniature* and low enough to allow fo
the organ gallery on top. Very ornate front towards the chance
The apse is decorated with blank arcading and three paint
ings on metal in evident imitation of the Trecento, a rar
thing, even for 1873, their date. They look in fact older.
FONT. Round, with gloriously thickly carved flowers an
leaves. – PULPIT. Of alabaster. – PLATE. Paten on foot, 1716

CASTLE. Half Hastings Castle is down in the sea. What remains in recognizable ruins is the N and E curtain wall and the collegiate church of St Mary, replaced finally in the C19 by the present St Mary at the foot of the cliff and for which more cliff had to be scooped out. The castle had been built by Robert Count of Eu shortly after 1069, and of his time the smaller masonry of the N wall of the nave of the church may date which became part of the curtain wall. The church was begun before 1094. Much building was done by Henry II in the early 1170s, including the building of the keep in 1172, and on in the eighties and nineties. The present entrance is immediately by the chancel of the church. The most easily understood piece of architecture is the arch, which led from the nave into a central tower preceding the chancel. It is rebuilt, but with the old materials, and must be of the early C13. The central tower is of the C11, as the remaining herringbone work shows. Attached to it is a spiral staircase. Off the chancel to the N was a rib-vaulted room, off to the S a chapel with an altar projection and a doorway to the W. This led into a S aisle, or rather S cloister, as there seems to have been solid wall between it and the nave. To the W of the nave was apparently a narthex, and beyond that stands a small square tower, duplicated perhaps on the S side of the narthex. Otherwise there is curtain walling, rising up the mound in the corner NE and coming down to the main gatehouse with its two towers round to the outside. This is C13 work. S of this a fragment of the wall walk is preserved, and another tower. The main living quarters were no doubt on the S side. Outside the walls by the present entrance is a series of narrow tunnel-vaulted corridors with recesses, called the Dungeons, and built, it is suggested, as store-rooms.

TOWN HALL, Queen's Road. 1880 by *Henry Ward*. Gothic and very modest. A narrow front; E.E. – REGALIA. Two Maces, given in 1710; Punch Bowl, 1727; Water Bailiff's Oar, 1737.

BRASSEY INSTITUTE, Claremont. 1878 by *A. Vernon*. A squeezed-in Gothic job with Venetian touches. Asymmetrical tower. To the r. a range of three equally squeezed-in bays with giant brick piers, appropriate scenes in tiles and sgraffiti, and a projecting veranda right at the top.

RAILWAY BRIDGE, across Braybrooke Street. Of c.1850. Iron with pairs of thick fluted sub-Doric columns, i.e. without entasis and with freely varied capitals. Quite a capital piece.

PERAMBULATION

OLD HASTINGS

Now that the small streets and passages round Bourne Road have been sacrificed to traffic and the widened street supplied with nice healthy housing – the Rape of Hastings indeed – the main streets, the High Street and All Saints Street, are separated by a gulf. We walk up All Saints Street first, then down the High Street, and up the remaining streets further w. But first at the foot of BOURNE ROAD just behind the Royal Standard Inn, in WINDING STREET, the very scanty remains of the SEA WALL of Hastings, built in the late C14 to protect the town from the French.

ALL SAINTS STREET starts from the sea-front (of which anon) in a nicely transitional way by a phony Gothic house with half-timbering and a big Gothic stone window. Most of the noteworthy houses, as we go on, are timber-framed, and first No. 70 on the r. Then high up EAST HILL HOUSE, really in TACKLEWAY, a fine reminder of the differences of level, as the old town grew up the slopes of the two hills in the C18 and early C19. Four storeys, two bow windows, an often recurring theme. The house is said to have been built in 1762* (and has a good staircase; VCH). More timber-framing r. (58–60: C15, and 51: C16) and l. (121). No. 29 (r.) has an oriel, 27 (r.) is made super by alterations. Nos 135–137 (l.) have an oriel under a gable. Then up another steep lane and at its end EBENEZER CHAPEL of 1817, three bays, rendered, with a pediment and the window details oddly debased for so early a date.

Now down the HIGH STREET. Here the interest is more varied. There is also more townscape interest in that the street, although narrow, for whole stretches has the w pavement elevated. The start is really *ante portas*, two large detached houses facing the church of All Saints: TORFIELD HOUSE, long, low, and white, of five bays, with tripartite windows and a deep Tuscan porch, probably *c.*1780 or so, and OLD HASTINGS HOUSE, tall, of chequer brick, three storeys, seven bays. Blunt top ending. The date probably *c.*1750. Tuscan porch. Opposite the fine former Stables of Old Hastings House, now the STABLES THEATRE. They must be of *c.*1700. Red brick. Three-bay centre, two-bay projecting wings. Wooden cross-windows. Hipped roof, the wings half-hipped. Down the

* Which would make the two bows improbably early.

street, many houses have C18 doorways with straight hoods on brackets. No. 4 (r.) has them carved. No. 6 (WELLINGTON HOUSE) is Georgian too, grey brick with red trim. No. 112 (l.), very small, timber-framed. No. 106 (l.) has a more ambitious Georgian front with two canted bay windows and steps leading up to the doorway from l. and r. No. 105 again has carved brackets. Nos 101–104 is a Jacobean group of timber-framed houses. Opposite, No. 23, grey and red, early C18. Doorway with fluted Ionic pilasters and entablature, the middle window on the two upper floors singled out by a basket-arch. No. 97 (r.) is dated 1668 and has its oversailing upper floor on carved brackets. No. 91 very nice, about 1800, with a bow for the two upper storeys and Venetian windows bent round it on both. No. 46, according to the VCH, may be the earliest house in Hastings. It was a hall-house at r. angles to the street and still has a kingpost truss. No. 38 (l.) has the same motif as No. 91. Nos 78–81 (r.) was one composition, though the l. part has lost its shallow bow. In the middle a bust of Nelson. Opposite is the OLD HASTINGS CLUB, early C19, of three bays only, but with Ionic columns on the upper floors. Rusticated ground floor, all nicely painted now. After that only the OLD TOWN HALL, rebuilt in 1828. Stuccoed. Five ground-floor arches, originally open. Five windows above. Quite unpretentious. Nothing after that.

Above the High Street up the slope of West Hill one or two more streets, tiered up. In THE CROFT is CROFT HOUSE, yellow brick, three-storeyed, with two canted bay windows and an additional third, late C18 no doubt. More nice, tall, four-storeyed houses with bows and doorways with broken pediments, early C19. In CROFT ROAD at its E end more such houses (55–59), with bows this time. Croft Road then curves down to St Clement's Church, and here is a specially charming group with bows and iron balconies (Nos 21, 27, 29, 31), also early C19. The continuation of Croft Road is HILL ROAD, back in Old Hastings, with the timber-framed and closely studded Nos 1–3. At once however into the early C19 again with the end house, HILL HOUSE, with two bows (and a Victorian doorway), and EXMOUTH HOUSE, up at the top of Exmouth Place.

This part of the perambulation ends in GEORGE STREET, where the commercial Victorian town with its shops takes over. There are, however, still two early C19 and Early Victorian houses to note: No. 10, the former MARKET, with the word Market in

Grotesque carved in stone and in Egyptian on the cast-iron gates, and Nos 15–16 with giant pilasters and balconies.

The fishing harbour of course belongs to the old town as well, but it is now inextricably part of the sea-front.

SEASIDE HASTINGS

Visitors seem to have come from about 1775 onwards, but architecturally the first event is PELHAM CRESCENT of 1824–8, by *Joseph Kay*, an enterprise of the first Earl of Chichester. The crescent rises as it curves, and its apex and climax is St Mary. A pity the houses of the crescent are not a storey lower. As it is, the church is not helped by the houses. The houses have wide shallow first-floor bows with balconies and roofs, smaller ones on the second floor, and lunette windows on the third.

If one turns E first, one passes the CINEMA, built as the Marine Palace of Varieties in 1897–9 (by *Runtz*), a long terracotta front, with two corner eminences and garland and similar decoration. After that the much more irregular houses of the fishing harbour, monstrously deprived of all their atmosphere by the Playland in front. Weatherboarding appears, and only occasionally a more ambitious house such as the EAST CLIFF GUEST HOUSE, at the corner of All Saints Street, Early Victorian, with a centre and two canted bays. Yellow brick, the ground floor stuccoed and rusticated.

Then soon the NET STORES, perhaps the most remarkable piece of architecture at Hastings, or rather piece of building, resulting as it happens in an architectural ensemble worthy of Louis Kahn. The stores are all weatherboarded and tarred. They differ in height and they differ in the direction of their saddle-back roofs, but only the two main directions occur. It is splendid basic geometry. The stores had all to be rebuilt recently after a fire.

If one walks W from Pelham Crescent, there follows at once BREEDS PLACE, with the familiar seaside bows and iron balconies. It dates from 1828 and is soon to be demolished. Then some recent building which is at Hastings remarkably tactful. We turn inland for a moment past the CASTLE HOTEL with its four storeys and four canted bays, said by the VCH to have been built before 1824, to WELLINGTON SQUARE, large and rising and of about the same date. It has a humbly Grecian centrepiece at the far end and otherwise no strict regularities or symmetries. At its foot on the l. side the BAPTIST CHAPEL of 1838, stuccoed, with giant arches embracing the two tiers of

windows. Wellington Square borders on the Victorian centre
of Hastings. Shopping streets, not many, centre on the ALBERT
MEMORIAL CLOCK TOWER of 1863 (by *E. A. Heffer* of
Liverpool, with sculpture by *Edwin Stirling*). Holy Trinity, the
church near by (*see* p. 522), is of the 1850s, and the Gothic
DRINKING FOUNTAIN, with its canopy, of 1861. Again of
mid C19 stylistic character, in Robertson Street, as is Holy
Trinity, the CONGREGATIONAL CHURCH, debased Italian
if ever there was and commercially squeezed in so that half the
ground floor is an archway into another street. In fact the
building is as shockingly late as 1884–5 (by *H. Ward*). Back to
the sea-front, where the QUEEN'S HOTEL by *F. H. Fowler*
dates from 1858–62. It is Italianate, but with a first-floor cast-
iron veranda, and not showy. The terraces of *c.*1850–60, similar, say, to those N of Hyde Park in London, are interrupted by
ALBANY COURT, flats of 1961–3 by *Sir John Burnet, Tait,
Wilson & Partners*, very tactfully done. This cannot be said of
the former PALACE HOTEL, now Palace Chambers, much
higher than anything else, with a mixture of Renaissance and
Baroque motifs and a tower ending in a French pavilion roof.
It was built in 1886. The architect was *Arthur Wells*. In
WHITE ROCK back to the early C19, but no consistent architecture. Another interruption by a recent block of flats, four
storeys, a good design and fitting in well (NORMAN COURT
by *Ronald Salmon & Partners*). Then the PIER, an elaborate
affair, with many buildings, 1872 and after. Opposite it the
WHITE ROCK PAVILION, 1913–27 by *C. Cowles-Voysey* and
H. S. Morgan, in the Spanish Mission style of America,
nicely done, with allegorical medallions of faience. After that
an imperceptible transition from Hastings to St Leonards.
One ought now to look at the development from the St Leonards point of view.

ST LEONARDS

St Leonards is entirely a made place. James Burton, successful
builder of London, in 1828 bought an estate to lay out a
watering place, stimulated of course by Brighton. The frontage
he had available was about two-thirds of a mile. It was a
speculation, and it paid. The centre of the composition, for
which no doubt his son *Decimus Burton*, the architect of the
Hyde Park Corner screen and of work in Regents Park, was
responsible, is all stuccoed brick. It has as its centre the Royal
Victoria Hotel (the name of course is later). This, with its

giant Corinthian columns, made a fine centre, both monumental and cheerful. It is now altered in too many ways to play its part. Yet that part is necessary; for the terraces to the l. and r. with their forceful but gloomy Tuscan columns below do not keep up the cheer. They have giant Ionic columns above to mark the main accents, and development has eaten into them. But development has done worse. MARINA COURT, only a little to the E, knocks everything out of scale. It was built in 1937–8 to the design of *Dalgliesh & Pullen* and was the first modernistic (as against modern) affront to the English seaside. Poor Erich Mendelsohn, poor Wells Coates, what will you be made responsible for ? The block is thirteen storeys high with a 'promenade deck' on the top floor. It is steel-framed, but with concrete balconies, the lower three flat, and to the E a perfectly civilized accent by a vertical emphasis in the windows. This represents the restaurants. Above, the balconies sweep in a domineering rhythm round the w corner and make a curved E end too. With this block the Copacabana ideal got hold of the enterprising developers, and they have not let go since.

To return to Burton's well-mannered composition, it ends on the l. with one detached house, smaller and more elegant than the others. This was Burton's own villa and the first house to be completed: three bays and two storeys, with an upper order of coupled fluted Ionic columns. Nice sunk panels on the ground floor. The main composition continues behind in a very attractive way. There is first the MASONIC HALL, more suitable visually for this purpose than as an Assembly Room for which it was built; for it is severely Greek Doric, with massive columns detached in the front, attached at the back. This axis is then continued in the SOUTH LODGE to the St Leonards Gardens, also Greek Doric, but less formidable. The ST LEONARDS GARDENS were at once part of the scheme. The site was a quarry and lent itself to picturesque landscaping. Moreover, Burton placed along its fringes, in QUARRY HILL and MAZE HILL, detached villas of large size – all this inspired by Regents Park and the villas built and intended for it, but made fully picturesque, both in the rocky layout and in the style of the villas. One, CLOCK HOUSE, is frankly Gothic, the others are Tudor, but also castellated or more cottagey,* and the NORTH LODGE is castellated too,

---

* Mr G. Spain draws my attention to two villas in Maze Hill, referred to in *The Builder* on 11 August 1860 and 22 July 1865. Both by *F. H. Fowler*.

with an archway with four-centred head.* Burton has rightly
a MONUMENT in the park, even if it is only a small stele.
Raised a little above Maze Hill is THE UPLANDS, a group of
semi-detached houses, each pair with a joint pediment.

That really is St Leonards. As the sea-front grows together with
that of Hastings, the style goes Early Victorian, or rather
fifties, and the only further effort at a composition is WARRIOR
SQUARE of 1853–64, uniform only to a certain degree, by
innumerable canted bays, but as architecture nil.

OUTER HASTINGS

Round BARLEY LANE, BELMONT ROAD, HIGH WICKHAM,
i.e. NE of the old town on East Hill, villas of c.1830–45.

From the N, down the Old Roar Gill, ALEXANDRA PARK was
designed by *Robert Marnock* in 1878 and opened in 1882. It
is a most effective feature, a long tongue of picturesque
landscaping, only very narrow, but nearly 1½ m. long.

CONVENT OF THE HOLY CHILD JESUS, Magdalen Road.
Founded by Cornelia Connelly (cf. Mayfield). The core by
Wardell, 1846–8. Much added to it, also a big detached chapel,
late C13 in style.

SILVERHILL WINDMILL. A smock-mill of 1866, the sails now
in a fragmentary state.

EYE CHAPEL, at the western outskirts of St Leonards, once the
parish church of Bulverhythe. What stands now in Hythe
Avenue is two fragments of the chancel N wall. No features.

FILSHAM FARM, Harley Shute Road. Dated 1683. Red brick
and still pre-classical, i.e. with a four-centred head to the
doorway and apparently originally mullioned windows. But
the doorway is central and the windows were probably symmetrically arranged. Typical of c.1675 or so are the circular
windows in the first and last bays.

HAYWARDS HEATH   3020

Large and quite amorphous. Shopping and offices near a main
station to London and housing tapering off in all directions.
There is after all something in the New Town idea.

ST WILFRID. Large; 1863–5 by *Bodley*, but apart from the
fine oblong central tower resting inside on two bold pointed
transverse arches no special features to make an architect of

---

* The date of the North Lodge is 1830. In the same year LAVATORIA
were built under that name.

rank recognizable. – STAINED GLASS. Some minor *Morris* glass in the S aisle; 1870. – The E window Expressionist by *A. Acket*, 1962–3.

ST PAUL (R.C.), Hazelgrove Road. Brick, round-arched, large, but architecturally indifferent. 1930 by *W. C. Maugan*.

HOLY CROSS CONVENT, Bolnore Road. Founded at Wapping in 1857 by Elizabeth Neale, sister of John Mason Neale (*see* East Grinstead). The move to Haywards Heath took place in 1872. The first wing was completed in 1887, the second in 1889. The chapel, externally of a rather fiery brick, is of 1902–6. It is by *W. E. Tower*, his *chef d'œuvre* as an architect. Tall, apsed, with a flèche and high, slender two-light windows. The interior is distinguished by transepts two narrow bays deep (not long). Rib-vaulted chancel. The vault is of concrete between the ribs. – By *Tower* also the long, ornate ROOD SCREEN and the REREDOS.

OAT HALL, Oat Hall Road. A three-bay villa with a handsome Greek Doric porch. Probably *c.*1830.

PRIORY OF OUR LADY OF GOOD COUNSEL, Franklyn Road, off Sussex Square. 1887–98. By *Edward Goldie*. Later additions.

ST FRANCIS HOSPITAL. One old house in the grounds, accessible from Hurstwood Lane. It is dated 1660 and conservative for the date. Brick and stone dressings. Two storeys, three bays. Mullioned windows. Doorway still with a four-centred head. The hospital itself is a large building of yellow brick with red-brick bands and round arches, 'Lombardo-Venetian' in style (Kelly). The S front is very long and symmetrical. The chapel lies behind. By *H. Kendall Jun.*, 1859, with additions of 1873–85.

In SUNNYWOOD DRIVE, W of Wood Ride, a group of eight two-storeyed, square brick cottages by *Lubetkin & Tecton*, 1934–6, an early date for the International Modern in England.

HEATHFIELD

ALL SAINTS, Old Heathfield, off the Battle road. Large, but not very interesting. Late C13 W tower, see the W window. Shingled broach spire. The windows all round the church renewed. Dec arches of four bays with standard details. The clerestory windows are quatrefoiled circles and placed above the spandrels, not the apexes, of the arches. – PLATE. Cup,

1565 (?); Cover, engraved 1572; Flagon, 1673; Almsdish, 1753; Paten on feet, 1772.

The entrance to the church is flanked by pretty cottages – weatherboarded and chequer brick.

HEATHFIELD PARK. Now largely by *Sir Reginald Blomfield*, 1898–1910, but incorporating the house begun in 1677 and remodelled by *Sir Robert Taylor* in 1766 for General Elliott, later made Lord Heathfield in recognition of the defence of Gibraltar in 1779–82. Blomfield has not made it easy to recognize what is old and what is his. On the garden side the old house was of seven bays with a three-bay projection. Blomfield repeated this latter motif and added another two bays. Bays six and seven of the old house became his centre and are distinguished by a big segmental pediment. The veranda is Blomfield's too, but replaces an old one in a slightly different position. On the entrance side, consequently, it is the r. part that is old, the l. part with the Venetian window that is Blomfield's. (In the hall fine chimneypiece with bearded caryatids.)

CADE STREET CHAPEL, ½ m. NE. 1809. A nice homely box with a keyed-in oval window in the façade. Inside and in the churchyard half a dozen of the pretty and naïve terracotta relief plaques by *Jonathan Harmer* of Heathfield; dates of death 1806–25.

PUNNETT'S TOWN. House and Surgery by *Bertram Carter*, 1950–1, a crisp job inside and out. (Also at Punnett's Town a WINDMILL, re-set from Biddenden in Kent. It is a smock-mill, brick below, weatherboarding above. No sails left. MHLG)

HELLINGLY

ST PETER AND ST PAUL. The W tower must be Georgian. This appears from the Y-tracery of the bell-openings, the intersecting tracery of the W window, the mouldings, and even the tooling. But the most remarkable part of the church is the chancel. Externally one sees just lancets, but, inside, the N windows are shafted, the shafts have a typically Latest Norman bobbin-ring, the capitals have crockets and foliage characteristic of the ending C12. Also, on both N and S sides, a fine palmette frieze runs along at their sill level. To this chancel belongs in its style the E respond of the N aisle with a main demi-column and pairs of subsidiary shafts with Late Norman capitals and even keeling. All this then is late C12, but what does the respond represent? The answer is probably the NW carrying pier of a crossing to which belongs the N transept, now late C13. Of that date the N window with intersecting tracery and the shafting inside the E wall, provided this can be trusted. The capitals here are stiff-leaf. The four-bay arcades have octagonal piers and arches with one chamfer and one hollow chamfer – C14, it seems. – FONT. Remains of a round Norman font with foliage built into the N transept wall. – PLATE. Cup and Paten, 1750; Paten and Flagon, 1807. – MONUMENTS. Fine Brass to a Lady with horned head-dress, c.1440, the figure 4 ft 1 in. long. – In the church-yard three head-stones with set-in terracotta ornaments, an urn, a vase of flowers, by *Jonathan Harmer* of Heathfield, late C18.

HORSELUNGES MANOR, ¼ m. SE. If this is now one of the most spectacular of Sussex timber houses, this is due to a certain extent to *Walter Godfrey*, who restored it c.1925. Yet he had good evidence for what he did, and the total effect is very probably near the effect achieved early in the C16, when the house was complete. It is a parallelogram now, facing E, but extended further N and S originally and may have been a courtyard house. Indeed Walter Godfrey thought that the house is later C15 and that the hall was not at all where it is now, but in another range, and was shifted in the early C16. The house has its entrance almost exactly in the middle. To its l. lies the hall, to its r. another room reached by a separate small doorway, and then an archway. The ground-floor windows are of eight arched lights with a transom and project in front of the wall. The upper windows are of six lights and without a transom. They also project in front of the wall, and the whole upper floor oversails. Only one of all the windows is original. The others are reconstruction on adequate evidence. The gables are an assumption only, if a well-founded one. The three doorways in the E front have carved spandrels with playing animals. Inside, the hall is one-storeyed only, with moulded beams. It has in the S wall an arched doorway to the demolished S range. In the N wall are three doorways, one leading to the entrance passage, another to the staircase. The staircase is of special interest in being an example of the earliest type of well-staircase, the well still with solid walls. It is assigned by Godfrey to the early C16, like the rest of the features of the house. But the two windows from the staircase to the entrance passage of five and four lights look Early

Elizabethan. The upper chamber has another doorway with carved spandrels.

BROAD FARMHOUSE, ⅜ m. NW. Mid C18. A specially fine piece of its date. Grey headers and red trim. Five bays, with a three-bay projection carrying a broken pediment. Hipped roof. Doorway with Doric pilasters, frieze, and segmental pediment. The frieze is carried on to run above a narrow window l. and r. The middle window above slightly decorated.

CARTERS CORNER PLACE, 1¾ m. E. The house dated 1602 above the doorway is only a part of the present house. This original part is the E front and what lies behind it. Red bricks mixed with black bricks. Centre and two gabled wings. Above the centre of the centre a dormer. This and the gables have ball finials. Mullioned and transomed windows on the main floors, mullioned windows in the gables.

HEMPSTEAD FARMSTEAD see FRAMFIELD

HERRON'S GHYLL
2 m. NNE of Maresfield

4020

ST JOHN (R.C.). 1904 by *F. A. Walters* (GR). Ashlar, with lancets and a N tower. – PULPIT. With Netherlandish C16 panels of Apostles and the Virgin.

OLDLANDS. By *Sir Matthew Digby Wyatt*, 1869. Ashlar, not the size of Possingworth. Symmetrical façade with attachments. A house like this is really in no style in particular, nor are motifs of different styles mixed with any gusto. The gables are Tudor, the rest is just clumsy and dull.

HERSTMONCEUX

6010

ALL SAINTS. The church is of *c*.1180–1200 and of the mid C15. The NW tower and N arcade come first. The tower has lancet bell-openings, one each side set in a triplet so that the l. and r. lancets are blank. Flat clasping buttresses with very shallow off-sets. Later shingled broach spire. The arch to the N aisle is pointed and has only a slight chamfer on simple imposts. The N arcade is of two bays. The pier and abacus are both octagonal, the responds and their abaci too, the arches are double-chamfered. The capitals of responds and pier have broad simple single leaves, really entirely pre-stiff-leaf. The s arcade on the other hand (three bays, slenderer piers) has the typical Sussex early stiff-leaf of one row of small leaves only showing much of the bell below. In the s aisle a cusped tomb recess and an E.E. capital by it. The aisle, as also the N aisle, is lit by dormer windows of the Victorian restoration. Straight-headed simple C14 windows. Rough two-storeyed s porch. The N chapel was built of brick about 1440 and the chancel at the same time all but rebuilt, also of brick. – FONT. A Norman bowl, decorated later with simple Gothic panelling (N aisle). – REREDOS. Stone and marble, with figure sculpture. 1893. – SCULPTURE. A cherub standing by an urn, on a base with attached colonnettes. What was it ? – PLATE. Cup, two Patens on feet, Plate, and Flagon, 1715. – MONUMENTS. First the large brass (chancel floor) of Sir William Ffiennes † 1402. Knight, 4 ft 11 in. long, under a canopy. The inscription offers 120 days of pardon to those who say a Pater Noster and an Ave for him. – Then the one really spectacular piece in the church, the monument to Thomas Lord Dacre † 1533 and his son Sir Thomas Fiennes. The twin recumbent effigies are earlier, and, as the arms are those of the Hoo family, they may represent Thomas Lord Hoo † 1455 and Sir Thomas Hoo † 1486, i.e. be of c.1480 and have come to Herstmonceux from Battle Abbey at the Dissolution to be used for the two Fiennes. The rest ornate Latest Gothic. Tomb-chest between chancel and N chapel with quatrefoils cusped and sub-cusped with gusto. Panelled arch, divided into two parts according to the two effigies below. Big tracery in the spandrels. Straight top, with, to the chancel, a swagger top-heavy cresting (of a different material ?) with three helmets, fluttering drapery, and big crests. – Georgiana Hare Naylor † 1806. By the Belgian sculptor *Kessels*. Tender, small-figured bedside scene. – (In the churchyard two tomb-chests and seven headstones of the early C19 with terracotta plaques by *Harmer*. SAC, 1962)

36a HERSTMONCEUX CASTLE. Herstmonceux Castle is the most striking proof of the extent which all-round symmetry had reached in England three generations before the coming of the Renaissance. It is true that Harlech and Beaumaris had – on French precedent – already been symmetrical before and about the year 1300, but Herstmonceux is much more domestic-looking and altogether, in spite of its moat, its battlements, and its turrets, a mansion rather than a castle. Licence to crenellate was granted to Sir Roger Fiennes in 1440. It was dismantled in 1777, and remained a ruin until restoration was taken in hand by Col. Lowther in 1913 and more seriously and indeed exemplarily by Sir Paul Latham in 1933. His architect was *Walter Godfrey*. Only in one way did the restoration radically deviate from the original. The four ranges of Herstmonceux had originally between them four courts of different sizes. There is now one large court-yard instead.

Herstmonceux is a splendid sight. The house is large, the moat wide, and the brick colour is a wonderfully soft red in the lush surrounding green. The fact that Herstmonceux is of brick is noteworthy; for, though occasionally brick had appeared in England throughout the Middle Ages, it became fashionable only at exactly the moment of Herstmonceux. Contemporary examples of similar scale in other counties are Tattershall in Lincolnshire, Caister in Norfolk, and Faulkbourne in Essex.

The castle is approached from the s. The outer arches of the bridge are restoration, the inner arches are original. To the N is a secondary entrance. It is preceded by a barbican which, however, was never completed. Both entries are in the middle of their walls. Both walls, and also the E and W walls, are accentuated by polygonal angle turrets, smaller intermediate projections also canted, and the centre motifs, again canted, which, on the E is the chapel apse, on the W the bay window of the C20 hall. The main GATEHOUSE has its turrets circular at the top, and circular still below the machicolations. Only lower down are they polygonal. Cross-shaped arrow-slits as well as gun-posts, the latter at entrance level. Between the turrets is a giant arch with a transomed two-light window below. The archway itself has a four-centred head. Otherwise most of the windows are later, i.e. Elizabethan to C20. Walter Godfrey did most of his work on the W and E sides, but on the latter, the tall two-light chapel windows with their transoms and arched lights as well as the Jacobean bow window are original.

The s GATEHOUSE has a handsome lierne-vault with diagonal ribs and ribs running straight across in pairs forming a Greek cross. Curiously enough the passage has a fireplace. The COURTYARD which one enters is impressive without question, more so than it can have been when it was so much smaller. At the back of this smaller courtyard lay the great hall. Of all this nothing can now be seen. The GREAT HALL of 1913 is in the W range and has sumptuous Gothic windows far from credible in their tracery. Opposite is the CHAPEL, which is entered by a doorway of Istrian marble. It is not large and never was. Horace Walpole in 1752 called it 'small and mean', and we do not know incidentally whether he did not consider the exposed brickwork mean too. He writes of the walls as 'in their native brickhood' without 'the luxury of whitewash'.

Other internal features of Herstmonceux are as follows. The main STAIRCASE lies to the r. of the gatehouse. It came from the Cecils' Theobalds and is indeed very similar to that of the Cecils' Hatfield. Square tapering balusters, some carved into caryatids. Tall posts with musical instruments, tools, etc., and with beasts on top. Another staircase, in the w wing, comes from Wheatley Hall near Doncaster. This must be of *c*.1675. It has gloriously rich openwork panels of cabbagey acanthus scrolls, much like those of the staircase of Dunster Castle, and posts with undersized vases. Two excellently detailed doorways with open segmental pediments. In the GALLERY in the N range is a sumptuous wooden Jacobean chimneypiece from Madingley Hall in Cambridgeshire. Coupled Ionic columns below, two tiers of caryatids and geometrical panels above.

Herstmonceux in 1948 became the home of the Royal Observatory, which had to move away from Greenwich because of too much disturbance there. For the observatory a number of new buildings had to be erected, none remarkable except for the Equatorial Group E of the castle (by *Brian O'Rorke*), completed in 1958. This is a group of six domes for equatorially mounted telescopes. They are of a most improbable beehive shape in the landscape, very successful indeed in their shapes and placing. The three northernmost are designed for reflector instruments – which involved planning things so that they should be interconnected and that the instruments themselves could be moved through trapdoors for re-silvering – the other three for refractor instruments. There is a balcony round each dome, necessary to watch for approaching clouds. The bases of the domes are of concrete and brick, the domes themselves of steel and copper. The details are elegant, not at all robust, as younger architects would no doubt do them now. The area of the six domes is formally landscaped.

HERSTMONCEUX PLACE, ½ m. NNW. A brick house with two faces, one, the entrance side, of about 1720, the other by *Samuel Wyatt* of 1777. The entrance side is wilful, a little

gaunt, and crowded with incident, the other is generously
spaced, at ease and even-tempered. The entrance side has three
storeys, the other for the same height two. On the entrance
side there are seven bays with a narrow three-bay centre. The
doorway has two shockingly detailed Ionic columns and an
open scrolly pediment. Narrow windows packed in l. and r.
Columns also closely flank the round-arched middle windows
on the first and second floors. There are two blank niches
l. and r. Brick frills above the upper windows. Round the
corner the windows are large, there are only seven bays, and
Coade stone plaques are set below the upper windows. Tuscan
porch, three-bay pediment. Again round the corner an ample
bow to which inside on the first floor corresponds a domed
oval room. Another such bow at the other end of this front.

WINDMILL HILL PLACE, 1½ m. NW. By *Willey Reveley*, the
architect of All Saints, Southampton, *c.*1790. Five bays, two
storeys, stuccoed, with one-bay, one-and-a-half-storey pavilions l. and r. Tripartite ground-floor windows. Inside, a
staircase with a delicate though simple iron railing starting
charmingly inside the hall and curving up to the first landing.
Also a three-bay room to the garden with an Adamish plaster
ceiling.

WINDMILL, NW of the above house and the A-road. A post-
mill without sails.

At BOREHAM STREET, 1¾ m. NE, several pleasant houses in
the village street and the WHITE FRIARS HOTEL with a
stepped C16 chimneybreast and next to it a Venetian window
with Ionic pilasters.

At CHAPEL ROW, 1⅜ m. N, a CONGREGATIONAL CHAPEL,
dated 1811 and pretty. Grey brick and red dressings with
arched windows and a broken pediment.

COWBEECH HOUSE at COWBEECH, 3 m. NNW, is dated 1731.
It is of five bays with a broken three-bay pediment and has to
the l. and r. of the doorway odd tall and narrow niches,
perhaps replacing windows in the Queen Anne tradition.

HICKSTEAD PLACE

2 m. SSE of Bolney

2020

On the A23 road. The house is in its general impression C18,
with tile-hanging, but on the S wall is a C15 or early C16
chimneybreast with brick gable, and inside one part has a
C15 roof. Opposite the S wall, quite close to the house, the
so-called CASTLE, probably a summer-house, but a startlingly

large one. Two storeys with stepped gables to N and S and one E projection from the staircase to the upper floor. The building is of brick and probably dates from the early C17.* The adjoining house, WESTOVERS, timber-framed and of the C15, has a C19 wing of brick in which the stepped gables of Hickstead Place are imitated.

3030 HIGHBROOK

ALL SAINTS. 1884 by *Carpenter & Ingelow*. Quite large, and a serious job, outside and inside. N tower with shingled broach spire. Windows with bar tracery, in the chancel a little more ornate. – (STAINED GLASS. E and W windows by *Clayton & Bell*.)

(BATTENS. The house has two medieval wings. That running N–S has a roof without kingposts or collar-purlins, i.e. dating perhaps from the late C13 or early C14. In this wing a two-bay hall. The other wing presumably C15. It may have contained the solar.)

HIGH CROSS *see* FRAMFIELD

4020 HIGH HURSTWOOD

HOLY TRINITY. 1870–2. Next to the dell with rhododendrons of the parsonage garden, Arcadia indeed. The church has a bellcote on the W end of the chancel and a lower apse. Lancet windows and, in the nave, plate tracery. The S tower with its half-timbered top storey is of 1903 (by *J. K. Christian*), and the W attachments are of 1935.

OLD MAYPOLE FARM, ⅝ m. S. C15, with close-studded timber-framing. Strong posts mark the division between hall, solar, and service wings, though the latter do not project. In the roof the kingposts and struts are still extant.

HOLLINGBURY HILL *see* BRIGHTON, p. 457

7010 HOLLINGTON

ST LEONARD. Away from the houses, between the trees. A medieval church, but restored almost out of existence. Small, aisleless, with a tile-hung bell-turret, looking from one side as if it were a pyramid on a truncated obelisk. Chancel of

---

* Inside the house itself, on the staircase a hunting wallpaper of *c.*1765. *See Country Life*, CIX, 1951, p. 1813.

1865. Nicely decorated, canted chancel ceiling. – SCULPTURE l. and r. of the altar by *Forsyth*. – STAINED GLASS. By *Capronnier*, 1873, the E window. Figure scenes, the coloured glass ending now with the top outline of the figures and continued in clear glass.

ST JOHN. 1865 by *E. Alexander Wyon*.

HOLMHURST *see* BALDSLOW

HOLMSHURST *see* BURWASH COMMON

HOLTYE COMMON
1¼ m. E of Hammerwood

3030

ST PETER. 1892. Recognized by Goodhart-Rendel as by *Lacy W. Ridge*. Nave with bellcote and chancel. Low lobby with two flying buttresses up to the W front. Bar tracery.

SUSSEX FARMHOUSE, 1 m. NE. Timber-framed. C15 N front with closely set studs. The r. hand gable with curved braces is C16. This front has three blocked original windows.

(KITFORD. Timber-framed C16 cottage with, on the S side, a large stone-stepped chimneybreast. MHLG)

HIGHLANDS (formerly Wilverley). By *Voysey*, 1906–7. Alterations to an existing house, also a coachman's cottage.*

HOMEWOOD HOUSE *see* BOLNEY

HOOE
8000

ST OSWALD. Perp W tower with higher stair-turret. Perp the nave too, and Perp the S porch. Entrance with big leaves in the spandrels. The most interesting part of the church is the E.E. N chapel, with tall narrow lancets to N and W, and an E end later replaced in brick. It must have been a shallow polygonal apse. – PULPIT. Only the sounding board demands notice, a fine piece with inlay, of *c*.1700. – COMMUNION RAIL. Later C17. – STAINED GLASS. In the E window small figures of a Coronation of the Virgin and yet smaller fragments. – PLATE. Cup and Cover, 1640.

COURT LODGE, ½ m. SW. A C17 house with Dutch gables, but the memorable thing about it is a room inside completely panelled with linenfold and friezes of heads in medallions

* I owe this reference to Mr Brandon-Jones.

surrounded by leaf and arabesques – i.e. typical work of
c.1530. It may not be *in situ*, but it is a perfect ensemble.

THE HOOKE see CHAILEY

HORAM

CHRIST CHURCH. 1890 by *Percy Monkton* (GR).
(MANOR FARM, ¼ m. w of the station. Late C16 or early C17.
Mainly ashlar. With mullioned windows. MHLG)
(BALLCOCKS, 1 m. ENE. C15, timber-framed. Kingpost roof
inside. MHLG)

HORSTED KEYNES

ST GILES. At the N end of the village in a dip. Cruciform with
a sharp shingled broach spire and otherwise all Norman, i.e. the
crossing tower, the nave masonry, the re-set plain N doorway,
and the chancel masonry. Then in the C13 the chancel
received lancet windows and a good stepped triplet of them
at the E end. The s transept also is C13 (see the lancets). The
N transept has disappeared, see its roof-line. Inside, the
Norman central space is interesting. The E arch is there, and
so are the much lower N and s arches, i.e. the crossing was
not a real crossing. The transepts must have been smaller and
lower, perhaps almost like Saxon *porticus*. The w arch is C14
and has re-cut foliage corbels. The N arcade is of the restoration of 1888 but the E arch is medieval.* – STAINED GLASS.
By *Kempe* the E window, 1895, and the W window, 1905. –
PLATE. Cup, 1622; Paten, Stuart; Flagon and Paten inscribed
1705; Dish, *temp.* George I. – MONUMENTS. Miniature
effigy of a cross-legged Knight, late C13 (chancel N). –
Brass to a Lady, early C15, headless, 16 in. long. – (Richard
Wyatt † 1753. By *R. Chambers*.)
(BROADHURST MANOR, 1 m. N. 1934, but with C16 parts.)
TREEMANS, 1¼ m. SSW. An interesting house, the result of
much changing. Much Tudor brickwork, some timber-
framing. Opposite the w front made uniform in 1693 with
five bays and three storeys of windows, chequer brick, and a
projecting wing of ashlar stone with mullioned windows.

HOVE see BRIGHTON, *passim*

* As the Rev. J. Eartham tells me, repairs in 1961 have brought to light
remains of a Norman and a lancet window in the nave.

HURST GREEN
1½ m. NW of Etchingham

7020

HOLY TRINITY. 1884 by *L. W. Ridge*. Red brick, with lancets and a two-tier bellcote.

GEORGE HOTEL. Early C19, with two canted bay windows, a porch or colonnade between of three pairs of Tuscan columns almost of Ledoux character, and above the name of the hotel in colossal Egyptian capitals.

Opposite a Georgian house with two bows.

HURSTPIERPOINT

2010

HOLY TRINITY. 1843–5 by *Sir Charles Barry*, large and prosperous, with a NW steeple, transepts, five bays of later-C14-looking piers, but windows with geometrical tracery, and a clerestory of three quatrefoils in a spherical triangle. The church replaces a sweet villagey one and contains many of the furnishings of this. – TILES. Ruinous, outside, in front of the W doorway. They are assigned to the late C13 and early C14. – STAINED GLASS. In the S aisle E window and one other many medallions of the C15 to C17 collected by Bishop Butler of Durham in the mid C18. – Much medievalizing glass of *c*.1850–60. – E window by *Kempe*, 1902. – PLATE. Silver-gilt Chalice, C17, probably Spanish. – Much Georgian plate: Paten, 1716; Cup, 1720; Paten, 1722; Flagon, 1725; Salver on feet, 1732; Almsdish, 1774; Paten, 1775. – MONUMENTS. Knight of the later C13, cross-legged (S chapel), and Knight of the later C14 (N aisle W), both badly preserved. Contemporary iron railings round the latter effigy. – Many minor tablets, e.g. one by *Flaxman* (Rev. C Dodson; 1800).

Near the church are a number of minor Georgian houses, e.g. one immediately SE of the church, another (LAMB HOUSE) at the start of Cuckfield Road. Off this, ⅜ m. NE of the church, is LITTLEMARK FARM, a brick house with a curiously fragmentary-looking two-bay W front of 1677 (rain-water head), conservative for its date; for it has two shaped gables, identical in design though not in size. The windows are all altered. To the r. side a big chimneybreast with stepped sides of a partial gable. Early C17 staircase.

To the E along the HIGH STREET not much of note: a nice Grecian cast-iron balcony on the r., a little three-bay Georgian brick house (WICKHAM HOUSE) on the l., a larger one again on the r. (Early Georgian, of five bays, two storeys, doorway with metope frieze on Doric pilasters). Further out detached houses of *c.*1830, especially the GOTHIC HOUSE, five bays and really standard Georgian, except that the lower windows are pointed, that there is a quatrefoil over the entrance, and that the top has battlements.

The KING'S HEAD is an oddly monumentally placed pub, where the village street reaches the A23. Centre with a copper-covered dome and a curved portico; wings at an angle. By *A. B. Peckham,* 1938.

ST JOHN'S COLLEGE, 1 m. NE. The first of the three Woodard schools in Sussex. It was built in 1851–3, designed by *R. C. Carpenter,* who also designed Lancing, which was started in 1854. Hurstpierpoint, if not as grandiose as Lancing, is also very large. The buildings are of knapped flint and look forbidding – that cannot be denied and may have been intentional. To the entrance there are two long projecting wings (as at Ardingly). Through a middle archway one enters an oblong inner courtyard and at the end of this the chapel and hall. The CHAPEL is by *R. H. Carpenter* and was begun in 1861. It has a T-shape with a tower over the meeting place – an Oxford conceit. It is tall, and the tower (it was built only in 1929) is taller. Long three-light geometrical windows. Arches high up to the N and S bays of the antechapel. – REREDOS. 1872 by *Forsyth.* With very richly carved large religious scenes. – STAINED GLASS. Apparently by *Clayton & Bell.* – The LIBRARY stands on an undercroft which was the dining hall. The library-and-chapel front is entirely asymmetrical. Otherwise much is done not to let the fenestration look too uniform. The windows are strange, mostly small, and many with ogee heads. Also two such lights with a quatrefoil over, but no arch to contain the whole. It is all severely economical in detail and careful in avoiding self-indulgence. By Carpenter also the Infirmary, the Gymnasium, and the Headmaster's House, the latter built in 1873.

THE HYDE *see* HANDCROSS

ICKLESHAM

ALL SAINTS. The oldest part of this interesting church is the N tower. It is Norman and early, see the very plain details on the ground floor inside, especially the unmoulded arch to the S and the plain imposts of blank arches. In the E arch one such plain impost has later been re-set. The N doorway into the tower has one order of columns, and their single-scallop capitals are early too. This work belonged to a cruciform church, where the tower took the place of a transept, for the N aisle ends in a Norman arch to the tower on very heavy semicircular responds, and the S aisle ends to the E in another Norman arch of about the same date (respond with volute capitals). This no doubt went into a transeptal chapel. Of the chapel one Norman W window is still visible inside. So the Norman church had aisles. But they must very soon have been replaced. The present three-bay arcades cannot be later than c.1175. Round piers, their capitals of typical Late Norman forms, a ring of small scallops, a ring of upright leaves, a ring of three tiers of upright leaves, a ring of leaves with inside them little fruit(?). The arches are round and have only two slight chamfers. The S aisle still has its small Norman windows. At the same time the tower was given a rib-vault inside. It is evident that this was an afterthought, and the capitals have waterleaf forms again of c.1170–80. Soon after that the N chapel was built and the S chapel begun. Both have blank arcading inside with crocket capitals of c.1200. The N chapel arcade goes with that (piers flat to the nave with thin filleted nook-shafts and semicircular projections to the arcade openings, pointed arches with two slight chamfers), and so does the remodelled arch from the tower to the chapel. The N chapel lancets go with it too (they have shafts between them inside with capitals just like those of the arcade), but the S chapel has geometrical tracery with unfoiled circles, i.e. a motif of the ending C13. The arcade also is later (standard elements). The PISCINA with its crocketed gable looks early C14 rather than late C13. Then the chancel – Dec with the flowing tracery and ogee foiling of its side windows. The E window is of *S. S. Teulon*'s restoration of 1848–9. The hexagonal W porch is of course his too. It was converted out of the porch of 1785, which was round. Dec also the PISCINA in the chancel (ogee arch; shelf). The chancel arch, however, though the responds have probably been removed later and replaced by the suspicious-looking corbels, belongs to the arcades – see the slight chamfers. The nave roof on its corbels with naturalistic foliage is of course *Teulon*'s. So is probably the FONT, round, with naturalistic leaves. – PLATE. Cup and Cover, later C17.

WINDMILL, Hog's Hill, ½ m. SE. A post-mill still with four sails and fan-tail.

IDEN

ALL SAINTS. Perp W tower with beacon turret.* W doorway
with angel busts as label-stops. C14 N arcade of standard
details, but responds of *c*.1200 with stop-chamfers. The S
aisle has been demolished. The remaining arcade is like the
N responds. Pier with stop chamfers, the arches only just
pointed. Perp N chapel, heightened probably in the C18. –
PAINTING. Return of the Prodigal Son, by *Hans Feibusch*,
1950. – PLATE. Cup and Cover, 1640. – BRASS to Walter
Seller † 1427, priest, a 28 in. figure.

OXENBRIDGE. C15, timber-framed, but painted all white.
Thatched. The eaves carried the Wealden way. L. part added
in the C18 and ending polygonally. (Inside, remains of the
kingpost roof of the hall. SCM, IV)

IFORD

ST NICHOLAS. Flint with an impressive, though not large,
Norman central tower. Original E, S, and N windows; later
shingled pyramid roof. The chancel also is Norman. Three
widely spaced round-headed lancets, as it were, and an oculus
above. Also Norman a plain round-headed PISCINA, if it is
original. The low wide arch to the former N chapel looks
c.1300. Norman again the W and E arches of the central space,
that to the W with a kind of crenellation motif with triangular
merlons, that to the E with a plain roll moulding. The N and
S walls have blank arches, which is worth noting. The nave
must be Norman too; for the former N aisle cannot have been
later than *c*.1200. The piers are chunks of the N wall, the
arches are pointed, but have only a slight chamfer. The nave
windows are simple Dec. – FONT. Of cauldron shape on five
supports; E.E. – PLATE. Cup and Cover, 1674.

SWANBOROUGH MANOR, ⅝ m. NW. The N range is a hall of
c.1200 altered in the C15, when a ceiling was put in to gain
an upper room. Of the earlier period a lancet window on the
N side, the doorway, and the oculus window in the W gable,
cut into by a C15 window. Three two-light windows of the
C15 on the N side. C15 also the great chimneybreast on the N
side and the remains of the gatehouse to the W. Attached on
the E to the hall and of the same period the former chapel
with an imitation Elizabethan four-light window. From the

* The rector of Iden tells me that the N wall of the tower is Norman.

hall into the chapel leads a doorway and a small quatrefoil peephole, both C15. C15 finally also the fine single-framed wagon roof of the upper room. A precious survival is the parts of the C15 SCREEN with pretty arched blank panelling.

ISFIELD

4010

ST MARGARET. Norman W tower, the buttressing of course later, and the top Victorian. The tower arch, pointed, with only a slight chamfer, seems late C12. So that may be the date of the Norman tower windows too. In the nave a C13 lancet. In the chancel a Dec PISCINA with gable with blank tracery. Also buttress-shafts and thick crocketing. Opposite a recess of the same Dec date. Here the tracery is now open-work, but was once blank too. The S chapel Dec too, see one finial of a PISCINA once probably of the same style. N aisle of 1876. – PULPIT. The tester of the former Jacobean pulpit is now a table-top in the N aisle. – STAINED GLASS. Some fragments, including a C14 canopy, in a S window. – In the S chapel linenfold PANELLING and BENCHES with poppy-heads, all said to be from the time of Sir John Shurley. – PLATE. Pewter Plate, inscribed 1675; Cup, 1806. – In the chapel also the Shurley MONUMENTS. Sir John † 1527. Grey Purbeck marble (Sussex marble?) recess with flat top. Tomb-chest with shields in cusped lozenges. – Edward † 1558. A similar recess, but with a shallow arch at the top. The effigies in brass against the back wall, he in late C15 armour. – Thomas † 1579. Stone aedicule with touch columns and a pediment, to be up-to-date. Brasses against the back wall. – Sir John † 1631. Big standing monument of alabaster. He and two wives in rising tiers. Dull faces. The children kneel small below. Deep coffered arch, two columns and two allegorical statuettes on top.

ISFIELD PLACE. A composite building. To the E some early C16 brick windows. To the W a two-storeyed frontispiece of *c.*1600. Doric columns below, fluted Ionic above. Top pediment with a motto. To the S a five-bay façade which looks late C17, see the upper upright two-light windows. To the N of the house a gatehouse, also partly C17. Four-centred arch. The house deserves investigation (cf. e.g. the Grimm water-colour).

ITFORD HILL *see* BEDDINGHAM

JEVINGTON

ST ANDREW. Flint, with a short, broad Anglo-Saxon w tower. The Saxon date is at once recognizable by the blocked N and s windows with tiles laid as if they were token voussoirs and by the turned baluster shafts with turned capitals of the bell-openings. In the spandrel a round opening and two more above the arch. They are not genuine, but could represent Saxon evidence. The arch to the nave has one step in jambs and arch. The s doorway seems of c.1200, very simple, just with one slight chamfer. E.E. N aisle, see the small (renewed) lancets and the arcade with circular pier and double-chamfered arches. In the nave kingpost roof. – SCULPTURE. Strange Late Saxon figure of Christ with only a loincloth, holding a long staff with a cross, placed on a tiny beast and by it and by Christ's foot bits of wild interlace of the Urnes style. – PLATE. Cup and Cover, 1687; Paten on foot, 1733. – MONUMENT. Charles Rochester † 1758. Big tablet with a lively bust in a medallion.

JEVINGTON PLACE. The house incorporates a pre-Reformation range, running N–S, recognizable by buttresses. One pointed-trefoil-headed window is also still there, though now *ex situ*.

FILCHING MANOR, I m. N. Timber-framed, C15, with close studding. Hall type with the two extensions for solar and services. They have oversailing gables, and from the wings the familiar curved braces run up parallel with the hall wall to support the roof eaves, i.e. the Wealden motif.

COMBE HILL. On the hill, I m. N of the church, lies a CAUSE-WAYED CAMP. It consists of an oval area defined by two concentric, U-sectioned ditches with internal banks, broken by a number of causeways. No earthworks are visible on the N sector of the hill, where the land slopes away steeply. The site is interesting in that it has produced sherds of Secondary Neolithic pottery from the primary ditch silting; in other British Neolithic causewayed camps, such pottery occurs only in a late context in the ditches. Also on the hill, I m. NE of the church, lies a small BOWL BARROW. In it, buried in the material of the mound, was found a hoard of three complete and one fragmentary Early Bronze Age flanged axes.

KEMP'S HOUSE see BALCOMBE

KEYMER

ST COSMAS AND ST DAMIAN. The dedication is said to occur

only three times in England (plus a fourth former one). 1866 by *E. E. Scott*, except for the Norman apse. Flint walling, crazy-paving fashion. SW steeple with a two-staged fancy spire. N aisle of 1890. – PLATE. Cup, 1635; Flagon, 1752.

OLDLAND WINDMILL, ¾ m. NNE. An C18 post-mill. Octagonal brick round-house. The sails are still there.

KIDBROOKE PARK
¼ m. SW of Forest Row

4030

The original house was a five-bay ashlar building, dated in the pediment 17.4.* The front has Gibbs surrounds to three of the ground-floor windows. Another round the corner in the bow window. This front also has a pediment, and the bow looks a later addition. At the back a third pediment. Here, later, a Tuscan colonnade was placed along the front. The porch on the entrance side is of course a Victorian addition. A Victorian wing has been demolished. Excellent STABLES by the side of the house, very cubic and solid, with lunette windows and a cupola. Too little is known about the architectural history of the house. The original architect is not recorded. The illustration in Neale's *Seats* differs from the present appearance. Neale says that *Robert Mylne* rebuilt Kidbrooke Park. He indeed worked at the house in 1805, *Dance* in 1814–15. Victorian alterations were made by *F. P. Cockerell*. The interior is not sufficiently recorded either. The Library could well be original, with its plaster ceiling (circular centre with three cherubs), and the Long Room looks certainly early C19. It is decorated in a Pompeian taste, with much dainty painting, also of the chimneypiece. The gardens were laid out by *Repton*.

KINGSTON
2½ m. SW of Lewes

3000

ST PANCRAS. Small, aisleless, and completely Dec, unless the W tower is a little earlier. Flint, the tower with a pyramid roof. The tower arch dies into the imposts, the chancel arch has continuous chamfers. – FONT. Round on a round foot, and heavily moulded without any enrichment. Is it C13 ? – PLATE. Cup and Paten, 1568; Almsdish, *c.*1700.

---

* Probably 1724, the year when, according to Neale's *Seats* (1822), the Earl of Aberconway bought the estate. There is also the date 1736 on the clock, and there are firebacks inside with the same date.

KINGSTON MANOR, W of the church. In the garden several carved fragments from Lewes Priory, a small head, a bit of zigzag, and a bit of dogtooth (these part of a mounting block), also a Norman capital, upturned. The front of the house itself is L-shaped, and, while the l. part is Georgian, the projecting part has a very large chimneybreast of ashlar stone, perhaps also from the Priory.

KITCHINGHAM FARM see ETCHINGHAM

KNELLSTONE see UDIMORE

LADYHEADS see WADHURST

6000
LANGNEY
part of Eastbourne

ST RICHARD, Priory Road. 1956–8 by *H. Hubbard Ford*. Small.

LANGNEY PRIORY, Priory Road. Attached to the house is a CHAPEL, perhaps of a grange of Lewes Priory which existed at Langney. Flint and stone, with simple, small windows, two with ogee heads. Above the chapel was a hall or living room. This still has a kingpost truss exposed.

BISHOP BILL'S SCHOOL, Priory Road. By *Oswald P. Milne*, 1957–9. Red brick, cubic blocks, no great expanse of glass.

LANGNEY POINT. Here one has the view of a number of MARTELLO TOWERS, extending as far as Pevensey Bay. On the Martello Towers *see* p. 490.

5010
LAUGHTON

ALL SAINTS. Pelham tower, Perp, with battlements and the Pelham buckle on the label-stops. C13 nave, see one lancet N, one S. The chancel must be of the later C18, i.e. early Gothick. The priest's doorway with its high ogee arch and the band of pretty little quatrefoils along jambs and arch are unmistakable. So are the diagonally set crocketed pinnacles at the E corners. But the S windows are odd. Their tracery is neither Perp nor C18. It is so bleak and so incorrect that it might well be C17. However, nothing is known of either C17 or C18 activity at Laughton. Inside, a Perp chancel arch and a single-framed roof with tie-beams and kingposts. – SCREEN. The tracery re-used in the chancel E wall. – HELMS. Two, above the chancel arch.

LAUGHTON PLACE. This was the original house of the Pelham family. It was rebuilt, according to tradition, in 1534, by Sir William and given up for Halland in 1595. All that survives, apart from the moat, is one tall and broad tower of red and black brick, on an irregular plan and with irregular details. The most interesting ones are the arched friezes at the top which are of terracotta and the terracotta window-jambs with Early Renaissance arabesques.* The arches of the windows have foliage in the spandrels. The tower was converted later in the C18 into a Gothick farmhouse, a charmingly incongruous idea. Three bays, two storeys, windows with four-centred arches, a perfectly normal classical pediment, but also Gothick windows above it in the tower including one characteristic quatrefoil.

LEASAM HOUSE see PLAYDEN

LEGH MANOR see CUCKFIELD

LEWES

4010

INTRODUCTION

Lewes has only about 14,000 inhabitants, but its character as a county town is unmistakable. It lies proudly and picturesquely on a hill, dominated not by a major church – for the churches of Lewes are minor – but by its castle. The town was of importance already in Saxon times. King Athelstan had two mints at Lewes. Lewes after the Conquest became the centre of William de Warenne's barony, which extended into Surrey and included lands in Norfolk. It was he who built the castle and he, with Gundrada, his wife, who created the Priory, the first Cluniac house in England. A merchant gild must have been granted to the town early; for it was restored to it about 1140 by William's grandson. The priory lies in the flat land s of the town. The Greyfriars settled down at Lewes before 1241 (see p. 560). No other friars came, which is curious. The High Street forms the spine of the town, sloping steeply down from the w, then running level and rising again to the E. In the High Street and altogether at Lewes the Georgian houses prevail, though there are plenty of older, timber-framed ones too. Defoe called Lewes 'a fine pleasant town, well built and situated', 'full of gentlemen of good families',

* For more such work, see Halland, p. 514.

but suffering from the bad roads around. Scarcely anything at Lewes has been spoilt and much has been preserved and exemplarily restored, thanks particularly to the work and influence of the late *Walter Godfrey*.*

CHURCHES

PRIORY OF ST PANCRAS. William de Warenne about 1075 travelled to Rome with his wife Gundrada. They visited the great abbey of Cluny in Burgundy on the way, the mother-house of the Cluniac order which just then was reaching the climax of its fame and influence. The then pope, Gregory VII, was a Cluniac. William decided to introduce the Cluniac reforms to England and in 1077 gave Cluniac monks a small church at Southover, s of Lewes, in the flat land. They must have begun the new large stone church at once; for in 1085 Gundrada was buried in it and in 1088 William himself. The first consecration in fact took place before 1098. The late C11 church is known only from excavations. The E end then found was considered by Walter Godfrey a late C12 addition. This is, however, not certain. In its final form the church was nearly 450 ft long, that at Cluny about 630. Like Cluny, Lewes Priory had an ambulatory with radiating chapels and two pairs of transepts, the more easterly one with one E chapel to each arm, the principal one with two. The aisled chancel between the sets was of four bays, the aisled nave of eight, and there was in addition a pair of W towers of which a fragment of the southern one can still be recognized. It can be found as follows. The site is approached from Cockshut Road, next to the South Down Tennis Club, but the original approach was from the N where, immediately W of St John Southover, the ruin of the Great Gate remains. This is of the C13, and largely of Sussex marble. The former pedestrian entrance was re-erected at the W end of Priory Crescent. The fragment of the SW tower of the church lies some 300 ft SE of the Great Gate. The cloister was oblong and, as usual, s of the s aisle. To its E, also as usual, was the apsed chapter house. The railway line now crosses this, the SE half of the cloister, and nearly the whole of the refectory, which lay, again as usual, s of the cloister. However, the vault below the lavatorium, which was round and which ran from the s cloister range into the garth, still exists, and so does, quite prominent, the SE corner of the refectory with herringbone

* Who also edited the *Official Guide*, a paragon of its kind.

LEWES

LEWES 551

masonry and double-splayed windows to the undercroft, i.e.
features clearly of the original building. The other parts of
the monastic quarters most easily visible are the undercroft
of the dormitory, formerly vaulted, and in its N parts late
C11, in its S parts late C12, and the infirmary chapel, also of
the late C12, which has a square chancel flanked by apsidal
chapels. The extended dormitory ended with a long building
across its S end which was the reredorter or lavatories. To the
NE of the priory site is an unexplained mount.*

ALL SAINTS, Friars Walk. An oddly elongated church, the
low W tower of flint out of scale with the rest. To it was added
by *Amon Wilds* in 1806 a long brick nave, with windows in
two tiers and a length of six of them, and to this *W. Basset
Smith* and *E. J. Munt* in 1883 added an E end with transepts,
again of flint. The interior still has its three galleries on thin
iron columns and with thin iron columns and a shallow
stucco vault for the nave. The W end of the work of 1883 shows
that it was meant to swallow up the Georgian nave. – FONT.
Basin on a baluster; *c.*1806 no doubt. – The REREDOS of
*c.*1806 now on the W gallery (columns and a segmental pediment) together with the former altar PAINTING. This represents St John Baptist in prison and is Italian. It was bought
in Italy by one of the earls of Chichester. – SCULPTURE. Two
stone Charity Children in Georgian dress now under the
tower. From the National Schools. – STAINED GLASS.
Windows of 1880 and 1884 by *Holiday*. – PLATE. Almsdish,
1674; Almsdish, given in 1733; Cup and Paten, 1744;
Flagon, 1780. – MONUMENTS. Two small kneelers from the
monument to Robert Hassard † 1624 and wife, and two
bigger kneelers from that to John Stansfield † 1627 and wife.
ST ANNE, High Street. High up and open to the S and the
Downs. Flint. Norman W tower and long, narrow Norman
nave, Norman S transept. The tower is evidently Norman, in
the nave one S window appears above the S arcade (visible
only from the aisle), in the S transept the E window is Norman.
Moreover, in the shallow N porch a Norman doorway is re-
set, no doubt the former N doorway. E.E. chancel, the external
details all imitation (1889). But inside, in the four corners,

* Figured capitals of the priory dating from *c.*1140 are now in the
British Museum and the Lewes Museum, and stones from the priory have 13b
been re-used in the gardens of Southover Grange and Red House, Southover; Court House Farm, Barcombe; the tower of Beddingham church (?);
the front wall of Hangleton Manor House; Kingston Manor House; the
chancel arch and squint of Rodmell church; and at More Place, Wivelsfield.

four corbels indicating the intention of vaulting, probably in two bays. The wonderful thing about St Anne is the s arcade, of the late C12. Round piers with square abaci. Flat stiff-leaf capitals on stiff-leaf sprays at the corners. Pointed arches with only a slight chamfer, but the last bay, where the Norman transept was, round-arched. The transept received a quadripartite rib-vault when the arcade was made. The boss is small and has stiff-leaf similar to that of the arcade. The powerful nave roof with tie-beams, queenposts, and carved raking struts is of 1538. – FONT. Norman, drum-shaped, without any stem. Basket-weave decoration, with a band of plait below, of pellets above. – PULPIT. Given in 1620. Two tiers of panels with lions' heads as their centre. Angle columns also in two tiers. – WEST GALLERY. C18. – COMMUNION RAIL. C18. – STAINED GLASS. s transept, by *Capronnier* of Brussels, 1889, still entirely Continental mid-century, and very terrible. – PLATE. Chalice and Paten, dated 1765. – MONUMENT. Chancel N. Tomb recess, over-restored. Tomb-chest and ogee canopy.

ST JOHN-UNDER-THE-CASTLE, St John's Hill. 1839 by *George Cheeseman*. Flint and red brick dressings. Short w tower with castellated turrets. Tall side windows with ignorant tracery. Short apsed chancel. Good, solid barn roof with tie-beams. The three-sided gallery has not been ripped out. The old church of St John-sub-Castro stood a little to the N, and from it came the Late Anglo-Saxon doorway, now attached to the E of the church. Unmoulded and undecorated jambs and arch, but outside them three demi-shafts and demi-rolls, a typical, unstructural way of adorning a portal. Instead of capitals just a slab across all three. Also from the old church the chancel arch with a restored inscription in Lombardic script commemorating a Magnus of royal Danish stock who chose to be an anchorite here. The arch is now on the s side. – PAINTING. Christ and the Children, large, probably Venetian, *c.*1600. – PLATE. Almsdish, 1728; Cup, 1750; Paten; two Flagons. – MONUMENTS. Tablets with urns; late C18 to early C19. – In the churchyard good C18 headstones, including one of 1747 by the carpenter *Mark Sharp* which represents all his tools.

ST JOHN BAPTIST, Southover High Street. This was originally the *hospitium* at the gates of Lewes Priory. For the gatehouse itself, *see* p. 550. The oldest part of the existing church is the s arcade, four bays with short round piers and unmoulded arches. They do not look in correct condition. Originally they were perhaps the columns dividing the men's from the women's part of the hospitium. The Perp E bay, followed by an identical Victorian one, is not *in situ*. The arch to the tower looks C14. The tower itself was rebuilt of brick in 1714–38. Brick chequer below. Top with battlements and cupola. The chancel dates from 1885, the horrible neo-Norman s chapel (*see* below) from 1847. It is by *J. L. Parsons* of Lewes, who was advised by Ferrey who should have known better. – In the chapel the memorable MONUMENTS to the founders of the priory (*see* p. 550), William de Warenne and Gundrada. They are two cists of lead *c.* 34 in. long and are placed in the two s recesses. In the opposite N recess a mutilated Sussex marble effigy of a Knight; late C13 (John de Braose ?). – In the middle large and beautiful black (Tournai marble ?) slab to Gundrada, with palmettes symmetrically l. and r. of a middle staff. Long inscription band. The slab is of the later C12. – STAINED GLASS. The N windows by *Kempe*, 1882–91. – PLATE. Late C17 Cup and Paten; Paten, 1709; Almsdish, 1826.

ST MICHAEL, High Street. Here is a round tower in the middle of Lewes. It is assigned to the C13, a puzzlingly late date. It has a shingled spire and is at present covered with pebbledash. The s arcade of three bays is C14. The arches have two hollow chamfers. But the E bays to the chapel and the whole N arcade are of 1748, of wood, with odd columnar capitals to the octagonal piers, and panelled arches. The street front is of the same date, but the windows were made correctly Gothic in 1885. However, the arrangement of the two doorways with the roundels over is typically Georgian. – STAINED GLASS. In the s chapel and s aisle of the 1880s, good for its date, and judging by its style, by *Powell's*. – PLATE. Cup and Paten, 1664; Paten, 1734; two Cups and Paten and Flagon, 1753. – MONUMENTS. Brass to a Knight, early C15, now headless, originally 3 ft long. – Brass to John Braydford, priest, † 1457, demi-figure. (Both N aisle w.) – Sir Nicholas Pelham † 1559. Tablet with kneeling parents and children, the children below. Touch columns l. and r.

ST PANCRAS (R.C.), High Street. Large, of red brick, without a tower. 1939, by *E. Walters* (GR).

ST THOMAS BECKET, Cliffe High Street. Flint. Perp w tower with w doorway (leaf spandrels). The external details of the church all over-restored. Inside, C14 arcades with hollow-chamfered arches. Former clerestory windows above the spandrels, not the arches. Elaborate squint ending to the chancel in a broad foiled ogee arch. – PAINTING. Ascension, Netherlandish, C17, given in 1779 by B. van der Gucht, art dealer and restorer in London.

BAPTIST CHURCH, Eastgate Street. 1843. In the Norman style, with one asymmetrically placed tower.

FRIENDS' MEETING HOUSE, Friars Walk. 1784. Meeting House and cottage under one roof. To the street timber porch with pairs of Doric pilasters and a pediment.

UNITARIAN CHAPEL, High Street. 1700. Knapped flint. Doorways and an E window still of that date.

WESTGATE CHAPEL. Behind the Bull Inn, with access from the High Street. The W side of the passageway from the entrance to the chapel consists of masonry from the West Gate of Lewes. The chapel dates from 1700 and is quite plain. The mullions and transoms of the windows are re-used material from the former S range of the Bull Inn (see p. 557). They are of three lights, mullioned and transomed, and no doubt Elizabethan. – (PULPIT. The tester is now a table at the back of the chapel.)

PUBLIC BUILDINGS

CASTLE. Lewes Castle was founded by William de Warenne and first built of flint (not of wood) about 1100. It covers an area of about 450 ft by 380 ft and is distinguished by the strange feature of two mounds, both artificial. The castle is approached from the S by a BARBICAN of the early C14, one of the mightiest barbicans in England. It is faced with squared flints and has two rounded turrets to the outside and formerly had two to the inside. The windows are cross-slits. The arch of the archway is moulded, and above the archway at the top are machicolations. The portcullis groove is preserved. The barbican is followed by the Norman GATEHOUSE (just as at Arundel), and the archway of this has plain arches, clearly Early Norman. The masonry of the gatehouse contains herringbone coursing. There is some contemporary walling to its l. and r. too. More substantial curtain walling further E (i.e. E of Castle Gate House). On the W mound stands the KEEP, a shell-keep, again Early Norman, though strengthened by two polygonal C13 turrets (again as at Arundel).* As one

* Inside the shell-keep a Serlian doorway with moulded bands at frequent intervals. Is it of the early C17? There are also some Gothick windows from the time when the keep was used as a summer-house.

ascends the path from the entrance to the keep one passes the
angle of an oblong intermediate tower, now part of Castle Gate
Lodge. The only other remains are some walling and a tunnel-
vault, N of the keep, belonging to a house along the path W
of Castle Banks, and some chalk masonry of the other mound,
which was called Brack Mount. Originally there was a second
shell-keep here.

TOWN WALLS. Built about 1266–9, and more money made available in 1314. They are visible in many places, especially behind
the houses on the E side of Keere Street. They ran from there
to Grange Road, then E along Grange Road, Southover Road,
and Lansdowne Place, curved N along Friars Wall and N
along Green Wall. The N side is N of the churchyard of St
John-sub-Castro, and there the wall turns S and SW, along
the castle and S along Pipes Passage back to Keere Street.
On the Westgate *see* below, p. 557.

COUNTY HALL, High Street. 1808–12 by *John Johnson*. Not
detached. Of Portland stone. Five plus two bays and two and
a half storeys. The five bays arranged with a middle loggia of
Tuscan columns. Originally the whole ground floor was open.
Above these bays in the half-storey three panels of *Coade*
stone representing Wisdom, Justice, and Mercy.

TOWN HALL, High Street. 1893. By *S. Denman* of Brighton.
Very red, and easily the least attractive building in Lewes.
The original town hall of Lewes stood in the middle of the
street opposite the White Hart. Inside, the staircase from the
Elizabethan Slaugham Place, a splendid piece carved elegantly
and with an exceptional variety of little figures in relief:
Greek Gods, the Continents, the Senses, Virtues, also musical
instruments and scenes of industry – a woman spinning, a
man loading bales on to a ship. Openwork tapering balusters.
High newel posts. Below the town hall is a tunnel-vaulted
undercroft. This and the archway halfway up are C14 work.
– REGALIA. Silver-gilt Steeple Cup, given in 1611. – Two
Constable's Staves, presented 1760. – Town Crier's Staff
1760. – Constable's Staves, twenty, from George IV onward.
– Tankard and Cover *c*.1820. – Cup and Cover, presented
1830. – Cup and Cover, presented 1831. – Many Victorian
pieces.

NEWCASTLE HOUSE. *See* p. 558.

(COUNTY GRAMMAR SCHOOL FOR BOYS, Mountfield Road.
New chapel by *Sir E. Maufe*.)

PRISON, Brighton Road. 1850–3 by *D. R. Hill* of Birmingham.

Additions 1868. Long symmetrical front of flint with red-brick dressings. Round-arched windows, low towers, machicolations.

OLD PRISON (Territorial H.Q.), North Street. 1793. By *James Fentiman* of Stoke Newington. Outer wall with heavy archway in a Vanbrughian mood. The building behind large, three-storeyed, of brick, with a canted centre projection. All windows barred.

PERAMBULATION

There is no obvious start for a walk through Lewes; so, as the HIGH STREET is the principal thing, one might just as well set out from St Anne, i.e. at the w end of the High Street. It starts descending at once, but first gently, until in its main stretch it is level. Later on it goes down steeply to the river. As one starts on the walk, the main themes are at once heard: grey and red brick chequer,* mathematical tiles over timber-framing (No. 120), tile-hanging, weatherboarding (No. 115), and also re-georgianizing (the shop-front of No. 128). The first house to be noticed is No. 118 (s), five bays, two storeys, nice doorway, C18. Then the SHELLEY HOTEL (N), with an E front of mathematical tiles, black and red trim, and an Elizabethan street front (porch dated 1577).‡ The GRAMMAR SCHOOL of knapped flint (another Lewes material) is a rebuilding of 1851. ST ANNE'S HOUSE opposite (No. 111; s) is dated 1719 and has five bays, two storeys, and a parapet. The Ionic porch must be early C19. No. 139 opposite is knapped flint for a change. The date 1654 on the rain-water head has nothing to say. No. 107, again s, has again mathematical tiles. In No. 141 (N) the knapped flints are squared and coursed. The house is Late Georgian. (No. 104, s, ANTIOCH HOUSE of five bays has C17 painting on a chimneybreast inside. No. 103 has an C18 GAZEBO in the garden. NBR) So to the BOOKSHOP, the first timber-framed house. It dates from the C15 and is very picturesque, with irregularly jutting upper storeys.

Now first down KEERE STREET, steep and for pedestrians only. Nice cottages on the r. On the l. ST MICHAEL'S COURT, formerly almshouses. The building dates from 1846.

---

* Mr Clifton-Taylor has pointed out that some of the Lewes grey brick-work is red-brick coated so that the surface turned grey in the firing.

‡ Garden terraces designed by *Alfred Waterhouse*. In one bedroom mid C16 decorative painting.

From here and lower down good views of the TOWN WALL.
At the bottom Southover Grange, *see* later (p. 560).
Up again and further along the HIGH STREET. On the N the
FREEMASONS' HALL, 1868 and very High Victorian Gothic.
Inside, parts of the rounded N tower of the former WESTGATE.
It stood across the High Street, and the S bastion was just W
of the Bull Inn. But first, on the S side, WESTGATE HOUSE
(No. 93), with a particularly pretty doorway. Adamish columns
and a broken pediment. Next the BULL INN, C15, with late
C16 additions (e.g. the overhang on carved brackets). Then
some Georgian shop-fronts and two houses with pairs of
shallow bow windows, as they will occur again later. Now
ST SWITHUN'S HOUSE (No. 82), late C18, three storeys, of
ashlar rendered, five bays, with a doorway with Ionic pilasters
and a lunette window in the middle of the top floor. Good
interiors. This is opposite CASTLE PLACE (No. 166), 1810
by *Amon Wilds*, three bays, with his unmistakable ammonite
capitals to the giant pilasters – they occur here for the first
time, i.e. before he introduced them to Brighton – a heavy
Ionic porch, a thin cast-iron balcony, and a top balustrade.
Its r. hand neighbour is a sweet little thing, one bay only with
a doorway set off-centre and black-tile facing. Opposite is No.
74, timber-framed and as early as the C14. Round the corner
a three-light window, straight-headed with pretty Dec
tracery. This house faces more or less CASTLE GATE. The r.
corner of this access lane to the castle is BARBICAN HOUSE
(No. 169), with a Georgian red brick front to the High Street.
Inside (the house is now a museum) one ground-floor room
with a fireplace dated 1579, one upper room with mixed C16
panelling from Bishopstone Manor House, a handsome late
C17 staircase with twisted balusters, and a good Georgian
fireplace in another ground-floor room. Up Castle Gate and
on the l. BARTHOLOMEW HOUSE, with black mathematical
tiles, and then the access to the castle. Then through the
barbican (see p. 554) and on the l. CASTLE LODGE, early
C19, rough flint, three bays, with battlements and Gothic
glazing bars and the inner corner of a former tower of the
castle, on the r. CASTLEGATE HOUSE of *c.*1830 with a Greek
Doric porch. The house has in the garden a summer-house
with a Doric portico and a pediment. Also a big lump of the
curtain walling of the castle appears here. CASTLE PRE-
CINCTS is Georgian of five bays, faced with red mathematical
tiles. The top storey is later. (In the house some Norman

flint walling of the castle and some old vaulting. VCH) The next house to the r. has chalk masonry of Brack Mount (*see* Castle, p. 555).

Back to the HIGH STREET and on. No. 173 (NATIONAL PROVINCIAL BANK) was Moat House and is now of 1928, by *Palmer & Holden* and *Walter Godfrey*, keeping in Georgian keeping. (Old materials were re-used; see especially at the back.) Nos 174–175 are tile-hung and gabled and C16 behind the front. Then NEWCASTLE HOUSE, by *Sir Reginald Blomfield*, 1928, in good Portland stone, with its ten windows' width, steep pediment, and its doorway with open segmental pediment a copy of the Newcastle House of 1717 that stood here.* Inside, the original staircase (thin wrought-iron railing with lyre-like motifs) and one fine panelled room with columns.

Opposite, down ST ANDREW'S LANE to PELHAM HOUSE, externally mostly late C18, though in the bones of the N façade Elizabethan, and internally with rich panelling dated 1579. Pilasters and an upper tier of caryatids. Overmantel with two big shields in blank arches. The arms are those of the Gorings (cf. Danny, Hassocks). Handsome S front of Elizabethan plan but all Georgian in elevation. Doorway with pediment. The windows l. and r. tripartite under blank arches.

Again back to the HIGH STREET, and on the S side No. 61 with a fine Georgian shop-front. Doorway with pediment on Adamish columns. Arched windows l. and r., separated by columns. Then the WHITE HART, Georgian, of five bays and three storeys, with a fourth above the cornice outside, but with some Elizabethan panelling inside. This was the Lewes house of the Pelhams. Then past the County Hall and into FISHER STREET. Here, on a house two handsome early C19 friezes with oxen. Then the Town Hall and after that a fork. The High Street continues straight, Market Street turns off half-left. We do this bit first, with the CROWN HOTEL, five bays, black mathematical tiles, minimum Venetian window in the centre, then the MARKET TOWER, the belfry of the town in the sense of the Belgian belfries, 1792, red brick. Then back and on in the HIGH STREET, which now runs down to the Ouse pretty steeply. Soon on the r. two of the stateliest houses, SCHOOL HILL HOUSE (No. 33) and LEWES HOUSE (No. 32), both of five bays, both of grey

---

* The Pelhams became Dukes of Newcastle in 1756.

headers with red dressings, both early C18. The first has a parapet, a later doorway, and a nice staircase with carved tread-ends, the second a more spacious façade. Opposite Nos 199–200, red brick, with two bow windows and in the middle a double entrance with one large segmental fan arch. On the same side No. 203, again five bays, but smaller. It is dated 1735 (rain-water head), but has a late C18 doorway. No. 29, across, is an undeniably ugly Victorian triplet of three storeys. The half-timbered Cinema which follows is in its own way as irredeemable. No. 208, back on the N side, is early C19 with a Greek-Doric doorway. Into ALBION STREET for a long terrace perhaps of c.1830 with a good cast-iron balcony. Nos 211, 212, and 213, back in the HIGH STREET, again Georgian of five windows, as is No. 14 opposite.

Under the railway bridge – an irritating interruption – and to No. 10, the former LIBRARY, 1862 by *Sir G. G. Scott*, Gothic of course, small, of red brick, with a symmetrical façade. The Library stands at the corner of Friars Walk, but the High Street and its continuation must first be explored. A little further E, on the N side, Nos 220–221, a wide stone front probably of c.1740 with a three-bay pediment. Perhaps originally a centre entrance. Later in the C18, it looks, the two bows were added and the two doorways with their Adamish columns and segmental pediments. The sundial has the date 1824. Soon now the BRIDGE, 1727 by *Nicholas Dubois*, but rebuilt in 1932, curving up and down.

The continuation is CLIFFE HIGH STREET. At the start, at r. angles, BRIDGE HOUSE, seven bays wide, overlooking the Ouse. Then No. 18, with a recessed early C19 shop-front and the upper part of the façade carried by Tuscan columns. Opposite, a house with an early C19 cast-iron balcony. The continuation of Cliffe High Street out of Lewes is MALLING STREET. Here again nice doorways, again mathematical tiles. On the l. the JIREH CHAPEL of 1805, red brick with an over-broad Tuscan porch. On the r. COMBE HOUSE, early C19 too, stuccoed, with a centre bow with attached Tuscan columns and two one-bay walls continuing the front l. and r. So to South Malling and Church Lane on the l.

Now back to the former Library, on to the lower-lying S part of Lewes and into Southover. In FRIARS WALK consider the former STATION of 1846. Yellow brick, five bays wide, with four Corinthian giant pilasters set oddly against half-pillars which carry the entablature. Soon on the r. the ARCH-

WAY which is the one survival of the GREYFRIARS from which the street derives its name. Perp, two-centred, with shields in the spandrels. Friars Walk continues as Lansdowne Place, and the corner of this and Southover High Street is SOUTHOVER GRANGE, built in 1572 for the Earl of Dorset's steward. The front is to the W and has two short wings connected by a recent porch. Mullioned, mullioned and transomed, and cross windows; gables. John Evelyn lived at the Grange as a boy. (Inside, the original staircase and some chimneypieces, one dated 1572, and two of the early C16, probably from the Prior's Lodging in the Priory.) SOUTHOVER HIGH STREET runs S first, then turns W. At the turn PRIORY CRESCENT of c.1835–45, perhaps by *George Harman*, townish and out of place, twenty bays long, of three storeys, yellow brick and stucco, a shallow curve, with pilasters to the angle two bays and the centre four, which gives you, alas, a pilaster right in the middle of the composition. Between this crescent and the Southover church, squeezed in, the remains of the gatehouse of the priory (*see* p. 550). Along the street many nice minor houses, including some timber-framed ones with narrowly spaced studs. (Nos 49–51; C16) and some early C19 ones such as No. 56 (THE GABLES) with honeysuckle capitals on giant pilasters. Specially interesting only ANNE OF CLEVES'S HOUSE, wrongly so called. The front part is early C16, the back wing Elizabethan. In the front wing the hall has an Elizabethan two-transomed window of five lights but the original roof construction with kingposts. The porch again is Elizabethan (dated 1599). Underneath the hall a tunnel-vaulted cellar, probably (see the doorway) of the C14.

ASHCOMBE HOUSE, 1¾ m. W of Lewes Castle, on the Brighton Road. Georgian, of five bays, grey and red brick, with a pedimented columnar porch. In front of the drive a TOLL HOUSE, probably of c.1800, one of a pair originally, round and domed, and looking exactly like a lock-up.

(CONYBORO', 2¾ m. N, on the Barcombe Road. By *Decimus Burton, c.*1850.)

BARROWS, 1 m. NW of the town. A large, flat-topped round barrow surrounded by a ditch with external bank lies near two small bowl barrows.

ROMAN ROAD. The road runs NE from Lewes over Malling Down, descending by a marked terrace. Its N course can be seen by hedgerow alignments and lanes, with occasional fragmentary remains of the *agger* and scatter of iron slag used in the metalling of the road. Just outside the w corner of Five Hundred Acres Wood the *agger* is plainly visible between small ditches 62 ft apart.

LEYSWOOD see GROOMBRIDGE

LINDFIELD 3020

Although so close to Haywards Heath as to be almost part of it, Lindfield has entirely its own personality of a large, house-proud village with its half-mile long High Street on which everything is concentrated. It is without any doubt the finest village street in East Sussex. Mr Bloe (VCH; unpublished) counts about thirty-five ancient buildings along it, about half of them of medieval origin.

ST JOHN BAPTIST. Mainly *c.*1300 and into the C14. w tower with shingled broach spire. The w window Dec, the arch to the nave of two continuous chamfers. Two-storeyed Dec porch. Arcades of two bays, N and S, also Dec, as are the arches from the aisles to the transepts and from the transepts to the nave. Dec, and this time very outspokenly, the (much restored) chancel E window with its flowing tracery. N and S chancel chapels Late Perp, with the typical thin piers (four-shafts-and-four-hollows moulding) and four-centred arches. Perp windows in the S transept and the N chapel. In the S chapel inside two pretty angel corbels (S wall). – FONT. Octagonal, with cusped ogee panels. – PLATE. Paten, 1690; Chalice and Paten, 1710; Paten, 1724.

As one leaves the church one should first turn N. Close to the church CHURCH COTTAGE, C15, timber-framed, with solar and buttery wings and the Wealden arrangement of the roof. Behind lies OLD PLACE, a spectacular, timber-framed and brick-nogged house of *c.*1590, spectacular largely owing to *Charles Eames Kempe*, who lived here and added considerably. The house was built in the C15 (E wing roof). The most original side externally is to the w. Three gables with moulded bressumers and bargeboards, two with bay windows under, the third with a porch. The large S wing is Kempe's. Fine late C17 iron GATES to the Garden Court, and a large, fanciful garden PAVILION by Kempe. Inside, two chimneypieces are still of *c.*1590. The entrance to the house from the street is screened by the THATCHED COTTAGE, a delightful C15 piece with close studding. The elevation is again of the

Wealden type with the curved braces. Then LINDFIELD HOUSE, early C18, five bays, two storeys, parapet, red brick. The doorway has an open pediment with a bust of Shakespeare set in. A little further N on the other side another five-bay red brick house, LINDFIELD PLACE, Early Georgian, with a canted centre in which the doorway is placed. It has a broken pediment with curvy decoration in it. The oriel above has a pediment too.

This alternation of timber-framing and stately Georgian brick is the leitmotif, as one goes down S from the church. It is in fact explicable (VCH; unpublished) by the older houses having originally been spaced very generously, and the later houses being infill. First opposite the church TOWNLANDS, a detached Georgian house faced with mathematical tiles and looking townish indeed, tall and just a little forbidding. Three widely spaced bays, three storeys, tripartite windows, no parapet or visible roof. Then on the l. THE TIGER (Church House), five-bay red brick to the front, but timber-framed to the side, still with the kingpost roof of the C15 hall. At the back a stone building of the C17 perhaps originally connected with the church. On the other side of the road BOWER HOUSE, tile-hung, but also timber-framing to the side. This also is a hall-house, and the kingpost roof is perfectly preserved inside. A little further S across the road, the BENT ARMS, consisting of a lower tile-hung part and a taller part of brick, three bays with a Venetian window to the N, no doubt the Assembly Room. Lower down the High Street widens. On the l. MALLING PRIORY, Early Georgian, brick, five bays, with a very odd doorway, on the l. BARNLANDS, C15 to C16, timber-framed and very spectacular. Closely set studs. Overhanging gable on the l., transomed windows on the r., and three oriels over. The next five-bay brick house is NASH HOUSE, again on the r., then on the same side the MANOR HOUSE, lying back, with three even gables. Porch with pediment. Venetian window. Two canted bays l. and r. (The house behind this C18 front is early C17. VCH) Again a five-bay brick house after that (THE POPLARS), then, opposite, the RED LION with two bow windows and a Tuscan porch. After that on the r. HUMPHREYS, conspicuous by a charming curved shop window, but memorable as a well-preserved early hall-house with an interesting roof. It dates probably from the late C14.

The High Street ends appropriately with a modest three-bay

brick house closing it to the eye. However, the continuation curves round a little and leads to the large village POND. Beyond to the W the COMMON and facing it the humble ranges of cottages and the verandaed villa of William Allen, a Quaker, who built them in the hungry 1820s as a colony for distressed workers. A school with schoolmaster's house formed part of it. It is now known as PELHAM PLACE and LITTLE PELHAM.

(SUNTE HOUSE, 1 m. WSW. Early C18. Five bays, the doorway in a typical way flanked by narrow windows.)

(SPRING COTTAGE, 500 yds N. C15, a hall-house with wings. The hall roof-truss is intact. VCH)

PRESTON COLLEGE (Parkhill Park), 1 m. ENE. There is an old core of 1606, but it became the present large mansion in 1865. Symmetrical W front of E-shape, but at the SW angle a polygonal Gothic turret, and then the front goes on to the S. The architect of 1865 seems unknown.

EAST MASCALLS, 1¼ m. E. Early C16 and 1578, but enlarged c.1896. On the original front a porch with a mullioned and transomed window and a bargeboard gable. To the r. some struts in the panels arranged decoratively to form what in medieval tracery is called reticulation units. This must date from c.1600 and is a form of decoration not at home in Sussex.

WAKEHURST. Large symmetrical neo-Tudor mansion with gables.

LITLINGTON

¾ m. SE of Alfriston

5000

CHURCH. At the N end of a flint village off the Cuckmere river. Norman nave and chancel and a weatherboarded bell turret. Norman two chancel N, and traces of two nave N, windows and the plain S doorway. Other details c.1300–50. But the SEDILIA with a C13 shaft, and the Easter Sepulchre with a Perp arch. Perp also the chancel roof. – PLATE. Cup, 1760.

NEOLITHIC LONG BARROW, 1 m. SE of the village. One of the smallest long barrows in Sussex. The site now measures some 60 ft in length, and it is 30 ft broad and 8 ft high. There are no traces of side ditches on the ground.

LITTLE COMMON *see* BEXHILL, p. 416

LITTLE HORSTED

4010

ST MICHAEL. Stately Perp W tower of ashlar with (altered)

higher stair-turret. The doorway has carved spandrels, one
with a Green Man. The chancel is Norman and has on the N
side the most remarkable motif of external blank arcading
without any capitals. There are four arches, and they hold two
windows. The other windows seem C19, except for the
easternmost aisle windows. *Scott* restored the church in 1863.
He can hardly have been responsible for these windows. But
the N doorway, the chancel arch, and the S recess in the chancel
are no doubt his. They are correct E.E., but why E.E. here?
– SCULPTURE. Small Continental statue of the Virgin; C18.
– PLATE. Cup, Paten on foot, Flagon, and Almsdish, 1738.

HORSTED PLACE. By *Samuel Dawkes*, 1850–1. Red and blue
bricks and a lot of chimneystacks. Early Tudor windows, i.e.
with transoms but arched heads to the lights. The porch
with its turret is right at a corner, an extraordinarily uncon-
ventional arrangement. The staircase with intricate panels
was partly exhibited in Pugin's Medieval Court at the 1851
Exhibition. Indeed Dr Girouard has recently suggested that
Pugin designs may have been used inside the house; for its
builder was *Myers*, Pugin's favourite builder. Much of the
inside fitments and furnishings are still in their original state.

LULLINGTON
5000
½ m. E of Alfriston

CHURCH. The present church is no more than the chancel of
the medieval building, and not even quite that – see the
position of the S low-side window. The details are most
probably early C14. The approach is informal indeed. It will
not easily be forgotten. – PLATE. Paten on foot, 1721; Cup,
1721 (?).

LYE GREEN see GROOMBRIDGE

MAPLESDEN see TICEHURST

MARESFIELD
4020
ST BARTHOLOMEW. Over-restored. In the nave one Norman
S window. The basic shape of the N doorway could be Norman
too. Perp W tower. Dec N porch with some bold tracery.
Transepts and chancel are by *J. Oldrid Scott*, 1875–9. He re-
used the old chancel arch as his arch to the N transept and
the old E window in the S transept. But the N transept N

window, which is circular with completely un-period tracery, is Scott's. – PULPIT. Jacobean, with little carving. The sounding board, dated 1621, was made into a table. – COMMUNION RAIL. Jacobean, with vertically symmetrical balusters and big knobs on the posts. – STAINED GLASS. The two-light chancel N window no doubt *Powell's*, and very good. – PLATE. Cup, 1634. – MONUMENT. Edward Kidder_{See} † 1817, tablet with a medallion on which a Turkish soldier. _{p. 691}

Opposite the church the free-Gothic GATEHOUSE to Maresfield Park, a house mostly demolished. The gatehouse seems late C19. The CHEQUERS INN is Georgian, of brick, five windows and two and a half storeys. Clumsy doorway.

PACK FARM HOUSE, S of the Recreation Ground, has a square, ashlar-built OASTHOUSE dated 1755 and not at all looking like other oasthouses.

MARSHALLS MANOR, 1¼ m. NW. Elizabethan. Not a Sussex-looking house, rather the type one calls vaguely Cotswold. Stone, L-shaped, with a gable at the end of the projecting wing and mullioned windows. Warm yellow sandstone. (At the back a C14–15 timber-framed part. MHLG)

MARK CROSS
₅₀₃₀

MAYFIELD COLLEGE. 1868 etc. by *E. W. Pugin*.
ST JOSEPH'S COLLEGE. 1868–9 by *E. W. Pugin*. The chapel by *Goldie*, c.1875. A wing by *J. S. Hansom*, 1903.

MARSHALLS MANOR see MARESFIELD

MAYFIELD
₅₀₂₀

ST DUNSTAN. A large church W of the palace, very largely hidden from the High Street and so to the N looking into the country. Short C13 W tower with later shingled broach spire. C13 also the W lancet of the N aisle. Otherwise Perp (after a fire of 1389), especially the two-storeyed S porch. Triple-chamfered entrance, vault with diagonal and ridge-ribs and a boss. The arcades inside are of four and a half bays, Perp, with octagonal piers and four-centred arches. The S chapel goes with them. What necessitated the half-arches? Fine ceiling with moulded beams in the S chapel. – FONT. 1666, octagonal, i.e. basically Gothic, but with the typical plain initials and minimum geometrical motifs of so many post-Commonwealth fonts. – PULPIT. Jacobean, with flat arabesque carving. – SCREEN. Part of the dado is Perp. Above the dado panels frieze of pierced quatrefoils. – COMMUNION RAIL. C18. – STAINED GLASS. Chancel windows 'Munich Glass'; one date of commemoration 1867. Terrible anyway. – CANDELABRA. Two of brass, large, and in two tiers. 1737 and 1773. – PLATE. Cup, 1694; two C18 Patens. – MONUMENTS. Thomas Aynscombe † 1620. Tablet with small kneelers and on the sides of an open curly pediment two angels. – Iron tomb slabs, one of 1668 with writing across, not along the slab, the other of 1708 even with a coat of arms, as if it were black marble. – Michael Baker † 1750 and his wife † 1796. Tablet with woman by an urn. By *Charles Regniart*. – Thomas Baker † 1782. Larger tablet with a woman by a draped urn. – In the churchyard ten headstones and one tomb-chest with little terracotta plaques by *Harmer* of Heathfield.

ST THOMAS OF CANTERBURY (R.C.). 1957 etc. by *H. Bingham Towner*. Flint, a blunt design with a low-pitched roof and a tower with the same roof-pitch. Windows with arched lights.

CONVENT OF THE HOLY CHILD JESUS. This comprises the remains of a palace of the Archbishops of Canterbury including one of the most spectacular medieval halls of England, now the chapel of the convent, and to its E a group of rooms round a courtyard not sufficiently investigated. Among that group there are C13 walls and details, especially in the E and N ranges.* But the hall belongs to the C14 and, according to its style, the first half. It is 68 by 38 ft in size and crossed by three spectacular pointed stone arches carrying a timber roof. The arches rest on sumptuous leaf brackets which in their turn rise from busts or figures. The mouldings of the arches are of big and smaller sunk quadrants. The windows are tall, of two lights with a transom, and have cusped trefoils with ogee details in their heads and arches to the lights below the transoms. Outside there are round relieving arches above the windows and big buttresses with gabled set-offs between them. The entrance is in the W bay and is protected by a big porch. The plain convex mouldings of the entrance to the porch have leaf capitals. In the porch is a quadripartite vault with corbels in the form of crouching figures and a large leaf boss. The doorway has many mouldings, both towards the porch and the

32a

* There is here also an Elizabethan chimneypiece. This dates from the time of Sir Thomas Gresham. The palace was surrendered in 1545 and first went to Sir Edward Rich, from whom Gresham bought it.

hall. There are also tall shafts to the hall, and the windows
are shafted to the hall too. Two minor doorways at the high
table end, i.e. the E end, in the SE corner. One corner shaft
serves them both. To the N of the high table is a bay window
and on the E wall (behind the archbishop's seat) an arched
recess with stone diapering. High up in the same wall is a
window in the form of a spherical triangle set in a blank
normal window surround. The W end was clearly the screens
passage. The usual three doorways to kitchen, buttery, and
pantry survive. They have plain continuous chamfers. *E. W.
Pugin* in 1863–6 made an excellent job of converting the
hall into a chapel. The altar end is the former dais end, and
the bay window serves as a chapel. Here is the MONUMENT
to Cornelia Connolly, the foundress of the order, who died in
1879. – SCULPTURE. Excellent Netherlandish Madonna of
c.1460. – PAINTING. Italian C14 Crucifixus.

To the W of the Hall the C14 work continues a little and
comprises a square tower. Further W a small C15 WELL-
HOUSE, and to the S the C15 GATEHOUSE, giving access to
the palace from the village street.

The Convent school operates mostly in red-brick buildings
of 1896 etc. (by *P. P. Pugin*). The new Concert Hall built by
Adrian Scott in 1929–31 repeats the motif of the cross-arches
of the hall very successfully.

Leaving the Convent by the gatehouse one stands in the High
Street. To the N a few houses, to the S the street proper. To
the N, on the E side, YEOMANS, an early C15 hall-house,
originally of the Wealden type. The hall was of two bays,
solar and services of one each. Another bay was added at the
E end *c*.1600. Good original kingpost roof inside. Then, E,
POUND HILL COTTAGES, C16 with curved braces. Also E
YEW TREE FARMHOUSE of *c*.1700. Five bays, grey-brick
headers and red-brick dressings.

Down the HIGH STREET to the S first (w) STONE HOUSE, five
bays, two storeys, Tuscan porch, but the windows adapted to
the palace by giving them vaguely Gothic basket arches. Is it
early C19? Opposite first WALNUT TREE HOUSE, C15, with
close timber studding and overhang on a moulded bressumer,
and then the MIDDLE HOUSE HOTEL, dated 1575 and
almost West-Country-looking with its many lozenge-braced
panels. Two symmetrical gables with decorated bressumers
and bases, but not otherwise symmetrical. Ground floor with
close studding. Under the l. gable a bay window, in the r.

gable an oriel. Another bay window to the r. of the entrance.
Inside, a late C17 chimneypiece of wood from the College of
Physicians. It seems to be made up of parts not originally
belonging together, and the overmantel may even have been
a doorhead. The volutes curving forward l. and r. of the
opening are very strange anyway. After that, opposite, the
BREWHOUSE, timber-framed and assigned to the early C17.
Then once more on the E side OLD COTTAGE with a timber-
framed gable, then LONDON HOUSE on the W side, large,
weatherboarded, with two bay windows, later C18, but at the
back early C17 gables, and so finally to AYLWINS, stone, large,
and now all imitation C17, but at the back some original
mullioned windows.

MAYFIELD COLLEGE. *See* Mark Cross.

MAYS *see* SELMESTON

5000

MICHELHAM PRIORY
2⅛ m. W of Hailsham

Founded in 1229 for thirteen Augustinian Canons. What remains
is part of a private house, except for the GATEHOUSE, by
which it is approached. This is tall and broad, of the C15, and
has a four-centred head to the archway. Above to the outside
twice two two-light windows with a transom, i.e. two on the
first, two on the second floor. To the inside, strangely enough,
no windows at all, only the stair-turret. To understand the
remains incorporated in the house one must realize that one
arrives in the former cloister with the church on the open
side. Consequently, in the usual claustral way, the refectory
lay opposite the church and the store-rooms etc. in the other
wing of the house, i.e. the W range of the cloister. Of this W
wing the part adjoining the church is now just a wall. What
stands upright is a cross wall further S in which, to the N, the
springers of a heavy single-chamfered rib-vault can be
observed. Beyond the wall the only complete survival: a
vaulted room with a circular middle pier and eight single-
chamfered ribs branching out towards the wall each into two,
i.e. a so-called tri-radial arrangement. Very strange is the
corridor to the E of this room, which has a tunnel-vault with
heavy single-chamfered arches. What was its purpose? Above
the vaulted room is the room called the Prior's. This has a
two-light C15 window to the S and a big chimneypiece with a
hood. The window shows that no high building can have

existed immediately to the s. That is curious; for this is the
corner w of the refectory where usually the offices and the
kitchen or access to the kitchen are. At Michelham, this cannot have been so even in the c13; for the refectory had to this
side a large, quite monumental w window of five stepped
lancet lights under one arch – a motif incidentally which
dates the refectory as well in the second half of the c13. Of
the tall closely set lancet windows of the refectory much can
still be traced in the s wall, something also in the n wall on
the present upper floor. Doorways lead into the refectory, one
from the s, one larger opposite from the cloister (two hollow
chamfers dying into the imposts), and a smaller one, separated
from the larger one by the lavatorium, a handsome two-bay
composition with stiff-leaf capitals to the shafts.

As regards the CHURCH, excavations have recently been
undertaken, but no report was published at the time of
writing. Close to the main buildings also a weatherboarded
BARN with a tie-beam and queenpost roof and the so-called
DOVECOTE, built, so the MHLG suggests, in the c18 with
medieval materials. The gatehouse is reached by a c16
BRIDGE across the large moat.

MOONHILL PLACE see CUCKFIELD

MOULSECOMB see BRIGHTON, p. 458

THE MOUNT see WADHURST

MOUNTFIELD

7020

ALL SAINTS. Very low w tower, its shingled broach spire
starting below the ridge-line of the nave roof. Norman nave
and chancel, as shown by two nave n windows, the outline
of the doorway, and the narrow chancel arch with the plainest
imposts and an unmoulded arch. The present chancel is E.E.
with a pointed-trefoiled PISCINA on E.E. capitals as brackets.
E.E. also the tower. In it stairs of venerable age. c14 s porch
of heavy timbers. Wagon roof in the nave. – FONT. Drum-
shaped, with single motifs in panels: square leaf, three shells,
etc. Perp carving on a Norman body. – COMMUNION RAIL.
c18. – PLATE. Cup, Cover, and Paten on foot, 1700. –
MONUMENTS. (In the churchyard two headstones, † 1806,
† 1810, with terracotta plaques by *Harmer*. SAC, 1962)
MOUNTFIELD COURT. Early c18. Nine bays, two storeys,

segment-headed windows, cemented giant pilaster strips dividing the windows 2–2–1–2–2. Parapet and hipped roof with alternatingly pedimented dormers. To the w a Late Georgian addition of five bays, the middle three recessed. No decorative details. Hipped roof. (Inside a staircase of 1730. VCH)

MUDDLES GREEN see CHIDDINGLY

7010

NETHERFIELD

ST JOHN BAPTIST. By *S. S. Teulon*, 1859. In the E.E. style, with bar tracery. s tower with the clock under a crocketed gable sticking up into the bell-openings. Interior without any of Teulon's perversities. – REREDOS by *Teulon*, very spiky, with marble columns and mosaic bits; highly 1860. – PULPIT. Also designed by *Teulon*. With stone stories. – STAINED GLASS. In the chancel side windows scenes all drawn in outline only, a very unusual thing.

4000

NEWHAVEN

The name records the fact that the Ouse in the 1560s had made itself a new mouth instead of that at Seaford. It was not where it is now, but the river finally settled for the present place before 1620. So what had been Meeching became Newhaven. A harbour was started later in the C17 and gradually improved, until the serious works of today were put in hand between 1860 and 1900. Yet the town remained small (population 1961: 8,300). The old centre has an intricate street pattern up the hill. The only building noticed individually is the BRIDGE HOTEL, because it is in a key position, but that also is irregular.

ST MICHAEL. On the hill, as so many old St Michael's churches are. And old the church is, with its Norman central tower and Norman apse, a fine sight from the E. The tower carries a later short shingled broach spire. The bell-openings have twin arches, and one still has the original shaft, actually with a shaft-ring. The corbel table has heads, monsters, etc. The rest of the church is Victorian (1854, by *Habershon*; GS), nave and wide aisles. Timber posts for the arcades with traceried spandrels. Roof with tie-beams. The Norman parts internally have for the tower a W arch, simple to the W, but with two orders of columns to the E, and between tower and apse another arch with two orders of columns. The capitals have slightly decorated

scallops. – MONUMENT. In the churchyard obelisk to Capt.
James Hanson, who, after a 'four-year voyage of danger and
difficulty round the world on discoveries with Capt. Van-
couver', was wrecked with his crew in 1800. The inscription
plates overhung by sprays of carved weeping willow. – Also
in the churchyard gravestone to Thomas Tipper † 1785,
brewer of Tipper Ale. The inscription* reads:

> Reader, with kind regard this grave survey,
> Nor heedless pass where TIPPER'S ashes lay,
> Honest he was, ingenious, blunt and kind,
> And dared do, what few dare do, speak his mind.
> PHILOSOPHY and HISTORY well he knew,
> Was versed in PHYSICK and in SURGERY too;
> The best old STINGO he both brewed and sold,
> Nor did one knavish act to get his Gold.
> He played through life a varied part,
> And knew immortal HUDIBRAS by heart.
> Reader, in real truth, such was the Man,
> Be better, wiser, laugh more if you can.

CHRIST CHURCH, South Street. 1881 by *E. P. Loftus Brock*.
Yellow and red brick, lancets, bell turret.

BAPTIST CHURCH, South Street (now Boys' Club). 1835.
Gothick.

The one farmhouse of Newhaven to which the MHLG allotted
Grade II has been duly pulled down (Fort Road).

NEWHOUSE FARM *see* ARDINGLY

NEWICK

ST MARY. Perp sandstone tower. W doorway with big heads as
label-stops. The W part of the nave is Norman, see one S window. The nave was lengthened in 1886–7 and the chancel rebuilt. Its details are late C13 (bar tracery). The restoration was
done well by *J. Oldrid Scott*, and he was no doubt also responsible for the excellent decoration of the chancel. Rich tiling on
the walls, stencilling above the tiled zone, gesso frieze with
flowers, wagon roof. – FONT. Square, with three blank cusped
ogee panels each side. – PULPIT. Jacobean, not large, with
back panel and sounding board. – STAINED GLASS. Bits in the
tops of the chancel S windows. – PLATE. Cup, *c.* 1565 (?);
Paten, 1726.

* Kindly conveyed to me by the Rev. R. G. G. Hooper.

On the triangular Green a PUMP of 1837, the step like a capital, the pump itself heavily Grecian, the spout an iron lion's head.

OLD RECTORY, E of the church. Georgian, red brick, five bays, two storeys, Tuscan porch. Nice wrought-iron rail of the stairs up to the front door.

FOUNTHILL, ⅜ m. S. Early C16 timber-framed oblong house with closely set studs.

LADY VERNON'S SCHOOL (now School Cottage), S of the former. Built in 1771. Small, of brick, a two-bay, two-storey centre with one-bay, one-storey wings.

NEWICK PARK, ¼ m. S of the church. An interesting late C17 S front, brick, with giant pilasters, originally no doubt all along. The E front has two later C18 bow windows. PINNACLE LODGE, the lodge to the estate, is a charming Late Georgian folly, a little block with big ogee gables enclosing oversized quatrefoils.

NEWTIMBER

2010

ST JOHN BAPTIST. Under the South Downs, which close in on the church from E and S. Pretty Gothick W tower, though as late as 1839. The rose window of course is Victorian. Nave and chancel are E.E., but all original features are restored out of existence (by *Carpenter & Ingelow*, 1875). – PULPIT. Jacobean. – PLATE. Paten, 1709; Pewter Almsdish, engraved 1719. – MONUMENTS. Doreen Fitzroy † 1923. Small group of mother and child by *W. Reynolds-Stephens*. – Lady Buxton † 1955. Slate tablet with exquisite inscription in italics. By *Reynolds Stone*.

To the W the OLD RECTORY, a comfortable Early Victorian box with a Tuscan porch, and then a Victorian house with gables to which *Peter Farley* added a square modern timber-framed extension on metal posts.

NEWTIMBER PLACE, ¼ m. NW. In a wide moat. The main front is late C17 and very impressive in its utter restraint. Nine bays, two storeys, hipped roof. Flint walls and flush window surrounds of rose-coloured bricks. (The N wing is older, of the late C16.)* Octagonal late C17 DOVECOTE with pyramid roof, also flint and brick.

NINFIELD

7010

ST MARY. Small, but exhibiting all kinds of materials: white

* Inside, some Etruscan decoration (Croft Murray).

weatherboarded bell turret, brick s porch of 1735, cemented nave, crazy-paving-laid stone in chancel and N aisle (*Sir Arthur Blomfield*, 1885–7, or some unworthy assistant?). – FONT. Plain, small, square, moulded piece. It might well be of the 1660s. – The tiny, still Jacobean-looking COVER anyway fits it (N aisle). – READER'S DESK, Jacobean or a little later, of bold, generous outline. – PANELLING. Behind the altar, Jacobean, very tapering flat pilasters and four-centred blank arches; big leaves in the spandrels. – WEST GALLERY. A sweet surprise, high up at the W end, with flat wavy balusters, only accessible by using a ladder. It is assigned to the C17, but the balusters are by *Adrian G. Scott*, 1923. – PLATE. Cup and Paten, 1699; Flagon, 1754.

STOCKS, N of the church, by the main road, under fir trees. They are entirely of cast iron, Sussex-wise.

STANDARD HILL FARMHOUSE, ⅜ m. NW. With three gables, canted bay windows under the outer ones, mullioned windows, a date 1659, and several inscriptions.

LOWER STANDARD HILL FARMHOUSE. Opposite the former. Dated 1702 and typical of that date. Flat front with symmetrical fenestration, the windows still mullioned (no doubt originally wooden mullions), but the doorway with bolection moulding.

TANYARD HOUSE, I m. SW. Georgian. Five bays, two storeys, chequer brick, the doorway with pilasters and a broken pediment.

NORTHIAM

8020

ST MARY. The lower part of the tower is Norman, see the round-headed window arches inside. They are set in large blank arches, also round of course. The pointed arch to the nave is set into a round arch too, i.e. is a later alteration. Above, the tower turns E.E. The single-lancet bell-openings are set in three-bay blank arcading. Perp buttresses and recessed stone spire, one of the few in Sussex. In the s aisle one small lancet, the other windows Dec and straight-headed. But the E end of the church is of 1837, ashlar-faced and with big lancet windows. It was given by Thomas Frewen Turner, who also, in 1846, added the family mausoleum. The architect of this was *Sydney Smirke*. Inside the church, the arcades are of three bays, E.E., with slim round piers and double-chamfered arches. The clerestory windows are small and above the spandrels. The details of the two arcades differ; s seems to come

before N. – PULPIT. C18, with a leaf-frieze at the foot. – A
FAMILY PEW. – COMMUNION RAIL. Three-sided. Bulgy
colonnettes carry arches with pierced spandrels. Given in
1638 by Thankful Frewen. The Frewens (*see* below) were lords
of the manor. They appeared at Northiam in the late C16. –
Also of *c.*1640 the PANELLING round the altar. Geometrical
as well as blank-arched motifs. – The ALTAR TABLE with
very bulgy legs belongs to the same gift too. – CHANDELIER.
Of brass. Dated 1727. – PLATE. Paten on foot, 1634; Almsplate, 1724; Cup, Paten, and Flagon, 1740. – MONUMENTS.
Brasses in the chancel to Robert Beuford, priest, † 1518 (18 in.
figure) and Nicolas Tufton † 1538, civilian (24 in. figure.). –
In the Frewen Mausoleum: Mrs Frewen † 1844. By *Behnes*,
with a white marble bust. – Thomas Frewen † 1870, large
Gothic tablet. – The GATE to the churchyard is Georgian,
with the overthrow for the lantern.

CHURCH HOUSE, N of the church. Early C18 brick front of
eight windows. Doorway with fluted pilasters. Dormers in the
roof, two with triangular and between them one with a segmental pediment. This was a Frewen house. It was built
originally by the puritan John Frewen, rector from 1598 to
1628. Thankful Frewen was his son.

BRICKWALL, ⅜ m. s. A large timber-framed house. Jacobean N
front with three gables, quite symmetrical. Under the gables
canted bay windows, except that in the centre, early in the C18,
a shell-hooded doorway was inserted. There are (still) closely
set studs. The gables with daintily carved bargeboards and
finials. Two dates: 1617 (l. gable) and 1633 (middle gable).
Inside, in the NW corner room on the first floor, is a stone
chimneypiece of the same time. Far more spectacular however is the interior work of the late C17: the staircase in the
W wing with strong twisted balusters and a richly stuccoed
domed ceiling over, and an even richer stucco ceiling with
foliage, fruit, and birds in the entrance hall. There is more
minor stucco work of the late C17 too. The later history of
Brickwall is confusing and would deserve to be elucidated.
Late C17 bricks in the W wing and the extension to the s. But
the chimneystack is dated 1832, and this is the time when
Sydney Smirke built the STABLES (on which his name is recorded) and the GATEPIERS, entirely Victorian in style. Then
Devey is reported to have designed the garden front about the
middle of the C19, with its half-timbered gables of various
sizes and its Elizabethan details below (canted oriels, mul-

lioned and transomed windows). The E wing is said to be of 1873.*

The VILLAGE remains in one's memory for white weather-boarding. The Green by the church has even a three-storeyed weatherboarded house. HAYES FARM HOUSE faces the church with close C15 studding, but away from the church with an Early Victorian range with canted bay windows. It also faces the triangular Green. Of houses along the HIGH STREET only one deserves singling out. It is of chequer brick with a tile-hung upper floor and carries the date 1747. Doorway on brackets. Further N one gets into the bungalows. Still one nice three-bay house with Gothic glazing bars, and at the end the BRIDGE, half in Kent, which dates from 1706, but looks older. Three chamfered round arches and cutwaters.

GREAT DIXTER, ¾ m. NW. As one approaches Great Dixter, one is faced by a fabulous piece of half-timbering on the r., all narrowly set uprights, and a restrained tile-hung piece on the l. Much of this is the work of *Lutyens* for Nathaniel Lloyd, carried out 1910, one of his most successful domestic jobs, combining sensitivity to the old with quite some daring, discreetly concealed. The old house was built about the third quarter of the C15. The date is controversial. One enters by a substantial porch, two bays deep. The porch leads to the hall. The gable beyond the hall setting up some balance to the porch gable represents the chamber with solar over. Trefoil-cusped bargeboards to the gable. The hall has a bay window to the front and one to the back. They are Lutyens's, but the canted posts at their start were evidence of their existence. Evidence for arched lights to the windows came from the chamber window. The arched lights look in fact a little later than the date of the house, say, Early Tudor. The hall has a roof in which hammer-beams alternate with tie-beams. In the solar a chimneypiece with dainty carving and a kingpost truss. The view of the house from the back, i.e. the S, is a surprise; for here Lutyens re-erected a complete timber-framed house from Benenden across the Kent border. This also is closely studded. Its hall has a kingpost truss too. Against the end wall a crenellated cornice half-way up the wall. It oddly returns and juts into the room, forming a kind of lobby. One two-light window in the S wall. This has a transom; the other windows have mullions only. Doorway with four-centred head. Lutyens's own work, to say it again, is very retiring. The only gayer bit is the corner

* Or do these two dates refer to the same campaign?

between the Dixter and the Benenden houses with its lively roof-line. By Lutyens also the big roof on the Benenden house, and of course by Lutyens the fanciful garden with its unmistakable motifs.

DOMONS, E of Great Dixter. Early Victorian front, with bargeboarded dormers and hood-moulds to the first-floor windows. The house itself is C16 with a fine cluster of polygonal chimneyshafts on the roof. The shafts have star-shaped tops.

STRAWBERRY HOLE FARMHOUSE, ¾ m. SW. The gable-end closely studded from top to bottom. The front instead has the Wealden arrangement. (Kingpost roof inside. MHLG)

SILVERDEN MANOR, ⅜ m. N. Timber-framed and thatched. Partly C15, with close studding and the Wealden arrangement. One window tripartite, of a type characteristic of c.1670. (Kingpost roof inside. MHLG)

WELLHOUSE, 1¼ m. S. C15; timber-framed. The façade with the Wealden arrangement of bracing. Thatched roof. The gable at the l. side of the front has decorated bargeboards. On the r. side of the front is the big, two-transomed hall window. Also other original windows. Inside, the hall is open to the roof, a kingpost roof.

4020 NUTLEY

ST JAMES. 1845 by *R. C. Carpenter* (GR); N aisle 1871. Nave with bellcote and chancel; lancet windows; uneventful. Inside an unusually steep roof.

SHELLEY ARMS. C18, of five bays and two and a half storeys. Grey brick, red brick, and stucco dressings.

WINDMILL, 1 m. NE. A post-mill with its four sails.

NYMANS *see* CUCKFIELD

3010 OFFHAM

ST PETER. 1859 by *Ewan Christian*. Quite a powerful design, Early Dec in style, with a tower on the chancel, an apse, and a vault under the tower. – STAINED GLASS. Two W windows by *Capronnier*, 1862. By the same SW 1876. One N window by *Kempe & Tower*, 1910.

COOMBE PLACE. The E front of 1730, seven bays with a recessed three-bay centre and a hipped roof. Coursed knapped flint and stone dressings. In the entrance hall a restrained Rococo ceiling (and a fine chimneypiece with open pediment).

Contemporary staircase too. The STABLES are cobbled and have a middle archway of grey and red brick with pediment and cupola. (Octagonal Gothick SUMMER-HOUSE with battlements and pyramid roof. Octagonal DOVECOTE. SCM, II, 1928)

OFFHAM HOUSE. Rain-water heads 1749. Seven-bay front of square knapped bricks with brick dressings. Three-bay pediment. Hipped roof. (Good entrance hall and staircase. MHLG)

(PICKETT'S COTTAGES. With a fine Elizabethan staircase with flat cut balusters. VCH)

OLDLAND WINDMILL see KEYMER

ORE

8010

ST HELEN. Of the medieval church only a ruinous fragment stands. Against the tower the outline of what seems a Norman or Saxon upper doorway or window and to its r. a circular window, both of course blocked by the tower. Chancel E.E. with a Dec E window. In it a cusped tomb recess. The church ruin stands close to Ore Place, SW of the NEW CHURCH. This is by *Habershon & Brock*, of 1869, and has an extremely fussy SE tower with spire. The interior is ugly too, with short round columns with rope rings and fancy capitals. – BRASSES to a Civilian and his wife, c.1400. Bracket brasses, with the bracket lost. The figures are 2 ft 6 in. long and set under canopies.

OTTEHAM COURT see POLEGATE

OVINGDEAN

3000

ST WULFRAN. A small Norman flint church with a W tower perhaps a little later. The church has Norman windows in the chancel on all three sides and in the nave on the N side. The blocked N doorway is Norman too. In the tower the windows are lancets, and the arch to the nave is also pointed, but has only one slight chamfer. The church had a two-bay S aisle which has been destroyed. The details of the arcade are not recognizable. A very puzzling fact is a pointed blank arch in the chancel N wall visible inside a chapel of 1907 which replaces a medieval one. This arch is cut into by the Norman window and includes below a low-side lancet. How can that be? Only if there had been an intention to open the wall for the chapel, and if the intention had then been given up.* Nor-

* Canon B. J. Scott suggests that it may all be connected with hurried repairs after the French raids in 1377.

19—S.

man chancel arch of the plainest details. The two side arches
are of course recent. To the l. of the l. one fragments of a former E.E. reredos which covered the wall l. of the chancel arch.
– SCREEN. Simple, Perp. – PLATE. Cup, 1726.

Several cobble-faced houses by the church including the REC-
TORY (with a Tuscan porch).

(OVINGDEAN HALL. Late C18. Six bays, two storeys. Two-bay
pediment. Pedimented porch on Doric columns. MHLG)

PASHLEY see TICEHURST

PATCHAM see BRIGHTON, p. 458

4000
PEACEHAVEN

63   What is one to say? Peacehaven has been called a rash on the
countryside. It is that, and there is no worse in England.
Peacehaven derives its name from the end of the First World
War. Whose haven was it? Whose haven is it? Architecturally
here may lie the source of the Australian or South African little
man's suburb. When first built, indeed, it was called New
Anzac on Sea. Small plots (or stands), yet nothing semi-
detached, let alone in terraces. Every man his own house,
even if only a few feet from the neighbours'!

8020
PEASMARSH

ST PETER AND ST PAUL. Norman core, i.e. the nave w wall
with a window high up, now blank, the chancel arch of dark
red ironstone, round, with chip-carved decoration of the imposts and two animals on the jambs,* and the arcades, two
bays plus a third. The two have square piers with stop-chamfers, the third is transeptally distinguished by nook-shafts with
E.E. rather than Norman details. Finally Norman also the s
doorway with one continuous roll moulding and a small re-set
window to its E. The W tower is a little later, and with it goes
the N aisle W lancet. E.E. chancel with lancets. Dec s aisle
windows. – MONUMENT. Elizabeth Delves † 1819. By *Bacon
Jun.* Oval inscription plate and a branch of weeping willow.

PEASMARSH HOUSE, ⅜ m. NW. Built as the Rectory in 1839 by
Donthorne. Three bays, two storeys, with a three-storeyed
middle porch. The porch gable has finials, the gable window

---

* Two more of the same style re-set outside, one in the chancel s wall,
the other in the SE buttress, below ground level.

an ogee-arched head. On the first floor windows with hood-moulds – i.e. generally Gothic, C14 to Tudor.

WOODSIDE, 1 m. NW, on the A-road. Late C18, of five bays, faced with mathematical tiles. Porch with thin Tuscan columns.

PEELINGS see WESTHAM

PEKE'S HOUSE see CHIDDINGLY

PELL GREEN see WADHURST

PENHURST

6010

ST MICHAEL. An unrestored or, as the VCH puts it nicely, 'conservatively restored' church is nearly always a delight. Penhurst is no exception. Perp W tower, cut short and finished by a bit of tile-hanging and a pyramid roof. Nave and chancel, the former with a kingpost, the latter with a wagon roof. The Norman-looking arch to the N chapel is, like the whole chapel, C17. – PULPIT and READER'S DESK. Jacobean, with the usual stumpy blank arches. – BOX PEWS and PANELLING all round the nave. – SCREEN. The simple tracery looks C14, though the uprights are muntins, not shafts. – STAINED GLASS. Bits in the E window. – PLATE. Cup, 1610.

COURT FARMHOUSE. Mid C17 probably. Of ashlar, high, with its two storeys on a half-basement. Five bays wide. Cross-windows on the ground floor, mullioned on the upper floor.

COURT LODGE, ¾ m. W. Brick, early to mid C17. The front is not symmetrical and has under its gable mullioned and tran-somed windows.

ASHBURNHAM FURNACE, close to the above, was the last iron smelting works in Sussex. It worked still in 1825.

PETT

8010

ST MARY AND ST PETER. 1864 by *B. Ferrey*.* Dull. Plate tracery. The only curious feature is the way the square NW porch tower develops by broaches into an octagonal bell-stage. – FONT. Octagonal bowl, dated 1753, on a fluted baluster stem. – PLATE. Chalice and Paten, Carolean. – MONUMENTS. Cordelia Sayer † 1820. Said to be by *Westmacott*. With corn ears and a sickle at the top. – George Wynch † 1836. By *Samuel Nixon*. Grecian with two slender urns flanking the

* Cost £2000 (GS).

inscription, but a sentimental ivy frieze below and a lily and a butterfly above.

PEVENSEY

ANDERIDA. The Roman fort was built in the late C3 as part of the Roman defensive network of forts in south-east England, designed as a bulwark against invading Saxons. The fort is the finest Roman monument in Sussex, with its ten great bastions supporting walls which still stand to a height of 20 ft in some places. Excavations within the fort revealed a well from which came a wooden bucket and rope which had survived along with the wooden lining of the well. The *Anglo-Saxon Chronicle* records how the fort was overthrown by the Saxons and its defenders slaughtered to a man.

9 PEVENSEY CASTLE. Nothing is known of the fort between the evacuation of the legions and the Norman Conquest. Then William gave Pevensey to his half-brother Robert of Mortmain, and he or his successor at Pevensey after 1101, Richer of Aquila, built a stone fortress in the NE corner of the fort, using the Roman walls of the fort as the walls of his outer bailey and part of them even as part of his KEEP. This keep is unique among Early Norman keeps in that it is not, like the others, simply oblong with flat buttresses, but the basic rectangle (of 55 by 30 ft internally) is strengthened in all directions and not at all regularly or systematically by long and broad solid spurs ending, on the Roman example, semicircularly.* The only explanation can be an inflated faith in massive masonry. The keep is in the extreme SE corner, and its SE walls, including the Roman parts except for one bastion, have collapsed. Access to the keep was on the first floor, and it is assumed that the ground floor was always filled in solidly with clay. Above the first floor nothing is preserved, so that we cannot say how high the keep was. On top of the remains is a concrete strongpoint of 1940, and another is among the fragments to the E. Of the early period are repairs to the Roman wall, specially noticeable by the herringbone laying N of the Roman Eastgate. Access to the inner bailey from the outer bailey is by a GATE-HOUSE to the w. This is early C13, of fine ashlar-work, and has semicircular towers to the w. The rooms in the basement l. and r. of the gateway are tunnel-vaulted. By the early C13

---

* Apsidal buttresses as such exist in the keeps of Allington (Kent), Bungay, and Lavardin (Renn: *J.B.A.A.*, xxiii, 1960).

Pevensey had become one of the Cinque Ports. The curtain wall of the INNER BAILEY is partly mid C13 and has three semicircular towers. Each of them has a narrow staircase to the basement, a branch staircase off it into the ditch round the inner bailey, a room and a garderobe at ground-floor level, and an upper room only accessible from the wall-walk. The basement of the N tower is rib-vaulted in two bays, with keeled ribs on stiff-leaf corbels. In the middle of the inner bailey was the CHAPEL, a plain small building of nave, narrow N aisle, and straight-ended chancel. It is attributed to c.1300. The OUTER BAILEY remained essentially Roman, but a new WEST GATE was apparently built about 1100 between the bastions of the Roman gate. Fragments of the jambs are still *in situ*. The archway of the EAST GATE was also rebuilt. Soon after the inner bailey was in its final form, the port must have begun to silt up, and Pevensey lost its importance. The castle decayed and was, except for a short moment in the memorable year 1587, not repaired or kept up.

ST NICOLAS. E of the castle, off the High Street of the former little town. The earliest evidence is two arches out of the present chancel to the N and S. The imposts, the slight chamfer, the pointed shape of the arch, all imply c.1200 or a little earlier. They must have led out of a central space, but it cannot have been a square one. Were they then more in the nature of side chambers or *porticus*? Otherwise the church is mostly E.E. It has a N tower with lancets (the bell-stage is of 1877–9 by *G. G. Scott Jun.*), a chancel with lancets (two on the S side are shafted inside), a N chapel with lancets (rebuilt by Scott), and a clerestory with lancets. And in addition the arcades are E.E. too. Five bays on the S side, piers alternating between quatrefoil and octagonal, double-chamfered arches. On the N side there are only three bays because of the tower. The chancel arch (much renewed) has mature stiff-leaf, i.e. is of c.1230–40. The N chapel is accessible from the chancel by one wide arch. The details are again E.E. The clerestory windows are above the spandrels of the arcade. Later kingpost roof. – PLATE. Chalice and Cover, engraved 1568; Paten, 1716. – Also the Corporation Regalia, i.e. a silver-gilt Mace on which the earliest name is of 1676 and a Constable's Staff of c.1825. – MONUMENT. John Wheately † 1616. Standing alabaster monument. He lies on his side. Two lions, facing outward, on the floor. Black columns carrying allegorical figures; back arch with cartouche and pediment.

COURT HOUSE, in the High Street, a few houses from the E
entrance to the castle. With an oriel. Of no architectural
interest, but it was the town hall of the incorporated town of
Pevensey with the council chamber on the upper floor and the
prison on the lower.

At PEVENSEY BAY are still two MARTELLO TOWERS. A third
w of Normans Bay. On Martello Towers, *see* p. 490.

PIDDINGHOE

4000

ST JOHN. Right by the Ouse, Piddinghoe being the last village
before Newhaven. The church is of flint and has one of the
three Norman round towers of Sussex. Shingled octagonal
spire. Unmoulded arch to the nave. Otherwise outside worth
mentioning only the odd priest's doorway with windows l.
and r. and the windows opposite on the N side. The church
was restored in 1882 (by *Philip Currey*; PF), but are these
features not *c*.1850? The tiled nave roof reaches right low
down over the N aisle. The interior has much of interest.
First a Norman N arcade, with the wall of the earlier Norman
nave left standing and unmoulded round arches cut in. Then
the s arcade of *c*.1200, treating the wall in the same way, but
with pointed, slightly chamfered arches. The aisle was rebuilt in 1882, as were the N and S chapels. They must have
been of the early C13. Round piers, round abaci, double-
chamfered arches. The chancel between is a C13 addition to
the Norman church too – see the triplet of single-stepped E
lancets with an oculus in the gable. The lancets have thin roll
mouldings inside. The chancel arch seems over-restored, but
original. It has a moulded arch on triple shafts with developed
stiff-leaf capitals. – PLATE. Pre-Reformation Paten, and Cup
of 1568 on a pre-Reformation foot. – CURIOSUM. An early
C19 BARREL ORGAN.

LONG BARROW, on a spur overlooking the Ouse, 2 m. w of
Newhaven. The barrow is orientated E–W. It is 120 ft long,
and 60 ft wide at its broader E end. No side ditches are now
visible. An unaccompanied inhumation burial, almost certainly secondary, was found in the body of the mound.

PILSTYE see CUCKFIELD

PILTDOWN see FLETCHING

PLAYDEN

ST MICHAEL. A church essentially of *c.*1200. Central tower with an elegant later shingled broach spire. The bell-openings are single lancets. Nave long, and with aisles embracing the central tower but not forming transepts. Blunt W front. In the N wall doorway with a typical heavy quadrant moulding and, W of it, one still entirely Norman window. Inside, the crossing piers simply stepped (not shafted) with slight stop-chamfers. The W arch to the W and the E arch to both sides have a keeled roll moulding. The arcade arches have the same motif. The piers alternate between round and octagonal. But whereas the tower arches are pointed, three of the four arcade bays have round arches. The W bay alone is pointed. Above the arcade remains of a former clerestory. One round window N, one S. Did they belong to a Norman nave with Norman aisles ? – SCREEN to the N chapel. Dec, i.e. remarkably early. Remarkable also by the combination of coarseness and richness. Shafts, not mullions, ogee arches, and in the spandrels ogee spherical triangles and mouchette wheels. – SCREEN to the chancel. Perp; coarse. – PULPIT. A plain C18 piece with two candleholders. – How old is the LADDER in the tower? – PLATE. Cup and Cover with arabesque ornament, 1568. – MONUMENT. Incised slab to Cornelis Roetmans. The inscription is in Flemish, and a barrel is added* (N aisle).

LEASAM HOUSE, ⅝ m. W. Built *c.*1800 of red brick with three storeys. The façade has a pedimented three-bay centre, but the pediment is set against the attic storey, an awkward arrangement. It makes the attic look a later alteration. On the ground floor a porch of six unfluted Ionic columns. The E side has three bays, the side windows tripartite on ground floor and first floor and of lunette shape on the top floor. The view over Rye is specially good from here.

PLUMPTON

ST MICHAEL. Small, Norman (see one N window and the simple S doorway), with a C13 chancel (see the two S lancets). The short W tower (with shingled broach spire) C13 too (one small lancet). Of the C14 the tower W details. – PAINTINGS. Wall paintings in the Clayton–Hardham style were found within the last ten years and recorded by Mr Clive Rouse. They are on the N wall high up and only dimly recognizable. Most

* Was he a brewer, asks Mr McHardy, who drew my attention to this slab.

easily seen are the scrolls in the reveals of the Norman window.
Above and E of it Christ seated in the Heavenly Jerusalem, an
enclosure of low arcading as at Clayton. To the l. of the window St Peter with the keys, further l. several figures.* –
PLATE. Chalice and Paten, 1734.

PLUMPTON PLACE. An enchanted place due to *Lutyens* and
rare birds. The house is of the C16 and early C17, but now
essentially the work of Lutyens, done in 1927–8 for Edward
Hudson, the owner of *Country Life*, for whom he had done
Deanery Garden, Sonning, and Lindisfarne Castle some
twenty-five years before. The C16 work is timber-framed
and shows on the N side. The W front is of *c.*1600, E-shaped,
of flint with red brick dressings. Lutyens added a music
room at the NE corner with large square multi-transomed
bay windows to N and S overlooking the moat and lake –
Lutyens's Mill House. Moreover, as one approaches the
house in its moat, one first crosses a Lutyens bridge and
then passes through a typical Lutyens composition: an archway, on the inner side treated like a Venetian window, but l.
and r. weatherboarded cottages, with formal fenestration,
three windows l., three windows r., the whole under one big
roof. BARN to the W of the house. Probably C17, partly timber-framed, partly weatherboarded. Queenpost roof.

ALL SAINTS, Plumpton Green, 2 m. N. 1893 by *Samuel Denman*.
Plain funny, with its octagonal tower and the way the octagon
is accomplished.

LATE BRONZE AGE SETTLEMENT, on Plumpton Plain, ¾ m.
SW. The settlement, the most famous of the period in Britain,
consists of two principal sites. Site A comprises four embanked enclosures linked by trackways. Three of the enclosures have been excavated, and each was found to contain the
remains of a circular timber hut about 20 ft in diameter. A
second, similar site, Site B, lying ¾ m. SE of the former, appears to have been occupied after the abandonment of the first
site.

S of Site B is a well-marked FIELD SYSTEM, possibly associated with the settlements.

POLEGATE

ST JOHN. 1874–6 by *R. K. Blessley* (GR). Low NW tower with
broach spire. Lancets and geometrical tracery. Brick-faced

* In 1964 wall paintings were discovered on the E wall of the nave as well.

inside. Big timber roof with arched braces and collar-beams.
Nothing of architectural value at Polegate. The only remark
worth making is that flats are beginning to appear (cf. Eastbourne, four miles away).

WINDMILL, to the S. A tower mill of 1817. The four sails survive.

OTTEHAM COURT, ¾ m. NNE. A chapel of the early C14 survives here, with two very prettily double-cusped windows and
the SEDILIA and PISCINA, both gabled. It belonged to a
grange of the Premonstratensians, founded in the late C12 and
soon after coming under Bayham.

SAYERLAND, 1 m. N. Quite a nice C18 front with three canted
bay windows, the middle one serving as a porch on the ground
floor, i.e. with two columns.

PORTSLADE see BRIGHTON, p. 459

POSSINGWORTH
1¼–1½ m. NW of Waldron

OLD POSSINGWORTH MANOR. Dated 1657. Only the N part
is of that date, and seems even conservative for it.* Mullioned
windows, gables with ball finials. However, the part of 1921
represents what had been there. At the back, where three wings
project, a doorway which must be of pre-Reformation date.
Small blank panels on the uprights, carving in the spandrels.

POSSINGWORTH MANOR (Holy Cross Priory). Built in 1866
for Louis Huth, member of a City family and art collector,‡ by
Sir Matthew Digby Wyatt at a cost of £60,000. It is almost
beyond belief how joyless it is for that money, in spite of a
great variety of motifs and bulk and height. The house is of
dull red brick with stone dressings and Gothic in style. On the
entrance side plenty of turrets and nothing very high. The
garden side on the other hand, owing to the fall of the ground,
is four-storeyed. It is of course asymmetrical, and the most
curious thing is one thin tall turret more than halfway down,
which houses a staircase only right at the top. At least as perverse the fact that the only access to the garden is by a small
doorway and down two flights of steps. The great hall is on
the entrance side, filling the recessed centre between two far-
projecting wings. It is reached by a big, very ornately Gothic

---

* The MHLG reports a rain-water head of 1620 on a part of the offices.
‡ His brother Harry Huth, however, was the more famous collector.

portal set diagonally in the l. corner of the centre. To it on the r. corresponds a normal tall bay window. Very ornately Gothic fireplace too. The staircase runs right up in the hall and is in a Gothic so free that the general impression is 1670 rather than 1470. The picture gallery is in one of the wings. It is sky-lit and has a big stucco coving in which you can even see Gothic buttresses bending forward to follow the curve of the coving.

POYNINGS

HOLY TRINITY. The first impression is of a C13 church, uniform and aisleless. Soon, however, one recognizes that this is a unified, consistent Early Perp job, even if one may perhaps presume that existing foundations were used. The church was built under the will of Michael of Poynings who died in 1369. It is faced with squared flint. The chancel is nearly of the same length as the nave, the windows are all Perp, including the five-light E window with tracery a little out of the ordinary, but matched at Alfriston and West Tarring. Only the s transept s window is an exception. This was brought from Chichester Cathedral, corresponds to a s window of the chancel aisle there, and is probably of c.1643 (see p. 139). The crossing tower has remarkably few and small windows. The interior is spacious, and dominated by the crossing arches with heavy, not very high semi-octagonal responds, all identical. SEDILIA and PISCINA with ogee arches. – FONT. This might well be of the time of the church, octagonal bowl, stem and foot all one, with blank ogee arcading. – SCREEN. To the s transept, three-light divisions, but each three again with mullions up to the top and no arches of more than one light. – PULPIT. Jacobean, with flatly carved panels and back panel with the crudest of caryatids. – Two single FAMILY PEWS. – COMMUNION RAIL. Three-sided, of early C17 style, with vertically symmetrical balusters, the main posts crowned by (recent) high finials. – TILES. A number of the later C13 on the sanctuary steps. – STAINED GLASS. C15 glass in the nave N, the nave S, and the N transept E tracery, in the latter an Annunciation. – PLATE. Cup and Cover, 1567.

RECTORY. Reassuring, solid three-bay house, with widely spaced windows and a Tuscan porch, probably of the 1830s.

ROYAL OAK. The jollity of 1880 or so, with its plenitude of garlands, is enterprisingly in contrast with the bleak neighbouring ZION CHAPEL of 1843.

PRESTON *see* BRIGHTON, p. 460

PRESTON COLLEGE *see* LINDFIELD

PUNNETT'S TOWN *see* HEATHFIELD

PYECOMBE

2010

CHURCH. A small church, facing the Downs, flint, pebbledash and few windows. Low c13 w tower with pyramid roof, Norman nave and chancel, as recognizable now only in the chancel arch, an unmoulded arch on the plainest imposts. The side openings are c19, as are the c13-looking chancel windows. – FONT. Of lead, drum-shaped, c12. Not as delicate as some, yet admirably civilized in its ornamental restraint. The lead was cut flat and then bent. There is only one seam. The main strip of decoration has double scrolls in arcading, the scrolls resembling a figure of eight. Above a small decorative band, then a band of low trefoil-arched arcading, and at the top a small band of fluting. – PULPIT. 1636. With flat ornamental carving. – Similar pieces worked into the READER'S DESK. – PLATE. Cup, c.1660, with a stem, probably of c.1568, and foot, c.1720; Cover, perhaps Elizabethan.

RATTON *see* EASTBOURNE, p. 485

RINGMER

4010

ST MARY. The flint w tower and w extension of the nave of 1884–5 by *Ewan Christian*. The two sandstone chancel chapels are Perp. So are their two-bay arcades to the chancel (four-centred arches). But the aisle arcades are earlier. They have very tall unmoulded bases, and on these there are on the N side c13 bases. But the piers and arches, like those of the s arcade, are rather c14. Heavy original timbers in the s porch. The s chapel probably the one built c.1500, the N chapel the one to which a will of 1535 refers. But the s chapel doorway and s window must be re-used c14 material. The N chapel has a good Jacobean plaster ceiling with decorated beams. – ARCHITECTURAL FRAGMENTS. Norman bits in the sw buttress. – PLATE. Cup and Paten, 1704.* – MONUMENTS. Harbert Springett † 1620. Alabaster tablet, with kneeling figure between two obelisks. – Sir William Springett † 1643. Tablet

* The SWORD is from the first World War.

with frontal bust in an oval recess. – Sir Harbert Whalley † 1689. Tablet with garlands and two cherubs at the top. These three in the s chapel. – Richard Wynne † 1679. Handsome cartouche, in the chancel. – In the N chapel. Elizabeth Jefferay, c.1620, but no date recorded. Tablet with kneeling figures with an obelisk between. – Ensign H. D. Crunden † 1793. With a frontal figure of Fortitude looking like Bellona. Ascribed to *Westmacott* in an old guidebook; good (s aisle).

LITTLE MANOR, s of the church on the A-road. Five-bay brick house with a lively brick frieze under the eaves.

WILLINGHAM HOUSE, 1¼ m. NW. Late Georgian, of brick, three bays with a Tuscan porch. The two lower pedimented three-bay pavilions l. and r. were added in 1961. (In the garden a GAZEBO, octagonal with a shell-grotto beneath. MHLG)

5010

RIPE

ST JOHN BAPTIST. A Pelham tower, i.e. substantial, Perp, and with the Pelham buckle on the doorway. Battlements; no spire. The chancel E window of five lights has flowing tracery. If that is correct restoration, a Dec date is certain. Otherwise the details of the church are Perp. A puzzle is the recess to the l. of the chancel arch. It seems of a piece with the chancel arch, and certainly Perp. But the arch is a Dec arch, re-used, and moreover, if the recess was to hold the reredos of a nave altar, how could the rood screen and rood loft cut so into it ?* – STAINED GLASS. In the E window many fragments of Dec glass, green and yellow. No figures.

ECKINGTON MANOR, w of the church. Chequer-brick, c.1700. Five bays, two storeys, hipped roof, dormers with alternatingly triangular and segmental pediments. Arched chimneystacks. The doorway is late C18.

ECKINGTON LODGE (or House), ⅝ m. NW. Early C17. With four-light mullioned windows and two dormers. There is a subtle difference in size between the former hall window and its counterpiece on the other side of the doorway.

OLD COTTAGE, on the way to the Manor House. Timber-framed with brick nogging and a mighty lot of bits and pieces of old woodwork.

MANOR HOUSE, ½ m. WNW. Behind the brick front of 1686 with its two symmetrical porches lies a C15 or early C16 house.

* Mr McHardy noticed that the mysterious arch matches the single SEDILE in its entirety.

At the N end some exposed timber-framing with closely set studs.

RIVERHALL *see* WADHURST

ROBERTSBRIDGE   7020

No church; the church is at Salehurst, across the river Rother.

The HIGH STREET has no great events. What distinguishes it is a little more exposed timberwork with closely set studs than in other places. Coming from the bridge there is such a house on the r. (Nos 25–27), then opposite the BETHEL CHAPEL of 1842 with pointed windows, then the SEVEN STARS, much altered but still showing the Wealden bracing, and after that the truly horrible CONGREGATIONAL METHODIST CHURCH of 1881, by *Thomas Elworthy* of St Leonards, whose name is recorded on it. It is in the most dissolute Italianate with some Gothic details. Opposite a Georgian house of three storeys with two bows, then again on the r. side a bigger C17 timber-framed house (Nos 55–59), then cottages ramble off into a bottom dip, and across the end stands the GEORGE HOTEL, Georgian, tile-hung, and of five bays.*

ROBERTSBRIDGE ABBEY. This was a Cistercian abbey founded in 1176. What survives is not at once easily placed. The ruins to the E of the house are of the refectory, including a round-headed doorway in the W wall. The E wall borders on the warming room, and this on the dormitory undercroft, of which the vaulting springers in its W wall survive. The ribs are hollow-chamfered. The present house is the abbot's house projecting W of the W range of the cloister (which does not exist), just as at Battle Abbey. Of the house an undercroft is complete, probably of the hall. It is of six bays of rib-vaulting, with two round piers, hollow-chamfered arches, and simply chamfered ribs. Above, the W window is still *in situ*, large and shafted, with stiff-leaf label-stops and a small recess by its side. All this is of the mid C13. The roof of the hall is of the kingpost type.

RODMELL   4000

A small flint village of one street. The prettiest house is the REC-TORY, Early Victorian, lightly medievalizing, the parapet with little gablets.

* Mr R. T. Mason has recorded Nos 23–5 East Street as a hall-house with single-bay hall and solar and service wings (SAC 96, 1958).

ST PETER. Small, with an early C13 W tower with pyramid spire.
Attached to the tower to the S another early C13 room (for the
date, see the lancets). For the rest, it looks as if windows have
been changed round freely. The interior is more enlightening.
This is a Norman church, even if the chancel arch is heavily
Victorian, though copying the rich Late Norman geometrical
motifs of a pointed arch previously there and said to have been
made up from stones of Lewes Priory.* But in the chancel is a
Norman window,‡ and the S aisle was thrown out not later
than c.1200. It is of two bays and has a round pier and a square
abacus and a low single-tier stiff-leaf capital resting on corner
sprays (and one corbel head) – exactly as at St Anne Lewes and
Beddingham. The arches are round with a slight chamfer. But
what complicates matters is that the aisle has Norman round
arches also to W and E. The E responds at least are right, and
the W arch. The E arch leads into a two-bay chapel with an
extremely short round pier with round abacus and pointed,
slightly chamfered arches. The tower arch finally is the same.
How does this work out as a development ? Were round arches
and pointed arches used indiscriminately ? And square and
round abaci ? – FONT. Square, of the Purbeck type, with very
flat blank arches. – SCREEN. Between chancel and S chapel part
of a C14 screen, ogee-arched openings and instead of tracery
simply a row of quatrefoiled circles pulled out into ogees at
the foot. – ARCHITECTURAL FRAGMENT. A shaft with vertical zigzag and a base with spurs, probably from the monks'
lavatorium of Lewes Priory. – STAINED GLASS. In a N window small C15 Crucifixus. – E window by *Powell's*; 1859. –
PLATE. Cup and Cover, 1568; Paten, 1680.

ROEDEAN

The school was founded by the Misses Lawrence in 1885 and
operated in houses in Brighton till the new building became
available. It was built in 1898–9 and is designed by *Sir J. W.
Simpson*.§ The style is a free Jacobean. The whole originally
was one long block with a deeply recessed centre. The centre
has two symmetrical towers, straight gables, and a raised porch
feature in the middle. The wings come forward, again with

---

* Some of them now in the Rectory garden, and two under the tower.
‡ The E window is Perp, but there are externally signs of an earlier group
(cf. perhaps Iford).
§ Mr G. Spain tells me that the tender was for £44,957.

gables, and then continue parallel to the centre with more, much bigger gables. It is a most ambitious scheme, combining under one roof the teaching and the residential parts, staff as well as girls' quarters. School House forms the centre, with the Hall behind. Four 'houses' occupy the wings. The most prominent additions are the Chapel (NW) of 1906, the Art School and Library (NE) of 1911, and the Junior School and the Sanatorium of 1908, some distance away to the NE. All these are by Simpson too. A new Dining Room is under construction at the time of writing. This projects to the W and was designed by *Sir Hubert Worthington*.

ROTHERFIELD   5030

ST DENYS. Early C13 with Perp contributions. The latter are quite prominent; for they are the ashlar-faced W tower with stair-turret (and a recessed shingled spire), the aisle windows, and the two-storeyed N porch with a rib-vault inside. Early C13 the three-bay aisle arcades of the wide nave, N before S, the former with round, the latter with octagonal piers and capitals, and both with slight double chamfers to the arches, the W lancets of the aisles before the Perp widening, the chancel with its tall lancets high up, and the N chapel also with tall lancets high up and with a two-bay arcade to the chancel, in style closely similar to the aisle arcades. The W arch on the other hand looks rather more primitive, but it is difficult to explain this. The E window is Perp. At the E end of the S aisle a plain arch, now also blocked. This and some masonry indicate that there was a SE tower here, before the Perp tower was built. Simple SEDILIA in the chancel. Wagon roof in the nave, single-framed open roof in the chancel. – FONT COVER. Dated 1533. In the churchwardens' book it is called the Tabernacle of the font. It was repaired in 1816 and is of the closed polygonal type which folds back by doors (cf. Ticehurst). The panels are Early Renaissance. – PULPIT. An exceptionally splendid Laudian piece. The back panel with enormous front halves of eagles in profile l. and r. The sounding board large, the pulpit itself with tapering pilasters at the angles and panels filled with the simplest geometrical motifs but in strong relief. – SCREEN. To the N chapel, actually parts of two different, quite dainty, Perp screens. – BOX PEWS. Rising a little at the W end. – REREDOS. Of alabaster, shrine type, cutting alas into the E window. – STAINED GLASS. E window. By *William Morris*, the figures by *Burne-Jones*, outstandingly good. Single

figures in beautifully interwoven foliage.* – WALL PAINT-
INGS. The paintings on the E wall of nave and N aisle are at
least partially well enough preserved to show their quality.
They represent the Doom, and Christ and angels appear high
up. Lower down the exquisite figure of St Michael weighing
souls. These paintings look c.1300. To the l. Doubting
Thomas, a little earlier. Also an Archangel Gabriel in the l.
jamb of the E window of the N chapel. – MONUMENT. Nicholas Fowle † 1656. The tablet addresses you, *studiose lector*, and
explains itself by a military still-life. – (In the N aisle a cast-
iron ledger-stone.)

To the NE of the church a nice triangle of houses – brick, tile-
hanging, weatherboarding.

The OLD MANOR lies just behind a shop at the main road junction in the centre. Late C17, of five bays, with wooden cross
windows. The first floor tile-hung. Across the railway, past
the station and up the hill on the l., OAKDENE, a house by
Barry Parker, 1907. Pretty front with one roof running over
two canted bays and a middle bow. All quite small.

ROTHERFIELD HALL, ¾ m. SW. Some C16 features at the N end,
made the occasion for a symmetrical neo-Elizabethan house by
Inigo Thomas in 1897.

(BLETCHINGLY, 1¼ m. ENE. Early C15. The centre was the hall
of two bays. The mid-truss survives. VCH)

(BROOK HOUSE. Brick-faced centre, timber-framed wings. One
chimneystack with star tops. Old features inside. NBR)

ARGOS HILL WINDMILL, 1½ m. SE. A post-mill with its sail.

3000   ROTTINGDEAN

ST MARGARET. A flint church with an impressive central
tower. The nave is Norman, as part of one N window shows
inside. Foundations of a S transept have been found, and these
are probably Norman too. There is in addition a stone with
zigzag carving. Otherwise it is an E.E. church. The tower has
long lancets, single even for the bell-openings. The W and E
arches are triple-chamfered, all chamfers being slight. In the
chancel the priest's doorway has C13 mouldings too. The rest
is all of the restoration (*Sir G. G. Scott*, 1856), including the
whole S aisle and the chancel E lancets. – TRIPTYCH (by the

_____
* Mr McHardy has told me that the original drawing is in the vestry and
carries the date 1874.

font). Small; Spanish, C16. – STAINED GLASS. Much by
Burne-Jones, who had a house at Rottingdean from 1880 to his
death (i.e. by him and *William Morris*'s firm). The E window
was given by him in 1893, but the finest are the tower N and S
windows, the Tree of Jesse and Jacob's Ladder. They are of
1897. Two in the nave are by *Morris & Co.*, but after the death
of both Morris and Burne-Jones. – PLATE. Cup and Paten,
1719. – MONUMENT. Thomas Redman Hooker † 1838. With
a bust as the principal motif.

Behind the church an agglomeration of half-timbering, gables,
and brick chimneystacks, picturesque and essentially of between the World Wars.

In front of the church an exceptionally pretty green with a pond
and houses in no special arrangement. At the S end THE
GRANGE, now the Library and originally the Vicarage. It has
a seven-bay front with a doorway of pairs of unfluted Ionic
columns not in the centre. At the back, nice, informal additions by *Lutyens* (1920s).

On the W side the green is touched by the HIGH STREET, and
here is NORTH END HOUSE, Burne-Jones's house, which is
an adaptation of two separate houses by means of a link with
the upper floor glazed and at the r. end extended with a Norman-Shavian oriel. The link was designed by *W. A. Benson*. A
little further N three more good houses:

HILLSIDE. Dated 1724, of red brick. Five bays and two storeys,
the ground-floor windows with lintels of fine rubbed brick.
The porch has Tuscan columns.

COURT HOUSE. Also five bays and two storeys, but coursed
flint with brick dressings and a thin porch.

DOWN HOUSE. Flint and brick too, but six bays and a doorway
with broken pediment.

WINDMILL, ¾ m. W. An C18 smock-mill with its four sails.

ST DUNSTAN'S, ¼ m. W. 1937–9 by *Francis Lorne* of Sir John
Burnet, Tait & Lorne. 'International Modern', and for that
reason memorable still. However, compared e.g. with the Bexhill Pavilion this is a conventional composition using traditional materials. Strictly symmetrical, of yellow brick. Owing
to the contours, the entrance side has more storeys than the
back. The entrance is in fact in the basement, and the chapel
lies yet lower down in axis with the entrance. The centre of
the façade then builds up with a middle projection, largest in
the basement, less in ground floor and first floor, and only a
glazed semi-tube above. The latter is a motif familiar from

winding staircases, but there is here no staircase to justify it. The Dining Hall is on the ground floor behind the principal range. This range has long bands of windows separated by bands of brick.

(BALSDEAN CHAPEL, near Norton Farm. No road leads to the hamlet of Balsdean, 2¼ m. NNE of Rottingdean. Remains of a C12 nave, used as a stable. One small window in the N wall. VCH)

ROWFANT HOUSE see WORTH

RUSHLAKE GREEN see WARBLETON

9020

RYE

INTRODUCTION. Hill towns are rare in England. In Sussex Lewes is one, Winchelsea another, but Rye, its sandstone rock rising out of the total flat of the fen, makes its statement yet more unmistakably. The houses building up to the low tower of the church are reminiscent of the north of France. The medieval confinement to the hill – walls and gates survive to a certain extent – has been kept. The main through roads keep to the flat. All streets in the town proper rise and fall and undulate, and many are cobbled. The main plan is regular on paper with a spine street, the High Street, along the hill and streets at r. angles, but one does not feel it all the time as at Winchelsea. The E part of the town has largely disappeared, owing to the action of the sea. Rye became a royal manor under Henry III, and it was one of the Cinque Ports, though it assumed full stature as a member only c.1336. The town suffered severely from French raids. There was one in 1339, another, much more disastrous, in 1377, a third in 1448. The prosperity of the town, which made it so desirable a target for the French, is attested by the establishment of houses of the friars (Sack c.1263, Austin before 1350). It began to diminish in the second half of the C16, when the harbour silted up. But as a country town it evidently had still quite a comfortable existence in the C18.

ST MARY. That there was a cruciform Norman church here is at once visible. The N transept has a Norman doorway with one order of colonnettes. In the S transept S wall Norman and slightly post-Norman (dogtooth) bits have been re-set, and inside, the transepts are still essentially Norman. Blank arcading on the W walls, on the N side with a crenellation frieze, on the S side with thick zigzag at r. angles to the wall. Above on the N side another row of big blank arches, these on corbels. The N transept shows traces of this same arrangement on the E wall. Then N and S complete windows, shafted, with shaft-rings. This Norman church had aisles; for the arches into them from the transepts exist, that on the S in good condition. Tripartite responds. Leaves in the capitals. The arch has a fat half-roll as its centre moulding. These Norman aisles were replaced soon; for the present arcades are of the early C13. Five bays, piers round or octagonal. Arches with rolls and chamfers, the two westernmost ones decidedly more pointed. Hood-mould with dogtooth. Clerestory of single windows re-built in 1882. Is the motif of the wall-passage correct? Fully E.E. the two chancel chapels. They have lancet windows. Those of the S chapel are in pairs with an oculus over and are shafted inside. In the S chapel wall also the re-used head of a small lancet. Inside, the chapels have a wall-passage at the level of the sill of the lancets. Of the three-bay arcades of the chapels only two bays on the N side are E.E. Crocket capitals on piers with four main shafts and four keeled ones in the diagonals with thin hollows between. The rest of the arcades was re-done in the C15, at the same time as the crossing with its tower was re-done. The piers are Perp. So are the arches, the W arch lower than the others. The tower is low, with battle-ments and a pyramid roof. Perp also the flying buttresses at the E end of the church and the main transept windows. An-other, very attractive Perp addition is two-storeyed and W of the S transept. The ground floor has a quadripartite rib-vault with a flat leaf boss and a large, circular, quatrefoiled window on the S. On the upper floor a circular window of similar size to the W. This was probably a sacristy with the priest's room over. The spirelet over the crossing tower with its wind-vane is of 1702. – PULPIT. With early C16 linenfold panels. – SCREENS. From the transepts to the N and S chapels. Simple, Perp. – CHANDELIER. Of brass, two tiers, inscribed 1759. – CLOCK. Outside, high up, on the N transept, visible from the High Street. With quarter-boys and a jolly framework. All of c.1760, but the clockwork made at Winchelsea in 1561–2. The pendulum, seen inside the church, is 18 ft long. – STAINED GLASS. S aisle W by *Kempe*, 1896; another S aisle window, 1889. – N aisle one by *Morris & Co.*, 1897, senti-mental. – PLATE. Two Cups, 1635; Pewter Flagon, c.1685; Paten on foot, 1704; Paten, 1722; Flagon, 1732. – MONU-MENTS. Catherine Owens † 1797, by *Flaxman*. Urn and branch; nothing special (N aisle). – John Woollett † 1819. Signed *J. Bacon* inv., *S. Manning* ft. Two allegorical women in front of an obelisk (crossing). – There are also unusually many tablets.

PERAMBULATION. It starts in CHURCH SQUARE, not a square at all, but rows of houses surrounding the church and church-yard on all four sides. Inside the enclosed area just NE of the church the WATER HOUSE, built in 1733–5 of brick, oval with a truncated dome, an upper storey, and a full dome. It served as a public cistern. The houses along the square with white weatherboarding, tile-hanging, or timber-framing exposed are of course of brick, and the recurrent theme of the whole of Rye. Another theme also appears at once, on the E side of the square: the open view into the plain. At the SE corner the first interruption, the YPRES TOWER, built as the castle of Rye in the C13 and used as a prison from 1518 to the early C19. The tower has four round turrets and remains of machicolation. It is continued by part of the C14 town WALL to the E. Back to the square and at the SE corner the METHODIST CHAPEL of 1901, much remodelled in 1942 etc. On the S side of the square Nos 22–30 etc. are a pic-turesque group of timber-framed houses with several gables. This is followed by a house whose oversailing, tile-hung upper floor is supported by three thin Late Georgian iron columns. No. 40 is all that remains of the house of the FRIARS OF THE SACK, founded c.1263 and dissolved c.1305. In the N gable an upper window of two pointed-trefoiled lights with a quatrefoiled circle over – i.e. later C13. (C14 roof inside. VCH) Continue along WATCHBELL STREET again towards a view into the open. On the r. the former INDEPENDENT CHAPEL of 1817, red brick with arched windows and door-way. The front is of three bays. Back to the square, and at the corner of Watchbell Street No. 48, a good, long timber-framed C15 house with oversailing upper floor. Doorway with four-centred head and leaf carving in the spandrels. After that another C15 house, now Nos 54–60, but no longer recognizable as such. No. 60 has a door-hood with carved brackets. Not much along the N side, except that the distance between church and houses narrows.

In the middle of this N side turn down LION STREET. The timber-framed house on the l. is FLETCHER'S HOUSE, three storeys, of the C15. At the end, at the bottom you see the Old Grammar School in the High Street, but that will come later.

First turn E, halfway down into Market Street and to the
TOWN HALL. Market Street is not a market square. It
widens only slightly, and the town hall is placed discreetly,
unmonumentally. Yet in design it could stand up to a detached
and axial position. It was designed in 1743 by *Andrews Jelfe*,
a successful London mason, and stands on the site of an
earlier court and market house. It is of brick with stone
dressings including quoins. The ground floor has arcading
of five bays on square piers, the upper floor (still) segment-
headed windows. The doorway under the arcade has fluted
pilasters and a metope frieze. At the top a parapet and a
cupola. Panelled council chamber with raised platform. Graceful balustrade. The chimneypiece with heavy Tuscan columns
is of French stylistic derivation, i.e. the so-called architecture
of the French Revolution. It may date from *c.*1800.* E of the
Town Hall the FLUSHING INN, C15 on a C13 cellar with
tunnel-vault and hollow-chamfered transverse arches. Timber-
framed and within, in the ground-floor hall, WALL PAINTING
dated 1536–7. Inscriptions in black letter held by putti and
below large rustically done leaf scrolls with animals disporting
themselves in them. Then DURRANT HOUSE, *c.*1800, three
storeys, white, with tripartite windows, and down EAST
STREET with CHEQUER on the r., four bays, three storeys,
Tuscan porch. Again view down to the High Street, and
again it is too early to join.

So back once more to Church Square and now off its NW
corner into WEST STREET. This has a dog-leg course, and
the house facing one as one comes from the square is Henry
James's house, LAMB HOUSE, clearly of the early C18 with
its panelled parapet and its angle pilaster strips. It is of four
bays and brick chequer. On the way down, West Street
widens with a break so that, looking from the High Street, the
view is closed by another red-brick house. This is No. 1
MERMAID STREET, dated 1789, of three storeys and again
with the typical tripartite windows. Before turning into Mermaid Street the remainder of West Street. TOWER HOUSE
opposite has an excellent carved door surround of *c.*1700.
Flat hood on carved brackets. Some timber-framed houses on
the l., especially THOMAS HOUSE with two concave-sided
lozenges in the decoration of the r. overhang.

* In the Council Chamber a Gothic CHEST with blank traceried windows. – REGALIA. Two silver-gilt Maces inscribed 1767, two smaller
Maces, parcel-gilt. One of the shafts is of 1570.

3a Back and now down MERMAID STREET, down indeed. On the
r. the MERMAID INN with a vaulted C13 cellar (tunnel-vault
with hollow-chamfered transverse arches). Above, the inn is
of c.1500, with a long upper-floor overhang and a small
courtyard inside. The three back ranges are later C16.
Opposite, Nos 5–6 with a close-studded overhang. The door
29b is early C18. Again on the N side the OLD HOSPITAL, C15
and C16. A date 1576 is on one of the three gables. Of these,
two project beyond the third, but the third is bigger. Beneath
the latter a canted bay window, on the first floor of the others
two three-light windows typical in their design of about 1670.
More nice Georgian doorways with flat hoods on brackets.
Then on the l. TRADERS PASSAGE, a walk above the WALL
with the WAREHOUSES in the STRAND below and the river
beyond. At the end of Mermaid Street one reaches the bottom
for the first time, where the relief roads are. At the bottom
corner the BOROUGH ARMS, white, weatherboarded, and
reached up fifteen steps. It lies on the town WALL.

From here at last the HIGH STREET can be entered, or that
part of it which is called THE MINT. The street is No Entry
this way, and, as this is a perambulation, this is the direction
in which one should see it. On the l. at once houses partly
built on the WALL. On the r. a green, i.e. not yet quite
seriously a street. Nos 45–46 are C15, with oversailing studded
upper floor. No. 43 is C15 too, but the cusped quatrefoil
studding must be early C19, or Early Victorian. Opposite an
attractive early C18 door surround. Then a cobbled passage
up to Mermaid Street. The High Street now becomes the
High Street. It climbs and winds, though gently. On the r. a
house of four bays, all arched windows with rusticated
surrounds, as if it were a chapel. A house near by (No. 85)
has a generous Georgian bow and a thin Tuscan porch.

40 Then PEACOCK'S SCHOOL, a brick building of more than local
interest. It was built in 1636. Five bays, the first and last
blank except for the small doorways. Giant pilasters on high
bases. Dormers with Dutch gables, the middle one bigger
with an open segmental pediment. The interest of the façade
lies in the use of Dutch gables and giant pilasters. The former
began to appear shortly before 1620 (former house in Holborn,
c.1618, Blickling 1624, Dutch House Kew 1631), the latter
not before the 1630s (former houses in Great Queen Street
c.1637, Lindsey House Lincoln's Inn Fields 1640). So both
motifs are remarkably early here. Inside, two rooms and an

attic. Opposite the GEORGE HOTEL, white, of c.1719, of five bays, with a Tuscan porch. The middle window above must be a re-set door-surround. To the r. of the hotel the Assembly Room with two upper bows and a nice stucco ceiling. This dates from 1818. Again on the other side the MIDLAND BANK with a doorway with fluted pilasters and a metope frieze. Then, once more on the s side, at the corner of East Street, the APOTHECARY'S SHOP, with a handsome curved Georgian shop front. After that nothing more in need of comment in the High Street, but down CONDUIT HILL to see what remains of the AUSTIN FRIARS. It is the chapel, C14, with windows still with flowing tracery, although the order moved to this site only in 1378.* At the bottom you are on the flat once again. Turn l. into CINQUE PORTS STREET, and you will see on the l. more of the WALLS. Then turn r. to the end of Tower Street and on again to end this perambulation where most people will enter Rye, at the LANDGATE, C14, earlier below, later above. Two round towers to the outside. Remains of machicolation between. Archway with continuous chamfers and the portcullis groove.

Outside the old town to the W a WINDMILL of smock type, brick and weatherboarding, and a MARTELLO TOWER (see p. 490) with its roof in the original state.

On the way to Playden on the l. is MOUNTSFIELD, yellow brick, c.1775, three bays, porch of pairs of thin Tuscan columns, the ground-floor windows in blank arches, then on the r. SALTCOTE PLACE, neo-Restoration to neo-Georgian, with hipped roof, balustrade, and cupola, by *Sir Reginald Blomfield*, 1900–2, and then again on the l. HILL HOUSE HOSPITAL (former WORKHOUSE), 1846, Tudor with gables. (*Blomfield* designed between c.1895 and the first years of the C20 a number of other houses around here as well: They are WESTWICK, LAVENDER WALK, THE CROFT, POINT LODGE, POINT HOUSE, THE POINT, and, for himself and his wife, POINT HILL. This house he altered five times. The estate belonged to his wife's family.)‡

(STARLOCK, Military Road, 1 m. NE on the way to Appledore. By *Frank Scarlett*, 1929–30, i.e. a very early example, as England goes, of the International Modern style. White, cubic, with a symmetrical three-bay front. Horizontal

* Mr Bagley thinks the windows belonged to the preceding establishment and were transferred.

‡ Information kindly given me by Mr Austin Blomfield.

window. The staircase window in one of the side façades is long and thin like Le Corbusier's at Vaucresson.)

RYE HARBOUR
1¼ m. SE of Rye

HOLY SPIRIT. By *S. S. Teulon*, 1848–9. Altered and enlarged by *C. Spooner*, 1912 (GR). Apsed, with pointed-trefoiled lancets and a N porch tower in which the transition from square to octagon is handled in a Teulon way. Big arched braces inside. – Round stone PULPIT with black colonnettes and mosaic, and FONT with some black marble, no doubt also Teulon's.

MARTELLO TOWER, to the SE. On the Martello Towers, *see* p. 490.

SADDLESCOMBE
⅝ m. ESE of Poynings

Site of a preceptory of the Templars.

SADDLESCOMBE FARM has a timber-framed S wing of the C16 or earlier. Close to it a square, weatherboarded WELLHOUSE with a pyramid roof and the donkey-wheel inside.

ST JOHN'S COLLEGE *see* HURSTPIERPOINT

ST LEONARDS *see* HASTINGS, pp. 518, 520, 521, 522, 527

SALEHURST

ST MARY. The W tower was begun early in the C14. The doorway is round-headed with one order of shafts. Perp top with chamfered angles. E.E. also the W lancets of the aisles, yet the long, somewhat gaunt arcades of six bays with their low octagonal piers and double-chamfered arches are Dec. They must be a replacement, as the clerestory windows do not tally with them at all and as the straight-headed aisle windows are Dec. The clerestory is of 1861 (*D. Brandon*), a symmetrical composition of lancets, two, one, three, one, two. The chancel has E.E. side lancets, and the E window has cusped intersecting tracery; so that will be *c*.1300. N chapel Dec, with reticulated tracery in the E window. The S porch of heavy timbers might well be as early too. Finally the W porch with a niche above the entrance and a quadripartite rib-vault without boss inside. This again looks C14, though it may be post-Dec. – FONT. The base is C13, with four salamanders round it. – STAINED GLASS. In the SE and SW windows, in the tracery, birds drawn in brown on the green glass, eminently interesting, the type of draughtsmanship one finds in the late C14 Pepysian volume at Magdalene College in Cambridge. – S aisle by *Kempe*, 1901 (with his wheatsheaf signature). – PLATE. Two Pewter Flagons, engraved 1705. – MONUMENTS. In the S aisle, front of a tomb-chest with three shields in quatrefoils. – In the N chapel, tomb recess with crocketed ogee gable, i.e. of the time of the chapel itself. – Several cartouche tablets, late C17 to early C18. – Several cast-iron tomb-slabs (W end of aisles) of 1661 to 1713, the inscriptions across, not along the slab. – Anne Peckham † 1758. With a woman by an urn, better architecturally than sculpturally. – Jane Micklethwait † 1819. By *P. Rouw Jun.* Urn in front of obelisk. – (In the churchyard two tomb-chests and three headstones with terracotta plaques by *Harmer*. SAC, 100, 1962.)

On three sides of the church houses pleasant to look at.

VILLAGE HOUSING. A consistent group, built by the Battle Rural District Council, *c.*1947–8. Architecturally irrelevant, but as a composition following the up-to-date principles of after the war. Alternation of white, red, and white and red (i.e. with tile-hanging) groups of two, three, four, outbuildings connecting or nearly connecting the groups.

GREAT WIGSALL, 2 m. NE. Dated on the main door 1641, but on one initialled fireplace inside 1625. It is a stone house with an impressive, completely symmetrical front. Three gables, cross-windows, central porch. Above the doorway a fluted frieze. The chimneys underline the symmetry forcefully. (Inside, an open-well staircase with turned balusters. It is evidently of the date of the house.)

SALTDEAN

3000

Minor seaside gaiety and a cosy housing chaos. The *clou* is BUTLIN'S CAMP with its modernistic buildings (futuristic, they would have called it then). The entrance building dates from 1938. It is in Lagrange Avenue, and off this runs WICKLANDS AVENUE, where to the E, forlorn among their conformist brothers and sisters, stand three white, cubic, by now perhaps a little dispirited, houses by *Connell & Ward*, pioneers of English Corbusianism. The houses date from 1934. They cost £550 each.

SAYERLAND see POLEGATE

2010
SAYERS COMMON
1½ m. NW of Hurstpierpoint

CHRIST CHURCH. 1880 by *Banks & Barry*. The chancel is later. The earlier work is of big lumps of flint with red brick dressings. Lancet windows, and a bell-turret with spirelet placed perkily on the ridge, diagonally and not at the W end. – STAINED GLASS. Many small medallions in a N window. C16 and C17, of the Netherlandish type, the same collection no doubt as in Hurstpierpoint church (*see* there). – PLATE. Cup, 1829.

3020
SCAYNES HILL

ST AUGUSTINE. 1858 by *Habershon* (GR). Red brick. Thin w tower with pyramid roof. The tall S windows with dormers. The chancel windows smaller.

4090
SEAFORD

Seaford is the least gay of the chain of south coast seaside places S of London. It has no pavilion, no amusement arcade, and a short ESPLANADE, which, at the time of writing, appears far from thriving. There is the ESPLANADE HOTEL, neat and quite large, of 1907. To its r. a decaying terrace, to its l. a substantial Gothic one, probably of about 1875. The E end is the MARTELLO TOWER of 1810, with a Victorian top.*

But what Seaford possesses in greater numbers than probably any other seaside place is schools, starting from what was the Ladies' College, now TRAINING COLLEGE, the most dignified building in the town. It was a private house, perhaps of *c.*1800, seven bays, two storeys, balustraded and stuccoed with a columnar porch, and has since been extended much at the back. And then there are plenty of private schools, mostly of Edwardian or slightly later date, clean and cheerful-looking.

Of the old Seaford hardly anything has been kept, and if it is true that the fireplace of *c.*1300 in the Plough Inn and the undercroft of No. 27 Church Street with two bays of quadri-partite vaulting (single-chamfered ribs, foliage boss) have been allowed to disappear, then there is nothing left, and one

* On Martello Towers *see* Eastbourne, p. 490.

can only blame the Urban District Council. Both were just s of the church.

ST LEONARD. This is a large and monumental medieval church, and it tells of the time when the Ouse reached the sea at Seaford and the town was one of the Cinque Ports. The story of the church begins unexpectedly with a Norman nave, of which the s w bay is now visible outside and the n w bay from the vestry. One arch with shafted responds on either side. It would not have made a normal bay of an arcade. Above it a Norman clerestory window on either side. The w doorway into the tower, with one order of colonnettes, is not *in situ*. Above the s clerestory is a higher E.E. clerestory window, handsomely shafted. This is continued to the E by two more, and to them correspond the N and s arcades inside, of the early C13. Two-bay arcades, round piers, round abaci, pointed arches with two hollow chamfers. The capitals are very low. They have one row of early stiff-leaf, except for one with scenes in small figures: Baptism of Christ, Harrowing of Hell, Daniel in the Lions' Den, Massacre of the Innocents, Crucifixion. These arcades must have replaced a Norman arcade; for there are two small Norman windows. They, and some herringbone masonry, prove an Early Norman N aisle. The w tower was set inside the Norman nave; hence the position of the two arches. It has a C14 arch to the nave, with two big, continuous chamfers, and is Perp above. Finally, the whole E part with transepts and polygonal apse is of 1861–2 (by *John Billing*, who carefully recorded the state of the church before the alterations). – SCULPTURE. An excellent St Michael with the Dragon, of *c.*1130–40, in the style of the Chichester reliefs. – STAINED GLASS. One s window by *Kempe*, 1903. – Chancel by *Powell*, 1862. – PLATE. Cup, 1824; Two Patens on feet, 1824.

CONGREGATIONAL CHURCH, Clinton Place. 1877 by *W. F. Powlton*. In a handsome lancet style, but with a turret so funny and so daring that it can only be High Victorian. It develops out of two angle-buttresses and is very thin.

(SURREY CONVALESCENT HOME, Clinton Park. By *Ewan Christian*. Opened in 1891.)

HILL-FORT. An Iron Age fort lies on a promontory 1 m. SE of the town. The site, which is of roughly triangular plan, is defended on two sides by a low bank and ditch, traces of which can still be seen on the NE, and by the cliff on the third. Two entrances occur on the E side and one on the NW.

It is uncertain if all these are contemporary with the construction of the site.

Outside the NW entrance of the fort is a low ROUND BARROW, 40 ft in diameter and 3 ft high. In the C19 a hoard of flint axes and other tools was found in two pits dug into the material of the barrow.

SEDLESCOMBE

7010

ST JOHN BAPTIST. C14–15 W tower with battlements and higher stair-turret. The rest of the exterior all of the restoration by *Norman & Billing*, 1866–74. N arcade of standard details, Perp, partly also of the restoration. Kingpost roof, one tie-beam dated 1632 and given pretty decoration. – Typical High Victorian furnishings: stone PULPIT, low iron SCREEN. – FONT COVER. Polygonal, with doors to fold back. Linenfold panels, i.e. early C16. – STAINED GLASS. Original bits in the NW window. – Chancel windows N and S by *Kempe*, 1890. – HELM and GAUNTLETS with the Sackville crest. – PLATE. Paten on foot, 1697; Cup, c.1700; Cup, given 1714; Pewter Flagon, before 1726; Almsdish, 1798.

Nice village GREEN, with a well-house like a market cross and a pump, dated 1900.

DURHAMFORD MANOR, ½ m. W. Large, C15, with close studding. Gable at the l. end of the front.

MANOR HOUSE (now Manor Cottages), at SEDLESCOMBE STREET. A large house, the front with close studding on the r., then a small gable and beneath it the concave-sided lozenges typical of c.1600, and a large gable with scalloped bargeboard, pendants, and the date 1611.

PESTALOZZI VILLAGE, 1¼ m. SE. A plan was made by *Sir Hugh Casson & Neville Conder* for development of the estate round the Victorian-Tudor OAKLANDS. The Warden's House and the International House were built, but then, in 1963, shortage of funds called a halt.

SELMESTON

5000

CHURCH. Flint. Nave with bell-turret and chancel. The S aisle dates from the restoration of 1867 (*E. Christian*). The S arcade is of three bays with oak piers, C14 in style, but apparently replacements of the original ones. They are octagonal and carry instead of arches curved braces. In the chancel Late Perp Easter Sepulchre, a recess with a depressed

almost straight arch and a cresting. – STAINED GLASS.
Chancel N, *Kempe*, 1905. – PLATE. Cup and Cover, 1632;
Flagon, 1674.

MAYS, 1 m. SE. Georgian brick house, grey headers and red
dressings, three bays only, but with handsome forward-
curving walls l. and r. The windows are widely spaced. The
house has two and a half storeys and a Tuscan porch.

COBB COURT, 1¼ m. SE. The typical five-bay brick house.
Doorway with Doric pilasters and pediment.

MESOLITHIC SITE. In a sandpit SE of the church were found
a number of Mesolithic pits or working hollows, two of which
were excavated in 1933. In the pits were found traces of fires,
pot-boilers, and a large number of flint implements and waste
flakes. After their initial use by Mesolithic groups and when
the pits had been almost filled with wind-blown sand, one
was re-occupied by Secondary Neolithic peoples, who left
behind them sherds of their characteristic cord-impressed
pottery and the remains of hearths.

SELSFIELD HOUSE see WEST HOATHLY

SHALESBROOKE see FOREST ROW

SHAVER'S GREEN see TICEHURST

SHEFFIELD PARK

4020

Built for John Baker Holroyd, first Earl of Sheffield, before
1779 by *James Wyatt*. Among major Gothic Revival mansions *See*
p.
691
Sheffield Park is thus early. It is a large house with three
main fronts. The entrance (S) side is of nine bays, punctuated
by buttress-shafts and pinnacles or turrets. The porch is later.
So is the service extension on the l. Round the corner to the
r. (E) a large chapel-like window under a stepped gable. Then
a canted bay and a straight-sided bay. Again round the corner
the chief garden front with a somewhat ungainly combination
of pointed arches below stepped gables. The house is rendered
on an ashlar base. Inside, the staircase hall is higher than
the rest, i.e. already something like Wyatt's much later
arrangement at Ashridge. Round the first-floor level
clustered Gothic shafts. The staircase rises in one flight, then
divides and breaks by ninety and again ninety degrees.

Glazed dome on pointed segmental lunettes. At the NE corner
an oval room with niches, classical in taste. The SE room is
oblong with a tripartite window under a segmental tympanum.
This classical detail is tellingly out of keeping with the Gothic
detail outside the same window (ogee arches on shafts).
Delightful frieze inside the room with sphinxes and lions in
elliptical medallions. Very discreet Adamish stucco ceiling.
But the finest room lies behind the canted bay window. The
corners have charming fan motifs just faintly Gothic. In the
cove lions, tigers, and cheetahs. Painted segmental ceiling.
The paintings are by *C. Catton*, R.A., who was much appreciated as a painter of animals. – Superb gardens, laid out by
Repton before 1794 (see his *Sketches* of 1794).

<h2 style="text-align:center">SHELLEY'S FOLLY see BARCOMBE</h2>

<h2 style="text-align:center">SIDLEY see BEXHILL, p. 416</h2>

<h2 style="text-align:center">SILVERDEN MANOR see NORTHIAM</h2>

<h2 style="text-align:center">SILVERHILL see HASTINGS, pp. 521, 529</h2>

<h1 style="text-align:center">SLAUGHAM</h1>

2020

ST MARY. Low C13 W tower, its upper part and pyramid roof
Victorian. Norman nave, see the simple blocked N doorway.
Late C13 S aisle, much widened in 1857–60 (*Joseph Clarke*).
This widening is clearly visible on the W face, where the
lancet window is original and the rose window of course
Victorian. The S (Covert) chapel is of 1613, but has vic-
torianized windows. Nice early C14 chancel E window. Wide
interior and curiously wide two-bay arcade between nave and
S aisle. Octagonal pier, double-chamfered arches. The arcade
to the S chapel has taller octagonal piers and also double-
chamfered arches. – FONT. Square, C12, of the Purbeck type.
Two sides have the usual shallow arcading, the third a long,
naïvely stylized fish, the fourth three upright sprays. –
PULPIT. C17, with columns, not English. Presented in 1890.
– WOOD PANELS. Early C16. Next to the pulpit, four with
linenfold, two with small standing saints, perhaps from the
Lower Rhine or Holland. A yet smaller panel of the same
style in the vestry. – WALL PAINTINGS. Recorded in illustrations under the tower, but not preserved. They were of the
early C12 and represented scenes from the Passion. – STAINED
GLASS. By *Kempe*, early 1890s, one N, one S, and the aisle W

windows. That of the rose is particularly agreeable. – PLATE.
Cup, 1586; Flagon, 1809; Paten, 1816. – MONUMENTS. In
the s chapel is a brass to John Covert † 1503, a 26 in. figure
under a brass canopy. – In the chancel is a Late Perp recess
of the standard type with brasses against the back wall. They
are of Richard Covert † 1547 and his three wives. There is
also a representation of the Resurrection. – Next to it Jane
Covert † 1586, this one against the back wall of a surround,
but now with columns and a pediment. – In the s chapel, of
far higher and indeed exceptional quality, Richard Covert
† 1579. Big standing wall-monument. Corinthian columns,
straight top (with three funeral HELMS). Delightfully delicate
panels against the base. Small kneeling figures – much too
small, yet somehow just dainty and not preposterous. They
all kneel in the same direction, and the first letters of their
Christian names are placed above their heads: four men,
three boys, two wives, six daughters. The sculptor is known.
He was called *Flynton*, and was paid £30 for the monument.
– George Matcham † 1833. Gothic recess against the outer E
wall.

The church faces a triangular green, which then narrows funnel-
wise to the N. No telephone wires, you will notice. Col.
Warren, the Lord of the Manor, paid for them being laid
underground as early as 1937. To the r. (E) is BOSWORTH'S
FARMHOUSE, timber-framed, C15 and C16.

SLAUGHAM PLACE, ¼ m. SE, below, in the gentle valley. Of
the Elizabethan house only a ruin is standing, but John
Thorpe drew the house, probably as it had been built by Sir
Walter Covert, son of Sir Richard. It was a courtyard house,
and what one recognizes most clearly now is the front of the
hall range, i.e. the W range. This had a middle doorway (with
Serlian banded columns), to the l. mullioned and transomed
windows and then a bay, to the r. the same – and this was the
side of the hall – and at the l. end the kitchen with the big
fireplaces. In front of the façade an arcade of three bays now
decoratively isolated. This seems to have belonged to an
arcading of the entrance range open towards the courtyard,
just as it is e.g. at Kirby Hall. Another, bigger arcade, formerly
of five bays, to the N. This is not indicated in the Thorpe
drawing. What was it? The staircase of the house is now in
the town hall at Lewes (*see* p. 555). The approach to the
house was from the E, and there was, as e.g. at Montacute, a
front garden with angle pavilions l. and r.

Higher up to the s the house replacing the old one, built in 1901 by *W. E. Tower*, Kempe's partner. Red brick, Tudor, not quite symmetrical. Doorway with open semicircular pediment.

At SLAUGHAM COMMON, overlooking the lakes which once all belonged to Slaugham Place, is LOWER ASHFOLD, large, half-timbered Tudor, 1904 by Mr *L. E. Smith*, the banker, who was his own architect.

BELL'S FARM, 1¼ m. w of the church, is a restored timber-framed C15 house.

SOCKNERSH MANOR see BRIGHTLING

SOUTHEASE

4000

CHURCH. Small, of flint. Round tower (one of the three of Sussex) with Norman windows and shingled conical roof. Norman also the nave, which included the present chancel. The original chancel and also aisles of some kind have gone. Norman in the nave a N window higher up than the others and probably earlier. Other Norman windows one blocked to the N, one open to the s, one to the N in the present chancel. Norman also the jambs of the former N doorway. The C13 is represented by the jamb of an opening with a stiff-leaf spray at the foot of a hollow moulding. This is *ex situ*, in the infilling of the arch to the former s chapel. The division of chancel from nave is done ingenuously by a wooden arch and timber-framing above. – BOX PEWS. Jacobean, a few. – PAINTINGS. A pale survival. On the N wall, below a zigzag frieze, scenes from a mid C13 Life of Christ (Entry into Jerusalem, then traces of a later St Christopher (staff and hut), then Christ before Pilate, the Scourging of Christ, the Crucifixion). On the w wall Christ in Majesty and the Signs of the Evangelists; late C13. – BELL. Of *c.*1280, the third-oldest in Sussex. – PLATE. Cup on pre-Reformation foot with traces of an engraved Crucifix; Paten of *c.*1500 with the Vernicle in the centre, on a foot of 1568.

SOUTH HEIGHTON see DENTON

SOUTH MALLING

4010

ST MICHAEL. Built in 1626–8. John Evelyn, then a child, laid a foundation stone. He was at school in Lewes. However, not the entire church is of that date. The w window of the tower is Dec, the responds of the tower arch also or a little earlier, and in the E wall are two small stiff-leaf capitals as though from the window shafts of a preceding E wall. Altogether the C17 church is entirely traditional. Short w tower with pyramid roof; nave and chancel in one. – STAINED GLASS. One s window by *Kempe*, 1894. – PLATE. Cup, engraved 1628.

THE DEANERY. Large, square, impressive late C17 house of red brick, seven by seven bays, with giant pilasters, set back at the angles to allow for brick quoins – cf. Albourne Place of the mid C17. The house itself is older than the encasement, see the early C17 staircase with flat, openwork balusters, and some panelling.

MALLING HOUSE, ¼ m. E. 1710; grey brick with red-brick dressings, of nine bays and two storeys, i.e. stretching comfortably. Doorway with fluted Doric pilasters; altered. Fine staircase with three banisters to the tread, two twisted, one columnar. Contemporary STABLES, and also a nice C18 SUMMER HOUSE, wood, with a stone front of three open bays with two Tuscan columns and a pediment.

OLD MALLING FARM, ½ m. NW. In the garden a big piece of walling of Malling College, a secular college;* also a pointed window. Grimm, in his late C18 drawing, shows a C12 archway in the wall. (Inside the house a C14 carved stone corbel.)

LONG BARROW, on CLIFFE HILL. A Neolithic long barrow, 120 ft long and 60 wide at its broader E end, at which point it is some 6 ft high. The quarry ditches on the two long sides of the barrow are clearly visible.

SOUTHOVER *see* LEWES, pp. 550, 552, 560

SPITHURST
4010

2 m. NNE of Barcombe

ST BARTHOLOMEW. 1879–80 by *Henry Card* of Lewes. Flint, with a bellcote, lancets, and barren plate tracery. Foliage capitals for the N arcade and foliage too for the chancel arch.

SPRAYSBRIDGE FARM *see* WESTFIELD

STANDEN *see* EAST GRINSTEAD

STANMER *see* BRIGHTON, p. 460

* Dated by the VCH C11.

STAPLEFIELD

St Mark. 1847 by *Benjamin Ferrey*. With lancets, a three-tier bellcote, and a lower chancel. Pretty Morrisite WALL PAINTINGS in the chancel. By *Kempe*, of the 1870s.* Figures against trees. – STAINED GLASS. w window by *Kempe*, 1897. The church lies by an extensive green with few houses. Across to the w STAPLEFIELD PLACE, big, brick, with half-timbered gables. The architect seems unrecorded.

STARLOCK see RYE

STONE CROSS
2 m. w of Pevensey Church

St Luke. 1924. A cosy church, brick, with wooden windows and some tile-hanging. Central tower.

Memorial Hall. 1921 by *B. Stevens*. A curious splayed front with a convex centre enriched by two columns, flanking the entrance.

Windmill, E of Stone Cross, 2 m. w of Pevensey. A tower-mill with ogee cap and partly preserved sails.

STONEGATE
1¾ m. sw of Ticehurst

St Peter. 1904 by *Grenville Streatfeild*. Nave and chancel, lancet windows, but a fancy N tower with weatherboarding and a spire.

STONEHILL HOUSE see CHIDDINGLY

STONELANDS see WEST HOATHLY

STRAWBERRY HOLE FARMHOUSE see NORTHIAM

STREAT

Church. On the s a beautiful view to the calm line of the South Downs. All the details of the church are over-restored, and the s aisle is of 1854. Flint laid crazy-paving-wise. Shingled bell-turret with steep pyramid roof. – PLATE. Paten, 1693, another, 1701(?); Cup, 1709. – MONUMENTS. Two cast-iron slabs on the nave floor, with inscriptions, one † 1731,

* The Rev. E. F. Hollobon tells me that the artist was paid £74.18.0. for them.

the other with deaths of 1732–54. – William Dobell † 1752, and Mary Dobell † 1764, two large, elegant tablets in marbles of various colours, different in details, but the same in style. Both have cherubs' heads at the foot.

STREAT PLACE. The front is monumental, even, and probably Jacobean. It faces E and is of knapped flint, E-shaped, with three floors and lugged gables carrying finials. The wings have against their ends the usual canted bay windows. But the recessed centre is not symmetrical. The porch is in the middle, but the square hall bay window in the r. corner has (functionally of course rightly) no counterpart in the l. corner. Mullioned and transomed windows, except on the top floor, where they have no transoms. The hall fireplace has a nicely carved lintel, and the S room panelling with pilasters, a frieze with Latin mottoes, and a decorated overmantel.

SUMMERTREE FARMHOUSE see WARBLETON

SUNTE HOUSE see LINDFIELD

SWANBOROUGH MANOR see IFORD

TANYARD HOUSE see NINFIELD

TARRING NEVILLE

4000

ST MARY. E.E. S arcade of two bays; round pier, round abaci, double-chamfered arches. The chancel lancet windows indicate the same time. The church has nave and aisle under one tiled roof, a short W tower with pyramid roof, and is rendered. – PLATE. Cup (re-shaped later) and Cover, pre-Reformation and repaired in 1569.

TELSCOMBE

4000

The village is in a dip of the Downs, sheltered by beech screens. It keeps close to the small church.

ST LAWRENCE. Flint, with an unbuttressed W tower. Nave and chancel Norman, though the only evidence is the jamb of a chancel S window. But the N aisle and the N chapel were both added as early as the late C12. The chapel is of two bays, and though the pier cannot be trusted, the imposts can. One still has a multi-scalloped capital, the other already one with crocket-leaves. That (in Chichester terms) means c.1185–90.

The arches are round and unmoulded. The N arcade has round piers already with round abaci, but the arches are still round and unmoulded. Similarly, the tower has lancets on the one hand, but they are round-arched inside, and the tower arch is unmoulded, though pointed. – LECTERN and READING DESK, with parts late medieval and later. The sides of the desk are re-used stall ends. – PLATE. Elizabethan Cup on a pre-Reformation foot.

TICEHURST

6030

ST MARY. Mostly C14. W tower with embattled stair-turret and a short shingled broach spire. The big doorway with characteristic C14 mouldings. Big Perp W window. Very tall, impressive Perp arch to the nave. The aisles were originally narrower than they are now, see their C13 W faces. But Dec the N and S windows of the aisles, all renewed. They have segmental arches and reticulation units with the ogees only at the bottom, i.e. a drop-shape. The same form for the chapel windows. The same form also occurs at Wadhurst. The Perp E window is of 1856, of the restoration by *Slater*. His is also the responsibility for the big and crude Dec clerestory windows, arch-shapes with a big circle inside and within these circles a variety of oversized flowing tracery forms. Perp N porch of two storeys. The entrance however has a re-used C13 arch. Pretty little niche above it. Quadripartite inside. Four-bay arcades of the C14 (octagonal piers, double-chamfered arches). The same type of arcades for the chapels (two bays). – FONT COVER. A splendid piece, of the octagonal closed type with doors that fold back. Flamboyant tracery panels inside as well as outside. – REREDOS (N chapel). Four small Netherlandish Mannerist panels. – STAINED GLASS. In the chancel on the N side substantial fragments of the original glass, including figures, some evidently from a doom. Medieval fragments also in the N aisle NW window. – The E window by *Margaret Holgate Foster*, 1879, the central panel painted for the Paris Exhibition of 1878. – PLATE. Cup, 1567–8; large Flagon, 1684; Paten on feet, 1713; Almsdish, 1733. – MONUMENTS. Brass of a Knight, later C14, 2 ft 10 in. long, appropriated for John Wybarne † 1490. His two wives are 1 ft 6 in. effigies. – In the S chapel an iron tombstone. – George Courthope † 1714. Lively cartouche without figures; by *Green* of Camberwell.

BAPTIST CHAPEL, Shaver's Green, 2¼ m. w. Probably c.1820. Tile-hung. Plain front of three round-headed windows.

SCHOOL. 1899 by *Aston Webb*. A nice cheery, asymmetrical composition with a cupola.

TICEHURST HOUSE, ¼ m. NW. The front part is rather grim. Early Victorian. Behind it the early C19 house where Dr Newington started a mental home. In the garden originally some ornamental buildings such as a Chinese Gallery, a Gothic Conservatory, and aviaries (Horsfield).

FURZE HOUSE (former WORKHOUSE), 1½ m. NE. 1836 by *Sampson Kempthorne*, still classical, but visibly weakening. No tension left. Nine-bay front with three-bay pediment.

PASHLEY, 1½ m. SE. A delightful early C17 façade with the timber-framing exposed. Much close studding. Three even gables, the middle one on carved brackets, all three with carved bargeboards. On the side of the house a big chimney-breast. The back early C18 brick, with urns on the parapet.

(WARDSBROOK, ¾ m. S. C15 wing with close studding. Queen-post roof. MHLG)

MAPLESDEN, 2½ m. WSW. Good early C18 N front. Chequer brick, five windows, two storeys, hipped roof. The porch can hardly be original.

WHILIGH, 2¼ m. WNW. S front of 1586. Centre and two gabled side pieces. First-floor overhang and another for the gables. E façade and alterations by *Vulliamy*, 1836. Ten bays long, faced with mathematical tiles. The MHLG notes that the timbers for Westminster Hall were cut on the Whiligh estate in the late C14.

(DUNSTERS MILL HOUSE. C15. The interior is interesting. It belongs to the type christened by Mr Mason quasi-semi-aisled, i.e. with a hall roofed over with one truss but with single-aisled divisions of the hall end walls. The arrangement is similar to Homewood House, Bolney.)

TICKERIDGE *see* WEST HOATHLY

TIDEBROOK
2 m. SE of Wadhurst

6020

ST JOHN BAPTIST. 1856 by *Rushforth*, and a remarkably good job. Lancet style with a bellcote over the w end of the chancel. Owing to the fall of the ground the w end has an undercroft, and this has small horizontal three-light windows. The nave has four windows, the E end faces the road with five stepped lancets, and the interior has big arched braces sweeping up to high collar-beams – the same spirit as the exterior.

TOTEASE see BUXTED

TREEMANS see HORSTED KEYNES

3030

TURNERS HILL
1½ m. ssw of Crawley Down

St Leonard. 1895–7 by *Lacy Ridge*, the tower and porches by *Sir Aston Webb*, 1923 (GR). Rock-faced, the tower not in any way enterprising. – (REREDOS. Said to have been brought from St Mildred Poultry when that City church by Wren was pulled down in 1872. According to Mr McHardy, this is a composite piece, the caryatids mostly from one source, the upper reliefs – German or Netherlandish C17? – from another, and the principal relief probably from yet another. Two of the caryatids must be Victorian.) – STAINED GLASS. E window 1897, chancel side windows 1903 and 1905, all by *Kempe*.

2020

TWINEHAM

St Peter. Alone, close to the little river. A brick church, entirely Early Tudor. W tower, nave, and lower chancel. The w tower has a low shingled broach spire. Timber s porch. The windows are entirely of brick too and have depressed-arched lights. – PULPIT. Jacobean. – In the REREDOS some probably French or Flemish panels with Flamboyant tracery. – FONT COVER. Lovable minimum-Jacobean. – GALLERY in the tower arch; elementary. – FAMILY PEW with Jacobean panels. – PAINTING. An early copy of *Camillo Procaccini*'s Holy Family at Dresden. – STAINED GLASS. In the E window an early Annunciation by *Kempe*. – PLATE. Cup of 1667, the lower parts probably Elizabethan; Paten Cover probably of 1667; Flagon and two Alms Plates of 1722. – One part of the CHURCHYARD was given over to the Quakers from 1694 to 1732 – a remarkable fact.

Slipe, ¼ m. E. Compact timber-framed farmhouse of the C15 with a very big roof and a conspicuous chimneystack.

4020

UCKFIELD

Holy Cross. 1839 by *William Moseley*. Chancel and tower

were left of the old church, but no features show this. The
tower has a shingled spire. The windows of the church are
tall, of two lights. Plain piers inside without capitals; four-
centred arches. Three galleries. Low-pitched roof with tie-
beams and pendants. Across the chancel two pointed arches.
– PLATE. Cup, 1717; Flagon, 1766 and Paten, probably of
same date. – MONUMENTS. One brass of 1610 and one cast-
iron slab of 1707 with the inscription across, not along the
slab.

OUR LADY AND ST PHILIP NERI (R.C.), s of the station. By
the Rev. *C. P. Plummer*, 1957–61. – STAINED GLASS by
Alexander Klecki. An effort to make figure-work semi-
abstract.

HIGHVIEW HOUSE (the former WORKHOUSE), 1¼ m. SSE. By
Kendall, a workhouse specialist, 1839. Brick. Nine-bay front
with three-bay pediment. Classical going coarse.

Uckfield is disappointing. Opposite the church is not a bad
beginning and, down CHURCH STREET, CHURCH HOUSE
is a nice five-bay job of grey brick with red-brick dressings.
Then the OLD GRAMMAR SCHOOL, with a humble Early
Victorian front of three bays, two of them bows, but, behind,
a timber-framed early C17 wing. So to the junction with the
HIGH STREET. The corner is marked by a good, smooth
recent flush-frame job, shops and offices by *H. Bingham
Towner*, three to four storeys. From there to the s, down the
hill, nothing for the eye (though Nos 122–124 behind its
unpromising exterior hides a C15 hall-house with a tie-beam-
kingpost-and-struts truss. VCH)

N of the junction with Church Street a little more, especially
the MAIDEN'S HEAD HOTEL, Georgian, three-storeyed,
with two bows and some nice doorways to its l. and r. and at
the N end.

HOOKE HALL. Finest early C18, chequer brick, five bays,
hipped roof, with a door hood with some carving.

THE ROCKS, ½ m. w. 1838 by *Sydney Smirke*. Red brick, Tudor,
with shaped gables. Of no great merit.

UDIMORE   8010

ST MARY. Norman nave of which one blocked N window high
up is witness. Also two blocked doorways, sign probably of a
lengthening. On checking inside one finds indeed a two-bay s
arcade lengthened by a third, w, bay. The aisle has been
pulled down, but the arcade is recognizable. Two bays with

round piers with simple stiff-leaf or not quite stiff-leaf capitals. Pointed arches with two slight chamfers. The third bay is only a little later. The arch chamfers are still slight; the responds still have stop-chamfers. The chancel arch must have been rebuilt then too; stop-chamfers and moulded brackets with dogtooth. But the chancel itself is decidedly early C13, an even, as it were, classic piece: lancets and, at the E end, three widely spaced stepped lancets. On the S side one was a 'low-side,' but the lower part has been blocked. Short E.E. w tower with rectangular stair-turret. Pyramid roof. – ARCHITECTURAL FRAGMENT. Part of a spiral-fluted shaft in the porch (PILLAR PISCINA?). – STAINED GLASS. Some bits in a S window.

KNELLSTONE, 1 m. E. L-shaped C15 house, quite big, all closely studded.

UPPER DICKER
2½ m. w of Hailsham

5000

HOLY TRINITY. By *W. J. Donthorne*, 1843. Flint, in the Norman style. Nave with bellcote; short chancel. Nave roof with tie-beams and wind-braces. – FONT. 1663. Octagonal, with initials – a typical, uncostly post-Commonwealth job. – PLATE. Flagon, 1632.

UPPER PARROCK *see* FOREST ROW

WADHURST

6030

ST PETER AND ST PAUL. The church has a Norman w tower, as one lower window and one twin bell-opening show. Pretty broached and shingled needle spire. That the tower was un-buttressed originally goes without saying. The tower is followed chronologically by the provision of C13 aisles to the Norman nave. Of these the arcades, both S and N, bear witness. They have piers alternatingly round and octagonal, and double-chamfered arches. The N arcade is a little higher and (according to Godfrey) a C14 remodelling. Early C14 chancel, some of the windows shafted inside. C14, a little later, the over-restored N and S aisle windows (restoration by *Slater*, 1858; GS). They have segmental arches and reticulation units with the ogees only at the bottom, not at the top, i.e. drop shapes (cf. Ticehurst). Perp S aisle E window and Perp two-storeyed porch with a vault of diagonal and ridge-ribs inside.

Wide and high nave, its roof C15; that of the s aisle is dated
1592. – FONT. A round C13 capital on a C13 base plus some
mouldings. – TOWER SCREEN. By *Duncan Wilson*, 1957. Of
thin scrolls with occasional leaves and a whimsical top, but
unquestionably pretty in its position. – STAINED GLASS. In
the s aisle w window glass by *Morris & Co.*, after Morris's
death; decidedly feeble. – PLATE. Cup, 1568; Almsdish, 1634;
Paten, 1669; Cup, 1684; Paten and Flagon, 1748. – MONU-
MENTS. Some thirty cast-iron tomb-slabs on the floor,
ranging from 1617 to 1799.* The earliest have just six shields
with initials and the date as their only decoration, later they
have writing in lines across, not along the slab. – Mary
Dunmoll † 1651. Small alabaster tablet with kneeling figure.
– John Barham, 1730, large tablet with obelisk-shaped
inscription in front of drapery. Columns l. and r., also cherubs.
By *William Palmer* of London.

CHURCHGATE HOUSE stands by the churchyard. It is timber-
framed and tile-hung with a first floor oversailing on brackets.
The doorway is Georgian and the pediment is very sweetly
attached to the overhang.

In the main street much that is pretty, but only two houses
to be mentioned individually, both C18, both of three bays,
both with hipped roof. The VICARAGE is Early Georgian and
has doorway and windows with rusticated (or quoined)
surrounds. Narrow windows l. and r. of the doorway. HILL
HOUSE is tile-hung, an incorrect but piquant effect. Roman
Doric porch.

The buildings outside will be taken clockwise starting from the
w.

WADHURST COLLEGE, 1 m. w. Originally called South Park.
Asymmetrical, with a tower with dormered saddleback roof.
By *Arthur Croft*, 1888.

(WADHURST CASTLE, ⅜ m. WNW. By *E. B. Lamb*, as an enlarge-
ment of a 'modern' house with four octagon towers. So *The
Gardener's Magazine*, VIII, 1842, writes, and so Mr John
Harris tells me.)

LORIEN, at Best Beech, 1½ m. WSW. Originally called Vespers.
Built by *William H. Bidlake* for himself in 1924. Handsome,
varied Tudor.

HOUNDSELL PLACE. 1912–16. By *Alwyn Ball* (1884–1918),
and his only major work. Neo-Georgian, of red brick, strictly
axial and uncommonly elegantly done. Front with short pro-

* The latter in the churchyard.

jecting wings and a central semicircular bow containing on the ground floor the porch with two heavy Tuscan columns. On the l. and r. of the forecourt two pyramid-roofed pavilions. To the garden the porch has excessively long stone windows, and the wings project further but are of one storey only. Segment-headed windows, hipped roof behind a parapet which is actually flush with the façade. Ball was an assistant of Smith & Brewer, but also clearly inspired by Lutyens. The certainty of his touch at a mere twenty-eight years of age is remarkable.

STATION. This little minimum brick job with a middle pediment and lower half-pediments l. and r., under which the entrances have a kind of domestic Gothic details, is by *W. Trees* and was illustrated in *The Illustrated London News* in 1852.

THE MOUNT, 1½ m. NE. An Italianate Victorian house became the novitiate house of the Fathers of Charity. In 1881 *Bernard Whelan* added a tall brick tower and an octagonal brick chapel like a chapter house. It is rib-vaulted in brick. E.E. details (stiff-leaf capitals, geometrical tracery).

RIVERHALL, 2½ m. ENE. The tile-hung front with a three-bay centre and gabled two-bay outer parts all C18. Doorway on carved brackets. But round the corner Elizabethan star chimneys.

GREAT SHOESMITHS, 2 m. NW. Up along a long approach. The house of the Banhams. A long late C17 front with hipped roof. The windows, with wooden crosses, are not regularly placed.

REHOBOTH CHAPEL, Pell Green, ¾ m. NE. Dated 1824. Weatherboarded, two doorways and three round-headed windows, in the rhythm W–D–W–D–W.

LADYHEADS, Lower Cousley Wood, 2 m. NE. Small but pretty, three bays, two storeys, chequer brick, dated 1707. Big hipped roof.

WHILIGH, *see* Ticehurst, p. 613.

WALLAND, 1 m. S. C15 centre and two wings of c.1620. Three gables with original bargeboards and pendants. Close studding on the first floor. Inside, a chimneypiece dated 1621 with a fine wooden overmantel with four closely decorated stubby blank arches.

WENBANS, 1½ m. SSW. (Inside the house a fireplace dated 1612. VCH) Attached a timber-framed barn of the C16 with much diagonal bracing.

WAKEHURST PLACE see ARDINGLY

WALDRON

ALL SAINTS. Mostly E.E., see the chancel E wall with two
blocked lancets, probably of a former group of five stepped
ones. See also the W tower (with later, higher stair-turret and
later W doorway and window), the N aisle W window, a cinquecusped lancet, the N windows with simple bar tracery, and
the N arcade of four bays with standard details. The aisle is
remarkably wide for a C13 aisle. The nave is wide too. The
S aisle dates from 1859–62 (*R. C. Hussey*). – Two very tall
CANDLESTICKS of bronze; Italian? But what date? There
are C16 and also C18 motifs. The candlesticks were given by
Louis Huth of Possingworth. – PLATE. Chalice, 1611; Cup
and Paten, 1638; Paten and Flagon, 1707. – MONUMENTS.
Major John Fuller † 1722. Standing grey and white marble
monument. Straight-sided tapering sarcophagus, tall obelisk
with a shield and garlands. Urns on pedestals l. and r. No
figures at all. A very up-to-date and a metropolitan piece.
The Fullers were ironfounders. – In the churchyard two of
the little terracotta plaques by *Harmer*.

TANNERS MANOR. Brick. Jacobean. Only two-thirds of the
former façade. Gable at the l. end of the front. Five-light
mullioned and transomed windows.

(HERONSDALE MANOR, ⅝ m. SW. Tile-hung, with an imposing
cluster of polygonal chimneyshafts. Inside, a fireplace dated
1634. SCM, IX)

WALLAND see WADHURST

WAPSBOURNE FARMHOUSE see CHAILEY

WARBLETON

ST MARY. With wide view to the SW. E.E. chancel with lancets,
one made later into a low-side window. Dec N aisle and S
windows, the former under segmental arches. Perp W tower,
the top with big heads sticking out. Perp chancel E and
chapel E windows. Perp N arcade of four bays. – FONT. C13,
round, just very boldly moulded. – SQUIRE'S PEW. Set
happily in the middle of the N aisle, high up on posts and
accessible by a staircase in the aisle. The squire must have
felt in full command here. – STAINED GLASS. Original bits
in a N aisle window and the chapel E window. – By *Kempe* the
W window, 1882, i.e. early. – By *Hornwood Bros.* of Frome

the E window (TK). – PLATE. Paten on foot, engraved 1666;
Paten, c.1670; Cup, 1774; Paten and Flagon, 1775. – MONU-
MENTS. Brass to William Prestwick, Dean of St Mary's
College, Hastings, † 1436, figure, 4 ft 5 in. long, under an
ogee canopy. Biblical passage up the orphreys. Long marginal
inscription in Latin hexameters. – Handsome cartouche, date
of death 1688. – Sir John Lade † 1740. By *Rysbrack*, and at
once unmistakably of the highest order. It ought to be re-set
in a worthier position. Sussex has little like it. White, grey,
and variegated marble. The centre is the outstanding bust on
a scrolly pedestal. It and the grey back wall have the most
skilful floral decoration. Reredos background with columns
and a broken pediment, its underside coffered. Sir John was,
we read, not only a supporter of royalty and the established
church but also 'without acrimony to dissenters'. – (In the
churchyard a headstone with a terracotta tablet by *Harmer*.
Date of death 1813. SAC 100, 1962)

Opposite the church the original WORKHOUSE, now a row of
cottages. The r. half is the original, five bays, two storeys,
with wooden cross-windows and a date 1739 on the central
chimney.

KINGSLEY HILL, ½ m. E. Timber-framed, of five bays with cross-
windows. The ground floor is chequer brick, the upper floor
tile-hung. It looks later C17, but is dated 1720.

CRALLE PLACE, 1¼ m. S. Built by Sir John Lade (*see* above) in
1724. Seven bays, two storeys, angle pilaster strips, parapet.
Later doorway. (The staircase is dated 1724.)

STONE HOUSE, Rushlake Green, 1¾ m. E. The best house in the
parish. To the S Jacobean, with three even gables and mullioned windows, regular, except for the placing of the doorway. To the W of 1778, brick, two canted bay windows and a
doorway in the middle with Tuscan columns and pediment.

(SUMMERTREE FARMHOUSE, 2½ m. SE. With a C15 N range
and a kingpost roof inside. MHLG)

WARBLETON PRIORY, 2 m. E. A small priory of Augustinian
Canons, transferred here by the offices of Sir John Pelham in
1413. What remains is now a farmhouse with an outbuilding.
The outbuilding E of the house has a doorway with two-
centred head and a blocked round-arched doorway further l.
The farmhouse has to the S a buttress. This S front is now
C17, ashlar, symmetrical, with mullioned windows. Round
the corner to W and E transomed windows. Behind, the N
wing has C15 close-studded timbering.

WARDSBROOK see TICEHURST

WARNINGLID
1¼ m. s of Slaugham

2020

St Andrew. 1935 by *F. G. Troup*. Small (cost £1,200). Brick,
with groups of round-headed lancets. Inside, quite dramatic,
steep groin-vaulting, tent-like. – STAINED GLASS. E and a
one-light s window, mildly Expressionist, by *J. H. Hogan*
of *Powell's*.

WARTLING

6000

St Mary Magdalene. Small, with a weatherboarded bell-
turret. Short Perp N and s arcades of two bays, not in line
and neither starting at the w end. The elements are standard,
but the details differ.* The chancel must have had a s chapel
(see the blocked arch). – PULPIT. Nice plain C18. – BOX
PEWS. – PLATE. Cup, Paten on foot, and Flagon, 1747; Almsdish, 1753. – MONUMENTS. Many tablets of Curteises from
the later Georgian decades, with the usual motifs: an urn (by
T. Gaffin), a cherub by an urn, a woman by a sarcophagus
(by *E. Gaffin*), an urn with weeping willow branch (by *Mc-
Swiney*). – (In the churchyard some of the terracotta work by
Jonathan Harmer, see p. 67n.)

Near by a whole group of radar installations performing their
mechanical motions.

(COMPHURST, Windmill Hill. Partly of mid C15 brick.)

WELLHOUSE see NORTHIAM

WENBANS see WADHURST

WEST BLATCHINGTON see BRIGHTON, p. 461

WESTDEAN

A delightful Downs village, sheltered and secluded.

All Saints. The striking thing is the broad, oblong w tower,
Norman below, early C14 above, with its curiously half-
hipped spire. The arch to the nave has shafts, starting relatively high up. These are C14 too. The w doorway is Victorian.
The nave, as proved by one tiny N window, is Norman again.

* Outside the s aisle a Pelham buckle.

Other windows point to the early C14, a date confirmed by the monuments in the N wall of the chancel. – PLATE. Paten, 1721; Flagon, 1792; Cup, 1793. – MONUMENTS. The l. one in the chancel late C13, interfered with, the r. one clumsily Dec, with big, heavy buttress-shafts. – Other monuments as follows: William Thomas † 1639. Alabaster and touch. Large, standing wall-monument. Two kneeling figures. Columns l. and r. and outside them two angels. – The two big-headed cherubs with spade and torch on the tablet to Mrs Susanna Tirrey † 1637 are decidedly funny. – Sir Oswald Birley, the painter, † 1952, a bronze head by *Clare Sheridan*. – Lord Waverley † 1958, also a bronze head, by *Epstein*.

RECTORY. A late C13 house with the hall on the first floor and a solar next to it. The partition is timber-framed. The hall has two-light windows with pointed-trefoiled lights, the solar single lights with shouldered lintels. The same simple type in the room below the hall. In the hall a fine fireplace. The jambs curve out and up to the hood and have broad fillets. The hall end wall has a small staircase projection next to the chimneybreast, the solar end wall a garderobe projection. The windows of the room below the solar are the simplest, just small rectangles.

MANOR HOUSE and DOVECOTE, both medieval and both in ruins.

CHARLESTON MANOR, ⅝ m. NW. A perfect house in a perfect setting. The part of highest architectural interest is the S wing, which is of *c*.1200 and has a hall on the upper floor. One two-light window in the end wall, abundantly shafted. The arch is round, but the capitals are leaf crockets clearly not earlier than 1200. In the opposite gable-end a tiny lancet. The manor also possesses two fine BARNS, nearly but not quite in line, one thatched, the other tiled. They total 177 ft in length. There is a circular medieval DOVECOTE too.

WESTFIELD

ST JOHN BAPTIST. A Norman church, as is shown by two chancel windows, the narrow chancel arch with one order of nook-shafts with decorated capitals, and two nave S windows originally no doubt Norman. The chancel was remodelled in the C13, see the lancets. The W tower probably a little later, short, with a Dec moulding to the doorway. Heavy buttressing. One buttress with a date plate 1624. Dec S windows. Victorian N aisle of 1860 (*C. E. Davis*; PF). – PULPIT. Square, Jacobean, with flatly carved short blank arches. The sounding board with a star in inlay is c18. – PLATE. Cup, 1735; Paten and Flagon, 1736; Paten, 1761; Cup, 1764.

SPRAYSBRIDGE FARMHOUSE, 1 m. NW. Dated 1690, and interesting for that. Symmetrical, but pre-classical. The one-storeyed porch still has a kind of shaped gable, and the fenestration distinguishes the hall side by five lights from the other side, which has four.

GREAT MAXFIELD, 1⅜ m. E. A visually perfect timber-framed house. One side with close studding and a big ashlar chimney-breast; round the corner first a gable with an oriel under, then, recessed, wider timbering and two original windows.

WEST FIRLE

4000

ST PETER. One token of an earlier church is the N doorway, *ex situ*, of c.1200, round-arched with two slight continuous chamfers. Then the story begins properly with the c13 chancel (lancets) and W tower (arch with double-chamfer on broaches) and nicely moulded S doorway. The doorway again is *ex situ*. Dec three light aisle E windows with good tracery, that on the N side re-set when the Gage Chapel was built in the c16. Dec also the arcades of four bays and the clerestory with cinquefoiled windows. They are above the spandrels, not the apexes, of the arcade arches. The two-bay arcade of the Gage Chapel is Late Perp, the pier with a typical moulding, largely continuous. – STAINED GLASS. In the S aisle E window some original glass. – PLATE. Cup and Cover, 1680. – MONUMENTS. Brass to Bartholomew Bolne † 1476 and wife, 25 in. figures; good. N aisle E. Their daughter married William Gage, father of Sir John. – There are also brasses to Thomas Gage † 1590 and wife and another Gage of about the same date. – In the nave floor Mary Howard † 1638, in her shroud. – Then in the Gage Chapel, three alabaster monuments made in 1595 by *Gerard Johnson* (Janssen). The drawings survive at Firle Place. The one to Sir John Gage † 1557 is an outstanding piece, fully detached, a very plain tomb-chest, but on it two telling effigies, he on a half-rolled-up mat, a characteristic Dutch motif. In the other two monuments the design of the tomb-chest is repeated, although they are shorter and set against the wall. On one the date 1595 is recorded. On both are brasses, one to Sir Edward Gage † 1569 and wife, the other to John Gage † 1595 and two wives.

FIRLE PLACE. Built for the Sir John Gage who died in 1557. He was Vice-Chamberlain to Henry VIII, Captain of the Royal Guard, Constable of the Tower, Comptroller of the Household, Chancellor of the Duchy of Lancaster, and later Queen Mary's Chamberlain. The Gages remained Catholics to the late C18. They are still possessors of Firle Place now, in direct male succession. What little remains of Sir John Gage's house will be seen when the perambulation reaches it. The house is large, with a complicated plan, arranged round two courtyards. Symmetrical E front of c.1745 with the main entrance. Five bays, hipped roof. The centre bay has the archway with a rusticated surround, a Venetian window with Ionic pilasters over, and a crowning pediment. The archway leads into the main courtyard and has here a Gibbs surround. Facing the visitor is the modest doorway to the great hall. Pediment on Ionic columns. The GREAT HALL is that of the Tudor house, and above the present ceiling still has its hammerbeam roof. This hall comprised what is now the staircase hall, as is proved by the one dainty doorway with four-centred head and leaf in the spandrels. It was probably originally approached from the opposite (W) side; for here are the external Tudor features of the house: a gable facing S with straight-headed windows also below on the ground floor, and a miniature gable on the N side disturbing the regular Georgian composition. As for these regular façades, or rather façades attempting to be regular, they are as follows: to the N one return bay of the E façade, then six plain even bays, then a composition in itself of a recessed six-bay centre, not quite even, and two projecting wings with bow windows and above them Venetian windows.* To the S there is also first the return bay of the E façade and then an arrangement of two shallow projections with irregular Georgian windows between. The l. projection houses the principal staircase. After that some more Georgian windows and then the Tudor gable referred to.

Now inside. Apart from the early features already mentioned there is in a private room SW of the great hall and E of the Tudor gable an Elizabethan chimneypiece and an Elizabethan wall painting over it. Otherwise the GREAT HALL, now entrance hall, is in its present form of c.1740–50. Tall, with coved ceiling, a pedimented doorway to the staircase

* Behind the r. bow lies the old KITCHEN, and in this is yet another Early Tudor survival: part of a blocked arch.

hall, and a heavy architectural fireplace with volutes, below at r. angles to the wall, above parallel to it. The STAIRCASE HALL is the only really splendid room in the house. Stair balusters decorated at the foot, stucco panels on the walls, stucco on the ceiling. The other principal room on the ground floor is the DRAWING ROOM. This has screens in front of the end walls with fluted Ionic columns. E of the drawing room is the LIBRARY, with a lively Rococo ceiling. On the upper floor are a number of rooms decorated in the Dixhuitième style in the late C19.

The STABLES are of white brick and not big. They date from c.1800 and have a recessed centre with cupola and projecting wings with coupled pilasters. The adjoining RIDING SCHOOL is of red brick with lunette windows.

DAIRY, SW of the house. Small, of flint and red brick. Tiled walls inside.

LODGE. White brick like the stables, and also of c.1800. But ogee-arched windows and wooden verandas on three sides.

BARROWS. On Firle Beacon Ridge are more than fifty Early Bronze Age bowl barrows. Most appear to have been excavated, although there is no record of this work. From one of the group came a bronze pin of Central European type (since lost).

NEOLITHIC LONG BARROW, 1¼ m. SE of the village. The barrow, which has a magnificent view over the surrounding countryside, is over 100 ft long and over 8 ft high. The side ditches completely enclose the barrow, except for a narrow causeway at the SE corner.

IRON AGE AND ROMAN SETTLEMENT, 1½ m. SE, on CHARLESTON BROW. On the SE side of the promontory is a small enclosure with a rectangular hut and storage pits. Among the finds from the hut, which suggest a date in the latter part of the C1 B.C. and early C1 A.D., was a fine imported 'thistle' brooch. A second settlement on the E side of the spur, again consisting of a hut and storage pits, appears to have continued in use after the Roman occupation.

The LYNCHETS surrounding these two settlements are probably to be ascribed to the same period.

WESTHAM

ST MARY. Flint and stone. Norman nave, demonstrated by three S windows in a row, above a string-course, and Norman s transept, see the arch inside. But the N and S transepts have traces of arches in their E walls which must have belonged to apses. The church was probably the church of the Hospital of St Cross outside the W gate of Pevensey. That could explain its plan, cruciform with transept apses and no doubt a chancel apse. Perp W tower, broad and low, with battlements, Perp most windows, those of the N aisle specially large. C14 N arcade with octagonal piers and double-hollow-chamfered arches. – SCREENS. Perp, of one-light divisions to chancel and to S transept. – STAINED GLASS. In the tracery heads of the E window a series of complete C15 figures; also smaller fragments below. – PLATE. Cup and Cover, 1632; Flagon, 1662; Paten, 1756.

By the church two C15 houses, both timber-framed with close studding. One has curved braces as well and an original oriel. Also in the High Street the PEVENSEY CASTLE, a Victorian Gothic pub.

PEELINGS, 1½ m. W. Externally a small symmetrical C17 house of stone, two gabled wings, a recessed three-bay centre with two dormers, and a central doorway; all mullioned windows. The symmetry suggests a date as late as the mid C17. But internally there is still the hall of a timber-framed hall-house and the complete and characteristic big timbers of the wall between the hall and the service part of the house.

DOG HOUSE, Hankham, ⅜ m. N of the former. Of c.1600, timber-framed with brick infilling. Two symmetrical gables with bargeboards and pendants. Narrow bay windows under them.

HANKHAM HALL, ⅝ m. ENE of Peelings. A charming Late Georgian house of grey and red brick. Only three bays wide, but the doorway and all the windows Gothick, i.e. pointed.

3030

WEST HOATHLY

ST MARGARET. A simple, not a small church. Perp W tower with the usual shingled broach spire, and Norman nave and chancel, see one nave N window and perhaps one chancel N window lengthened into a lancet. Later C13 E end with lancets and plate tracery. The S chapel E window of the same type as the chancel E window (three stepped and cusped lancets under one arch; renewed). The chancel windows and this chapel window are shafted inside. SEDILIA and PISCINA go with them, though they could be a little earlier. Then follows the S aisle, which is Dec. But this was clearly only a widening; for the S arcade of two bays with fat short round pier and double-chamfered arches is no later than early C13. The s chapel arcade, also of two bays, has a more normal octagonal pier. The nave and the more enterprising chancel roof of *Slater & Carpenter*'s restoration of 1870. – FONT. Square, plain, C13, on the usual five supports. – PAINTING. In the rere-arches of the chancel N windows C13 leaf trails in red. – STAINED GLASS. The SW window of one light is by *Kempe*; 1902. – PLATE. Cup, 1716; Flagon, possibly same date. – MONUMENTS. Two cast-iron tomb-slabs, one of 1619 with the inscription round the rim, in the medieval tradition, the other of 1624 with the inscription in three lines along the slab. There is also a brass inscription plate of 1635 mounted on a plain iron slab.

The village street has no houses of special interest, except the MANOR HOUSE, facing the church, a stone front of 1627, nearly symmetrical, with two gables and mullioned windows, only that on the ground floor the r. window has six, the l. window four lights. This indicates where the hall was. To the s of the Manor House the PRIEST'S HOUSE, timber-framed, of the C15. Doorway with two-centred arch. The first-floor windows are in their original state.

CHIDDINGLYE (formerly Rockhurst), ⅝ m. w. Built in 1866 by *William & Henry Godwin*, and since a little simplified. The size no more than a well-endowed rectory, and as Gothic as any, i.e. with plenty of stop-chamfered window details. Stone with red sandstone bands.

STONELANDS, w of the former. By *E. W. Mountford*, c.1887. Standard, gabled Tudor, and standard asymmetry. However, behind that front some C16 timber-framed as well as stone parts.

SELSFIELD HOUSE, 1¼ m. NW. Early Georgian stone front of five bays, angle pilaster-strips. The parapet curves up to their vertical continuation. Doorway reached by an open stair. Next to the house traces of former quarrying.

GRAVETYE MANOR, 1 m. N, in large grounds. Late Elizabethan s front of four bays with mullioned and transomed windows and four even gables with lugs and finials. One-storeyed porch. Three groups of brick chimneys. There is a date 1598 on one fireplace, a date 1603 on an overmantel. The owner then was Richard Infield, an ironmaster. The house belonged to *William Robinson*, the garden reformer, in the early C20, and he not only added the NE wing but also re-did the gardens as a pattern of their kind (*Country Life*, XXXII, 1912, p. 409). – Below the house, formerly on an island in a hammer pond, THE MOAT, timber-framed of *c.*1500.

TICKERIDGE, just N of Kingscote Station. Externally the house looks much like the many around of London commuters; internally it is of high antiquarian interest, a house of the C14 and perhaps the early C14, consisting of the hall of two bays with a splendid truss over the centre (collar-beam on large curved braces almost like crucks, kingpost) and the end walls of the hall with free-standing posts forming aisle-like passages l. and r. Beyond these walls the solar and the service wings. The solar wing now C16, with oversailing W and E gables.

WESTMESTON
3010

ST MARTIN. Flint, with a shingled bell-turret. Plain Norman N doorway. C14 W wall and S arcade of two bays. To the C14 also the heavy original timbers of the N porch are assigned. Most of the church is over-restored. – PAINTINGS. In 1862 wall paintings of the C12 were discovered; but they have not been preserved. They belonged to the C12 group of Hardham and Clayton and were on the nave E wall, the lamb in a quatrefoil between angels above the chancel arch, scenes from the life of Christ to the l. and r. The descriptive *tituli* or captions were specially interesting. – STAINED GLASS. E window by *Capronnier*, 1873, as terrible as only Continental mid C19 glass can be. – W window by *Kempe*, 1890. – PLATE. Cup and Paten, 1718; Flagon, 1746.

WESTMESTON PLACE. On the W side of the house a three-light mullioned window and a two-light window of *c.*1500. In the porch also an arched stone window. Where do they come from ? In front of the house a handsome *Coade* stone urn.

MIDDLETON MANOR. Much of the house is by *G. S. Repton*, *c.*1830,* e.g. the three-bay S front with its Tuscan colonnade and the E front with a canted bay and tripartite windows. Repton used red mathematical tiles as his facing material.

WHATLINGTON
2010

ST MARY MAGDALENE. Small, with an unfortunate Victorian steeple and an apsidal vestry, both by *S. W. Tracey*, 1862

* The drawings at the Royal Institute of British Architects, so Mr John Harris tells me, are on paper with the watermark 1829.

(PF). Nave and chancel are E.E., with lancets. Plain SEDILIA recess. – PULPIT. On three angels; exhibited at the 1851 Exhibition. – CHANDELIER. Of brass. C18. – PLATE. Later C15 Paten; Cup, 1624.

THATCHED COTTAGE, by the stream. White weatherboarding. Gothick windows and a veranda on wooden posts between two projecting wings. All quite small.

WHILIGH see TICEHURST

WICKHAM FARMHOUSE see WINCHELSEA

WILLINGDON

5000

ST MARY. The tower of the church stands NW of it, only touching it at an angle. It is E.E., and the roof-line of a former nave is visible to its E. The short shingled broach spire is of course later. Then, in the early C14 a new nave was built. Straight-headed windows with ogee-headed lights. The E.E. s doorway must be re-set. Two orders of shafts, fine arch mouldings. The N arcade is of standard elements, also early C14. Kingpost roof. – FONT. Square, with panelled stem; Perp. – PLATE. Paten, 1670; Cup, engraved 1693; Flagon, 1736; two Almsdishes, 1757. – WEST GALLERY. In the Wren style. By *Blacking*, 1953. – MONUMENTS. To Parkers of Ratton. Mrs Elinar † 1598. Tiny kneeling figure. – Sir John † 1617. Alabaster, larger kneeling figures. – Sir Nicholas † 1619. Standing monument, also alabaster. Recumbent effigy, kneeling children, black columns l. and r., straight top, two obelisks. – Thomas † 1663. Standing monument with a high base and a big urn. But can it be so early? It must be of the early C18. The inscription does in fact include references to deaths in 1691 and 1708. – Good, lively cartouches of † 1700 and † 1727. – Sir George † 1726. Architectural, with an urn and no figures.

THE HOO, opposite the church. By *Lutyens*, 1902. A curiously intricate group, deliberately not all one. The l. part has a pebbled wall to the curving street and behind on the upper floor tall, thin oriels – out of Norman Shaw. The r. part has a small courtyard screened from the street by a wall with two round windows. Only towards the pretty stepping-down garden is there a symmetrical, formal front. Five-bay classical wings and a recessed centre with three weatherboarded gables, reminiscent of Webb's Standen.

(RATTON GATE HOUSE. The gatehouse to the manor house of the Parker family. It is timber-framed and of the C15. Two storeys with overhang. One ground-floor window on brackets is original. MHLG)

WILLINGHAM HOUSE see RINGMER

5000

WILMINGTON

ST MARY AND ST PETER. To the N of the church stands an enormous yew tree. The church has a pretty weatherboarded and shingled bell-turret. The chancel is Norman, with two preserved windows and part of a frieze of little triangles. It looks as if the windows may have been placed in a blank arcading as at Little Horsted. Inside the chancel along part of the wall stone seating. E.E. s aisle, see the E lancet and the two-bay arcade of standard details. The chancel arch looks more elaborate E.E., but is Victorian (1883, *Paley & Austin*). Kingpost roofs. – PULPIT. Jacobean, with back panel and sounding board. Jolly openwork obelisk on the latter, jolly brackets for the book-rest. – SCULPTURE. Small seated figure, male and C13, it seems (chancel). – PLATE. Paten, inscribed 1679 and Cup, probably same date; Paten, 1721. – MONUMENT. At the W end of the S aisle the top of an Elizabethan monument, with a fluted frieze and a steep pediment.

PRIORY. It was founded for Benedictines from Grestain in Normandy before 1100. It cannot have been a thriving community; for they seem to have been satisfied with the parish church and never built a proper claustral establishment. Instead there is a group of rooms not making any architectural sense. Coming from the church there is first the masonry of a room with a vaulted undercroft under. It has an octagonal pier and four bays of rib-vaulting with single-chamfered ribs dying into the pier – C14 evidently. Then there is a small courtyard with a wall, and to its W the E.E. doorway into a larger room. The doorway has sturdy triple responds. Much more elegant is the doorway from the S into the same room. This must have been the main entrance. It has three orders and moulded capitals. A porch was added to it probably in the C14, see the sunk quadrant mouldings and the way the vault cuts into the doorway. The keystone is a big face. Also of the C14 is the bigger hall built to the W of this porch. Its S wall stands high up with two polygonal turrets. The large window however is of course Elizabethan or later (three

lights, two transoms). Above the porch is the room called the
Prior's Chapel. In it part of a three-light E window of the C14
can be seen. It is stepped and has ogee-headed lights. On the
way to the chapel one passes up an C18 staircase of the present
house with a nice Chippendale fretwork balustrade, and sees
traces of a window and a doorway.

LONG BARROWS AND FLINT MINES. ½ m. SE of the village
lies a fine long barrow, 190 ft long and 75 ft broad at the S
end. The side ditches are clearly visible. They continue round
the S end of the barrow, giving a U-shaped plan. ¼ m. SE of
the long barrow, on the S slope of WINDOVER HILL, is a
group of Neolithic flint mines marked by a series of depressions representing the filled-in shafts and low mounds of
material from the galleries. S of the mines is another well-
preserved long barrow, 180 ft long and 50 ft wide at its
broader NE end. The side ditches, which are still visible, are
slightly inturned at their ends.

THE LONG MAN OF WILMINGTON. On the N face of WIND-
OVER HILL, overlooking the village, is a gigantic figure,
226 ft high, cut in the turf. The figure, holding a staff or
spear in each hand, has been carefully designed so as not to
appear unduly foreshortened when viewed from below. The
date of this hill figure is obscure, the earliest reference to it
being in an C18 manuscript, but it is probably not of very
great antiquity.*

ROUND BARROWS. S of the Long Man is a very large bowl
barrow, over 120 ft in diameter, which covered a cremation
in a collared urn. Further round barrows are to be seen on
the ridge S and E of the Long Man.

WINCHELSEA

9010

The original Cinque Ports were Hastings, Romney, Hythe,
Dover, and Sandwich, but Rye and Winchelsea had become
members by 1191. Winchelsea at that time lay on the E side of
the estuary of the Rother near Camber. A storm damaged the
town in 1252, in 1266 the war between the barons and Edward I
did further damage, and in 1288 a yet greater storm all but
ruined Winchelsea. But already in 1280 the king had acquired
the manor of Iham to build a new town there, a new town in
the sense of the French bastides and the Villafrancas, Castel-

* Although a similar figure appears on the silver cauldron from Gundes-
trup, Denmark, dating from the C1 BC.

francos, etc., of Italy, i.e. a planned town. It was laid out in 1283 by the then Warden of the Cinque Ports in consultation with Henry de Waleys, Mayor of London (and later of Bordeaux), and *Itier Bochard* of Angoulême, builder of bastides, who was summoned from Bordeaux. The purpose was not military, but commercial: to help the wine trade with Gascony

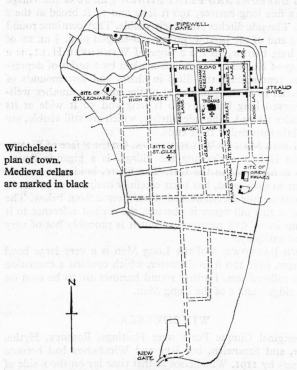

Winchelsea:
plan of town.
Medieval cellars
are marked in black

by an up-to-date, workable settlement this end. The plan is a grid inside an irregular triangle, but it is not complete. The s half with a town hall and market place was never built. Two of the churches of the old town were re-founded, St Thomas and the since demolished St Giles. A third, St Leonard, has also disappeared. The Greyfriars were transferred from the old to the new town too, and much later, in 1352, the Blackfriars built premises as well. There were also three hospitals. But the town was not a success. By the mid C14 holdings had become vacant.

There were several French raids from 1337 to 1380, and in the time of Queen Elizabeth I the harbour silted up. So the present Winchelsea is confined to twelve blocks out of the originally laid-out thirty-nine.

Visually the outcome of this history is very curious. Here is a hill town like Rye or like Lewes, but it never succeeds in looking like a town. The plots leased were quite large, and each original house had ample space. As the population never grew, the spaces never closed up, and so today Winchelsea with its green grass verges flanking the streets is more like a formally planned garden suburb than like a town. Moreover, though there are plenty of medieval houses, their medieval parts are mostly confined to the cellars and so do not contribute anything for the perambulating visitor. For him Winchelsea is partly Georgian and partly a pretty neo-C17 and C18 of the early C20. The visual surprise of today was already felt by earlier visitors. Defoe about 1725 calls Winchelsea 'rather the skeleton of an ancient city, than a real town'. Celia Fiennes in 1697 writes: 'I rode up a middle street and saw the others run across of good breadth ..., but ... there are but a very few houses and ... grass grows now where Winchelsea was, as was once said of Troy.' Lord Torrington in 1788 wrote virtually the same ('The town seems to have been laid out on a regular plan, ... but few houses remain'), in 1790 John Wesley spoke, like Defoe, of 'that poor skeleton of Ancient Winchelsea', and *The Beauties of England and Wales* in 1813 more originally described Winchelsea as 'the shadow of a shade'.

ST THOMAS. The church was intended to be on the proudest scale. With its churchyard it fills one whole block of the plan of the town. However, in the end only the chancel with its side chapels remained intact. The transepts have gone, and so has the nave, if this was indeed ever finished. Gone also is a big square tower (of stone and wood) which may have been a watch tower anyway and not a campanile. This was demolished only in 1790, the rest probably by the French. The style of the chancel is consistently that of the early C14, still externally without any ogees. Instead the large windows – in the chapels three and five lights, in the chancel two and five – have Kentish tracery, i.e. barbed trefoils, set in spherical triangles or not (cf. e.g. Chartham, Kent),* and in the chancel grossly overcusped tracery. Openwork parapets. Beneath the

* The E window is a replacement of a Perp window, made in 1850.

chancel is a vaulted undercroft of two bays, divided by a transverse arch. The bays oddly enough have tripartite rib-vaults. The interior of the church is now, as far as the transepts are concerned, exterior. One can still read the fact that the E window was set in very deep recesses with strong jamb-shafts, and that the end and the w windows had narrow blank arches l. and r. The crossing piers were of five shafts, the middle one filleted. On the N side the arch to the future N aisle again with five shafts is the end. One enters what is now inside by a w porch and w entrance, both Late Perp and coarse. But the impression inside is grand and rich, grand architecturally, rich decoratively. The scale is almost that of a cathedral. Three bays. Tall piers of four main shafts and four subsidiary shafts of Sussex marble. The shaft-rings not of marble. Arches with typically Dec mouldings (sunk quadrants). The windows are all marble-shafted. They are set with a narrow blank arch l. and r. and a somewhat depressed super-arch over the three, not a happy conceit. Single-framed roofs with tie-beams. Walls skinned except in the sanctuary.

Now the enrichments. First the chancel SEDILIA and PISCINA. One composition with crocketed gables and buttress-shafts and cinquecusped arches. Diapered back wall. No ogees. Then the s chapel SEDILIA and PISCINA, at first sight seemingly very similar, but now with plenty of ogees. Ogee-cusped and subcusped arches. Ogee spherical triangles in the spandrels. Fine head-stops, the first of many to come. Adjoining the chapel sedilia, but separated by the fragment of an IMAGE on a bracket supported by a splendid crouching figure, the first two of the monuments. – PLATE. Elizabethan Cup, c.1568; Paten on foot, 1726; Paten, 1807.

MONUMENTS. Two in the s, three in the N chapel, all of c.1310–20, and all with plenty of ogees. The N group one composition, the s group two different ones. The first of the latter is tripartite with canted sides and three gables. In the main spandrel a Green Man. Effigy with crossed legs. He is holding his heart. Two angels were originally by his pillow. A lion stands by his feet. Diapered back wall. Even the tomb-chest or base with its canopies leaning forward is all diapered. Again excellent head-stops, especially for the middle gable. This monument is suggested to commemorate Gervase de Alard † 1310, first Admiral of the Cinque Ports. The smaller adjoining monument then could be Stephen Alard † 1330, also an Admiral of the Cinque Ports. Stephen Alard had indeed

founded a chantry in the church in 1312. The monument is
also tripartite but flat. The effigy is similar, except for the
motif of the hands and the position of the shield. The lion at
his feet seems ready to pounce. The centre gable on very big
heads. All spandrels of the cusps filled with leaf. In the gable
a small grinning head in leaves. The monuments opposite
are divided by pairs of buttress-shafts with a niche between.
The recesses are low here, i.e. the arches close above the
effigies. The arches have a pronounced ogee shape. The effigies
are of Sussex marble and represent a Knight, a Lady, and a
Civilian. In the big gables of the l. and r. monuments are
enormous trefoil leaves and an excessively raised boss in the
middle. The leaf motifs in the centre gable are arranged to
fit triangular, diaper-like shapes. Again plenty of head-stops.
– In one of the recesses WALL PAINTING of an angel holding
a soul in a napkin. The second angel is destroyed. Early C14
too. – ORGAN CASE. Wrenian. By *Macartney*, completed in
1931. – (SCULPTURE. Wooden Virgin, Continental, C17, N
aisle E.) – STAINED GLASS. Some medieval glass in the chancel
N window. Otherwise all by *Douglas Strachan*, 1928–33,
moderately Expressionist, with very close black lead lines,
rather streaky and decidedly sentimental. – BRASS. Civilian of
c.1440, 26 in. figure (chancel floor).

STRANDGATE. The NE gate. Strand, because it lay originally
by the bank of the river Brede. Early C14. With four round
angle towers. The interior was vaulted. Stair-turret to the
outside.

PIPEWELL GATE. The NW gate. A rebuilding of *c*.1400. Archway with four-centred head. Segmental tunnel-vault inside.

NEW GATE, at the S end, far out of the present town. Archway
also with four-centred head. Tunnel-vault also segmental,
but with a transverse arch.

GREYFRIARS, Friars Road, at its S end. The house was built
in 1819 but looks Victorian now. In the garden the ruin of
the FRANCISCAN CHURCH, built *c*.1310–20. The nave has
disappeared, and only the chancel survives. Considering the
dearth of Franciscan remains in England, this is one of the
most impressive there are. Polygonal apse, large windows
deprived of their tracery. Chancel arch with tripartite
responds. One roll in the arch itself. To the S of the chancel
arch a stair-turret. To the immediate W of the N wall of the
chancel are the remains of the doorway into the customary
steeple space, which was divided by a wall from the nave.

Something also still stands of the E wall of the N aisle and the
S wall of the S aisle. The residential quarters were to the S.
A small doorway once belonging to the Greyfriars precinct
has been re-set in BACK LANE.

COURT HOUSE, High Street. Of stone, C14, heightened in the
C15 and much restored in the C19. The building was larger
originally to the E, and to the W (see the springers of ribs) as
well. Inside, a C15 kingpost roof. In the garden wall to the E
a re-set C13 doorway with segmental head and a re-set C13
niche. – REGALIA. Mace of *c.*1485, silver on an iron core;
Mace of *c.*1550; Serjeant's Mace 'of uncertain date' (VCH).

STREETS

A perambulation cannot be prescribed. The pattern is too
uniform, and there is nothing outstanding to note.

There are still over thirty medieval VAULTS, mostly with direct
access from the street. They served probably as wine cellars
for the barrels of wine imported from Gascony. Their location
is marked on the plan on p. 632, though few of them are
easily accessible. In addition to the thirty there is evidence of
another sixteen. They all seem to date from the years between
the foundation of Winchelsea and the early C14. The majority
are tunnel-vaulted, pointed or round or segmental, and with
transverse arches, single-chamfered or hollow-chamfered.
There are from two to eight such arches, though the majority
have four and five. In some cases two interconnected chambers
have survived. A few are more elaborate in that they have
25b   quadripartite rib-vaults. Such are that of the former SALU-
TATION INN at the NW corner of Castle Street and Mill
Road. This has three bays, hollow-chamfered ribs standing
on corbels with figures, at the W end a group of niches with
the middle one higher, and a doorway with two-centred head
and continuous mouldings. Even more interesting is one in
RECTORY LANE below a barn belonging to Mill Farm
House and lying between High Street and Back Lane on the
W side. Here there are three chambers, two with two bays of
rib-vaulting each, but the middle one tunnel-vaulted. The ribs
rest on corbels. Under the NEW INN at the SW corner of
High Street and German Street is a square cellar with four
rib-vaults.

Otherwise the following houses deserve comment. The streets
in which they lie are listed in alphabetical order.

In CASTLE STREET is THE WELLHOUSE, 1831, but with

three medieval archways and buttresses at the W angles, and THE ARMOURY, a C14 house (W range) with C15 addition (E range). Buttresses at the ends of the front, a kingpost roof inside, and a tunnel-vaulted cellar of *c.*1300.

FRIARS' ROAD. Nos 1–2 have a kingpost roof.

In GERMAN STREET is the NEW INN, C18 white-rendered brick, and a nice group to its S, facing the churchyard. For the cellar *see* above. The houses in German Street are partly C18-looking, partly early C20. Further S MARITEAU HOUSE, late C18, of five bays with a three-bay pediment on Ionic pilasters.

HASTINGS ROAD. Outside the town to the S on the way to the New Gate was ST JOHN'S HOSPITAL. Only one gable of one range remains.

NORTH STREET. A chunk of the medieval TOWN WALLS in a garden close to the street. The walls were built, it seems, from 1295 onwards.

RECTORY LANE. The METHODIST CHURCH is of 1785, red brick and quite simple. Opposite a BARN, now roofless and ruined. For the cellar beneath this, *see* above. Beyond this a WINDMILL, a tarred post-mill of *c.*1760, without sails. Remains of the TOWN WALLS in the gardens of PIPEWELL FARM and MILL FARM. Below the latter another vaulted cellar.

Between the few houses here named and in the other streets plenty of attractive, charming, cosy houses, white, tile-hung or of brick. But they do not demand comment.

WICKHAM FARMHOUSE, ¾ m. SW. Early C16, of stone, with mullioned windows.

WINDMILL HILL PLACE *see* HERSTMONCEUX

WINDOVER HILL *see* WILMINGTON

WITHYHAM

ST MICHAEL. In quite a high position above the main street. The medieval church was struck by lightning in 1663 and rebuilt immediately. It was completed in 1672, except for the Sackville Chapel, which was finished only in 1680. C14 parts were re-used and are recognizable, e.g. in the broad W tower and the chancel (one S window). The E window and the windows of the Sackville Chapel with their depressed arches are clearly C17. The arcade of the Sackville Chapel to S and w is purely Gothic, which deserves notice. The s aisle of the church was built in 1841, the N arcade removed perhaps at the same time, and much else victorianized. – FONT. 1666. Octagonal and merely moulded, the mouldings still being in the Gothic tradition. – WALL PAINTING. Last Judgement over the chancel arch by *Earl de la Warr*, rector of the church, shortly before 1856. – PAINTINGS. Polyptych in the s aisle. Italian Trecento, the predella Quattrocento. – Three panels of the Life of Christ, also Trecento and inspired by Giotto. These pieces were bought in Italy by the pioneer of the appreciation of Italian Primitives, William Young Ottley, and reached the church via the chapel of Buckhurst (*see* below). – STAINED GLASS. In the s aisle by *Kempe*, 1904 and 1905. – PLATE. Chalice, 1707. – MONUMENTS. The Sackville Chapel is of course what matters in the church. It was built as such, as has been said, and the iron RAILINGS are original. The monument for which the chapel was erected is that of Thomas Sackville, who died in 1677 at the age of thirteen. The monument was commissioned in 1677. It is by *C. G. Cibber*, who was paid £350 for it to be 'artificially produced' and to 'ye well liking of Mr Peter Lilly, his majesty's painter'. Cibber has indeed produced a monument different from any seen in England up to that time, inspired clearly by the Italian Baroque though perhaps by way of Holland. The monument is placed free standing in the middle of the chapel and is of the traditional tomb-chest type. The material is white and grey marble. The boy reclines on a half-rolled-up mat, definitely a Netherlandish and Elizabetho-Jacobean motif, and holds a skull, and his parents, the fifth Earl and Countess of Dorset, kneel life-size on cushions placed on the steps of the tomb-chest. They look at him disconsolately. As if they had only that moment decided to kneel there, their figures make part of the representations of other children invisible which are placed against the side of the tomb-chest, again a traditional motif. These children kneel or lie in a variety of poses, some holding skulls. The whole has a directness of feeling and expression unprecedented in England (but cf. Ashburnham, p. 401). – Large tablets to the following: John Frederick, third duke. By *Nollekens*, 1802. Three putti hang a garland over an urn with the portrait. The group has a charming, almost dancing rhythm. – George John Frederick, fourth duke, † 1815, By *Flaxman*. Seated Greek woman by an urn. Above, an excellent portrait medallion. – Arabella

Diana, third duchess, † 1825. By *Chantrey*. Two young women by an urn. – George John, Earl de la Warr, † 1869 by *William Tyler*. A kneeling sentimental young lady holds a wreath above the waves. – William Alfrey † 1610 (1630?). Iron slab on the s buttress of the chancel E end. The inscription runs across the top. – V. Sackville-West † 1962. Beautiful slate plaque by *Reynolds Stone*.

ST JOHN, 2½ m. SSE. 1839 by *W. L. Blaker*, the apsidal chancel of 1870. Ashlar, lancets, bellcote. – STAINED GLASS. By *Kempe*, all between 1895 and 1902. – PLATE. Chalice and Paten, 1707; Flagon, 1825; Almsdish, 1825.

OLD BUCKHURST, ½ m. SSW. Of the former Sackville mansion the principal survival is the Early Tudor gatehouse. This is of stone, with a higher stair-turret and an archway with four-centred head. To the inside two tiers of three-light windows with arched lights. Buttress-shafts and finials; battlements. Behind is the principal range of the house, low and comfortably spreading. This is mostly by *Cecil Brewer* (illustrated in *Country Life* in 1919), but incorporates old timber-framed parts at the l. end. Brewer connected this end by a loggia with the converted oast-houses on the l. From the gatehouse down to the river ample foundations. But the grand courtyard mansion which Thorpe drew was apparently never built.

BUCKHURST, ½ m. SE. 1830–*c*.1835 by *Repton* and then called Stoneland Hall. The house is large and lies high up. Tudor front with the porch not in the middle. Mullioned and transomed windows; gables; very prominent chimneys. (Inside in the chapel oak panelling from Bolebrooke, *see* p. 517.)

In the short, scattered village street the DORSET ARMS, white, weatherboarded, with decorated bargeboards of the early C19, and further E, on the same side, DUCKINGS, timber-framed, with close studs, said to be of 1507. Close to the house is a hammer pond; so the house was an ironmaster's.

WIVELSFIELD

3020

ST PETER AND ST JOHN BAPTIST. The small N doorway, re-set in the C19 N aisle, is witness of an C11 past of the church. The reeded arch and hood-mould recur at Bolney and Stopham. *Slater & Carpenter* built the aisle in 1869, with small lancets arranged symmetrically and ungothically l. and r. of the doorway. The s arcade of two bays with its short round pier and double-chamfered arches must be early

C13. The chancel was rebuilt late in the C13, see the E window of three stepped lancets under one arch, re-set in the C19 at the E end of the N aisle. The S chapel, with a roof higher than that of the S aisle, is also late C13. It has an E lancet and arches to aisle and chancel with continuous chamfers. In the E wall a reredos recess. Finally the W lengthening of the nave and the building of the SW tower; C14 to C15. In the tower two tiny windows built up of very large stones, probably re-set and perhaps C11. A tower window and the S doorway have entertaining label stops including an owl. – (PULPIT. Jacobean carving on the base, which was originally the sounding-board.)

MORE HOUSE, ¼ m. E, on the main road. A C16 core, but a tile-hung Georgian front. In the garden a square GAZEBO with a pyramid roof, C18 or a little earlier.

CONGREGATIONAL CHAPEL, ½ m. SE. Founded in 1778 and built in 1780 by Selina Countess of Huntingdon, who lived at Great Ote Hall. A small box with a hipped roof. Front of two windows and a doorway between, all three arched.

GREAT OTE HALL, ¼ m. SW. An impressive but very puzzling house, not at all large. C16 and 1600. As one approaches it from the S, there is a recent wing on the l. and in front a timber-framed structure of narrowly set uprights with two dormers and a big brick chimneybreast with four stacks. Round the corner, the E is the main front. This is also timber-framed of narrow uprights, but symmetrical with a (former) middle porch. Above the former entrance a flat oriel with a pediment and the date 1600. The windows here are mullioned and transomed. The NBR, however, has a reproduction of an old drawing, where the porch has no pediments and the windows have arched lights and no transoms. This range contains the hall to the r. of the porch, the kitchen to the l. The big chimneys of the S front belong to the kitchen. Again round the corner one sees a window behind the high-table end of the hall and the hall chimneybreast (three stacks) and a porch (not old) with a three-light oriel over. Finally once more round the corner (W) a yet bigger chimneybreast which has five stacks. They belong to a kitchen built together with this whole back range a little after the E range. The former kitchen was then no doubt put to another use.

(THEOBALDS, ¼ m. NW of the former. A Georgian front of grey brick and black mathematical tiles with red and white brick dressings. MHLG)

WOODSGATE PARK *see* BEXHILL, p. 417

WOODSIDE *see* PEASMARSH

WOOTTON PLACE *see* FOLKINGTON

WORTH   *3030*

ST NICHOLAS. Worth church is one of the most powerful of
Anglo-Saxon churches, large in scale and bold in conception.
It is cruciform with a wide and high nave, lower transepts
rather than *porticus*, not exactly in line with one another, and
a lower apsed chancel. The exterior is decorated with lesenes
or pilaster strips throughout, a motif of the late Anglo-Saxon
time, and so the church is most probably of the C11 and not
earlier. The pilaster strips carry a horizontal course, but the
walls go on above it. This course is higher in the nave, lower
in the chancel. In the nave above it are two-light windows 11b
with mid-wall shafts or rather thick, stumpy mid-wall
columns, a type of opening usual in towers but in nave
windows so far unique. One remains on the S side, two on the
N. The nave doorways are also recognizable, though the S
doorway only internally. They are very tall and very narrow.
It is unfortunate, at least from anywhere near by, that in 1871
Salvin added a NE tower. It has the usual shingled broach
spire. In 1869 the plan had actually been more sweeping and
included the destruction of the chancel. But protests defeated
this. The interior hits one at once by its dimensions and the
blunt force of its details. Mighty chancel arch with big semicircular responds and cushion capitals. Unmoulded arch, and
one outer band up outside jambs and arch, as was a Saxon
custom. The transept arches are much lower and narrower
(cf. Sompting, Climping, Oving, in West Sussex). The capitals
are not original, the arches again unmoulded. In the S transept
is a Gothic reredos recess below a wider and higher arch
which cannot be the former opening to a chapel or apse,
because the pilaster strips do not allow it. In the N transept is
a similar but pointed recess with a lancet window in it. –
FONT. Square, of stone, C13, but with simple tracery patterns
cut in flatly about 1300. – PULPIT. With a German inscription and the date 1577. Angle columns, and in niched panels
Christ and the four Evangelists. – LECTERN. 1896. With two
standing angels. – COMMUNION RAIL. Foreign, like the
pulpit. The figures of the posts are Mannerist, i.e. probably

21—S.

of *c*.1600, the pierced panels are of *c*.1700 or later. – WEST
GALLERY. Dated 1610. With vertically symmetrical balusters.
– PANELLING. Bits, probably Jacobean, in the s transept. –
CHANDELIERS. Of brass, apparently late C17. – PAINTING.
A little ornamental painting in the arch of the window by the
lectern. – STAINED GLASS. In the s transept, by *Willement*,
date of death 1849. Typical of the date. Three large figures. –
PLATE. Cup and Paten on foot, 1635; Paten, 1692; Flagon,
1704; the first three silver-gilt. – MONUMENTS. Many, but
all minor. Good Grecian piece with sarcophagus and urn to
James Norman † 1837. – John Ewart † 1834 with a kneeling
angel, and his wife Catherine † 1835 with a female figure
standing by an urn. Both by *Peter Rouw Jun.*

CRABBET PARK, ¾ m. NNE. Built in 1873 and, if this date is
correct, the unexpected and memorable case of a neo-Queen-
Anne in the true (not the Norman-Shaw) sense of the word
at so early a date. Soft-coloured rose brick with stone dressings.
Nine-bay front with a slight pedimented three-bay projection. Curved open stairs up to the doorway which carries a
semicircular pediment. The same motif repeats on the less
regular garden side. Hipped roof behind a balustrade. To its
w are the ORANGERY and TENNIS COURT, supposed to have
been added early in the C20. A high range with lower projections along both sides, nine bays to the N, seven to the s.
These have arched windows, and attached Tuscan columns
with a balustrade. But to the N from this even range projects
yet further a porte-cochère-like porch or veranda consisting
of a more-than-semicircle connected with the range by further
quarter-circles, a strangely indistinct form. Who were the
architects of this building and of the house?

ROWFANT HOUSE, 1⅝ m. ENE. The s front has a l. part which is
Late Elizabethan and was probably built for Robert Whitfield,
an ironmaster. It is symmetrical, with a porch and gables
crowned by finials. In the entrance hall a simple fireplace
dated 1597. Behind this remains evidence of the preceding
late C15 timber-framed house, especially kingpost trusses. The
w front of brick is a paraphrase on the original façade. It
dates from 1759 (rain-water heads), but the top parts were re-
elizabethanized, in 1848. The r. part of the s front is C19 too.

WORTH PRIORY OF OUR LADY HELP OF CHRISTIANS, 1½ m.
SE. The principal building is PADDOCKHURST, the vast
imitation Tudor mansion of Mr George Smith, 1869–72 by
Salvin. Architecturally the most rewarding part of the house

is the addition at the E end of the S front made for Sir Weet-
man Pearson by *Sir Aston Webb* in 1897. This is much
prettier externally with its fanciful gatehouse motif, and has
inside a super-room of that date, 45 by 20 ft in size. Alabaster
and pavonazzo fireplaces, stucco ceiling, and stucco frieze
signed by *Walter Crane*, representing in a lively, sketchy way 61b
the history of locomotion from the ox-wagon to the motor-
car, alluding to the source of the wealth of the client. Canoe,
stage-coach, railway, bicycle, perambulator are all there. A
large addition by *Francis Pollen* of Brett & Pollen is to be
started in 1964.

GLOSSARY

ABACUS: flat slab on the top of a capital (q.v.).

ABUTMENT: solid masonry placed to resist the lateral pressure of a vault.

ACANTHUS: plant with thick fleshy and scalloped leaves used as part of the decoration of a Corinthian capital (q.v.) and in some types of leaf carving.

ACHIEVEMENT OF ARMS: in heraldry, a complete display of armorial bearings.

ACROTERION: foliage-carved block on the end or top of a classical pediment (q.v.).

ADDORSED: two human figures, animals, or birds, etc., placed symmetrically so that they turn their backs to each other.

AEDICULE, AEDICULA: framing of a window or door by columns and a pediment (q.v.).

AFFRONTED: two human figures, animals, or birds, etc., placed symmetrically so that they face each other.

AGGER: Latin term for the built-up foundations of Roman roads; also sometimes applied to the banks of hill-forts or other earthworks.

AMBULATORY: semicircular or polygonal aisle enclosing an apse (q.v.).

ANNULET: see Shaft-ring.

ANSE DE PANIER: see Arch, Basket.

ANTEPENDIUM: covering of the front of an altar, usually by textiles or metalwork.

ANTIS, IN: see Portico.

APSE: vaulted semicircular or polygonal end of a chancel or a chapel.

ARABESQUE: light and fanciful surface decoration using combinations of flowing lines, tendrils, etc., interspersed with vases, animals, etc.

ARCADE: range of arches supported on piers or columns, free-standing: or, BLIND ARCADE, the same attached to a wall.

ARCH: round-headed, i.e. semicircular; pointed, i.e. consisting of two curves, each drawn from one centre, and meeting in a point at the top; segmental, i.e. in the form of a segment;

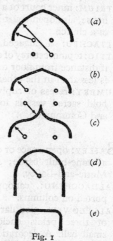

Fig. 1

pointed; four-centred (a Late Medieval form), see Fig. 1(a); Tudor (also a Late Medieval form), *see* Fig. 1(*b*); Ogee (introduced *c.*1300 and specially popular in the C14), *see* Fig. 1(*c*); Stilted, *see* Fig. 1(*d*); Basket, with lintel connected to the jambs by concave quadrant curves, *see* Fig. 1(*e*) for one example; Diaphragm, a transverse arch with solid spandrels carrying not a vault but a principal beam of a timber roof.

ARCHITRAVE: lowest of the three main parts of the entablature (q.v.) of an order (q.v.) (*see* Fig. 12).

ARCHIVOLT: under-surface of an arch (also called Soffit).

ARRIS: sharp edge at the meeting of two surfaces.

ASHLAR: masonry of large blocks wrought to even faces and square edges.

ATLANTES: male counterparts of caryatids (q.v.).

ATRIUM: inner court of a Roman house, also open court in front of a church.

ATTACHED: *see* Engaged.

ATTIC: topmost storey of a house, if distance from floor to ceiling is less than in the others.

AUMBRY: recess or cupboard to hold sacred vessels for Mass and Communion.

BAILEY: open space or court of a stone-built castle; *see* also Motte-and-Bailey.

BALDACCHINO: canopy supported on columns.

BALLFLOWER: globular flower of three petals enclosing a small ball. A decoration used in the first quarter of the C14.

BALUSTER: small pillar or column of fanciful outline.

BALUSTRADE: series of balusters

supporting a handrail or coping (q.v.).

BARBICAN: outwork defending the entrance to a castle.

BARGEBOARDS: projecting decorated boards placed against the incline of the gable of a building and hiding the horizontal roof timbers.

BARROW: *see* Bell, Bowl, Disc, Long, *and* Pond Barrow.

BASILICA: in medieval architecture an aisled church with a clerestory.

BASKET ARCH: *see* Arch (Fig. 1e).

BASTION: projection at the angle of a fortification.

BATTER: inclined face of a wall.

BATTLEMENT: parapet with a series of indentations or embrasures with raised portions or merlons between (also called Crenellation).

BAYS: internal compartments of a building; each divided from the other not by solid walls but by divisions only marked in the side walls (columns, pilasters, etc.) or the ceiling (beams, etc.). Also external divisions of a building by fenestration.

BAY-WINDOW: angular or curved projection of a house front with ample fenestration. If curved, also called bow-window: if on an upper floor only, also called oriel or oriel window.

BEAKER FOLK: Late New Stone Age warrior invaders from the Continent who buried their dead in round barrows and introduced the first metal tools and weapons to Britain.

BEAKHEAD: Norman ornamental motif consisting of a row of bird or beast heads with beaks biting usually into a roll moulding.

BELFRY: turret on a roof to hang bells in.

BELGAE: Aristocratic warrior bands who settled in Britain in two main waves in the C1 B.C. In Britain their culture is termed Iron Age C.

BELL BARROW: Early Bronze Age round barrow in which the mound is separated from its encircling ditch by a flat platform or berm (q.v.).

BELLCOTE: framework on a roof to hang bells from.

BERM: level area separating ditch from bank on a hill-fort or barrow.

BILLET FRIEZE: Norman ornamental motif made up of short raised rectangles placed at regular intervals.

BIVALLATE: Of a hill-fort: defended by two concentric banks and ditches.

BLOCK CAPITAL: Romanesque capital cut from a cube by having

Fig. 2

the lower angles rounded off to the circular shaft below (also called Cushion Capital) (Fig. 2).

BOND, ENGLISH or FLEMISH: see Brickwork.

BOSS: knob or projection usually placed to cover the intersection of ribs in a vault.

BOWL BARROW: round barrow surrounded by a quarry ditch. Introduced in Late Neolithic

times, the form continued until the Saxon period.

BOW-WINDOW: see Bay-Window.

BOX: A small country house, e.g. a shooting box. A convenient term to describe a compact minor dwelling, e.g. a rectory.

BOX PEW: pew with a high wooden enclosure.

BRACES: see Roof.

BRACKET: small supporting piece of stone, etc., to carry a projecting horizontal.

BRESSUMER: beam in a timber-framed building to support the, usually projecting, superstructure.

BRICKWORK: *Header:* brick laid so that the end only appears on the face of the wall. *Stretcher:* brick laid so that the side only appears on the face of the wall. *English Bond:* method of laying bricks so that alternate courses or layers on the face of the wall are composed of headers or stretchers only (Fig. 3a). *Flemish Bond:* method of laying

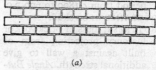

(a)

(b)

Fig. 3

bricks so that alternate headers and stretchers appear in each course on the face of the wall (Fig. 3b).

BROACH: see Spire.

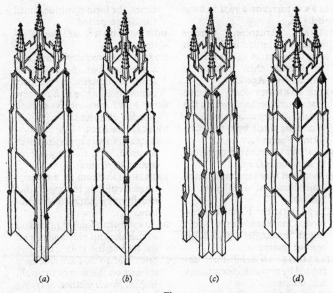

(a)   (b)   (c)   (d)

Fig. 4

BROKEN PEDIMENT: *see* Pediment.

BRONZE AGE: In Britain, the period from *c.*1800 to 600 B.C.

BUCRANIUM: ox skull.

BUTTRESS: mass of brickwork or masonry projecting from or built against a wall to give additional strength. *Angle Buttresses:* two meeting at an angle of 90° at the angle of a building (Fig. 4*a*). *Clasping Buttress:* one which encases the angle (Fig. 4*d*). *Diagonal Buttress:* one placed against the right angle formed by two walls, and more or less equiangular with both (Fig. 4*b*). *Flying Buttress:* arch or half arch transmitting the thrust of a vault or roof from the upper part of a wall to an outer support or buttress. *Setback Buttress:* angle buttress set slightly back from the angle (Fig. 4*c*).

CABLE MOULDING: Norman moulding imitating a twisted cord.

CAIRN: a mound of stones usually covering a burial.

CAMBER: slight rise or upward curve of an otherwise horizontal structure.

CAMPANILE: isolated bell tower.

CANOPY: projection or hood over an altar, pulpit, niche, statue, etc.

CAP: in a windmill the crowning feature.

CAPITAL: head or top part of a column.

CARTOUCHE: tablet with an ornate frame, usually enclosing an inscription.

CARYATID: whole female figure supporting an entablature or other similar member. *Termini Caryatids:* female busts or demi-figures or three-quarter figures supporting an entablature or other similar member and placed at the top of termini pilasters (q.v.). Cf. Atlantes.

CASTELLATED: decorated with battlements.

CELURE: panelled and adorned part of a wagon-roof above the rood or the altar.

CENSER: vessel for the burning of incense.

CENTERING: wooden framework used in arch and vault construction and removed when the mortar has set.

CHALICE: cup used in the Communion service or at Mass. *See also* Recusant Chalice.

CHAMBERED TOMB: burial mound of the New Stone Age having a stone-built chamber and entrance passage covered by an earthen barrow or stone cairn. The form was introduced to Britain from the Mediterranean.

CHAMFER: surface made by cutting across the square angle of a stone block, piece of wood, etc., usually at an angle of 45° to the other two surfaces.

CHANCEL: that part of the E end of a church in which the altar is placed, usually applied to the whole continuation of the nave E of the crossing.

CHANCEL ARCH: arch at the W end of the chancel.

CHANTRY CHAPEL: chapel attached to, or inside, a church, endowed for the saying of Masses for the soul of the founder or some other individual.

CHEVET: French term for the E end of a church (chancel, ambulatory, and radiating chapels).

CHEVRON: Norman moulding forming a zigzag.

CHOIR: that part of the church where divine service is sung.

CIBORIUM: a baldacchino.

CINQUEFOIL: *see* Foil.

CIST: stone-lined or slab-built grave. First appears in Late Neolithic times. It continued to be used in the Early Christian period.

CLAPPER BRIDGE: bridge made of large slabs of stone, some built up to make rough piers and other longer ones laid on top to make the roadway.

CLASSIC: here used to mean the moment of highest achievement of a style.

CLASSICAL: here used as the term for Greek and Roman architecture and any subsequent styles inspired by it.

CLERESTORY: upper storey of the nave walls of a church, pierced by windows.

COADE STONE: artificial (cast) stone made in the late C18 and the early C19 by Coade and Sealy in London.

COB: walling material made of mixed clay and straw.

COFFERING: decorating a ceiling with sunk square or polygonal ornamental panels.

COLLAR-BEAM: *see* Roof.

COLONNADE: range of columns.

COLONNETTE: small column.

COLUMNA ROSTRATA: column decorated with carved prows of ships to celebrate a naval victory.

COMPOSITE: see Order.

CONSOLE: bracket (q.v.) with a compound curved outline.

COPING: capping or covering to a wall.

CORBEL: block of stone projecting from a wall, supporting some feature on its horizontal top surface.

CORBEL TABLE: series of corbels, occurring just below the roof eaves externally or internally, often seen in Norman buildings.

CORINTHIAN: see Order.

CORNICE: in classical architecture the top section of the entablature (q.v.). Also for a projecting decorative feature along the top of a wall, arch, etc.

CORRIDOR VILLA: see Villa.

COUNTERSCARP BANK: small bank on the down-hill or outer side of a hill-fort ditch.

COURTYARD VILLA: see Villa.

COVE, COVING: concave undersurface in the nature of a hollow moulding but on a larger scale.

COVER PATEN: cover to a Communion cup, suitable for use as a paten or plate for the consecrated bread.

CRADLE ROOF: see Wagon roof.

CRENELLATION: see Battlement.

CREST, CRESTING: ornamental finish along the top of a screen, etc.

CRINKLE-CRANKLE WALL: undulating wall.

CROCKET, CROCKETING: decorative features placed on the sloping sides of spires, pinnacles, gables, etc., in Gothic architecture, carved in various leaf shapes and placed at regular intervals.

CROCKET CAPITAL: see Fig. 5. An Early Gothic form.

CROMLECH: word of Celtic origin still occasionally used of single free-standing stones ascribed to the Neolithic or Bronze Age periods.

Fig. 5

CROSSING: space at the intersection of nave, chancel, and transepts.

CROSS-WINDOWS: windows with one mullion and one transom.

CRUCK: big curved beam supporting both walls and roof of a cottage.

CRYPT: underground room usually below the E end of a church.

CUPOLA: small polygonal or circular domed turret crowning a roof.

CURTAIN WALL: connecting wall between the towers of a castle.

CUSHION CAPITAL: see Block Capital.

CUSP: projecting point between the foils in a foiled Gothic arch.

DADO: decorative covering of the lower part of a wall.

DAGGER: tracery motif of the Dec style. It is a lancet shape rounded or pointed at the head, pointed at the foot, and cusped inside (see Fig. 6).

Fig. 6

DAIS: raised platform at one end of a room.

DEC ('DECORATED'): historical division of English Gothic architecture covering the period from c.1290 to c.1350.

DEMI-COLUMNS: columns half sunk into a wall.

DIAPER WORK: surface decoration composed of square or lozenge shapes.

DIAPHRAGM ARCH: see Arch.

DISC BARROW: Bronze Age round barrow with inconspicuous central mound surrounded by bank and ditch.

DOGTOOTH: typical E.E. ornament consisting of a series of four-cornered stars placed diagonally and raised pyramidally (Fig. 7).

Fig. 7

DOMICAL VAULT: see Vault.

DONJON: see Keep.

DORIC: see Order.

DORMER (WINDOW): window placed vertically in the sloping plane of a roof.

DRIPSTONE: see Hood-mould.

DRUM: circular or polygonal vertical wall of a dome or cupola.

E.E. ('EARLY ENGLISH'): historical division of English Gothic architecture roughly covering the C13.

EASTER SEPULCHRE: recess with tomb-chest, usually in the wall of a chancel, the tomb-chest to receive an effigy of Christ for Easter celebrations.

EAVES: underpart of a sloping roof overhanging a wall.

EAVES CORNICE: cornice below the eaves of a roof.

ECHINUS: Convex or projecting moulding supporting the abacus of a Greek Doric capital, sometimes bearing an egg and dart pattern.

EMBATTLED: see Battlement.

EMBRASURE: small opening in the wall or parapet of a fortified building, usually splayed on the inside.

ENCAUSTIC TILES: earthenware glazed and decorated tiles used for paving.

ENGAGED COLUMNS: columns attached to, or partly sunk into, a wall.

ENGLISH BOND: see Brickwork.

ENTABLATURE: in classical architecture the whole of the horizontal members above a column (that is architrave, frieze, and cornice) (see Fig. 12).

ENTASIS: very slight convex deviation from a straight line; used on Greek columns and sometimes on spires to prevent an optical illusion of concavity.

ENTRESOL: see Mezzanine.

EPITAPH: hanging wall monument.

ESCUTCHEON: shield for armorial bearings.

EXEDRA: the apsidal end of a room. See Apse.

FAN-VAULT: see Vault.

FERETORY: place behind the

high altar where the chief shrine of a church is kept.

FESTOON: carved garland of flowers and fruit suspended at both ends.

FILLET: narrow flat band running down a shaft or along a roll moulding.

FINIAL: top of a canopy, gable, pinnacle.

FLAGON: vessel for the wine used in the Communion service.

FLAMBOYANT: properly the latest phase of French Gothic architecture where the window tracery takes on wavy undulating lines.

FLÈCHE: slender wooden spire on the centre of a roof (also called Spirelet).

FLEMISH BOND: see Brickwork.

FLEURON: decorative carved flower or leaf.

FLUSHWORK: decorative use of flint in conjunction with dressed stone so as to form patterns: tracery, initials, etc.

FLUTING: vertical channelling in the shaft of a column.

FLYING BUTTRESS: see Buttress.

FOIL: lobe formed by the cusping (q.v.) of a circle or an arch. Trefoil, quatrefoil, cinquefoil, multifoil, express the number of leaf shapes to be seen.

FOLIATED: carved with leaf shapes.

FOSSE: ditch.

FOUR-CENTRED ARCH: see Arch.

FRATER: refectory or dining hall of a monastery.

FRESCO: wall painting on wet plaster.

FRIEZE: middle division of a classical entablature (q.v.) (see Fig. 12).

FRONTAL: covering for the front of an altar.

GABLE: *Dutch gable:* A gable with curved sides crowned by a pediment, characteristic of c.1630–50 (Fig. 8a). *Shaped gable:* A gable with multi-curved sides characteristic of c.1600–50 (Fig. 8b).

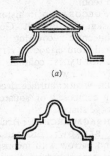

(a)

(b)

Fig. 8

GADROONED: enriched with a series of convex ridges, the opposite of fluting.

GALILEE: chapel or vestibule usually at the w end of a church enclosing the porch. Also called Narthex (q.v.).

GALLERY: in church architecture upper storey above an aisle, opened in arches to the nave. Also called Tribune and often erroneously Triforium (q.v.).

GALLERY GRAVE: chambered tomb (q.v.) in which there is little or no differentiation between the entrance passage and the actual burial chamber(s).

GARDEROBE: lavatory or privy in a medieval building.

GARGOYLE: water spout projecting from the parapet of a wall or tower; carved into a human or animal shape.

GAZEBO: lookout tower or raised

summer house in a picturesque garden.

'GEOMETRICAL': see Tracery.

'GIBBS SURROUND': of a doorway or window. An c18 motif consisting of a surround with alternating larger and smaller blocks of stone, quoin-wise, or intermittent large blocks, sometimes with a narrow raised band connecting them up the verticals and along the face of the arch (Fig. 9).

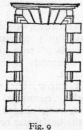

Fig. 9

GROIN: sharp edge at the meeting of two cells of a cross-vault.

GROIN-VAULT: see Vault.

GROTESQUE: fanciful ornamental decoration: see also Arabesque.

HAGIOSCOPE: see Squint.

HALF-TIMBERING: see Timber-Framing.

HALL CHURCH: church in which nave and aisles are of equal height or approximately so.

HAMMERBEAM: see Roof.

HANAP: large metal cup, generally made for domestic use, standing on an elaborate base and stem; with a very ornate cover frequently crowned with a little steeple.

HEADERS: see Brickwork.

HERRINGBONE WORK: brick, stone, or tile construction where the component blocks are laid diagonally instead of flat. Alternate courses lie in opposing directions to make a zigzag pattern up the face of the wall.

HEXASTYLE: having six detached columns.

HILL-FORT: Iron Age earthwork enclosed by a ditch and bank system; in the later part of the period the defences multiplied in size and complexity. They vary from about an acre to over 30 acres in area, and are usually built with careful regard to natural elevations or promontories.

HIPPED ROOF: see Roof.

HOOD-MOULD: projecting moulding above an arch or a lintel to throw off water (also called Dripstone or Label).

ICONOGRAPHY: the science of the subject matter of works of the visual arts.

IMPOST: bracket in a wall, usually formed of mouldings, on which the ends of an arch rest.

INDENT: shape chiselled out in a stone slab to receive a brass.

INGLENOOK: bench or seat built in beside a fireplace, sometimes covered by the chimneybreast, occasionally lit by small windows on each side of the fire.

INTERCOLUMNIATION: the space between columns.

IONIC: see Order (Fig. 12).

IRON AGE: in Britain the period from c. 600 B.C. to the coming of the Romans. The term is also used for those un-Romanized native communities which survived until the Saxon incursions.

JAMB: straight side of an archway, doorway, or window.

KEEL MOULDING: moulding whose outline is in section like that of the keel of a ship.

KEEP: massive tower of a Norman castle.

KEYSTONE: middle stone in an arch or a rib-vault.

KING-POST: see Roof (Fig. 14).

KNEELER: horizontal decorative projection at the base of a gable.

KNOP: a knob-like thickening in the stem of a chalice.

LABEL: see Hood-mould.

LABEL STOP: ornamental boss at the end of a hood-mould (q.v.).

LACED WINDOWS: windows pulled visually together by strips, usually in brick of a different colour, which continue vertically the lines of the vertical parts of the window surrounds. The motif is typical of c. 1720.

LANCET WINDOW: slender pointed-arched window.

LANTERN: in architecture, a small circular or polygonal turret with windows all round crowning a roof (see Cupola) or a dome.

LANTERN CROSS: churchyard cross with lantern-shaped top usually with sculptured representations on the sides of the top.

LEAN-TO ROOF: roof with one slope only, built against a higher wall.

LESENE or PILASTER STRIP: pilaster without base or capital.

LIERNE: see Vault (Fig. 21).

LINENFOLD: Tudor panelling ornamented with a conventional representation of a piece of linen laid in vertical folds. The piece is repeated in each panel.

LINTEL: horizontal beam or stone bridging an opening.

LOGGIA: recessed colonnade (q.v.).

LONG AND SHORT WORK: Saxon quoins (q.v.) consisting of stones placed with the long sides alternately upright and horizontal.

LONG BARROW: unchambered Neolithic communal burial mound, wedge-shaped in plan, with the burial and occasional other structures massed at the broader end, from which the mound itself tapers in height; quarry ditches flank the mound.

LOUVRE: opening, often with lantern (q.v.) over, in the roof of a room to let the smoke from a central hearth escape.

LOWER PALAEOLITHIC: see Palaeolithic.

LOZENGE: diamond shape.

LUCARNE: small opening to let light in.

LUNETTE: tympanum (q.v.) or semicircular opening.

LYCH GATE: wooden gate structure with a roof and open sides placed at the entrance to a churchyard to provide space for the reception of a coffin. The word lych is Saxon and means a corpse.

LYNCHET: long terraced strip of soil accumulating on the downward side of prehistoric and medieval fields due to soil creep from continuous ploughing along the contours.

MACHICOLATION: projecting gallery on brackets constructed on the outside of castle towers or walls. The gallery has holes in the floor to drop missiles through.

MAJOLICA: ornamented glazed earthenware.

MANSARD: see Roof.

MATHEMATICAL TILES: Small facing tiles the size of brick headers, applied to timber-framed walls to make them appear brick-built.

MEGALITHIC TOMB: stone-built burial chamber of the New Stone Age covered by an earth or stone mound. The form was introduced to Britain from the Mediterranean area.

MERLON: see Battlement.

MESOLITHIC: 'Middle Stone' Age; the post-glacial period of hunting and fishing communities dating in Britain from c. 8000 B.C. to the arrival of Neolithic communities, with which they must have considerably overlapped.

METOPE: in classical architecture of the Doric order (q.v.) the space in the frieze between the triglyphs (Fig. 12).

MEZZANINE: low storey placed between two higher ones.

MISERERE: see Misericord.

MISERICORD: bracket placed on the underside of a hinged choir stall seat which, when turned up, provided the occupant of the seat with a support during long periods of standing (also called Miserere).

MODILLION: small bracket of which large numbers (modillion frieze) are often placed below a cornice (q.v.) in classical architecture.

MOTTE: steep mound forming the main feature of C11 and C12 castles.

MOTTE-AND-BAILEY: post-Roman and Norman defence system consisting of an earthen mound (the motte) topped with a wooden tower eccentrically placed within a bailey (q.v.), with enclosure ditch and palisade, and with the rare addition of an internal bank.

MOUCHETTE: tracery motif in curvilinear tracery, a curved dagger (q.v.), specially popular in the early C14 (Fig. 10).

Fig. 10

MULLIONS: vertical posts or uprights dividing a window into 'lights'.

MULTIVALLATE: Of a hill-fort: defended by three or more concentric banks and ditches.

MUNTIN: post as a rule moulded and part of a screen.

NAIL-HEAD: E.E. ornamental motif, consisting of small pyramids regularly repeated (Fig. 11).

Fig. 11

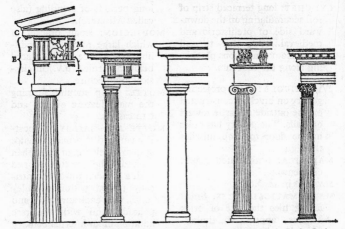

Fig. 12. Orders of Columns (Greek Doric, Roman Doric, Tuscan Doric, Ionic, Corinthian) E, Entablature; C, Cornice; F, Frieze; A, Architrave; M, Metope; T, Triglyph.

NARTHEX: enclosed vestibule or covered porch at the main entrance to a church (*see* Galilee).

NEOLITHIC: 'New Stone' Age, dating in Britain from the appearance from the Continent of the first settled farming communities c. 3500 B.C. until the introduction of the Bronze Age.

NEWEL: central post in a circular or winding staircase; also the principal post when a flight of stairs meets a landing.

NOOK-SHAFT: shaft set in the angle of a pier or respond or wall, or the angle of the jamb of a window or doorway.

NUTMEG MOULDING: consisting of a chain of tiny triangles placed obliquely.

OBELISK: lofty pillar of square section tapering at the top and ending pyramidally.

OGEE: *see* Arch (Fig. 1c).

ORATORY: small private chapel in a house.

ORDER: (1) *of a doorway or window:* series of concentric steps receding towards the opening; (2) *in classical architecture:* column with base, shaft, capital, and entablature (q.v.) according to one of the following styles: Greek Doric, Roman Doric, Tuscan Doric, Ionic, Corinthian, Composite. The established details are very elaborate, and some specialist architectural work should be consulted for further guidance (*see* Fig. 12).

ORIEL: *see* Bay-Window.

OVERHANG: projection of the upper storey of a house.

OVERSAILING COURSES: series of stone or brick courses, each one projecting beyond the one below it.

OVOLO: convex moulding.

PALAEOLITHIC: 'Old Stone' Age; the first period of human culture, commencing in the

Ice Age and immediately prior to the Mesolithic; the Lower Palaeolithic is the older phase, the Upper Palaeolithic the later.

PALIMPSEST: (1) *of a brass:* where a metal plate has been re-used by turning over and engraving on the back; (2) *of a wall painting:* where one overlaps and partly obscures an earlier one.

PALLADIAN: architecture following the ideas and principles of Andrea Palladio, 1518–80.

PANTILE: tile of curved S-shaped section.

PARAPET: low wall placed to protect any spot where there is a sudden drop, for example on a bridge, quay, hillside, housetop, etc.

PARGETTING: plaster work with patterns and ornaments either in relief or engraved on it.

PARVIS: term wrongly applied to a room over a church porch. These rooms were often used as a schoolroom or as a store room.

PATEN: plate to hold the bread at Communion or Mass.

PATERA: small flat circular or oval ornament in classical architecture.

PEDIMENT: low-pitched gable used in classical, Renaissance, and neo-classical architecture above a portico and above doors, windows, etc. It may be straight-sided or curved segmentally. *Broken Pediment:* one where the centre portion of the base is left open. *Open Pediment:* one where the centre portion of the sloping sides is left out.

PENDANT: boss (q.v.) elongated so that it seems to hang down.

PENDENTIF: concave triangular spandrel used to lead from the angle of two walls to the base of a circular dome. It is constructed as part of the hemisphere over a diameter the size of the diagonal of the basic square (Fig. 13).

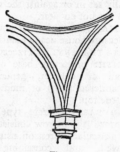

Fig. 13

PERP (PERPENDICULAR): historical division of English Gothic architecture covering the period from c.1335–50 to c.1530.

PIANO NOBILE: principal storey of a house with the reception rooms; usually the first floor.

PIAZZA: open space surrounded by buildings; in C17 and C18 England sometimes used to mean a long colonnade or loggia.

PIER: strong, solid support, frequently square in section or of composite section (compound pier).

PIETRA DURA: ornamental or scenic inlay by means of thin slabs of stone.

PILASTER: shallow pier attached to a wall. *Termini Pilasters:* pilasters with sides tapering downwards.

PILLAR PISCINA: free-standing piscina on a pillar.

PINNACLE: ornamental form crowning a spire, tower, buttress, etc., usually of steep pyramidal, conical, or some similar shape.

PISCINA: basin for washing the Communion or Mass vessels, provided with a drain. Generally set in or against the wall to the S of an altar.

PLAISANCE: summer-house, pleasure house near a mansion.

PLATE TRACERY: see Tracery.

PLINTH: projecting base of a wall or column, generally chamfered (q.v.) or moulded at the top.

POND BARROW: rare type of Bronze Age barrow consisting of a circular depression, usually paved, and containing a number of cremation burials.

POPPYHEAD: ornament of leaf and flower type used to decorate the tops of bench- or stall-ends.

PORTCULLIS: gate constructed to rise and fall in vertical grooves; used in gateways of castles.

PORTE COCHÈRE: porch large enough to admit wheeled vehicles.

PORTICO: centre-piece of a house or a church with classical detached or attached columns and a pediment. A portico is called *prostyle* or *in antis* according to whether it projects from or recedes into a building. In a portico *in antis* the columns range with the side walls.

POSTERN: small gateway at the back of a building.

PREDELLA: in an altarpiece the horizontal strip below the main representation, often used for a number of subsidiary representations in a row.

PRESBYTERY: the part of the church lying E of the choir. It is the part where the altar is placed.

PRINCIPAL: see Roof (Fig. 14).

PRIORY: monastic house whose head is a prior or prioress, not an abbot or abbess.

PROSTYLE: with free-standing columns in a row.

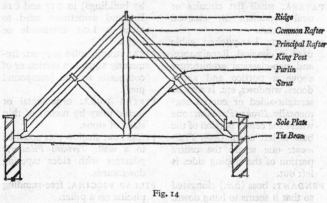

Ridge
Common Rafter
Principal Rafter
King Post
Purlin
Strut
Sole Plate
Tie Beam

Fig. 14

PULPITUM: stone screen in a major church provided to shut off the choir from the nave and also as a backing for the return choir stalls.

PULVINATED FRIEZE: frieze with a bold convex moulding.

PURLIN: see Roof (Figs. 14, 15).

PUTHOLE or PUTLOCK HOLE: putlocks are the short horizontal timbers on which during construction the boards of scaffolding rest. Putholes or putlock holes are the holes in the wall for putlocks, which often are not filled in after construction is complete.

PUTTO: small naked boy.

QUADRANGLE: inner courtyard in a large building.

QUARRY: in stained-glass work, a small diamond- or square-shaped piece of glass set diagonally.

QUATREFOIL: see Foil.

QUEEN-POSTS: see Roof (Fig. 15).

QUOINS: dressed stones at the angles of a building. Sometimes all the stones are of the same size; more often they are alternately large and small.

RADIATING CHAPELS: chapels projecting radially from an ambulatory or an apse.

RAFTER: see Roof.

RAMPART: stone wall or wall of earth surrounding a castle, fortress, or fortified city.

RAMPART-WALK: path along the inner face of a rampart.

REBATE: continuous rectangular notch cut on an edge.

REBUS: pun, a play on words. The literal translation and illustration of a name for artistic and heraldic purposes (Belton = bell, tun).

RECUSANT CHALICE: chalice made after the Reformation and before Catholic Emancipation for Roman Catholic use.

REEDING: decoration with parallel convex mouldings touching one another.

REFECTORY: dining hall; see Frater.

RENDERING: plastering of an outer wall.

REPOUSSÉ: decoration of metal work by relief designs, formed by beating the metal from the back.

REREDOS: structure behind and above an altar.

RESPOND: half-pier bonded into a wall and carrying one end of an arch.

RETABLE: altarpiece, a picture or piece of carving, standing behind and attached to an altar.

RETICULATION: see Tracery (Fig. 20e).

REVEAL: that part of a jamb (q.v.) which lies between the glass or door and the outer surface of the wall.

RIB-VAULT: see Vault.

ROCOCO: latest phase of the Baroque style, current in most Continental countries between c.1720 and c.1760.

ROLL MOULDING: moulding of semicircular or more than semicircular section.

ROMANESQUE: that style in architecture which was current in the C11 and C12 and preceded the Gothic style (in England often called Norman). (Some scholars extend the use of the term Romanesque back to the C10 or C9.)

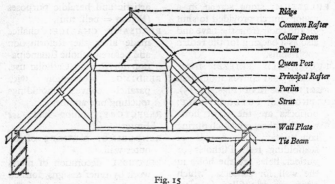

Ridge
Common Rafter
Collar Beam
Purlin
Queen Post
Principal Rafter
Purlin
Strut
Wall Plate
Tie Beam

Fig. 15

ROMANO-BRITISH: A somewhat vague term applied to the period and cultural features of Britain affected by the Roman occupation of the C1–5 A.D.

ROOD: cross or crucifix.

ROOD LOFT: singing gallery on the top of the rood screen, often supported by a coving.

ROOD SCREEN: *see* Screen.

ROOD STAIRS: stairs to give access to the rood loft.

ROOF: *Single-framed:* if consisting entirely of transverse members (such as rafters with or without braces, collars, tie-beams, king-posts or queen-posts, etc.) not tied together longitudinally. *Double-framed:* if longitudinal members (such as a ridge beam and purlins) are employed. As a rule in such cases the rafters are divided into stronger principals and weaker subsidiary rafters. *Hipped:* roof with sloped instead of vertical ends. *Mansard:* roof with a double slope, the

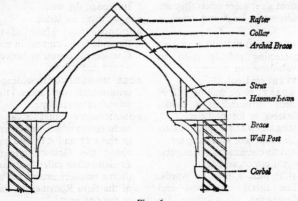

Rafter
Collar
Arched Brace
Strut
Hammer Beam
Brace
Wall Post
Corbel

Fig. 16

lower slope being larger and steeper than the upper. *Saddleback:* tower roof shaped like an ordinary gabled timber roof. The following members have special names: *Rafter:* roof-timber sloping up from the wall plate to the ridge. *Principal:* principal rafter, usually corresponding to the main bay divisions of the nave or chancel below. *Wall Plate:* timber laid longitudinally on the top of a wall. *Purlin:* longitudinal member laid parallel with wall plate and ridge beam some way up the slope of the roof. *Tie-beam:* beam connecting the two slopes of a roof across at its foot, usually at the height of the wall plate, to prevent the roof from spreading. *Collar-beam:* tie-beam applied higher up the slope of the roof. *Strut:* upright timber connecting the tie-beam with the rafter above it. *King-post:* upright timber connecting a tie-beam and collar-beam with the ridge beam. *Queen-posts:* two struts placed symmetrically on a tie-beam or collar-beam. *Braces:* inclined timbers inserted to strengthen others. Usually braces connect a collar-beam with the rafters below or a tie-beam with the wall below. Braces can be straight or curved (also called arched). *Hammer-beam:* beam projecting at right angles, usually from the top of a wall, to carry arched braces or struts and arched braces. (*See* Figs. 14, 15, 16.)

ROSE WINDOW (or WHEEL WINDOW): circular window with patterned tracery arranged to radiate from the centre.

ROTUNDA: building circular in plan.

RUBBLE: building stones, not square or hewn, nor laid in regular courses.

RUSTICATION: *rock-faced* if the surfaces of large blocks of ashlar stone are left rough like rock; *smooth* if the ashlar blocks are smooth and separated by V-joints; *banded* if the separation by V-joints applies only to the horizontals.

SADDLEBACK: *see* Roof.

SALTIRE CROSS: equal-limbed cross placed diagonally.

SANCTUARY: (1) area around the main altar of a church (*see* Presbytery); (2) sacred site consisting of wood or stone uprights enclosed by a circular bank and ditch. Beginning in the Neolithic, they were elaborated in the succeeding Bronze Age. The best known examples are Stonehenge and Avebury.

SARCOPHAGUS: elaborately carved coffin.

SCAGLIOLA: material composed of cement and colouring matter to imitate marble.

SCALLOPED CAPITAL: development of the block capital (q.v.) in which the single semi-circular surface is elaborated into a series of truncated cones (Fig. 17).

Fig. 17

SCARP: artificial cutting away of the ground to form a steep slope.

SCREEN: *Parclose screen:* screen separating a chapel from the rest of a church. *Rood screen:* screen below the rood (q.v.), usually at the W end of a chancel.

SCREENS PASSAGE: passage between the entrances to kitchen, buttery, etc., and the screen behind which lies the hall of a medieval house.

SEDILIA: seats for the priests (usually three) on the S side of the chancel of a church.

SEGMENTAL ARCH: see Arch.

SET-OFF: see Weathering.

SEXPARTITE: see Vault.

SGRAFFITO: pattern incised into plaster so as to expose a dark surface underneath.

SHAFT-RING: motif of the C12 and C13 consisting of a ring round a circular pier or a shaft attached to a pier.

SHEILA-NA-GIG: fertility figure, usually with legs wide open.

SILL: lower horizontal part of the frame of a window.

SLATEHANGING: the covering of walls by overlapping rows of slates, on a timber substructure.

SOFFIT: underside of an arch, lintel, etc.

SOLAR: upper living-room of a medieval house.

SOPRAPORTE: painting above the door of a room, usual in the C17 and C18.

SOUNDING BOARD: horizontal board or canopy over a pulpit. Also called Tester.

SPANDREL: triangular surface between one side of an arch, the horizontal drawn from its apex, and the vertical drawn from its springer; also the surface between two arches.

SPERE-TRUSS: roof truss on two free-standing posts to mask the division between screens passage and hall. The screen itself, where a spere-truss exists, was originally movable.

SPIRE: tall pyramidal or conical pointed erection often built on top of a tower, turret, etc. *Broach Spire:* a broach is a sloping half-pyramid of masonry or wood introduced at the base of each of the four oblique faces of a tapering octagonal spire with the object of effecting the transition from the square to the octagon. The *splayed foot spire* is a variation of the broach form found principally in the south-eastern counties. In this form the four cardinal faces are splayed out near their base, to cover the corners, while the oblique (or intermediate) faces taper away to a point. *Needle Spire:* thin spire rising from the centre of a tower roof, well inside the parapet.

SPIRELET: see Flèche.

SPLAY: chamfer, usually of the jamb of a window.

SPRINGING: level at which an arch rises from its supports.

SQUINCH: arch or system of concentric arches thrown across the angle between two walls to support a superstructure, for example a dome (Fig. 18).

SQUINT: a hole cut in a wall or through a pier to allow a view of the main altar of a church from places whence it could not otherwise be seen (also called Hagioscope).

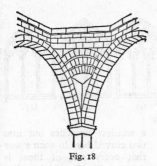

Fig. 18

STALL: carved seat, one of a row, made of wood or stone.

STAUNCHION: upright iron or steel member.

STEEPLE: the tower of a church together with a spire, cupola, etc.

STIFF-LEAF: E.E. type of foliage of many-lobed shapes (Fig. 19).

Fig. 19

STILTED: see Arch.

STOREY-POSTS: the principal posts of a timber-framed wall.

STOUP: vessel for the reception of holy water, usually placed near a door.

STRAINER ARCH: arch inserted across a room to prevent the walls from leaning.

STRAPWORK: C16 decoration consisting of interlaced bands, and forms similar to fretwork or cut and bent leather.

STRETCHER: see Brickwork.

STRING COURSE: projecting horizontal band or moulding set in the surface of a wall.

STRUT: see Roof.

STUCCO: plaster work.

STUDS: the subsidiary vertical timber members of a timber-framed wall.

SWAG: festoon formed by a carved piece of cloth suspended from both ends.

TABERNACLE: richly ornamented niche or free-standing canopy. Usually contains the Holy Sacrament.

TARSIA: inlay in various woods.

TAZZA: shallow bowl on a foot.

TERMINAL FIGURES (TERMS, TERMINI): upper part of a human figure growing out of a pier, pilaster, etc., which tapers towards the base. See also Caryatid, Pilaster.

TERRACOTTA: burnt clay, unglazed.

TESSELLATED PAVEMENT: mosaic flooring, particularly Roman, consisting of small 'tesserae' or cubes of glass, stone, or brick.

TESSERAE: see Tessellated Pavement.

TESTER: see Sounding Board.

TETRASTYLE: having four detached columns.

THREE-DECKER PULPIT: pulpit with Clerk's Stall below and Reading Desk below the Clerk's Stall.

TIE-BEAM: see Roof (Figs. 14, 15).

TIERCERON: see Vault (Fig. 21).

TILEHANGING: see Slatehanging.

TIMBER-FRAMING: method of construction where walls are built of timber framework with the spaces filled in by plaster

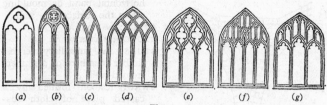

(a)   (b)   (c)   (d)   (e)   (f)   (g)

Fig. 20

or brickwork. Sometimes the timber is covered over with plaster or boarding laid horizontally.

TOMB-CHEST: chest-shaped stone coffin, the most usual medieval form of funeral monument.

TOUCH: soft black marble quarried near Tournai.

TOURELLE: turret corbelled out from the wall.

TRACERY: intersecting ribwork in the upper part of a window, or used decoratively in blank arches, on vaults, etc. *Plate tracery: see* Fig. 20(a). Early form of tracery where decoratively shaped openings are cut through the solid stone infilling in a window head. *Bar tracery:* a form introduced into England *c.*1250. Intersecting ribwork made up of slender shafts, continuing the lines of the mullions of windows up to a decorative mesh in the head of the window. *Geometrical tracery: see* Fig. 20(b). Tracery characteristic of *c.* 1250–1310 consisting chiefly of circles or foiled circles. *Y-tracery: see* Fig. 20(c). Tracery consisting of a mullion which branches into two forming a Y shape; typical of *c.* 1300. *Intersecting tracery: see* Fig. 20(d). Tracery in which each mullion of

a window branches out into two curved bars in such a way that every one of them is drawn with the same radius from a different centre. The result is that every light of the window is a lancet and every two, three, four, etc., lights together form a pointed arch. This treatment also is typical of *c.* 1300. *Reticulated tracery: see* Fig. 20(e). Tracery typical of the early C14 consisting entirely of circles drawn at top and bottom into ogee shapes so that a net-like appearance results. *Panel tracery: see* Fig. 20(f) *and* (g). Perp tracery, which is formed of upright straight-sided panels above lights of a window.

TRANSEPT: transverse portion of a cross-shaped church.

TRANSOM: horizontal bar across the openings of a window.

TRANSVERSE ARCH: *see* Vault.

TRIBUNE: *see* Gallery.

TRICIPUT, SIGNUM TRICIPUT: sign of the Trinity expressed by three faces belonging to one head.

TRIFORIUM: arcaded wall passage or blank arcading facing the nave at the height of the aisle roof and below the clerestory (q.v.) windows. (*See* Gallery.)

TRIGLYPHS: blocks with vertical

grooves separating the metopes (q.v.) in the Doric frieze (Fig. 12).

TROPHY: sculptured group of arms or armour, used as a memorial of victory.

TRUMEAU: stone mullion (q.v.) supporting the tympanum (q.v.) of a wide doorway.

TUMULUS: *see* Barrow.

TURRET: very small tower, round or polygonal in plan.

TUSCAN: *see* Order.

TYMPANUM: space between the lintel of a doorway and the arch above it.

UNDERCROFT: vaulted room, sometimes underground, below a church or chapel.

UNIVALLATE: of a hill-fort: defended by a single bank and ditch.

UPPER PALAEOLITHIC: *see* Palaeolithic.

VAULT: *Barrel-vault: see* Tunnel-vault. *Cross-vault: see* Groin-vault. *Domical vault:* square or polygonal dome rising direct on a square or polygonal bay, the curved surfaces separated by groins (q.v.). *Fan-vault:* late medieval vault where all ribs springing from one springer are of the same length, the same distance from the next, and the same curvature. *Groin-vault* or *Cross-vault:* vault of two tunnel-vaults of identical shape intersecting each other at r. angles. Chiefly Norman and Renaissance. *Lierne:* tertiary rib, that is, rib which does not spring either from one of the main springers or from the central

boss. Introduced in the C14, continues to the C16. *Quadripartite vault:* one wherein one bay of vaulting is divided into four parts. *Rib-vault:* vault with diagonal ribs projecting along the groins. *Ridge-rib:* rib along the longitudinal or transverse ridge of a vault. Introduced in the early C13. *Sexpartite vault:* one wherein one bay of quadripartite vaulting is divided into two parts transversely so that each bay of vaulting has six parts. *Tierceron:* secondary rib, that is, rib which issues from one of the main springers or the central boss and leads to a place on a ridge-rib. Introduced in the early C13. *Transverse arch:* arch separating one bay of a vault from the next. *Tunnel-vault* or *Barrel-vault:* vault of semicircular or pointed section. Chiefly Norman and Renaissance. (*See* Fig. 21.)

VAULTING SHAFT: vertical member leading to the springer of a vault.

VENETIAN WINDOW: window with three openings, the central one arched and wider than the outside ones. Current in England chiefly in the C17–18.

VERANDA: open gallery or balcony with a roof on light, usually metal, supports.

VESICA: oval with pointed head and foot.

VESTIBULE: anteroom or entrance hall.

VILLA: (1) according to Gwilt (1842) 'a country house for the residence of opulent persons'; (2) Romano-British country houses cum farms, to which the description given in (1)

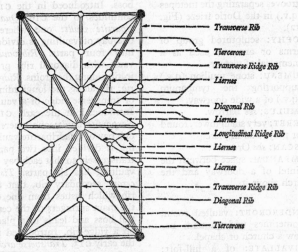

Transverse Rib
Tiercerons
Transverse Ridge Rib
Liernes
Diagonal Rib
Liernes
Longitudinal Ridge Rib
Liernes
Liernes
Transverse Ridge Rib
Diagonal Rib
Tiercerons

Fig. 21

more or less applies. They developed with the growth of urbanization. The basic type is the simple corridor pattern with rooms opening off a single passage; the next stage is the addition of wings. The court-yard villa fills a square plan with subsidiary buildings and an enclosure wall with a gate facing the main corridor block.

VITRIFIED: made similar to glass.

VITRUVIAN OPENING: A door or window which diminishes towards the top, as advocated by Vitruvius, bk. IV, chapter VI.

VOLUTE: spiral scroll, one of the component parts of an Ionic column (see Order).

VOUSSOIR: wedge-shaped stone used in arch construction.

WAGON ROOF: roof in which by closely set rafters with arched braces the appearance of the inside of a canvas tilt over a wagon is achieved. Wagon roofs can be panelled or plastered (ceiled) or left uncovered.

WAINSCOT: timber lining to walls.

WALL PLATE: see Roof.

WATERLEAF: leaf shape used in later C12 capitals. The water-leaf is a broad, unribbed, taper-ing leaf curving up towards the angle of the abacus and turned in at the top (Fig. 22).

Fig. 22

WEALDEN HOUSE: timber-framed house with the hall in the centre and wings projecting only slightly and only on the jutting upper floor. The roof, however, runs through without a break between wings and hall, and the eaves of the hall part are therefore exceptionally deep. They are supported by diagonal, usually curved, braces starting from the short inner sides of the overhanging wings and rising parallel with the front wall of the hall towards the centre of the eaves.

WEATHERBOARDING: overlapping horizontal boards, covering a timber-framed wall.

WEATHERING: sloped horizontal surface on sills, buttresses, etc., to throw off water.

WEEPERS: small figures placed in niches along the sides of some medieval tombs (also called Mourners).

WHEEL WINDOW: see Rose Window.

INDEX OF PLATES

INDEX OF ARTISTS

INDEX OF PLACES

ADDENDA

(NOVEMBER 1964)

p. 69 [Brighton, Annunciation.] The church is by *William Dancy*.

p. 224 [Fishbourne, Roman Villa.] The most recent excavations, reported in *The Times* (5 November 1964), have produced further evidence from all the building periods. Of the work of c. A.D. 43 and c. A.D. 55 a large timber store building of military character and an unusually elaborate masonry bath house have been discovered. The mosaics of the bath house, which was incorporated into the villa built in c. A.D. 75, are the earliest known in Britain. An unfinished masonry structure of c. A.D. 55 has also appeared, indicating that the decision to build the villa represents a sudden change of plan. The word villa is in fact now thought to be an inadequate description of what amounts to nothing less than a palace. It was some 500 ft square and had four wings surrounding a great central court. Much of the s wing now lies under the main road. The sea, probably in the form of an artificial inlet, reached right up to it. There were probably also other domestic ranges. About eighty-five out of perhaps a hundred or so of the rooms in the palace have been examined; nearly all of them appear to have had mosaic floors. Much painted wall-plaster has also been recovered. The building was destroyed and demolished c. A.D. 270–300.

p. 430 [Brighton, Annunciation.] Mr Nicholas Taylor tells me that the architect is *William Dancy*. Wooden piers had also been used a little earlier in St Mary Magdalene.

p. 433 [Brighton, St Martin.] Built by Father Wagner and his two half-brothers.

p. 434 [Brighton, St Michael.] When the text for St Michael was already in page proof, Mr Anthony Symondson very kindly gave me some more details which I am glad to be able to summarize here. STAINED GLASS. W window. The archangels at the bottom were designed in 1861, St Michael and St Uriel by *Ford Madox Brown*, the other two by *Morris*. The Virgin and angels in the rose above is by *Burne-Jones*. He also designed the windows in the s chapel. The window in the E wall of the chapel is by *Morris*. The s aisle w window is by *Burne-Jones*, but the two l. angels re-drawn by *Webb*. – PAINTING. The St Michael and also the Annunciation above the s door to the choir vestry are by Mr *Frank Holford*, churchwarden. – PLATE. Also by *Burges* (made by *Charles*

Hunt) a silver-gilt Flagon, 1862. – TEXTILES. Set of Mass
Vestments and white Frontal by *Burges*. – Two sets of Mass
Vestments by *Kempe*.

p. 435 [Brighton, St Paul.] The tower and spire are by *R. H.
        Carpenter*.

p. 466 [Buxted.] ST MARY. By *Edmund Scott* and *F. T. Cawthorn*,
        1885–6. Built at the expense of Father Wagner of Brighton.
        A simple church in the traditional Sussex style, flint with
        stone dressings, Late Gothic in style. Tower with pyramid
        roof. Aisleless nave. Lavish furnishings.
            ST MARY'S HOUSE, ½ m. N (now under St Mary's
        Wantage), and ST MARGARET'S HOUSE, opposite St
        Mary's House. Both were built at the same time, and also
        for Father Wagner.
            The whole story had completely escaped my notice and
        that of my assistants. I am grateful to Mr Nicholas Taylor
        for having told me about it.

p. 565 [Maresfield, St Bartholomew.] Under the tower a cast-iron 24b
        tomb slab; date of death 1667.

p. 605 [Sheffield Park.] The position about date and architect is this.
        In W. Watts's *Seats of the Nobility and Gentry*, 1779, the N
        front is shown, Gothic, but without the name of an archi-
        tect. In W. Angus's *Views of Seats . . .*, 1791, the E and S
        fronts are illustrated and called improved by *Wyatt*.

NOTES

NOTES